CADOGAN GUIDES

"One of the most attractive of all general guides series published in recent years is Cadogan Guides. The elegant jackets, the literate cultural texts and the balanced practical information make these enlightening companions for the independent traveller and the luxury tourist alike."
—*The Bookseller*

"The quality of writing in this British series is exceptional . . . From practical facts to history, customs, sightseeing, food and lodging, the Cadogan Series can be counted on for interesting detail and informed recommendations."
—*Going Places* (US)

"Standouts these days are the Cadogan Guides . . . sophisticated, beautifully written books."
—*American Bookseller Magazine*

"Entertaining companions, with sharp insights, local gossip and far more of a feeling of a living author . . . The series has received plaudits worldwide for intelligence, originality and a slightly irreverent sense of fun."
—*The Daily Telegraph*

Other titles in the Cadogan Guides series:

ABOUT THE AUTHOR

Part Scottish, part English, Richenda Miers is a novelist, freelance journalist and travel writer, who has lived and worked for many years in Scotland. Her husband was in a Highland regiment, her son was born in Inverness, two of her daughters went to school in Aberdeen and two went to Scottish universities. The family shares a home in the Outer Hebridies.

ACKNOWLEDGEMENTS

This book is for my husband Douglas, with thanks for his patience during its creation and subsequent updating.

I would also like to thank the staff of the Scottish Tourist Board and the Area Tourist Boards who have given me invaluable help, advice and information, particularly: John Hutchinson, Catriona M. Earons, Jackie McKenzie, Charles Currie, Ken Walton, Iain F. Clason, Scott K. Armstrong, Andrew Llanwarne, Patrick Laughlin, Paul Buchanan, Gordon E. Henry, Anne Burgess, Sheena Andrew, Colin Simpson, Moira Ewen, Alison Connell, Riddel Graham, Helen Lang, Christine Irving, Michael Ambrose, Ann Jones, Liz Allan, Winnie Dick, F. Macleod, E. MacLennan, Alan Reid, Michael Blair, Moira Dyer, Clive Good and all their assistants.

Others to whom I am indebted for their invaluable help and advice on how to improve the second edition include: Richard Agnew, Leonie de Barros, Duncan and Jilly Bengough, Sue Brown, Nairne Cross, Eileen Eaton, Angus Fairrie, Mike Thorne, John MacInnes, Alasdair MacLean, Charles MacLean, Francis Pearson, Clive Hardcastle, Grenville Johnston, Sara Low, Christoper and Anne Thompson.

Finally I should like to thank Paula Levey whose tireless good humour and diplomacy have enlivened the writing of this edition.

PLEASE NOTE

Every effort has been made to ensure the accuracy of the information in this book at the time of going to press. However, practical details such as opening hours, travel information, standards in hotels and restaurants and, in particular, prices are liable to change.

We will be delighted to receive any corrections and suggestions for improvement which can be incorporated into the next edition, but cannot accept any responsibility for consequences arising from the use of this guide.

CADOGAN GUIDES

SCOTLAND

RICHENDA MIERS

CADOGAN BOOKS
London

THE GLOBE PEQUOT PRESS
Chester, Connecticut

Cadogan Books Ltd
Mercury House, 195 Knightsbridge, London SW7 1RE

The Globe Pequot Press
138 West Main Street, Chester, Connecticut 06412

Copyright © Richenda Miers 1987, 1989, 1991
Illustrations © Pauline Pears 1987, 1991
Maps © Cadogan Books Ltd 1989, 1991

Cover design by Keith Pointing
Cover illustration by Povl Webb
Maps by Thames Cartographic Services Ltd
Index by Meg Davies

Editor: Victoria Ingle
Series Editors: Paula Levey and Rachel Fielding

First published in 1987
Second Edition 1989
Third Edition 1991

A catalogue record for this book is available from the British Library

Library of Congress Cataloging-in-Publication Data

Miers, Richenda.
  Scotland / Richenda Miers: illustrations by Pauline Pears.—3rd ed.
    p.   cm.—(Cadogan guides)
  Includes bibliographical references and index.
  ISBN 0–87106–351–4
  1. Scotland—Description and travel—1981- —Guide books.
I. Title.   II. Series.
DA870.M54   1991   91–11290
914.1104′859—dc20   CIP

Photoset in Ehrhardt on a Linotron 202
Printed on recycled paper and bound in Great Britain by
Redwood Press Limited, Melksham, Wiltshire

CONTENTS

v

Part VI: Lothian: excluding Edinburgh *Pages 127–57*

Part VII: Edinburgh *Pages 158–85*

Part VIII: Strathclyde: Excluding Glasgow *Pages 186–242*

Part IX: Glasgow *Pages 243–60*

LIST OF MAPS

INTRODUCTION

Caledonia! Stern and wild,
Meet nurse for a poetic child,
Land of brown heath and shaggy wood,
Land of the mountain and the flood,
Land of my sires! What mortal hand
Can e're untie the filial band
That knits me to thy rugged strand.

—Sir Walter Scott

Even Scotland's most ardent advocate failed to capture the essence of his native land. No poem can perfectly evoke the evening sun, dipping below the horizon beyond islands that stand out in dark relief against a blazing sky, nor the heart-stopping sound of a lone piper playing a grave-side lament in a remote highland glen. And no artist, not even McTaggart, has yet done full justice to the scenery: smoke-grey hills; stark mountain ranges; wild moorland carpeted with mulberry-red heather; mossy glens shaded by rowans and gnarled oaks; rivers and burns swirling over slabs of granite, and slicing through steep-sided gorges into lochs where peat-coloured water is overlaid by fragments of mist.

Ceud Mile Failte! You'll see this poster all over Scotland; it means A Hundred Thousand Welcomes! But don't expect the Scots to gush over you; their hospitality comes from the heart, with quiet dignity tempered with shrewd wit. To find their true nature, you must peel away layers of tartan, haggis, monsters and whimsical blether. The Romans called them Caledonians, failed to subdue them, and went away. Brave, proud and fiercely independent, they have been fighting for freedom from England since their earliest history; yet when Bonnie Prince Charlie swept through Scotland, rallying the clans to his father's standard and offering them an alternative to Hanoverian rule, far more fought against him or remained neutral than fought with him.

The Scots defy classification—they are canny, yet generous; taciturn, yet eloquent; dour, yet witty; realistic, yet unashamedly romantic. A piper, decked out in kilt and plaid, will serenade a captive audience in a loch-side lay-by, and expect a tip, but if you break down and a Highlander comes to your rescue with a tractor, petrol or make-shift fan-belt, reward him with a dram or a bottle, don't insult him with a fiver. A Gaelic-speaking bard will sit on a bench outside his cottage surrounded by picture-postcard scenery, beguiling you with Celtic tales, while, round the back there's a tangle of rusting machinery, and empty cans and bottles lie strewn like confetti in the heather.

Whatever sort of holiday you want, you'll find it in Scotland. You can climb in the Cuillins with crampons and ropes, or reel in a salmon as it thrashes about in the Spey, or play golf at St Andrews. You can sail among the islands on the west coast at the helm of a sturdy ketch, anchoring for the night in a sheltered sea-loch, and fall asleep to the eerie wailing of seals. You can explore the blanket bog of the Flow Country, spotting rare birds and insects and carnivorous plants. You can sit in a croft-house kitchen, pungent with acrid peat-smoke, and listen to Gaelic songs and stories of the past that have been handed down verbally over many generations. You can gaze at paintings in Edinburgh's 'finest small gallery in the world', or marvel at priceless tapestries in Glasgow's Burrell Collection. If you are a gourmet you can dine on smoked salmon or local oysters, followed by a succulent lobster, fresh from the Minch, or an inch-thick Aberdeen Angus steak, and finish off with raspberries from the Carse of Gowrie. And for your picnic lunch, you can buy scampie off one of the fishing boats, boil them up in a billycan over your camping-gaz fire, and eat them still warm with wholemeal bread. You can go north and look for that illusive cosmic stunt, the Aurora Borealis (Northern Lights), when shafts of coloured lights, mostly green and red, flash across the sky like a pageant of searchlights.

If none of these attractions are to your taste, you can rent a bothy on a remote island and curl up in front of a peat fire with a glass of whisky and your favourite companion (or, failing that, the complete works of Sir Walter Scott). *Ùine gu leòr* is Gaelic for 'time enough' and the word 'whisky' comes from *uisge beatha*—water of life.

The Best of Scotland

Ruins: 13th-century *Castle Tioram* in Loch Moidart, reached across the sands at low tide, echoes with memories of its Jacobite past. John Knox's voice still rings out in dramatic *Castle Campbell*, high above the Burn of Care and Burn of Sorrow, backed by the Ochil Hills. *Tantallon Castle*, in Lothian, perched on a sheer cliff lashed by the sea, was seat of the audacious Red Douglases and finally 'dinged doun' by Cromwell after 12 days' pounding. Bleak and isolated, the bloodstained history of *Hermitage Castle* in the Borders is tempered by an incident of romantic folly. *Linlithgow Palace* still waits for James IV to return from Flodden.

Antiquities: *Maes Howe*, a Stone Age burial cairn in Orkney, is remarkable for its Viking graffiti as well as its older history. *Mousa Broch*, in Shetland, is an almost perfect example of the 2000-year-old towers whose purpose can only be guessed at. *Callanish Standing Stones*, by a sea loch in Lewis, are as important as Stonehenge and in a far more romantic setting. The massive mound of *Traprain Law*, rearing from the Lothian plain, was once the capital of the Vortadini. The *Iron Age hill fort* on top of Barry Hill near Alyth, where romantics believe Queen Guinevere was imprisoned by King Arthur for infidelity, is impressive for atmosphere rather than substance. *Ruthwell Cross*, near Annan, has exceptional carvings and Runic inscriptions, including extracts from The Dream of the Rood—the oldest poem in the English language.

Preserved castles and mansions: Mediaeval *Cawdor Castle* near Inverness is a gem, with a lovely walled garden. *Eilean Donan Castle*, on a craggy island in Loch Duich, surrounded by hills, is understandably one of Scotland's most photographed buildings. *Blair Castle*, a majestic white baronial pile, splendid rather than beautiful, has played its part in many historic events. *Floors Castle*, in the Borders, Scotland's largest inhabited

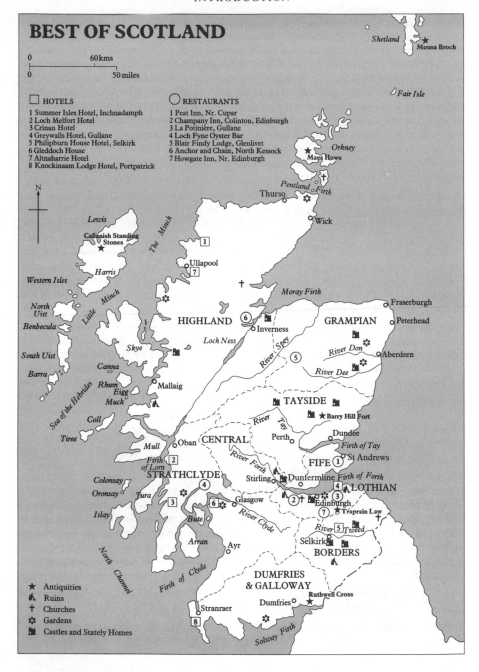

BEST OF SCOTLAND

0   60 kms

0   50 miles

☐ HOTELS
1 Summer Isles Hotel, Inchnadamph
2 Loch Melfort Hotel
3 Crinan Hotel
4 Greywalls Hotel, Gullane
5 Philipburn House Hotel, Selkirk
6 Gleddoch House
7 Altnaharrie Hotel
8 Knockinaam Lodge Hotel, Portpatrick

○ RESTAURANTS
1 Peat Inn, Nr. Cupar
2 Champany Inn, Colinton, Edinburgh
3 La Potinière, Gullane
4 Loch Fyne Oyster Bar
5 Blair Findy Lodge, Glenlivet
6 Anchor and Chain, North Kessock
7 Howgate Inn, Nr. Edinburgh

★ Antiquities
⚒ Ruins
† Churches
❀ Gardens
🏰 Castles and Stately Homes

xi

castle, must also be its most flamboyant: a triumph of astonishing minarets, cupolas and pavilions. Magnificent *Glamis Castle* has an unrivalled reputation for ghosts. *Fyvie Castle* in Grampian, was once described as the 'crowning glory of Scottish Baronial architecture' and is full of treasures. *Crathes Castle*, in Grampian, is one of the finest examples of Scotish domestic architecture built after the need for fortification and the gardens are magnificent. *Edinburgh and Stirling Castles* are both spectacular for position and history. *Traquair House* on the Tweed, the oldest mansion in Scotland to have been continuously inhabited by the same family, is crammed with historical memorabilia. *Hopetoun House* near Edinburgh is unsurpassed for classical beauty and elegance. *Abbotsford*, where Sir Walter Scott lived and died, is so well preserved in his memory that he is almost physically present. *Fasque*, in Grampian, home of the Gladstones, contains an unforgettable collection of Victoriana.

Gardens: *Finlaystone*, on the Clyde, is indisputably the most beautiful in Scotland. The charming gardens of *Castle of Mey* are owned by the Queen Mother. *Crathes Castle gardens* in Grampian, are a series of small interlinked gardens, each with its own delightful character. *The Botanic Gardens*, in Edinburgh, display a magnificent variety of horticulture: herbaceous, alpine, aquatic, and hot-house. *Crarae Woodland Garden*, on Loch Fyne, has pretty walks along the banks of a cascading burn. *Inverewe Garden*, near Poolewe, is a triumph of ingenuity. *Pitmedden Garden*, in Grampian, is memorable not so much for beauty as for intricate formal design. *Threave Gardens*, near Castle Douglas, are the training college for potential gardeners.

Churches: *Croick Church* near Bonar Bridge is a simple kirk with poignant memories of the Clearances. *The Italian Chapel* in Orkney is a miracle of faith, built from scraps by Italian prisoners of war. *Dalmeny Church* in Lothian is tiny gem of Norman architecture. *Ladykirk*, in the Borders, is one of Scotland's least austere, and therefore most welcoming, houses of God.

Art galleries and collections: the newly restored *National Gallery of Scotland* in Edinburgh has rightly been proclaimed 'the finest small gallery in the world'. *The Scottish National Gallery of Modern Art*, also in Edinburgh, has an excellent collection and exciting exhibitions. *Glasgow (Museum) and Art Gallery* has Salvador Dali's 'St John of the Cross', and the *Hunterian Art Gallery* has hundreds of Whistlers. *The Burrell Collection*, near Glasgow, is world-famous.

Museums: *The Royal Museum of Scotland*, in Edinburgh, including its separate Antiquities collection and *Glasgow Museum (and Art Gallery)* are both excellent. *The Highland Folk Museum*, in Kingussie has an outstanding display of Highland life, culture and folklore. Picturesque terraced cottages house the imaginative *Angus Folk Museum* in Glamis village. *Gairloch Heritage Museum* gives intriguing glimpses into all aspects of Highland life. *Strath Naver Museum*, in Bettyhill, tells the emotive story of the Clearances.

Dogs: Border Terriers are, without doubt, the aristocrats in Scotland's canine hierarchy—for charm, character, courage and manners.

Festivals: Edinburgh is famous for its Festival in August. Running a close second is Glasgow's Mayfest. Jedburgh, Selkirk and Hawick have the biggest Common Riding Festivals in the summer.

Activities: *Sheep dog trials* and *piping competitions* are worth looking out for; so are *Highland Games and Gatherings*, particularly the rural ones such as at Glenfinnan. *Curling* is played on most ice rinks. *The Malt Whisky Trail* in the Grampian Highlands tours eight distilleries with a free dram in each.

Restaurants: Peat Inn, Fife. Champany Inn, Linlithgow. La Potinière, Gullane. Loch Fyne Oyster Bar, Cairndow, Loch Fyne. Blairfindy Lodge, Glenlivet. Anchor and Chain, North Kessock on the Beauly Firth. Howgate Inn in Lothian.

Places to Stay: Excluding famous luxury hotels like Gleneagles. The Summer Isles Hotel, Auchiltibuie. Inchnadamph Hotel, Loch Assynt. Loch Melfort Hotel, Arduaine. Crinan Hotel, Greywalls, Gullane—where the food is so outstanding that the King of Jordan pinched their last chef. Philipburn House Hotel, Selkirk. Gleddoch House, Langbank. Altnaharrie Hotel, Ullapool. Knockinaam Lodge Hotel, Portpatrick.

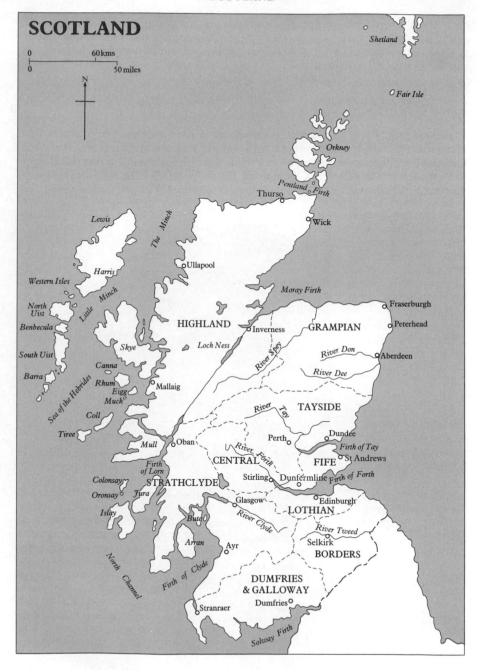

SCOTLAND

0   60kms

0   50 miles

N

Shetland

Fair Isle

Orkney

Pentland Firth

Thurso

Wick

The Minch

Lewis

Ullapool

Harris

Moray Firth

Western Isles

Fraserburgh

Little Minch

North Uist

HIGHLAND

Inverness

GRAMPIAN

Peterhead

Benbecula

Loch Ness

River Spey

River Don

Aberdeen

South Uist

Skye

River Dee

Barra

Canna

Mallaig

Rhum

Sea of the Hebrides

Eigg

Muck

River Tay

TAYSIDE

Coll

Tiree

Perth

Dundee

Mull

Oban

River Forth

Firth of Tay

CENTRAL

FIFE

St Andrews

Firth of Lorn

Stirling

Dunfermline

Firth of Forth

Colonsay

STRATHCLYDE

Glasgow

Edinburgh

Oronsay

Jura

River Clyde

LOTHIAN

Islay

Bute

River Tweed

Arran

Ayr

Selkirk

BORDERS

North Channel

Firth of Clyde

DUMFRIES & GALLOWAY

Stranraer

Dumfries

Solway Firth

Part I

GENERAL INFORMATION

Dee Valley Bridge

Before You Go

A Guide to the Guide

In 1975, amid bitter controversy, Scotland was divided into regions, some of which are obvious, others less so. This book is similarly divided. Now and then, the reader must therefore turn to a different section that crosses a regional boundary.

For tourism purposes, Scotland is divided into regions covered by Area Tourist Boards; each has its own Tourist Information Centre and publishes its own free brochure with local information and a comprehensive accommodation guide. They will advise on routes, sporting permits and local events and will book accommodation.

Anyone starting from London should visit the Scottish Tourist Board's Scottish Travel Centre, 19 Cockspur Street, London SW1 5BL, tel 071 930 8661 (open Mon–Fri throughout the year). As well as providing a full range of information, advice and literature, they help with route planning and have a travel agency where you can make reservations for accommodation and book tickets for various events such as the Edinburgh Military Tattoo.

Also in London is British Travel Centre, 12 Regent Street, Piccadilly Circus, tel 071 730 3400 (open daily, no telephone service on Sundays). Here, the British Tourist

Authority, British Rail, American Express and Roomcentre combine to provide a comprehensive booking service covering rail, air and sea travel, sightseeing tours, theatre tickets and accommodation. They also change currency.

For drivers using the M6 route north, Southwaite Tourist Information Centre, in the Southwaite Service Station a few minutes south of the border near Carlisle, offers full information on all areas in Scotland, and accommodation services.

The head administrative office of the Scottish Tourist Board is at 23 Ravelston Terrace, Edinburgh EH4 3EU, tel 031 332 2433.

Getting to Scotland from abroad

By air

Scheduled flights serve Scotland from all over the world, some direct, some via London.

From the USA, there are direct services with Northwest Orient to Prestwick Airport in Scotland, 30 miles or so south of Glasgow. Free coaches run to the station for a frequent rail link with Glasgow.

From Canada, Air Canada flies from Toronto and Halifax to Prestwick.

European airlines with direct scheduled services to Scotland include: British Airways, from Milan, Paris, Frankfurt, Dusseldorf, and Munich; Air UK, from Amsterdam, Bergen, Copenhagen, Oslo, Stavanger; KLM Royal Dutch Airline, from Amsterdam; SAS from Copenhagen, Oslo and Stavanger; Lufthansa, from Dusseldorf; Scandinavian Airways from Oslo, Stavanger and Copenhagen; Icelandair Airways, from Copenhagen and Reykjavik; JAT Yugoslav Airlines from Dubrovnik.

Visitors from other countries must travel via England.

Tours

A number of tour operators offer travel-inclusive packages to suit all tastes: golfing holidays, fishing holidays, historic trails, scenic tours, etc. Consult your travel agent for details. For example, for Americans, Abercrombie and Kent, tel 800 323 3602, run tours through lovely Highland scenery in a restored steam train, The Royal Scotsman. The tours last from three to six days with sleeping berths in luxury Victorian and Edwardian coaches and gourmet food. Caravan Tours, tel 800 621 8338, offer a 15-day holiday for Americans which includes the air fare from New York, escorted motorcoach tours of Scotland and Ireland, free entrance fees, evening entertainment, first-class hotels, all breakfasts, a lunch and 11 dinners.

Alternatively, there are any number of package tours arranged from all over Britain. Luxury coach tours with scheduled itineraries and first-class accommodation, or cheaper tours with less ritzy accommodation. National Holidays operate from all over the country with an extensive choice of tours, tel 0924 383838 (West Yorks) or 0942 44246 (Lancs). The Scottish Tourist Board publish a free brochure *Scotland* with details of over 300 good-value holidays all over the country, all of which can be booked at an ABTA Travel Agent.

Special holidays

If you like to build your holiday round a theme or particular activity, the Scottish Tourist Board publishes an excellent brochure: *Adventure and Special Interest Holidays in Scotland*, free, with details of dozens of ideas for 'different' holidays, and addresses to contact. Write for a copy to Scottish Tourist Board, PO Box 15, Edinburgh EH1 1UY.

You can, for example, go on an Archaeological holiday (Dumfries and Galloway Tourist Board, tel 0387 53862), and be introduced to the many prehistoric sites on the Solway Coast, and the Early Christian remains at Whithorn.

For creative people there are any amount of arts and crafts courses that offer instruction as well as relaxation. Prices vary, not necessarily depending on standard of tuition and accommodation. Subjects range from painting and music to woodcraft, silversmithing and stone-cutting.

Outdoor enthusiasts can choose from a wide range: birdwatching, camping, canoeing, climbing and walking, cross-country and downhill skiing, cycling, diving, fishing, gardening, geology, gliding, golf, riding, shooting and stalking, skiing, swimming and all watersports.

If you've always wanted to see the west coast of Scotland from the sea, haven't got your own boat, and prefer an experienced hand on the helm, try STA Schooners, tel 0705 832055. They run week-long voyages in the Tall Ship *Malcolm Miller*, a 300 ton topsail schooner, and part of the experience is that you are one of the crew—a pleasure for which you pay quite a lot. There are many more, smaller and mostly cheaper: Sinbad Charters, for instance, tel 0346 84 2247, or Yacht Corryvreckan, tel 0631 64371.

Hebridean Island Cruises, tel 0756 701338, offer a variety of cruises to many of the most beautiful spots on the western seaboard in the *Hebridean Princess*, a floating luxury hotel with a crew of 30 serving 40 passengers. If you are lucky with the weather and can afford luxury prices, this is an ideal holiday for hedonists. There are plenty of opportunities for a 'run ashore'. Serenissima, tel 071 730 9841, do a cruise in MS *Caledonian Star*, starting from Edinburgh and going up the east coast to Orkney and back down the west coast via the Outer Hebrides to Greenock.

There are various 'working' opportunities, such as Farmhouse Holidays where you can help with anything from peat-cutting to cheese making: try Hi Line House, tel 0349 63434. Or you can go on a conservation project, learning drystone walling, fencing, tree-planting and lots more. Tel 0786 79697. For impoverished students, a fruit-picking holiday in Perthshire can be fun and lucrative. With free accommodation and acres of strawberries and raspberries to pick, there are worse ways of making holiday money. Tel 0250 3707.

There are any amount of Touring Holidays to choose from, ranging from luxury transport and accommodation to spartan. Try Landrover Expeditions, tel 03552 30385, which give you a good selection of Scottish scenery and attractions and you can choose from hotel, farmhouse and camping for your accommodation. Other tours include Scottish Heritage tours of castles and historic sites, Whisky Tours—where someone else drives you home, and scenic tours.

There are also special holidays for those who prefer a more cerebral break. English language courses, for example, with outdoor activities laid on, such as English Écosse,

3

run by Fiona Wyllie, Arduaine, Oban, Argyll, tel 085 22 227. Or, if you really want to stretch yourself, The College of Sabhal Mor Ostaig, in Skye, runs short courses in Gaelic at all levels and in piping, as well as courses in fiddle, clarsach, accordion, song and dance. Tel 07414 373.

For an outdoor Activity Holiday try Garry Gualach Country Holidays, Invergarry. In a wonderfully relaxed family atmosphere, you can do a variety of things including pony-trekking, sailing and windsurfing, fishing and field sports. There are boys' and girls' dormitories, and two family rooms, and the rates are cheap. Holidays here are unique and never forgotten. Contact Jane Isaacson, tel 08092 230.

Getting to Scotland from England

By air

British Airways and British Midland Airways fly direct to Edinburgh and to Glasgow (Abbotsinch), from London's Heathrow Airport. British Airways also fly to Inverness via Glasgow. Air UK fly to both cities from Gatwick Airport. Flights take just over an hour and there are frequent buses and plenty of taxis into Edinburgh or Glasgow. DanAir fly direct from Heathrow to Inverness. All airlines offer special economy fares with conditions, such as having to book and pay ahead, with no cancellation refund and you must spend Saturday night. For example, British Airways offer a return fare, London to Edinburgh or Glasgow, booked at least 2 weeks in advance, for from £94.

Fully flexible, refundable fare £194. Standby, £64 each way. London to Inverness, booking 14 days ahead, no refund and you must spend a Saturday night, £128. Fully flexible and refundable, £214. Offers change frequently so it is always worth checking.

There are also many special 'package' offers, some of which include return fare, self-drive car, insurance and a tank of petrol: well worth enquiring about.

Useful telephone numbers
British Airways 0345 222111.
British Midland 071 589 5599.
Air UK 0293 517654.
DanAir 081 759 1818.

By train

British Rail run regular train services to Scotland. You leave from Kings Cross Station, London, to Edinburgh, and from Euston Station, London, to Glasgow. The journey takes about 5 hours and there are at least 15 trains a day to both cities. Special-offer tickets, with all sorts of extras such as free parking, a free dram and free breakfast, are frequently available. A Supersaver—not travelling on a Friday—costs £55 return London to Edinburgh or Glasgow. Normal return, £65. Supersaver, London to Inverness, costs £70, £78 normal return. The inter-city trains are modern and comfortable and it is a good idea to book seats in advance during the tourist season. In addition, there are direct trains to other big towns in Scotland from London, or convenient connections from Edinburgh and Glasgow. Overnight sleeper connections from

London and Bristol operate to Edinburgh, Glasgow, Dundee, Perth, Aberdeen and Inverness. A second-class sleeper costs £20 (First, £25 but you must then have a first-class ticket). During the holiday season you should book well in advance.

Special tickets include Freedom of Scotland Rover tickets for set periods: maximum period of 15 days costs £92 and you can travel anywhere in Scotland. There are other travel passes worth enquiring about. North Americans can buy a Brit Rail Pass through their travel agents.

There is also a motor-rail service to the main cities.

Useful telephone numbers
Kings Cross Station, London, 071 837 4200.
Euston Station, London, 071 387 9400.
Waverley Station, Edinburgh, 031 556 2451.
Buchanan Street, Glasgow, 041 332 9811, Central Station 041 204 2844.
Aberdeen Station, 0224 594222.
Inverness Station, 0463 238924.

By bus/coach

Several coach companies operate between London and Scotland, usually running at least one day coach and at least one overnight. The journey from London to Edinburgh or Glasgow takes about 8 hours, with 40-minute stops at (at least) two service stations. The coaches are reasonably comfortable, with toilets. Most have a snack service and show a film. Prices vary and there are often special offers. Average midweek single, London to Edinburgh or Glasgow, costs from £16.50.

Useful telephone numbers
Eastern Scottish Coaches, Victoria Coach Station, London, tel 071 730 0202.
Scottish City Link, Victoria Coach Station, London, tel 071 730 0202. Glasgow, tel 041 332 9191.
Caledonian Express, tel 071 226 6262, Victoria Coach Station, London.

By car

An excellent network of motorways means that you can drive comfortably from London to Edinburgh in 7 hours, sticking to the 70 mph limit. The M1, A68 and A1(M) are the quickest routes to Edinburgh, and the M1, M6 and A74, to Glasgow.

What to take

Clothes obviously depend on what sort of holiday you intend to have and when. Because of the unpredictability of the weather, sweaters and waterproof clothing are essential all year round if you are to enjoy the country to the full, as are comfortable, sturdy shoes. Remember Scotland is famous for its woollen industry so if you intend to buy Fair Isle, Shetland, Cashmere and tweed, pack the minimum. Rubber boots are useful if you are not pressed for luggage space, but uncomfortable for walking long distances and cheap to buy locally if wet weather looks relentless. Go prepared for rain and cold; the chances are you will have hot sunshine and drought. Scottish waters are cold but if the sun shines you might regret not bringing bathing things. Very summery clothes are seldom needed.

Good **maps** are essential if you are to enjoy your holiday to the full. Bartholomew's half-inch maps are good but you need many of them and they are expensive. There is a very adequate *Ordnance Survey Motoring Atlas* (£3.25), 3 miles: 1 inch (Scottish Highlands and Islands, 7 miles: 1 inch), available from most garages and bookshops.

A 'tourist map' of the whole of Scotland, marking special attractions, is useful. There are several, including the *Scotland Touring Map*, published by Geographia Ltd, 63 Fleet Street, London EC4Y 1PE. This has more than 20 different classifications of tourist information including castles, historic houses, forests, parks, golf courses, skiing, picnic sites, camping/caravan sites and beaches. Available from most map centres. There are usually excellent maps of each region, obtainable from the relevant Tourist Board.

If you plan to walk or climb then you should get the appropriate Ordnance Survey sheets, scale 1:50000.

One of the best places to get maps and travel books is Stanford's, 12–14 Long Acre, London WC2E 9LP, tel 071 836 1321.

On Arrival

The main Tourist Information Centre for the whole of Scotland is Edinburgh Marketing in Waverley Market, 3 Princes Street, Edinburgh (open daily, except Sundays, Oct–May, personal callers only). Run in partnership with American Express and Europcar, they offer advice to tourists in all areas, accommodation and travel booking, route planning, a Scottish bookshop, currency exchange and car hire.

Getting around

Trains run as far as Thurso and Wick via Inverness and Lairg, in the far northeast, and to Oban, Fort William, Mallaig and Kyle of Lochalsh in the west. There is a network of inter-island ferries, and an island-hopping air service. Alternatively, it is easy to hire a car or join one of the many coach tours.

By air

British Airways and Loganair operate various internal services around the mainland and out to the islands.

Useful telephone numbers
Loganair:
Aberdeen Airport, 0224 723306.
Glasgow Airport, Abbotsinch, 041 889 3181.
Inverness Airport, 0463 62332.
Kirkwall Airport, Orkney, 0856 3457.
Lerwick Airport, Shetland, 059 584 246.
Stornoway Airport, Lewis, 0851 3067.

British Airways:
Aberdeen Airport, 0224 722331.
Edinburgh Airport, 031 333 1000.
Glasgow Airport, Abbotsinch, 041 887 1111.
Inverness Airport, 0463 232471.
Wick Airport, 0955 2215.

By train

As well as the main inter-city routes, branch lines run through the very best of highland scenery. Aberdeen–Inverness, Glasgow–Stranraer, Glasgow–Oban, Perth–Inverness are all very attractive journeys. The Kyle Line runs from Inverness across Scotland to Kyle of Lochalsh, a lovely stretch of country which links up with the 5-minute ferry to Skye. The famous West Highland Line from Glasgow up to Fort William and on to Mallaig is worth doing just for the beauty of the journey, particularly for railway enthusiasts. The trains on this route are preserved locomotives and coaches, authentically decorated in the style of the old trains.

British Rail offer all sorts of excellent bargain tickets and it is worth checking at any station for full details.

By bus

Buses serve most of Scotland. In very rural areas there is usually a 'postbus' service in the mail mini-bus—an experience often memorable for the social outing as much as for the transportation. There are large numbers of bus companies: enquire locally or at the tourist information offices.

By car

Car hire firms operate from the airports and stations, and there are always local firms: the more rural, the better the bargain usually.

You drive on the left in Scotland as in the rest of the British Isles and it is law in Britain for all drivers and front seat passengers to wear seat belts. Road signs are similar to those in Europe. There is a mandatory speed limit of 70 mph on all motorways. Parking in towns is usually restricted to parking meters and car parks. A single yellow line by the kerb means you can't park by day; a double yellow line, and zigzag lines by pedestrian crossings, mean no parking at any time.

Main roads are generally good, although many are not dual carriageways which can be frustrating for faster drivers. For exploring the country properly, get to the area on main roads and then take minor roads. In rural areas there are many single-track roads with frequent passing bays. These should not be used for parking; they are also for slow cars to pull into, to allow faster ones to overtake. When touring in the far north, remember there are not many petrol stations and some close on Sundays.

Hitch-hiking

It is neither more nor less chancy to thumb a lift in Scotland than anywhere else: maniacs and rapists exist all over the world. In populated areas, be extremely wary. In the islands, however, locals will invariably stop and offer a lift without being thumbed; it is part of their instinctive hospitality.

Ferries

Caledonian MacBrayne provide a steamer service to the Western Isles, with roll-on, roll-off car ferries, restaurants, bars, and, in some, sleeping accommodation. They offer mini cruises, driveaway, island hopscotch, or car rover tickets. There are also day excursions, family tickets and excursion returns. They publish a comprehensive brochure with details: schedules, prices and special offers change seasonally as well as annually. For full information write to Caledonian MacBrayne, The Ferry Terminal, Gourock PA19 1QP, tel 0475 33755.

Suggested itineraries

For first-time visitors to Scotland, planning a holiday can be a daunting prospect. It is worth remembering that it is a small country with, on the whole, an excellent network of main roads. It is therefore possible to explore much of the country from one base. These are a few suggestions of tours from the main towns or tourist centres, to be used in conjunction with the guide. The tours can be driven in a day, but if you stop off to visit each of the attractions along the way you may have to take several bites at each cherry.

Day trips from Edinburgh

1. **Drive east** along the coast taking in Dirlton Castle where the witches were imprisoned, Yellow Craig with its Treasure Island association, North Berwick and the Bass Rock, then on to Dunbar Castle and harbour via spectacular Tantallon Castle. Head back towards Haddington with its many interesting buildings, taking in Traprain Law, Hailes Castle and Lennoxlove House on the way.
2. **Drive west** along the Forth to Dalmeny House where Queen Victoria admired the view and the plumbing. Go on to Hopetoun House, one of Scotland's finest stately homes and then to House of the Binns where Tam Dalyell gambled with the Devil. Even if your appetite for history is sated, continue on to the haunting ruin of Linlithgow palace where Mary, Queen of Scots was born. While you are here it would be criminal to miss out on a meal at Champany Inn.
3. **South of Edinburgh**, among the lovely Pentlands, you can follow Mary, Queen of Scots, to Crichton Castle and on to Borthwick Castle. Have lunch at the Howgate Inn and visit Roslin Chapel with its Prentice Pillar. Finish with a stroll in the hills up to Castlelaw Fort.

4. **Further south**, in the Borders, making an early start from Edinburgh or based in one of the Border towns, there are any amount of day trips. From cliffside St Abbs and towering St Abbs Head, travel down along the Tweed via the enchanting church at Ladykirk to Coldstream and The Hirsel, on to Kelso with its abbey, and Floors Castle, the largest inhabited castle in Scotland. Finish at Mellerstain House, another stately home with fine grounds.

5. **Walter Scott fans** must spend at least half a day at Abbotsford and can then visit the abbeys at Melrose and Dryburgh.

6. **Jedburgh** deserves several hours followed by a visit to Hermitage Castle, steeped in history and romance.

7. **Around Peebles**, visit historic Traquair House, followed by Neidpath Castle, perched above the Tweed, and then go on to the John Buchan Centre in Broughton and look at the pictures in Broughton Place.

8. **North from Edinburgh**, the coast road round to St Andrews—through the attractive East Neuk villages of Elie, St Monans, Pittenweem, Anstruther and Crail—makes an excellent outing on a fine day. St Andrews has lots to offer, followed by a visit to Earlshall. Try and include a meal at the Peat Inn, and squeeze in Falkland Palace if you can.

9. **Also north of Edinburgh**, via Dunfermline Abbey, peer into the awesome gorge at Rumbling Bridge and then climb to one of Scotland's most romantic castles, Castle Campbell. Spend the rest of the day climbing in the Ochils and exploring the Hillfoots.

10. **Stirling** deserves a day to itself.

Day trips from Glasgow

1. **Go west**, hugging the Clyde and visit Finlaystone, Scotland's most beautiful garden. If you are a Burns lover, take the shortest route on to Ayr and adjoining Alloway, (via Mauchline if you want to see more of his haunts), where there is enough nostalgic memorabilia to keep you busy for the day. If your enthusiasm for Burns is only luke warm, pay a quick visit to Alloway and go on to Culzean Castle and Country Park. Golfers and gourmets should finish up at Turnberry.

2. North of the Clyde, as well as plenty of historic sites to visit, the scenery alone merits innumerable outings. Travel up west Loch Lomond, (in company with plenty of other sightseers), turn off at Tarbert, up the Rest and be Thankful, round Loch Fyne to Inveraray Castle, and on to Crarae Gardens. At Lochgilphead, go up to Crinan, look at the canal and eat at the hotel. Or, on the way back up Loch Fyne, eat at The Oyster Bar at the head of the loch, near Cairndow.

3. **East of Loch Lomond**, Queen Elizabeth Forest Park would take a day to explore, particularly if you enjoy walking and climbing.

Day trips from Dumfries

1. **Go east** to Gretna Green via Caerlaverock Castle and the magnificent Ruthwell Cross. Drive up the lovely Esk valley, round St Mary's Loch with its literary associations, branching west at Cappercleuch on a spectacular route across to the

Tweed. Go south, pausing to peer into the Devil's Beef Tub, and back down Annandale, taking in Ecclefechan if you are a Thomas Carlyle fan.

2. **Drive up the Nith valley**, visiting Lincluden Abbey and Drumlanrig Castle, and taking a detour into the Lowther Hills to visit Scotland's two highest villages, Wanlockhead and Leadhills, and walk in the Covenanter-haunted hills. Go on up to New Cumnock and return via Dalmellington and The Glenkens.
3. **Take the road south** to Sweetheart Abbey where Queen Devorguilla Balliol lies at rest with her husband's heart in a casket. Visit the gardens at Arbigland, birthplace of dashing John Paul Jones; the Motte of Mark, and unique Orchardton Tower. On round the coast to Dundrennan with its tragic memories of Mary, Queen of Scots. Have lunch in attractive Kirkcudbright before going on along the coast to Wigtown with its martyrs, and down to Whithorn, cradle of Christianity. Depending on time and your stamina, you can either go to fascinating Glenluce Abbey and back via Newton Stewart and New Galloway or retrace your steps.
4. **The Rhinns of Galloway**, with gardens and spectacular views, should be a separate trip, taking in some of the above, and Clatteringshaws Loch and Galloway Forest Park on the way there or back.

Day trips from Perth

If beautiful scenery is what you are after, there are plenty of good tours from Perth.

1. **Go west** to Crieff, around Loch Earn with its water sports, up to pretty Killin, round beautiful Loch Tay under the lee of Ben Lawers and back through Aberfeldy, Pitlochry and Blairgowrie. Or come back through Dunblane to see its cathedral and Little Houses.
2. **Go north** to Scone Palace and then on to the ancient stones in Meigle and on again to Glamis Castle which, with the Angus Folk Museum next door, won't leave you much time for anything else.
3. **Dundee** needs a day of its own, including Broughty Ferry.
4. **Arbroath**, with its abbey, St Vigeans with its fascinating pictish stones, Montrose and the lovely Palladian House of Dun, make a good tour, back via Brechin Tower. Or go on up to Edzell Castle and its spectacular gardens.
5. **The main route north** from Perth takes you, with detours, via Dunkeld, Pitlochry Festival town, historic Killiecrankie and Blair Atholl with its magnificent castle. Retrace your steps to Killiecrankie and go west along Loch Tummel and Loch Rannoch, returning along the south side and back via Aberfeldy.

Day trips from Aberdeen

1. **Probably the most popular** is the drive west along the Dee, taking in Crathes Castle with its glorious gardens and Balmoral, and returning on the other side of the river.
2. **Go south** to Stonehaven and the sinister ruin of Dunnottar Castle, perched on a rock above the sea. Continue south-west to Glenbervie and visit the graves of Burns' ancestors. Go through Howe of the Mearns on the back roads to Fettercairn and Fasque with its Gladstone associations and memorable Victoriana. Return up the B974 to Banchory, pausing to admire the view from Cairn o' Mount.

10

3. **West** of Aberdeen through Howe of Alford takes you to A97. Go left to Kildrummy Castle and gardens, on to Glenbuchat Castle and on again to Corgarff Castle with its grim history. Continue on the hazardous Lecht Road to the ski centre and on to Tomintoul, one of the highest villages in the highlands. Look in at the Glenlivet Distillery and then stagger on to the Glenfiddich Distillery for further comfort, at Dufftown. Finish up at Leith Hall with its lovely gardens, and return through Inverurie.

4. **Take the coast road north** to Cruden Bay, for Slains Castle and Bullers of Buchan, both with memories of Johnstone and Boswell. North of Peterhead go left at Inverugie to visit Aden Country Park and Old Deer Abbey. Go south-west to lovely Haddo House and back via the amazing Pitmedden garden with its intricate heraldic designs.

5. **The coast road along the north of Grampian** to Inverness takes in some charming fishing towns and villages, each with its own quaint character. Go as far as the mouth of the Spey and return inland, to Keith and across to Turriff and down via spectacular Fyvie Castle.

Day trips from Inverness

1. **East of Inverness** go to Culloden battlefield and visitor centre and Clava Cairns. Visit Cawdor Castle and gardens and take the back roads across the River Findhorn, to Pluscarden Priory. Return via Forres, Brodie Castle and Fort George.

2. **Follow the Caledonian Canal** down the west side of Loch Ness, keeping a weather eye out for Nessie, visiting the exhibition centre at Drumnadrochit and Urquhart Castle. At Invermoriston go west through Glen Moriston, past Mackenzie's Cairn, and return through spectacular Glen Garry to Invergarry. A short detour south to the Well of Seven Heads and then back north to Fort Augustus and up the east side of Loch Ness to Inverness.

3. **Go west** along the southern shore of the Beauly Firth, buy your tweeds from Campbells in Beauly, and then drive up the west side of the River Beauly to Cannich and back on the minor road on the other side, through Eskadale—a very scenic drive. All the glens around Beauly are lovely and worth visiting if you have time.

4. **The A9 south** from Inverness offers a number of interesting attractions including Aviemore Centre, the Highland Wildlife Park near Kincraig, and Kingussie and its excellent Folk Museum. Travel back via Ruthven Barracks and memories of the tragic aftermath of Culloden, Rock Wood Ponds, charming Insh Church, the whisky centre at Coylumbridge, and out to the chair lift on Cairn Gorm for a panoramic view. If you have time, do a big circle back down the Spey.

5. **A day can be spent exploring the Black Isle**, driving over the Kessock Bridge and right round the coast.

6. **Northwest to Dingwall** and then Strathpeffer. Take the A832 at Gorstan through Strath Bran to Kinlochewe and the Beinn Eighe National Nature Reserve. Go up Loch Maree to Poolewe and visit Inverewe Garden, and return via Little Loch Broom and the Corrieshalloch Gorge.

11

7. **Another good trip via Dingwall** takes you back as far as the Corrieshalloch Gorge and then north up Loch Broom to Ullapool. Go on north through wonderful scenery to Ledmore and back through Strath Oykel and Bonar Bridge.
8. **For more spectacular scenery**, go north over the Kessock Bridge on A9 to Tain, crossing the Dornoch Firth on the new road. Visit Dornoch and its cathedral, and Dunrobin Castle. Take the back road along Golspie Burn and go west through Strath Fleet to Lairg. Take the minor road south along the River Shin, visiting the waterfall, and return along Kyle of Sutherland, taking A836 through Struie. (If you have time, detour at Ardgay, west to Croick with its poignant church.)

Day trip from Wick

North to John o' Groats and Duncansby Head with a detour to the Arts Centre in Lyth. West along the north coast to Thurso, south through the Flow Country to Lybster and back up the east coast to Wick.

Day trip from Thurso

West to Melvich and Bettyhill with its Clearances Museum, down Strathnaver to Syre, across to Kinbrace, down Strath of Kildonan to Helmsdale, up the coast to Latheron, then due north back to Thurso.

Day trips on the north coast

Because of the scarcity of roads you will usually find yourself backtracking. Cape Wrath is a must, and any of the north–south glens, each with its memories of the Clearances. The road south from Loch Eribol along Loch Hope, under the lee of Ben Hope to Altnaharra and back up to Tongue is beautiful. So is the trip from Durness to Rhiconich and out to the west coast on any of the side roads. Anywhere you drive down this western seaboard is staggeringly beautiful, and it is better to do it progressively rather than to try and do day trips.

Day trip from Lairg

Go west along Loch Shin to Laxford Bridge and then out to Scourie. East to Kylestrome, follow the coast down to Drumbeg and Lochinver. Then up the Inver to Loch Assynt and Ardvreck Castle with its memories of gallant Montrose; on through Inchnadamph Nature Reserve to Ledmore, east to Oykel Bridge and falls; along Strath Oykel to Cassley Waterfall and back to Lairg.

Day trip from Kyle of Lochalsh

Up the coast to Plockton, along Loch Carron to Strathcarron, west to Loch Kishorn. Detour west up the dramatic Pass of the Cattle from Tornapress Farm. North to Shieldaig, east along Upper Loch Torridon to Torridon, up to Kinlochewe, east to Achnasheen, down Glen Carron to Strathcarron. Retrace your steps along Loch Carron and then go due south to Auchtertyre and detour to Eilean Donan Castle before returning along Loch Alsh to Kyle.

Day trips in Skye

Ideally, Skye should be a holiday of its own, with each day spent exploring one small area. If you have only one day then you must choose between two tours. From Kyleakin, hug the east coast up to Portree, Loch Mealt and Flodigarry, across to Duntulm Castle, down the west to Dunvegan Castle, back to Sligachan and then retrace your steps, with a quick sprint out to Elgol from Broadford. Or explore the Sleat Peninsula with its staggering views across the Sound of Sleat. It would be possible to do both trips in one day, but only if you never got out of your car.

Day trips from Fort William

1. **Go west** along Loch Eil to Glenfinnan with its Jacobite memories, on to Lochailort. Detour along Loch Nan Uamh, to the monument where Prince Charlie landed in 1745 and whence he departed, defeated, in 1746. If you can fit it in, go on to Arisaig and Mallaig. A cul de sac, the whole detour adds nearly 40 miles to your tour, but the scenery on this road is special. Then hug Loch Ailort down to Glenuig and Kinloch-moidart. You are at the heart of Jacobite country here. Carry on down to Acharacle, Salen, along Loch Sunart to Strontian, on to Kingairloch, up Loch Linnhe and back round the south side of Loch Eil.
2. **Take the A82 down Loch Linnhe** to Ballachulish, Glencoe village and through Glen Coe, haunted by memories of the massacre. Go on to Tyndrum and then west to Connel and then hug the coast northwards back to Fort William. Alternatively, at Tyndrum continue on to Crianlarich and then through Glen Dochart to Killin, along Loch Tay to Fearnan, and take the back road north across the River Lyon to B846 and up to Loch Tummel. You've another choice here: either west to Dunalastair and up through Glen Errochty on a minor road with lovely views, or east along Loch Tummel to historic Killiecrankie and Blair Castle. Either way, go on north on the A9 and branch left on the A889 to the A86, along Loch Laggan, through Glen Spean to Spean Bridge and Fort William.

Day trip from Oban

Follow the coast south to Lochgilphead, then up Loch Fyne to Inveraray, north up Glen Aray to Cladich. Here you can choose between turning left and driving all the way round beautiful Loch Awe and up Glen Nant to Taynuilt, or going on to the A85 and back on the main road.

Day trip in Mull

As in Skye, Mull should be a holiday in itself, explored in small sections. If you've only a day, start at Tobermory, take the B8073 to Dervaig, turn left to Salen where you join the B8035, go round the south side of Loch Na Keal to Gribun, through Gleann Seilisdeir. Go east, through Glen More to Castle Duart and back up the east coast along the Sound of Mull.

Day trips from Lochgilphead

1. **Go south on the** A83 to Inverneill and then turn right on the B8024 and follow the coast right round beautiful Knapdale and back up Loch Fyne.
2. **Go north** to ancient Dunadd Fort and on to see the standing stones as far as Kilmartin. Backtrack and take the B8025. Detour to see Crinan and then explore Loch Sween, both sides of which are cul de sacs.
3. **Go south** on the A83 right down Kintyre Peninsula to Campbeltown, and carry on south to Southend and then west to Mull of Kintyre. Head back to Southend and east on the minor road, and follow the east coast all the way up, round Campbeltown Loch, and up the B842 along the coast up to Tarbert.

Public Holidays

New Year's Day is the only statutory public holiday in Scotland. Bank Holidays are mainly for banks only and include: 2 January, the Friday before Easter, the first Monday and last Monday in May, the first Monday in August, 30 November (St Andrew's Day), 25 December (Christmas Day), and 26 December.

Most towns and districts have local public trades' and other holidays which vary from place to place and from year to year. It is worth asking at one of the Area Tourist Board Information Centres for the annual leaflet, *Public Holidays in Scotland*.

Shopping

Tweed and wool: As well as tourist-traps, there are little sheds and cottage parlours where weaving is still done on hand looms, mostly in the islands and parts of the highlands. They are invariably signposted from the road. Hardwearing Harris tweed is acclaimed all over the world: to be authentic it should be woven in the home of the crofter on a hand loom with Scottish wool (but not necessarily wool from Harris). Most of the textile mills in the borders have their own shops and some, like Pringles, have centres further north. Perhaps the most tempting of the first-class establishments is Campbells of Beauly, Inverness-shire (q.v.).

Glass: Some Scottish glass is beautiful. At Edinburgh Crystal, in Penicuik and Caithness Glass in Perth, Oban and Wick, factory tours show all the processes of glass-blowing, moulding and engraving, and there are shops selling the finished products.

Hoots memorabilia: Traditional accessories to Highland dress, set with cairngorms and amethysts, in wrought silver and gold, can be bought from most jewellers. Hamilton and Inches, George Street, Edinburgh, are probably the most reliable and respected. Jewellery made from local stones can be found in workshops and craft shops throughout the country. With such a large deer population, both decorative and functional objects carved from horn are made all over Scotland. Take home a shepherd's crook, called a *crommach*, with a handle carved from ramshorn or, if your luggage isn't designed to take something of 5 ft or more in length, go for a horn salt spoon or drinking bowl.

Food and drink: Try and squeeze a side of smoked salmon into your suitcase but make sure it is well wrapped. It isn't cheap: for good quality and the most reasonable price go to Clark Brothers, The Harbour, Musselburgh, tel 031 665 6181.

Buy shortbread, oatcakes and Dundee cake, in tins. They keep for ever and are a good reminder of a Scottish holiday.

In the duty-free shop at the airport, your choice lies between the malt whisky you have adopted as your 'special' (if in doubt, Glenfiddich won't let you down) and Drambuie, Scotland's whisky liqueur.

Tracing your ancestors

For many reasons, not least the Highland Clearances in the 17th and 18th centuries, a large number of exiled Scots, and descendants of exiled Scots, return to the land of their origins hoping to trace their family history.

First, write to Keeper of the Records of Scotland, Scottish Record Office, Her Majesty's General Register House, Princes Street, Edinburgh EH1 3YY, tel 031 557 1022. Send all the information you have on your ancestors.

Alternatively, try a good researcher. Probably the best in Britain, who will set your feet on the right path, is Census Searches, The Lady Teviot, 12 Grand Avenue, Hassocks, West Sussex BN6 8DA tel 07918 4471.

Sports and activities

Angling
(see 'Fishing').

Canoeing
This is possible all round the coast and on many of the rivers, where the fast flow is often ideal for 'white water' canoeing. There are many water-sport centres where canoes can be hired. The Scottish Sports Council, 1–3 St. Colme Street, Edinburgh, tel 031 225 8411, runs outdoor training centres where courses include canoeing. Canoeing can be dangerous.

Climbing
Climbing in Scotland can be an energetic scramble, suitable for anyone who is reasonably fit and sensible, or skilled rock-climbing which should only be undertaken by experts with proper equipment. There are more than 270 mountains over 3000 ft (914 m) high and nicknamed 'Munros' after Sir Hugh Munro, who collated these hilltops in his 'Munro's Tables'. It has become a popular sport to climb as many Munros as possible. The Cuillins, in Skye, have provided a testing training ground for some of the world's top mountaineers. From Glasgow and Edinburgh there are several high hills within easy reach by car for a day's outing. The Arrochar Alps, the peaks northwest of Loch Lomond, and particularly the Cobbler, 2891 ft (867 m), are an example. The Trossachs Hills are popular, and also Ben Vorlich, 3231 ft (969 m), near Lochearnhead. North of Loch Tay, Ben Lawers, with exceptional alpine flowers, is another Munro at 3984 ft (1195 m), looked after by the National Trust for Scotland. Perthshire has a number of hills, including Schiehallion, 3554 ft (1066 m), near Loch Rannoch. The hills around Glen Lyon are also good and Glencoe has a variety of challenging peaks.

Further north, Ben Nevis, 4406 ft (1322 m), is Scotland's highest mountain, with several routes up including a well marked tourist route. There are a number of other high hills in Lochaber. To the northwest, the highest peaks of the Grampians are truly arctic in the winter, but splendid for experienced climbers. The eastern edge of the Grampians, around Glen Clova, and the Lochnagar area, accessible from Deeside, are also popular. North of the Great Glen, Torridon, in the west, offers spectacular rock scenery, equalled only by the peaks of the Inverpolly Nature Reserve north of Ullapool and including the distinctive Stac Polly, 2009 ft (603 m), Canisp, 2779 ft (834 m) and Guilven, 2399 ft (720 m). Ben Hope, southwest of Tongue, is Scotland's most northerly Munro, at 3042 ft (913 m).

The following advice may seem nannyish and bossy to those accustomed to hill-climbing: nevertheless, there are a great many idiots whose ignorance has put the lives of Mountain Rescue teams at risk. However settled and fine the weather may look, there are certain precautions that should always be taken if you are going any distance off the road. Bear in mind that the weather changes rapidly in the hills and that other lives can be lost if you get into difficulties and have to be rescued. Always tell someone where you are going, what time you are leaving and what time you expect to return. Display a note in your parked car with this information. Consult someone local about your planned route and keep an eye on the weather. Carry a compass and a good map. Wear warm, waterproof clothing and suitable footwear. Wellington boots are not comfortable for long-distance walking and climbing.

Curling

Scotland's traditional winter game is usually played on indoor rinks these days. It has been played in Scotland for over 450 years and is described as 'a sort of bowls on ice'. For information on where you can go to watch or participate, ask the Scottish Sports Council, 1–3 St. Colme Street, Edinburgh, tel 031 225 8411.

Diving

Sub-aqua is very popular. The wonderful clarity of the sea around the coast, full of highly coloured sea animals and plants, makes Scottish waters among the best in the world for diving.

There is a wide choice of good places where you can dive. The four places listed here are outstanding. In the north there is Scapa, in Orkney. Four ships of the sunken German fleet, scuttled at the end of the First World War, lie untouched below the clear waters of this huge anchorage and offer marvellous scope for wreck diving. You can charter boats from several places around the coast and get air.

On the east coast, St Abbs Head is well known among divers for its exceptional sub-aqua quality. This stretch of coast, down to Eyemouth, is good for beginners, being reasonably shallow with lovely marine life. The weather can be bad, so you must be prepared to hang around sometimes.

On the west coast the waters around Oban are excellent for diving, with a good air supply and plenty of boats to charter in Oban. The Sound of Mull is littered with wrecks, and there is good sub-aqua cliff scenery. Ailsa Craig and the Firth of Clyde are also good diving sites.

The Summer Isles, in the northwest, are also ideal for diving. For more information contact Scottish Sub-aqua Club, 16 Royal Crescent, Glasgow, tel 041 332 9291.

Fishing

Lord, suffer me to catch a fish,
So large that even I,
When talking of it afterwards,
May have no need to lie.

A Fisherman's Prayer, Anon

We are most grateful to Michael Wigan for the following guide to fishing in Scotland. Michael is a fisherman based in Sutherland, and the director for Luss Estates Company with responsibility for the fishery on Loch Lomond, the river Leven, and the loch's west-side spawning rivers. He manages a well-known trout loch on his estate, Borrobol, in Sutherland. A regular contributor to UK national newspapers and country magazines, he is also author of The Scottish Highland Estate *(pub. 1991).*

In the first half of the 19th century southern fishermen began making the stagecoach trek to Scotland to ply for salmon with rod and line. The industrial revolution had begun to pollute England's great salmon rivers, and was to wipe the salmon out in many of them by the turn of the century. The Scottish lairds had been accustomed to sending forth their 'scalgairs' (hunters) to procure fish and game for them, frequently disdaining such activities themselves. They were amazed and delighted to be paid by these newcomers for the right to dangle their baits in the water.

Much has changed since Scotland made its name as the world's best fishing venue. The night-time revellers who hunted spawning salmon in their breeding places with lamps and pronged spears have been replaced by fishermen and women throwing out high-tech fishing lines with rods made of supremely light, flexible and strong new materials. Where once the huge bulk of Scottish salmon were caught by estuary nets, now salmon nets (challenged by the low price of farmed salmon) are becoming uneconomic; many have fallen into disuse, or been bought up and laid to rest by the rod angling

17

fraternity. The silver king of the river is chiefly valuable as a game fish, and the value of fishing rentals to Scotland, apart from the benefits fishing brings to many sideline economies, is enormous. The capital value of salmon fishing in Scotland has been calculated at close to £1 billion.

It is no exaggeration to say that in the valleys of some of the great rivers like the Spey and Tay, the way of life is chiefly determined by the fishery. Fishing hotels and lodges occupy strategic positions above the precious waters, and ghillies' and water bailiffs' houses are never far from the fish that sustains their livelihood. In many villages on rivers the focal point is the tackle shop, not only trading in fishing paraphernalia, but also in gossip about pools in which fish have been caught and flies that have caught them. The news of big hauls is particularly influential with trout fishermen, and round any little loch in which someone has struck lucky large concentrations of anglers are to be observed days later, trying in vain to repeat an individual's one-off glory.

The joy of a river is that its course connects contrasting parts of the country. The sources of many of Scotland's great rivers are swampy spring-fed patches in hanging valleys high in the mountains, or even springs in the floors of lochs. Many Scottish rivers can be fished from the mountain burns near the headwaters right through to the wide sleepy stretches flowing through farmland nearer the coast.

In some places fishermen use rod and line to spin for migratory fish in the sea off the river mouths, usually for seatrout. Seatrout are the members of the native brown trout family which choose to migrate to sea, but unlike the Atlantic salmon which forage as far as the Greenland shelf to feed, seatrout winter offshore, generally returning in spring and early summer.

In seeking enjoyment from duping fish many methods have been devised to balance the challenge of a catch with applications of physical dexterity and manual skill. Fishing is an outwitting art, and man delights in playing the deceiver.

Salmon fishing in Scotland is classically associated with the wet fly, a contraption of feathers and other titbits which need bear no resemblance to any known insect or creature, but for certain well-tested reasons rouses fishes' aggressive urge. On the bigger rivers spinning is practised in slow, wide pools; but fly fishing is in the ascendancy, and spinning increasingly frowned on. The ancient practice of worming, which is suited to the tails of deepening pools where the worms twirl enticingly in the current, is discouraged even more.

Dapping is a technique developed for catching seatrout and brown trout in windy conditions on lochs. By deploying a loose silky cord from a pole-like rod the fly can be made to dance over the surface like an insect blown from land and trying unsuccessfully to rise. Nymph fishing employs a wingless body in imitation of the fly at larval stage. When a trout takes a nymph it is capitalising on the momentary opportunity offered by a fly as it rises from the river-bed prior to hatching on the surface. Dry fly, like nymph, is imitative, and although in most Scottish salmon rivers the water is too cold for dry fly to be successful, trout fishermen use it productively on warm evenings on the lochs, when the puffed-up wings of the dry fly keep it popped up on the surface.

The water surface to all fishermen is a hypnotic thing, always moving, always changing with the shifting light in the sky. Cunliffe Pearce has written evocatively of 'the top of the water, that magic looking-glass through which trout and man mysteriously make acquaintance with each other'. In Scotland there is the extra factor of supreme scenery. The Highland lochs—Loch Lomond, Loch Awe—are famed for beauty, yet also loved in a different way by the connoisseurs for the fishing they offer. Some of the far north rivers—Helmsdale, Brora, Naver, Dionard—open out through heather moorland, and become faster as they drop through rocky passages before entering the sea. The outer isles have magnificent salmon and seatrout fishing, and it is on the magical Grimersta, where running fish can steam in in a seemingly endless flow, that the British record catch by one man in a day was recorded—52 salmon.

Some of the most exciting trout lochs are those gem-like bodies of water in the far north, famous for being dour and uncooperative in one mood, then exploding into action the next. A hundred fish in a day to two rods is not unimaginable.

Scottish rivers come in all styles and sizes. The Tay and Tweed fishermen waddle to the bank in chest-waders, bearing aloft 18-foot rods capable of throwing 45 yards of line, to brave the heavy waters. If the width of the river completely defeats them, ghillies row the boat to the most productive lies. Alternatively there are the restricted lies of smaller, more intimate and secretive rivers, like the Stinchar in the southwest, or the Laxford in the northwest. Fishermen speak with bated breath and condign respect of these illustrious names; rivers more remarkable in their great catches for the small water the fish have come out of.

Scottish salmon fishing is not, as is sometimes said, the preserve of rich tenants on famous water. There are thousands of miles of fishing in Scotland, and many opportunities for those who seek them out. The game fishing magazines, *Trout and Salmon* and *Salmon Trout and Seatrout*, advertise plenty of rentable fishing, and once embarked on the salmon fishing circuit, chances spring up for keen fishermen through contacts made along the way. Some local councils own water, and many rivers are open to day-ticket fishermen either through angling associations, fishing hotels, local river boards, or private riparian owners. Salmon fishing permits start at around £10 per day.

Trout fishing is available in greater supply than is ever utilised, particularly in the far north and west of Scotland, and some of the famous fishing hotels have access to numerous remote lochs which never see a fisherman year-round. A boat on a loch costs around £10 a day, bank fishing around £8. Tourist information centres circulate fishing information, and details of self-catering accommodation which is accompanied by trout fishing. The more expensive salmon fishing possibilities are marketed through the main sporting agencies, and often sold in exclusive packages based in neighbouring fishing lodges.

The salmon fishing season varies from river to river; starting from January in some places and as late as March in others. Trout fishing is from 15 March to 6 October.

Sea fishing is extensive, with such a length of coastline. Porbeagle shark, halibut, cod, bass, hake, ling, skate and turbot are but a few of the many species of fish you can expect to find. There is never a shortage of charter boats or, in most places, of experienced locals to take you out. There is no closed season: weather and availability are the only limitations. Again, ask at your hotel, or in the tourist information centre.

19

Useful addresses for fishermen

Central Scotland Anglers Association, 53 Fernieside Crescent, Edinburgh, tel 031 664 4685.

Scottish Anglers National Association, 307 West George Street, Glasgow, tel 041 221 7206.

Scottish Federation for Coarse Angling, TighnaFleurs, Hill o' Gryfe Road, Bridge of Weir, Renfrewshire, tel 0505 612580.

The Scottish Federation of Sea Anglers, 18 Ainslie Place, Edinburgh, tel 031 225 7611.
Scottish Sports Council, 1–3 St Colme Street, Edinburgh, tel 031 225 8411.

Gliding

Gliding is possible in some areas and most clubs offer temporary membership and instruction. Consult the Scottish Sports Council, 1–3 St Colme Street, Edinburgh, tel 031 225 8411.

Golf

Royal & Ancient Golf Club

We are most grateful to Bruce Critchley for this expert guide to Scotland's golf courses. Bruce is one of television's golf commentators, following a successful amateur international career in the 1960s. Now a consultant to golf-course developers, he also, in association with his wife's company, Critchley Pursuits, arranges tours of British, Irish and Continental courses for both English and American enthusiasts.

The origins of the game of golf are lost in the mists of time. Some say golf, or a form of it, was first played in Holland; but no one denies that the Scots nurtured the peculiar habit of knocking along a pebble with an old stick and are mainly seen as the founding fathers of the game we know today.

Fortunately the best terrain for golf is usually land of little use for agricultural purposes. So it is that many of the oldest courses evolved along the sea shore on salt-laden land reclaimed from the sea; in other words, links.

Golf on this sort of terrain is almost unique to the British Isles and traditionally our major championships, including the Open, are played on links courses and the majority of them in Scotland. That said, there are some pretty spectacular inland courses as well.

The Borders and Lothian

The area between Edinburgh and the border with England contains some beautiful rolling countryside, but is not to the forefront of Scotland's golfing heritage. However, there are one or two gems, none more so than **Hawick** where the views from the higher parts of the course are breathtaking. **Minto** and **St Boswells** are two others worth taking in should you be in the vicinity.

On the other hand, **Lothian** positively teems with courses and East Lothian in particular contains some of the finest links courses to be found anywhere.

Furthest to the east is **Dunbar,** not as widely known as some of the more famous championship venues, but the 14 holes that ran along the sea shore are on a par with the best. While at Dunbar, and if looking to play 9 holes after tea, pop inland to **Gifford** and sample one of the least known delights in this part of the world.

Moving north and east, **North Berwick** is the next port of call. A collector's item for any acquisitive golfer, the West Links probably isn't very different from when it came into being in 1832. Shots over ancient walls and across bays confirm that courses in those days materialised rather than were designed, and at least two of the holes here have been copied elsewhere in the world.

Five miles closer to Edinburgh lies **Muirfield**, the home of **the Honourable Company of Edinburgh Golfers** and for many the best seaside course of all. The Open Championship has been coming here regularly since the course was founded towards the end of the last century. For those wishing to play, a letter to the secretary beforehand is a must, preferably endorsed by the applicant's own club secretary.

Muirfield lies on the eastern edge of the town of Gullane, which has 3 courses of its own. **Gullane No 1** is a fine test and, like North Berwick, is used as one of the qualifying courses when the Open is at Muirfield. **Nos 2 and 3** get progressively shorter and easier, but all are a stiff test when the wind blows.

As if all this wasn't enough, alongside the three Gullane courses lies **Luffness New**. Perhaps not as visually striking as the Gullanes and Muirfield and certainly flatter, it is nevertheless quite a test and is more exposed to the wind, such an important element of seaside golf.

The courses round Gullane are the cream of those situated on the southern shores of the Firth of Forth. But moving ever closer to Edinburgh, this seam of golfing country continues unabated with **Kilspindie** and **Longniddry** upholding the area's reputation almost to the city boundary.

Just when you might think that nothing more of importance could exist in the urban fringes, the traveller will come upon Musselborough Race Course. The original links at **Musselborough** was on the site of the race course and the 9 holes still exist. The second home of the Honourable Company (the first being in Leith), Musselborough was one of the early venues for the Open until Muirfield was developed in the late 1800s.

Two other clubs which shared the Musselborough Links with the Honourable Company, have established courses of their own in Edinburgh. The **Bruntsfield Links Golf Society** and **The Royal Burgess Golfing Society** have adjacent parkland course in the western suburbs of the city, and a joy to play they are too.

To the west of Edinburgh are a number of mostly parkland courses and undoubtedly the best is **Dalmahoy**. The scene of several national and international tournaments, Dalmahoy has 36 holes and is the centre of a fine new hotel and leisure complex.

Fife and Tayside

Across the Firth of Forth from Gullane and its surrounds lies the Kingdom of Fife, as blessed as East Lothian both in the quality and the quantity of its golf courses. Also, if golf did start in Scotland, then it probably began somewhere along the shores of Fife or Tayside.

St Andrews is the golfing capital not only of Fife, but of the world. It is from their clubhouse overlooking the first and last holes of the Old Course that the **Royal & Ancient Golf Club** look after the customs of the game and mastermind the world's premier golf event, the Open Championship.

The **Old Course** is unique. There are huge double greens; the 17th, the Road Hole, is probably the most famous hole in golf; and the massive shared fairway of the opening and closing holes is seemingly in the middle of the 'Old Grey Toun'. The other courses of St Andrews, **the Jubilee**, **the Eden** and **the New**, lie deep in the shadow of their famous sister, but are all well worth a game if the pilgrimage has been made.

A few miles to the south are a number of fine links courses, some whose origins go back over 200 years. The nearest is the **Crail Golfing Society** who play over the Balcomie Links, a course built over sloping terrain and looking out over the Firth of Forth towards North Berwick.

On round the corner, and perhaps best known after St Andrews, lies **Elie** where the members of **the Golf House Club** play. No par 5s and only two par 3s make this a tough course to score on, but once again the knowledgeable golfer can only marvel at the way holes have been conjured out of the sandy humps and hollows left by the departing sea.

Further west still and you come to the links of **Lundin** and **Leven**. Lundin is the more links-like in character and, to be honest, more fun. Also Lundin is good enough to be one of the final qualifying courses when the Open is at St Andrews.

To the north and over looking the Firth of Tay towards Dundee, **Scotscraig** is another course good enough to have helped sort out those anxious to play in the Open proper. More trees than are usually found on links courses gives a somewhat inland atmosphere, but that in no way disguises the quality of the golf.

The inland courses of Fife should not be ignored and amongst the likes of **Glenrothes** and **Dunfirmline, Ladybank** stands out as a course that has evolved from its 6-hole inception in 1879 into a first class heathland course.

Across the Tay and **Carnoustie** is to Tayside what the Old at St Andrews is to Fife. On the Open Championship rota until 1975, when lack of sufficient good hotel accommodation caused its removal, Carnoustie is one of the toughest championship layouts of them all. There are five more links course within the proverbial 'drive and pitch' of Carnoustie, with the longer **Monifieth** and **Panmure** being the pick of the bunch.

Further up the coast, **Montrose** is a must should you be on the way to or from Aberdeen. One of the oldest of the lot, the current layout is largely unchanged since the middle of the last century.

Of inland character the **Downfield Club** at Dundee is a fine, relatively modern course and is a most pleasant change from the staple diet of links golf. To the north, **Forfar** has an excellent 18 holes, not very long, but full of interest.

While on the subject of inland courses, it is vital to take a swift drive to the west and visit the glorious rolling hills of **Perthshire**.

Rosemount at Blairgowrie is ranked amongst the most beautiful courses in the world, set as it is amongst heather and pine. Another in a stunning setting is **Pitlochry** and while not very long, its hill-top situation gives panoramic views of the surrounding hills and valleys.

But the monarch in these parts is **Gleneagles**. Set as if by nature in the lee of the Ochil Hills and dominated by the great hotel, the **Kings** and the **Queens** are as fine a pair of courses as you will come across in a day's march. A third course, designed by Jack Nicklaus, is on the point of completion and provided you have the wherewithal to fund a couple of days there, the combination of great golf and good living is hard to beat.

The Highlands

Golf in the Highlands is concentrated around the east coast, the rest being somewhat too hilly even for this ardent golfing nation!

Moving northwards from Tayside, Aberdeen is soon reached and boasts 11 courses. Of these, **Royal Aberdeen** and **Murcar** stand out, both classic links and right next door to one another. Some 20 miles on up the coast is **Cruden Bay** and this is a truly splendid seaside course and, while the locals would shudder to contemplate it, were it a little longer and more accessible, could be a great test for a full blown professional tournament.

Up to the north-facing Grampian coast and we find a stretch of golfing country as prolific as any in the country. Starting with **Fraserburgh** on the eastern tip, the fanatic could have a fortnight of golf before he got to Inverness, without ever playing the same course twice. While Fraserburgh is a pure links and great fun, Banff sports a couple of titled courses in **Royal Tarlair** and **Duff House Royal**. Neither are really links courses but should not be bypassed if the itinerant golfer is taking his time about sampling all the delights of Highland golf.

Into Morayshire and a clutch of courses of which **Moray (Lossiemouth)** and **Forres** are the pick next to the sea, together with **Elgin** some 12 miles inland. Still moving west, and at **Nairn** there's a highly regarded links course, which on more than one occasion has played host to the Scottish Championships.

Some 40 miles to the south, in the Spey Valley and not far from Aviemore, lies **Boat of Garten** a relatively short course, but an absolute joy to play. James Braid designed the course and his holes, coupled with the superb views of the mountains, make a diversion here an absolute must.

North of Inverness and the courses continue to come thick and fast. **Fortrose and Rosemarkie, Muir of Ord** and **Strathpeffer Spa** all offer a pleasant 18 holes, but **Tain** is the choice if time doesn't permit all to be visited.

However, the reason the avid golfer continues ever northwards is just a few miles further on—**Royal Dornoch**. A new bridge at Tain has cut an hour from the journey north and made this magnificent links just that little bit more accessible. But for its location, Dornoch would be the choice for the most important championships and indeed the Amateur Championships was taken there for the first time in 1985.

By now you are very near the top, and carrying on through **Wick** to **Thurso** and **Reay** will enable the collector to say he has played the most northern courses on the British mainland. As for the Islands, **Orkney**, **Shetland**, **Skye** and **Lewis** all have courses and well worth playing if the weather's good.

Strathclyde, Dumfries and Galloway

In the west, the Ayrshire coast is as blessed as Fife and East Lothian both in terms of quality and quantity. Once again, standards are measured in terms of the Open Championship. The top of the heap are those that host the Open, followed by the courses that are used for the final qualifying rounds.

This great golfing stretch begins just south of the town of Irvine with **Western** and **Glasgow Gailes**. Of the two, Western Gailes just has the edge, perched as it is on a narrow strip of land between the Glasgow to Ayr railway line and the sea. Glasgow Gailes is flatter, but both have served with distinction in the qualifying stages when the Open is held at Troon.

Immediately south is **Barassie**, also a 'qualifier' but perhaps a little gentler than the Gailes courses. It may not be quite so high on the golfer's shopping list, but it would be a mistake to miss it out.

Barassie is just to the north of Troon, a town positively ringed with courses, both private and public. **Royal Troon** is the Championship course and typical of many old links courses in that it runs straight out and back along the sea shore, with the 9th at the farthest point. Flattish at start and finish, the best holes are through the dunes around the turn. It also has the distinction of having the longest and shortest holes in British Championship golf, the 6th measuring nearly 600 yards and the 8th, the 'Postage Stamp', just 126 yards.

Moving ever southwards, indeed just across the Pow Burn beyond Troon's 9th green, you come to the exception to the championship rating rule. **Prestwick** is neither on the Open Championship rota nor is it used in the qualifying events. It no longer has the space to cope with the paraphernalia of big tournaments and has anyway done its share as the venue for the first dozen Opens when it all started in the middle of the 19th century.

Prestwick remains one of the pearls in Scotland's golfing heritage and should be the first choice of any golfer visiting these parts. Right from the start along the railway line, you can see these holes being played over the centuries with gutty ball and hickory shaft. At the end, the final four holes; well, you really feel they should be preserved behind glass in a museum.

While in the town of Prestwick, don't miss the opportunity of playing another fine links, **Prestwick St Nicholas**, which, but for its more famous sister, would be the choice course in this town.

Finally, some 20 miles to the south of Ayr, you come to the splendidly isolated **Turnberry Hotel**. A wonderful structure looking out over the **Ailsa** and **Arran** courses, it is very much a Gleneagles by the sea; indeed both Turnberry and Gleneagles were the creation and, for most of their lives, the property of the railway companies. The Ailsa is the senior course and takes its name from the rock standing proud out in the bay.

While in this part of the world, golf on the islands should not be ignored. **Arran** has 7 courses of which **Blackwaterfoot**, **Lamlash** and **Brodick** are the pick. Then there's **Machrihanish** on the **Mull of Kintyre** and the **Machrie** on **Islay**. Islay has just the one course and 8 distilleries, so care is needed with your priorities if the golf is to be enjoyed! A few days on these islands, using Caledonian MacBraynes ferries to get about is a glorious mixture of uncluttered golf and spectacular scenery, all stirred in with great Scottish hospitality.

With all this wealth of quality golf, the courses round Glasgow are left somewhat in the shadows. Back up the coast from Irvine, **Greenock**, **Gourock** and **Largs** are all fine courses in their own right and the sheer volume of courses close to the city almost defy selection. If pressed, **Haggs Castle** and **Pollock** would be two not to miss.

A review of Scottish courses would not be complete without turning briefly south once more. Dumfries and Galloway is not thought of as being somewhere to go in pursuit of the game. However, along the northern shores of the Solway Firth there are some absolute gems. Close to where the ferry departs for Northern Ireland at Stranraer is **Portpatrick**, a little fishing port with a stunning golf course. Long it is not, but with the west winds constantly blowing, the course is a test for the very best; that is if they can avoid being distracted by the views. A few miles east and next to the village of Port William is **St Medan**, just 9 holes, but a must if you are in the area.

Finally, and almost due south of the town of Dumfries, lies **Southernes**, just maybe the best seaside course of the lot. Only opened since the war, it is a true mixture of links and heathland, with heather and gorse standing alongside wispy grass-covered dunes.

So the journey is complete. Scotland has more to offer the golfer than perhaps any country on earth. Most of the courses are not too difficult to get on, but the more famous they are, the more crowded they are likely to be during the summer months. Go out of season and you will have them almost to yourself.

Any golfing trip should be carefully planned beforehand, with letters to the secretaries of the clubs you intend to visit. This way starting times will be guaranteed and caddies, if required, booked in advance. For addresses and telephone numbers, the *Golfers Handbook* is invaluable, though all the local tourist boards will have them as well.

One other piece of advice. Plan to take lunch at the clubhouses you visit. There are no better places to sample the best of local Scottish fare at reasonable prices and in an atmosphere almost untouched by time. Good golfing, I wish I was coming with you.

Useful Telephone Numbers

Club	Tel	Secretary
Hawick Golf Club	0450 72293	G. A. Rennie
Minto Golf Club	0450 87220	I. R. Welch
St Boswells Golf Club	0835 22359	G. B. Ovens
Dunbar Golf Club	0368 62317	A. J. Poole
Gifford Golf Club	062 081 267	D. A. Fantom
North Berwick Golf Club	0620 2135	R. Russell
Hon Comp Edin Golfers Muirfield	0620 842123	Gp Capt J. Prideaux
The Gullanes	0620 843115	Mrs S. Montgomery
Luffness New Golf Club	0620 843114	Lt Col J. Tedford
Bruntsfield Links GS	031 336 2006	M. W. Walton
Royal Burgess GS	031 339 2012	J. P. Audis
Dalmahoy Golf Club	031 333 2055	Mrs I. Auld
St Andrews Golf Courses Links Management Commtee	0334 75757	A. Beveridge
Crail Golfing Society	0333 50278	Mrs G. Penhale
Golf House Club (Elie)	0333 330327	G. A. Forgie
Lundin Links Golf Club	0333 320202	A. C. McBride
Leven Links Golf Club	0333 23509	M. Innes
Scotscraig Golf Club	0382 552515	K. Gourlay
Glenrothes Golf Club	0592 754561	L. D. Dalrymple
Dunfermline Golf Club	0383 723534	J. A. Gillies
Ladybank Golf Club	0337 30320	D. Downie
Carnoustie Golf Club	0241 53789	E. J. C. Smith
Moniefieth Golf Links	0382 532767	J. A. R. Fraser
Panmure Golf Club	0241 53120	Capt J. C. Ray
Montrose Golf Club	0674 72932	Mrs M. Stewart
Downfield Golf Club	0382 825595	R. S. Imrie
Blairgowrie Golf Club	0250 2622	N/A
Pitlochry Golf Club	0796 2114	D. C. M. McKenzie
Gleneagles Hotel	076 46 3543	T. A. K. Younger
Royal Aberdeen Golf Club	0224 702571	G. F. Webster
Murcar Golf Club	0224 704345	R. Matthews
Fraseborough Golf Club	0346 28287	J. W. Love
Royal Tarlair Golf Club	0261 32548	Mrs E. Black
Duff House Royal Golf Club	026 12 2062	M. Pierog
Moray Golf Club	034 381 2018	J. Hamilton
Forres Golf Club	0309 72949	G. A. Reaper
Elgin Golf Club	0343 2338	W. McKay
Nairn Golf Club	0667 52103	D. Patrick
Boat of Garten Golf Club	047 983 351	J. R. Ingram
Portrose & Rosemarkie GC	0381 20529	Mrs M. Collier
Muir of Ord Golf Club	0463 870825	Mrs C. Muir
Strathpeffer Spa	0997 21219	N. Roxburgh

Royal Dornoch Golf Club	0862 810219	A. S. Kinnear
Wick Golf Club	0955 2726	Mrs M. Abernethy
Thurso Golf Club	0847 63807	G. Bailey
Reay Golf Club	084 781 288	N. H. McDonald
Western Gailes Golf Club	0294 311649	J. A. Clement
Glasgow Gailes Golf Club	0294 311347	I. A. D. Mann
Kilmarnock Barassie GC	0292 311077	R. L. Bryce
Royal Troon Golf Club	0292 311555	J. D. Montgomerie
Prestwick Golf Club	0292 77404	D. Donaldson
Prestwick St Nicholas GC	0292 77608	J. R. Leishman
Turnberry Hotel	0655 31000	C. L. Rouse
Blackwaterfoot Golf Course	077068 226	J. R. Liddell
Lamlash Golf Club	07706 296	J. Henderson
Brodick Golf Club	0770 2349	H. M. Macrae
Machrihanish Golf Club	0586 81213	Mrs A. Anderson
Machrie Golf Club	0496 2310	M. Macpherson
Greenock Golf Club	0475 20793	E. J. Black
Gourock Golf Club	0475 31001	C. M. Campbell
Largs Golf Club	0475 673594	F. Gilmour
Haggs Castle Golf Club	041 427 0480	A. R. C. Alexander
Pollock Golf Club	041 632 1080	A. Mathison Boyd
Portpatrick Golf Club	0776 81273	J. A. Horberry
St Medan Golf Club	098 87 358	D. O'Neill
Southerness Golf Club	0387 88677	W. T. Train

Golfing holidays
A number of tourist organizations organize specialist holidays. The Scottish Tourist Board, 23 Ravelston Terrace, Edinburgh, tel 031 332 2433 will send full details.

Ornithology: for a number of reasons, including terrain, climate and vast tracts of land both unpopulated and remote, Scotland's birdlife is unsurpassed. Some regions harbour birds so rare many people have never even heard of them. There are dozens of nature reserves and bird sanctuaries all over the country. Fair Isle, staging post on a number of migratory routes, is probably the best place for serious ornithologists. For details, write to Fair Isle Lodge and Bird Observatory, Fair Isle, tel 03512 258. Other ornithological information is available from RSPB Scottish Office, 17 Regent Terrace, Edinburgh, tel 031 556 5624.

Pony trekking is a pleasant way of seeing the country and you don't have to be an experienced rider. There are hundreds of pony-trekking centres, offering a choice of day trekking or trekking and camping. The local tourist information centres will give you addresses: most tourist maps mark them with a horseshoe. The Scottish Tourist Board publishes a leaflet called *Pony Trekking and Riding Centres in Scotland*.

Shinty or Shinny, is Scotland's version of Irish Hurling and is said to derive from cries used in the game: shin ye, shin t'ye. It's like hockey, with a leather ball and curved sticks.

Skiing resorts, with groomed runs and lift networks, are developing rapidly but first-timers should note that picture-postcard conditions are less common in Scotland than the Alps. At times only the more experienced skier will enjoy this sport, when the slopes are icy, balding and pitted with rocks, visibility is nil and a piercing wind invades even the most thermal of clothing. The main centres are at: Cairngorm, Glencoe, Glenshee and The Lecht, with cross-country as well as downhill skiing. The Scottish Tourist Board booklet, *Ski Holidays in Scotland*, gives details of the many skiing packages on offer and you can book in London, at 19 Cockspur Street, London SW1Y 5BL, tel 071 930 8661.

There are dry-ski slopes at: Hillend, in the Pentlands, just outside Edinburgh— the largest in Britain—Aviemore, Glasgow, Aberdeen, Bearsden, Cairnwell and Polmont.

Shooting and stalking are ideal for trigger-happy sportsmen, with farmland, mixed woodland and moorland, and Scotland has a long tradition of good game management. The estuaries and marshes provide excellent scope for wildfowlers, and there are plenty of *Monarchs of the Glen*. Stalking, for the uninitiated, involves spending all day wriggling through wet undergrowth until your prey is within range and then, at a signal from the keeper, missing it, or wounding it and spending the night following it to administer the coup de grâce. Game-shooting species include pheasants, snipe, grey partridge, wood-cock, grouse, capercailzie and ptarmigan. Permitted wildfowl species include many varieties of duck and geese. Rough shooting is for wood pigeon, rabbit and hare. Deer species include red deer, roe, fallow and sika. All other species of wildlife, both bird and mammal, are strictly protected in Scotland by the Wildlife and Countryside Act.

No game shooting is allowed on Sundays and a certificate is required by anyone owning or using either a rifle or a shotgun. Before you shoot game you must get a game licence, which is available in all main and branch post offices throughout the country. Some hotels will arrange shooting and stalking and local tourist boards will advise on contacting estates and on shooting seasons.

Surfing in Scotland

We are grateful to **Chris Hines**, *an experienced surfer, freelance sports writer and former associate editor of* Surf Scene *for the following personal account. Chris also wrote on surfing in the* Cadogan Guide to Bali.

Surfing in Scotland hardly conjures up images of Hawaiian shores and hot weather, but the north of Scotland can lay claim to some of the best surfing waves in Europe. In fact, the European Amateur Surfing Championships were held here in Thurso, in 1981.

Any exposed part of Scotland's long coastline has the potential for excellent waves; but the northernmost section, from Bettyhill almost to John O'Groats, has a reputation for the most consistent swells and variety of breaks. There are waves to suit everyone from gentle beachbreaks to massive reefs, point breaks and river mouths. This is wild-frontier surfing against stunning back-drops of mountains and castles.

The water is a slightly off-putting brown, but don't be alarmed because it's only coloured by peat washed down from the hills. Not surprisingly there are very few local surfers but those there are are really friendly.

Walking: There are coastal footpaths, nature trails, woodland trails, city strolls and long-distance footpaths.

Long-distance footpaths include the **West Highland Way,** which runs for 95 miles from Milngavie on the outskirts of Glasgow to Fort William on the south end of the Great Glen. It includes a marvellous range of lowland and highland scenery, on the old drove roads, forestry tracks, an old military road and a railway track bed.

The **Speyside Way** runs for 30 miles, from Tugnet to Ballindalloch, then a further 15 miles to Tomintoul, with splendid and very varied scenery along the route.

The **Southern Upland Way** runs from Portpatrick in Dumfries and Galloway, east to Cockburnspath in the Border Region, and is 212 miles long. It is signposted and well marked all the way and there are leaflets to make it more interesting.

Ski lifts for walkers are available at Cairngorm, Glencoe and Glenshee. These chair-lifts are open for hill walkers in the non-skiing season only and give easy access to some of the higher terrain.

Scotland: Walks and Trails, £2.80, gives details of a selection of walks needing no special equipment and suitable for children. *Scotland: Hillwalking* gives details of over 60 more difficult, higher level walks. Both can be got from Scottish Holidays, Telelink, 56 Belhaven Road, Wishaw M12 7BN.

Water sports are available all over the country, including sailing, windsurfing, waterskiing and swimming. Coastal resorts invariably have sailing clubs where you can get tuition and hire boats and equipment. There are a large number of inland water sport centres on the lochs. For full details get the *Scotland Holiday Afloat* booklet from the Scottish Tourist Board or tel 0382 21555 or 0577 62816.

Leisure centres are springing up all over Scotland. They include facilities for playing squash, tennis, badminton, bowls, table tennis, ice hockey, etc. Some also provide aerobic dancing, judo, karate, skating and a whole lot more.

Tourist offices will tell you which centre is open in your area.

Glen Orchy

29

National Trust for Scotland

Many of Scotland's historic buildings and conserved land are under the care of the National Trust for Scotland (NTS), a charity formed in 1931 to promote the preservation of the country's heritage. Over 100 properties, including castles, small houses, islands, mountains, coastline and gardens come under the protection of the NTS, visited by more than 1.5 million people each year. Most are open from April to October, and admission charges vary. Membership for £13.50 a year admits one person free to all NTS properties, and to 300 National Trust properties in England, Wales and Northern Ireland. For further information, write to the National Trust for Scotland Head Office, 5 Charlotte Square, Edinburgh EH2 4DU, tel 031 226 5922.

Historic Scotland

Historic Scotland is a division of the Scottish Development Department, responsible for the care and upkeep of many of the country's historic ruins, buildings and sites.

Some castles and historic houses open to the public are privately owned: each has its own opening times and admission charges. Wherever possible, this book gives an idea of opening dates but these change from year to year and should always be checked if possible.

There is an 'open to view' ticket which entitles you to free entrance to 563 places of historic interest: castles, abbeys, stately homes, famous gardens, etc., in Scotland, England, Wales and Northern Ireland. These can be bought from major tourist information centres. Tickets are valid for a month, starting from the date of your first visit. Included with the ticket is a large illustrated map showing all the places together with information about opening times and free or reduced entry to many museums, as well as discounts at certain museum shops.

Americans who are flying with British Airways can get a voucher for one of these when they buy their air ticket. This can be exchanged at the tourist information centres at Prestwick Airport, Waverley Market in Edinburgh, or Murray's Green in Jedburgh.

It is worth remembering that many castles, historic houses and smaller museums close for the winter, as do some hotels.

Where to stay

The choice of accommodation in Scotland is enormous, ranging from (a few) superb, luxury hotels to simple bed and breakfasts, or self-catering. The price is not always a reliable guide. The accommodation guides in the local brochures give full details of price and facilities, and many give photographs. As already mentioned, tourists should always try and get one of these publications for each area they want to visit.

As little as £10 a night can buy bed and breakfast in a clean house, with a warm welcome and a thumping good breakfast. £120 can buy a night in a four-poster bed or £150, a suite with a jacuzzi. You can rent a whole house or cottage for as little as £60 a week, or over £600. There are an enormous number of 'packages' on offer, including fishing, golfing, skiing, pony trekking, shooting, stalking and boating. Specialist holidays include heritage trails, whisky trails, castle trails, and Taste of Scotland trails. Details of all these are given in the brochures. See below for the Scottish Tourist Board's Accommodation Gradings.

Prices often vary seasonally: single rooms are usually more expensive, per head, than double. You can get good value in a hotel for as little as £15 a night in some areas. A static caravan costs from £40 a week upwards, and camp sites charge from about £3 a night for visiting caravans. Camp site facilities vary enormously. Some are good, others are not, but often the scenery makes up for primitive plumbing. The one at Braemar is excellent.

Many bed and breakfast places serve an evening meal and all hotels provide full service.

In the more rural areas, and indeed in the towns, don't be put off by the lack of en suite bathrooms in the smaller hotels. What they lack in modern facilities is invariably made up for in the friendly hospitality of the staff. Very often 'public bathroom' means sole use of a bathroom across the passage.

Price categories

Prices change frequently. In this guide accommodation is loosely graded in three categories, based on the price of bed and breakfast for one person in a single room—double rooms are almost always cheaper per person—as charged in 1991. Many hotels, however, do special bargain breaks, so it is well worth enquiring about these.

Expensive
You won't see much change from £60 at the bottom end of this range, and the ceiling is high.

Medium/moderate
From about £30–50 should buy you a very comfortable night.

Cheap
As little as £10 a night, if you are lucky, up to about £25 and some of the cheapest are often surprisingly good.

Scottish Tourist Board accommodation gradings

An impartial team of inspectors, employed by the Scottish Tourist Board, visits hotels, guest houses, bed and breakfast, and self-catering establishments, to assess their quality. They award classifications ranging from 'Listed' to five crowns, and gradings from 'Approved' to 'Highly Commended,' depending on the standard and facilities. Full details can be obtained from the Scottish Tourist Board, 23 Ravelston Terrace, Edinburgh EH4 3EU, tel 031 332 2433. Visitors should be aware that these awards are based on a set range of standards and facilities such as: TV, shoe-cleaning kit, full-length mirror, trouser press, luggage stand, hospitality tray, etc., as well as the more obvious requirements such as heat and towels. They do not apply to character and soul. It is therefore possible to opt for a Highly Commended, five-crown hotel only to find yourself in an sweltering, double-glazed bedroom crammed with gadgets and electric goodies, totally lacking in atmosphere. Equally, an old fashioned, slightly shabby ex-shooting

31

lodge, as full of highland character and hospitality as you could ever wish for, with blazing log fires instead of central heating, pure cotton sheets, early-morning tea brought to you, and delicious home cooking, may be excluded from the Scottish Tourist Board's list because of its lack of tangible 'Facilities'.

As well as the individual publications you can get free from Area Tourist Centres, the Scottish Tourist Board publish a number of useful brochures covering the whole country, with details of accommodation, sports, special holidays etc.

Youth hostels

There are 80 youth hostels in Scotland, marked on most maps by a triangle. They fall into three grades, A, B and C, some having central heating, hot showers, carpets, etc., and all offering dormitory accommodation and self-catering facilities. Anyone over the age of five may use a youth hostel. For full details, write to SYHA, 7 Glebe Crescent, Stirling FK8 2JA, tel 0786 72821.

Eating out

You can choose between 'haute cuisine' that will satisfy any gourmet; good plain cooking at a reasonable price; and fast-food.

In the cities, meals are served at fairly flexible hours, but in smaller places you should aim to have lunch between 12.30 and 2, and dinner between about 7 and 9. If you know you will be late it is wise to make arrangements in advance. 'High tea' is an alternative to dinner, usually served between 4.30–6.30, and is an extremely sustaining meal consisting of a main course (usually fried) followed by bread, cake, biscuits, etc., washed down by cups of tea—a very British meal.

Some of the country's best restaurants are to be found tucked away in out-of-the-way places. These are mentioned in the relevant sections within this book. Examples are: The Peat Inn, Fife, La Potinière, Gullane, Champany Inn, Linlithgow, and Blairfindy Lodge, Glenlivet.

National dishes

> *Fair fa' your honest, sonsie face,*
> *Great chieftain o' the puddin-race!*
> *Aboon them a' ye tak your place, Painch, tripe, or thairm:*
> *Weel are ye wordy of a grace, as lang's my arm.*

> —from *Address to a Haggis*, by Robert Burns

Scotland has an unmatched reputation for salmon, both fresh and smoked. The development of fish farming has increased the availability but it has to be said that 'wild' salmon is unquestionably more delicious than that which has been reared in a farm, which tends to be rather fatty.

Apart from the salmon, national dishes include trout, sea fish, shell fish, game, beef and lamb. Almost without exception you should go for these served in the traditional ways without too much 'dolling up'. Poached salmon with mayonnaise, new potatoes and cucumber; a freshly caught mackerel, fried so that its skin is crisp and curling, with wedges of lemon and watercress; an Aberdeen Angus fillet steak, medium-rare, an inch thick, with a green salad of just lettuce, chives and a hint of garlic; well-hung roast grouse with game chips, fresh petit pois, fried breadcrumbs, bread sauce, and gravy. These will linger on the taste buds as well as in the memory long after any dish wrapped up in an exotic sauce and given a pretentious name.

Everyone should try haggis—if only once. It is made of the heart, liver and lungs of a sheep, mixed with suet, oatmeal and onion, highly seasoned and sewn into the sheep's stomach. Traditionally, it is eaten with 'bashed neeps' (mashed turnip or swede) and washed down with neat whisky. Try black pudding, too: its unusual flavour is strangely addictive.

Arbroath smokies are fresh haddock, dry salted and smoked in pairs; a delicate, mild flavour makes them particularly delicious and the best way to eat them is cold, with brown wholemeal bread and butter, a generous squeeze of lemon juice and plenty of freshly ground black pepper.

Porridge is no longer a national habit but you can always get it in hotels if you ask. The popular myth that Scotsmen eat their porridge with salt, standing up or walking about, is quickly disproved when you discover how many of them sit down and tuck into it heaped with sugar and cream and sometimes, even treacle!

Scottish cheeses are various and worth pursuing. Crowdie is unique to Scotland, a creamed cottage cheese, made from skimmed milk. Dunlop cheese, originally made in an Ayrshire village of the same name, is now also made in Orkney, Arran and Islay. Caboc is a rich double-cream cheese rolled in pinhead oatmeal. Galic and Hramsa are both soft cream cheeses flavoured with wild garlic and herbs. Pentland and Lothian cheeses are like Camembert and Brie.

Oatcakes are unsweetened biscuits made with oatmeal. Brand-named oatcakes can be dull but local and home-made varieties that crumble and melt in the mouth are delicious. Best eaten with cheese, honey or marmalade.

Shortbread originated in Scotland and is known all over the world. You will find many local variations of the standard buttery biscuit: Yetholm Bannock, for instance, a very rich shortbread with crystallized ginger, to be found in the Borders.

Dundee cake is a rich, dark fruit cake with split almonds on top, indispensable for cold, wet picnics.

Soups include Cock-a-leekie, made with chicken and leeks; Scotch Broth, made with mutton stock and barley; Cullen Skink—delicious—made with smoked haddock, and Partan Bree, made with crab.

Scotch pies are to be found all over the country; small round pies made of hot water pastry filled with minced meat, eaten hot.

Bridies are pies made with a round of pastry folded over, filled with meat, sometimes padded with potatoes and vegetables.

Cranachan, if properly made, is memorable; double cream, and sometimes crowdie, is mixed with toasted oatmeal, sweetened and eaten with fresh soft fruit, preferably raspberries—another of Scotland's specialities.

The Scottish Tourist Board brings out a *Taste of Scotland* booklet every year offering details of over 200 hotels and restaurants specializing in good Scottish cooking.

Drinking in Scotland

Inspiring, bold John Barleycorn!
What dangers thou canst make us scorn!
Wi' tippeny, [ale] we fear nae evil;
Wi' usquabae, [whisky] we'll face the Devil!

—from *Tam o' Shanter*, by Robert Burns

Among the myths that need to be taken with a pinch of salt is the whisky myth. The average canny Scot will go for the two bottles of cut-price blended whisky that he can get for the price of one bottle of vintage malt. On the whole, except among the very rich, malt whisky is kept for special occasions, bought as presents for other people—or exported. There are hundreds of brands and every connoisseur will swear to the unquestionable superiority of his particular fancy. However, experiments involving the transfer of a 'favourite' malt into a bottle with a rival label will often prove that it is the eye rather than the taste buds that dictate preference.

Traditionally, malt whisky should be drunk neat, without ice—any additions are believed to spoil the flavour. No other country in the world has the essential ingredients for that unique taste that makes Scotland's whisky so special: a blend of snow melt, peaty water, and carefully malted barley. A true Scotsman drinks whisky, or asks for 'a dram'; he will never ask for 'Scotch'—unless he is abroad and in danger of being served with a foreign imposter.

Drambuie is a whisky liquer, very drinkable for those who enjoy 'stickies'. Gingermac is a delicious mixture of whisky and ginger wine which slips down very easily on cold, outdoor occasions.

Scotsmen prefer to do their drinking seriously, in bars, though chic wine bars and English-type pubs are mushrooming in the towns. You may hear, in a true bar, someone ordering 'a pint of heavy and a chaser'. This will turn out to be a pint of bitter and a dram of whisky—the accepted way to spin out the precious *uisge beatha*—Gaelic for 'water of life'. And the dram is not sipped and savoured, it is tossed down in a single reviving gulp. In the old days, when the licensing laws were very restrictive, there was no time for leisurely drinking.

Now, licensing laws in Scotland permit public houses to stay open for 12 hours a day or longer with special extensions, but not all of them choose to do so. Generally, a bar will be open from 11 am to 2.30, and from 5 to about 11, with reduced hours on Sunday. Most city centre bars will stay open till at least midnight. Residents in licensed hotels can buy drinks at any time. Minors (children under 18) may not be served drink in a public house or restaurant, nor may they be sold alcohol in a shop. Some establishments provide special family rooms where children can join their parents, but they must not drink alcohol here. Landlords stand to lose their licences if they break the law in this respect.

Most of the distilleries are on Speyside, northeast of Aviemore, in the north, or on the islands of Islay and Jura and a large number of them run guided tours showing the process of whisky making, culminating in a free dram. The Malt Whisky Trail, on Speyside, is a 70-mile voyage of discovery, taking in eight distilleries. Guided tours last about an hour and you can get details from the tourist information centres.

Sláinte, pronounced Slarnge, is Gaelic for 'cheers'.

34

Part II

TOPICS

Climate

A popular postcard shows someone sitting in a deck chair under an umbrella in pouring rain, with the caption 'Having plenty of weather here in Scotland'. In fact, with a bit of luck, you can return from a holiday in Scotland with a deep tan not entirely inflicted by the wind, and a packet of photographs showing idyllic blue skies and brilliant sunshine.

Unpredictability is the main drawback. When the weather is good, there is no country more perfect. When the weather is bad and people struggle against piercing winds and relentless rain and a damp chill pervades to the marrow, Siberia would be preferable. It is worth remembering that places in the north of the country have an average of 18 to 20 hours of daylight in the summer, and resorts on the east coast are noted for their hours of sunshine. In the far north, in the middle of the summer, it is never completely dark. In spite of the Gulf Stream, whose warm waters are alleged to lick the western shores of Scotland, the sea is gelid.

In general, the west is wettish, and mild enough in some coastal regions, to support palm trees and tropical vegetation. The east is drier with a more bracing climate and colder winds. (Edinburgh has almost exactly the same rainfall as London and Rome.) Winter, in the Highlands, when the precipitation is mainly snow, can be very beautiful, with clear skies and sun, though temperatures may seldom rise above freezing.

An unfortunate side-product of the moist, mild weather in the west is the 'midge', a particularly virulent breed of gnat unequalled in persistence anywhere else in the British Isles. Grown men have been reduced to gibbering wrecks under their vicious attacks.

They are at their worst in warm, humid conditions; they hide when it is windy and sometimes, though not always, in very bright sunshine. Anyone contemplating camping or picnicking during the midge season should have lots of the strongest possible repellent. In truth, midges can completely ruin an outdoor holiday; even the natives retreat indoors when they are marauding. The only good thing about them is they won't follow a boat off-shore.

Religious differences

In the Highlands and Islands, where communities tend to be slow to change, there are areas predominantly Catholic, untouched by the Reformation, while others, following the laird, became Protestant. On the whole, Catholics and Protestants live together perfectly happily with few of the sectarian problems experienced in Ireland. The football field proves an occasional exception, such as when fans of the two Glasgow teams, traditionally Catholic Celtic and Protestant Rangers, meet. Sometimes, too, an innovation conflicts with the strict Sabbatarian beliefs and practices of a small proportion of Presbyterians and invariably the media manage to stir up an 'incident'.

In the Outer Hebrides, South Uist, Eriskay and Barra are almost entirely Catholic. In their belief God belongs to every day and Sunday is for celebration, both in church and out. North Uist, Harris and Lewis are Presbyterian and the most rigid Protestants in Britain. Their interpretation of the Fourth Commandment is stringently enforced by the Lord's Day Observance Society, who exert moral, social and political pressure. Sunday is for long sermons in church, full of the threat of damnation; for reading the Bible and holy tracts; for dark clothes and solemn faces. No work must be done, not even cooking; the washing must come in off the line; the fishing boats must lie at anchor and swings are padlocked.

Until recently, no ferries ran to the islands on Sundays. Then Caledonian MacBrayne announced a changed schedule including some Sunday sailings. The uproar was clamorous and still goes on. There are huffings and puffings and threats of barricades and everyone has sent everyone else to Coventry. It will all be forgotten soon, as it was when the same thing happened in Skye some years ago, but until it is, relations between north and south are uncomfortable.

Running in tandem with this dispute, there was friction over a new £12 million school, built at tax-payers' expense, on the island of Benbecula, mid-way between the Catholic south and Protestant north and serving both. The predominantly Protestant Western Isles Council would not employ supervisory staff on Sundays, so no one could use the school's leisure facilities—swimming pool, cafeteria, games hall, library, etc. Catholics protested that their beliefs allowed them to have fun on Sundays and they saw no reason why Sabbatarian rules should prevent them. The situation was satisfactorily resolved in the end, but not without lasting damage to the hitherto dignified, laissez-faire attitudes that enabled such extreme creeds to live side by side in harmony.

The Free Presbyterian Church of Scotland (Wee Frees) is a tiny, fundamentalist sect who believe that the Pope is 'Antichrist' and the Mass ... 'the most blasphemous form of religious worship that Satan ever invented; an offence unto God and destructive of the souls of men.' In 1989, Britain's Lord Chancellor, Lord Mackay of Clashfern, a member of this strict sect, was castigated by fellow members of his congregation because he attended requiem masses for two of his Catholic friends. The Free Church Synod suspended him from his position as a senior Elder of the Kirk, and from Communion. Lord Mackay, who once said his church gave 'the most tender love that has ever been described' was forced to resign from it.

Clans and tartans

The Scottish clan system was once an integral part of the Highlands and Islands. Every member of the clan bore the name of the chief, whether related by blood or by allegiance, and each was an equal member of the clan family (Mac means son of). The chief was the father, ruler and judge and the strength of the clan lay in his justice, kindness and wisdom, and in the loyalty of the members of the clan, to him and to one another. Rents were mostly paid in kind or man-rent, and in return for his patronage and protection, the chief could call on his people at any time to form an army and fight for him.

It is known that Highlanders wore some sort of brightly coloured, striped and checked material as far back as the 13th century, though whether the designs, or 'setts', were related to clans or to territories is not known for certain.

The Suppression of the Highlands after Culloden in 1746 broke up clans, forbade tartan and led to the death of the clan system. During the 36 years Highland dress was banned, many of the old setts were lost or forgotten. It was not until Hanoverian George IV appeared at Holyrood in 1822 in an astonishing Highland outfit, that the fashion for tartan was revived. In a wave of enthusiasm, a large number of tartans were hastily designed, and adopted by clans who had for many years been kindred in name only. They were also keenly worn by Lowlanders whose ancestors would have died rather than be seen in Highland dress. It is these relatively modern patterns that make up most of today's enormous range of tartans which can be seen all over the world, not only in cloth but also adorning luggage, footwear and a staggering range of knick-knacks. The average Scotsman doesn't stride over his native hills swathed in tartan. On the whole, kilts are kept for ceremonial or formal occasions and a great many Scotsmen don't even own one.

Clan feelings still run strong, especially in the veins of expatriates, but the clan name is now no more than an umbrella for historical museums, annual gatherings and ceremonial, with the chief as a figurehead, appearing in a tartan costume redolent of moth balls.

The mystique that has grown up round clan tartans is put into perspective by the apocryphal story of the irate chieftain, towering over one of a coach party, visiting his ancestral castle:

'By what right are you wearing my tartan, my man?'
'By the ri' o' purrchis, at fifteen pounds a yard, my lord.'

See also section on Clans at the end of the book.

The Highland Clearances

The Clearances are an emotive subject and it has to be remembered that the first emigration ship sailed out of Fort William as early as 1773, almost 20 years before *Bliadhna nan Caorach*—the year of the sheep. There were several contributory reasons for the depopulation of the Highlands after Culloden. Some Jacobites who had escaped execution found it expedient to go abroad for a few years; others were transported. Many Catholics, unable to practise their religion publicly at home, sought liberty across the ocean. The suppression of the Highlands and the breaking up of the clan system deprived chiefs of their hereditary status as patriarchs, and many drifted south to become London Scots. Away from the womb of the clan and the benefits of feudality, however, they felt the pinch financially. Vast, infertile estates in the north, overpopulated by impoverished peasants, brought in little or no revenue. Rents paid in kind were of little use to those trying to keep up with society in fashionable Assembly Rooms or pay off gambling debts in gentlemen's clubs. Sheep farmers from the south offered good rent for sheep-runs in the north but they wanted land free of people. Highland landowners, desperate for money, began to evict their tenants. Some built resettlement towns and villages for them and established new livelihoods such as fishing; some merely served eviction notices and employed agents to enforce them; some offered to assist with fares to new countries. Hundreds of crofting communities—those which relied entirely on their smallholdings for a living—broke up and scattered. Those who didn't emigrate flocked to the cities in the hope of finding work or to settlements, mainly on the coast, where the land was unsuitable for sheep.

Meanwhile, in the islands, landlords basked in a false prosperity from the kelp industry. Seaweed, of which there was an inexhaustible supply, was collected after each tide, burned in kilns, processed into valuable fertilizer and exported. All that was needed was a huge labour force to cut, carry and burn it. Island proprietors with an eye to the main chance offered tiny plots of land to dispossessed crofters from the mainland. They charged high rent and deliberately ensured each tenant had not enough land for self-sufficiency, forcing them to work at the kelp. By 1812 the islands were crammed with people entirely dependent on kelp for their living. After the Napoleonic Wars, import duty was abolished and cheap foreign kelp flooded the market: prices plummeted; people starved. Proprietors and politicians, faced with the problem of destitute multitudes, offered inducements to encourage emigration and many people went.

The final blow came in 1846. The potato famine which had already decimated Ireland, drifted across the sea in wind-born spores and descended on Scotland, half of whose population lived on potatoes. For the already starving Highlanders and Islanders, the effect was catastrophic. Many of those who had managed to stay on, often surviving several evictions, were now forced to join their compatriots in Canada, America, Australia and New Zealand. By the end of the 19th century, the rural Highlands and Islands were almost deserted.

Gaelic

Gaelic is still the first language in the Outer Hebrides, but even there, with an influx of non-Gaelic speakers, the children are growing up speaking English among themselves. Elsewhere it is no longer a living language, though it is self-consciously paraded in some places, often by people who themselves are converts, to impress visitors. Recently, a crop of very grand new notices appeared in some of the islands, proclaiming place names in Gaelic. They must have cost a fortune: local people don't need them, and visitors can neither understand, nor pronounce them.

Gaelic stems from the Goidelic branch of Celtic languages which were an offshoot from the Indo-European language widely used in early times. Scottish Gaelic became a distinct dialect separate from Irish around the 13th century, and there are still many similarities. There are Gaelic colleges and Gaelic slots on Scottish radio and Gaelic publications. It is an almost impossible language to 'pick up' by ear and eye because the spoken word bears little resemblance to the written.

If you want to hear Gaelic, go to church in the Outer Isles on a Sunday when there isn't a visiting priest from the mainland. Locals are too courteous to speak it among themselves when they know that they have a non-Gaelic speaker in their midst.

Crofting

A croft is a smallholding in the Highlands, with a few acres, as many sheep as the land will support, sometimes a few cows and poultry. If there is arable land it will be tilled. In the old days, *feannagan*, or inappropriately named lazy-beds, were dug, for potatoes, involving much hard work, deep digging and carting heavy creels of seaweed for fertilizer. Some of the work on the croft is still done communally—sheep-dipping and shearing for instance, and cutting the peat and haymaking.

Peat is still used as fuel in some areas. Composed of partially rotted vegetation, compressed in waterlogged conditions in temperate or cold climates, it takes 3000 years to form a depth of one foot, so peat-bogs are getting scarce. It is cut in the spring, in oblong slabs with a special digger and stacked in situ, on end like miniature wigwams, until dry. In a wet summer the peat can still be lying late into the year. Once dry, it is carted down to the house, often some distance away, and built into neat beehives. As recently as the 1970s, hay was cut by hand, with scythes, and it is still turned with pitchforks until dry.

The family dwelling is the croft-house—often mistakenly called the croft. Less than 50 years ago, many Highlanders still lived in a *taigh dubh* or Black House, now almost extinct except as a folk museum or byre. It had thick, double walls, about six foot high, made of local stone and packed with earth and rubble. Unlined on the inside, it had rounded corners, no gables, and a reed- or heather-thatched roof anchored by boulders tied to ropes of plaited heather. Inside, the furniture was functional: a dresser, box-beds, a bench, stools, rat-proof meal chests, coffers and a spinning wheel. A peat fire was laid on a stone slab on the earthen floor in the middle of the room, the smoke escaping out of a hole in the thatch. Light came from a *cruisgein*—a lamp fuelled with fish liver oil burning on a wick of plaited rushes. Even within this century, in some island communities, the beasts shared the family house, penned at one end with the floor sloping down towards them and the effluent running out through holes in the wall.

The crofter is the owner or tenant of the croft. Most crofters have a subsidiary job as well: fishing, building or public works. Since the Clearances (see p. 37), the Crofting Commission has kept very careful control of crofters' rights.

Ceilidh

Ceilidh, pronounced kayly, is a Gaelic word meaning visit. In winter, when nights were long, crofters used to gather in one of the houses when darkness fell, packed in round the central fire. One of the older members, often a bard or musician, acted as the master of ceremonies and everyone was expected to contribute to the entertainment. The women knitted or spun, men repaired fishing nets or whittled wood; everyone listened. Stories, songs, poems, proverbs and legends were recited, passing their history, folklore and tradition from one generation to the next. Their music stirred the soul: mouth-music, straight from the heart; Gaelic songs; pipe, harp and fiddle music. Stories reached down into the roots of everyone's existence. Children grew up steeped in the past and could tell you who their great, great, great grand-uncle was and whose sweetheart he had run off with. The practice is dying now, thanks to television. Nowadays *ceilidhs* tend to be commercial shows, staged in halls and hotels.

Piping

Few people are indifferent to the sound of the bagpipes: they love it or they hate it. For those who love it, their passion will extend even to listening in a tiny, low room, where the sound is so intense that it takes over the entire consciousness. Light pipe music includes jolly reels, strathspeys, jigs and marches. *Pibroch* is the classical music of the bagpipe. Every piece, and they can be very long, is intricate, with a basic melody or groundwork which has three or four variations, finishing with the original theme.

Sorcerers and superstition

Communities lived in terror of Devil-worshippers and sorcerers, whom they believed could control the elements and cause plague, famine, drought, miscarriage and crop failure.

In the Middle Ages, fertile Celtic minds were fed by inherited paganism, folklore, ignorance and religion. This was particularly so in Galloway and the Highlands, where remote communities were separated by vast tracts of moor, hill and loch, far from urban influence, schools and the steely eye of the church. Every act, from pre-birth to death was hedged with portent, and the power of evil had to be propitiated. Offerings of food, herbal potions, benisons, gestures, talismans and rites were employed in the hope of warding off supernatural ills. Curiously shaped stones had magic properties.

Certain lakes and wells were thought to be especially efficacious. Pilgrims brought their sick and their petitions and tied votive offerings to trees and bushes. People still go to some of the *Clootie Wells* as they are called. There is one at Culloden where coachloads of people arrive on or around May Day, the Celtic Beltane, and throw money into the well. Superstition or not, when the Highland Division was being pounded on the beaches of Dunkirk in the summer of 1940, the Culloden Clootie Well attracted throngs of petitioners. Another, on a back road in Ross-shire, is so festooned with squalid old rags it looks like a tinkers' tip, yet even today, no one removes them for fear of reprisals from the god of the well.

It was by no means just ignorant peasants who believed in sorcery. Macbeth's encounter with the three witches was not a figment of Shakespeare's rich imagination. His source for the story was Holinshed, the 16th-century chronicler, who describes 'three women in strange and wild apparell, resembling creatures of eldritch world', who 'vanished immediatlie' having delivered their prophecies. King James VI/I was terrified of witches. He believed his political enemies hired them to try to kill him and comforted himself with the theory that the sacred oil with which he was anointed at his coronation made him immune from their sorcery. One of his enemies was half-mad Francis Stewart, Earl of Bothwell, nephew of Mary's Bothwell, commonly believed to be the Satanic overlord of several covens of witches. When the king nearly drowned in a freak storm off the Bass Rock, he claimed to have seen one of Bothwell's covens sailing round his foundering ship in a sieve. He ordered their arrest and they were discovered in the graveyard of the Auld Kirk in North Berwick, having an orgy presided over by their 'Devil' Bothwell. James attended their mass trial and wrote a learned treatise on witchcraft.

The last execution for witchcraft in Scotland was believed to be in Dornoch in 1727, when a mother was found guilty of riding upon her daughter, who had been transformed into a pony and shod by the Devil. She was burned in a barrel of pitch having first warmed her cold feet at the fire that was to consume her.

Seers

Second sight, *taibh-searachd* in Gaelic, goes hand in hand with sorcery and among the many seers who emerged from the Celtic mists were Thomas the Rhymer and the Brahan Seer. Thomas, born in 1220, lived for nearly 80 years, earning himself the title True Thomas. He predicted the death of Alexander III and the Battle of Bannockburn. Traditionally, he had a passionate affair with the Fairy Queen and went off to live with her for three years in Elfland, deep in the Eildon Hills.

The Brahan Seer, Coinneach Odhar, is an enigmatic figure from the 17th century, known throughout Scotland for the uncanny accuracy of many of his prophecies about the Highlands, some of which are still to be fulfilled. He fell asleep, so it is said, on an enchanted hillside and when he woke he was clutching a stone with a hole in it, through which he could only see the truth and the future. Among the things he foretold that have already happened are the depopulation of the Highlands, the demise of crofting, the arrival of rich landowners, and the making of the Caledonian Canal. He said that when it was possible to cross the River Ness in Inverness, dryshod, in five places a terrible disaster would strike the world. There were four bridges over the Ness until a temporary suspension bridge was erected to replace an older one about to be demolished. This fifth bridge was opened at the end of August 1939: on 1 September Hitler marched into Poland.

The Brahan Seer met his death by antagonizing his patroness, the Countess of Seaforth. The Earl visited France, soon after the Restoration of Charles II in 1660, and had not returned. The Countess sent for the Brahan Seer and asked what her husband was doing. When he was reluctant to say, she pressed him until he revealed that the Earl was in a sumptuous gilded room, grandly decked out in velvet, silk and cloth of gold, with a voluptuous lady on his lap. The Countess was furious, accused him of malice and ordered him to be burnt in a barrel of tar at Fortrose. Before he died he predicted the downfall of the Seaforth Mackenzies, whose line came to an end after a chain of dramatic events precisely following the prophecy, within a hundred years.

The Stone of Destiny (Stone of Scone)

Traditionally, the Stone of Destiny was the pillow on which Jacob laid his head when he dreamt about the ladder of angels reaching from earth to heaven. Its subsequent history is shadowy. It floated round the world carrying mystical powers of sovereignty until it arrived in Ireland, whence it was brought to Dunadd by early missionaries and used as a throne in the coronation of Scottish kings.

In those days, *mormaers* owned their kingdoms and the High King was their overlord, King of the Scots but not of Scotland. At the coronation, each *mormaer* filled a shoe with earth from his kingdom and poured a little into a footprint carved into a rock. The King sat on the Stone of Destiny and put his foot over this cocktail of Scottish soil.

From here the Stone was moved to Dunstaffnage. In the 9th century, Kenneth Macalpine took it to Scone where it continued to be a coronation throne for the united Scots and Picts. Edward I, believing firmly in its mystical powers, pinched what he thought to be the Stone of Destiny, during one of his ravages of the north and whisked it off to become part of the Coronation Chair in Westminster Abbey. It has been there ever since, except for a brief hiatus in 1950 when Scottish Nationalists kidnapped it and hid it for about three months in Arbroath. However, the canny Scots had almost certainly hidden the original stone and the one in London, a rather dull lump of plain sandstone, is not even a replica, because the true stone was intricately carved. It is safe, in a secret cavern, and will be brought out by its hereditary guardians when the time is right.

Two enlightened men

Walter Scott (1771–1832) was a remarkable man. A woman who knew him as a child described him as sweet and intelligent and 'the most extraordinary genius of a boy'. One of his tutors described him as an incorrigibly idle imp but never a dunce. In maturity he was worldly, genial, magnanimous, never jealous or petty, fiercely patriotic and loyal. He was a delightful combination of romantic and practical and his integrity was much admired.

Scott was one of 12 children, six of whom died. His father was a Writer to the Signet, in Edinburgh, his mother the daughter of an eminent physician. A serious illness when he was 18 months old affected his right leg. From the age of three he spent much of his youth at his grandparents' farm, Sandyknowe, in the Tweed valley in the heart of the Borders. His grandparents tried every sort of cure for his lameness, such as wrapping his leg in the fleece of a newly killed sheep, but without success, and he was lame for the rest of his life. He sat for hours listening to the Border shepherds and country people and to the songs his grandmother sang for him, and her endless fund of legends. The essence of the land seeped into his soul to become his inspiration.

When stronger, he was sent to Edinburgh High School, where, though lazy, he excelled at Latin. In spite of his deformity, he was physically brave and was renowned for climbing around on the dangerous crags on the castle rock. He was also quick to square up to the 'town boys' who used to taunt their more privileged peers. Growing too fast in adolescence, he became weak and was sent to Kelso for six months convalescence. Here he read Percy's *Reliques*, a collection of ancient ballads, songs, sonnets and romances discovered, restored and edited by Percy and these, together with the romances of 16th-century Torquato Tasso, and Spenser's *Faerie Queene*, fired his imagination.

He also studied the old romantic poetry of France and Italy, and modern German poetry. Even in his teens he had the gift of spinning a good yarn and he would ramble over Arthur's Seat, in Edinburgh, swopping stories with a friend.

He went to Edinburgh University where he was no less idle, but continued to collect material to feed his passion for romantic ballads and songs. By the time he was a law clerk in his father's office, he was tall and strong, with a graceful figure and 'the chest and arms of Hercules.' His features were 'not handsome but singularly varied and pleasing', with bright eyes and a 'brilliant complexion'. He fell deeply in love with a girl of 16 called Williamina Belsches, but because of her age her father forbade their friendship. His friends believed this was the strongest passion of his life and that Williamina appears in several of his novels.

He was called to the Bar in 1792 and travelled the country extensively, always listening, observing, absorbing. His first visit to the Highlands, second only to the Borders as background for his stories, was while he was on a case, directing one of the evictions of the Clearances. In 1796 he published, anonymously, a collection of translations of German ballads. On holiday in Cumbria, near Hadrian's Wall, he met Margaret Charlotte Carpenter, the daughter of a Royalist émigré from the French Revolution, who was taking the waters at Gilsland Spa. She was high spirited and beautiful with an entrancing French accent, dark brown eyes, masses of black hair and a 'fairy-like figure'. He fell in love with her, 'raved' about her and they were married in Carlisle Cathedral on Christmas Eve 1797. (Some stones by the river where he 'popped the question' are known locally as the Popping Stones.)

Two years later he was appointed Sheriff of Selkirkshire, a position he held for 27 years, during which time he wrote the majority of his books. To begin with he stuck to ballads and romantic poems. His first publication was *Border Minstrelsy*, three volumes of ballads he had collected and edited, and this was followed by his first original work, the romantic poem 'The Lay of the Last Minstrel'. He became a partner in James Ballantyne's printing business. In 1811, with the money rolling in from his (still anonymous) prolific output and his post of Sheriff, he bought land on the Tweed and built himself a fanciful baronial castle, described by Ruskin as an incongruous pile. The place was originally called Clarty Hole—*clarty* being the Scots word for 'a lump of something unpleasant'—so he changed it to the more dignified Abbotsford, in memory of the days when it was just that.

About this time, Byron hit the headlines with 'Childe Harold' and Scott, recognizing without rancour a greater talent than his own, decided to turn his pen to prose. He was self-deprecating about his poetry: when someone asked his daughter if she had read 'The Lay of the Last Minstrel' she shook her head and answered demurely: 'Oh no, Papa says there is nothing so injurious for young people as reading bad poetry.' Indeed, when he was offered the laureateship, in 1813, he turned it down, suggesting Southey as an alternative, although many would argue that his loose, flowing verse was preferable to Southey's rather stilted, plodding style.

Waverley was Scott's first novel, published in 1814, a stirring Jacobite tale in which the turncoat hero is rescued from reprisals after Culloden by an English colonel whose life he had saved. In the following 16 years he published 29 stories. When he had milked Scottish history dry, he turned to England in the Middle Ages, and rattled off *Ivanhoe*. Among the many places and periods he wrote about was 15th century France, in *Quentin*

Durward, and he frequently returned to his beloved Scotland as in *Redgauntlet*, the imaginative story of Prince Charlie's abortive return, some years after 1745, to have another crack at the throne.

Scott entwined his extensive knowledge of the minutiae of history with romance and adventure and he brought the past vividly to life by endowing it with the present. He was not always strong on character, though some of his simple country people were brilliant, and his plots were a bit shaky, but his sense of place was outstanding and his passion for history gave him a limitless supply of stories. His books were good clean fun and as such were loved by the reading public. As well as novels, he wrote and edited a number of learned publications including histories, essays, biography and the delightful children's history: *Tales of a Grandfather*.

Scott's influence as a novelist was unquestionable. He established the form of the historical novel and was a model to such other novelists as Mrs Gaskell, George Eliot and the Brontës. *The Two Drovers* and *The Highland Widow* were, in themselves, a new form of short story.

Abbotsford became a popular meeting place for all the learned men of the day. Scott was liked and admired and had many friends. In maturity he was described as a straightforward man who got on equally well with dukes and peasants, a delightful companion not only to his contemporaries but to his children. Growing up as he had during the Scottish Enlightenment (see p. 62), his circle included many of the great men who created Scotland's Golden Age. He contributed to the *Edinburgh Review* until its Whiggish leanings outraged his Tory heart, when he promoted the rival *Quarterly Review*. In 1818 he instigated a successful search for the 'Honours of Scotland' as the Crown Jewels were called. Tucked away ignominiously in a chest at the Union of Parliaments in 1707, they had been forgotten. Scott's passion for history embraced a passion for the trappings of the past and the Scottish Regalia were the oldest in Europe. In 1820, he was created a baronet and in 1822 he had an enthusiastic hand in George IV's flamboyant visit to Edinburgh. He was always surrounded by a crowd of dogs and thoroughly enjoyed gentlemanly sport. It was a period of prosperity and happiness until 1826, when disaster struck.

Due partly to the inefficiency of James Ballantyne the printer and partly to rash borrowing, the firm went bankrupt, together with Scott's publisher, Constable. As a partner, Scott himself was liable for some £114,000. Determined to repay every penny to his creditors, he threw himself into an even greater frenzy of work, breaking his health and shortening his life. In 1827, no longer Sheriff of Selkirkshire, he emerged from the anonymity he had previously sheltered behind and poured a torrent of words into several more books, some of which reflect the rapid decline in his health. Scott's own pathetic *Journal* shows how anguished his last few years were. He died in 1832 at the age of 61, within sight and sound of the River Tweed, surrounded by his family. All his debts were paid as a result of his labours, and Abbotsford, which had been restored to him by his creditors, was preserved as a monument. It is an apt memorial to a man whose passion for Scotland was unrivalled and who himself epitomized the things he admired most about his beloved country.

Perhaps the most informative biography of Scott is *Memoirs of the Life of Sir Walter Scott* by his son-in-law, John Gibson Lockhart, a comprehensive account full of personal anecdotes but perhaps a little too tender in some details.

Robert Burns (1759–96).

> *Immortal Robert Burns of Ayr,*
> *There's but few poets can with you compare;*
> *Some of your poems and songs are very fine:*
> *'To Mary in Heaven' is most sublime;*
> *And then again in your 'Cottar's Saturday Night',*
> *Your genius there does shine most bright,*
> *As pure as the dewdrops of night...*

—tribute from Scotland's worst poet, William McGonagall

Burns, the ploughman-poet, came from a very different background to that of Walter Scott, but he was no less a remarkable product of the Scottish Enlightenment.

He was a genius. He cut through elegant devices and rhetoric and went straight to the heart of mankind. No subject was sacrosanct: 'Holy Willie's Prayer' is a blueprint for satire. Nothing could be more tender than his 'To a Mouse', that 'Wee, sleekit, cowrin', tim'rous beastie' he turned up in her nest with his plough, nor more romantic than his love who was 'like a red, red rose, that's newly sprung in June'. Nationalism blazes in 'Scots wha hae wi' Wallace bled' and the revolutionary spirit was so strong in 'A man's a man for a' that' it had to be published anonymously.

Burns' admirers shroud him with an almost mawkish sentimentality, personified in the statue in Dumfries High Street of a languishing beau clutching a posy of flowers. In fact he was an earthy man with a wicked sense of humour, contemptuous of the hypocrisy of Kirk and officialdom, as his satirical poems show. He was sensitive and perceptive and his heart frequently ruled his head, but he was not sentimental. On the contrary, he was extremely down to earth. He was fiercely humanitarian; loathed oppression; despised privilege through birth and wealth; hated cruelty. His easy wit and natural charm endeared him to peasant and noble alike. He was convivial and thoroughly enjoyed tavern life and a night out with the boys, but was by no means a reeling drunkard. James Currie, three years his senior, was a reformed alcoholic and his biography of Burns was strongly influenced by his vehement abhorrence for the Demon Drink. Burns liked his dram but most of the time poverty and a weak heart kept him fairly abstemious. He was extremely good-looking with dark hair, large dreamy eyes, a straight nose and a quirky, sensual mouth. Sir Walter Scott said of him: 'There was a strong expression of sense and shrewdness in all his lineaments: the eye alone, I think, indicated the poetical character and temperament. It was large and of a dark cast, which glowed, I say literally glowed, when he spoke with feeling or interest. I never saw such another eye in a human head, though I have seen the most distinguished men of my time.' Women found him irresistible and fell like skittles. He fathered 15 children, six of whom were bastards, but he made no distinction and was a good father to them all. He had an easy morality, believing that 'the light that led astray was light from Heaven'. But in spite of his many infidelities and the rough passage of their early years together, he loved Jean Armour more than any of his mistresses and their marriage was happy. He farmed for all but the last five years of his short life and was far more at home on the end of a plough than in an Edinburgh drawing room. Tough work on the land when he was undernourished and still growing led to recurring bouts of rheumatic fever which strained his heart.

Oldest of the seven children of an impoverished market gardener, he grew up hungry, always labouring, barely subsisting at times. He went to the village school when he was six and his retentive memory impressed his teachers. He learnt some Latin and French and devoured any book he could lay hands on. *The History of Sir William Wallace*, borrowed from the blacksmith, 'poured a Scottish prejudice into my veins which will boil along there till the floodgates of life shut in eternal rest.'

He wrote his first song, 'Handsome Nell' to Nelly Kirkpatrick, a 'bewitching creature' who worked in the fields with him and probably initiated him into that 'delicious passion which I hold to be the first of human joys.' In 1775 he went to Kirkoswald to study surveying but 'a charming filette who lived next door to the school overset my Trigo-nometry and set me off on a tangent from the sphere of my studies.' It was here he developed a liking for tavern life and learned 'to look unconcerned on a large tavern bill'. His cronies in the Inn were Douglas Graham of Shanter Farm—model for Tam o' Shanter, and John Davidson the cobbler—Souter Johnnie.

When he was 18, he joined a dancing class at Tarbolton, against his father's wishes, 'to give my manners a brush'. A year later he helped found the Tarbolton Bachelors' Club, and he and his friends sat debating long into the night.

These were exciting times to be growing up in and his sharp mind was uncluttered by received opinions and prejudices. The French Revolution was 10 years ahead but its labour pains were starting. Poverty made him sympathetic towards any movement against oppression. The Scottish Enlightenment was in full bloom: new ideas were burgeoning. Men were arguing, inventing, abandoning moribund conventions. Burns was ripe for rebellion.

When he was 26 he met Jean, one of 11 children of stonemason James Armour, and declared her his common-law wife. At the beginning of the following year, however, desperate for money, he made plans to emigrate to Jamaica to work on a plantation. Before departing, he arranged for some of his poems to be published in Kilmarnock. James Armour renounced him as a son-in-law, and issued a writ against him although Jean was by now pregnant. Robert in his turn renounced Jean and went into hiding. In July 1786, *The Kilmarnock Poems* was published. Six days later he was hauled up before the Kirk in Mauchline and ordered to sit on the Penitential Stool in chastisement for his irregular marriage. (He stood, defiantly, beside it and such was his magnetism that no one insisted on the full humiliation.) For all his failings, he was a religious man, but his clear, revolutionary mind despised the hypocrisy of strict Calvinistic discipline.

Three weeks later he exchanged a pledge of marriage with Mary Campbell of Auchnamore, near Dunoon. A wistful apotheosis has left the impression that Highland Mary was a pure, virginal maiden whose tragic death, five months later, left him heartbroken. In fact if rumour is to be believed she was little more than a local floozie and a number of writs and claims for paternity settlements, soon after her death, indicate he was not slow to seek solace in other arms. In September, Jean Armour gave birth to twins, Robert and Jean, who did not survive long.

The Kilmarnock Poems was an instant success. Burns cancelled his plans for Jamaica and went to Edinburgh where he was lionized by Society and the *literati*. After a second edition of his poems appeared, he was asked if he would help collect old Scottish songs for the Scots Musical Museum. He threw himself into this venture and during the last 10 years of his life collected, edited and wrote over 200 songs. He travelled in the Highlands and the Borders to find material and accepted no payment, saying it was his patriotic duty. In January 1787 the Grand Lodge of Scotland (Masonic) hailed him as 'Caledonia's Bard'. That same year he met Mrs Agnes McLehose and started a passionate correspondence of high-flown letters, addressing her as Clarinda and signing himself as Sylvander.

In February 1788, he left Edinburgh, bought Jean Armour a mahogany bed and set up house with her in an upper room in Mauchline, publicly declaring them to be married (again). Just over a week later, Jean gave birth to another set of twins, neither of whom survived the month. The couple moved to Ellisland and while trying his hand at experimental farming, Burns trained as an excise officer. The Kirk Session finally acknowledged the authenticity of the marriage but eight months after the birth of the twins, a Jenny Clow bore him a son and claimed paternity settlement.

In 1790, Burns was posted to Dumfries as Excise Officer. He moved his family to the town and for the last six years of his life, continued to write, procreate, and pay up for his indiscretions. An inquiry was launched at the end of 1793, to look into his revolutionary leanings. He was acquitted, and when the French declared war on Britain in 1795 he was the first to join the Dumfries Volunteers and he wrote several patriotic songs. He died in July 1796 at the age of 37, from a heart defect contracted after rheumatic fever. On the day of his funeral Jean, with not a shilling in the world, gave birth to his son Maxwell.

Part III

HISTORY

Scotland, wild and fiercely independent, was always a thorn in England's flesh. No one wants hostile neighbours and inevitably Scotland's history has been a continual struggle to remain independent. The Romans tried to occupy it for a few years, found it invincible and slunk away. The English spent centuries trying to annex it until eventually they had to accept a Scottish king on their throne. Intrepid younger sons, black sheep, political exiles and the dispossessed sailed from Scotland to leave their mark on the world.

John Logie Baird invented television; Alexander Bell invented the telephone; Alexander Fleming discovered penicillin; James Watt invented the steam engine. James Clerk Maxwell, the Scottish physicist, claimed the existence of radio waves in 1873, before Marconi pioneered their use for communication; Lord Reith of Stonehaven greatly influenced the early development of the BBC and was its first General Manager. John Paul Jones founded the American Navy. David Hume, the 18th-century philosopher and historian, has influenced thought up to the 20th century. Patrick Gordon was a General to Tsar Peter the Great; James Keith was a Field-Marshal to Frederick the Great. 'Adam' is a household word used to describe the style of architecture designed by brothers Robert and James Adam. Thomas Telford's bridges, roads and canals, Robert Stevenson's lighthouses, Carnegie's benevolent institutions, are all renowned.

Gladstone, Ramsay MacDonald, Harold Macmillan and Alec Douglas-Home each served as Prime Minister of Britain. Eleven of America's presidents were of Scottish descent, as were 25 of the 73 Americans honoured in their Hall of Fame, a third of their secretaries of state and half their secretaries to the treasury. John McDouall Stuart was the first man to cross Australia, through the central desert, in 1866; John Macarthur laid the foundations of Australia's agricultural system; Lachlan MacQuarie was responsible for turning the penal colony of Botany Bay into Sydney.

These are but a few of the Scots who spread their talents across the world.

Pre-history

The Ice Age eradicated evidence of any previous habitation in Scotland. **Stone Age** settlers, at least 7000 years ago, were the first to leave clues to their existence. Burial sites and middens (rubbish heaps) from those times have thrown up enough to tantalize archaeologists, but not enough to leave more than a shadow of the identity of those nomadic tribes. They came from Asia and Europe, through England and Ireland, wave after wave of them, creeping up the coast in dug-out canoes, settling for long enough to leave traces of their culture and way of life, before vanishing into obscurity. They lived off the flesh of deer and wild boar, fish and crustaceans. Some only stayed a short time, living in caves. A recently excavated house in Grampian dates from 7000 BC, a round stone building about 25 feet across. Later, farmers came over from the continent and introduced agriculture. People settled for longer periods, burning forests and enriching the land with potash.

After the hunters and gatherers came the **Beaker People**, who laid beakers in the tombs of their dead. They were skillful engineers and historians puzzle over their mysterious stone circles and monoliths, and over the true purpose of their brochs (massive stone towers built near the sea in the far north, about 2000 years ago).

Metal was introduced about a thousand years before Christ, and with it the sword and shield. Scotland, on the trade route between Ireland and Scandinavia, was able to barter food and hides for bronze and copper. During this millennium the Celtic-speaking Britons arrived, a sturdy, fair-haired race, combative and quick to attack in order to acquire precious land. The local people built defensive forts, with ditches and ramparts, such as the ones on Berry Hill and Finavon, and skirmishing became part of life.

The Romans: AD 82–4th century

The Romans arrived in AD 82 and with them came the first record of Scottish history, written by the historian **Tacitus**. Tacitus describes how his father-in-law, **Agricola**, defeated an army of tall, red-haired men on an unidentified hillside in the northeast, in the **Battle of Mons Graupius**. The exact location of this battle is debatable, but it was somewhere in today's Grampian, so called from a misprint of 'Graupius' by a 16th-century chronicler.

The Romans called their victims *picti*, the painted ones, from which the name 'Picts' is thought to derive, and failed to subdue them. Highly trained legionnaires could not compete with hostile tribes who faded into the mountains and forests and marshes, refusing to fight army-to-army, preferring to lay cunning ambushes for their aggressors. The Romans fell back having, it has long been believed, lost the entire Ninth Legion in a savage massacre. In fact evidence of their having been merely posted elsewhere was unearthed recently when traces of their later existence were found around the Danube.

In 121 **Hadrian** built a wall between the Solway and the Tyne, hoping to contain the barbarians in the north, but the wall was so frequently attacked that another was constructed between the Forth and the Clyde in 141–2—the **Antonine Wall**. This proved to be no more effective and was soon abandoned.

Exasperated, the Romans withdrew to Hadrian's Wall. In 208, **Emperor Severus** sailed into the Firth of Forth and laid waste Fife and the land around the Tay. In spite of the devastation he caused, the barbarians refused to be conquered. The old emperor died, the Romans withdrew again and an uneasy peace existed between the north and south until the middle of the fourth century. The Picts then resumed their ferocious attacks while Saxons began to invade from the northeast. The Roman empire was in decline: more and more legions were being recalled to fight nearer home. By the end of the fourth century the Romans abandoned Scotland completely, leaving the untamed Picts to defend themselves against new invaders. Not only had they failed to subdue their foes, but they failed to impose any of their sophisticated culture on them. The only evidence of their occupation is a few straight roads, a number of forts and the remains of the Antonine Wall.

The coming of Christianity: 397–7th century

Four races dominated Scotland, then called Alba, or Alban. The **Celtic Picts** were the most powerful, occupying the land from Caithness to the Forth; the **Teutonic Angles**, or **Anglo-Saxons**, occupied Bernicia, south of the Forth; the **Britons,** another Celtic race, occupied the western lands south of the Clyde. Finally there were the **Scots**: Celts who had come over from Ireland during the third and fourth centuries and settled north of the Clyde, establishing the **Kingdom of Dalriada** and eventually giving their name to all Scotland.

St Ninian founded the first Christian centre at Whithorn, near the Solway Firth, in 397, and started the daunting task of converting the pagans. Then came **Columba**, a clever man of royal birth, who was exiled from Ireland and arrived in Scotland in 563. He established himself on the island of Iona, continuing St Ninian's work, and sent missionaries to the mainland and to the other islands. These penetrated further and further into Pictland. Columba's influence was political as well as religious and he did much to consolidate the strength of the Scots.

For those who believe there is some historic truth in the Arthurian legends, King Arthur led his army north at some time in the fifth or sixth century and had a crack at the Picts and Scots. That intrepid romancer, Geoffrey of Monmouth, in his *History of the Kings of Britain* describes the **Battle of Loch Lomond** in graphic detail. The loch, with its islands, streams and crags, and its eagles who foretold 'any prodigious event which was about to occur in the kingdom by a shrill-pitched scream emitted in concert', provided sanctuary for the barbarians. They fled to the islands where Arthur besieged them for 15 days until he had reduced them to such a state of famine that they died in their thousands. The Irish arrived with a fleet and a 'huge horde of pagans' to help the Scots, but Arthur cut them to pieces mercilessly and forced them to return home. He then continued to massacre the barbarians until they 'fell on their knees and besought him to have mercy'. The king was moved to tears and pardoned them. True or false, it is stirring stuff and well worth a read.

By the end of the 7th century the four kingdoms of Alban were nominally converted to Christianity—a Celtic Christianity, not yet in line with that dictated by Rome.

Norse invasion: 8th century

At the end of the 8th-century Norsemen began to attack from the north conquering Orkney and Shetland, the Western Isles, Caithness and Sutherland, while the four kingdoms continued to fight amongst themselves, weakening their resistance to outside attack.

The birth of Scotland: 843–1034

In 843 **Kenneth Macalpine,** King of the Scots, achieved some sort of union between Scots and Picts, making himself king over all the territory north of the Forth and Clyde, which then became Scotia. The Picts, who had been dominant for more than 1000 years, vanished for ever. They remain an enigmatic people whose history is unrecorded and unknown; an elusive ghost-race who will perhaps never be fully understood. It was not until 1018, however, that **Malcolm II** defeated the Angles and brought Bernicia, or Lothian, into the kingdom. He was succeeded, in 1034, by his grandson **Duncan I** who already ruled the Britons, and so the four kingdoms were finally united into one Scotland, except for those parts occupied by the Norsemen. The country was divided into seven main kingdoms, of which Fife was the strongest, plus a few smaller ones, each ruled by a *mormaer*. The *Ard Righ* or High King was their overlord—King of the Scots, but not of Scotland, for each *mormaer* owned his land (see 'Stone of Destiny', 'Topics'). In those days, under a remarkable clan system in which no one was subservient and each played an important part, Scotland was truly democratic.

The Norman influence: 11th century

Duncan I was killed in 1040 by **Macbeth,** the last Celtic king. Shakespeare's Macbeth was a weak man, with a domineering wife, but, in fact, he ruled for 17 years and his reign was chronicled as a time of plenty. He was eventually killed by Duncan's son, **Malcolm Canmore**, with the help of the English, in 1057. *Ceann Mor* is Gaelic for big head, referring to Malcolm III's status rather than to any anatomical defect, or conceit.

It was Malcolm Canmore's second wife, **Margaret**, who made his 36-year reign memorable. She was an English princess, sister of Edgar Atheling—Edward the Confessor's heir, usurped by William the Conqueror. She and her brother had taken refuge in Scotland after the Norman Conquest, in 1066. Margaret, who was extremely pious and later canonized, set about Anglicizing the Celtic church. She brought in English clergy and established an English court, and it was her influence that civilized Scotland and transformed it into a kingdom similar to Norman England. It was now that the Lowland clans gave up their democracy: *mormaers* became earls and established a feudal system, while the Highlands and Islands retained the old, patriarchal clan.

Inspired by the presence in his court of his English brother-in-law, Malcolm coveted the English throne. He made several border raids into Northumberland and Cumbria, forcing William the Conqueror to invade Scotland to subdue him. In order to prevent the subsequent destruction of Scotland, Malcolm was then forced to pay homage to William at Abernethy in 1071. He continued to harass the English until he was treacherously killed while laying siege to Alnwick Castle in 1093. Queen Margaret, already mortally ill, survived him by only three days. She died thanking God for her grief, believing that it purified her soul.

David I: 1124–53

David I, ninth son of Malcolm Canmore, inherited the throne in 1124 from a succession of unremarkable monarchs and ruled for nearly 30 years, bringing many beneficial changes to Scotland.

He had been brought up in England and most of his friends were Norman. His wife was a Norman heiress: his sister, Maud, was married to King Henry I of England. He gave large Scottish estates to his Anglo-Norman friends among whom were the ancestors of the Balliols, Robert the Bruce and the Stewarts. Old Celtic families merged with French-speaking incomers, establishing families in the Lowlands and the northeast, whose names are common throughout Scotland today: Frasers, Maxwells, Gordons, Crichtons and many more. The Highlanders retained their traditional clan system and took little notice of these southern interlopers.

David led an army against England in 1138. Although the outcome of the **Battle of the Standard**, at Cowton Moor was inconclusive, subsequent negotiation won him Northumberland and Cumbria. He encouraged Flemish weavers to settle along the east coast, granting them special privileges, rights and monopolies. These ancestors of the Flemings and the Taylors introduced new fabrics and taught new skills, and their foreign ways were absorbed by their new neighbours.

David had little time for vows of poverty: he founded a number of lavish cathedrals, churches and monasteries, including the Border abbeys, importing religious communities from Europe and urging the monks to establish commercial interests to the glory of God. He granted royal charters to towns, permitting markets and fairs; he tried to establish a national judiciary; he encouraged foreign trade and selected a body of advisers from his court to help him. He died in 1153, heartbroken from the death of his son and heir the year before.

The Auld Alliance: 12th century

Malcolm IV was only 13 when he inherited the throne from his grandfather David I. Known as Malcolm the Maiden, he was nevertheless a brave young man, whose courage inspired many of his followers. Gentle and deeply religious, he ruled for only 12 years before he died, to be succeeded by his brother, **William the Lion**. William was ambitious and ruthless in his desire to recover parts of his kingdom annexed by England. He established an alliance with France in 1165, 'The Auld Alliance', and tried to invade England. He failed, was taken prisoner and sent to Normandy, where he was forced to sign the humiliating **Treaty of Falaise**. This placed Scotland under feudal subjection to England. Fifteen years later, when the English king, Richard Coeur de Lion, needed money for a Crusade, he agreed to annul the Treaty of Falaise in return for 10,000 marks.

The end of the Norse occupation: 13th century

England and Scotland were at peace, then, for more than 100 years. **Alexander II** succeeded to the throne in 1214, and directed his attention to the Western Isles, whose lords gave their allegiance to Norway. It was his son, **Alexander III**, however, who managed to expel the Norsemen from the Hebrides. He did this by defeating old **King Haakon IV** of Norway in the **Battle of Largs** in 1263. The Hebrides became part of the Kingdom of Scotland again, though the Lords of the Isles paid little heed to any authority but their own.

Alexander continued to foster prosperity in Scotland, along the same lines as his great-great-grandfather, David I. He married the English Princess Margaret, daughter of Henry III. Their daughter, also Margaret, married King Eric of Norway and thus links were forged with both countries. Alexander had a long and successful reign. He outlived his first wife and three children and married again in an attempt to father an heir. He was, however, killed six months later, in 1286, when thrown from his horse, leaving his grand-daughter **Margaret of Norway** to succeed him, under the regency of John Balliol. Balliol was a powerful Norman-Scot whose wife, Devorguilla, founded Balliol College in Oxford.

Wars of independence: 13th century

Edward I of England, determined to unite Scotland to England, immediately proposed a marriage between his son Edward and the 8-year-old **Maid of Norway**. This poor little queen died of seasickness on her way to Britain, and Edward declared himself to be overlord of Scotland. There were several claimants to the Scottish throne, the strongest being those of **John Balliol,** son of the regent, and **Robert Bruce**. Both were Anglo-Norman nobles with estates in England and Scotland, given to their ancestors by David I. They were descended from David's youngest son and had both fought in Edward's army.

Edward came north in 1291 and awarded the crown to John Balliol in Berwick Castle, believing him to be more easily manipulated than Robert Bruce. He then ordered Balliol to pay homage to the English throne and accept himself (Edward) as Scotland's overlord. He also insisted that Scotland should contribute to English defence costs and join with them in an invasion of France. Balliol was a weak man, known to his subjects as 'Toom Tabard', Empty Coat, but these demands were too much even for him and he prepared to invade England. Edward was supported by many of the Scottish nobles who owned estates in England, including Robert Bruce, and he defeated Balliol who was forced to renounce his crown.

Edward, 'The Hammer of the Scots', progressed through Scotland, compelling nobles and lairds to sign a roll, **The Ragman's Roll**. This acknowledged him to be their king. He then returned to England, taking with him what he thought to be the Stone of Destiny, brought from Ireland seven centuries earlier and believed to embody special powers of sovereignty. It had always been used in the coronation of Scottish kings (see 'Topics'). Edward was convinced he had finally conquered Scotland.

William Wallace: 1274(?)–1305

William Wallace was a young Scot from the southwest, outlawed in 1297 for killing the Sheriff of Lanark in revenge for the murder of his wife. In exile Wallace became the leader of a fast-expanding resistance movement against English repression. In September 1297 he led a resounding defeat of the English at the **Battle of Stirling Bridge**, kindling new hope in Scottish hearts, and paving the way to freedom from English tyranny. The following year he was defeated by Edward and had to go into hiding, while Edward ravaged Scotland in his attempt to crush further resistance. Wallace evaded capture for seven unhappy years before he was betrayed. He was paraded through the streets of London, tried on a series of trumped-up charges and condemned to death. It was a particularly vicious execution. He was hanged, drawn and emasculated, his entrails being burnt before his eyes as he died. Quarters of his body and his head were displayed throughout Britain.

Robert Bruce: 1306–1329

Robert Bruce, son of John Balliol's rival, had served Edward in his youth. Like his father, he had a claim to the throne, as did Balliol's nephew, **Red John Comyn**. These two men met at Greyfriars Kirk, in Dumfries, presumably to discuss plans for ridding their country of English domination. A quarrel arose between them and Bruce killed Comyn, in the kirk, thus committing sacrilege as well as murder. Excommunicated by Rome and hounded by the Comyns, he went to Scone and had himself crowned King of Scotland, in May 1306.

Edward hurried north and defeated Bruce, a month later, at Methven.

Outlawed, his friends and allies dead, Bruce went into hiding. During this time of exile, probably on the island of Rathlin, off the Irish coast, he encountered the legendary spider, whose determination and persistence finally enabled it to swing from one rafter to another on its frail homespun web. If the spider could succeed, then so could he. Bruce returned to Scotland in 1307 on the death of Edward I, overcame all other claimants to the throne and defeated Edward II at **Bannockburn** in 1314.

Excommunicated by the Pope, Bruce's sovereignty was not recognized by Europe. In 1320 his Council met and decided to send a petition to the Pope, asking him to tell Edward to leave Scotland in peace, and to acknowledge Bruce as the rightful king. An elaborate Latin document was drafted, probably by the Abbot of Arbroath, Bernard de Linton, who was the Chancellor, and signed by eight earls and 38 barons. This Declaration of Independence is a passionate plea for freedom from English harassment, emphasizing the ancient Celtic line of the Scots and playing down the Anglo-Norman blood that had infiltrated their veins. It states 'as long as but a hundred of us remain alive, never will we on any conditions be brought under English rule.' The Pope was sufficiently impressed by the spirit of the appeal and advised Edward to leave Scotland alone. Edward, however, was not so easily deterred. He marched his army across the Tweed but Bruce's army, retreating, so devastated the land that the English army died like flies of famine and dysentery. They fled back to England, sacking and desecrating abbeys, killing priests and monks. The Pope finally acknowledged Bruce's claim to the Scottish throne. He reigned for a further 15 years and died of leprosy, at Cardross Castle on the Clyde in 1329. It is said that he always wore a hair shirt in penance for his act of sacrilege.

Struggle for power: 14th century

Bruce was succeeded by his five-year-old son, **David II**, with **Thomas Randolph, Earl of Moray**, as regent. The 42 years of David's reign were troubled times for Scotland. Encouraged by Edward III of England, the Scottish nobles, who had been disinherited earlier by Bruce for backing the English, tried to put Toom Tabard's son, **Edward Balliol**, on the throne. Moray was killed, as was his cousin the Earl of Mar, who succeeded him as Regent. Balliol was crowned King of Scotland, at Scone, but not for long: irate Scottish nobles rose up in fury and chased him from the country.

David, who had been sent to France for safety at the age of 10 with his child-wife Joan, was brought back to Scotland in 1341. He was captured by the English at the **Battle of Neville's Cross,** however, and spent the next 12 years in England. He was very content with the easy life of Edward III's court, while his regent, **Robert Stewart**, grandson of Robert Bruce, continued to harass the English. Beguiled by his love for England, David consented to name Edward III's son as his heir. However, Scotland was not in favour of such a betrayal and when David died in 1371, they put Robert Stewart on the throne, the former Regent and the first Stewart king.

The Stewarts: 14th–15th century

Robert was better as a regent than a king. Anarchy, rebellion and internal squabbles disturbed the peace he strove for. Border raiding was rife, causing continual devastation in the south, and the whole country seethed in a turmoil of lawlessness. Robert II died in 1390 and was succeeded by his son, **Robert III**.

Crippled by a kick from a horse, Robert was in poor health. He allowed his brother, the **Duke of Albany**, to assume power and he abdicated in 1399 because of his disabilities. For the next 25 years Scotland was ruled by regents, including Robert's son, **David, Duke of Rothesay**. Rothesay disappeared in mysterious circumstances, allegedly starved to death by his uncle, the Duke of Albany, who once again took office—this time as Regent.

The ailing Robert III sent his grandson and heir, **James I**, to France, in 1406, fearing that Albany had plans to remove him from succession. The young prince was, however, captured by pirates and handed over to the English. Too shocked to go on living, Robert died a month later, leaving Albany in full power for 18 years while James was held hostage. Powerful nobles in Scotland seized the opportunity to consolidate their strength. They expanded their estates and built up private armies, many of them becoming as powerful as kings. Most notable among them was the **Douglas** family, whose lands and subjects rivalled those of the king. Meanwhile, in the northwest, the Lords of the Isles allied themselves with the English and continued to live their own lives with little regard for central government.

Anarchy: James I, 1406–1437

James I returned to his throne in 1424, at the age of 29, with an English bride, Joan Beaufort, cousin of Henry VI. Reared and educated in England, he had had a good grounding in statesmanship and in military strategy. He found his country in turmoil. His nobles were far too powerful, and anarchy, poverty and lawlessness were rampant. His first step was the wholesale execution of the Albany family, in 1425, and the seizure of their considerable estates. In 1427 he summoned the Highland chiefs and arrested 40 of them: Alexander of the Isles retaliated by burning Inverness. Further rebellion from the west was subdued and James managed to redress the balance of power in the Lowlands by annexing many of the earldoms that had threatened his supremacy.

James achieved a great deal for Scotland, restoring law and order and introducing a number of much-needed reforms. Inevitably, his decisive methods won him enemies and in 1437 three of them stabbed him to death, leaving his six-year-old son **James II** as his heir.

The Douglases: 15th century

Scotland was once again ruled by regency, and once again the nobles, in particular the Douglas family, became too powerful. In 1440, the Regent, Sir William Crichton, invited the 14-year-old Earl of Douglas and his younger brother to dine with the eight-year-old King at Edinburgh Castle. This came to be known as the **'Black Dinner'**: a black bull's head, symbol of death, was brought into the Great Hall, and the two Douglas youths were murdered, in front of the boy-king. For a while, the Douglas family were subdued.

James II came to his throne in 1449 at the age of 19. He continued to establish the reforms so dear to his father, but was threatened by an alliance between the Douglases, Crawfords and John of the Isles.

Perhaps remembering the 'Black Dinner' of his youth, he summoned the Earl of Douglas to Stirling Castle and stabbed him to death. With English help the Douglases attempted revenge and James defeated them completely at the **Battle of Arkinholm,** killing three of the murdered earl's four brothers. The power of the Douglas family, known as the Black Douglases, was squashed. James was killed in 1460 when a canon exploded during the siege of Roxburghe.

James III: 1460–1488

His son, James III, was nine years old and so Scotland was once more ruled by regents, until his accession at the age of 19. He married the King of Norway's daughter who brought with her the islands of Orkney and Shetland as part of her dowry.

James was an intellectual, better fitted for an academic life than for a crown. He antagonized his nobles, who rose against him. They hanged his favourites and proclaimed his son, James IV, to be king in his place. James III tried to regain power, fighting the rebels at Sauchieburn, near Stirling, in 1488. His horse bolted and threw him. Badly injured, he begged for a priest and the man who stepped forward to administer the last rites stabbed him to death.

James IV: Renaissance, 1488–1513

James IV, the most popular of the Stewart kings, was 15 when he came to the throne. He was clever and charming, a good leader, pious and energetic, generous, flamboyant and sensual. His mistresses bore him a number of bastards. His reign brought the Renaissance to Scotland: the arts and education blossomed and James led the way. He authorized the building of beautiful palaces and churches. His court was elegant and cultured and the country was at peace, growing in prosperity. But the peace was not absolute: on the doorstep the Lords of the Isles continued to live as they always had, fiercely patriarchal, their loyalties all directed to their own clans and chieftains. James, who had taken the trouble to learn Gaelic, decided to visit the Western Highlands and Islands, hoping to win the friendship of the clans. His attempts were viewed with suspicion, thus he desisted and appointed overlords to rule them. This resulted in an uprising of the Macdonalds and the Macleans, in 1503: they stormed Inverness and burned it.

In 1503, James married 12-year-old Margaret Tudor and signed a treaty of perpetual peace with England. But in 1511, his brother-in-law, Henry VIII of England, joined the Pope, the King of Spain and the Doge of Venice in a Holy League against France. James passionately desired a united Europe. Determined to maintain a balance of power, therefore, he renewed the Auld Alliance with France and tried, in vain, to mediate.

In 1513, threatened from all directions, France appealed to Scotland for help. James in turn appealed to Henry, who replied with insults. Against all advice, in August 1513, James led a Scottish army across the Tweed, to **Flodden Field**, where they were massacred by the superior forces of the English. The king, his nobles and most of Scotland's best men were killed in a battle that was as pointless as it was valiant: it was perhaps Scotland's greatest tragedy. The country was left leaderless, its army slain, its new king **James V**, a toddler and its regent, Margaret Tudor, with divided loyalties.

James V: 1513–1542

There followed a period of more turmoil and intrigue until the king was old enough to take office and try to restore order to his country. Ignoring several offers of brides, he chose French Madeleine, who only lived for two months after their marriage. The following year he took a second French wife, **Marie de Guise Lorraine**, who bore him two sons, both of whom died.

James was an ingenuous man. He liked to disguise himself as a commoner and mingle with his subjects, posing as the Guidman of Ballangeich, fooling no one but himself, and getting into several unfortunate escapades.

He squabbled with the English, aggravated his nobles, and tried to invade England. His pathetic, mutinous army, quarrelling amongst itself, was defeated by Henry VIII's army, at **Solway Moss**, in 1542. Sick and despairing, James returned to Falkland Palace where he heard that his wife had just given birth to a daughter. The news was too much for him and he died, leaving as his heir Mary, Queen of Scots, only a few days old.

Mary, Queen of Scots: 1542–1567 (died 1587)

Henry VIII, determined to take Scotland into his realm, proposed a marriage between Mary and his delicate son, Edward. A marriage treaty was arranged with the Regent, Earl of Arran, but the Queen Mother, Marie de Guise, had other plans. Mary was crowned

Queen of Scotland, at Scone, with the approval of the Three Estates (the Church, the nobles and the burghers). Furious to be thus snubbed, Henry set about what became known as the **Rough Wooing**. He devastated the south of Scotland and earned the bitter hatred of the Scots.

Mary was sent off to France for safety at the age of five, where she stayed for 15 years, marrying the French Dauphin. While she was away, learning French ways, Protestants were gaining power in Scotland, resenting the Catholic French influence. The Regent, now Marie de Guise, backed by the French, denounced all Protestants as heretics. This so enraged **John Knox**, a powerful and energetic reformer, that he incited his followers to destroy the Catholic churches and religious houses. The Regent Queen was deposed in 1559 and Catholicism was abolished. At this point, Mary's French husband died and she returned to her country as queen; no longer Mary Stewart, but Mary Stuart because the French have no 'w' in their alphabet.

Mary was not yet 20 when she landed in Scotland in 1561. French in education and attitude, a devout Catholic, high-spirited, passionate, sensual and beautiful, she had the best intentions. She had no desire to tangle with the Protestants. She was not a bigot; she merely wished to be allowed to practise her own religion in peace. This horrified John Knox and his followers, who found her light-hearted ways obnoxious.

In 1565, she married her cousin, **Henry Stewart, Lord Darnley**, a dissipated Catholic youth, four years her junior, and mistrusted by all. Within a year, when Mary was six months pregnant, Darnley became jealous of her Italian secretary, **Rizzio** and murdered him, with the help of his friends, in Mary's presence. She never forgave him. When he himself was murdered, the following year, some hinted that Mary may have known of the plot. Eight weeks later, she married **James Hepburn, Earl of Bothwell**, a buccaneering Protestant of great charm and little honour. He had abducted and allegedly raped Mary in order to force the marriage, having hastily divorced his wife. Some say that Mary was passionately in love with Bothwell and that there was no question of rape.

Bothwell had been heavily implicated in the murder of Darnley and this ill-advised marriage sparked off an inferno of protest from both Catholics and Protestants. Mary, publicly humiliated, was forced to abdicate in favour of her baby son, **James VI**. Her half-brother, **James Stewart, Earl of Moray**, bastard son of James V, was proclaimed Regent. Mary fled to England and threw herself on the mercy of her cousin, Elizabeth I. But they never met. Elizabeth, without an heir, could not forget Mary's claims to the English throne. Mary was imprisoned for 20 years, and then beheaded.

James VI/I: 1567–1625

After another spell of regency, James proclaimed himself king in 1583 and found himself to be the head of a country divided between Catholics and Protestants. He aspired to be an impartial king, thus incurring the animosity of both factions. A Protestant himself in name, if not belief, James had no wish to antagonize his Protestant cousin Elizabeth of England and spoil his chances of inheriting her throne. He concluded an alliance with England and made no more than a formal protest when Elizabeth agreed to the execution of his mother in 1587.

The new, Protestant religion in Scotland now presented problems. It was divided between the extreme Presbyterians, who wanted a religion of the purest simplicity with equality of ministers and no bishops or elaborate ritual, and James' English form of Protestantism, with bishops appointed by the crown and a formal liturgy. He tried to impose his will on the Kirk, but failed. Presbyterians grew more and more averse to Episcopacy and their religion became less and less formal, with extempore prayers replacing those in the prayer book.

In 1603, Queen Elizabeth I died, appointing James as her heir. Thus, he became James VI of Scotland and I of England. He hurried to London and only returned to Scotland once, preferring the pomp and magnificence of the English court, and the ritual of the Church of England. But he still tried to foist Episcopacy on his northern subjects and to reinstate formal worship. He died in 1625 and his son, **Charles I**, succeeded him.

The Last of the Stewarts: 1625–1688

Charles, reared in England and a devout Anglican and Episcopalian, had no love for the Kirk. When he went north for his Scottish coronation, his subjects were scandalized by the 'Popish' practices he brought with him. He authorized the revision of the English prayer book in an attempt to produce one for Scotland that might replace extempore prayer. This act produced violent opposition, riots and protest. Important men and nobles rebelled against the enforcement of the use of the new prayer book. Thousands flocked to Greyfriars Kirk in Edinburgh in February 1638 to sign the **National Covenant**, a document that condemned all Catholic doctrines and upheld the 'True Religion'. Copies of the Covenant were carried all over the Lowlands and signed amidst strong national feeling. The Covenant, however, was somewhat ambivalent: its signatories swore, not only to uphold the True Religion, but also to be loyal to a king who demanded the Episcopacy they shunned. Thus, loyal subjects of the crown found themselves torn between obedience to the king and obedience to their new religion.

When civil war broke out in England, the Covenanting Scots agreed to go to the aid of the English Parliamentarians, on condition that Presbyterianism was adopted throughout England and Ireland, as well as Scotland.

In 1649, Charles I was defeated by Cromwell and executed. The Scots grasped this opportunity to advance their quest for stability and invited his exiled son, **Charles II,** to Scotland where he was crowned king, on the condition that he supported the Covenant. Furious, Cromwell invaded Scotland. Charles went back into exile and Cromwell ruled both countries until the **Restoration of the Monarchy** in 1660.

Charles II now ignored all the promises he had made, and sought to reintroduce Episcopacy. This rekindled the fervour of the Covenanters, who fled into the hills and worshipped in secret 'Conventicles'. In 1670, these conventicles were declared to be treasonable, and there then followed the **Killing Times**, when thousands of fanatical Covenanters were slaughtered, retaliating with brutal reprisals.

Charles II died of apoplexy in 1685 and was succeeded by his brother, **James VII/II,** Scotland's first Catholic sovereign for 120 years. During his brief reign, James tried unsuccessfully to introduce tolerance for all religions. He was deposed in 1688 by his Protestant daughter Mary and her Dutch husband, William of Orange. He fled to France and **William and Mary** were crowned King and Queen.

Some Scots, mostly Highlanders, remained true to James, however. **The Jacobites,** as they were called, rose, under **Graham of Claverhouse** and almost annihilated William's army in a savage battle at **Killiecrankie** in 1689. But Claverhouse was killed, leaving them leaderless, and they lost heart and returned to their Highlands.

The Massacre of Glencoe: 1692

The government, uneasy about the rebellious Highlanders, issued a proclamation, ordering all the clans to take an oath of allegiance to the crown by the first day of 1692. Circumstances prevented **MacIan MacDonald of Glencoe** from taking the oath until after the deadline. This provided the government with a chance to rid itself of any likely threat from one of the most powerful clans. A company of Campbell soldiers, commanded by a relation of MacIan's, **Captain Robert Campbell of Glenlyon,** billeted themselves on the MacDonalds in Glencoe. Under orders from higher authority, they rose up at dawn and slaughtered their hosts. The barbarity of the Massacre of Glencoe produced public outcry, not so much because of the number killed—38 out of about 150—but because of the abuse of hospitality. The king denied all foreknowledge: as a gesture, he sacked his Secretary of State, the Master of Stair, who had instigated the deed.

The Union of Parliaments: 1707

In 1695 Scotland's economy was shattered by an unsuccessful attempt to colonize the Darien Peninsula, between North and South America. The failure of this **Darien Scheme** was partly due to fever and inhospitable Spaniards, and partly because England lost its nerve and withdrew promises of financial backing. Scotland, literally bankrupt, was forced to accept the **Treaty of Union,** in 1707, uniting the parliaments of England and Scotland. This carefully worded document brought advantage to both countries: in particular, it gave Scotland a badly needed boost to her economy and the right to Presbyterianism, and removed the threat of further war between the two countries.

Jacobite rebellion: 1708–1746

The signing of the Treaty of Union forced the Scots to accept a Hanoverian succession to the throne, but Jacobite loyalties still prevailed in the Highlands. **James Edward Stuart,** son of the deposed James VII/II, was regarded by many as Scotland's king. The Old Pretender, as he was called by Hanoverians, made three unsuccessful attempts to regain his throne. (Pretender is from the French *prétendre*—to claim, not from the English word for make-believe.) In 1708 he only got as far as the Firth of Forth. In 1715 he persuaded the Earl of Mar to rally an army of Highlanders. Mar raised the Scottish standard and proclaimed James king. The rising looked promising; a battle was fought at **Sheriffmuir** in which the result was inconclusive but The Old Pretender escaped to France, leaving the Highlanders to fend for themselves. In 1719, a final attempt was made, backed by the Spanish; but the supporting fleet was lost in a storm and the Highlanders dispersed.

Stringent measures were put into effect to quell the clans. **General Wade** built a series of military roads and forts, opening up the Highlands and linking strategic strong points, at Fort William, Fort Augustus and Fort George. He raised a regiment of clansmen loyal to the Whig government, the **Black Watch**, whose duty it was to keep order among the resentful clans.

George I came to the throne in 1714, an unattractive German who disliked the British as much as they disliked him. When he died, his son, **George II**, was equally Germanic and unsuitable to rule over those Highlanders who still clung to their Jacobite dreams. This was excuse enough.

Exiled in Rome, the Old Pretender's son, **Prince Charles Edward Stuart**, was a brave young man with a great deal of charm and magnetism. He pawned his mother's rubies and set sail for Scotland, landing in Eriskay on 2 August 1745, with the intention of winning the crown for his father.

At first his reception was daunting: Macdonald of Boisdale told him to go home. 'I am come home', he retorted. MacLeod, and Macdonald of Sleat, refused to help, but Macdonald of Clanranald stood by him. Cameron of Lochiel was reluctant to encourage what he believed to be romantic folly, but he was won over and on 19 August the standard was raised in **Glenfinnan** and the Old Pretender proclaimed King James VIII/III, with Prince Charles as his regent.

Subsequent events are well known. Clansmen flocked to the prince as he marched on Edinburgh, capturing Perth on the way. He held glorious court, at Holyrood, defeated General Cope's soldiers at **Prestonpans**, and gathered more and more support. He led his motley army south, hoping to attract more Jacobites on the way, with the intention of taking London. Meeting little resistance, they got as far as Derby, only 120-odd miles from their target, but at this point the prince's prudent advisers insisted that to go any further was madness. Furious, the prince had to give in and on 6 December 1745, the weary Highlanders turned round to march back to Scotland. Pursued by Hanoverian troops, they struggled north until, in April 1746, they were slaughtered in battle, on **Culloden Moor** near Inverness. They were starving, exhausted, untrained and ill equipped. The prince escaped, with a price of £30,000 on his head, and spent the next five months in hiding in the Western Highlands and Islands. Aided by brave **Flora Macdonald**, he escaped eventually to Europe, where he lived in pathetic and squalid exile for the rest of his life, dying in Rome in 1788.

The aftermath of Culloden: 1746–1860

The English and the Lowland Scots were determined to squash the rebellious Highlanders for ever. They enforced the **Act of Proscription** in 1747, banning Highland dress, the bearing of arms and even the playing of the pipes. Jacobites who had not died at Culloden were either executed or transported. The old way of life was dead. The act was repealed in 1782, but by this time it was no longer relevant; the **Highland Clearances** had begun (see 'Topics'). Between 1780 and 1860, thousands of crofters were evicted from their homes in the Highlands and Islands, to make way for sheep. Many others emigrated voluntarily, to escape persecution, to Canada, America, New Zealand and Australia. In the middle of the 19th century Ireland's potato famine reached the Highlands, resulting in appalling hardship and causing further emigration. By the end of the 19th century, the rural Highlands and Islands were almost deserted.

The Scottish Enlightenment: 18th/19th century

Meanwhile, the Lowland aristocracy drifted south, seduced by London, leaving room for a burgeoning middle class. Unfettered by the inhibitions of social mores, without the blinkered vision and moribund minds of a nobility which had grown complacent, a new intelligentsia emerged in a surge of genius to dazzle the world. Egalitarian social clubs became centres for debate and the free exchange of views. Philosophy and literature flourished. David Hume, Adam Smith, Thomas Carlyle were but a few of the great names that contributed to the Enlightenment. Sydney Smith, though not a Scot, taught in Edinburgh and helped to found the *Edinburgh Review*. Allan Ramsay the poet lived long enough to see the birth of the Enlightenment. Robert Burns was a product of the period, Sir Walter Scott was a leading influence. Others were: James Thomson the poet, Tobias Smollett the writer, James Boswell, biographer of Dr Johnson, James Watt the physicist who invented the steam engine. These remarkable men, and many more, achieved an astonishing record of success in all fields of human accomplishment. Scottish physicians, engineers and inventors led the world.

The Enlightenment spanned about a century, from after Culloden until Queen Victoria discovered Scotland in the mid-19th century and herds of nobility stampeded north to smother the piercing blasts of innovation with cosy convention.

A flourishing cotton industry collapsed in the 1860s when the American Civil War cut off supplies of raw cotton and heavy industry developed instead. Glasgow, once the biggest tobacco importer in Britain, led the world in shipbuilding. Expanding industries meant expanding labour forces; there were concentrations of population in industrial areas, fed by refugee Highlanders and Irish.

20th-century Scotland

Shipbuilding and engineering developed rapidly from the mid-19th century until, by the beginning of the 20th century, some 100,000 jobs were related to Clydeside shipbuilding alone. The Steel Company of Scotland, founded in 1871, replaced iron, and the entire economy of west and mid-Scotland depended on Glasgow's heavy industry. The First World War took its toll of Scottish manhood, but it needed a constant supply of arms and ships and machinery and there was more than enough work for those left behind. It was the Great Depression in the 1920s and 1930s that dealt Scotland a mortal blow. After the Wall Street Crash in 1929, the global wave of economic disaster washed over Clydeside and by 1936 the output from the shipyards had fallen from three quarters of a million tons to less than 60,000, with at least two-thirds of the workforce unemployed. In order to try to increase efficiency and generate more trade, firms merged and pruned their labour forces still further, resulting in more job losses.

Not surprisingly, socialism flourished, passionately fuelled by leaders like James Maxton and Emmanuel Shinwell. Public opinion favoured the plight of the workers and by the end of the 1930s, things were beginning to look up. The Second World War brought with it a fresh demand for armaments and ships: Clydeside boomed and Scotland grew prosperous again. But after the war, competition from abroad began to steal much of the trade. Instead of looking ahead and seeing the imperative need to modernize and revitalize old methods, the Scots, led by militant unions, grumbled and groaned and went on strike, refusing to accept innovations which could have kept them in the forefront of the world's industry. Strikes led to failure to meet deadlines and buyers went elsewhere for their goods. Shipyards, steelworks and factories closed. Less coal was needed so coalmines closed. Sullen Scots queued for their dole cheques and blamed their employers.

The oil boom in the 1970s has brought new prosperity to the east coast for a while and will probably spread to the west, but this is short-lived affluence. Recently, as demonstrated by Glasgow, a new generation of enterprising minds is turning the tide of apathy. Diversification has spread a rash of light industry throughout the country and workers are more inclined to negotiate for rights than to cripple their livelihood with strikes.

The Scottish education system is more democratic and more effective than that of England. When England had but two universities, Scotland had four. Until recently considerably more Scottish children received a secondary education. The legal system is also different, rooted in Roman and Germanic customary law, it is more logical than English law and is based on common law.

Politically, Scotland leans to the left and juggles with the idea of nationalism. Those in favour of autonomy hold that they are the poor relations of politicians at Westminster, whose survival-of-the-fittest policies make no allowance for Scotland's circumstances. But when, in 1979, they were invited to vote for Devolution, over 36% didn't bother to vote and the Nationalists lost through the nation's apathy but, genetically proud and fiercely independent by nature, Scotland bides its time. Who can say when the Stone of Destiny will be brought from its hiding place?

Part IV

BORDERS

Dryburgh Abbey

March, march, Ettrick and Teviotdale,
Why the deil dinna ye march forward in order!
March, march, Eskdale and Liddesdale,
All the blue bonnets are bound for the Border.

—Sir Walter Scott

Most of the routes into Scotland take you over a summit from which you look across a chequerboard of fertile farmland, laced with wooded river valleys within a rim of undulating hills. In dramatic contrast is the savage, rocky coastline with cliff-hung fishing towns and villages.

Every inch of this borderland was fought over, bitterly and often, from pre-historic times until the middle of the 17th century: many ruins bear witness to those violent times. Buildings and whole towns were sacked and hastily rebuilt: most settlements were fortified. The four magnificent abbeys, at Melrose, Jedburgh, Kelso and Dryburgh, built in the 12th century by David I, and within only a few miles of each other in the fertile river valleys, were destroyed and repaired many times before the Reformation led to their final decay.

It was not just the invading English who caused havoc: the Border Reivers were the powerful border families who warred amongst themselves, raiding each other's territory and stealing the cattle. Ballads and folk tales have romanticized them: in reality they were savage and barbaric.

The fast-flowing rivers, now internationally famous for their salmon and trout, were harnessed in the old days to drive woollen mills: today, though the mills may be powered by more modern means, the Borders are famous for their textiles. Farming and horse-breeding also play an important part in the economy of this fertile land and the annual agricultural shows provide robust local colour.

Much has been written in prose, poetry and song, trying to capture the elusive spirit of the Borders. Perhaps Sir Walter Scott, that son of Edinburgh who spent the last years of his life at Abbotsford and made the Borders his domain, wrote most.

The turbulent days of the Border Reivers are remembered today with annual **Common Riding Festivals**, in several of the towns, each with its own local variation, remembering the days when the men rode out from the town to check the boundaries. These celebrations are worth seeking out, transforming normally sedate communities into colourful carnival mood, decked out in period costume, providing lighthearted entertainment and pageantry. These Common Ridings take place throughout the summer months and last from a few days up to a week. They usually incorporate some special event in local history, as well as a 'ride' when a great cavalcade of riders streams out of the town to 'inspect the marches'.

You can pick up one of the free *What's on in the Borders* leaflets that are published monthly, from any Tourist Information Centre. Some of the Border Ridings and festivals to look out for in June include: the Peebles Beltane Festival, the Earlston Civic Week, Galashiels Braw Lads Gathering, Hawick Common Riding, Melrose Summer Festival, and Selkirk Common Riding. In July there are: Jethart Callants Festival, Jedburgh, Duns Summer Festival, Kelso Civic Week, Innerleithen St Ronans Border Games, and Lauder Common Riding. The Coldstream Civic Week usually takes place in August.

The Kelso Races are lively gatherings from October to May, and you get a good taste of Border atmosphere at the many agricultural shows, games and horse sales that proliferate. Several of the stately homes stage extravaganzas in the summer in an attempt to keep their stately roofs on.

SPORT
Game fishing is famous in the Borders. Permits and advice are available from tackle shops, some post offices, sport shops, hotels and the tourist information centres for river and loch fishing, not always as expensive as you might expect. The Tweed is most famous as a salmon river, but there is an endless variety of both game and coarse fishing, not only on other rivers such as the Ettrick, Teviot, Whiteadder and Till, but in many smaller streams and lochs. A large number of hotels offer fishing packages for all grades of fishermen, including beginners. The Scottish Borders Tourist Board publishes an inexpensive book, *Angling in the Scottish Borders*, which is available from any of its information offices. For further information about fishing see pp. 17–20.

Riding is popular in this land of horse-breeders. Most villages will have a pony trekking centre and a few hotels provide riding. Your hotel or the local tourist information office will have details. Some of the tourist maps show riding centres, marked with a horseshoe (see also p. 27).

Walking is rewarding in the Borders, and not too challenging, with an endless choice of routes. The Southern Upland Way is a footpath that meanders for 212 miles right across the Lowlands from the Irish Sea in the southwest up to Cockburnspath on the North Sea coast, through moor and hill, past rivers and lochs, with panoramic views.

BORDERS

N

| 0 | 10 kms |
| 0 | 10 miles |

St Abbs
1
Coldingham
Eyemouth
A1
Ayton
Whiteadder W.
2
Chirnside
Foulden
Duns
16
Ladykirk
Tweed
Blackadder W.
Lammermuirs
Lauder
15
A697
Greenlaw
3
Coldstream
West Linton
Penilands
Moorfoots
Gala Water
Leader W. A68
Eildeston W.
A703
Peebles
11
6
Earlston
Galashiels
Melrose
5
4
Kelso
Walkerburn
A72
Broughton
9
Innerleithen
8
Dryburgh
10
Tweed
Eildon
Hills
12
Drumelzier
St Boswells
Tweed
Dollar Law
2682
A708
13
Selkirk
Glenwhappen
Rig
2263
A701
Tweedsmuir
14
Yarrow Water
St Mary's
Loch
Ettrickbridge
Clyde Law
1790
White Coombe
2696
Hawick
Denholm
Jedburgh
2651
Hart Fell
Bonchester
Bridge
Teviot
A7
Cheviots
Teviothead
7
ENGLAND
Liddlesdale
Newcastleton

1   Fast Castle
2   Edinshall Broch
3   The Hirsel
4   Floors Castle
5   Smailholm Tower
6   Mellerstain House
7   Hermitage Castle
8   Abbotsford
9   Neidpath Castle
10 Traquair House
11 Glentress Forest
12 Roxburgh
13 Newark Castle
14 Bowhill
15 Thirlestane Castle
16 Manderston

Much of it crosses the Borders and the stretch that takes in St Mary's Loch is particularly rewarding. If you like solitude, the early morning of a fine day is ideal: you'll feel very close to nature there, by the still water, among the hills. Details of the best walks in each area are available from the tourist offices, as well as information about guided walks and hikes, organized by the Ranger Service.

Golfers will find plenty of good courses throughout the region, marked on tourist maps with a triangular flag.

Sub-aqua divers are catered for at St Abbs Head, one of Scotland's most famous stretches of coast for diving. From here, south to Eyemouth, is a maritime reserve, with abundant sea life to be found in glass-clear water. In places it is shallow—40 ft (122 m) or so—and therefore ideal for beginners. Because the weather is so variable here, you may have to wait around for calm.

TOURIST INFORMATION
The Scottish Borders Tourist Board, Municipal Buildings, High Street, Selkirk TD7 4JX, tel 0750 20555 is open all the year with a 24-hour answerphone service. The only other tourist office in the Borders region that is open all year is at Murray's Green, Jedburgh, tel 0835 63435/63688.
Local offices are at : Eyemouth: Auld Kirk, tel 08907 50678, open April–Oct; Coldstream: Henderson Park, tel 0890 2607, open April–Oct; Kelso: Turret House, tel 0573 23464, open April–Oct; Melrose: Priorwood Gardens, tel 089682 2555, open April–Oct; Selkirk: Halliwell's House, tel 0750 20054, open April–Oct; Galashiels: Bank Street, tel 0896 55551, open April–Oct; Peebles: High Street, tel 0721 20138, open April–Oct; Hawick: Common Haugh, tel 0450 72547, open April–Oct.

The Coast and Northeast Corner

Fishing and smuggling played an important part in forming the characters of those whose descendants live along the coastal fringe of the Borders. Some of the towns and villages are little changed since the days when smugglers teemed in the warrens of twisting wynds and closes, evading the excisemen in underground hideaways.

St Abbs

St Abbs, on the northeast corner of the coast, down the B6438, a cul-de-sac off the A1107, is a pretty village, almost Cornish in character, clinging tenaciously to the cliffs, with narrow zigzag streets running steeply down to the harbour, lined by brightly painted terraced fisher cottages, some of which still have their quaint 'doll's house' sheds in front. St Abbs is a holiday village now, with just a few lobster boats replacing the trawlers that used to go out for haddock, cod and turbot. Boats still come in during bad weather for shelter. Down in the harbour there are upturned boats, piles of nets, tottering stacks of creels and boxes backed by the old stone tackle-sheds. St Abbs has one of the few sandy beaches on this bit of coast.

St Abbs Head is a rugged promontory just north of the village—a towering headland of black volcanic rock, pounded by the sea, with a lighthouse at its tip. Parking is limited at the lighthouse but it is an invigorating walk, across cropped turf dotted with sheep, whins and wind-stunted trees, the restless sea in the background. You can go over the lighthouse at the keeper's discretion. This desolate headland is a wildlife reserve and there are many different species of sea-bird: guillemots, like a host of chattering waiters; razorbills, with their cut-throat razor beaks and their endearing courting ritual; shags, stretching out their black wings to dry their feathers, and many more. The air is vibrant with their noise. There is an excellent Visitors Centre at Northfield Farm Steading, with displays and information about all the things in the reserve.

Fast Castle, about three miles to the west, out on Wheat Stack, attached to the mainland by a terrifying gangway, is a lovely walk along the cliffs, but take care where you put your feet—the path approach is hazardous. All you can see now are the tattered remains of what was once a notorious fortress, used by wreckers and robbers, perched half-way up the cliff. It is easy to see why Scott used Fast Castle as the model for 'Wolf's Crag' in *The Bride of Lammermoor*. It is accessible, with care, from the cliff above. Its origins are not known: it was a stronghold of the Home family (pronounced Hume) by the end of the 14th century. Margaret Tudor, Henry VIII's sister, stayed there on her way to marry James IV, leaving her entourage of 1500 attendants at Coldingham Priory. She was fourteen years old at the time. What can have been her thoughts as she stood in her bedchamber, fresh from the magnificent English court, and looked out across that bleak sea with her heavy-lidded eyes. The year was 1503: in ten years time in an upstairs room in Linlithgow, she was to weep for her faithless husband, one of the many flowers of the forest that were 'a' wede awae' on Flodden Field.

Coldingham

Coldingham, a mile inland to the southwest on the A1107, is an attractive, twisting village with the remains of a 13th-century priory, the choir of which is now the parish church. A soaring arch rises with splendid dignity from the ruined foundations, ancient gravestones and fragments of carved masonry scattered at its feet. Making an impressive foreground to a distant seascape, the priory was mostly demolished by Cromwell in 1648. It bore the right of sanctuary for lawbreakers, the boundary within which they were safe being marked by crosses. On the beach you can collect pretty coloured pebbles which make unusual ornaments, polished and displayed in glass jars.

Eyemouth

Just down the coast, Eyemouth is a small seaside town with a busy commercial fishing industry that includes the export of shell-fish. When James VI/I granted it a Free Port Charter, in 1597, it became a thriving centre for smugglers. The intricate design of the older part of the town provided a maze of hiding places and escape routes and many of the houses still have hidden chambers and secret passages: it is said that more than half of Eyemouth is underground! The cliffs around are honeycombed with caves.

Today, standing on the harbour wall, looking out to sea, you find yourself thinking back to Friday 14 October, 1881—a day that dawned too bright and too still, with the barometer reading too low. The fishing fleet sailed out to sea: at noon there was a terrifying dark stillness, followed by a sudden storm—a tornado that devastated the fleet. Many drowned at once; others, struggling home, were smashed on the rocks outside the harbour in sight of their helpless families. Only six boats got back safely; 23 were lost; 129 Eyemouth men were drowned, leaving 107 widows. Other fleets up and down the coast suffered in the same way. Not an event one can easily forget.

The Eyemouth Museum (open daily April–Oct), is in the converted Georgian Auld Kirk, in the Market Place down near the harbour. It was opened in 1981 as a centenary memorial to the fishing disaster. Look out for the tapestry, a most striking piece of contemporary work with pictures of the storm, sea scenes and the names of all the boats that were lost and of the men aboard them. There is also the wheel-house of a modern fishing boat as well as the fishing and farming history of this region.

Eyemouth Harbour, recently improved and enlarged, is long and narrow and teeming with maritime life. Fish boxes are stacked in open-sided sheds surrounded by all the clutter of the sea: nets and derricks and craft of all sizes, and great ribbed skeletons of hulls propped in cradles. For those who find the North Sea rather chilly, there is a swimming pool with sauna and sunbed at The Shore, as well as trampolines, one of those huge outdoor chess and draughts boards and a children's playground. **Gunsgreen House**, opposite the harbour, is alleged to have secret passages leading to the water.

Every July, Eyemouth holds a Children's Picnic and Herring Festival.

WHERE TO STAY AND EAT
There are several not very inspiring hotels and guest houses in Eyemouth, some overlooking the harbour, all quite cheap. You won't find much in the way of haute cuisine around this unpretentious area, but if you want a warm welcome and local atmosphere, try **The Contented Sole,** in Harbour Road, Eyemouth, tel 08907 50268. It's open all day and you can get bar meals. If you like to try local food, 'Eyemouth Pale' is a lighter, more delicate version of smoked haddock, and Eyemouth Tart is a delicious confection made with walnuts, currants and coconut.

Ayton

Ayton is a crossroad village, southwest of Eyemouth. Prominent here is **Ayton Castle** (open 2–5 on Sundays in the summer, or by appointment, tel 08907 81212), a vast red Victorian pile, clearly seen from the road. This architectural extravaganza is so ostentatious that it is easy to believe the local legend that it developed from its foundations without plans or architect, its creator crossing the river each day to order the erection of yet another tower or turret or crow-stepped gable according to his mood. This splendid example of Scottish Baronial at its most fanciful was in fact designed by Gillespie Graham in 1846, on the site of an ancient fortalice that was destroyed by the English in the 15th century.

Beyond the church, near the imposing entrance to the castle, in a graveyard that is a carpet of snowdrops in early spring, are the ruins of a pre-Reformation church. Among these ivy-covered stones, perched above a chattering river, emissaries of Scots and English kings often met to arrange short-lived truces during the years of the border wars. Many ancient bones lie buried far below the present layer of graves in this tranquil resting-place, and the huge castle, standing high on the skyline, seems to intrude like a brash newcomer on the ancient ruin.

Foulden

Foulden, to the south, is little more than a brightly painted row of cottages on a cobbled terrace on one side of the road, facing a green beyond which the land falls gently away to the Cheviot Hills on the southern horizon. The Flemish-style cottages seem to be gazing out over the magnificent view, their gabled eyebrows for ever raised in surprise. To the left of the row, in the old school house, the door to the post office is set back behind four delightfully incongruous fluted columns.

By the church is a restored two-storey **tithe barn,** with an outside stair and crow-stepped gables, where the minister stored the grain given him by his parishioners as a stipend.

Chirnside

Chirnside, due west of Foulden, is where the racing driver Jim Clark was born and is buried. The **church** has a 12th-century Norman doorway on the south wall. Inside you will see a plaque, dated 1572, telling you to 'Helpe the Pur'. In 1674, the Chirnside minister's wife was buried in this churchyard, wearing a valuable ring. The wicked sexton, returning at night to rob the grave, tried to hack off the ring with a knife. The corpse sat up, screamed and rushed to the manse, yelling: 'Open the door, open the door, for I'm fair clemmed wi' the cauld'. (She later mothered two sons who founded the Original Secession Church!)

Manderston

Manderston (open Thursday and Sunday afternoon, mid May–Sept: adm) is two miles east of Duns, and is one of the finest Edwardian stately homes in Scotland, with 56 acres of gardens. The rhododendrons are especially worth seeing. In the house is what is believed to be the only silver staircase in the world: spare a thought for whoever has to keep it clean. Presumably, to judge by the 56 bells in the servants' quarters, each with a different tone, there were plenty of silver cleaners when the house was built.

Duns

Heading inland towards the heart of the Borders you come to the small county town of Duns, straggling uphill from a solid-looking church on a green mound with narrow streets behind, where buildings seem to jostle each other, all set at odd angles in no apparent order.

Duns has a horse show in May, a Summer Festival in July, which is their Common Riding Celebration, and the Berwickshire Agricultural Association Show in August.

Duns Nature Reserve is reached by a footpath from the top of Castle Street. It has pleasant walks and a short, steep climb up **Duns Law**. The town used to cling to the southwest slope of this hill until the English completely destroyed it in 1545 as part of

Henry VIII's revenge for being refused Mary, Queen of Scots as a daughter-in-law: it was rebuilt in its present position within 50 years. On top of the Law is a stone with a hole in it: a Covenanting army flew its standard here, in 1639, awaiting a battle that never took place. Their general, Leslie, is thought to have had his headquarters in the elegant **Duns Castle**, at the foot of the hill. The stone at the castle gate was erected by Franciscans, claiming Duns to be the birthplace of Johannes Duns Scotus, a great medieval scholar who questioned the teachings of Thomas Aquinas.

The Jim Clark Memorial (open in the summer: adm) is clearly signposted on the west side of the town. Its trophy room displays the trophies of the world champion racing driver who was killed in 1968.

Crumstane Farm Park (open daily except Tuesdays, May-Sept: adm), two miles east of Duns, offers farm walks with many rare breeds of farm animals and poultry.

Edinshall Broch

For anyone interested in antiquities, Edinshall Broch is four miles north of Duns on the northeast shoulder of Cockburn Law, the sturdy remains of one of those Iron Age towers, unique to Scotland and rare so far south. The 20–30-minute climb from a pine wood by the road is clearly marked. It crosses a suspension bridge over Whiteadder Water, which cascades down over gleaming slabs of granite below, the sound of its turmoil carrying far across the bleak moorland. Scattered piles of stones on the grassy slopes are relics of those settlers who roamed the desolate hillside with their beasts, huddling for refuge within the tall, double-walled tower, honeycombed with chambers and galleries. The massive walls were the base of a tapering tower about 40 ft (122 m) high, its one passage-entrance easily defended.

Greenlaw

Greenlaw, a little town seven miles southwest of Duns on the Blackadder, has a remarkable **church** whose tower was built to resemble a church spire but which contained the prison. Known locally as **Hell's Hole**, it has a sinister grid-iron gate, or *yett*, and barred windows. Originally the courthouse was also joined to the church as if to emphasize the connection between the wrath of God, and justice.

WHERE TO STAY AND EAT
All the following will give you bed and breakfast for less than £30. **Barniken House Hotel**, 18 Murray Street, Duns, tel 0361 82466, is a Georgian house in its own grounds in the town, family-run, with only a few bedrooms. There is a putting green in the garden and you can get bar-food all day. **The Black Bull,** in Black Bull Street, and the **White Swan,** in the Market Square, both have a few bedrooms for those who like to be at the centre of things. Greenlaw has several hotels of which **The Castle Hotel**, tel 03616 217, a Georgian coaching inn, family-run, is friendly, and **Bridgend Guest House** in West High Street, built in 1861, is by the river and has trout fishing. There is also the **Waterloo Arms Hotel** in Chirnside, tel 089081 520, a village inn with a mention in the *Good Pub Guide.*

The Tweed Valley

The River Tweed is one of Scotland's most famous salmon-fishing rivers, and also one of its most delightful. It rises in the hills above Moffat, quickly gathering strength to meander through a wide, mostly wooded valley until it reaches the sea at Berwick-on-Tweed, across the border in England. (The name 'tweed', incidentally, comes not from the river but from a printing error by an English clerk employed by James Locke of London in 1829, who misread a blotted word—tweels—on a consignment note, 'tweels' being the Scots word for cloth.)

Ladykirk

Ladykirk, a few miles southwest of the mouth of the Tweed, is just a handful of houses surrounding a cruciform **church**—a pale rose-coloured church that is worth travelling a long way to see. Built in 1500, its solid buttresses, topped by carved finials, support the tremendous weight of an overlapping slabbed-stone roof, and a curiously oriental tower that was added in 1743 by William Adam. The delicate blush of the exterior seems to glow in daylight as if lit from within translucent walls.

James IV was almost drowned crossing the Tweed here and he vowed to build a shrine, dedicated to Our Lady, in gratitude for his survival. Ladykirk was the fulfilment of his promise: a magnificent rarity in a land where the house of God, since the Reformation, is so often grimly austere.

Inside this well-restored gem, a spiral stair leads up to the original living-quarters of the priest, with a small window from which he could watch the altar. James often visited Ladykirk, and he knelt at prayer here before the Battle of Flodden in 1513. Sit in one of the pews for a moment, and you can almost catch an echo of that poignant lament, composed by a woman over two hundred years after Flodden, that enshrines the whole tragedy of the battle:

> We'll hear nae mair lilting at the ewe-milking
> Women and bairns are heartless and wae:
> Sighing and moaning on ilka green loaning—
> The flowers of the forest are a' wede awae.

Coldstream

Literally a border town, Coldstream clings to the banks of the Tweed a few miles southwest of Ladykirk, seeming to ignore the rumble and grind of the traffic that thunders continually up its narrow main street. The Tweed, winding through its broad valley, casts a spell over this area, each bend and pool and cascade having its own special character and beauty. The fast, dark currents slide and whirl seawards carrying memories of the past when the mingled blood of Scots and English so often stained the water. Coldstream was the first place where it was easy to cross the river: many armies passed this way and camped on the banks.

The Common Riding Celebrations take place at the beginning of August, during Coldstream Civic Week. There is also the Borders Country Fair at The Hirsel, every June.

In the middle of the bridge that spans the Tweed is a plaque marking the spot where Robert Burns first put a foot across the border into England in 1787.

On the north side of the bridge is a tiny 'marriage house', much used by fugitive lovers from England in the 18th century. The figure in a frock-coat, just beyond, who stands Nelson-like on a fluted column, dispatch papers in hand, lightning-conductor pointing heavenwards from the back of his head, was a popular Victorian MP—Charles Marjorie-banks.

Henderson Park is a formal garden overlooking the river off the Main Street. Look for the engraved stone, erected by the Coldstream Guards, recording how, in 1660, their predecessors crossed the Tweed nearby, following their beloved General Monk, to crush Cromwell and establish Charles II on the throne. Although they were not raised here, they later adopted their title of Coldstream Guards in honour of this historic event.

Coldstream Museum (open Whitsun to Sept, Mon, Fri and Sun, 2–5, Sat, 10–1: adm) is in General Monk's Headquarters in the town's asymmetrical Market Square, rebuilt in 1863. It is a simple building, with iron gates across a large door, and it houses regimental and local history exhibits.

Abbey Road leads down from the Main Street to where a Cistercian priory stood for four centuries until it was destroyed by the English in 1545. No trace remains today but human bones were excavated in 1834, some of which may have been the sad remains of bodies that arrived here, piled on waggons in 1513: Flodden's dead, brought to the Lady Abbess for burial.

The Hirsel, seat of the Douglas-Home family, is signposted by a white board pinned to a tree on the western edge of the town. Lord Home (pronounced Hume) of the Hirsel was Prime Minister when President Kennedy was assassinated in 1963. He made history by renouncing his peerage and fighting a by-election at Kinross, during which, although Premier, he was technically not a member of either the House of Lords or the House of Commons. The house is not open to the public but visitors can walk in the park at any time of the year, leaving a donation in the honesty box in the car park. A picturesque stableyard has been converted into a Homestead Museum, craft centre and workshops, each stall containing domestic displays under such headings as: wash house; joiner's shop; forestry; archaeology. Maps and guides are sold and there are toilets and a coffee shop.

WHERE TO STAY AND EAT

The sober truth is that, with one exception, the best hotels around Coldstream are across the river—in England! The exception is **Wheatsheaf Hotel** in Swinton, tel 089086 257, an attractive country inn with only three bedrooms. They won the Scottish Tourist Board Competition for Best Eating Place in the Borders in 1990 so even if you can't get a room it's worth eating there. Otherwise, if you want to spoil yourself you are advised to sneak back over that bridge to Cornhill-on-Tweed in Northumberland: it is still a Coldstream telephone number, if that makes it feel better. Moderately priced, **Till-mouth Park Hotel**, in Cornhill-on-Tweed, tel 0890 2255, is an imposing Victorian baronial pile in 1000 acres with salmon fishing. Antique furniture gives a country-house atmosphere and the food is good. **The Collingwood Arms,** also in Cornhill-on-Tweed, tel 0890 2424/2556/2265, is cheap, and a nice old inn. At Crookham, just outside Cornhill, and also cheap, **The Coach House,** built round a sunny courtyard, is very comfortable with good home cooking. There's not much in the way of gourmet restaurants around here, apart from the Wheatsheaf.

Kelso

Two famous border rivers, the Teviot and the Tweed, meet under the walls of Kelso, a compact market town facing south across green plains towards the Cheviots. Originally called Calkou (Chalk-hill), Kelso was never strongly fortified, relying on its status as an abbey town for immunity from attack. However, being on the threshold of Scotland, it was in fact frequently sacked by the English; it was also the last staging post for Scottish armies on their way south. The Old Pretender was proclaimed king in the market place in 1715 and his son, retreating north after his march on London in 1745, stayed here.

In spite of shocking architectural vandalism in the 19th century, when the town hall's piazza was filled in and a monstrous bank was built on a corner, the elegant Georgian square is still very fine, almost Flemish in style, its spaciousness a marked contrast to the narrow streets of most border towns, crammed behind defensive walls.

The Kelso Races take place in the winter months, from October to May. The Berwickshire Hunt has its point-to-point in Kelso in February, and the Buccleuch and Jed Forest point-to-point takes place in April. April is also the month for the Kelso Horse Sales. The Great Tweed Raft Race takes place in May, followed by the Kelso Dog Show in June. July is usually the month for the Kelso Games, and also Kelso Civic Week, which celebrates the Common Riding Festival, followed by the Border Union Agricultural Show. The Scottish Horse Driving Trials take place at Floors Castle during the summer and in September there are the Kelso Ram Sales. (These dates should be checked, as some of them vary from year to year.)

Kelso Abbey

Kelso Abbey (open daily: free) was founded by David I in 1128, the monks having been moved there, inexplicably, from Selkirk. All that can be seen today is the façade of the northwest transept, the tower and a small part of the nave. This was once the most powerful ecclesiastical establishment in the land and one of the most wealthy, collecting revenue from dozens of parishes, manors, granges, mills and fisheries. The infant James III was crowned here in 1460. In 1523 the English began their attacks on the abbey, tearing off the roofs and firing the monastic buildings. In 1545 they completed the work, slaughtering a hundred brave defendants, including twelve monks.

Kelso Museum (open April–Oct: adm) is in one of Kelso's oldest buildings, Turret House, Abbey Court, off Bridge Street, owned by the National Trust for Scotland. The museum concentrates on Kelso's history as a market town whose main industries were skinning and tanning—good for anyone interested in local knowledge.

By 29 Roxburgh Street a horseshoe has been set into the road, marking the spot where Prince Charlie's horse cast a shoe in 1745, during his progress south to Derby.

The graceful five-arched bridge over the Tweed was built by Rennie in 1801 as a model for the now demolished Waterloo Bridge, two of whose lamps adorn it.

Floors Castle

Two miles northwest of Kelso, Floors Castle (castle and grounds open Easter; May, June, Sept, Sun–Thurs inclusive; July–Aug, daily; Oct, Sun and Wed; adm) is the home of the Duke of Roxburghe. Built by William Adam between 1721 and 1725, and added to by William Playfair in 1849, this immense castellated mansion, flanked by vast pavilions, with minarets and cupolas, has an almost Eastern look and is best appreciated from a distance. A tree in the grounds marks the spot where James II was killed by an exploding cannon in 1460. Inside, there is a magnificent collection of tapestries, porcelain and paintings.

Floors Castle, the largest inhabited castle in Scotland, used to advertise itself as being the 'ancestral home of Tarzan' having been the location of the film *Greystoke*. Its more romantic claim to fame is that it was the setting for the formal proposal of marriage by Prince Andrew to Miss Sarah Ferguson, now the Duke and Duchess of York, in the spring of 1986.

Mellerstain House

Seven miles northwest of Kelso, Mellerstain (open Easter and 1 May–30 Sept, daily except Sat: adm), the home of Lord Haddington, was partly built by William Adam in 1725 and finished by his son Robert in 1778. It is one of Scotland's finest Georgian mansions, approached down a mile-long avenue of giant beeches, oaks and firs, with formal Italian terraced gardens at the back sloping down to an ornamental lake. Inside, you can see the original Robert Adam ceilings and plaster work, especially in one of the two libraries. The furniture includes pieces by Chippendale, Sheraton and Hepplewhite. Among the paintings are works by Gainsborough, Allan Ramsay, Constable and Veronese.

A brief liaison between a son of the house, Robbie, and Pippin, a lady of easy virtue who lived in one of the estate cottages, resulted in the birth of a jaunty, wolfish Borderer known as Tam o' Shanter. Picaresque tales of his life as a maverick hunter became legend, even in his lifetime.

Smailholm Tower

Smailholm Tower (open daily in summer: adm) is a couple of miles south of Mellerstain, off the B6404, and it would be difficult to find a better example of a 15th-century Border peel tower anywhere. Very well restored, it stands, gaunt and forbidding, 57 ft (174 m) high on a turf-carpeted crag above a small, weed-choked loch. The views over the surrounding flat arable land are extensive; the peak that dominates the horizon to the south is Muckle Cheviot, guardian of the border with England. Monks from Dryburgh Abbey were given these lands in 1160 and grazed their sheep here. In 1799, the tower was a complete ruin. Walter Scott, who had spent many holidays with his grandparents at Sandyknowe Farm just to the east, made a deal with the owner, Scott of Harden, who agreed to save the tower if Sir Walter would write a ballad about it. *The Eve of St John* was the result and Smailholm also got a mention in *Marmion*. It seems incongruous that such a stern-faced fortress should contain a museum of dolls and tapestries, but the theme of the display is Scott's *Minstrelsy of the Scottish Border*. With piped 'atmospheric' music to fuel the imagination, it isn't difficult to picture the five storeys as they were, with store rooms below and living quarters above, despite the present exhibitions. When the wind is howling outside one almost hears the war-cries of marauding clans and the clash of broadsword and pike.

Kirk Yetholm

Before going on up the Tweed Valley, pay a visit to Kirk Yetholm, about seven miles southeast of Kelso on the B6352. This was the gypsy capital of Scotland, where all gypsy queens were crowned, until 1883, when the last one, Esther Faa Blythe, died.You can still see the Gypsy Palace, a tiny cottage in the village. Many of Flodden's dead were buried in the churchyard here, in 1513, around an earlier church.

WHERE TO STAY AND EAT
If it is self-indulgent luxury you are after, then it has to be **Sunlaws House Hotel**, Heiton, Kelso, tel 05735 331. It's expensive but worth it. Owned by the Duke of Roxburghe, Sunlaws is an 18th-century baronial residence in 200 acres of gardens and parkland on the banks of the Teviot. Conversion to comfortable hotel has not spoiled its family home atmosphere, with antique furniture and excellent food and wine. They offer fishing on the Tweed and the Teviot, shooting, tennis and even croquet.

In contrast, moderately priced **Cross Keys Hotel**, The Square, Kelso, tel 0573 23303, is one of Scotland's oldest coaching inns, completely modernized, right in the middle of the town overlooking the square. Much more peaceful, and slightly cheaper, **Ednam House Hotel,** in Bridge Street, Kelso, tel 0573 24168/9, is an 18th-century mansion overlooking the Tweed. Modern extensions haven't spoiled the original ceilings, fireplaces and woodwork of the old bit and it is extremely comfortable. It is weighed down with stars from the leading good-food, good-hotel guides. If you are interested in a very cheap farmhouse holiday, with pony trekking, shooting, fishing and walking, good home cooking, a cosy open-fire atmosphere, on a 1350-acre sheep farm, try **Bowmont Centre and Guest House**, Belford-on-Bowmont, Yetholm, tel 057382 362.

If you stay in any of the above hotels, it would be silly not to eat their food. For a lunch out, try the restaurant in the old stable courtyard at **Floors Castle**, Kelso, tel 0573 23333, overlooking the Tweed. Try Floors Kitchen Pheasant Pâté, or the fresh or smoked local salmon. Good home baking from the castle kitchen, too, and none of it expensive. A local speciality to look out for is Yetholm Bannock, a very rich shortbread with crystallized ginger.

Dryburgh Abbey

Returning to the Tweed, Dryburgh Abbey (open daily; adm), ten miles west of Kelso, is one of the quartet of 12th-century Border abbeys founded by David I, all within a few miles of each other. Built in 1150, it is a beautiful ruin, in a loop of the Tweed. Its cloister buildings are more complete than those of other Scottish monasteries, though little remains of the church itself, which is all in the pinkish, warm-coloured local stone. In common with the other abbeys, Dryburgh was continually ravaged by the English until 1545 when Hertford, acting for Henry VIII, left it a smoking ruin. It was robbed of its usefulness, but not of its tranquil beauty, or its atmosphere of sanctity. Look out for Walter Scott's tomb, behind a railing: his great-grandfather owned the abbey lands at the beginning of the 18th century. Earl Haig, the First World War leader, is also buried here. The stately cedars of Lebanon that throw their shade across the grass were brought back from the Holy Land during one of the Crusades.

Scott's View

A detour from Dryburgh, five miles north up the B6356, to Earlston, takes in Scott's View from below the crest of Bemersyde Hill. This very typical Borders' panorama, across a chequerboard of woods and fields, to distant hills, with the Tweed sparkling below, was such a favourite of Sir Walter's that when his mile-long funeral cortege passed by on the way to Dryburgh Abbey, his horses paused here of their own accord! For the history of the Eildon Hills, the three nearest to the southwest, see Denholm and Rubers Law, below, p. 90. Legend has King Arthur and his knights sleeping below the Eildons, awaiting summons back to the world.

Earlston

Earlston (with a Summer Festival in June) was the home in the 13th century of Thomas the Rhymer, the seer who was given his gift of prophecy by the Fairy Queen and whose gift was so effective that he was known as True Thomas. There is a stone, worn almost bare, in the east wall of the parish church, with his name carved on it, and the chunk of ruined wall behind the café to the south of the village is said to be all that remains of his tower.

Sorrowlessfield, in Earlston, was so called because it was the only farm in the Borders to which all the men returned safely after the tragic battle of Flodden in 1513.

Lauder

Go on up the valley of Leader Water, six miles or so northwest to Lauder—a one-street town with its market place in the middle, once an important staging post in the days of coaches. The pink stuccoed church, built in 1673, is in the form of a Greek cross with each arm equal and the pulpit in the middle under the tower. Lauder Common Riding is in early August.

Thirlestane Castle

Thirlestane Castle (open May, June, Sept, Wed, Thurs and Sun only; July–Aug, daily except Sat, afternoons only: adm), home of the Maitland family for four hundred years, is on the outskirts of Lauder. This huge pile, built onto in many different styles over the centuries, was originally a 14th-century fortress, Lauder Fort, though most of what you see today is late Tudor and early Victorian. William Maitland, Secretary of State to Mary Queen of Scots, converted the original fortress into a home; John Maitland was Secretary and Chancellor to her son James VI. A lot of the rich decoration inside was the work of the architect Sir William Bruce in the 17th century, commissioned by John Maitland's grandson, the Duke of Lauderdale who was a close friend of King Charles II.

Among the treasures to see in the magnificent state rooms are paintings by Gainsborough, Lawrence, Hoppner and Romney. The nurseries are a delight, with all the old toys on display. There is a Border Country Life Museum in the grounds, giving an interesting record of life in the Borders from earliest times, as well as a tea room and gift shop.

Melrose

Melrose is an unpretentious little town best known for its ruined abbey, fragments of which can be seen incorporated into a few of the older houses in the town. The Melrose Summer Festival, in June, brings all the inhabitants out *en fête*: some of the ceremonies, re-enacting history, take place among the ruins of the abbey. The Southern Upland Way passes close to the north of the town and makes a delightful walk along the banks of the Tweed.

Melrose Abbey
Melrose Abbey (open daily: adm) was perhaps the most beautiful of the four abbeys founded by David I in the Borders in the 12th century. Established in 1136 to replace a Celtic monastery at Old Melrose nearby, it was, like its sisters, sacked frequently by the English and as frequently rebuilt by its monks. Much of its mellow stone still remains, soaring upwards, a triumphant harmony of arches, towers and windows, all most splendidly decorated. Don't miss the enigmatic carving of a pig playing the bagpipes. Robert Bruce's heart is believed to be buried here in its casket, having failed to make it to the Holy Land. In fulfilment of a vow that he had made to the king before he died, his friend Sir James Douglas cut out his heart and set off to the Holy Land, where it was to be buried. But Douglas was killed on the way, fighting against Moors, in Spain, and the heart was returned to Scotland and buried in the abbey. An embalmed heart, excavated in this century and hastily reburied, is claimed to be the royal organ. The Abbey has its own **Museum**, in the Commendator's House, at the entrance, with local history and a room devoted to excavations from the Roman fort at Trimontium.

The Melrose Motor Museum (open daily in summer: adm) is 200 yards from the Abbey going towards Newstead. This private collection of about 20 vintage cars as well as motor cycles and cycles, old signs, posters and memorabilia will fascinate the mechanically-minded members of the family. While the motor enthusiasts are sighing over vintage cars, horticulturalists should slip across to **Priorwood Gardens** also by the Abbey (open daily April–Oct, and 7 Nov–24 Dec: adm). Priorwood belongs to the National Trust for Scotland, and all the flowers you see here are suitable for drying. For anyone who has tried to grow everlasting flowers and then attempted to tease them into one of those chic, expensive arrangements that are fashionable these days, there is a wealth of inspiration in these gardens. If you feel daunted, however, there is a shop where you can buy them. There is also an NTS Visitor Centre and shop, an orchard walk and picnic area.

Abbotsford House

Abbotsford House (open daily late March–31 Oct: adm) lies less than two miles west of Melrose and was Sir Walter Scott's home for the last 20 years of his life. He bought a farm here in 1811 but wasn't happy with its name—Clarty Hole—'clarty' being a Scots word meaning dirty, smelly, with certain farmyard connotations; he decided on Abbotsford in memory of the monks from Melrose who used to cross the river nearby. He demolished the farmhouse and, bit by bit, as the money came in from his books, built the house which stands today. When financial disaster overcame him his creditors made him a present of the house. Mock Scots Baronial, it is Sir Walter's monument to himself with ideas of design borrowed from many sources: a cloister from Melrose; a porch from Linlithgow; a ceiling from Roslin. Now a museum, it is a compulsory pilgrimage for any true Scott enthusiast. Visitors can see his personal possessions, the rooms just as they were, and the extraordinary range of things he collected: a lock of Bonnie Prince Charlie's hair, for instance, and one of Robert Burns' drinking tumblers. All the most romantic names in history seem to be represented here, and when you've had enough of nostalgia you can inspect the library with 9000 volumes in it. There is also a teashop serving light refreshments, and a gift shop.

Before tracing the Tweed further, make a detour two miles southwest of Abbotsford, and follow the Yarrow Water a few miles down to Selkirk.

Selkirk

Selkirk means 'kirk-of-the-shieling', a peaceful, rural connotation that no longer applies to this sturdy little town on the hillside above the valleys of the Ettrick and Yarrow, its spires and gables visible for miles, its textile mills tucked away along the river banks. These valleys were once extensive forests, hunting ground for kings and refuge for fugitives. Selkirk men are still called 'Souters' (shoemakers) from the days when cobbling was the main occupation: Prince Charlie ordered 4000 shoes from Selkirk for his barefooted army.

Of the 80 Selkirk men who rode out to fight at Flodden in 1513, only one returned, throwing down a captured English standard at the feet of the waiting families in silent tribute to his fallen friends. The standard is preserved in the public library, and the Selkirk Common Riding, one of the most spectacular of these Border Festivals, in June, culminates in a poignant ceremony reenacting the 'casting of the colours.'

Most of the mills in and around Selkirk have their own mill shops, where you can buy lovely tweeds and woollen goods.

The Market Place, which is triangular, has a statue of Sir Walter Scott on a 20 ft (61 m) pedestal in front of the Town Hall. Scott was county sheriff here for 33 years. In the Town Hall (open weekday afternoons in summer or by arrangement) where Court Sessions were heard in the days of Sir Walter's jurisdiction, there are mementoes of him, and of many other famous 'Souters'.

Halliwell's House Museum and Gallery (open daily April–Oct; weekday afternoons, Nov–Dec, free) is off the main square in the town centre. This row of 18th-century houses has recently been renovated to create an imaginative display of Selkirk's rich history. You can trace the history of the buildings, too, including an ironmonger's shop with a listening post, and there is a video upstairs. The Robson Gallery has exhibitions of all sorts of art, which change frequently.

The statue at the east end of the High Street is of **Mungo Park,** the 18th-century explorer. He was born four miles away at Foulshiels and gave up medical practice to devote himself to exploring the Niger, in which he was finally drowned while escaping in a canoe from hostile natives. **The Flodden Monument** is just beyond Mungo Park's statue: a statue of a standard bearer, with the poignant inscription 'O Flodden Field'.

At **Selkirk Glass** at Linglie Mill, Riverside Road, off the A7 just north of Selkirk, there is a new Visitors' Centre (open all year; free); you can watch glass paperweights being made with all their range of patterns and colours.

There is a plaque over a shop doorway, in West Port, marking where Montrose lodged in 1645 before his defeat at the battle of Philiphaugh a couple of miles to the west. After the battle, General Leslie and his bloodthirsty Covenanter army butchered the remains of Montrose's army, including hundreds of women and children, without mercy, in the name of their God.

Newark Castle

Newark Castle, further west of Selkirk (to visit, apply to the Buccleuch Estates, tel 0750 20081), is where a hundred of these luckless victims were shot. Even without its grim history—and you may find yourself looking for bloodstains and shot-scars on the walls, and listening for the echo of the screams—it is an impressive ruin. It stands five storeys tall, a tower house within a curtain wall on a green mound above the fast flowing river, once a royal hunting seat for the Forest of Ettrick, with the 15th-century arms of James I on the west gable. This castle was the setting for Walter Scott's *Lay of the Last Minstrel.*

Bowhill

Bowhill (grounds open daily in the summer, except Fri, house only open for a few weeks in July and Aug: adm, ring 0750 20732 to avoid disappointment) is three miles west of Selkirk, on the way to Newark. This sumptuous Georgian mansion, built in 1812, is the Borders home of the Scotts of Buccleuch, surrounded by wooded hills that dazzle the eye in autumn. Here, in a truly gracious setting, are works of art including paintings by Leonardo da Vinci, Gainsborough, Reynolds, Claude, Canaletto, Guardi and Raeburn; proof copies of books by Walter Scott; relics of the Duke of Monmouth, and a good deal more. While the culture vultures are sighing over these treasures, this enterprising stately home provides its more philistine visitors with an adventure playground in the park, nature trails, a riding centre, as well as an audio-visual show, mountain-bicycle hire, a gift shop and a licensed tea-room.

St Mary's Loch

Before returning to the Tweed, follow the Yarrow Valley down to St Mary's Loch, 14 miles southwest of Selkirk. This delightful three mile stretch of reed-fringed water among gentle hills is a popular spot for sailors and for fishermen. You can stop for refreshment at Tibbie Shiel's Inn, on the southeast shore of the loch, called after the innkeeper who used to serve Walter Scott, Thomas Carlyle, Robert Louis Stevenson and James Hogg (the poet who was Scott's protégé, known as the Ettrick Shepherd). These literary giants used to come here for convivial gatherings. Hogg lived nearby and his statue can be seen on the wooded hillside overlooking the inn on the other side of the loch. A service is held each year in the churchyard of **St Mary's of the Lowes** overlooking the loch on the northwest. The church has gone now and this annual service celebrates the Blanket Preaching, when the preacher delivered his message from a tent made from a blanket.

One of the most beautiful stretches of the Southern Upland Way skirts the eastern shore of the loch and the walk north from here, about eight miles, to Traquair House (see p. 83) is not too stiff and well worth the effort. There is also a beautiful route from Cappercleuch, on the west side of the loch about nine miles to Tweedsmuir, steep and twisting and remote, with panoramic views. This takes you past **Megget Reservoir**, long and wide, cradled below the hills and winner of a major design award. This valley was once part of the Forest of Ettrick, a favourite hunting ground in the days of David I.

WHERE TO STAY AND EAT

You won't go far wrong in moderately priced **Philipburn House Hotel**, a mile out of Selkirk on the A708 to Peebles, tel 0750 20747/21690. This homely 18th-century country house in five acres of grounds, with its own swimming pool, has a cuisine that has won acclaim in most of the good food guides and first prize in the dinner section of the Scottish Borders Tourist Board competition. Try saddle of roe deer in port wine and bilberry sauce. They offer special packages to include riding, mountain-biking, walking, fishing and excursions. Another hotel that offers fishing, riding and golf, has its own miniature farmyard, and is cheap, is **Woodburn House**, Heatherlie Park, Selkirk, tel 0750 20816. Moderately priced, **Ettrickshaws Hotel**, Ettrickbridge, tel 0750 52229, six miles southwest of Selkirk, is a family-run Victorian mansion in ten acres of the Ettrick valley beside the river. Salmon and trout fishing are included at no extra charge and there is also riding available. **Dryburgh Abbey Hotel**, St Boswells, tel 0835 22261, is an imposing pile in wooded grounds next to the abbey, on the banks of the Tweed; moderately priced and a bit genteel. **The Buccleuch Arms**, in St Boswells, tel 0835 22243, also moderately priced, is a restored 17th-century coaching inn overlooking the village green and they will arrange fishing, golfing, shooting and pony-trekking holidays for you. There are several hotels in Melrose, of which the recently refurbished **Bon Accord**, in the Market Square, tel 089682 2645, is probably the best value. More imposing is the moderately priced **Burts Hotel**, tel 089682 2285, also in the Market Square. **Black Bull Hotel**, Lauder, tel 05782 208, is a restored coaching inn, cheap, with good bar meals and a nice atmosphere.

For food, **Cross Keys Inn**, Selkirk, **Hoebridge Inn**, Gattonside, Melrose, and **Tibbie Shiels Inn**, St Mary's Loch were all runners up in the Scottish Borders Tourist Board Best Eating Place competition in 1990.

Galashiels

On another tributary of the Tweed, the Gala, six miles or so north of Selkirk, Galashiels (Shieling-on-the-Gala) is a busy town that concentrates on the manufacture of textiles. Plain and unpretentious, it lies snugly among green hills and fast flowing rivers. Involved in milling since 1622, Galashiels built the first Scottish carding machine in 1790 and is particularly famous for its tweed and woollen hosiery. The internationally renowned **Scottish College for Textiles** is in the town, launching pad for many aspiring designers.

Galashiels holds its Common Riding celebrations in June, with the Braw Lads Gathering.

The Galashiels **War Memorial** is a reconstruction of a peel tower with a death-roll engraved on a bronze tablet set into the wall, serving as a backdrop to a statue of one of the Border Reivers, sitting on his horse, proud and vigilant. The town crest is interesting and you can see it on the wall of the Municipal Buildings. It consists of a fox, reaching up for some plums, with the motto 'Sour Plums', and commemorates the incident in 1337 when men of Galashiels disposed of a band of English soldiers who were looking for wild plums in the woods.

Old Gala House has a visitor centre with the history of all the lairds of Galashiels, an art gallery and a permanent exhibition of sculpture. **Galashiels Museum** is attached to Peter Anderson's Woollen Mill. They run guided tours round the mill and have interesting displays tracing the history of Galashiels textile industry. At the **Borders Wool Centre** there is a collection of rare breeds of sheep, spinning demonstrations, and a display of all the different fleeces, as well as a shop where you can buy woollen goods.

WHERE TO STAY AND EAT
Kingsknowes Hotel, Selkirk Road, Galashiels, tel 0896 58375, is a moderately priced 19th-century mansion house full of good, solid Victorian character, overlooking the River Tweed and Abbotsford.

If you like a holiday with activities provided, **Tweed Valley Hotel**, Walkerburn, tel 089687 220, is the place for you. This Edwardian country house, also moderately priced, overlooking the River Tweed offers fishing, walking, bicycling, golf, bird-watching and wildlife, as well as courses in sketching and watercolours, a sauna and solarium. Try their Tweed Valley Game Casserole. There are a number of other hotels in Galashiels. If you want to eat out, try the **Redgauntlet Restaurant**, 36 Market Street, Galashiels, tel 0896 2098. Small and nicely furnished, in the centre of the town, they serve excellent local beef, lamb and fish as well as home-made soups and pâtés; Scottish puddings and cheeses.

Scottish Museum of Woollen Textiles

The Scottish Museum of Woollen Textiles (open weekdays all year, and daily in summer, free) is at Walkerburn, half way to Peebles on the A72 from Galashiels. The museum's somewhat uninspiring name houses an extremely interesting collection, showing the history of the wool industry, its development from a humble cottage industry, with the original wool and cloth patterns, through to the thriving activity it is today. There is a mill shop where you can treat yourself to some of the local products.

Innerleithen

When Walter Scott's *St Ronan's Well* was published in 1824, his readers identified the spa in the novel as the mineral spring above Innerleithen and flocked there to take the waters. The contemporary Earl of Traquair who owned the land, a canny Scot, built a pump room to exploit his natural resources and you can still buy a gulp of the water there today, and see the well. One of the earls, perhaps an urbanite at heart, named the streets in Innerleithen after more sophisticated places: Bond Street, The Strand, Princes Street, for example.

Robert Smail's Printing Works, in Innerleithen, has been restored by the National Trust for Scotland and is now a working printing museum with vintage machinery including a 100-year-old press once driven by water, amd a NTS Visitor Centre.

Traquair House

Traquair House (open Easter and daily May–mid-Sept; grounds and restaurant daily from Easter: adm) is three miles southwest of Walkerburn. The name comes from *Tra*—a dwelling or hamlet, and *quair*—winding stream. Dating from the 10th century, Traquair is said to be the oldest mansion in Scotland to have been continuously inhabited by the same family: William the Lion held court here in 1209. The house seems to hum with bustling domesticity as you walk round it, in pleasant contrast to the museum-like atmosphere of most stately homes. The grey harled walls rise to four storeys with corbelled turrets and a steeply pitched roof, not unlike a French château. Twenty-seven monarchs have visited Traquair, notably Mary, Queen of Scots, with Darnley and their infant son, whose cradle you can see, as well as Mary's rosary, crucifix and purse.

Prince Charlie was the last person to leave through the 'Bear Gates' that bar the entrance to the avenue, on his triumphant march to Derby in 1745. They were then clanged shut by the staunchly Jacobite Fifth Earl of Traquair, who vowed they would never be re-opened until a Stuart ruled Scotland again. Another version of this story is that in the days when Catholics were not allowed to own carriages, but continued to do so clandestinely, an unfriendly neighbour of the Catholic Earl of Traquair grassed on him. His carriage and horses were confiscated and he slammed his gates in protest. Whichever story is true, the gates remain closed. At one time the Tweed ran so close to the house that its owner could fish for salmon from his windows: finding, however, that he could also swim in his cellars, James Stuart, the 17th-century laird, diverted the course of the river so that it now flows a quarter of a mile away. The grounds offer woodland walks, a maze, craft workshops and exhibitions. Ale is still produced in the 18th-century brewhouse and there is an annual Traquair Fair, in August.

A beautiful stretch of the Southern Upland Way passes close to Traquair: see St Mary's Loch, p. 80.

Glentress Forest

Glentress Forest is about three miles northwest of Traquair on the way to Peebles, with several signposted walks, one of which leads to **Cardie Hill Fort**, with its grass-covered ramparts, and another to **Shielgreen Tower**, of which little now remains. At the entrance to the park look out for a trio of tall wooden figures, unornamented and wonderfully graceful in their simplicity, carved from local wood.

Peebles

Flanked by wide greens, the River Tweed hurries on its way through Peebles, a peaceful old town with narrow streets leading to quaint yards and buildings with carved lintels. The name is derived from an old word—*pebylls*—meaning tents: these were the tents of a nomad tribe, Gadeni, who were the first inhabitants of the town. You can still see traces of the wall that was built to protect the town from the ever-destructive English. Cromwell garrisoned his troops here and, as early as the sixth century, St Mungo came to Peebles, baptizing his converts from the well that bears his name.

The Beltane Festival in June has pagan roots and incorporates Peebles' celebration of the Common Riding of the Marches. There are sheepdog trials in June, an inspiring sight for anyone who has never seen these highly intelligent animals at work. In August there is an Agricultural Show, and in September, the Peebles Highland Games and an Arts Festival.

The **Tweed Bridge**, with five elegant stone arches, decorated with ornate lamp standards, dates from the 15th century.

The Chambers Institute (open weekdays: free) was once the townhouse of the Queensberry family, and was given to the town by William Chambers, the publisher. With the help of a grant from Andrew Carnegie, the institute was enlarged to house reading rooms, libraries, two museums and an art gallery. **The Cornice**, 31 High Street, is an intriguing museum of ornamental plasterwork, with a re-creation of a plasterer's casting shop. Crammed full of cornices, corbels, mouldings, gargoyles, statues, and all the tools of the craft, this should attract anyone interested in plastic art.

Cross Kirk (open daily: free, key from the custodian next door) is the 13th-century ruined nave and west tower of a Trinitarian friary, with the foundations of the cloister buildings. When the English burnt down the collegiate church of St Andrew, Cross Kirk was used as the parish church.

Neidpath Castle

Neidpath Castle (open Easter and daily in summer: adm), a 13th-century castle just west of the town, stands high on a green mound overlooking the Tweed. This L-shaped castle has been continuously inhabited for almost seven hundred years and is still lived in today. Its mellow ochre walls, nearly 12 ft (36 m) thick in places, withstood the bombardment of Cromwell's troops in the mid-17th century for longer than any other castle south of the Forth. You can still see the pit prison hewn out of the rock and some of the original vaults, and climb right up to the roof and look out over miles of wooded hills and valleys. Along the grassy path to this dramatic castle are a few yew trees. These are all that remain of a once famous avenue (the Neidpath Yews) from which bows were made for crusaders. The majority of the yews were cut down to pay the gambling debts of that debauched old reprobate, 'Old Q'—William Douglas, Duke of Queensberry, in 1795. Wordsworth was so shocked by this vandalism that, during his tour of Scotland in 1803, he wrote the sonnet 'Composed at Neidpath Castle' starting:

Degenerate Douglas! oh, the unworthy Lord!
Whom mere despite of heart could so far please,
And love of havoc, (for with such disease
Fame taxes him,) that he could send forth word
To level with the dust a noble horde
A brotherhood of venerable Trees.

Neidpath stages one of the ceremonies of the annual Beltane Festival, when the Warden of Neidpath—someone in high office—is proclaimed from the castle steps.

Kailzie Gardens

Kailzie Gardens (open daily: adm), two miles east of Peebles, cover 17 acres, including a rose garden, herbaceous border, shrubs, a 19th-century walled garden with greenhouses, and a 'laburnum alley'. There is an art gallery, gift shop and licensed tea room. You can walk in the woods surrounding the gardens, along a sparkling burn, where the ground is golden with daffodils in spring, and inspect the collection of waterfowl.

Dawyck Botanic Gardens

Dawyck Botanic Gardens (open daily in summer: adm), eight miles southwest of Peebles, were created by Sir James Nasmyth in 1720, under the influence of his mentor Linnaeus, a great Swedish botanist. Here visitors can walk through carpets of scented narcissi, among rare trees and shrubs from all over the world, twisting and climbing until you come to a pretty Dutch bridge over a waterfall. The little chapel in the woods was designed by William Burn whose 'restoration' of St Giles Cathedral in Edinburgh was such a disaster that it had to be undone.

Drumelzier

Merlindale, in Drumelzier, nine miles southwest of Peebles, is one of the legendary sites of the grave of Merlin, Britain's most elusive magician. Thomas the Rhymer, the 13th-century seer, said: 'When Tweed and Powsail meet at Merlin's grave, England and Scotland shall one monarch have.' The day Elizabeth I died, when James VI of Scotland inherited the English throne also, the River Tweed burst its banks and flooded across Drumelzier into the neighbouring Powsail. This seems conclusive proof!

Broughton

Broughton, ten miles southwest of Peebles, is a village in the valley of Biggar Water, below layers of gentle rounded hills. **Broughton Place** is a treasure which could be missed—look out for the signs, up a steep drive. It is a 20th-century castle, designed by Sir Basil Spence in the 1930s, in the style of the Border fortresses. It looks startlingly authentic against its background of blue-grey hills and inside is a first class art gallery which can be visited in the summer. Many contemporary artists and craftsmen show their work here and if you are lucky you may see some of the outstanding watercolours painted by its father-and-son proprietors, Ian and Graham Buchanan-Dunlop.

The **John Buchan Centre** (open afternoons Easter–mid-Oct: adm) is also in Broughton, in a converted chapel. There is a wealth of biographical information here for devotees of that remarkable writer, alias 1st Baron Tweedsmuir, who not only wrote more than fifty books (and created television's romantic Richard Hannay), but was also an eminent barrister, statesman and Governor-General of Canada. Buchan grew up here and, looking around at the wild, lonely hills, it becomes clear where he got many of the settings for his Scottish novels. You will reel out of here determined to re-read all his books.

Six miles to the south, on the right (west) of the A702, **The Crook Inn** is one of the oldest pubs in the Borders. John Buchan was a frequent customer here as were Walter Scott and his circle. As you drink your pint in the bar, cast your mind back to the 18th century when this was the kitchen: Robert Burns sat here then, drawn in no doubt by the charms of one of the kitchen staff, and dashed off one of his poems at the table!

Another mile south is the small village of **Tweedsmuir**, from which John Buchan took his title.

If you've never seen sheepdogs working, go to Tweedhopefoot,where Geoff and Viv Billingham run a small hill farm which incorporates **Tweedhope Sheepdogs** (open April–Nov: adm) a **Border Collie and Shepherd Centre**. Here, at 11 am, 2 and 3.30 pm shepherds put these highly intelligent animals through their paces. It's a joy to watch such perfect communication between a man and his dog. There is also a craft shop, and Scotland's smallest schoolhouse, late 19th century, complete with equipment.

A little further south on the left (east) of the A702 is **Tweed's Well**, the source of the River Tweed. It is hard to believe that this small beginning will so quickly develop into that great torrent that swirls its way through the Borders to the sea.

WHERE TO STAY AND EAT

Among the many hotels in the area, the huge, moderately priced, château-like **Peebles Hotel Hydro**, Innerleithan Road, Peebles, tel 0721 20602, might be up your street if you are more concerned with facilities available than cosy atmosphere. In 30 acres, with a backdrop of rolling hills, it has a swimming pool, jacuzzi, saunas, solaria, gym, games room for badminton, tennis and squash, golf, riding and pitch-and-putt. It also offers a wide range of theme holidays, such as Golfing, Walking, spring Reviver and Festival Packages. Also moderately priced, **Cringletie House Hotel**, at Eddleston, Peebles, tel 0721 3233, is a privately owned, personally run baronial mansion, festooned with turrets, two miles out of Peebles. It stands in 28 acres of garden and woods, with wonderful views from all the rooms, and serves imaginative food that has won praise in several guides. Try their poached salmon. **Drummore**, Venlaw High Road, Peebles, tel 0721 20336, perched up on a hill with panoramic views, is cheap. It specializes in mountain biking for those who like to get away from traffic. If castles appeal to you, try **Venlaw Castle Hotel**, Peebles, tel 0721 20384. Built in 1782 in the Venlaw Hills, with magnificent views, this baronial pile is family-run with a reputation for good home cooking and is cheap.

Kingsmuir Hotel, Peebles and **Kailzie Garden Restaurant**, Peebles, were both runners up, and **Riverbank Restaurant**, Innerleithen, was a winner in the Scottish Borders Tourist Board Best Eating Place competition.

The Teviot Valley

The River Teviot starts its life in the hills south of Teviothead, on the border of Dumfries and Galloway, descending rapidly to cut a beautiful path northeastwards through its valley to Kelso, where, as if exhausted by all its rushing, in a flurry of water it throws itself into the River Tweed.

Roxburgh

Roxburgh was once a mighty walled Royal burgh, built round the fortress of March-mount, about a mile southwest of Kelso, so large that in the 12th century, some of its inhabitants had to be re-housed outside the town. This great metropolis was so bitterly fought over and so frequently annexed by the English, that in 1460, the Scots decided the only way to keep it permanently from their enemies was to remove it from the map. They made a pretty good job of it: all that remains today are the earthworks of the castle, and you have to search around for them. (The present village of Roxburgh, further to the southwest, dates from more recent times.)

Jedburgh

Jedburgh lies in the valley of Jed Water, a tributary of the Teviot, surrounded by green fields and woods whose vivid autumnal colours are a delight. Its proximity to the border made it the target of many raids and its position on one of the main routes north brought a succession of armies through its streets. Built round its abbey, this beautiful little town is packed tight with history. The men of Jedburgh were renowned for their brave resistance to invasion, defending their town with gruesome tenacity. 'Jeddart Handba', a local game played with a hay-stuffed leather ball, is said to originate from when Jedburgh (or Jeddart) men returned from a successful routing of the English and played ball with the heads of their victims.

The Jedburgh Festival is held annually in July, a week of pageantry dominated by the Jeddart Callants—the young men of Jedburgh—who re-enact the Common Ridings of the past. The Jedburgh Border Games are also held in July.

Jedburgh Abbey

Jedburgh Abbey and Visitor Centre (open daily except Thurs afternoon and Fri, Oct–March: adm) has a history spanning several centuries. Fragments of Celtic carved stonework, found during the careful and effective restoration of the abbey, suggest that it was built on the site of a 9th-century church that appears in the records of Lindisfarne.

Founded as a priory in 1138, by David I, and raised to Abbey status in 1147, it was frequently sacked by the English, the most devasting attack being by Hertford in 1544 during his ruthless execution of the orders of Henry VIII. It stands now on a green sward, its mellow stone still supporting graceful arches and windows, including a rose window, called St Catherine's Wheel. You can dream of the past in this ruin, on a fine day when the sun picks up the colours of the intricately carved masonry and you can hear echoes of plainchant in the walls. Indeed it won't just be echoes that you hear, if you go to the

Visitors Centre. In this extremely well thought-out interpretation of the Abbey's history, you will not only see displays that give a fascinating insight to how the monks lived in those distant days but you hear their music and chanting.

Jedburgh Castle Jail Museum

The museum (open daily in summer: adm) was built at the top of Castlegate in 1823 as the county prison, on the site of a castle that was built around the same time as the abbey. It was a popular royal residence; Alexander III chose it as the place for his wedding feast when, desperate for an heir, he married his second wife Jolande in the Abbey in 1285. It was at this feast that the spectre of Death appeared, prophesying the death of the king: an event that happened six months later when he fell from his horse. Frequently occupied by the English and in fact ceded to them under the Treaty of Falaise in 1174, it was destroyed by order of the Scottish Parliament to keep it from the enemy. The museum contains reconstructed rooms showing the 'reformed' system of imprisonment in the early 19th century and gives a gruelling insight into the penal and social history of those days.

Mary, Queen of Scots House

Queen Mary's House (open daily in summer: adm) in Queen Street is haunted with memories of Scotland's tragic queen. Mary came here in 1556, still married to Darnley, to preside over the Court of Justice at the Assizes. She stayed in this house, reputedly because it was the only one with indoor sanitation. During her stay she heard that James Bothwell had been wounded and was seriously ill at Hermitage Castle, 20 miles away. Perhaps already in love with the attractive earl, she rode over to Hermitage and back again, all in the same day, to visit him. As a result she became critically ill of a fever from which she nearly died: her attendants opened the window at the crisis of her illness, to let her soul fly free. Years later she was to say: 'Would that I had died, that time in Jedburgh.' Darnley came to visit her while she was ill and when she was better she rode back to

Queen Mary's House

88

Edinburgh with Bothwell, now also recovered, in her entourage. The charming, ochre-coloured house has high crow-stepped gables and a turret stair; the steep roof was once thatched. It has been beautifully restored and is much as it was when Mary was there: you can see the great hall, withdrawing-room and fireplace and the stuffy little room where she lay so ill for a month, near to the chamber occupied by her famous four Marys: Mary Beaton, Mary Seton, Mary Carmichael and Mary Hamilton. The **Visitor Centre** was extensively up-graded to mark the 400th anniversary of her death in 1987, and presents an interesting interpretation of her life and times. Among the fascinating exhibits are one of the rare portraits of Bothwell, done in 1565; a facsimile of Mary's death-warrant, signed by her cousin Elizabeth, and her watch, apparently found in the marshy land near Hermitage Castle 200 years after she lost it on her impulsive visit to Bothwell. There is also a gift shop.

The Woodland Centre

Anyone interested in the cultivation of woodland might be interested in this exhibition, three miles north of Jedburgh, well signposted off the A68. Here forestry techniques are demonstrated, with slideshows. There are pleasant walks, a picnic area and playground for children.

Jedforest Deer and Farm Park (open daily May–Oct: adm), four miles south of Jedburgh, is an upland farm where you can see deer and many rare breeds of animals as well as a modern working farm. There is an adventure playground, walks, and information centre, cafe and shop.

Hermitage Castle

Although it is closer to Hawick than to Jedburgh, it is really from Jedburgh that you should visit Hermitage Castle, so that you can appreciate Mary's frantic ride, while you are still steeped in her history. (Open daily: adm.) 20 miles to the southwest and well signposted, it stands stark and indestructable, on a grassy platform surrounded by extensive earthworks; an angular fortress with fierce, frowning arches. On all sides, bleak moorland rises in peaks from where watch could be kept in every direction, including across the border into England. Even in sunshine, with the swift, sparkling Hermitage Water at its feet, it has a grim aura about it. A 14th-century tower, built round a small courtyard, can still be seen with the later additions of massive square towers and walls set with holes and corbels that once supported a continuous walkway, high on the exterior walls, reached through rectangular doorways. Close by are the ruins of St Mary's Chapel and traces of the medieval village that grew up round the castle.

Legends of such horror and cruelty surround this melancholy lump of history that it is no wonder locals believed the weight of its iniquities would eventually cause it to sink into Hades, though it shows no sign of doing so yet.

The first man to build on the site was Nicholas de Soulis, in the 13th century. He was so cruel and evil that his neighbours and servants carted him off to Ninestone Rig, a mile to the northeast, wrapped him in a sheet of lead, and boiled him to death.

The 11-foot-long grave outside the walls of the little kirkyard which lies beyond the castle, is believed to contain the mortal remains of the Cout of Kielder, a giant baron who came over the hills from Kielder Castle across the border in England, to Hermitage to slay de Soulis. He was drowned by his intended victim, in a deep pool in the river that is still known as Cout of Kielder Pool. A 'gallant Scottish patriot', Alexander Ramsay of Dalhousie, was lowered into the pit-prison still visible in the castle. He existed for many days on a trickle of grain that fell from the granary above, before eventually starving to death.

And here, to this lonely fortress, came Mary, galloping *ventre a terre* across the moors from Jedburgh to visit Bothwell when he lay wounded in a room above the bakehouse, after a battle. One can see her, flinging herself from her horse, running up the spiral stair and bursting impetuously into her lover's room. She could only stay to comfort him for a short time before hurrying back to Jedburgh, perhaps already aching from the fever that nearly killed her.

WHERE TO STAY AND EAT
Glenbank Hotel, Castlegate, Jedburgh, tel 0835 62258 is a Georgian house in attractive gardens, only five minutes walk from the town centre, and cheap. If it's history you are after, the **Spread Eagle Hotel**, Jedburgh, tel 0835 62870 and also cheap, is reputed to be the oldest in Scotland, and claims that Mary, Queen of Scots slept there. With such romance, you can't expect ritzy surroundings.

Denholm

Denholm, five miles southwest of Jedburgh, is a conservation village, its 18th-century houses built close together round a large green, in the style of earlier settlements when the beasts could be herded into the green when raids were anticipated, the narrow alleyways making defence easier. The elaborate monument on the green is to Dr John Leyden, who was born in the tiny thatched cottage just off the north side of the square, in 1775. This remarkable scholar, physician and poet was almost entirely self-taught, astounding his contemporaries including Sir Walter Scott, with the range and scope of his knowledge, though he was only 36 when he died.

The village is dominated by **Rubers Law** to the southeast, accessible from all sides and easily scaled to the remains of an Iron Age Hill Fort at the top. This was a Roman signal station, within sight of a similar one on nearby Bonchester Hill. There is a rock on the Law, known as Peden's Pulpit, from which the Pedan preached to huge congregations of Covenanters during the Killing Times.

It is said that the Devil used to get so irritated at being woken every morning by the chanting of the monks in Melrose Abbey that he decided to move three of the Cheviot Hills and plant them between Melrose and the rising sun. Unfortunately, during the move, he dropped the top half of the last one. This was Rubers Law, and explains why it would fit exactly on to the flat top of one of the Eildon Hills.

Hawick

Substantially built in a fold of the hills on the banks of the Teviot, Hawick (pronounced Hoyk) owes its prosperity to the thriving textile mills along the river, many with their own shops, and to the well-stocked timber yards in the area. The proud hub of this bustling town is a bronze statue in the High Street, an armoured youth on a charger, holding a standard above his head. In 1514 a band of English troops, looting their way through the Borders, were carelessly camped at nearby Hornshole, knowing that the death-toll from the Battle of Flodden the previous year had reduced the fighting strength of the Border towns to nothing but old men and boys. The Callants—teenaged youths—of Hawick rode out in a brave, ragged band, routed the English and returned with the enemy standard.

The Callants' routing of the English in 1514 is an event that is enthusiastically incorporated into the Common Riding Celebrations in June.

Rugby is the town's ruling passion; Hawick has contributed players to the Scottish International Team over many years. The Hawick Rugby Sevens take place in April. For two weeks in August the town also holds a Summer Festival.

Wilton Lodge Museum (open daily April–Sept, afternoons except Sat, Oct–March: adm) in Wilton Lodge Park on the western outskirts of the town shows exhibits related to the textile industry as well as displays of Border history and archaeology, and local natural history. It also houses an art gallery with monthly exhibitions. William Wallace visited here in 1297 and you can still see the tree where he is supposed to have tethered his horse. The park has walks, gardens and sports facilities.

If you are unlucky with the weather and the family is getting fractious, it is worth noting that Hawick has a particularly good **Indoor Leisure Centre**, north of the town on the A7, complete with swimming pool, restaurant and good entertainment such as puppet shows for children.

Teviothead

There is a poignant memorial nine miles southwest of Hawick in the village of Teviothead, on the A7. The memorial is a stone, set into the wall of the graveyard opposite the kirk and it is dedicated to the 16th-century freebooter, Johnnie Armstrong and his band of followers. Armstrong rode up to this bleak and lonely place from Langholm, further south, hoping to win the favour of his teenaged sovereign, James V. He offered the service and allegiance of his men and himself, but the young king, intent on cleaning up the lawless Borders, was not won over. Armstrong and his band were hanged from a makeshift gallows at Caerlanrig to the southwest.

Newcastleton

Newcastleton, by lovely Liddel Water, about five miles south of Hermitage Castle, was founded in 1793 by the Duke of Buccleuch and has an unusual, very symmetrical layout. Their Traditional Music Festival, in early July, is fun.

WHERE TO STAY
There are a number of respectable, genteel hotels around Hawick, where you will be reasonably comfortable and get what you pay for. Moderately priced **Kirklands Hotel**, in West Stewart Place, Hawick, tel 0450 72263, is probably the best of these, a comfortable if unexciting Victorian town house, mentioned in most guides. They have a croquet lawn, snooker room and library, to pass any spare time you may have.

For something a bit different, **Hazeldean Holidays**, Denholm, Hawick, tel 0450 087 373, has 12 self-catering log cabins and chalets dotted around 25 acres of lovely grounds on the Teviot. They have horses, a large indoor riding school, fishing, and golf nearby. Terms are weekly, on application. If you don't want to cook, **The Fox and Hounds** in the Main Street of Denholm is a cosy old coaching inn.

Old Forge, at Newmill on Teviot, south of Hawick, was a runner up in the Scottish Borders Tourist Board Best Eating Place competition in 1990.

Part V

DUMFRIES & GALLOWAY

Henry Moore's King and Queen

Dumfries and Galloway borders the northern shore of the Solway Firth with the dramatic hammerhead of the Rhinns of Galloway at its western tip. Apart from the extreme east, this is an isolated corner, off the main route to anywhere else, except Ireland, to which it is closer than to much of the rest of Scotland.

The name Galloway is derived from the Gaelic *gallgaidhel*—land of the stranger. It was here, early in the 6th century, that the Celtic Christian Scots from Ireland landed, driving out the aboriginal Picts, before moving northwards and establishing the Kingdom of Dalriada. Earlier still, St Ninian brought the first message of Christianity to Whithorn, in AD 397. Many churches and abbeys were built in the area, becoming places of pilgrimage for monarchs of Scotland and for people travelling from distant lands. Frequent wars, the Reformation and Henry VIII's 'Rough Wooing' in the 16th century reduced most of these to ruins, but you can still see the shells of their former splendour today. Towns near the border suffered their share of hammering from the English, and settlements on the coast had to be fortified against invasion from the sea. Mary, Queen of Scots, passed through during a triumphant royal tour of her kingdom, in 1563, escorted by a glittering train of nobles: a happy, lighthearted progress in contrast to her next visit, five years later, when she fled here after her defeat at Langside and embarked from Port Mary at Dundrennan in the hope of finding sanctuary in England.

This remote corner attracts little industry; fishing and farming are important to the economy as is tourism. In early days smuggling was rife, providing employment for, among others, Robert Burns who spent his last years in Dumfries as an exciseman.

As in the Borders, some of the towns and villages that lie close to the English boundary have annual **Common Riding Festivals**, in memory of the days when the men used to

93

go out and check the marches, to make sure that Border reivers hadn't been at work, stealing the cattle. These festivals, full of carnival fun, last for up to a week and incorporate events in local history, as well as plenty of colourful pageantry and entertainment. In June there is Dumfries' Guid Nychburris Festival, and Lockerbie's Common Riding Festival. In July there is Annan's Riding of the Marches and Moffat's Gala Week, and Langholm's Common Riding Festival. Sanquhar has a similar festival in August.

SPORT

Water sports. With the sea forming nearly half its boundary, Dumfries and Galloway is an ideal place for all kinds of water sports including **sailing, water-skiing, windsurfing, canoeing and swimming**.

Fishing is very popular, with some of Britain's best sea angling in Luce Bay and neighbouring waters, as well as good game fishing on the rivers and lochs. You can generally get permits from local tackle shops, post offices, tourist centres and some hotels. For detailed information, write for *'Castabout' Anglers' Guide to Dumfries and Galloway*, from the Dumfries and Galloway Tourist Board, Whitesands, Dumfries DG1 2SB. Or you can get leaflets on Sea Angling, and Fishing on Rivers and Lochs from any local tourist information centre.

Golf can be played on any of the 23 courses available, many of which provide lessons and open competitions.

Riding is a great way of exploring the region and you will find a number of riding and pony-trekking establishments such as at Beattock, Whithorn, Ringford and Sandyhills. Some of the self-catering houses provide horses, too.

Bird-watching and wildlife This is a naturalist's paradise! The mild climate of both coastal and inland habitats attracts countless numbers of rare species of birds, animals and plants. The tidal marshes are wintering grounds for barnacle geese and lots of other waterfowl. If you are lucky you may see peregrine falcons, whose breeding sites are carefully guarded by the police against avaricious crooks who sell their incubated eggs for hundreds of pounds. Of the many nature reserves you can visit, one of the best is **Caerlaverock**—a wildfowl refuge on the Solway shore, open from mid-September to April, or **Wood of Cree**, four miles north of Newton Stewart. The local RSPB group have produced a guide to 35 *Birdwalks in Dumfries and Galloway*, suitable for anyone interested in wildlife. You can get this at any of the Tourist Information Centres.

Walking is one the most rewarding activities in Dumfries and Galloway, whether you take a gentle, riverside stroll or a challenging scramble through rugged hills. There are countless marvellous walks, both coastal and inland, forest and hill-walking. **The Southern Upland Way** starts its 212-mile journey to the North Sea coast at Portpatrick on the west coast. If you don't feel the urge to follow its entire length, you can join it at any point as it meanders through the hills of the Galloway Forest Park—some of them quite high—eastwards over the Lowthers and then the Moffat Hills into the Borders. Views from the peaks are stunning. Though parts of it will stretch your muscles, all of it is within the capabilities of anyone who is reasonably fit. You can get *200 Walks and Climbs in Dumfries and Galloway* from local tourist information centres. For those who prefer company, there are also guided walks around many of the beauty spots. Tourist centres and most hotels will give you details.

DUMFRIES & GALLOWAY

STRATHCLYDE

BORDERS

1 Kinmount Gardens
2 Caerlaverock Castle
3 Devil's Beef Tub
4 Grey Mare's Tail
5 Lincluden Abbey
6 Sweetheart Abbey
7 Drumlanrig Castle
8 Maxwelton House
9 Threave Castle
10 Motte of Mark
11 Orchardton Tower
12 Motte of Urr
13 Dundrennan Abbey
14 Cardonnes Castle
15 Glenluce Abbey
16 St Ninian's Cave
17 Gilnockie Tower
18 Arbigland Gardens
19 Ardwell Gardens
20 Logan Botanic Gardens

Cycling has to be popular on the quiet country roads of Dumfries and Galloway because the world's first bicycle was invented at Keir Mill, near Thornhill, around 1840. Off-road routes are being set up in the forests, ideal for mountain bicyclists. You can hire bikes and there are good route leaflets availavle from the Tourist Information Centres.

TOURIST INFORMATION
The main Tourist Information Centre is at Whitesands, Dumfries, tel 0387 53862 (24-hour answering service); open all the year. The local centres, which are all open from Easter to mid-October are Gretna Green: tel 0461 37834; Kirkcudbright: Harbour Square, tel 0557 30494; Gatehouse of Fleet: Car Park, tel 0557 814212; Newton Stewart: Dashwood Square, tel 0671 2431; Stranraer: Port Rodie Car Park, tel 0776 2595; Langholm: High Street, tel 03873 80976; Moffat: Churchgate, tel 0683 20620; Sanquhar: Tolbooth Visitor Centre, 0659 50185; Castle Douglas: Markethill, tel 0556 2611; and Dalbeattie: Town Hall, tel 0556 610117.

The Solway Coast

Tidal mudflats and sandy beaches, fringed by woods and cut by river valleys, are bordered by a string of attractive towns. You can trace the history of this Solway coast through its many ruins and prehistoric stones.

Gretna Green

Coming from England, on the A74, you cross the Scottish border into Dumfries and Galloway at Gretna Green. From the romance that has grown up around this famous village it is difficult to untangle the squalid reality of an era when a great many innocent females were duped by men whose motives could not stand the test of a formal betrothal with parental consent. Runaway lovers, cheated of 'irregular marriages' in England by the 1754 Hardwicke Marriage Act, were able to cross the border until 1856 and be married by declaration before a witness. The union was 'forged' over an anvil by the blacksmith. Even in the 20th century couples came north because until the age of consent was altered in 1969, Scotland was the only place where parental consent was not required after the age of 16. The border villages of Gretna and Springfield, now by-passed by the A74, vied with each other for the considerable profit that could be made from these often disastrous unions. One blacksmith, called Rennison, is said to have performed 5147 ceremonies. Today they continue to exploit that dishonourable trade by displaying the marriage houses where the ceremonies took place. Springfield lost its trade to Gretna in 1830, when the building of the Sark Bridge caused it to be by-passed by the main north–south route. At the height of the marriage industry, rivalry between the 'priests' in the area was ferocious and each had his agent, promoting his superiority in hotels in Carlisle.

The Old Blacksmith Shop, or Smithy, at Gretna (open daily all the year: adm), behind Gretna Hall Hotel, is set back off an attractive cobbled yard, through a 'kissing gate'. Dating from 1710, it contains a museum where you can see the marriage room, anvil, and many photographs and documents relating to those days. If you are lucky, a kilted piper will welcome you to this rather tawdry display.

Lochmaben Stone

This stone, on the shore of the Solway Firth not far south of Gretna, weighs at least 10 tons and is thought to be the remains of a stone circle, possibly connected with a shrine to Maponos, god of youth and music: a very appropriate trysting place for runaway lovers! Fairs were held here in the Middle Ages and it was the site where border disputes were discussed and settled, under daylight truce.

Annan

Going west from Gretna Green you come to Annan on the northern shore of the Solway Firth. Once a busy main-road town, it is now mercifully bypassed by A75, making the town centre a more leisurely place to explore. Although its history goes back a long way, the town was too frequently torn apart in border disputes to show much sign of antiquity today. In 1317 it was recorded that 'the Vale of Annan lay so wasted and burned that neither man nor beast was left'. If you are lucky, you may see haaf-net fishermen, standing up to their chests in the water, holding out their awkward nets, framed like football goal-posts. This ancient tradition, dating from Viking days, protected by Royal Charter, and restricted by licence to the men of Annan only, is currently under threat from a time share company. These incomers, whose clients can pay up to £15,000 for an annual week's share of the salmon fishing, are seeking to have haaf-netting made illegal, on conservation grounds.

Shrimp-canning is one of the town's valuable industries, and in the 19th century the beautiful tea-clippers used to be made here. The blind poet Dr Thomas Blacklock lived here; a man who did an enormous amount to promote the genius of Robert Burns and who prevented him from emigrating when times were hard. Annan celebrates the Riding of the Marches in July.

Look out for the **Brus Stone**, built into the wall of the Town Hall—a carved tablet from a castle built by the Brus lords. It is inscribed with the name Robert de Brus, thought to be King Robert the Bruce. This poignant relic was stolen in the 19th century and lost for 100 years before someone found it in North Devon in 1916.

If you want to take something special home from Annan, Pinneys, at Brydhill, are high-class fish-smokers where you can get very good smoked fish pâtés as well as smoked salmon, trout, mackerel, etc.

Ruthwell Cross

Ruthwell (pronounced Rivvel) is six miles west of Annan on the coastal road B724, now the start of the Solway Coast Heritage Trail which takes you all the way to Stranraer. Stop off at the church, and in an apse built specially for it, you will find the 7th-century Ruthwell Cross, one of Scotland's greatest treasures, with incredibly clear sculpted figures and vine scrolls and birds and animals. The Runic inscriptions, the longest and perhaps oldest known in Britain, have been deciphered by scholars and are extracts from a devotional poem, 'The Dream of the Rood', the oldest poem in the English language, written by 7th-century Northumbrian poets. The arms of the 18-ft-high cross are modern, but this in no way detracts from the awe-inspiring grace and charm of this ancient relic. The reason why it is so well preserved is that it was buried some time in the 17th century by the minister, to protect it from the rabid iconoclasm of the Presbyterian reformers. The man who subsequently unearthed and re-erected it was the Rev. Henry Duncan, who also established Scotland's first savings bank, in Ruthwell in 1810. The cottage where this first bank was founded is now a **Museum** (open all the year round: free) in which those who are interested can learn all about the early days of the savings bank movement.

Comlongon Castle

At Clarencefield, just northwest of Ruthwell (open daily March–Nov: adm), Comlongon, in the process of being restored, is a particularly well-preserved 15th-century castle complete with spooky dungeons, kitchen, great hall, heraldic devices and bed chambers with privies. There is a picnic area, nature trail, woodland walks, and even some peacocks to add a touch of grandeur. See below for details of adjoining hotel.

The Caerlaverock Nature Reserve

West of Ruthwell, between Lochar Water and the mouth of the Nith, this reserve is a great tract of wild salt-marsh and mud-flats, belonging to the Wildfowl Trust, a marvellous sanctuary for nature-lovers. It is the most northerly breeding ground of the natterjack toad, an endearing little fellow whose hindlegs are too short to let it hop, so it has to run. You can visit the reserve between mid-September and April.

Caerlaverock Castle

Caerlaverock (open daily: adm) is a massive triangular-shaped ruin on the western part of the nature reserve, its moat still full, so you cross a footbridge to reach it. Its shape was governed by that of the rock on which it was built, just a few feet above the high-tide level at the mouth of the Nith. Aptly described by a medieval monk as 'shield-shaped', the castle managed to hold off 3000 English troops under Edward I for two days in 1300, defended by only 60 men. Adding considerably to its impregnability, it is surrounded by treacherous sinking-mud and swampland. Built in 1290, the castle was a Maxwell stronghold, and it has an elegant Renaissance interior designed by the first Earl of Nithsdale in the 17th century. There is something very French about its three-storey façade, surrounding the triangular courtyard, decorated with sculpted doors and windows. Sadly, the Covenanters destroyed it not long after the first Earl's improvements. You can still see the Maxwell crest and motto, above the door.

WHERE TO STAY AND EAT
Hotels around this area are rather ordinary, but there are plenty of them. Without doubt you should try and get into moderately priced **Warmanbie Hotel**, Annan, tel 04612 4015, an elegant Georgian country house in secluded woodland grounds overlooking the

River Annan with free fishing. The bedrooms are comfortable with private bathrooms and colour TV. Good food and wine, and special rates for weekend breaks and off-season holidays. If castles are your fancy, try **Comlongon Castle** at Clarencefield, just north of Ruthwell, tel 038787 283, open from March to December. Adjoining the original medieval castle (see above), this baronial pile, in 50 acres of parkland, is cheap and what you miss in vitality is compensated for in respectability and adjacent history.

Dumfries

Dumfries stands serenely on the banks of the Nith 16 miles west of Annan, surrounded by lush farmland, woods and beautiful gardens. Its history is as bloodstained as that of any border town, its inhabitants known for their brave opposition to invasion. William the Lion made it a Royal Burgh in 1186 and it was granted a charter in 1395 by Robert III. Bronze and Iron Age relics have been excavated nearby and it is almost certain that there was a Roman settlement with a Roman road up Nithsdale. Edward I captured the now vanished castle; Robert Bruce murdered Red Comyn here in 1306; Bonny Prince Charlie passed through in 1745. Robert Burns lived and died in Dumfries and described the town as 'Maggie by the banks of Nith, a dame wi' pride eneuch'.

The name Dumfries comes from *dun*, or *drum*, *phreas*—the fort, or ridge, in the brushwood. The town was home to Norwegian exiles during the Second World War.

There is an annual **Guid Nychburris Festival** (Good Neighbours) in June, a week-long celebration incorporating many historic events from the past including the granting of the charter and the Border Marches.

Dumfries Museum (open daily except closed Sun and Mon, Oct–March: free) adjoins a water mill—a round whitewashed tower, built about 1730 and recently restored in lovely grounds. Inside the museum, in 'period' rooms, you can see a wide range of local exhibits: archaeological, natural history, Roman altars, early Christian monuments and costumes and, of course, Burns memorabilia. There is a 'camera obscura' in the old mill (adm), giving you an ingeniously reflected bird's eye view of the town and surrounding countryside.

The Auld Brig, a six-arched footbridge above a tumbling caul (weir) created in the 18th century to provide power for grain mills, is a successor to a wooden bridge put up by Devorguilla Balliol in the 14th century (see 'Sweetheart Abbey', below). The present bridge dates from 1432 but was considerably restored after the 17th century when floodwater reduced it from nine, or even thirteen, arches, to the present six. This was once the gateway into Galloway. The quaint little **Old Bridge House** (open daily in the summer: free) at the end of the bridge, dating from 1662, is a folk museum with Victorian and Edwardian rooms giving a splendid insight into life in Dumfries over the centuries.

Robert Burns

Dumfries glows with Burns nostalgia. Listen for the echo of an ironic chuckle from that most earthy of romantic poets as you stand in the High Street, in front of Greyfriars Church where several roads meet, and look up at the splendidly sentimental statue of him. A white marble Adonis lounges against a tree-stump, hand on heart, clutching a posy of flowers, his dog resting its faithful head on his rustic boot. He stares out over the town wearing a rather vapid expression that does not quite match his colourful life, totally oblivious of the swirl of traffic at his feet.

The Globe Tavern and the **Hole in the Wa'**, two of the poet's favourite inns, are in the High Street. Both are crammed with Burns memorabilia and and it is hard to believe that he died nearly 200 years ago, so alive is his memory in these stones. It is said that his tragically early death at the age of 36 was brought about by collapsing in the snow after a 'night wi' the boys' in The Globe, and lying there long enough to catch a chill. In fact, the chronic heart complaint that carried him off could have done so at any time. The barmaid at The Globe bore one of his many children. Burns lived in Dumfries for the last four and a half years of his life, working as an exciseman and writing nearly 100 of his best known works including 'Auld Lang Syne'.

Burns House (open daily except closed Sun and Mon, Oct–March: adm) is a must for Burns enthusiasts. You will find this humble red-brick workman's cottage in what is now Burns Street but which was called Mill Vennel when he lived and died there. He called it 'Stinking Vennel' on account of the open drain that ran down the alley carrying effluent from the meat market to the river. Here you can see more mementoes of his short life; the house has recently been restored.

An elaborate **Mausoleum** in the grounds of St Michael's Church contains the body of Burns, and those of his wife Jean Armour and five of their children. Like the statue in the High Street, this splendid Grecian temple with the muse of poetry, sculpted by Turnerelli, coming on Burns at the plough, is somehow too mawkish for the man. This monument was erected early in the 19th century when it cost £1450.

Robert Burns Centre in Mill Road (open daily, April–Sept: free) is the latest tribute to the poet. In an 18th-century red sandstone mill on the banks of the Nith, this centre has a 70-seat theatre where you can see audio-visual shows, for a small charge. There is a scale model of 18th-century Dumfries as Burns would have known it, displays of Burns' life, a bookshop and a café—Jean Armour's Pantry.

In this welter of Burns memorabilia, it would be easy to miss the plaque in Castle Street, all that remains of the **Monastery of Greyfriars**. It commemorates the event which was one of the turning points in Scottish history, when Robert Bruce stabbed to death Red Comyn, his rival claimant to the crown, in a quarrel. Having thus disposed of opposition with the double crime of murder and sacrilege, Bruce was then able to seize the throne. His sins weighed heavy on his shoulders until he died at the age of 55.

The early 18th-century **Midsteeple**, in the middle of the town, is the former tolbooth with a plan on the wall of how Dumfries was in Burns' day. This imposing building was also the prison and ammunition store.

Lincluden Collegiate Church

Lincluden (open daily except closed Thurs afternoons and Fri in winter: adm) stands on the northern outskirts of the town on a grassy plateau within a bend of Cluden Water. It has somehow managed to retain its tranquillity in spite of the modern houses surrounding it. It was founded for Benedictine nuns in the 12th century: in 1339 the nuns were thrown out by Archibald the Grim and the church became collegiate. Archibald's son, the fourth Earl of Douglas, son-in-law of Robert III, was killed fighting for France against England. His wife, Princess Margaret, endowed a chapel in the south transept of

Lincluden in memory of her husband and was herself buried in the richly decorated and inscribed canopied tomb that you can still see in the ruins today. You can also see plenty of Douglas signatures on the walls in the form of coats of arms, shields, etc., as well as some carvings on the rood screen showing scenes from the life of Christ.

Sweetheart Abbey

Sweetheart Abbey (open daily: adm), at New Abbey, seven and a half miles south of Dumfries, is one of Scotland's most poignant monastic ruins. Roofless, its grass-carpeted nave is enclosed within soaring red sandstone arches. It was founded in 1273 by Devorguilla Balliol—mother of King John Balliol, the luckless 'Toom Tabard'—who also founded Balliol College in Oxford. Devorguilla was buried here with her husband's embalmed heart, which she had carried around with her in an ivory and silver casket, since his death: her 'sweet, silent companion'. The abbey became known as Dulce Cor, or Sweet Heart, and you can see Devorguilla's tomb, marked by a raised platform of turf with a cross cut in it, in front of the high altar.

The shell of the abbey dominates the pretty little village of **New Abbey** with its main street lined by single-storey whitewashed cottages, curving up to the gates of what used to be the precincts. You can still see part of the enormous boulder wall that once encircled the grounds. There is a beautifully restored 19th-century corn-mill with working water wheel, that you can look round. Criffel, the highest of the coastal hills, (1868 ft) can be climbed from here.

About 5 miles northwest, **Beeswing** village is so called after a 19th-century racehorse who won a fortune for a gambling butler. He used his winnings to buy an inn here and called it Beeswing; the village grew up round it. Today the inn is a private house, identifiable by the large yellow butterfly by the front door.

Arbigland

Arbigland Gardens (open 1st May–30 Sept, Tues, Thurs and Sun: adm) are 12 miles south of Dumfries. On a sandy bay overlooking the estuary of the Nith, you can wander in beautiful woodland, water-gardens and formal gardens. In 1747, John Paul Jones was born in a humble cottage south of the estate road, and grew up there. This flamboyant character, whose father, John Paul, was gardener at Arbigland, served a prison sentence for murder and then made his home in America. A brave, dashing sailor, he fought for the Americans in the War of Independence, helping to establish their navy, and led several daring raids on English and Scottish territory in command of an American brig. A true mercenary at heart, he fought for France and for Russia and died in Paris. There are many glamorized stories of his exploits, including one in which he returned some treasure, plundered by his crew, to its owner—a lady who lived on the Solway Firth.

Drumcoltran Tower

Drumcoltran Tower (open daily: free), eight miles southwest of Dumfries just off the A711, is a 16th century, simple oblong tower-house among farm buildings. It stands three storeys high with a wheel-stair in a projecting turret. A hoard of Bronze Age rapiers was found in a ditch nearby to set your imagination winging back to what it might have been like here in those distant times.

WHERE TO STAY AND EAT
There is a large choice of hotels and guest houses in this area, from castle to bungalow, and you will find most of them in the Dumfries and Galloway brochure. **Hetland Hall Hotel** at Carrutherstown, seven miles southeast of Dumfries along the A75, tel 0387 84201, is a large Georgian mansion, moderately priced, with panoramic views of the Solway coast and 'Sporting Breaks' for a minimum of three days. **The Station Hotel**, in Dumfries, tel 0387 54316, is cheap and not so prosaic as it sounds. For one thing, it's in Lovers Walk. For another, it is in a listed building—though they list anything from warehouses to underground stations these days—and it is extremely comfortable and the food is excellent.

Dalbeattie

Dalbeattie, 14 miles southwest of Dumfries, is in the Stewartry, so called from the time when Balliol lands were confiscated and placed under a royal 'steward'—hence also the origins of the Stewart/Stuart dynasty. Much of this small town is built with a glittering granite that is internationally acclaimed for its beauty and durability and has been used to strengthen buildings all over the world. The Eddystone Lighthouse, the Thames Embankment, lighthouses in Ceylon, paving stones in Russia and South America, are just a few instances in which this Galloway granite was used. Dalbeattie Civic Week, at the end of July, is a week full of entertainment and fun of all kinds.

The Motte of Mark and The Motte of Urr

Anyone interested in antiquities should go to The Motte of Mark at Rockcliffe, on the Urr Water. This 5th/6th century hillfort commanded such a spectacular view of the coast that few invaders could have slipped past unnoticed. The Motte of Urr, nearly three miles north of Dalbeattie, just off the B794, is another fortified hill—the most extensive motte and bailey earthwork castle in Scotland. It is an almost circular mound, rising in three tiers, on a platform surrounded by a deep trench; a splendid relic of Saxon-Norman occupation.

Colvend Coast

The coast south of Dalbeattie, around Colvend, Rockcliffe, and Sandyhills Bay, is attractive, with good walks, the bird sanctuary at Rough Island, and the picturesque harbour at Kippford. This was smugglers' territory in the old days. A good five-mile walk is from Kippford, southeast along the coast to Castle Point, passing Motte of Mark and back past Dalbeattie Forest.

Following the coast westwards on the A711 you come to **Palnackie**, three miles southwest of Dalbeattie. In the small, silted-up harbour here, in the summer, the World Flounder-tramping Championships are held. Competitors find the flounders in the mud with their bare feet and spear them, at considerable risk to their toes. Here also you can watch glass-blowing, welding and sculpting at the North Glen Gallery (open daily, but ring 055660 200 to check).

Orchardton

Orchardton Tower, less than two miles south, west of the Urr Estuary, just off the A711 (open daily: free; key from the custodian who lives in a cottage nearby), is a sturdy, 15th-century cylindrical tower built by John Cairns in an attractive wooded dip. This is the only tower of its kind in Scotland, modelled on a style common in Ireland.

Screel Hill

If you need to stretch your legs, Screel Hill, on the other side of the road from Orchardton, has a signed trail up through the forest to the craggy summit from which you will be rewarded with panoramic views of the firth and surrounding countryside.

Dundrennan Abbey

About six miles on down the coast on the A711, Dundrennan Abbey (open daily: adm) is a must for anyone with romance in their veins. There remains little of its former splendour but its roofless aisles and transepts, its pointed arches and blind arcades reverberate with the echo of yet another act in the tragedy of the life of Mary, Queen of Scots. Founded for Cistercians in 1142, and falling into ruin after the Reformation, the abbey provided the queen with her final resting place before she embarked for England from Port Mary. It is not known whether she slept here or merely rested. She arrived in tattered, shabby clothes, her head shorn for disguise, and sat somewhere in these ruins to write a final letter to her cousin Elizabeth of England, begging for sanctuary. It is heartbreaking to picture her tall, slender, elegant figure, passing through the exquisite 13th-century pointed doorway that you can still see, between two arched windows, into the chapter house, to receive the care of the abbot and his monks.

Kirkcudbright

Beware! If you first meet Kirkcudbright (pronounced Kir-coo-bry) on a sunny spring day when the blossom is out and the early flowers in bloom, you may find it impossible to move on and explore anywhere else in Scotland. Sturdy, gaily painted houses and old streets beside the water at the mouth of the Dee make this one of Scotland's most enchanting towns. It was a medieval port and a royal burgh, named after the Kirk of St Cuthbert, when the saint's bones rested there on the way to interment in Durham. With its mild, almost Mediterranean climate and glorious sea views, the town is popular with painters and has a thriving art colony. A large variety of boats lie peacefully at anchor reflected in the water of the attractive harbour.

The Kirkcudbright Summer Festivities, July–mid-August, provide Scottish Nights, a raft race, a puppet festival, sports, walks and a floodlit Tattoo in front of MacLellan's Castle.

MacLellan's Castle (open daily, except closed weekdays Oct–March: adm) is an impressive turreted ruin off the High Street, dating from 1582, and built by Thomas MacLellan with stones from a ruined friary which once stood here. The jagged fangs of this castellated mansion draw you to it from across the town. In the huge great hall, look for the remarkable single stone lintel that spans the 10½-ft (32-m) aperture, and also for the small closet behind the fireplace with a peephole, hinting at all sorts of intrigue and concealment in the past. MacLellan's extremely elaborate tomb is in the original 16th-century aisle of **Greyfriars Church**.

Broughton House (open daily in the summer, closed Sun mornings and Tues in winter: adm) in the High Street, was built in the 18th century. It was the home of E. A. Hornel, one of the first settlers of the Kircudbright artists' colony and a renowned artist himself. Hornel died in 1933 and left this lovely Georgian house to the town, with a marvellous collection of books and manuscripts on Galloway, a treasure-trove for the researcher. The colourful gardens slope gracefully down to the river.

The Tolbooth, also in the High Street, dates from 1627 with an outside stone stair. Several witches were imprisoned here, as was John Paul Jones (see 'Arbigland' p. 101), convicted for causing the death of a seaman, but later freed. Don't miss the 'jougs' with which miscreants were tethered by the neck for public humiliation.

The Stewartry Museum (open Mon–Sat, Easter–Oct: adm) is the place to go if you want to know more about the buccaneering life of John Paul Jones. It's in St Mary Street, where there is a special exhibition devoted to him. You can also see displays relating to everyday life in the Stewartrys, both historic and domestic, going back to prehistoric times. There are also works by local artists, especially Jessie M. King who was a contemporary of E. A. Hornel.

Before you leave Kirkudbright, visit **St Cuthbert's Churchyard** on the edge of the town. Here you will find a tombstone marking the grave of 'William Marshall, Tinker, who died in 1792 at the the advanced age of 120 years'. This remarkable man is alleged to have fathered four of his many children after the age of 100, which may account for the pair of ram's horns engraved on the reverse side of the headstone.

Gatehouse of Fleet

The Murray Forest Centre, northwest at Gatehouse of Fleet, has a Log Cabin Centre, an information office, picnic sites and signposted forest walks. There is also the **Fleet Forest Visitor Centre** to the south, a reconstructed Bobbin Mill and a display of town history.

Cardoness Castle

Cardoness Castle (open daily: adm), a mile southwest of Gatehouse of Fleet, is a 15th-century tower-house, a stark sentinel, four storeys high above a neat turf mound, with a vaulted basement. Although it lacks a roof it gives you a good idea of what it must have been like, with the original stairway, stone benches and elaborate fireplaces. In the Dark Ages, the owners, called de Cardine, got so carried away celebrating the birth of an heir that, it is said, they all went skating on the loch before the ice was strong enough to hold them and that was the end of them.

Anwoth

Near Cardoness on the fast A75 there is a turning to Anwoth less than a mile away. In the ruin of the old church here there is a fascinating gem for anyone who enjoys the study of old gravestones. You will see an elaborate Gordon tomb, inscribed with an epitaph to a lady of Cardoness who died in 1628, beginning:

> Ze gaizers on this trophee of a tombe
> Send out ane grone for want of hir whois lyfe
> Twyse borne on earth and now is in earthis wombe
> Lived long a virgine now a spotless wife.

If you manage to get to Glasgow Cathedral, you will find the tomb of the Hamiltons of Holmhead, inscribed in 1616:

> Yee gazers on this trophie of a tomb
> Send out ane grone for want of her whose life
> Once born of earth, and now lies in earth's womb
> Liv'd long a virgin, then a spotless wyfe.

There is an ancient Pictish stone near the church, carved with a cross, indicating that this was an early Christian settlement.

Skyreburn Aquarium

Like an underwater wildlife park, Skyreburn has a selection of species from local waters, fresh and salt, with information about them. This is a good way of amusing the children on a wet afternoon—though to some, fish do become rather similar after a while.

Dirk Hatteraick's Cave is on the shore just east of the mouth of Kirkdale Burn and quite tricky to get at, crossed by the A75 about seven miles west of Gatehouse of Fleet. It is the largest of several caves in this area. Hatteraick was a notorious smuggler and so caves were important to him.

Barholm Castle is in the wooded glen just to the northeast. This 16th-century ruin was one of John Knox's refuges in the days when he was a fugitive.

Half a mile up the glen of Kirkdale Burn you come to two great Neolithic burial tombs at **Cairn Holy**. The first is a stone cist with standing stones; the second has a double burial chamber. These ancient, lonely stones, silhouetted against an evening sky, have a primal mystery that stirs the imagination. What were they like, those mourners, 4000 years ago?

WHERE TO STAY AND EAT

There is a mass of accommodation in this popular tourist area, mostly listed in the Dumfries and Galloway brochure. If you are after a sumptuous setting you will be more than satisfied at the unfortunately named **Cally Palace Hotel**, Gatehouse of Fleet, tel 05574 341 (open March–Jan). Moderately priced, it is a vast Georgian mansion with original moulded ceilings, standing in 100 acres of parkland, with a heated swimming-pool, and every sort of leisure facility. Also moderately priced at Gatehouse of Fleet, **The Murray Arms Hotel** on the corner of Ann Street and the High Street, tel 05574 207, was one of the haunts of that discerning pub-crawler, R. Burns, and it was here that he composed 'Scots Wha Hae', inspired, no doubt, by their fine wine and excellent cuisine. Try their local beef. You'll get moderately priced comfort at **Barons Craig Hotel** at

Rockcliffe south of Dalbeattie, tel 055663 225, but it is only open from April to October. This imposing Victorian country house stands in 12 acres of wooded garden, over-looking the Solway Firth. Perhaps a little soul-less, but the food is good and the staff are efficient. Another imposing, moderately priced country house hotel, standing literally on the beach, is the **Balcary Bay Hotel** at Auchencairn, tel 055664 217, run by a family, closed December to February. The seafood is excellent.

Though not exactly the mansion it proclaims itself to be, **Clonyard House Hotel** at Colvend, tel 055663 372, is cheap, comfortable, serves excellent food and caters for disabled guests. They do scallops very well. Another cheap one is **The Selkirk Arms** in Kirkcudbright High Street, with excellent food and a friendly atmosphere. Burns wrote the Selkirk Grace here.

Some hae meat and canna eat,
And some wad eat that want it:
But we hae meat and we can eat
And sae the Lord be thankit.

Creetown

Following the coast on round for about six miles you come to Creetown on the eastern shore of the Cree estuary, the granite gateway to Wigtownshire, a peaceful village whose public image has recently had a face-lift. With hills, forests, lochs and sandy beaches all within easy reach, this is a good holiday base. Town and country walks are signposted from Adamson Square. Gemmologists should stop off here to see the **Gem Rock Museum and Gallery** (open daily: adm) up the road opposite the clock tower. This collection of gems and rocks from all over the world took 50 years to gather: it is awe-inspiring to be shown a rock that contains water two million years old! There is a gem-cutting workshop, a tea room and gift shop. Don't miss the **Craft Centre and Fragrance Shop** in The Square, or **Creetown Gold Silversmithing Workshop**, in St John Street where you can watch a craftsman making jewellery in gold, silver and semi-precious stones.

Newton Stewart

Another five or so miles along the A75, on the banks of the River Cree, Newton Stewart grew around the first easy place to ford the river. It is an attractive holiday centre and market town, surrounded by wooded moors and fertile farmland on the reclaimed mud-flats of the estuary. From here you can enjoy a marvellously varied holiday: walking, fishing, boating, bird-watching, sightseeing or just relaxing in the mild, often hot, sunshine. It is a good base from which to explore the enormous Galloway Forest Park, to the north.

Creebridge Mohair Mill visitors welcome to watch the mohair being woven and finished. The mill is open from Mon–Fri, with guided tours from Easter–October; the shop where you can buy a large range of mohair articles is also open on Saturdays. The privately owned, non-profit making **Museum**, in York Road (open Easter and Mon–Sat, May–June, daily, July–Sept; adm) displays local history.

106

Wigtown

Seven miles south of Newton Stewart on the western shore of Wigtown Bay, Wigtown is another pleasant little holiday resort. Here you will see two mercat crosses, the second, rather ostentatious, one having been erected to celebrate the victory at Waterloo in 1816. The railed enclosure in the large town square was for penning up cattle at night, a practice that was necessary not only to stop them straying, but also to keep them safe from reivers.

Wigtown will always be remembered for its two martyrs, Margaret McLachlan, aged 62, and Margaret Wilson, aged 18. In 1685, these two women were convicted of having attended 20 conventicles—the illegal Covenanter prayer meetings. They were tied to stakes in the estuary and drowned by the rising tide watched by a large, avid crowd. Margaret Wilson was deliberately placed so that she could witness the final throes of her older companion: she was then half-rescued and given the chance to 'repent'. She refused and was re-secured to her stake. The graves of these two women, the Wigtown Martyrs, together with those of six other Covenanter martyrs, are in the churchyard where you can see the ruins of two former churches beside the present parish church. These sad memorials are food enough for thought, as is the monument on the hill above the town, but it is not until you see the simple pillar on the shore where the drownings took place, and watch the tide rising over the estuary mudflats, that the full horror of that appalling event really hits you.

While you are here, visit the **Bladnoch Distillery**, the most southerly in Scotland, just south of the town on the A714. You can go on conducted tours and learn the secrets of distilling, with a dram of single malt to see you on your way!

Torhouse Stone Circle

The Torhouse Stone Circle, dating from about 2000 BC, is about five miles west of Wigtown, and is one of the best of this type in Britain. There are 19 roundish boulders forming a complete circle 60 ft (183 m) in diameter with three more in the centre. As with all other standing-stone circles, historians can only guess at their original purpose.

Galloway House Gardens at Garlieston, about six miles south of Wigtown on the coast (open daily: adm), is a woodland garden. Informal walks among gorgeous shrubs, borders, wild flowers, fine trees and exotica lead down to a quiet sandy bay. There is a walled garden with a camellia house. The 18th-century house, built by Lord Garlies, is not open to the public, but you can get tea in the village.

WHERE TO STAY AND EAT
Open from Easter to the end of December, Moderately priced **Hills of Burns Country House Hotel** at Creetown, tel 067182 487, is an 18th-century mansion with stunning views over the Cree estuary, in 9 acres of wooded grounds. It has a nice family atmosphere, with log fires, reasonable food and a snooker room. Newton Stewart has a number of hotels: **Creebridge House Hotel**, tel 0671 2121, is a nice house close to the town centre, moderately priced and comfortable, with special week-end and short-break rates. **Rowallan House Hotel** in Corsbie Road, tel 0671 2520, is an attractive country

house, five minutes' walk from the town centre, and cheap. It deservedly won a 'good room' award. **Ellangowan Hotel,** tel 0671 82201, is another cheap, family-run hotel with good food.

Whithorn

About 10 miles south of Wigtown you come to Whithorn (from the Anglo-Saxon *huit aern*—'white house'), the birthplace of Christianity in Scotland. Born nearby, some time in the middle of the 4th century, and of royal descent, St Ninian went to Rome on a pilgrimage and returned here in 397 as a consecrated bishop. He built a white stone church which became known as *Candida Casa*, and from here he set about converting the Britons and southern Picts to Christianity. Whithorn is the oldest Royal Burgh in Scotland, its first charter having been granted by Robert the Bruce in 1329.

Whithorn Priory and Museum
You go through The Pend to get to the Priory, a deep 17th-century arch flanked by 15th-century pillars with a stone panel above carved with the Scottish coat of arms as it was before the Union, in 1707.

The Museum (open daily: adm), through The Pend, is well worth visiting before doing anything else because it gives an excellent and very clear description of the significance of Whithorn and the vital part it played in the birth of Christianity in Britain. There are some fascinating early Christian crosses and stones with explanations that make you long to go and read up all the books about this significant time in British history.

A ticket includes entry to the Priory on the site of Candida Casa: you can still see the 13th-century nave and a doorway in the south wall that was built by Fergus of Galloway who founded the priory in 1126. It was a place of pilgrimage for more than 400 years, until 'idolatry' was made illegal in 1581 by the Reformers. Many of Scotland's monarchs paid regular visits to the shrine: James IV walked from Edinburgh on one occasion. Mary, Queen of Scots, was the last, in 1563, during her tour of the west.

Whithorn Excavations
At Bruce Street, off George Street (open April–mid-Oct: adm), you can watch archaeologists working on the extensive excavations of the original Christian community with buildings and graves going back as far as the 5th century, the remains of a Viking settlement with reconstructed buildings, medieval burials and even a medieval herb garden. This is almost more interesting than the museum. As you watch the experts sifting through the earth, it seems miraculous that they can reconstruct history from such fragments of material. There is an information centre and shop, a video interpretation of what you can see, and guided tours.

A mile west of Whithorn, **Rispain Camp** is a rectangular settlement defended by a bank and ditch, dating from the first century AD.

Isle of Whithorn

Isle of Whithorn, three miles southeast of Whithorn village, on the southeast tip of the peninsula, is a little port built on what was once an island, and is still a centre for fishing, with a variety of boats working out of the harbour. You can see here the ruin of a 12th-century chapel dedicated to St Ninian, built on the site of one that was probably for the use of the pilgrims who came from abroad, for whom special safe-conducts were granted.

St Ninian's Cave

St Ninian's Cave, three miles southwest of Whithorn, is believed to have been the saint's private oratory, with early Christian crosses carved on the rock, on your left as you look in, small and quite hard to spot. There is something very moving about this tiny corner of Galloway: whether you are a Christian or not, you cannot fail to wonder at the strength of the faith of those first missionaries, working among barbaric pagans, sowing the seeds that grew into the Christian church as we know it today. You can get to the cave by taking the minor road south off the A747, a mile east of its junction with the A746. There's a car park at Kidsdale Farm and the cave is signposted from there, 3 miles the round trip; a nice walk through Physgill woods, where daffodils carpet the ground in spring and the trees overhead form an enchanting canopy. Due to a rockfall, you have to be very cautious getting into the cave at the moment, but there is an information board.

Archaeological Sites

If archaeology interests you, the coast road northwest along Luce Bay from the Isle of Whithorn to Glenluce links up several antiquities on or near the shore.

The Wren's Egg Stone Circle is on the left after Craiglemine; another of those ancient remains whose purpose remains a mystery. **Barsalloch Fort**, an Iron Age fort, surrounded by a horseshoe ditch, on a cliff 60 ft (183 m) above the sea, is by Barsalloch Point. It's quite a steep climb up a cattle track, but worth it for a splendid example of how the ancient Britons defended themselves against attack. Archaeologists found the remains of Mesolithic fishermen here, over 6000 years old. (If you come in summer, the foreshore is a glorious blue carpet of saxifrage.) **Drumtrodden Stones**, less than 3 miles inland from Barsalloch, have Bronze Age cup-and-ring markings carved in the rock. These mysterious symbols, a foot in diameter, are found on stones scattered throughout the north as well as on the continent. **Druchtag Motehill**, to the north beyond Mochrum village, is a typical early medieval earthwork mound, very steep, with traces of the stone buildings.

The **Gavin Maxwell Memorial** is a very life-like sculpted otter on a cliff top overlooking Monreith Bay. The talented writer grew up in this area and it is fitting that his memorial should command an outstanding view.

Chapel Finian, little more than a few stones now, beside the A747, and five miles northwest of Port William, was a 10th-century chapel dedicated to St Finbarr. The chapel was built here in this little inlet for pilgrims landing from the sea on their way either to Whithorn or Glenluce.

Glenluce Abbey

Glenluce Abbey (open daily: adm) at the head of Luce Bay was restored during this century and is so interesting that you will want to return many times. Founded in 1190 by

Roland, Lord of Galloway, its 15th-century vaulted chapter house is almost intact, entered by a round, curiously carved doorway. Inside, a single octagonal pillar stands in the middle, supporting the stone vaulting-ribs on carved corbels, each arch being decorated with twined foliage, grotesques and emblems. All this is aesthetically satisfying, but of even greater interest to some will be the baked-clay water pipes and drains that have been excavated, laid by those monks so long ago and yet still sound today. These traces of early plumbing are fascinating, most expertly put together and possibly a great deal more durable than the unfortunate development of modern plastic drains.

A 13th-century wizard, Michael Scot, is said to have lived here and to have saved the community from extinction by luring the plague that had attacked them, into the abbey and shutting it up in a vault and starving it to death. He is also said to have occupied the witches who helped him at his work by commissioning them to spin the ropes of sand that you will see, south of the abbey at Ringdoo Point, revealed as broken strands of sand when the tide goes out.

Castle of Park, just west of Glenluce off the A75, is a very well-preserved castellated tower house built in 1590 by Thomas Hay of Park. You can't go in, but it's worth stopping for a look.

WHERE TO STAY AND EAT
There's quite a good choice around this area. For dependability, though not necessarily humming with vitality (they charge you for your dog!), moderately priced **Corsemalzie House Hotel** at Port William, tel 098886 254, should be your first choice. Open from March to mid-January, this country house, in 40 acres of wooded gardens, has good food, free golf, private fishing and rough shooting—and is extremely comfortable. Try their smoked fish. In the cheap range, peaceful **Castlewigg Hotel,** two miles from Whithorn, tel 09885 213, overlooks Galloway hills and has cosy log fires in the bar. Also cheap is **The Steampacket Hotel** overlooking the lively harbour in Isle of Whithorn, tel 09885 334, with excellent fish dishes.

The Rhinns of Galloway

Exploring the Rhinns of Galloway, that extraordinary hammer-head butt on the western extremity of Dumfries and Galloway, you will pull up in delight at the many panoramic views that unfold seawards from the rugged cliffs. In certain conditions, Ireland looks so close you feel it would make an easy swim! Seldom more than spitting distance from the sea, you can experience fierce storms here, as well as the mild gentle climate of the rest of the region. Try and catch a sunset from the Mull of Galloway.

Stranraer

Stranraer is a busy port and the market centre for the area, as well as being a popular holiday resort. Very sheltered, at the head of Loch Ryan, 10 miles west of Glenluce, it is the gateway to the Rhinns of Galloway. Although it isn't a beautiful town it can give you all the amenities you could ask for on holiday, with numerous hotels and guest houses, golf courses, good beaches, excellent trout and sea fishing, boating and exploring. Frequent car-ferries make the 2-hour crossing to Larne in Northern Ireland.

It is odd to think, as you walk about the bustling modern town, that below your feet lie the oystershells that were thrown out by Mesolithic settlers, 6000 years ago. Looking out across Loch Ryan you can picture it in Roman times when they used the sheltered anchorage for their galleys, in their expeditions against the Gallovidians, calling it *Rericonius Sinus*.

Old Castle of St John in Castle Street, is a 16th-century towerhouse, occupied by Claverhouse during his relentless persecution of the Covenanters in 1682: his victims were imprisoned in the dungeons where many of them perished. You can get a wonderful view from the parapet walk. This was also the police station and prison in the 19th century. There are exhibitions on the Castle, Covenanters and the jail, in the new Visitors' Centre (open Apr–Sept, daily except Sat; free).

Wigtown District Museum, London Road, Stranraer (open Mon, Wed and Fri afternoons, 1st May–30 Sept: free), will give you information about Sir John Ross (see below). It is a local history museum with emphasis on dairy farming.

North West Castle Hotel, opposite the pier in Stranraer, was the home of Sir John Ross, the 18th-century Arctic explorer who sailed in search of the Northwest Passage and discovered the true position of the magnetic North Pole. A passionate seaman, Ross built his house as much like a ship as possible, a flamboyant, castellated mansion with the dining room modelled like a ship's cabin with rounded stern. (Hotel details below.)

Castle Kennedy Gardens

Three miles east of Stranraer just off the A75 (open daily in the summer: adm), Castle Kennedy Gardens are well worth an unhurried visit. They were laid out by the second Earl of Stair, who died in 1747, having been Ambassador in France and been inspired by the gardens of Versailles. Not slow off the mark, the Earl used soldiers of the Royal Scots

Castle Kennedy, Stranraer

111

Greys and the Inniskilling Fusiliers (who were in the area to quell Covenanters) to build his garden for him around his home, Castle Kennedy, which you can now see as a ruin, softened by swathes of ivy, on an isthmus between two lochs. After the castle was burned down in 1715, the gardens were sadly neglected for years, until 1847, when they were rescued and restored to their original 17th-century design, with a sunken garden. The rhododendrons, azaleas, magnolias and embothriums are remarkable and the pinetum was the first one to be grown in Scotland. The monkey puzzle avenue is one of the longest in Scotland. The present Scots–French mansion, Lochinch Castle, home of Lord Stair, was built in 1867 to replace Castle Kennedy. There is a tea room and you can buy plants. If you are interested in the culture and use of herbs, you will learn a lot in the **Meadowsweet Herb Garden** also at Castle Kennedy, where they have over a hundred herbs with instructive tours.

Corsewall Point

Drive up to the northwest tip of the Rhinns. You get to Corsewall Point and the lighthouse along a rough track with the dominating cone of Ailsa Craig rising from the sea to the north. Robert Louis Stevenson's grandfather built the lighthouse. You are a lot closer to Belfast, on this tip, than you are to Edinburgh!

Portpatrick

Portpatrick, not quite half-way down the west coast of the peninsula, is a thriving holiday resort and fishing village. Only 22 miles northeast of Donaghadee, in Ireland, this was once the port for the main route west, but southwesterly gales frequently made docking hazardous, so the port was moved to sheltered Stranraer. Portpatrick is an idyllic holiday centre with lovely coastal scenery, sandy bays, a golf course, a picturesque little harbour. **The Southern Upland Way** starts here and the least taxing stretch of it is the first six or seven miles to Castle Kennedy. In summer you could easily be in some Mediterranean resort, without all that garlic and oil. The landscape is bright with flowers, the air deliciously scented. It is said that St Patrick landed here on a visit from Ireland.

Little Wheels Toy Transport Display and Model Railway, in Hill Street, (open daily except Fri, Easter–Oct, daily July–Aug; adm) is a unique collection for mechanics of all ages.

Dunskey Castle, a gaunt, jagged ruin dating back to the 16th century, stands on a cliff less than a mile to the south. It is one of those dramatic ruins that fire your imagination with pictures of pirates and wreckers and damsels in distress. Take great care walking on the cliff paths which are not suitable for young children.

Kirkmadrine Stones, eight miles south of Stranraer off the A716, will interest any archaeologist. The 5th/6th-century stones are to be found against the church wall, with a description that explains their significance. Some bear Latin inscriptions and the 'ChiRho' symbol, formed by a combination of the first two letters of Christ's name in Greek. These ancient stones prove that St Ninian managed to establish Christianity in this area; they are the earliest Christian memorials in Scotland after those at Whithorn.

Ardwell House Gardens

Ardwell House Gardens (open Easter–31 Oct: adm) are a couple of miles south of the stones off the A716. Go there not only for the almost tropical gardens round the 18th-century house, and the pond walks, but also for the sea views.

At **Ardwell Bay**, on the precipitous west coast, there is a narrow rock spit, cut off by a wall, where you can see one of the few brochs in the southwest, unusual in that it had two entrances, one to seaward and one to landward. Those early settlers would certainly have had the advantage of anyone trying to invade them by sea.

Logan Botanic Garden

About a mile south of Ardwell on the A716, turn right on to the B7065 to **Port Logan**, a picturesque, sheltered harbour with a stone jetty, lighthouse and small beach. Logan Botanic Gardens (open daily April–Sept: adm) are just over a mile to the north. A branch of the Royal Botanic Garden in Edinburgh, this is a compulsory stop for garden-lovers—a glorious riot of sub-tropical plants, tree-ferns, cabbage palms and the Brazilian *Gunnera manicata*, largest-leafed outdoor plant in Britain. Plants from all over the world flourish in the mild climate and you feel you are walking in some exotic foreign land.

There is an excellent licensed salad-bar restaurant, open from 10 to 5.

The Mull of Galloway

The Mull of Galloway, the most southerly point in Scotland, less than 25 miles from Ireland and the Isle of Man, is a dramatic headland with cliffs 200 ft (61 m) high on the southern tip of the Rhinns. You can stand here, buffeted by the wind and salt spray, and watch a boiling cauldron, far below, at certain times and conditions when seven currents meet and do battle together. You can see over the lighthouse at the keeper's discretion—well worth it for the views from the walkway at the top.

Double Dykes is the name of the trench across the western end of the point and is said to have been the last defence of the Picts, retreating from the Scots who had driven them down the peninsula early in the 6th century.

WHERE TO STAY AND EAT
By far the best hotel in this area is **Knockinaam Lodge Hotel** in Portpatrick, tel 077681 471. Open from March to December, and expensive, it is a proper country-house hotel in a secluded glen with a private beach, and glorious sea views across to Ireland. The grounds are lovely and include a croquet lawn. All the rooms are elegantly decorated and comfortable, and the food is excellent. It's just like staying in a private house—except for the bill. Apart from that, you have a large and varied choice. **North West Castle Hotel** in Stranraer, tel 0776 4413, is highly recommended if you like comfort combined with something out of the ordinary. See Stranraer for the reason why this amazing concoction is built to resemble a ship! On the seafront, with swimming pool, games room, saunas, sunbeds and even a curling rink, it is moderately priced: maddeningly, they don't take credit cards. The food is good. There are lots of other hotels in Stranraer, listed in the Dumfries and Galloway Tourist Guide. In Portpatrick, and also moderately priced, **The**

Fernhill Golf Hotel, tel 077681 220, stands high above the harbour overlooking the Irish Sea, 400 yards from the golf course. It is closed for the first three weeks in November. Family-run and comfortable, it has good food and every dish is cooked to order so there's no danger of instant microwave flannel. Also overlooking the harbour and moderately priced, **Portpatrick Hotel**, tel 077681 333, gives good value and welcomes families, but it is only open from March to November.

The Valleys

Dumfries and Galloway is cut by a number of valleys that bring the rivers cascading down into the Solway Firth from the hills and moorland in the north. If you have time as you go west along the coast, you will find many unexpected delights if you pause to trace some of these rivers up to their source.

ESKDALE

A network of streams rise in the wooded hills of Eskdalemuir Forest, to the north, joining together above Langholm to form the lovely River Esk, that hurries south, chattering and tumbling, through gorges and ravines until it steadies its pace and flows into the Solway Firth at Gretna.

Scotsdike

On the English border, Scotsdike has a 16th-century trench and dyke dug to mark the border in the days when the 'Debatable Lands' were hotly contested.

Gilnockie Tower

Recently restored Gilnockie Tower (viewable from the outside at all reasonable times or by appointment, tel 0541 80976), once called Hollows, or Holehouse, is five miles south of Langholm, off the A7. Dating from the 16th century this was one of Johnnie Armstrong of Gilnockie's strongholds—that hero of a number of border ballads; see Teviot, Borders (p. 91), for this colourful freebooter's history. Ruffian he may have been, but he was reputed never to do harm to any of his countrymen even though James V ordered his hanging in 1529, and it is easy to feel a twinge of affection for him, as you look up at this romantic tower, with crow-stepped gables and a carved parapet-walkway round the top, standing high above the Esk valley. He would certainly have approved of his descendant, Neil Armstrong, who was first man on to the moon in 1969.

Langholm

Langholm, about 10 miles north of the border, is a pleasant little mill-town where the Esk gathers up the waters of the Wauchope and Ewes. The narrow, twisting old town, with its market place and town house is quite different to the spacious, stately-looking quarter across the river that developed in the 18th century when Langholm became a flourishing textile centre. The town has its Common Riding celebrations in July, with a great charge of riders through a narrow bend and up the hill from the square—a very dramatic stampede.

If the poet Hugh McDiarmid is one of your heroes, visit the memorial to him two miles to the northeast on the Newcastleton road. A two-fold panel stands like a great open book overlooking Eskdale with carvings of wildlife and countryside, dramatic in their simplicity. Local feeling ran high when this memorial was first commissioned after McDiarmid's death in 1978. Although he had referred to his home town as 'my touchstone in all creative matters' he was not loved by many of his fellow Langholmites. Stuffy locals objected to some of his bawdy anecdotes and his veiled references to the sexual habits of a local citizen in his autobiography *Lucky Poet*. When the statue was finished, it was refused by a six to five vote from the Dumfries and Galloway Planning Committee. Fortunately, the small-minded have been overruled.

If you want to stretch your legs, there is a good walk from Langholm up to the **Malcolm Monument**—the obelisk that dominates the hill to the east. Start from the car park beside the A7, just north of the town, and go up past the golf course. The round trip is five miles, and the view from the monument makes the final steepish climb well worth it. (In case you didn't know, Malcolm was Sir John Malcolm who, in 1782, aged 13, was commissioned into the East India Company and became Governor of Bombay 45 years later.)

Scottish Explorers Museum, Craigcleuch

Craigcleuch (open Easter and daily, 1 May–30 Sept: or by arrangement, tel Langholm 80137: adm) is two miles northwest of Langholm on the B709, in sheltered parkland surrounded by trees and shrubs, overlooking the Esk valley. This 19th-century Scottish Baronial mansion contains an amazingly diverse collection of rare objects from all over the world gathered up by early Scottish explorers. While Neil Armstrong made history with a handful of moonrocks, his ancestors may well have helped to collect up the exquisite carved coral and ivory, African wood-carvings, pre-historic ornaments and implements, Chinese silk paintings, wall hangings, tribal art, hunting trophies and skins that can be seen in the museum. There is something here for everyone and you can even buy some of the pictures. Outside, you can walk and picnic by the river with lovely views between two hills known as the 'Gates of Eden' to the north.

Westerkirk

In 1757, Thomas Telford was born at Westerkirk, further northwest on the B709 and here, overlooking his beloved Esk, you can see a memorial to this giant of the Industrial Revolution, who built roads and bridges all over the country, serving his apprenticeship on his own local bridges.

Kagyu Samye Ling Tibetan Monastery

Whether Buddhism is your thing or not, there is something very inspiring about this largest Buddhist temple in Western Europe, just north of Eskdalemuir on the B709.

Founded in 1967 and completed in the mid-80s, in all the peace and tranquillity of this lovely setting, near the source of the Esk, it is a far cry from the persecution and atrocities of Communist Tibet. Whatever your creed, you won't regret taking one of their free conducted tours round the temple and monastery.

WHERE TO STAY AND EAT

If you don't mind being in the middle of the town, **Eskdale Hotel** in Langholm, tel 0541 80357, is a cheap, family-run former coaching inn whose rather stern exterior conceals an air of genteel respectability and good plain cooking. They can arrange shooting and fishing for you. Also in the middle of the town and cheap, the more attractive-looking **Crown Hotel**, tel 03873 80247, was a coaching inn in the 18th century and has a slightly less hushed atmosphere.

Gourmet restaurants don't abound in this area but the hotel meals are usually not too bad.

ANNANDALE

Follow the River Annan north along the back roads to its source just north of Moffat: the scenery gets progressively wilder and more impressive.

Kirkpatrick Fleming

Kirkpatrick Fleming, three miles northeast of Annan off the A74, has a cave where Robert Bruce hid for three months. Accessible now by path, it was then reached by swinging down the cliff on a rope. The cave was originally cut out of the rock by Stone Age men whose tools were found near the river. Locals will tell you that it was here, and not on Rathlin Island, or anywhere else making similar claims, that Bruce took courage from that persevering spider we were all brought up to emulate.

Kirtlebridge

If you enjoy antiquities, go to Kirtlebridge, three miles further on, off the A74, for the 15th-century Merkland Cross, 9 ft (27 m) high, with intricate carvings, erected in memory of a Maxwell who was killed in battle. There are people alive today who remember the shock of the train crash near here in the First World War, when over 200 people were killed.

Children should enjoy the **Clydesdale Horse Centre** at Robgill Tower near Kirtlebridge, where you can see the horses and all the old harness and implements.

Ecclefechan

Ecclefechan, about five miles north of Annan off the A74, was Thomas Carlyle's birthplace in 1795. He was born in the pretty white **Arched House**, now a museum (open daily, Easter–31 Oct, or by arrangement, tel 05763 666: adm), so called because of its arched gateway. The house was built by his father and uncle. His parents were simple, unpretentious people, god-fearing and exceptionally eloquent. (Carlyle's mother learnt to write so that she could answer his letters to her.) They sent Thomas to Edinburgh University to train for the Church in 1809. His inherited intelligence, fed by education, flowered: he developed a critical awareness and knowledge of books and men that set him apart from his peers. Among the many things he wrote was *Sartor Resartus* (Tailor Repatched) in which he describes a village, 'Entepfuhl' which is recognizable as Ecclefechan.

A mass of memorabilia is packed into the tiny cottage. The kitchen, with original fireplace, would have been the heart of the household and you can almost see the family, seated at the table, listening to long dissertations from the young student, surrounded by all the domestic clutter of country life now displayed. Upstairs, although the box-bed is not original, it is contemporary with that in which Thomas was born, in this bedroom. Other furniture and items come from Cheyne Row, Chelsea, where the Carlyles lived for more than 30 years. The museum is of interest for its social history as well as being a fascinating memorial to a complex man.

This great literary genius refused burial in Westminster Abbey and is buried below a simple sandstone slab in the churchyard behind the cottage, an unfussy monument to a brilliant man who loathed ostentation. He was a temperamental husband to intellectual Jane Baillie Welsh, with whom he shared a stormy relationship reflected in her caustic, witty letters. Although they were devoted to each other and Jane's death in 1866 'shattered my whole existence into immeasurable ruin' she left instructions that she was not to be buried with him, but with her father in Haddington, Lothian.

Hoddam Castle

This castle, two miles to the southwest, was built in the 16th century by John Maxwell, 4th Lord Herries, with a watchtower on Repentance Hill to the south. (Repentance, they say, because the noble lord threw his prisoners into the sea during a storm after a piratical raid on England.) There is a caravan park at Hoddam with a warden in the castle.

Lockerbie

At 6 on Wednesday 21 December 1988, as people prepared for Christmas, a Pan-Am Boeing 747 Jumbo Jet, en route from Frankfurt to New York, took off from London Heathrow. It carried in its luggage hold a transistor radio packed with explosives, planted by terrorists. The device exploded over Lockerbie, at 7.19, killing all the crew and passengers in the plane. The wreckage fell on and around the the town and on the adjacent motorway, flattening houses in a quiet crescent, killing the residents and a number of people driving up the motorway. In all, nearly 280 people died.

The town lives on, with Scottish guts and stoicism. Don't add to the cars that creep through the town, full of curious eyes, avid for sensation. There is nothing to see and the people need time to get over their tragedy.

By the end of the 18th century, Lockerbie, 10 miles north of Annan, was a substantial town, with lamb sales held annually on Lamb Hill. These sales were great occasions for the whole of Annandale: boisterous, colourful fairs, with sideshows and booths and noisy, jostling crowds. Perhaps, one day, the people will feel like rejoicing on their streets again: meanwhile, leave them in peace.

Birrenswark, or Burnswark as it is sometimes called, has a distinctive outline which can't be missed. It is a steep, flat-topped hill southeast of Lockerbie, visible for miles around. This commanding position was the site of a large fort, many centuries BC, with circular huts inside sturdy ramparts. Along came the Romans, besieged the inhabitants and moved in, leaving the foundations you can see today. It is well worth the 940-ft (286.5 m) climb, not just for the tremendous view from the top but for the great feeling of ancient history among those ancient ramparts and ditches. In 937 a ferocious battle took place here, the Battle of Brunanburh between the Saxon-English and the united Scots and Norse armies, with victory for the English.

Lochmaben

Lochmaben, four miles west of Lockerbie on the A709, is a small town with a history that goes back to the 12th century when Robert Bruce's forebears were powerful. It is one of the places claimed as the birthplace of King Robert himself, whose statue glowers down the main road. Many of the buildings were built with stone from 13th-century **Lochmaben Castle**, whose scant remains are on a promontory signposted down a track south of Castle Loch. The massive, ivy-clad walls and humpy arches, gap-toothed among saplings on a grassy mound with traces of a moat, are a pathetic travesty of what used to be a 16-acre concourse with four moats. It was one of James IV's favourite places in the 16th century though his preferences were often influenced by whatever female charms were available in the area. Mary, Queen of Scots, came here with Darnley and it is said that she introduced 'vendace' to the lochs—small rare fish, considered a great delicacy: they have to be netted because they won't take bait.

Spedlins Tower

Spedlins Tower, now a ruin, is three miles north of Lochmaben. It was once haunted by a rather gruesome ghost. In the 17th century the local miller, Porteous, was locked in the dungeon by the laird who then rode off to Edinburgh, forgetting about his prisoner. Porteous starved to death, eating his own flesh in an attempt to survive, and his ghost haunted the tower until they managed to confine it to the dungeon by laying a black-letter Cranmer Bible on the cellar steps.

Moffat

Take the B7020 from Lochmaben, through rolling farmland between the low, smooth contours of the Lowther Hills to the west and Eskdalemuir to the east, patched with forest. Moffat is an attractive town with a very wide High Street, dissected by a double avenue of lime trees. The Colvin Fountain, at the end, is a cairn of boulders with a huge bronze ram on top, underlining the town's importance as a sheep-farming centre. It's a shame they can't ban cars from this impressive town centre.

In 1633, Rachel Whitford, a bishop's daughter, tasted the water from a spring to the east and recognized the strong tang as that of sulphur. Within 100 years, peaceful little

Moffat, deep in its valley among the hills, became one of the most fashionable spas in Europe, attracting the ailing rich from far afield.

It was here in 1759, that James Macpherson produced his first 'Ossianic' Fragments, poems that he swore he had 'translated from the Gaelic of Ossian, the son of Fingal'. The authenticity of these poems was hotly debated by Dr Samuel Johnson, among others, and although many scholars were convinced that they were genuinely collected from oral tradition, others believed that Macpherson composed them straight from his own head when he was a student. The truth seems immaterial as they are excellent in their own right.

Moffat Museum, in a converted bakery, gives you all the town's history, from sheep to spa.

If you have a sweet tooth, visit the Moffat Toffee Shop—a first-class 'sweetie shop', renowned for its delicious Moffat toffee.

The Devils Beef Tub

The Devils Beef Tub, six miles north of Moffat, off the A701, is an incredible natural corral, where cattle thieves used to hide their stolen beasts. An electric fence borders the edge but there is a gate. As you peer down the steep grassy walls into the black abyss where swirling mist rises eerily from a tiny stream in the bottom, you can almost hear the thudding hoofs and the harsh calls of the Johnstone men, rounding up their Maxwell neighbours' cattle. Many stories are told: when prisoners from Culloden were being marched up here in 1746, one broke away and rolled down the almost sheer sides and escaped in a thick mist. Walter Scott met this man and used his story in *Redgauntlet*:

'It looks as if four hills were laying their heads together to shut out daylight from the dark hollow space between them. A d—d dark black blackguard looking abyss of a hole it is and goes down straight from the roadside as perpendicular as it can do.'

You are on the watershed here between the source of the Annan and that of the Tweed—high, wild country that can be cut off in winter. Covenanters used to seek shelter in these hills and a memorial grave to one of them, who was shot opposite, stands on the lip of the Tub.

Grey Mare's Tail

Grey Mare's Tail, one of the highest waterfalls in the country, is 10 miles northeast of Moffat on the A708. The corrie was gouged out by a retreating glacier in the Ice Age. Tail Burn pours in a single cascade, 200 ft down from Loch Skeen into Moffat Water. The part you can see from the road seems to hang motionless in the air, but when you approach, its spray fills the air like mist and the sound of its water becomes a roar. In winter it can freeze solid and climbers test their skills on it with crampons and ice-axes! The National Trust for Scotland owns the land around the falls—beautiful country rich in wild flowers and supporting a rare herd of wild goats. There is an excellent seven-mile walk from Birkhill on the A708. You can go just to the foot of the waterfall, or you can continue up its right side to Loch Skeen, a mysterious, mist-shrouded loch surrounded by hills. You should be very cautious walking here; there are some precipitous edges to fall over, and there have been several serious accidents including four deaths. (Sir Walter Scott and his horse fell into a bog-hole round here and had the devil of a job 'to get extricated'.) On the way back to Birkhill, go left up the narrow rocky gorge of Dob' Lin.

WHERE TO STAY AND EAT
Auchen Castle Hotel and Restaurant at Beattock, near Moffat, tel 06833 407, is a 19th-century baronial mansion with a modern extension, in 50 acres of gorgeous gardens and grounds, with splendid views and a trout loch. Moderately priced gracious living here, with excellent cooking using local ingredients. There is a big choice in Moffat, of which **Moffat House Hotel**, tel 0683 20039, is probably one of the best, in an Adam mansion in the town centre with over two acres of grounds. Cheap, comfortable and convenient, it is open from March to November. Another good one in Moffat is **Beechwood Country House Hotel**, tel 0683 20210, with very much a Victorian country-house feeling, in a lovely garden overlooking the Annan Valley. Open from February to December, it is moderately priced, very friendly, with good food and wines. For something a bit different, try **Corehead Farm** at Annanwater, Moffat, tel 0683 20182, open from April to October. This guest house is on a 2500-acre hill farm at the base of the Devil's Beef Tub. Marvellous home cooking, a Farmhouse Award, children and pets not only allowed, but welcomed. It has two double rooms and a family room, and if you have children you could forget them all day among the farm animals while you slipped off for some solitary bird-watching. Extremely cheap and an ideal away-from-it-all holiday.

NITHSDALE

The river Nith rises across the Strathclyde border, rushing down through the upper moors fed by many streams to descend at a more leisurely pace into Dumfries and on out into the Solway mudflats. It is hugged by the A76, but try to stick to the back roads where you can.

Twelve Apostles Stone Circle

Antiquarians should go to Newbridge, two and a half miles northwest of Dumfries off the A76, to see Scotland's widest stone circle, the 11 stones clearly visible from the gate. Possibly of sacrificial origins, these stone circles are shrouded in mystery.

Routin Brig

If you follow the road along the Cairn Water from Newbridge you come to Routin Brig, where the river cascades down through the woods in a series of waterfalls.

Ellisland

Six miles north of Dumfries off the A76, Ellisland Farm is another Robert Burns landmark (open at all reasonable times, but ring in advance, tel 038774 246, free). Burns took over the farm in 1788, built the house and made his last, abortive attempt to make a living from the soil, with new farming methods. Alas, his mind was too absorbed by poetry and the ladies, and it was a dismal failure. He auctioned the stock in 1791 and moved to Dumfries to be an exciseman. He wrote some of his most famous poems here, including 'Tam O' Shanter'. In the granary you can see Burns as a farmer! There is a walk along the river, said to be where he went to get inspiration.

There are several open farms in this area, where children can get a good idea of farming methods both modern and extinct, but they are fairly predictable for anyone brought up in the country. One is **The Barony**, eight miles northeast of Dumfries off the A701, which includes farm walks with a woodland bird hide, a fishery and nature reserve.

Maxwelton House

Maxwelton House (house, museum, chapel and lovely grounds open at varying times in the summer or by appointment: tel 08482 385: adm) is 13 miles northwest of Dumfries on the B729. It was the birthplace of Annie Laurie, for love of whom the ardent young Jacobite, William Douglas of Fingland, wrote the well-known poem, set to music and reshaped in 1835, in which he declared that for Bonnie Annie Laurie he would 'lay me doon and dee'. She didn't put him to the test and married Mr Ferguson of Craigdarroch. In this 14th-century house you can see Annie's boudoir, an early kitchen, and dairy and farming implements. The gardens are typically Scottish. **Moniaive**, 5 miles to the west on A702, is a particularly attractive village with brightly painted houses and narrow streets and wynds.

Thornhill

A 10th-century, Anglian cross-shaft 9 ft high can be seen at Nith Bridge, half a mile west of Thornhill along A702. **Keir Mill**, three miles southwest of Thornhill, signposted off the A702, is where the world's first pedal bicycle was built at Courthill Smithy in 1839. Kirkpatrick MacMillan, the inventor, rode his 'Dandy Horse' to Glasgow where he was fined for 'dangerous behaviour, furious driving and knocking down a girl ...' Macmillan, who never bothered to patent his invention, is buried in the churchyard.

Drumlanrig Castle

Drumlanrig Castle, about 18 miles northwest of Dumfries off the A76 (open most days in the summer: adm), is a gorgeous pink sandstone Renaissance palace, on a grassy dais beside the Nith among the Lowther Hills. Now home of the Duke of Buccleuch, this impressive pile, with its mass of turrets and windows, was built in 1689 for his ancestor, the first Duke of Queensberry. The Duke moved in, spent one night, didn't like it and moved out again, having virtually ruined himself paying for his folly. When the castle was inherited by the fourth Duke, the notorious 'Old Q', in 1778, he sold the beautiful avenue of lime trees to help pay his gambling debts. On his death the Duke of Buccleuch inherited the estate and it is now open to the public and well worth a visit. (It has an unaccompanied wheelchair lift.)

You will see state rooms panelled with carved oak, beautiful French furniture, many treasures, and among the paintings, works by Leonardo da Vinci, Rembrandt, Holbein, Murillo, Ruysdael and Rowlandson, and portraits by Kneller, Reynolds and Ramsay. There are nature trails and an adventure play area in the lovely grounds and a visitor centre in the old stable yard with gift shop and tea room. Also in the stables is a Craft Centre where you can see resident craftsmen at work.

Durisdeer

At Durisdeer, a pretty hamlet tucked away at the entrance to the Dalveen Pass less than five miles to the northeast of Drumlanrig, off the A702, don't miss the delightfully 'Baroque-Arcadian' Queensberry Aisle in the 17th-century church: (key from the cottage nearby). This mausoleum contains a white marble monument, designed by Van Nost, in memory of the second Duke and Duchess of Queensberry who died in 1711 and 1709, respectively. The duchess lies supine, with her husband propped on an elbow beside her, like lovers on a pastoral tryst, surrounded by twisted columns, garlands and cherubs. Above the romantic-looking couple there is a scroll, extolling their virtues: it doesn't mention their heir, Lord Drumlanrig, who in 1707 murdered and tried to eat a spit-boy, in Queensberry House, Edinburgh.

The A702 continues north through the dramatic scenery of the **Dalveen Pass**, towards the A74, and can be linked with a visit to Wanlockhead.

Wanlockhead

Wanlockhead is the highest village in Scotland, 1380 ft up in the moors. You get there on the B797, off the A76, climbing steeply up a narrow valley beside the Mennock Water, through curiously unreal-looking, mottled green and brown hills. The village is a wedge-shaped cluster of houses built on turf mounds, nestling in a bowl in austere moorland.

The Museum of Scottish Lead Mining (open daily, Easter–Sept: adm) is in a rebuilt miner's cottage, with mining artifacts and a beam-pumping engine outside. You can follow an open-air trail and see a mine-shaft if you don't suffer from claustrophobia. There are also separate miners' cottages, set out in period style.

Gold was once panned from the streams in the hills here; a piece weighing four to five oz (approx 130 g) is now in the British Museum. The lonely, heather-covered moorland was a haunt of Covenanters, who used to hold their illegal conventicles up here, with look-outs on guard on surrounding peaks to warn of approaching soldiers, during the 'Killing Times' in the 17th century.

The **Southern Upland Way** passes through Wanlockhead, one of its more lonely stretches with panoramic views.

(For Leadhills, Scotland's second highest village just a short distance on up the road across the regional boundary, see Strathclyde p. 202.)

Sanquhar

A small, main-road town about 27 miles up the A76 from Dumfries, Sanquhar's chief interest is historic rather than scenic. Two Covenanters' declarations were pinned to its mercat cross: the first, by Richard Cameron in 1680, the second, by James Renwick in 1685, both protesting against the Episcopalian leanings of Charles II during the Killing Times (see 'History', p. 59). An obelisk marks the site of the cross, and it is hard to conjure up now just what hysterical bitterness must have pervaded the atmosphere then, when crowds of angry Covenanters stood around, pledging their lives for the cause. Richard Cameron was killed but his followers were granted an amnesty by William III, and it was from them that the regiment of the Cameronians was founded—now disbanded. Renwick was also killed and you can see a memorial to him near Moniaive.

The Tolbooth designed by William Adam in 1735 is a visitor centre and local-interest museum. It has an attractive clock tower and double external steps.

Post a letter in the **Sanquhar Post Office**—the oldest in Britain, opened in 1763, 20 years before the introduction of the mailcoach service, and still in use today.

The Admirable Crichton—the 16th-century genius and child prodigy, not the castaway butler on the island—was born at Elicock Castle, two miles to the south, and killed in an unfortunate brawl in Mantua when he was only 22.

WHERE TO STAY AND EAT
Not a very inspiring choice: try **Trigony House Hotel**, Closeburn, Thornhill, tel 0848 31211, is cheap, with salmon and sea trout fishing; a cosy, family-run country house in secluded grounds with very adequate food.

THE GLENKENS

Bordering the eastern flank of the Rhinns of Kells and the Galloway Forest Park, The Glenkens is a string of rivers and lochs, descending through wild, windswept moorland to Loch Ken, which narrows to become the River Dee, flowing into the Solway Firth at Kirkcudbright. Loch Ken offers fishing, birdwatching and watersports.

Tongland

Two miles north of Kirkcudbright, **Tongland Power Station** has free conducted tours daily except Sundays in the summer for those more interested in modern engineering than in anecdotal history, tel 0557 30114 to book. If you aren't tempted to join the family, wait for them outside, overlooking the dam. While you try to spot salmon leaping up the man-made ladder, cast your mind back to the colourful history of Tongland Abbey which once stood here. One of its abbots was murdered as he knelt at the altar in 1235, and its most famous abbot was John Damian, an alchemist. Damian enjoyed the patronage of James IV, the king who would undoubtedly have been a leading entrepreneur today and whose enquiring mind encouraged many experiments. In an attempt to show the king that it was possible for man to fly, Damian leapt off the walls of Stirling Castle in his presence. He broke his thigh.

Castle Douglas

Nine miles northeast of Kirkcudbright, Castle Douglas's history goes way back to when Iron Age builders created two crannogs on pretty Carlingwark Loch below the town. These islets, built on wooden platforms and submerged in shallow water, provided extra protection for the inhabitants of the huts on top. Horseshoes, excavated from the shore of the loch which the Civic Park now covers, are thought to date from a shoeing-forge that served the horses of Edward I's army when he was hammering the Scots. The town was once the village of Carlingwark, changing its name in honour of a pedlar called William Douglas who made his fortune in Virginia and returned to his homeland in 1789, buying up the village and developing it into a prosperous cattle market.

Threave Castle

Threave Castle (open 1 Apr–30 Sept, daily except Sat: free, small charge for ferry) is one and a half miles west of Castle Douglas. Square and stark, it stands on an island in the river Dee, a Black Douglas stronghold dating from the 14th century. It was the last of their fortresses to surrender to James II in 1455, during his struggle to throw off their powerful grip on his kingdom. James won his victory with the help of Mons Meg, that mighty cannon that you can now see in Edinburgh. Contrary to general belief, local tradition claims that Mons Meg was forged especially for the battle by a Galloway blacksmith called McKim: Mons being a contraction of Mollance—the land he was given as a reward—and Meg being his wife. The 70 ft (213 m) tower had five storeys, each containing a single room linked by a spiral stair, surrounded by a curtain wall and four drum towers. You will see a stone projecting above the doorway; this was 'The Gallows Knob' and Archibald the Grim, the aptly named 14th-century Earl of Douglas, used to boast that it 'never lacked a tassel'. Covenanters stormed this sinister castle in 1640 and demolished the interior.

Threave Gardens (open daily, all the year round: adm) are a mile south of the Castle. This important National Trust for Scotland creation provides a school of practical gardening, whose fortunate students receive a 2-year training in gardening skills that might once have been learnt at the knee of that almost extinct breed, the head gardener. Students live in the Victorian house in the grounds and between them and their instructors, they maintain a garden that is a joy to walk in. You can also explore the National Trust for Scotland Visitor Centre and the Threave Wildfowl Refuge with its many species of wild geese and ducks. (Access to the nature reserve is limited in the breeding season: adm.)

New Galloway

Although it was only a village, 18 miles north of Kirkcudbright, New Galloway was created a royal burgh in 1633, the smallest in Scotland, so that the Gordon Laird of nearby Kenmure Castle (a private residence) could have easy access to a market. It is an attractive place, its steep main street flanked by freshly painted stone cottages. Surrounded by wild moorland and forest, the landscape was transformed in 1929 by Scotland's first hydro-electric development, with reservoirs where rivers and burns once ran, looking remarkably natural in spite of dams.

Kenmure Castle

Kenmure Castle is off the A762 just south of New Galloway, a huge shell on a hill, topped by tall chimneys, visible through trees and accessible only on foot. With 15th-century origins, this ruin is cloaked in nostalgic history: home of the staunchly Jacobite Gordons of Lochinvar, it opened its doors to Mary, Queen of Scots during her state tour in 1563, and later sheltered her when she was escaping to England, providing her with the disguise she was wearing when she arrived at Dundrennan.

Lochinvar

If you had to recite 'Young Lochinvar' as punishment for crimes in your youth, you might feel some sort of compensatory delight in finding traces of Lochinvar's birthplace—bringing reality to what may once have seemed legend. Go three miles northeast of Dalry, off the A702 and along a track to the left. When, in Scott's 'Marmion', brave Lochinvar came out of the west, to rescue fair Ellen from having to marry a 'laggard in love and a dastard in war', it could have been from the fragment of castle you can see on the islet that he set out.

Dalry is a charming, well-kept village a couple of miles north of New Galloway.

The Galloway Forest Park

Formerly Glen Trool Forest, the Galloway Forest Park covers 250 sq miles of magnificent terrain, owned by the Forestry Commission. You can walk the many trails, surrounded by exceptionally lovely scenery as well as a wealth of wildlife, including roe deer, red deer and wild goats. Lonely moorland, peat bog, hills, lochs and fast-flowing rivers and burns, all dominated by the great bulk of Merrick, 2765 ft (610 m), make a visit here unforgettable. In autumn the range of colours is staggering. It is a good idea to get one of the guide-books, sold locally, with information and details of the many walks as well as of the campsites, picnic areas and special view points. **Queensway** is the scenic drive between New Galloway and Newton Stewart on the A712 with lots of tourist attractions to detain you on the way.

One of these attractions is **Clatteringshaws Loch**, about five miles west of New Galloway. Here you will come to the Galloway Deer Museum, a converted farm steading (open daily, April–Sept: free). You can see and learn all about not only deer but all other aspects of wildlife in this area, with geology and history, wild goats and a live trout exhibition. An attraction in the Forest Park is **Bruce's Stone**, commemorating Bruce's victory over the English at the Battle of Rapploch Moss in 1307. It is reached either by following the National Trust for Scotland signs up into the moor northwest from Clatteringshaws Loch—quite a long haul—or from the A714, through Glentrool village. Another **Bruce's Stone** is a massive engraved boulder overlooking lovely Loch Trool, marking the site where Robert Bruce defeated the English by rolling massive boulders down on to them. If the stones were anything like this, you can see why.

WHERE TO STAY AND EAT
There's quite a wide choice. In Castle Douglas you will get good value at **The Imperial Hotel**, tel 0556 2086/3009; **The Urr Valley Country House Hotel**, tel 0556 2188;

and **Douglas Arms Hotel**, tel 0556 2231. They are all cheap and serve reasonable food. In New Galloway, and also cheap, are: **Ken Bridge Hotel**, tel 06442 211, a Victorian coaching house on the river bank (and the main road), with free fishing; **Cross Keys Hotel**, tel 06442 494; **Kenmure Arms Hotel**, tel 06442 240; and **Leamington Hotel** in the High Street, tel 06442 327, which offers sporting packages.

Part VI

LOTHIAN: EXCLUDING EDINBURGH

Tantallon Castle

Arriving in Lothian from the Borders on a clear day, you come over the Lammermuirs, Moorfoots or Pentlands and see the whole region laid out below you: an expanse of farmland punctuated with rust-red roofs and massive carbuncles of volcanic rock, with the glinting firth beyond and the blue hills of Fife on the horizon. Your eye is drawn towards Edinburgh, dark and dense in the distance, dominated by Castle Rock and Authur's Seat. There are 70-odd miles of coastline: sheer rock cliffs, wide golden sands, dunes tufted with marram grass, quaint little fishing harbours. Rivers and streams tumble down from the hills and clatter across the plain to the sea, bringing beauty and irrigation to the fertile land and once providing power to the mills.

Lothian's roots go a long way down into pre-history. Stone Age Man left traces of hill forts. When the Romans arrived it was inhabited by the Votadini with Traprain Law as its capital, and it may have taken its name from their King Loth. After they had faded into obscurity, it formed the northern part of Bernicia, inhabited by Britons. Lothian men were always independent; they kept aloof from the rest of Scotland until 1018 when Malcolm II defeated the Angles and drew Bernicia into his kingdom.

When Queen Margaret persuaded her husband to move the court to Edinburgh in the middle of the 11th century, Lothian's history became integral with that of the capital. Invading armies swept through it in both directions. When the monarchy was strong, so was the surrounding land; when anarchy prevailed, it was within range of the capital that the powerful lords were most aggressive. Much of Mary's brief reign was played out in

Lothian in the middle of the 16th century, and Bonnie Prince Charlie's even briefer appearance dazzled the citizens of Lothian for six weeks when his army camped out at Duddingston near Edinburgh. When Scotland finally took on the mantle of peace, houses no longer needed to be fortresses. The cultural renaissance that erupted in Edinburgh, in the wake of the suppression of the Highlands, spread outwards in ripples of fine architecture and collections of art. Great mansions were built on vast estates, close to the capital, often financed by fortunes made from coal.

Coal mining is Lothian's oldest industry, pioneered 800 years ago by medieval monks, whose primitive, shallow workings were the forerunners of today's deep mines. Coal was used to boil sea-water to make salt, essential as a preservative before the days of refrigeration, and provided fuel for castle and cottage as well as for industry. Whole families toiled in the pits, and miners were bought and sold with their mines, like slaves. Only one open cast mine is left now where once there were hundreds, but some of the closures have been cleverly exploited to create interesting colliery museums such as the Lady Victoria, at Newtongrange.

With some of the most fertile land in Britain, agriculture plays an important part in the economy. In the mid-18th century, landowners started to 'enclose' the land, turning the small uneconomic 'run rig' fields of the peasants into the larger fields used today. Farm steadings were built and whole new villages, such as at Tyninghame, were created to house the displaced peasants who became farm labourers. Some worked in textile mills built along the rivers, or went down the mines. Today, barley is the most important crop, used for malting and for feeding stock. Market gardening and potato- and vegetable-growing are lucrative, with the markets of the ever-hungry capital on the doorstep. On the less fertile hill pastures to the south, cattle are bred and sold to the farms on the plain to be fattened for market. Only sheep can be grazed on the higher moors, often being moved down for the winter.

Tourism is also important to Lothian's economy, and petro-chemical related industry abounds around the oil terminal at Grangemouth.

Although Lothian has Edinburgh for its centre, it is by no means just the city's dormitory. Out in the surrounding countryside there are dozens of exciting places to discover and explore.

SPORT

On the whole, sport in Lothian can be divided into walking and riding, preferably in the hills; playing golf, mainly on the plain, and swimming and boating in the sea.

Golf is Lothian's main sport with internationally renowned Muirfield at Gullane as well as a large number of other good courses to choose from. **Water sports**, including sailing, windsurfing, water-skiing, sub-aqua diving, and swimming, are all available round the coast. In spite of the good record of sunshine, wet suits are strongly advised. Although not on a par with the Borders, there is plenty of good **fishing** to be had on lochs, reservoirs and rivers and in the sea: permits are available locally for fly and bait fishing and it isn't expensive. **Skiing** is possible all the year round on the dry-ski runs at Hillend in the Pentlands. There are **riding and pony trekking** centres to suit all standards of rider, throughout the region. **Walks** in the hills and in the hidden corners, where narrow lanes twist through remote, pretty villages, can be an endless delight.

TOURIST INFORMATION
The region is divided into sections: East Lothian, Mid Lothian and West Lothian. The following Tourist Information Centres open all the year.

East Lothian Tourist Board, Quality Street, North Berwick, tel 0620 2197.
Town House, Dunbar, tel 0368 63353.
Granada A1 Service Area, Oldcraighall, Musselburgh, tel 031 653 6172.
Mid Lothian Tourist Bureau, 7 Station Road, Roslin EH25 9PF, tel 031 440 2210 extn 220.
West Lothian: Forth Valley Tourist Board, Burgh Halls, The Cross, Linlithgow EH49 7AH, tel 0506 844600.
There are local centres, usually open from Easter to the end of September, at Dalkeith Library, tel 031 663 2083; at Musselburgh, Brunton Hall, tel 031 665 3711; and at A1 Pencraig, east Linton, tel 0620 860063.

The Coast East of Edinburgh: Barns Ness to Musselburgh

This stretch of coast is a paradise for naturalists, with nature reserves, wonderful sandy beaches, rugged rocks and a wealth of birds. The seaside towns are like English resorts, with rows of villas staring out to sea, genteel and trim, now and then blind with salt-spray.

Barns Ness

You must make a small detour off the A1, about three miles east of Dunbar, to reach Barns Ness: the road runs straight out to the lighthouse on a rock promontory beyond a campsite. Here there is a wildlife preserve, a geology trail with an old lime kiln, and splendid bracing bathing from clean white sands.

Dunbar

Dunbar was an important fishing port 300 years ago, giving jobs to 20,000 workers. The harbour is quiet now, though it still has a small fishing fleet. Smuggling once flourished: in 1765, 8000 lbs of contraband tobacco passed through the port. Today it is a rapidly developing holiday resort with a record of the lowest rainfall and highest sunshine in Scotland. Edward I defeated the Scots here in 1295 and his son Edward II escaped from the harbour by sea, 19 years later, after his defeat at Bannockburn. In 1650, Cromwell fought and defeated the supporters of Charles II in Dunbar, killing 3000 and taking 10,000 prisoners. (What can he have done with them?)

The town sprawls round a wide High Street, squared off at the north end by **Lauderdale House**, built by Robert Adam and once used as a barracks. The 17th-century steepled **Town House**, in the middle of the High Street, is the oldest civic building in constant use in Scotland.

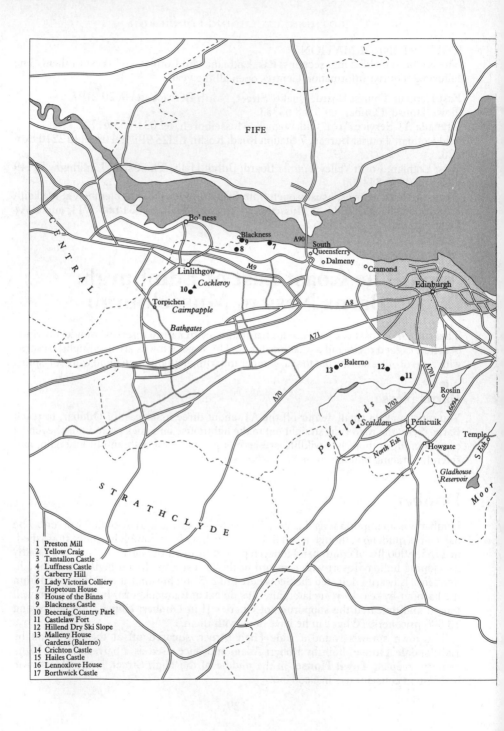

FIFE

CENTRAL

Bo' ness
Blackness
9
8 7
A90
South
Queensferry
Dalmeny
Cramond

Linlithgow
M9
Cockleroy
10
Torpichen
Cairnpapple
Bathgates

Edinburgh

A8

A71

Balerno
13 12
11
A701
Roslin
A70
Pentlands
A702
Scaldlaw
Penicuik
Temple
North Esk
Howgate
S Esk
Gladhouse
Reservoir
Moor

S T R A T H C L Y D E

1 Preston Mill
2 Yellow Craig
3 Tantallon Castle
4 Luffness Castle
5 Carberry Hill
6 Lady Victoria Colliery
7 Hopetoun House
8 House of the Binns
9 Blackness Castle
10 Beecraig Country Park
11 Castlelaw Fort
12 Hillend Dry Ski Slope
13 Malleny House
   Gardens (Balerno)
14 Crichton Castle
15 Hailes Castle
16 Lennoxlove House
17 Borthwick Castle

LOTHIAN

0 ___ 5 kms
0 ___ 5 miles

N

Fidra Island
Bass Rock
North Berwick
2
Dirleton
A198
3
Gullane
Whitekirk
Aberlady Bay
4
Aberlady
Gosford Sands
Athelstaneford
East Linton
1
A1
Dunbar
Barns Ness
Seton Sands
Cockenzie
Seton
Longniddry
15
Traprain Law
Stenton
Prestonpans
Haddington
Musselburgh
16
Tyne
Garvald
Oldhamstocks
5
Dalkeith
Gifford
6
A68
Lammermuirs
14
Whiteadder
A7
17
foots
BORDERS
Lauder

Dunbar Castle

The best view of the castle is from the edge of Lauderdale House barrack square. From here you can look down on it and read the detailed description of its history which is displayed on a board. Only one jagged, fang-like tower and a few scattered stones remain of what was once an extensive fortress guarding the gateway to the eastern plain, sprawled across menacing sea-lashed rocks, overhanging the narrow entrance to the harbour. The original castle was built in the 11th century for Cospatrick, Earl of Northumbria, deposed by William the Conqueror and made Earl of Dunbar by his cousin Malcolm Canmore. The focus of many battles, its most stirring claim on the imagination was a siege in 1339, when Black Agnes, Countess of Dunbar, and her ladies held it for six weeks against the English. This brave woman mocked the great siege engine, called a 'sow', which was used against the castle. She and her ladies leant over the battlements and wiped the walls with their dainty handkerchiefs where the sow's missiles had hit. When Bothwell abducted Mary, Queen of Scots, in 1567, he brought her to Dunbar Castle and it was here that he raped her, though many believe it was not rape. It was to Dunbar that they fled, less than six weeks later, playing out the final act in Mary's tragedy. The castle was demolished by her half-brother, Regent Moray, after her final defeat, and later, Cromwell used its stones to improve the harbour.

Picturesque **Dunbar Harbour** has cobbled quays round an outer and inner basin, restored warehouses, a coast-guard station, working fishing boats, piles of netting and lobster creels, pleasure craft and the ever-vigilant lifeboat. Kittiwakes throng the rocks, their cries echoing eerily above the ruined castle. In northerly and easterly gales, waves pour over the harbour walls. Picture it in the old days, the boats packed tight in the basins, men busy on deck, sorting and landing the catches, the quays alive with the chatter of the women, gutting great heaps of slithering silver herring.

The **John Muir Country Park**, on the western outskirts of the town, is called after a 19th-century conservationist, born in Dunbar, who founded America's national parks. Many acres of wild and beautiful coastland surround the mouth of the Tyne, where you can walk along the cliffs, go fishing, sailing, surf-riding or swimming, play golf, or just enjoy the abundant wildlife.

Whitekirk

Following the coast you take the A198, four miles west of Dunbar, and Whitekirk is a couple of miles further on. This was once the site of a holy well, now lost in the field opposite the church. Among the many pilgrims who visited it in the 15th century was a papal delegate, Enia Silvo de Piccolomini, who later became Pope Pius II. He walked there from Dunbar, barefooted in the snow, to give thanks for rescue from a shipwreck. This pilgrimage earned him rheumatism in his feet for the rest of his life. It is said that he found the Scottish lassies 'forthcoming and eager to kiss everyone in sight'. (An amusing epilogue to this story can be seen in Siena Cathedral: a picture in the chapel on the right, painted in memory of Piccolomini's travels, shows a wonderfully romantic, Italian idea of Scotland, full of fanciful flowers and fairyland scenery.)

The imposing red sandstone church dates from the 12th century, well restored after it was burnt by zealous suffragettes in 1914. The name Whitekirk for such a dominantly red building is explained by the use, in earlier times, of whitewash or harling to cover the sandstone.

Tantallon Castle

Tantallon (open daily, except closed Wed and Thurs, Oct–March: adm) is a mile or so beyond Whitekirk and however limited your time is in Lothian, try to visit it. Dramatic and sinister, this impressive ruin stands on the edge of a sheer cliff overhanging the booming sea, between two bays. Dating from the 14th century, it was a stronghold of the powerful Douglas family who leased it (when it was a much smaller fortalice in the 14th century) from the Earls of Fife—an unusual practice in those days. These were the Red Douglases, Earls of Angus, who 'rose upon the ruins of the Black' Douglases when they were finally subdued by James II. These Red Douglases became a menace to the crown, ruling their domains with a total disregard for authority. They flaunted their personal armies and lived just as they pleased, especially when Margaret Tudor, the devious widow of James IV, married their leader, the Earl of Angus in 1514, and they became arch manipulators in the power struggle over the boy king James V. They built on to, and strengthened, Tantallon and it provided a perfect stronghold for this arrogantly audacious, power-loving family.

The castle's massive curtain walls cut it off on its headland making it impregnable against the impotent battering of frustrated rivals, while supplies came in regularly by sea. It took Cromwell's artillery twelve days of devastating bombardment before Tantallon was eventually 'dinged doun'. The three ditches that you can see to landward were to repel siege engines and potential invaders. The walls are 14 ft thick and the well 100 ft deep, bored through the rock. Seen silhouetted against the sea, especially as the sun comes up out of the east, Tantallon is one of the most heart-stopping ruins in Scotland.

The Bass Rock

The Bass Rock, one of Lothian's volcanic plugs, is an island one and a half miles off-shore from Tantallon. Standing 350 ft high, a mile in circumference, its familiar, sheer-walled wedge shape, looming out of a mist, is a welcome landmark for sailors. You can take boat trips from North Berwick to cruise round it but special permission is needed to land, a feat not always possible in rough weather.

St Baldred, the hermit, died on the rock in the 7th or 8th century and you can just make out where his cell was, half-way up, on a terrace on the south side. Near the lighthouse you can also see the ruins of a castle owned by the Lauder family. In 1406, James I, the 12-year-old heir to the throne, sheltered on the Bass on his way to sanctuary in France. (His subsequent capture at sea and detention in London for 18 years proved to be greatly to Scotland's advantage, for he returned well educated and able to cope with the anarchy that was strangling his country.) Many Covenanters, a number of whom subsequently died, were imprisoned on the rock during the Killing Times in the 17th century. Later, four Jacobites held out against all attempts to capture them, provisioned by the French for four years.

The Bass Rock is now a famous gannetry as well as a haven for gulls, kittiwakes, puffins, fulmars and guillemots. You may even see seals. If you are sailing near its guano-whitened cliffs on a hot day you won't miss it!

133

SCOTLAND

North Berwick

North Berwick is about 10 miles northwest along the coast from Dunbar and was created a royal burgh by Robert III around the end of the 14th century. The town developed into a seaside holiday and golfing resort during the 19th century. It has lots of sunshine thus making it still popular today. A compact town flanked by two bays with a rocky headland between them, it is the main shopping centre for the area. Narrow, one-way streets, teeming with bustling holiday crowds in summer, lead down to the tiny, sheltered harbour, full of boats, surrounded by warehouses converted into flats. Lobster creels, nets and fish-boxes mingle on the quay with the spars of pleasure boats and hulls of sail-boards and, just beyond, an open-air swimming pool has been built into the rock, high above the sea.

North Berwick Museum (open daily, June–Sept and Fri–Mon Easter–end of May: free) is in School Road. It is a cosy little museum on the upper floor of the old school, where you can pick up a good idea of the local social history, archaeology, and wild life, with special exhibitions.

The Auld Kirk stands on a rocky spit near the harbour. All you can see of this notorious 12th-century ruin today is the whitewashed nave, south aisle and foundations. When James VI/I was nearly drowned in a freak storm off the Bass Rock, he blamed a well-established coven of witches in North Berwick, alleging that some of them had had the temerity to row round his foundering ship in a sieve! The witches were arrested one dark night as they performed some rather nasty rituals in and around the Auld Kirk, presided over by their 'Devil', Francis, Earl of Bothwell, nephew of Mary's Bothwell, who lived at Hailes Castle nearby. The subsequent trial of 94 witches and 6 wizards was based on confessions extracted by gruesome torture and attended by the king who was inspired to write a book on the subject.

North Berwick Law is the volcanic rock that towers 613 ft (184 m) above the town. If you have the energy you should climb the path up its steep flank for a wonderful view out to sea, over to the hills of Fife and across the Lothian plain to the Lammermuirs, Moorfoots and Pentlands, with a view indicator to help you get your bearings. This was once one of a chain of warning beacons, and in the Dark Ages it was crowned by a fort. Now it is occupied by a watchtower that was used to look for invaders during the Napoleonic Wars, and some other, more modern, buildings used in the First World War. There is also an arch made from the jawbone of a whale, a relic from the days of whale fishing in the North Sea.

Dirleton

Three miles west of North Berwick, Dirleton is one of the prettiest villages in the area. In medieval design, the pantiled cottages, 17th-century church, session house, old school and inns are grouped round two wide, tree-lined greens in this peaceful backwater.

Dirleton Castle (open daily: adm) is an impressive 13th-century ruin overlooking the upper green from a rocky mound right in the middle of the village. It was the last castle in the south of Scotland to resist Edward I and was finally demolished by General Monk, for Cromwell, in 1650. Surrounded by lawns, a garden and a 17th-century bowling green, it has a 17th-century dovecote containing 1100 empty nests. This is a relic from the days when pigeon meat was a valuable supplement to the diet in the lean winter months. As you wander among the mellow stones of this castle it is eerie to think of a coven of witches, possibly those of North Berwick, who were imprisoned here before being half strangled and publicly burnt at the stake on Dirleton Green.

Yellow Craig

Yellow Craig, a sandy beach studded with dunes and backed by woodland, is reached by a lane leading a mile seawards from the eastern edge of Dirleton. It has a caravan park, picnic sites and a nature trail and is a favourite haunt of dog-owners. If you climb the small hillock that rises from the trees you are ascending into fiction; this was the model for Spyglass Hill in Robert Louis Stevenson's *Treasure Island*. The sandy bay, fringed with buckthorn and marram grass, overlooks Fidra Island, a menacing lump of black basalt rock, eroded by wind and sea. There was a Celtic monastery on Fidra. Romanized in 1165, it was a popular place for pilgrimages and its ruins can still be seen. (Boat trips are available from North Berwick.)

Gullane

Gullane is a seaside golfing mecca about a mile west of Dirleton. Pronunciations vary, from Gillan and Gullan, to Goolan: Gillan was once considered 'posh' but Gullan and Goolan date from further back. It is an overgrown village with numerous hotels, guest houses and holiday flats, centering around attractive Goose Green. Church land until the Reformation, it developed more recently into a holiday centre for the wealthy-genteel, with Muirfield among its golf courses and a sandy beach to occupy the non-golfing members of the family. The Open Golf Championship is a great event at Muirfield every summer.

St Andrew's Collegiate Church is said to have fallen into ruin in the 16th century when James VI/I objected to the minister smoking tobacco, and transferred the parish two miles east to Dirleton.

Gullane Hill, on the west flank of the village, was formed by wind-blown sand, a process that still continues. Sand has silted up Aberlady Bay on the west side of the hill and created a well-known bird sanctuary and nature reserve, with over 200 recorded species of birds, including all five members of the tern family. A wooden footbridge leads from the roadside car park into the reserve. Many years ago, great sailing ships would have lain at anchor right up to the mouth of the river.

Luffness Castle (open to the public by appointment only: tel 08757 218, free) overlooks Aberlady Bay. It dates from the 16th century, with a 13th-century keep built on the site of a Norse camp. You can still see the moat, curtain walls and towers. The castle was built by the Scottish-Norman family, de Lindsay, one of whom was Regent of Scotland when Alexander III was a boy. He died on a Crusade, bequeathing land to the monk who carried his embalmed body home. The ruins of the monastery that was built on the promised gift of land are near the castle, with the tomb and effigy of the crusading Laird.

135

Aberlady

Aberlady is now no more than a straggling village on the southwest shore of the bay. It was once a thriving trading port, until the Peffer Burn silted up. Attractive pantiled cottages border the main street, with the Quill Gallery, pretty inns and a mercat cross that lost its top during the Reformation. In the church, with its 15th-century tower and vaulted stone basement, you can see part of an 8th-century Celtic cross with interwoven bird carvings. The original 'louping-on stane' at the gate was the mounting block.

Myreton Motor Museum (open daily: adm) is signposted, a mile to the east. Here, surrounded by farmland, is a varied collection of vintage cars, old road signs, advertisements, petrol-pumps, cycles, motor-cycles, military vehicles and memorabilia from early motoring days: fun for younger members of the family.

Gosford Sands are less than a mile beyond Aberlady to the southwest. Overlooking the Firth of Forth, they are cut by a network of tracks and picnic sites, backed by quaintly wind-sculpted trees behind the wall of Gosford Estate. This long, rock-strewn beach can be a bit scruffy but is ideal if you want to stretch your legs, exercise the dog or enjoy a good blow before reaching the suburbs of Edinburgh.

Seton

Seton Collegiate Church (open daily except closed Tues afternoons and Wed: adm) is just beyond Gosford Bay on the coast road. Built on the site of an earlier church, it was established as collegiate in 1492 and you can still see the ruins of the domestic buildings. Among the many ancient and interesting things in the church are effigies of the fifth Lord Seton and his wife: he was killed at Flodden in 1513; she built the transept and spire.

Seton Castle (private), an 18th-century building adjacent to the church, stands on the site of Seton Palace. This was frequently visited by Mary, Queen of Scots, the Setons having been loyal supporters of her cause. She came here with Darnley after Rizzio's murder and also the next year, with Bothwell, after Darnley's murder, when she took part in an archery contest, adding another nail to the coffin that was being built for her by her critics. The daughter of the house, Mary Seton, was one of the queen's Four Marys.

Seton Sands, nearby, is an extensive holiday park with permanent caravans and all possible facilities for those who prefer a holiday crammed with entertainment and bustle, rather than one designed to 'get-away-from-it-all'.

Prestonpans

Prestonpans straggles along the coast a couple of miles to the east, forming an almost continuous waterside township with Port Seton, Cockenzie and Longniddry. It took its name from the open-air salt pans in which 12th-century monks from Newbattle Abbey boiled sea-water from the Firth, fuelled by local coal, to make salt. It would be easy to drive through this apparently uninspiring sprawl without pausing to dive up the hill and discover its treasures, but the very name Prestonpans will draw keen Jacobites like a magnet.

Go first to Meadowmill, between Prestonpans and Tranent. Looking out from the viewpoint across grassland that now covers old colliery workings, it is hard to believe that you are on the front line of the Battle of Prestonpans, when Bonnie Prince Charlie defeated General Johnnie Cope in a fifteen-minute dawn battle in September 1745. Cope established his army with Preston, Cockenzie and Port Seton behind them, a deep ditch and a boggy marsh in front and the ten-foot wall of Preston House protecting their western flank. With local knowledge, and in spite of considerable disagreement among his staff officers, the Prince's army slipped in from the east as the sun rose, three men at a time down a narrow track, and overwhelmed the enemy by the sheer ferocity and speed of their surprise attack, hacking their way through the Hanoverian lines with broadsword and dirk. The Hanoverians fled 'eskaped like rabets,' as the Prince later reported to his father. The outcome so boosted the Prince's morale that he believed they were invincible. There is a cairn in a field beside the A1 commemorating the battle.

If you turn off the coastal road in Prestonpans and drive up into the heart of the village you will find relics of the prosperity of the former lairds who made their fortunes from coal. There is a ruined 15th-century tower with an attached lectern dovecote; 16th-century **Northfield** (a private house) with elegant corner turrets, and 17th-century **Hamilton House**, National Trust for Scotland (open by appointment only).

The 17th-century **Mercat Cross** is the most charming member of this group. It is the only complete and unaltered cross of its kind in Scotland. It has a unicorn-crowned shaft rising from a circular base with pilasters and niches, and a turnpike stair to a platform from which public proclamations were read. It is nice to think that perhaps the town crier in 1745 hurried to this platform to inform the townspeople of the victory of the Stuart prince just down the road.

Monks mined coal here as far back as the 12th century and established great open-air pans, heated by coal, for the evaporation of sea-water from the Firth, to extract valuable salt. **Prestongrange Mining Museum** (open Easter–Sept: free) is on the western outskirts of Prestonpans. Developed on a former colliery site, the museum covers 800 years of mining history. Outside, you can see an 1874 Cornish Beam Pumping Engine with its five-storey engine house. The former power house is an exhibition hall full of mining artefacts and documents. There are steam locomotives and various vintage exhibits. Special 'steam days' are held on the first Sunday of each month from April to September.

Musselburgh

Musselburgh, nine miles beyond Aberlady, is the next sizeable town southwest along the coast. It lies at the mouth of the River Esk whose tidal flats were once carpeted with mussel beds. A stream of A1 traffic pounds through the heart of the town, robbing it of its peace but not its history. The Romans had a fort here, to supply their camp at Inveresk, and 5000-year-old Bronze Age relics have been excavated locally.

Being on the direct route to Edinburgh, Musselburgh was often sacked by invading English armies. In 1332, Robert Bruce's nephew, Thomas Randolph, Earl of Moray and Regent of Scotland, fell ill and was given sanctuary from the English by the citizens of Musselburgh, until he died. The town was called The Honest Toun thereafter and Honesty remains its motto. **Honest Toun** celebrations are held every summer: a festival with plenty of pageantry and entertainment, both inside and out.

From its earliest beginnings, golf was played on **Musselburgh Links**, now more familiar as a race course, the Royal Musselburgh Golf Club having moved along the river to Prestongrange. James VI/I was an enthusiastic player and James IV is believed to have played here also. Cromwell stationed his troops on the Links in 1650 after his victory at Dunbar while he 'sorted out' the district. Now they are also the site for an annual shooting contest by the Queen's Bodyguard for Scotland, the Royal Company of Archers.

Fisherrow is Musselburgh's old harbour with terraces of fisher cottages round the harbour-basin on the waterfront. On the quay there is a wooden cabin, painted bright red. Inside it Mr Clark sells smoked salmon, done by him in a little cupboard just inside the door; it is the most succulent in Scotland and among the cheapest.

The Tolbooth, recently restored, and at the east end of Musselburgh High Street near the mercat cross, was once the town prison. Its unusual 16th-century spire was built from material taken from the chapel of Our Lady of Loretto, nearby, when the Reformation decreed its demolition. The chapel, founded by a hermit, Thomas Douchtie, in 1533, became a great healing centre for the sick, much as Lourdes is today. When its stones were recycled for secular use the pope was so outraged that he excommunicated the Honest Toun for 200 years! Today a boys' public school stands on the lands of Loretto.

The Battle of Pinkie was fought just southeast of the town in 1547, one of Henry VIII's victories during his 'Rough Wooing'.

Pinkie House (open to the public Tues afternoons during the summer and Christmas terms: free) is opposite Loretto and now part of the school. It is an early 17th-century building with later additions and it is well worth a visit. Go and see the magnificent painted gallery on the first floor. It is long and wide, its arched timber ceiling painted in tempera by Italian artists.

Inveresk Lodge Gardens (open all year except Sat: adm) are a mile south of Musselburgh in the attractive village of Inveresk. This garden of a 17th-century house (which is not open to the public) is run by the National Trust for Scotland and specializes in plants that are suitable for small gardens. It offers masses of tempting ideas for those of us who don't live in stately homes.

Just south of Inveresk is **Carberry Hill**, scene of the so-called battle that resulted in Mary, Queen of Scots' surrender and capture. Picture Mary, aged only 25, proud to the last, preparing to watch the series of chivalric encounters that were to decide the issue. No one of suitable rank among the rebel nobles stepped forward to take up Bothwell's challenge. There was no fight and Mary decided that her surrender and the promise of a safe conduct for Bothwell were the best solution. There, at Queen's Mount, on Carberry Hill, watched by those of her army who had not melted away, she embraced her new husband whose child she was carrying, and watched him ride off. She never saw him again. What can have been in her heart?

WHERE TO STAY AND EAT
Every other house along this popular holiday coast seems to be a hotel or guest house and the range is enormous. In Dunbar,**The Craigengelt Hotel**, Marine Road, tel 0368 62287, overlooking the harbour and ruins of Dunbar Castle, is moderately priced and offers golf packages. North Berwick is crammed with choice: From small, cheap, homely

guest houses like **Craigview**, tel 0620 2257, overlooking the sea, to comfortable, family-run hotels like **Point Garry Hotel**, West Bay Road, tel 0620 2380, moderately priced with good golf packages. **The Open Arms Hotel**, in Dirleton, tel 062 085 241, is an unexpected treasure in a smallish village, family-run for the last 40 years. Dating from 1685, it is on the edge of the green overlooking the castle. Moderately priced, comfortable and peaceful, with open log fires, it has long been acclaimed for its food. People drive out from Edinburgh to eat here.

For expensive luxury, try **Greywalls**, a Lutyens-designed country house in an attractive garden overlooking Muirfield at Gullane, tel 0620 842144. Only open from mid-April to the end of October, Greywalls is one of the best hotels in Scotland and it would be criminal to stay and not eat dinner here too. A couple of years ago, King Hussein and Queen Noor of Jordan were eating at Greywalls and were so impressed by the food that they pinched the chef: the replacement is just as good. Alternatively, stay somewhere cheaper and dine here.

La Potinière is at Gullane, tel 0620 843214. In what looks like a restored bus shelter on the main road, proprietors David and Hilary Brown serve lunch on Sunday, Monday, Tuesday and Thursday, and dinner on Friday and Saturday—six meals a week and you must book, though it is worth trying for a last-minute cancellation. There is no choice: Hilary cooks a set French country-style meal each day of a quality that is outstanding as well as being remarkably cheap. The wine list was runner-up in the 'Best in Britain' awards, and is not expensive.

The Coast West of Edinburgh: Cramond to Bo'ness

This stretch of coast is rich in stately homes linked by attractive walks along the shore and giving way to the industrial sprawl around Grangemouth to the west.

Cramond

Cramond, on the western fringe of Edinburgh, is a pretty 18th-century village at the mouth of the River Almond as it flows into the Firth of Forth. Cramond means literally fort-on-the-river. The fort was Roman, built in about AD 142 to guard the harbour. If you look by the church you can still see its foundations, with an excellent illustrated plan of how it was. (In the summer, free conducted walks round the village start from the Kirk at 3 pm every Sunday.) To the south, beside an older Cramond Brig than the present 17th-century bridge, James V was violently attacked. The king was given to wandering about the country dressed as a humble farmer, calling himself the Goodman of Ballengeich. He was thus disguised when he was attacked by robbers, or, some say, by the family of a peasant girl to whom he was making love. He was rescued by a local man called Howieson, who gave him water. The king rewarded him with a gift of land on condition that Howieson and his descendants should always have water ready whenever a monarch should pass. George IV, Queen Victoria, George V and the present Queen have all been offered water by Howieson's descendants.

Dalmeny

Dalmeny Village, about three miles west of Cramond, is a group of attractive cottages clustered round a green, tucked away below the A90 some distance from Dalmeny House. You won't regret making a detour to see the 12th-century **church** here, dedicated to St Cuthbert. Lovingly restored in this century, it must be one of the finest gems of Norman architecture in all Scotland. Its receding arches draw your eye magnetically towards a simple altar and east window. In the pulpit is a carved misericord, possibly unique, on which the weary preacher could surreptitiously perch his bottom between exhortations.

Dalmeny House is a good mile northeast of the village, on the Forth (open 1 May–29 Sept every afternoon except Fri and Sat: adm). This splendid example of Romantic-Gothic was built in 1815 for the Earl of Rosebery whose family has lived on the site for more than 300 years. Although it isn't old in terms of history, it is a splendid Baronial mansion with a Gothic hammerbeamed hall, vaulted corridors and classical main rooms. You can see the fabulous collection of 18th-century French furniture, tapestries and porcelain and there is a unique collection of Napoleonic memorabilia. Some of the paintings are very fine, especially the portraits. Queen Victoria stayed here with Prince Albert in 1842 and commented on the beauty of the setting—you can see why—and the 'excellent modern comforts' of the house, which might have had something to do with the plumbing. The grounds are lovely and you can walk along the shore to Cramond or South Queensferry.

South Queensferry

South Queensferry is nine miles west of Edinburgh, where the Firth of Forth narrows to little more than a mile. In the 11th century, Queen Margaret of Scotland established a free ferry here, to carry not only herself but also the many pilgrims she encouraged to visit the holy shrines at Dunfermline and St Andrews. She built two hospices for the weary pilgrims, one on each bank, and the ferry service continued (though latterly not free) until the opening of the road bridge in 1964, linking what became known as North Queensferry and South Queensferry.

You can often see naval ships as far up as the dockyard at Rosyth, and great oil tankers lying at anchor, waiting to take on oil from the man-made island just east of the rail bridge. This is the terminal of the pipeline from the North Sea oil fields. South Queensferry juts into the river between the feet of the two bridges, its main street no longer choked with traffic waiting to catch the ferry. Stretching away on either side are private estates with houses open to the public, farmland and woods with lovely views across the water to the hills of Fife.

The Burry Man Festival is the village's annual summer carnival, with plenty of parades and entertainment bringing colour and life to its picturesque streets.

The 16th-century **Hawes Inn** stands on the site of the southern hospice, facing the old ferry ramp. Its view out across the river is blinkered on either side by the two bridges—a very different aspect from the days of Walter Scott, who was often here and mentioned it in *The Antiquary*. In Robert Louis Stevenson's *Kidnapped*, young David Balfour first met Captain Hoseason at the Hawes Inn, in a bedroom 'heated like an oven by a great fire of coal', the captain having been 'carbonadoed in the tropic seas'!

LOTHIAN: EXCLUDING EDINBURGH

The Queensferry Museum (open Thurs and Fri afternoons, May–Sept) is in Burgh Chambers, and its exhibits give you a good idea of the local history including the problems of the building of the rail bridge.

Maid of the Forth sails from Hawes Pier to **Inchcolm Island** (see 'Fife', p. 289), throughout the summer; tel 031 331 1454.

At **Port Edgar**, west of the road bridge, a thriving yacht marina has been developed in the former naval station of *HMS Lochinvar*. Here, you can launch your own boat from the ramp, take part in races and regattas, water ski, or take lessons in sailing and wind-surfing.

Hopetoun House

Hopetoun House (open daily, 1 May–30 Sept: adm) is two miles west of Queensferry, a couple of miles along the shore if you have time to walk. Hopetoun is one of Scotland's most magnificent mansions, built for and still lived in by the Hope family. Originally completed between 1699 and 1704, by the architect Sir William Bruce (who rebuilt Holyrood), for the first Earl of Hopetoun, it was rebuilt and enlarged by William Adam and his sons Robert and John, between 1721 and 1754. There is a new exhibition on the building of Hopetoun, a tribute to the men who contributed to its creation. To get the best picture of its simple, classical beauty, you should go to the end of the avenue and look back at the house, a perfectly proportioned sweep of inspired architecture. Among its sumptuous furnishings and treasures are paintings by Van Dyck, Titian, Rubens, Rembrandt and Canaletto, some of which are hung on walls lined with silk and damask.

The gardens were modelled on those at Versailles and landscaped to give views across the Forth to the peaks of Ben Lomond. There is a deer park in the grounds, some rare St Kilda sheep and a nature trail, as well as walks along the river. In the stable block you can see an exhibition called 'Horse and Man in Lowland Scotland'. When you are exhausted with sightseeing, you can go to the licensed restaurant in the lovely tapestry room and indulge yourself with some smoked salmon, Aberdeen Angus beef, or the 'Hopetoun Delight' dessert; all is delicious home cooking. The Antique Dealers' Fair is held at Hopetoun in September, and is a marvellous chance for collectors to pick up a bargain.

Special arrangements for blind and disabled people with prior notice, tel 031 331 2451.

House of the Binns

The House of the Binns (open Easter and 1 May–30 Sept, daily except Fri, afternoons only: adm) is a couple of miles west along the river from Hopetoun and a very different sort of stately home. The curious name stems from *ben*, the Scottish word for 'hill'. The house, dating from 1630 with 19th-century Gothic embellishments stands above park-land with views across the Forth. The moulded ceilings are very fine, and the rooms are beautifully furnished.

But by far the most intriguing aspect of a visit to the Binns is the memorabilia of the notorious Tam Dalyell (pronounced Dee-el) who raised the Royal Scots Greys here in 1681 and whose father built the house. Stories about General Tam, whose mortal remains were popularly believed to have been removed from the family vault at Aber-corn, nearby, and carried to a far warmer resting place by the Devil himself, are as

141

spine-chilling as they are apocryphal. Known to his troops as the 'Bluidy Muscovite', he was alleged to hold flagellation parties, to munch wine glasses and to have conversations with the Devil—stories that were richly embroidered by his Covenanting enemies. In the house you will see a heavy carved table that was recovered from a muddy pond where it had lain for 200 years, having, it is said, been hurled there by the Devil, a bad loser in a game of cards with Tam. Among the relics of this legendary man are his sword and his Bible and the comb with which he groomed his beard, having sworn after the execution of Charles I never to cut a hair of his head until the restoration of the monarchy. His contemporary descendant, also Tam Dalyell, is a well-known Labour M.P.

Blackness Castle

Blackness Castle (open daily, but closed Mon afternoons and Tues, Oct–March: adm) is a mile or so north of the House of the Binns. The castle juts into the River Forth, its northern walls pointed like the prow of a massive battleship, lapped on three sides by the river. The original date of this grim fortress is unknown. The present tower was built in the 15th century when it was one of Scotland's most important fortresses. Besieged by Cromwell, it has in its time been a royal castle, a prison for Covenanters, a powder magazine and a youth hostel. When Scotland and England were joined by the Acts of Union in 1707, Blackness was one of the four fortresses to be maintained at full military strength. If you stand looking out across the water through the gun-slits in the sturdy curtain wall, you can almost hear the roar of cannon fire and smell the acrid tang of spent gunpowder.

The quiet riverside village of **Blackness**, just along from the castle, was a bustling medieval seaport, with wharves and warehouses and teeming with all the noise and smell and colour of a busy port which supplied the Royal Burgh of Linlithgow.

Bo'ness

Bo'ness or Borrowstownness, a couple of miles further west, is of historic rather than scenic interest. The **Antonine Wall** started a mile to the east, at Bridgeness. This wall was built by the Romans in AD 142 between the Forth and the Clyde in an abortive attempt to protect the south from the barbarians in the north (see 'History', pp. 49–50).

Bo'ness is also the home of the **Scottish Railway Preservation Society,** and steam enthusiasts can visit the Bo'ness and Kinneil Railway where they can take steam train rides at weekends and on certain weekdays in the summer.

Kinneil House

Kinneil House (open daily except closed on Tues afternoons and Fri Oct–March: adm) is a mile west of Bo'ness, up a steep zigzag drive above the Forth. It was built in the 16th and 17th centuries and saved from demolition in 1936 when workmen uncovered original wall paintings and decorated ceilings that are among the finest in Scotland. Next to the house is **Kinneil Museum** (open daily except Sun, May–Oct, Sat only

Nov–April: free). The 17th century stables have been converted and you can see Bo'ness pottery and cast-iron work, as well as an exhibition of the estate's history going back 2000 years. Among things to see is an excavated fortlet from the Antonine Wall. Don't miss the bothy (hut) at the back where James Watt built the first steam engine while trying to help solve the problem of flooding in a nearby mine in 1765.

WHERE TO STAY AND EAT
There's nowhere very special to stay along this stretch so if you are after top quality, go into Edinburgh. But there are plenty of adequate hotels and guest houses. For history and character, go to **Hawes Inn**, South Queensferry, tel 031 331 1990 (see pp. 140–1 above). A traditional inn, moderately priced, it serves pub food as well as haute cuisine and if you can get one of the few bedrooms, you lie awake listening to the hushed voices of Queen Margaret's pilgrims, and the tramp of sailors' feet. You may even catch an echo of David Balfour's voice yelling for his uncle Ebenezer from the rails of the brig *Covenant*, as it carries him off to sea. At Bo'ness, **Richmond Park Hotel**, also moderately priced, has good views over the firth to the Fife hills and is comfortable if somewhat lacking in character.

The Hinterland: Linlithgow to Haddington

You will find plenty to interest you, both historical and aesthetic, as you make your way back eastwards, skirting the southern outskirts of Edinburgh. Don't be put off by built-up areas, they often conceal gems just around the corner.

LINLITHGOW AND ENVIRONS

Linlithgow

Linlithgow, three miles south of Bo'ness, is not far inland. When you see it, in its oasis of rural tranquillity, surrounded by smoothly rounded hills and remote farming communities, you forget the ugly sprawl of industrial and mining development that lies just out of sight beyond the horizon.

There was a Pictish settlement here before the Romans came and the first royal palace was recorded in the 12th century. Edward I had his headquarters in the town in 1301 and David II built a royal manor which was destroyed by fire, along with all the town, in 1424. The following year work began on the present palace. Since then this thriving, compact little town has watched over much of Scotland's history.

In June, the town celebrates the Riding of the Marches, in memory of the days when the men had to check the boundaries against cattle reivers. The celebration consists of a parade, with bands, decorated floats, flutes and drums, and plenty of fun.

Linlithgow Palace

The Palace (open daily: adm) must be one of the country's most poignant ruins. Only pigeons now inhabit the empty shell that stands on a gentle slope of grass overlooking its own loch. Mellow pinkish-ochre walls rise to five storeys, supported on the lower edge by flying buttresses: a roofless square with many of its rooms so well preserved that only a little imagination is needed to see how they must have been. Through its gateway in 1513, James IV rode out, against the advice of his lords, to lead his gallant army to tragic defeat at Flodden. His widow, Margaret Tudor, peered in vain from one of the turret window slits. The elaborate fountain in the quadrangle is said to have run with wine when James V gave it to Mary of Guise as a wedding present in 1538 and it was not many years afterwards, in 1542, that their daughter was born in one of the upper chambers. She was the ill-fated Mary who was proclaimed Queen of Scots within a week of her birth. Over-enthusiastic fuelling of domestic fires, possibly with bedding straw, by Cumberland's troops who were garrisoned there on the night of 31 January 1746, reduced the palace to a smouldering shell. The swans on the loch add a royal touch: it is said that they flew away when the Roundheads arrived and returned the day Charles II was crowned at Scone in 1649. Perhaps the best view you can get of the palace is at night, as you drive past on the M9, from where it looks almost ethereal, floodlit against the dark sky.

St Michael's Church is so close to the palace that from a distance it seems to be part of it. As well as providing a place of worship for many of Scotland's monarchs, this large pre-Reformation church has had to endure much harsh treatment since its consecration in 1242. It was rebuilt after the fire of 1424; John Knox's followers despoiled it; Cromwell's soldiers stabled their horses in the aisle and left shot-holes in the walls. While praying for guidance and victory before Flodden, James IV saw a ghost which stood by the altar and warned him of his coming defeat. An open stone crown on the tower was replaced, after the Second World War, by the present astonishing laminated wood-and-aluminium 'crown of thorns', an unfortunate flight of fancy that gives a somewhat stage-set appearance.

Cockleroy Hill

Cockleroy Hill is on your right, along a little country lane due south of Linlithgow, which is signposted to Preston. It is not a great feat of mountaineering to climb—a pleasant 15-minute stroll through dense pines and up a gentle slope of turf and vivid green moss. Some say the name is derived from 'cuckold le roi', and hint at an indiscretion by Mary of Guise, getting her own back for the philanderings of her husband James V. Others, more prosaic, will tell you that the name stems from the Gaelic *cochull ruadh*, meaning red-capped hill. The keenness of your eyes is the only limit to the horizon from here. A view indicator points out 36 landmarks including Goat Fell, 66 miles away on Arran. You can see the ramparts of a Pictish hill fort beyond the indicator: their look-outs would have been able to give plenty of warning of attack.

Torphichen Preceptory

Torphichen Preceptory (open daily in summer, closed in winter: free) lies two miles further south. It was founded as the community of the Scottish Order of the Knights of St John of Jerusalem, in 1153. The 15th-century tower and vaulted transepts are all that remain, together with the nave which was rebuilt in the 17th century, and it is now the parish kirk. It stands on the outskirts of the pretty little village, among lawns backed by bracken-covered hills and is a good example of fortified church architecture. There is a folding green-baize table in one of the box pews in the Kirk, hinting at a less than spiritual attitude among past parishioners. One of the tombstones in the rather spooky churchyard is thought to be pre-Christian, and there are several with ancient primitive carvings.

Cairnpapple

Cairnpapple is less than a mile south again, in the Bathgate Hills. It is a bleak summit aptly known as 'windy ways', with a wonderful panoramic view, coast to coast, from the Bass Rock to Goat Fell. Follow the Historic Scotland signs which will point you to a parking bay and a short, easy climb over turf to a lofty site that was used for ritual and burial from possibly 2500 BC, until the first century. An underground **cist**, or tomb (open daily, except closed Mon mornings and Fri, Oct–March: adm), has been cleverly reconstructed so that you can go down into it and see exactly how it was. A taped commentary is available to explain it all. It is an eerie feeling, standing on that windswept plateau, trying to picture those ancient ceremonies and those 4500-year-old tragedies and tears. (When the cist is shut you can get the key from the curator of the preceptory in Torphichen.)

Beecraigs Country Park

Beecraigs Country Park (open all year: free) is also in the Bathgate Hills, between Linlithgow and Bathgate. The park covers 657 acres of lovely grounds, where you can indulge in pretty well every sort of outdoor activity as well as look at exhibitions in the Park Centre. There are woodland walks, a deer farm, a trout farm, water sports on the lake, fly fishing, archery, a keep-trim course, orienteering and even rock climbing. For further information, tel 0506 844516.

WHERE TO STAY AND EAT

Houston House at Uphall just off the A89, tel 0506 853831, is a 16th-century fortified tower where Mary, Queen of Scots' advocate once lived. It has a pleasant garden and excellent food in a panelled dining room—they cure their own salmon, and the venison with orange and brandy sauce is mouthwatering—and a good wine list. Expensive but worth it.

If that seems rather over the top, try **Belsyde Farm**, Linlithgow, tel 0506 842098, a late 18th-century house on a sheep and cattle farm beside the Union Canal with views over the Forth to the Ochils. It's cheap and you'll find the Duke of Hamilton's crest on one of the walls to give grandeur (he didn't live here, just owned it). For a family, you could do a lot worse than one of the **Craigs Holiday Lodges** at Williamcraigs,

Linlithgow, tel 0506 84 5025. These are fully equipped A-frame chalets, on a wooded hillside with panoramic views over the Forth Valley. They are cheap and you even get linen and a colour telly.

Champany Inn, Champany Corner, tel 050683 4532, is just off the M9, and surely the best steak house in Britain. Don't expect instant microwave service here: lobsters glare out from a bubbling tank; cuts of raw meat, hung to full maturity, are laid out for inspection; whole salmon, fresh from the river, gleam on a slab; mouthwatering vegetables tempt from a huge wicker basket. The steaks make anything in America seem bland and flaccid. Passed through a house marinade, they are seared on charcoal: the combination of method, marinade and perfect maturity make them food fit for the gods. Expensive, and no one could grudge a penny of it.

PENTLANDS, MOORFOOTS AND ESK VALLEY

The Pentland Hills run southwest from Edinburgh, sprawling across a width of four to five miles; high, wild moorland carpeted with heather, bracken and deer-hair grass and laced with reservoirs and tumbling streams. There are dozens of lovely walks, some taking you along the old cattle-drove routes south. The highest peak is Scaldlaw, 1898 ft (569 m). The Moorfoots run more or less parallel to the east, equally lovely with attractive little villages nestling at their feet. The River North Esk starts in the Pentlands, the River South Esk in the Moorfoots: they tumble out of their separate hills and rush into a turbulent marriage beyond Dalkeith and enter the sea as one.

Malleny House Gardens

The Malleny House Gardens (open daily: adm) are in Balerno, about seven miles southwest of Edinburgh off the A70, lapped by the Water of Leith. Although the 17th-century house is not open to the public, it is a perfect focal point for the formal gardens, where you can see rare shrub roses and clipped yews, rhododendrons and a variety of other shrubs and plants. The saddle-backed dovecote behind the house has not been inhabited since 1961 when its residents perished from a surfeit of treated grain.

Hillend Dry Ski Slope

Hillend Dry Ski Slope (open all the year) on the northern slope of the Pentlands is the largest of its kind in Europe. If you are keen on skiing, whatever the season, it has a beginners' slope as well as the main run, and you can hire equipment and instruction.

Castlelaw

Castlelaw Iron Age Fort (open at all times) is clearly signposted off the west side of the A702, and is easily reached by a short climb through gorse scrub from the road. There is a souterrain, or earth-house, with a stone passage and chamber, surrounded by three ramparts, occupied in the second century by Romans. To counteract the slightly fake appearance given by recent restoration, visit Castlelaw at dawn, and then walk to the top of Woodhouselee Hill, beyond. The sun, rising over the Moorfoot Hills to the southeast, bathing the land in a pinkish light, with the mist still clinging to the valley, is well worth the early rise: for a breathtaking moment time seems to collapse, fusing pre-historic with present.

Flotterstone Inn is just south of Castlelaw on the A702. Here you can sit in the garden in summer beside the swift-flowing Glencorse Burn. (At the inn there is a good selection of dishes on the menu at reasonable prices.) From the inn you can walk up beside the burn for about a mile to the **Glencorse Reservoir**, an attractive pine-fringed stretch of water reflecting the surrounding hills. Like most of the reservoirs in the Pentlands, it is stocked with brown and rainbow trout, and day permits are available for both bank and boat fishing.

The naked mud shore and receding water-line too often indicate a shortage of rainfall. You would never guess, as you gaze across the water, that it covers the remains of the Chapel of St Katherine in the Hopes, drowned when the valley was flooded to make the reservoir. In the 13th century Sir William St Clair of Roslin had a bet with Robert Bruce. He wagered his head against this Glencorse valley, that his hounds would kill a certain deer that had eluded all huntsmen, before it reached the Glencorse Burn. The deer was brought down at the burn, St Clair won his land and built the chapel on the site in thanksgiving. (He was later killed, with James Douglas, on the way to the Holy Land with Bruce's heart in 1330—see 'Dunfermline', pp. 285–7).

Penicuik

In Penicuik you can go on a conducted tour of the Edinburgh Crystal Glass Factory, tel 0968 75128. Here you can see the whole process of glassmaking: blowing, cutting, engraving, etc. There is a small charge for tours and no children under ten are allowed. The tours run from Mon–Fri; the shop, and restaurant are open Mon–Sat all the year round.

The Penicuik to Bonnyrigg Walkway

The railway that used to link Penicuik with Bonnyrigg has been transformed into an attractive five-mile walk, following the course of the River North Esk, taking you through **Roslin Glen**. Here part of the wooded valley of the River North Esk is preserved as a countryside park, full of wildlife and wild flowers. You pass the remains of what was once Scotland's biggest **Gunpowder Mill**, supplying munitions for the Napoleonic Wars as well as for the First and Second World Wars.

Glencorse Kirk

Built in 1665, a mile northeast of Penicuik, Glencorse Kirk is now roofless except for the tower which was a 19th-century addition. In his youth, Robert Louis Stevenson was a fairly regular attender, having walked over the Pentlands from Swanston. In a letter from the South Seas, he wrote to the local minister and novelist, S. R. Crockett, one of the Kailyard School of writers: 'Go there and say a prayer for me. See that it is a sunny day; I would like it to be a Sunday. Stand on the right bank just where the road goes down into the water, and shut your eyes; and if I don't appear to you . . .'

Roslin

Roslin, or Rosslyn, is three miles east of Castlelaw, in the lee of the Pentlands. A fairy-story castle rises from trees above an historic chapel. To see it from the outside, park by the chapel and walk round the graveyard and over a narrow footbridge (once a drawbridge) that spans the River North Esk, dizzyingly, far below. The castle stands high over Roslin Glen, with dripping dungeons, an ancient yew tree and legends of buried treasure. Dating from 1304, when the Lantern Tower was built, it was the home of the St Clair family who came to England with William the Conqueror and were lured north by offers of land from Malcolm Canmore. Sir William St Clair, who lived here in sump-tuous state, in the 15th century, ate off gold plate, waited on by dozens of lords and ladies, and minted his own coins. When his wife, Elizabeth, went visiting, her mounted escort numbered two hundred.

The castle was burnt and bombarded many times. In 1447, one of the dog-loving women of the household scrambled under a bed to help a whelping bitch. Her candle set the bedding on fire and the old part of the castle was gutted. The castle suffered badly in the 16th century, when Hertford was obeying his king's order to 'put all to fire and sword' in Scotland. Part of the castle has been restored and you can rent it. It sleeps eight people and can be taken for as long as you like for an unforgettable holiday in wonderful surroundings. If interested, contact The Landmark Trust, Shottesbrooke, Maidenhead, Berkshire, tel 0628 82 5925.

Roslin Chapel (open daily, 1 April–31 Oct: adm) was the creation of the flamboyant Sir William St Clair above, in the 15th century. Worried, perhaps, that he might have used his great wealth too self-indulgently, he decided towards the end of his life that he'd better atone for some of his extravagances before going on to meet his Maker. He therefore started building a church. The St Clairs are hereditory Grand Master Masons, and the church was to be the world's High Temple of Masonry. Dedicated to St Matthew and founded in 1446, the chapel was designed to be an enormous cruciform collegiate church. It was never finished. When William died in 1484 enthusiasm for the project dwindled and all that was completed was the present chapel, a chancel and part of the transept, with a vault below. A number of St Clairs are buried in the vault, some, it is said, still in armour. The interior is so richly carved that you get visual indigestion, looking at it. Nearly every inch has been decorated with men and animals, birds and foliage, flowers and insects: there are the Seven Cardinal Virtues, the Seven Deadly Sins, the Dance of Death and a lot more besides, all created by the finest craftsmen of the day.

Your eye will be drawn inevitably to the famous **Prentice Pillar** on the south side of the Lady Chapel. The pillar's carving is so delicate that it makes the rest seem almost crude. Legend has it that the pillar was intended to enshrine the spiritual concept, rather than the material form, of the Holy Grail and that for such an important monument St Clair sent his master mason to Italy to find an appropriate design. When the mason returned to Roslin he found that one of his apprentices, inspired by a dream, had carved the pillar that you see today. Incensed with jealous rage, he killed the boy.

Roslin Inn, now the curator's house, beside the chapel, dates from 1662 and has had many illustrious visitors including Boswell, Johnson, Burns, Scott, the Wordsworths and Edward VII, who engraved a memorial to his visit on a window in 1859 when he was Prince of Wales.

Next door there is a gift shop and café, and it is here you get tickets for the chapel.

Not far to the west, in the Pentlands, the Battle of Rullion Green took place in 1666, when troops under General Tam Dalyell, Commander of the King's army in Scotland, defeated an uprising of Covenanters. Dalyell subsequently resigned his commission in disgust at the appalling reprisals that were inflicted on the prisoners and their families.

Howgate

The Howgate Inn, a couple of miles south of Roslin, is another inn with literary associations: Walter Scott, Allan Ramsay, Dr John Brown, Henry Mackenzie and Robert Louis Stevenson were among its better known customers. Dr John Brown immortalized the area when he wrote his lovely if sentimental book *Rab and His Friends* about the dog who goes to Edinburgh every day with the Howgate carriers. (You can see the grave of the carrier and his wife, in the churchyard of St Mungo's in Penicuik.) The Howgate Inn's smorgasbord, open sandwiches and fondues are acclaimed locally, it has a cosy little bar and when the weather is fine you can eat outside in the attractive terraced gardens.

Temple

Temple is a tiny hamlet about four miles east of Howgate as the crow flies—an attractive six-mile drive for the earthbound. Here, in a tranquil churchyard on a hillside beside a cascading burn, you will find the roofless ruin of a 14th-century church. It is on the site of one built by the Knights Templar, the soldier-monks of the Crusades who had head-quarters here until the pope decided they were becoming too powerful and suppressed them in 1312.

Dalkeith

Dalkeith, six miles north of Temple and six miles southeast of Edinburgh on the A68, is a compact, busy town, with a wide, cobbled main street, embraced by the North Esk and the South Esk before they unite further north for their final sprint to the sea. In spite of being the junction of several main roads, it has a stately feeling about it, enhanced perhaps by its palace and the historic castles that surround it.

In **Dalkeith Park** (open daily from Easter to the end of October and at weekends in November: adm) you can roam along the river among the trees taking one of several nature trails. There is a 'tunnel walk', a woodland adventure play area, an 18th-century bridge and an orangery. Although the palace is not open to the public it makes a splendid background to the park. Seat of the Scotts of Buccleuch since the 12th century, it is a large, reddish, neoclassical mansion. Designed in the 18th century by Sir John Vanburgh around an older castle, it has a recessed centre and two projecting wings, modelled on the Dutch Loo Palace. Here, in 1572, when the palace was known as the Lion's Den, the notorious James Douglas, Earl of Morton, lay on his sick-bed and held the council which plotted to bring Mary, Queen of Scots, to trial. George IV stayed here in 1822, during his State Visit to Scotland and Queen Victoria, in 1842, when she remarked in her diary that she had 'tasted oatmeal porridge, which I think very good'.

The Collegiate Church of St Nicholas, dating from the 12th century and much restored, is on the north side of Dalkeith High Street. In the roofless ruin of the 14th-century choir and apse you can see a double tomb which is believed to contain the remains of the first Earl Morton and his wife Johan, daughter of James I. It was here, in 1445, that Aeneas Silvius, a papal diplomat, later Pope Pius II, was astonished to see 'black stones' being given to the poor as alms. Much travelled as he was, the Italian had never seen coal before!

Dalkeith Arts Centre (open daily, except Tues and Sun: free) has art exhibitions and musical recitals.

The Edinburgh Butterfly and Insect World (open March–Oct daily: adm) is on the A7 two miles north of Dalkeith. Naturalists will be enchanted by this exotic rainforest, landscaped with tropical plants, cascading waterfalls and lily ponds, with butterflies from all over the world flying freely around. There are displays of insects, a tearoom, garden centre, playground and picnic area. There is also a tropical fish shop, though live fish might present a problem for the rest of your holiday.

Newbattle Abbey (conducted tours on written application to the Warden) lies a mile southeast of Dalkeith and you can see it clearly from the gate. Newbattle was founded for the Cistercians in the 12th century: after the Reformation it became the family seat of the Kerrs, later Marquesses of Lothian, who gave it to the nation as an adult education centre. In its heyday it was frequently visited by royalty: a murdered mistress of David II was buried here; James IV met his 14-year-old bride, Margaret Tudor, here; James V stayed here and George IV came, on his famous Scottish bonanza. The monks of Newbattle were among the first to work the local coal mines.

Lady Victoria Colliery, Newtongrange

Just south of Dalkeith, Lady Victoria Colliery was built by the Lothian Coal Company in 1890 and pioneered many techniques in the mechanization of coal cutting and haulage. It has been imaginatively converted into a **Mining Museum** (open daily Easter–Sept, 11–4: adm), and its award winning displays really bring to life what it must have been like for the people who worked and lived here. Even if the workings of the colliery don't interest you, the interiors of the pit village are most interesting and evocative. Look out for the miner, pale and exhausted, slumped in front of the fire in his kitchen after his shift in the mine, a blanket round his shoulders, his long-johns drying on a rail. There is even a licensed Victorian tea-room.

Vogrie Country Park

A couple of miles east of Newtongrange, on Tyne Water, the Vogrie Country Park (open daily: free) is a picturesque estate with wooded glens and gardens round a great mansion and a nine-hole golf course. Vogrie House was built in 1876 and now contains an Interpretive Centre with details of the park's history. In the grounds there are a variety of gardens, including the Garden of Peace and Friendship where foreign visitors can plant trees as a token of friendship. Lime in the soil encourages such beauties as wild thyme and quaking grass. The Rhododendron Walk, leading to the house, is glorious in the spring when the rhododendrons and azaleas are in full bloom on a sea of daffodils, with an attractive pond, waterfall and rockery at the end, in front of the house. There is a Tree Trail, as well as Nature Trails where you could see roe deer and even badgers. Over 70 species of birds have been recorded: on the river bank look out for the enchanting dippers, bobbing up and down on the stones. For children there is an orienteering course and adventure playground. A nine-hole golf course is about to open. This is a good place to take the family on a fine day.

Arniston House, Gorebridge

Arniston is a fine mansion built in 1726 by William Adam, for Robert Dundas, later Lord President of the Court of Session. (Open Tues, and the 1st Sun of the month, June–Sept, 2–5, or by apt: adm.) Walter Scott was a frequent guest and recorded in his diary in 1828: 'I am always happy in finding myself in the old Oak Room at Arniston where I have drank many a merry bottle...' Home-baked teas now replace the merry bottles and there is clay pigeon shooting.

Borthwick Castle

Borthwick Castle is five miles south of Dalkeith in a tiny hamlet in the Moorfoot Hills, just off the A7. More than 500 years old and the largest complete twin-towered keep in Scotland (sadly somewhat over-restored), it is now a private hotel where guests dine in a stone-vaulted Great Hall with Minstrels' Gallery and hooded fireplace, and can sleep in the bedchambers once occupied by Queen Mary and Bothwell. The ill-fated couple came here a month after their marriage, looking for peace, but not for long. Insurgents surrounded them, and Bothwell escaped through the postern gate, followed later by Mary, disguised as a man. It is said that prisoners were invited to jump the four-metre gap between the two towers at a height of twenty-four metres. If they succeeded, they were allowed to go free. There is an information centre beside the lodge at the gate, where you will find details of the history of this area.

There is a right of way linking Borthwick to Crichton Castle. It is a lovely walk and takes about an hour.

Crichton Castle

Crichton Castle (open daily except weekends, Oct–March: adm) stands within sight and signalling distance of Borthwick, two miles to the northeast on a grassy plateau, high and isolated above a steep valley. Now a ruin, this was Bothwell's seat and it is said that he kept his divorced wife here after his marriage to Mary. This, however, does not tie in with the belief that Mary came here for refuge after she escaped from Borthwick, on her way to meet up with Bothwell and run to Dunbar.

The castle dates from the 14th century, and in the courtyard you can see a delightful memento of Bothwell's nephew, Francis Stewart, Earl of Bothwell, the half-mad demonist (see 'North Berwick', p. 134). He travelled widely in Italy in the 16th century and brought back the idea for this astonishing Italianate piazza. Its walls are of a classical diamond design over pillars, making a remarkable contrast to the more sturdy structure of the rest of the castle. Certainly Mary came here as a guest of Bothwell when she was newly arrived in Scotland, to dance at the wedding of his sister to her half-brother. The chapel-like ruin beyond is a fortified stable.

Crichton Collegiate Church, half a mile north, has been in continuous use since it was built in 1449 and has marvellous barrel vaulting.

Soutra Aisle

From Crichton, go east on the back road for a mile and a half to the A68 and then three miles or so southwest to Soutra. The B6368 climbs into the hills from here, taking you to Soutra Aisle, a small stone building with a mossy roof, so simple that you might pass it off as a byre. In 1164, Malcolm IV founded a hospice here and it was used as the parish church in the 16th century. A service is still held here once a year. An archaeological dig has revealed the remains of a huge medieval hospital on this site. Let your imagination carry you back to the sad processions of sick people, being carted up to this lonely spot to be subjected to unthinkable medical practices that inevitably led to death. You can almost hear the screams and feel the pain as those unskilled surgeons wielded their rusty knives!

Haddington

Haddington is 12 miles northeast of Dalkeith, mercifully by-passed by the A1, and peacefully spread along the banks of the River Tyne. This compact and very beautiful little town was extensively restored by an enterprising town council a few years ago, with a lot of help from local inhabitants: the results are outstanding. The wedge-shaped market square is divided at one end by the fine William Adam Townhouse whose church-like steeple was added by Gillespie Graham in 1831, and has a clock that still strikes the curfew at 10 pm and 7 am. Bright colour-washed houses front the main streets with quaint wynds and courtyards leading off, affording charming little vistas through into another, older way of life. Flood water from the river has been known to reach the steps of the mercat cross.

There are over 130 buildings in Haddington listed as of special architectural or historic interest, and there is an excellent illustrated booklet, *A Walk Round Haddington*, which is sold locally. There is also an architectural trail map, on the wall of the Townhouse.

The Church of St Mary, a medieval church, is one of Haddington's greatest treasures. Built by the river in the 14th century on the site of at least two previous churches, its chancel and transepts were roofless for 400 years after the Reformation until it was restored to its full glory in 1973. Concerts are often performed here now, honoured by such musicians as Yehudi Menuhin and Louis Kentner. The size of the church gives you an idea of the early prosperity of this area. John Knox, who was born nearby in 1505, worshipped in St Mary's. Look out for a plain slab on the floor with a very moving inscription on it by Thomas Carlyle, to his wife Jane Welsh, daughter of a Haddington doctor. They were married for 40 years and she is buried in the churchyard, having left instructions that she did not wish to be buried with her husband with whom she shared a tempestuous though loving relationship.

Haddington House, 1680, in Sidegate, is now the headquarters and library of the Lamp of Lothian Trust, which is responsible for much of the restoration of the church and the cultural life of the town. You can reach its restored 17th-century garden (with lovely roses, herbs and a charming paved sunken garden) from Pleached Alley.

The Poldrate Corn Mill, a three-storey 18th-century mill, is situated beside the Tyne at Victoria Bridge. Its undershot water-wheel and cottages were also restored by the Lamp of Lothian Trust and it is now a community and arts centre. East of the river is called the Nungate: malefactors used to be hanged from the hump-backed bridge, a gruesome thought as you look at the attractive river scene where a swan breasts the current and an artist dabs peacefully at a canvas. The bridge led to the now vanished Abbey of Haddington, once known as the *Lucerna Laudoniae*, the 'Lamp of Lothian', for its reputation as a lamp of spirituality and learning, until the Reformation.

Traprain Law

Traprain Law dominates the plain east of Haddington, a massive whale-backed hump, part of a volcanic seam that includes North Berwick Law and the Bass Rock. Traprain, 734 ft (220 m) high, was the capital of the North British Votadini tribe, overlooking the 'Scottish Sea' whence invasion frequently threatened. The people lived on the rich, fertile lands below, in times of danger retiring to the summit, where you can still see the remains of a fort. Traces of their occupation on the lower slopes include standing stones and souterrains. In 1919 a fabulous hoard of 4th-century Christian and pagan treasure possibly buried by pirates, was excavated from the top of Traprain. You can see this fascinating collection in the Royal Museum of Scotland, (Antiquities), in Queen St, Edinburgh. It includes 160 silver-gilt bowls, goblets and clasps. Conservationists have managed to arrest the stone-quarrying operations at the east end of the Law and it is hoped that the huge, ugly gouged-out wedge will eventually be restored.

Hailes Castle, an open monument, is below Traprain on the northern side. The extensive ruin dates from the 13th century and was once a feudal stronghold. Built by the Hepburns, later Earls of Bothwell, and demolished by Cromwell, it was strategically sited on what was then the main north–south highway and used to charge extortionate tolls from passing travellers. The ruin stands beside a fast-flowing burn on a grassy bank carpeted with snowdrops and daffodils in spring. You can still see the water gate, bakehouse and vaulted pit prison into which prisoners were lowered and left to perish. The 29-year-old lover of the wife of one of the lairds was incarcerated here and it is said that his spirit lingers on, begging for a Christian burial.

Lennoxlove House

Lennoxlove House (open Wed, Sat and Sun afternoons, 1 May–30 Sept, or by arrangement, tel Haddington 3720: adm) is a mile south of Haddington on the B6369. Home of

Preston Mill, East Linton

the Duke of Hamilton, it stands in pretty woodland, overlooking the Lammermuirs. The 15th-century keep has parapet gargoyles, bartizans and a watchtower penthouse. In the keep and 17th- and 18th-century house you can see many good paintings including some by Raeburn, Van Dyck, Janssens, Lely, Augustus John and de Lazlo, as well as exquisite porcelain and furniture. Look out for the death mask of Mary, Queen of Scots, and her silver casket in which were found the letters (possibly forged) incriminating her in the murder of Darnley. The house got its present name from the beautiful 17th-century Duchess of Lennox, Frances Teresa Stuart. She was a favourite of Charles II and possibly the model for the original Britannia on the pre-decimal coinage.

Preston Mill

Preston Mill (open daily, 1 April–31 Oct and weekends in Nov: adm) lies about five miles northeast of Haddington on the outskirts of attractive East Linton. This really delightful mill, which has been restored by the National Trust for Scotland, stands in a picture-postcard setting, on a green beside the Tyne, where muscovy ducks and mallards bask in the shade of apple trees. It is probably the only mill of its kind in working order. Built of warm red sandstone and mellow pantiles, it has a quaint polygonal kiln with a ventilator, a working water-wheel and wooden machinery. Next door there is a small museum in an outbuilding.

Athelstaneford

Athelstaneford is a tiny hamlet on a whinstone ridge a few miles north of Haddington. Immediately noticeable is the St Andrews Cross flying proudly from a flag pole high above a brass mural in the kirkyard. The mural is engraved with a scene from a battle between an invading Northumbrian army and the combined forces of the Picts and Scots, in the Dark Ages. Legend states that the temporarily allied kings, normally at loggerheads, prayed for victory and were answered by seeing a saltire—the diagonal cross of St Andrew (diagonal at St Andrew's request because he did not wish to emulate Christ)—etched in cloud against a blue sky. When they then won their battle, the two kings agreed to make the saltire the national flag of their united kingdoms, with St Andrew as their patron saint; a resolution that was to be broken many times before it became reality. The head of the defeated Athelstane was stuck on a spike on Inch Garvie, a tiny island near the Forth Bridge.

Stenton

Stenton, six miles east of Haddington, just off the A1, is a delightful, well-preserved small village with a reputation for being one of the last places to have burnt witches. You can see a restored tron (a tall timber weighing scales, used for measuring out wool at the wool fairs) on one of the two tiny greens. Pretty red sandstone cottages with pantiled roofs surround the greens, one with its original outside stairway. The old joiner's house lies below, with a picturesque courtyard, and beside it stands a farm with a wheel house. Near the school is the Smiddy and the Oak Inn which incorporates a picture gallery with frequently changing exhibitions by contemporary artists. Here, you can sit at cosy tables enjoying an excellent light lunch (home-made soups, vol-au-vents with creamy fillings, pâtés, fish creams and cheese washed down with wine) surrounded by the paintings you came to see and possibly buy. It is hard to believe that Stenton was once notorious for the number of witches it burned.

Rood Well is easy to miss. It is on the right as you enter the village from the A1. This 16th-century well, once a popular place for pilgrims, is in a hollow carpeted with St John's Wort. Nearby, the ruins of the old kirk, with crow-stepped tower and dovecote, lie in the shadow of the tall pinnacles of the present church.

Pressmennan Glen

Pressmennan Glen, is a mile south of Stenton, and is reached by forking left at Stenton school. It is a long, wooded hanging valley. Bennet's Burn was dammed in 1819 to form this artificial loch, a lovely deep, dark snake of water and haunt of wildfowl and trout. There is a forest trail that takes about two hours, depending on how often you pause to enjoy the peaceful beauty of the glen.

WHERE TO STAY AND EAT
If you want to spoil yourself, you will be torn between two expensive castles with an almost equal claim on your delight and your pocket. One is **Borthwick Castle**, Gorebridge, tel 0875 20514, see above. Every stone of the castle drips with history, and you can lie in your bed listening to the wind moaning outside, picturing Mary and Bothwell, so recently married, perhaps enjoying one of their few moments of happiness together.

Only a few pounds cheaper, **Dalhousie Castle Hotel** at Bonnyrigg, tel 0875 20153, is a massive keep, 800 years old, not quite so romantic but every bit as impressive with turrets and battlements and a great round tower. You eat in the dungeons and the food is sublime; if you don't want to spoil your appetite, don't think about the ghastly tortures that went on down here. In the wine cellar there are marks on the walls made by prisoners who were hung upside down to die! There are ghosts, of course, including a walled-up Grey Lady, but the canny manageress won't say where in case honeymooners are frightened away! Four-poster beds in some of the rooms, a spring well (under the bridal suite!), and a crypt are some of the features of this excellent establishment. Clay pigeon shooting, croquet, riding and archery are all available.

Johnstounburn House in Humbie, tel 087533 696, is not a castle, but it is a very high class, elegant 17th-century country house nestling at the foot of the Lammermuirs and surrounded by 40 acres of park and gardens. It's comfortable, moderately priced and the food is excellent—for example, fresh crayfish with smoked salmon, or roast rack of border lamb. At the other end of the scale, you could do a lot worse than the pleasant **Laird and Dog Hotel** at Lasswade, tel 031 663 9219. A small, cheap family hotel, it has a cosy atmosphere and is comfortable. Nice, but on the main A68, **The Stair Arms Hotel** at Pathhead, tel 0875 320277, is also comfortable, has reasonable food and is moderately priced.

Brown's Hotel in West Road on the outskirts of Haddington, tel 062082 2254, will give you a comfortable stay in pleasant surroundings, moderately priced. It's an elegant 19th-century town house with a nice garden and a good reputation for food.

For excellent food, go to **Howgate Inn** (see p. 149). If you want something a bit different, **Bridge Inn**, Ratho, tel 031 333 1320, is on the canal, with a canal-boat restaurant, cruises and dancing.

LAMMERMUIRS

South and east of Haddington, deep valleys cut into the smoothly rounded summits of the high, wild moorland of the Lammermuir Hills. In summer, sheep graze among wine-red heather, whins and cascading burns; skylarks sing and wild thyme scents the air as you walk. In winter the roads are often blocked with snow; all is white, even the hares, and tractors go out from remote farmsteads to feed the sheep.

Garvald

Garvald, three miles south of Traprain Law, is a small redstone village nestling in a fold of the hills beside the fast flowing Papana Water. Behind a grille on the church wall and below a sundial dated 1633, you can see a metal neck-collar (the 'jougs') the height of a small man, where they used to tether petty criminals for punishment.

Nunraw is set back in a fringe of trees above the village to the southeast. It is a 15th-century tower house with later additions. This massive red pile, founded as a nunnery in the 12th century and abandoned during the Reformation, was bought by Irish Cistercians in 1946. It was their monastery while they built their new abbey. Now, the gentle monks in their white and black habits welcome all visitors who come here seeking God.

The new abbey, **Sancta Maria**, is further on up the hill on the right, a starkly simple, pale stone building, high on the hillside. In the long plain church, the many clear-glass windows look out over desolate moorland. When the wind moans outside and the clouds race across the sky, it is perhaps easy to feel closer to the God people come here to seek.

Gifford

Gifford, four and a half miles south of Haddington, is a lovely 17th-century village straggling round a wide main street. You can see the entrance to Yester House (private) at the end of an avenue, a graceful wrought-iron and gilded arch between redstone gatehouses with columned pillars topped by urns. It's a pity you can't go in, for on the estate there is the Goblin Ha', a mighty underground hall with a high vaulted roof. This was built in the 13th century by (as tradition has it) Sir Hugo Gifford who was known to be a wizard. Sir Walter Scott could not resist putting such a romantic place into *Marmion* ('Of lofty roof and ample size, beneath the castle deep it lies').

In **Gifford Kirk** you can see the 'laird's loft' or withdrawing room, with a fireplace for the pampered laird and his family. There is an interesting illustrated history of local buildings on a wall in the main street.

Whiteadder Reservoir lies, dark and mysterious, in a bowl of the Lammermuirs just inside the Lothian border eight miles to the southeast. There is a sheltered picnic site below the dam surrounded by clumps of trees, and there is a choice of good walks up into the hills.

Oldhamstocks

Oldhamstocks, still on the border, is eight miles northeast of the reservoir. This very attractive village, on a plateau above a valley, has its cottages clustered round a wide green with a pump and cross. The curious name comes from the Saxon for 'old settlement'. As in Gifford, there is an illustrated board in the middle of the village giving the history of local buildings. The **Watch Tower**, 1824, in the kirkyard was used to watch over the graves in order to protect them from the lucrative practice of body-snatching. The 15th-century chancel of the kirk has a stone-slabbed roof. Don't miss the proclamation hanging in the porch, granting the village 'two frie fares yeirlie . . . and . . . a werklie mercat for buying and selling of horse nolt, sheip meil, malt and all sort of grane, cloath, linnings etc'. What an easy life our ancestors had, before spelling was standardized!

WHERE TO STAY AND EAT

Tweeddale Arms Hotel in Gifford, tel 062081 240, moderately priced, is a Georgian listed building beside the Reformation church. It seems to combine an 18th-century atmosphere with thoroughly modern comforts and the food is good. Also in Gifford, **Goblin Ha' Hotel**, tel 062081 244, is a cheap, cosy, old-fashioned place known for its friendly staff. The cooking is country-style with bar suppers and special Sunday lunches, and they have a beer garden and boule court. Apart from these two, you would be advised to try one of the hotels in the previous sections, none of which are far away and some of which are worth driving a long way to stay in.

Part VII

EDINBURGH

Edinburgh Castle

Beautiful city of Edinburgh!
Where the tourist can drown his sorrow
By viewing your monuments and statues fine
During the lovely summer-time.
I'm sure it will his spirits cheer
As Sir Walter Scott's monument he draws near,
That stands in East Prince's Street
Amongst flowery gardens, fine and neat...

—William McGonagall

Edinburgh is a beautiful, fascinating city dominated by a castle built high on a craggy ridge at the centre. Known as 'The Athens of the North', the capital has a violent, romantic history, enormously versatile culture, architecture—both medieval and Georgian—to rival that of its Grecian counterpart, and a fiercely proud people. It also has some terrible warts: 1960s architecture at its worst defaces some of the suburbs and the more recent St James Centre, at the east end of Princes Street, is a monstrous, brown, concrete nightmare.

Once the cultural capital of the north, a century of complacency lulled Edinburgh into a dangerous lethargy. Recently, Glasgow stole that title and Edinburgh has had to get off its backside and try to regain its reputation. It won't be easy but a growing band of enthusiasts are making headway, fighting off the repressions of grudging, kill-joy councils and breathing vitality back into an almost moribund society. Outsiders are often jealous: some say Edinburgh is 'stuffy, stuck-up, pompous'. Perhaps it is: it is also a lively city once more, bursting with enterprise and spirit.

Built on and around a crop of hills, ancient Edinburgh stares down across a well-controlled sprawl of suburbs to an horizon smudged with mountains beyond the Lothian plain and the Firth of Forth. Its strategic, elevated position, guarding the route to the north, with the river at its feet and easy access to the south, made it an obvious choice for capital in the days when defence was paramount.

History

The unwritten history of Edinburgh goes back to the ancient British tribes who existed in clusters of wooden huts on the rocky slopes of the castle crag, choosing the windy heights for greater security. Recent excavations on the castle rock revealed Roman artefacts dating from the first centuries after Christ, when the Romans were busy trying to conquer Britain. They built a fort at Cramond, west of the town, and a naval harbour from which the Emperor Severus embarked on his northern campaigns. When the Angles of Northumbria invaded Lothian in the Dark Ages, their King Edwin built a ruined fortress on the rock, Dun Eadain, meaning literally 'Fortress-on-a-hill'. This became Edwin's Burgh and more excavation revealed traces of their occupation.

Small communities settled around the castle walls, tradesmen supplying the needs of those in the garrison, but it was not until the 11th century, in the reign of Malcolm Canmore, that Edinburgh began to develop as a town. Queen Margaret persuaded her husband to move into Edinburgh Castle and from then on, buildings flew up.

Queen Margaret's youngest son, David I, moved the capital to Edinburgh from Dunfermline when he came to the throne in 1124, founding Holyrood Abbey in 1128. Robert Bruce granted the town a Royal Charter in 1329. A city wall was built in 1436. The 16th century saw the building of a palace at Holyrood, and the hasty erection of the Flodden Wall, in 1513, to stem the anticipated advance of the conquering English. Shortly after this, the city suffered a dreadful battering from Henry VIII's 'Rough Wooing' after his marriage proposal for the infant Queen Mary and his sickly son Edward had been turned down. Mary spent most of her short, tragic reign based in Edinburgh, riding out from its walls on frequent excursions. When her son James VI inherited the English throne in 1603, he moved his court down to London, only returning once to his native land. For a while, then, Edinburgh retreated into the shadows, with brief leaps into the daylight, such as when the National Covenant was signed at Greyfriars in 1638, and when Cromwell occupied the city in 1650. The Act of Union, in 1707, pushed it still further into oblivion until Prince Charlie marched into the town in 1745 and took over Holyrood Palace and the hearts of the townspeople, for five crazy, unreal weeks of feasting and triumph, before his march south and his sad, ignominious retreat to the bloodbath of Culloden.

From the death-throes of the Jacobite rebellion, peace finally emerged and with it, the Scottish Enlightenment, that glorious explosion of culture and science that was born in Edinburgh and spread its tentacles throughout the world (see 'History', p. 62).

Walter Scott, a product of the Enlightenment, was largely responsible for the success of the triumphal visit to Edinburgh of the Hanoverian King George IV, in 1822,

SCOTLAND

resplendent in tartan. This was the first royal visit for more than 100 years, discounting that of Prince Charlie.

In the middle of the 19th century, Victoria and Albert discovered what the Queen called 'my dear, beloved Scotland' and the country became socially acceptable to other southerners. Edinburgh began to attract more and more eager Scotia-philes: tartan, porridge and bagpipes were the rage.

Old Town and New Town

One of the innovations of the Enlightenment was the building of Edinburgh New Town. In the 18th century, Edinburgh consisted of a warren of ancient buildings in the shadow of the castle rock; tall tenements, stacked together for want of space, teeming with people, vermin and disease. At the northern foot of the rock lay Nor' Loch, a stinking pond of effluent. Both Dr Johnson and Sydney Smith commented on the filth and smell of Edinburgh's streets. In 1767, the city fathers held a competition for a design to improve the town. The winner was 23-year-old James Craig, with his plan for a gracious, spacious town, north of the castle—today's New Town. Building began at once, and continued well into the 19th century when the Nor' Loch was drained, and turned into gardens. Edinburgh New Town is a masterpiece: elegant crescents, squares and gardens, lined with splendid Georgian buildings, all recently cleaned to reveal, beneath the black filth of pollution, their former pure stone. Only from the air is it possible to appreciate the perfect symmetry of Craig's formal design (described by some contemporary conservatives as 'windy parallelograms').

Edinburgh gained its affectionate sobriquet, 'Auld Reekie', in the days when *reek* (smoke), from the *lums* (chimneys) of the Old Town, lay over the city like a pall.

The large university, founded in 1582, attracts students from all over the world. Twice host to the Commonwealth Games, Edinburgh's sporting facilities are second to none. Murrayfield is a powerful magnet for rugby enthusiasts: the Murrayfield Roar can be heard from miles away and on big match days crowds in the streets reflect the fortunes of the opposing teams.

The stones of the city are honed by a pervasive east wind: they say you can always spot a native of Edinburgh—when he rounds a corner anywhere in the world, his hand will fly instinctively to clutch at his hat.

Listen to the shrewd cynicism of the Edinburgh taxi-driver; talk to the walnut-faced lollipop man who has shepherded children across the road in all weathers with the same rough humour for years; sit on a bench in Princes Street Gardens beside the neat, ordinary-looking old woman who is about to go into hospital and is worried about who will look after her cat. These are the real people of Edinburgh, just as much as the professionals for whom the city is renowned: the doctors, the lawyers, the bankers and accountants.

The Edinburgh Festival

The Edinburgh International Festival of Music and Drama, born in 1947, was conceived out of a desire to shake off the drabness of the post-war years. Its fathers were the Lord Provost, Sir John Falconer, Harry Harvey Wood of the British Council, and Rudolf

Bing, the first artistic director. In that first year, Bing collected up an amazingly glittering cast, including: the Glyndebourne Opera Company, the Hallé Orchestra, the Vienna State Orchestra, the Old Vic Theatre Company, the Sadler's Wells Ballet Company and many more, with Kathleen Ferrier among the artistes. No wonder it was an instant success.

The Festival takes a theme each year and many of the performances and exhibitions relate to this. For three weeks, in August and September, the city goes a little mad. Accommodation is booked for months ahead and people dash about in a frenzy, trying to cram as much as possible into the time.

The Fringe started at the same time and has mushroomed to such an extent that it is now the world's largest arts festival, with 500 performances each day, by some 450 companies, sharing about 150 stages. Every spare inch is used: redundant kirks, halls, back rooms, basements, attics, schools, pavements. Students and drama companies come from all over Britain and from overseas to perform anything from monologues, poetry readings, street shows and acrobatics to full-scale drama and opera. Shows are staged all day and most of the night but it is impossible to see them all. Among the literally dozens of stars who were first launched through the Fringe, Tom Stoppard, Rowan Atkinson and Billy Connolly are but a few.

The Military Tattoo takes place every night of the Festival on the castle esplanade, with some matinees, and is one of the most popular attractions, year after year. Lasting an hour and a half, against the dramatic back-drop of the floodlit castle, it is a pageant of military skills, with massed bands, pipes and drums, dancers, displays, precision drills and tableaux. Each year the organizers manage to find something different, as well as the set favourites, and you can never be sure whether the climax is going to be a Bulgarian belly-dancer or a parade of Indian elephants.

The Edinburgh International Film Festival runs at the same time as the main Festival with over 70 new feature films, documentaries, shorts, etc. There are discussions and conferences and the festival is attended by some of the leading film makers of the world.

The Edinburgh Book Festival is a biennial event (odd years) in August, a great literary bonanza spread through seven pavilions specially erected in Charlotte Square Gardens.

McEwan's Edinburgh International Jazz Festival presents top performers and bands from all over the world, with 80 hours of jazz daily throughout the city during the main Festival.

The Edinburgh International Folk Festival is a 10-day event in March with concerts, ceilidhs and cabarets. During the festival there are lectures and tuition on piping, playing the harp, fiddle, guitar and other folksy instruments.

TOURIST INFORMATION
Edinburgh Tourist Centre, Waverley Market, 3 Princes Street, tel 031 557 1700.
Tourist Desk, Edinburgh Airport, tel 031 333 2167.
Festival Offices, 21 Market Street, tel 031 226 4001.
Fringe Office and Society, 170 High Street, tel 031 226 5757.
Tattoo Office, 1 Cockburn Street, tel 031 225 1188.
Guides and Help (for specialized tours and walks), 9 Jordan Lane, tel 031 447 7190.

SCOTLAND

EDINBURGH

Holyrood Park

THE QUEEN'S DRIVE

1 Castle
2 City Art Centre
3 Georgian House
4 Gladstone's Land
5 Huntly House
6 John Knox's House
7 National Gallery of Scotland
8 Royal Museum of Scotland:
  (National Museum
  of Antiquities)
9 National Portrait Gallery
10 Palace of Holyroodhouse
11 Royal Scottish Academy
12 Royal Scottish Museum
13 St. Giles Cathedral
14 Scott Monument
15 Scottish Centre
16 Scottish National Gallery
  of Modern Art
17 Edinburgh Tourist Centre
18 Festival Office
19 Tattoo Office
20 Filmhouse
21 Fringe Office
22 Waverley Station
23 Bus Station
24 Car Parks
25 Camera Obscura
26 Canongate Tolbooth
27 Wax Museum
28 Lady Stair's House
29 Kings Theatre
30 Lyceum Theatre
31 Playhouse Theatre

162

Leisureline (for a selection of the main events of the day, 1 May–30 Sept), tel 031 246 8041.

Getting to Edinburgh

By air: Edinburgh Airport is eight miles from the city centre with frequent coach connections to Waverley Bridge as well as a fleet of taxis. A shuttle service operates between Edinburgh and London Heathrow. Booked two weeks in advance, a return fare costs from £79.

By train: Waverley Station, in the middle of the town, has frequent inter-city trains linking it with London Kings Cross in about five hours, as well as all other main towns in Britain. British Rail offer various special tickets which vary from month to month and are well worth asking about. Normal, off-peak returns cost from £53.

By coach: a number of coach companies operate day and night between Edinburgh and London, taking about eight hours, with at least two 40-minute stops on the way. This is far the cheapest way to travel and not too uncomfortable. A mid-week return costs from £22.

Getting around Edinburgh

Edinburgh is notorious for its lack of parking spaces and its abundance of traffic wardens. Feet are unquestionably the best form of conveyance in the very compact city centre. There are plenty of taxis and a good public bus service, with frequent buses to all areas and maps displayed so you can plot your route. There are also a variety of conducted tours that leave Waverley Bridge, by the station, frequently throughout the day from 9.30 am. This is an excellent way to orientate yourself before a more detailed exploration. Several different companies have established walking tours of the city; popular themes are spooks, witches and crime—much better than you might expect. Details from the Tourist Information Centre.

City Sights

If your stay is limited, don't try and see the whole city: you won't manage to and you won't enjoy what you do see. If you only have one day, for instance, your best bet is to confine your sightseeing to the Royal Mile. Start at the Castle, which takes a good two hours, and then wander down towards Holyrood, lunching at one of the many places on the way and looking in at some of the dozens of attractions you pass. Finish up at Holyrood Palace and Abbey. By now, you and your feet will be more than ready to go back to your hotel to freshen up before hitting the night-spots. If, however, you still have any energy left, climb Arthur's Seat from the Holyrood car park, for a glorious panorama of the city. (It doesn't take long: 822 ft and you can drive most of the way if you want to cheat.)

If you have two days, you should explore the New Town on the second day, including a couple of the art galleries or museums, with perhaps an hour or so browsing among the shops in Princes Street and George Street. If you have three days you should certainly devote most of a morning or afternoon to the National Gallery, or to the Modern Art Gallery if you prefer modern paintings: half a day at the National Gallery is excellently counterbalanced by spending the other half in the Royal Botanic Gardens.

The Old Town

Edinburgh Castle

(Open daily, with guided tours: adm.)

The history of the castle is the history of the city and its position makes it the focus of attention. Allow plenty of time—at least two hours, more if possible—and try to go on a reasonably clear day to get full advantage of the lovely views. The castle guides, in dark green uniform, many of them ex-servicemen, are a limitless fund of knowledge; they take you way back into the history of every corner and stone, as you toil upwards on the rough, cobbled pathways. If you prefer to be independent (and you will miss a lot of good anecdotes if you dispense with a guide) the following itinerary gives the castle's main attractions.

The Esplanade, below the castle gate, slopes surprisingly steeply upwards: it is here, during the Edinburgh Festival, that the Military Tattoo is staged, drawing vast crowds night after night, year after year, always combining displays of British military skills with those of other countries. The Tattoo ends with that most moving of all Scotland's performances: the lone piper, floodlit on the battlements, his haunting music reaching out across the darkened arena to echo in your heart for ever. Most Wednesday and Saturday evenings, in May and June, the ancient ceremony of Beating the Retreat is performed on the Esplanade, with pipes and drums and plenty of stirring ceremony.

Just through the entrance on to the Esplanade, **The Witches Well** is on the right, near where more than 300 witches were burned, between 1479 and as late as 1722.

At the top of the Esplanade a drawbridge crosses a dry moat through a massive gateway, flanked by statues of Robert Bruce and William Wallace. Ahead, the path slopes up to the right, towards the **Portcullis Gate** which dates from 1574. Just before this, up on the left, is a memorial stone to Sir William Kirkcaldy of Grange, a colourful, 16th-century character who helped to murder the notorious Cardinal Beaton (see St Andrews, p. 298) and was a leader of the Lords of the Congregation in the Reformation. Kirkcaldy was an accessory to the murder of Rizzio, Mary, Queen of Scots' Secretary. Later, he received her surrender at Carberry Hill and was mainly responsible for her final defeat at the Battle of Langside. After her imprisonment in England, he changed his loyalties, went over to her side and held Edinburgh Castle in her cause until he was forced to surrender, after which he was hanged.

Above the impressive Portcullis Gate is **Constable's Tower**, later known as Argyll's Tower because the Marquess of Argyll was held in the dungeon here before his execution in 1661. The mixed construction of the steep path, a seam of cobbles between smooth stones, allowed grip for the horses and free-running tracks for the vehicles they pulled. The path snakes upwards past the Argyll Battery, to the tourist administration area with a postcard and souvenir shop. Beyond this is the **Regimental Museum** of the Royal Scots, Britain's oldest infantry regiment, full of regimental trophies, uniforms, flags, weapons, documents, pictures and memorabilia. The Royal Scots are known as Pontius Pilate's Bodyguard: there was a dispute with some French officers about which was the oldest regiment. 'We were on duty at the Crucifixion' declared the French. 'Had we been,' retorted the colonel of the Royal Scots (then called Le Regiment de Douglas), 'we should not have been asleep on duty.'

Saint Margaret's Chapel, the oldest roofed building in Scotland, is at King's Bastion, the castle's highest terrace. This tiny Norman gem is thought to have been built by Margaret after she moved to the castle, in 1076, though some believe it may have been built in her memory, by her son David I. Although it has often been restored, this simple little chapel must look much the same now as it did when it was built. It is possible to hold extremely economical weddings and baptisms here.

Beside the chapel, on King's Bastion, is **Mons Meg**, a mighty 15th-century cannon about whose history people disagree. Some say she was forged in Mons, in Belgium, others will tell you that she was hastily cobbled together by a local blacksmith and his family, to help James II when he took Threave Castle in 1455 and finally subdued the Black Douglases. This story has some credence as the land that was given to the blacksmith as a reward was called Mollance, or Mons, and his wife's name was Meg. Whatever the true story, Mons Meg was taken to the Tower of London in 1754, but returned to its present home at the insistence of Sir Walter Scott.

Crown Square is signposted to the right, off the path up to King's Bastion. The buildings round the square are: the Scottish National War Memorial, the Crown Room, Queen Mary's Apartments, the Old Parliament or Banqueting Hall and the Scottish United Services Museum.

The Scottish National War Memorial, on the right, is perhaps one of the most dignified and poignant in the world. Designed by Sir Robert Lorimer in 1927, it contains a Gallery of Honour, divided into recesses, each containing a roll of Scottish soldiers, sailors and airmen who gave their lives for their country. Stained glass windows, by Douglas Strachan, depict war as part of man's destiny and carved reliefs illustrate all the different services. There is a tranquil shrine, opposite the entrance, built out of the rock, embodying the freedom these brave people bought with their lives.

The Crown Room in the 15th-century Old Palace is further round on the east side of the square. The regalia in the glass case have their origins in medieval times and are thus older than the English Crown Jewels in London, which are almost all post-Restoration (Cromwell having destroyed the earlier ones). The crown, made of Scottish gold, decorated with 94 pearls, 10 diamonds and many other precious stones, is said to have been used by Robert Bruce in 1306. (It was set on his head by a brave woman, Isobel of Fife, Countess of Buchan, acting for her brother whose hereditary right it was to crown the king, but who was too frightened to do so. This lion-hearted woman was captured by the English and hung up in a cage from a wall in Berwick, as a punishment.) The crown was last used when Charles II was crowned at Scone in 1651. The glittering Sword of State was given to James IV by Pope Julius II. During the troubled times of the Civil War, the Scottish Regalia were hidden for safety (see Dunnottar Castle, Grampian, p. 351). After the Act of Union in 1707, they were packed away in a chest and forgotten for about 100 years, until along came that tireless patriot, Walter Scott. He organized a search and the regalia were discovered, in the same room in which they are now displayed.

Queen Mary's Apartments are also in the Old Palace, with the tiny cupboard of a room in which Mary gave birth to James VI, in 1566. An intriguing mystery hangs over that accouchement and it doesn't take a lot of imagination to picture what could have happened in this airless little room, where the young queen endured her labour pains so long ago. A tiny oak coffin was discovered behind panelling in a recess in the room, in 1830, during restoration work. The coffin contained the remains of an infant, wrapped in silk, with a 'J' worked into the shroud. No one will ever know the story behind this pathetic little relic: it was re-interred, carrying its secret with it and leaving our minds seething with speculation. It is worth remembering that it was thought to be crucial, for Scotland's security, that the queen gave birth to a live son. Mary had suffered some nasty shocks during her pregnancy, including the murder of her Secretary, Rizzio, before her eyes. The room in which she laboured was so tiny that her loyal women could easily have blocked the view of the bed from the carousing nobles next door, gathered to witness the birth. It has been remarked that portraits of James VI show a definite similarity to portraits of John, second Earl of Mar, whose mother looked after the infant king after his birth.

The 15th-century **Banqueting Hall**, once the Old Parliament Hall, is on the south side of Crown Square. Extensively rebuilt by James IV, it is a vast chamber with a high open-timber roof and displays of weapons on the walls. It is still used for social gatherings on ceremonial occasions. In 1440, this was the setting for the infamous 'Black Dinner'. The Black Douglases were becoming altogether too powerful for the liking of those who ruled Scotland on behalf of the 8-year-old King, James II. They summoned 14-year-old William, Earl of Douglas, and his younger brother, to attend a banquet in the presence of the boy-king in this room. A black bull's head was brought in, signifying a death sentence, and the two young Douglases were murdered, in front of the king.

In one of the dungeons below the Banqueting Hall, the ninth Earl of Argyll was held before his execution in 1685. He was a staunch Protestant who supported Monmouth's rebellion against James VII/II, but he was defeated and executed. French prisoners were also imprisoned here during the Napoleonic wars.

On the west and east side of Crown Square, the Scottish United Services Museum covers the history, dress, weapons and equipment of all three Services.

On the way out, look over the northern and southern walls of the Esplanade: to the north you see Princes Street, the New Town, Leith and the Firth of Forth backed by the grey-blue hills of Fife. To the south lie the Pentlands, Moorfoots and Lammermuirs and, on a clear day, the distant shape of Ben Lomond to the west.

The Royal Mile

A walk down the Royal Mile from the Castle to Holyrood could take days if you explore every historic or interesting feature on the way. There is not space to mention more than just a few features here and you are well advised to get hold of Bartholomew's excellent *Visitor's Map of Central Edinburgh and the Royal Mile*, from any bookshop and many of the tourist souvenir shops. This gives a numbered map of the Royal Mile with each feature described. There are plenty of coffee shops, restaurants and wine bars for refreshment along the way.

The Royal Mile offers cameo glimpses into the past. From the 11th century onwards this area became a warren of close-packed houses, struggling upwards, shouldering each other for light and air, a maze of wynds, yards and twisting stairways: a steaming, stinking, cauldron of humanity. During the 18th and 19th centuries, when the rich crossed the putrid Nor' Loch and began to build the New Town, the Old Town became the poor quarter, with many families to each tenement, huddled together in overcrowded squalor. Today, many of these houses are being restored and re-inhabited by the descendants of the original occupiers: a social reversal that can be seen in cities all over the world.

Castle Hill leads down the Royal Mile from the Esplanade. From here, Castle Wynd Steps on the right descend to the Grassmarket. At the top is **Cannonball House**, so called from the ball embedded in its western gable, which is said to have been fired from the castle towards Holyrood during its occupation by Prince Charlie in 1745.

The Scottish Whisky Heritage Centre, also here (open daily: adm), is a new venture showing the history of whisky. A series of ingenious tableaux with life-like models, sounds and even smells, progress from the illicit still, smuggling and evasion of the redcoats, through to the laird with his decanter. An audio visual show explains (in seven languages) the process of whisky making and blending.

Outlook Tower is opposite, on the left (open daily: adm). From here you can look at the city through the Camera Obscura, a cunning contraption of mirrors that gives an intriguing, reflected bird's-eye view. There are also view-finders and telescopes round the roof, and special exhibitions.

The Assembly Hall of the General Assembly of the Church of Scotland is next to the Outlook Tower, past Semple's Close, and is not always open to the public. It is on the site of a palace where Mary of Guise, mother of Mary, Queen of Scots, lived in the 16th century. Plays are staged in this magnificent hall during the Edinburgh Festival.

Castle Street runs into **Lawnmarket**. Not far down on the left is **Gladstone's Land** (open daily 1 April–31 Oct, weekends in Nov: adm). Dating from 1617, with its original arcaded front, this is a splendid example of a typical tenement of those overcrowded days, expanding upwards to six storeys. Originally the home of a wealthy burgess, Thomas Gledstanes, it is furnished in the style of the period with remarkable painted ceilings.

Lady Stair's House (open daily except Sun: free) is beyond Gladstone's Land. Dating from the early 17th century, it is now a museum, with relics of those three literary giants: Burns, Scott and Stevenson. Lady Stair was a leading hostess of Edinburgh society in the 18th century.

Brodie's Close, opposite Lady Stair's House, was the home of the model for Robert Louis Stevenson's character Jekyll-and-Hyde. Deacon Brodie was a respectable citizen by day and a notorious thief by night. He was hanged in 1788.

On the corner of Lawnmarket and George IV Bridge, three brass studs in the road mark the site of the last public execution, in 1864.

It is city tradition to spit on the heart-shaped stones in front of Parliament Square, a little further down. These, called the **Heart of Midlothian**, mark the site of the old city jail, demolished in 1817. It was here, in 1650, that the head of gallant Montrose was displayed on a pike.

St Giles Cathedral lies within Parliament Square, which covers the old churchyard. John Knox is buried somewhere here, near his statue behind the cathedral. Everyone must form their own impression of St Giles: for some, its unadorned Presbyterian gloom seems to have banished all trace of the God whose house it claims to be. Correctly, it is The High Kirk of St Giles, and it seems strange that a church that was once the centre of anti-Episcopal rioting, where clergy were physically assaulted for trying to retain Episco-palian ritual, is still referred to as a cathedral—a word that means the seat of the bishop. A church is thought to have stood here as early as the 9th century, but the present Gothic building dates from the 15th century. It has been much restored, not always to advantage, and contains many interesting relics and monuments. Near the entrance to the side chapel, south of the nave, a tablet marks the spot from which Jenny Geddes flung her stool at the clergyman, striking a blow for the Covenanters in the 17th century.

The Regimental Colours of the Scottish regiments hang above the nave—historic banners embroidered with the battle honours of the regiments. These Colours are treated with enormous respect and honour: people stand up and men salute them, when they are paraded.

The Chapel of the Thistle (adm), in the east corner of the cathedral, was designed by Robert Lorimer in 1911. It is tiny and ornate, in honour of The Most Ancient and Most Noble Order of the Thistle—deliciously out of place among these dark, forbidding walls.

Parliament House (open all year, Tues–Fri: free) is just behind St Giles. Now the home of the Scottish Law Courts, it was the home of the Scottish Parliament until after the Union in 1707. The Great Hall has a splendid hammerbeam roof and lovely stained glass. A Greek façade, added in 1808, hides the original front, but you can see how it once looked from George IV Bridge, round the corner.

The Wax Museum, a little further down on the same side of the road (open 1 April–30 Sept: adm), contains over 150 costumed models of prominent figures in Scottish history, including Mary, Queen of Scots, Bonnie Prince Charlie, Robert Burns, William Wallace. Colourful tableaux with sound effects bring history to life. There is a Chamber of Horrors (Burke and Hare, and Deacon Brodie), and a fantasy corner for children.

In the High Street, leading on from Lawnmarket, 17th-century **Tron Church**, is a little way down past St Giles, so called because of the *tron*, or weighing beam, that stood nearby. This tron served to check the weights used by the merchants: those found using under-weight measures were nailed to the tron by their ears. Many locals have hazy recollections of storming up the Mound at Hogmanay, just before midnight, and staggering down the High Street to touch the tron, in salute to the New Year.

John Knox's House (open daily except Sun: adm) is on the left-hand corner where the High Street narrows before Netherbow Port. It dates from 1490 and still has an outside stair. Recently restoration revealed its original walls, fireplaces and painted ceilings. John Knox is believed to have lived here from 1561 to 1572 and it is thought that he died in one of the upstairs rooms. Inside are many relics of his life, with pictures of Edinburgh as it was in the past. Somehow, his dynamic personality is stamped into the soul of the building. It is easy to dismiss him as a dark, melancholy fanatic, breathing fire and brimstone and everlasting damnation, but there was much more to him than that. He had a sharp wit and a shrewd worldliness, and presumably had charm for, at the age of 51, he took as his second wife a girl of 16 who gave him three daughters.

The Museum of Childhood is opposite John Knox's House (open daily except Sun: free). It holds a fascinating collection of objects related to childhood in the past; not just toys and games, but books children used to read and medicines they were given. It is of as much, if not more, interest to adults as to children.

After Netherbow Port, High Street becomes **Canongate**—the road up which the canons, or clerics, walked from Holyrood Abbey through Netherbow Gate into the walled town. Canongate was once the smart residential quarter of the aristocracy.

Canongate Tolbooth, 1591 (open daily except Sun: free), contains the **People's Story Museum**, with temporary exhibitions throughout the year. **The Brass Rubbing Centre** is in Trinity Apse on the ground floor (open daily except Sun, and including Sun during the Festival: free entry, charge for each rubbing). A collection of replicas moulded from Pictish Stones, rare Scottish brasses and medieval church brasses are available for amateur brass rubbers, with experts on hand to instruct and supply materials. A shop sells ready-made rubbings, kits, booklets, etc.

Canongate Church, beside the Tolbooth, was built in 1688 for the congregation that James VII ousted from Holyrood Abbey. Opposite, 16th-century **Huntly House** (open daily except on Sun: free), is a museum showing Edinburgh life through the centuries. Next door in **Acheson House**, 1633, is the **Scottish Craft Centre** (open daily except Sun: free).

17th-century **Queensberry House** is further down on the right. As you pass, spare a thought for the poor little kitchen boy who used to turn the spit there. While the second Duke of Queensberry was busy accepting a bribe to help push through the Act of Union in 1707, his oldest son and heir, a homicidal lunatic, was equally busy roasting the kitchen boy on his spit. He was caught, but not before he had begun to eat his victim. The house is now a private hospital.

Holyrood Abbey

The history of Holyrood Abbey, at the foot of the Royal Mile, runs in tandem with that of the Castle. It was founded in 1128 by David I, on the spot where, tradition has it, he was saved by a miracle from being gored to death by a wild stag. The name Holy Rood (or Cross) is said to come from a fragment of the True Cross, brought to Scotland by saintly Queen Margaret in the 11th century and incorporated into the new abbey by her son David. If this story is true, the holy relic did not survive (perhaps it was carried off by Edward I, at the beginning of the 14th century, when he took away the Stone of Destiny from Scone). Only a shell now, with a soaring Norman arch, the abbey makes a beautiful silhouette against the evening sky, its ghosts reaching out from the ancient stones. It was a favourite royal residence: James II was born and crowned here in the 15th century; he and his two successors were married in the church, as was Mary (to Darnley in 1565). Several monarchs were buried at Holyrood and Charles I was crowned here as well as in London.

Holyrood Palace

Holyrood Palace, or the Palace of Holyroodhouse, now the Queen's official residence in Edinburgh, is open to the public when she isn't there (open daily, except Sun in the winter: closed for Royal and State visits: adm). It was built during the reign of James IV, around 1500. With the abbey, it took a severe bashing during the 'Rough Wooing' in 1544. The ghost of Queen Mary bewitches you in every corner. She came here, a bright-eyed, high-spirited, sensual young widow of 19, fresh from the French court, accustomed to French ways. Here she received Knox, and was berated by him for attending mass in her chapel. Here, in 1565, she married the dissolute Darnley, four years her junior, a vicious youth who suspected her of infidelity with her Italian

Secretary, Rizzio, and helped to murder him in front of her when she was six months pregnant. It is easy to imagine Mary, starting up from the table, in the small supper room, cumbersome with her unborn child, staring down at Rizzio who clawed at her skirt, abject and cowering, begging her to save him. And then hearing his screams as they dragged him away, followed by an awful silence. Finally, it was here that Mary married Bothwell, a squalid, hole-in-the-corner business that brought a swift end to her tragic reign.

Of happier memory, although only lasting for a short time, were those five weeks in 1745, when Prince Charles Edward Stuart held court at Holyrood: riding out in the morning to review his troops, spreading his magnetic charm at the magnificent Court levees in the evening, the darling of Edinburgh society, the dazzling focus of all female eyes.

In the 150 ft (457 m) long picture gallery is one of Scotland's best practical jokes. The gallery holds 89 of the original 111 portraits of Scottish monarchs, commissioned by the government in 1684 and completed in two years by a Dutchman called James de Wet. Many of the portraits are of fictitious characters and many of them, as Walter Scott commented when he saw them, 'lived several centuries before the invention of oil paints'. De Wet was paid £120 per annum for this daunting commission of monarchs 'in large, royall postures' and had to provide his own materials. One can only guess at the emotion of the official who received and hung these astonishing portrayals at a rate of more than one a week.

The quaint, turreted lodge on the edge of the palace grounds, on the left approaching from Canongate, is Queen Mary's Bath-house. Some say the queen bathed here in white wine. True or not, she was liable to catch pneumonia, walking back to her apartments through the cold Edinburgh wind.

South of The Royal Mile

The Grassmarket lies at the foot of Castle Wynd Steps, or down Victoria Street, off George IV Bridge just before the Central Library. Victoria Street has an excellent print shop and tempting antique and bric-à-brac shops. The Grassmarket, a long, wide rectangle, was once the scene of several ignoble events. Among parked cars and trees, there is an innocent-looking cross in a railed enclosure at the foot of Victoria Street. This marks the site of the gallows where more than 100 Covenanters were hanged in the 17th century for refusing to give up their right to worship God in their own way.

Another of the Grassmarket's victims was a certain Captain Porteous, who died in circumstances that could easily be dressed in 20th-century clothes. In 1736, a crowd became restless after an unpopular execution, just up the hill in the Lawnmarket. Porteous ordered the Guard to fire: some people were killed: Porteous was tried for murder and acquitted. The angry mob dragged him from the Tolbooth Jail and administered their own rough justice, hanging him from a dyer's pole in the Grass-market.

The Traverse Theatre looks down the Grassmarket from West Bow. Recently smartened up, this is Scotland's leading 'experimental' theatre. Like all experiments, trial and error play their part.

Part of the **Flodden Wall** can still be seen if you climb the steps in the Vennel (*vennel* meaning 'alley') from the southwest corner of the Grassmarket up to Heriot Place. This wall was hastily built to protect the city after the awful defeat at Flodden in 1513, when the victorious English army seemed too close for comfort.

A quick strengthener in the 17th-century **White Hart Inn** might encourage you to finish off your tour of the Old Town, all of which lies within a few minutes walk. Both Burns and Wordsworth are known to have stayed here.

The National Library of Scotland, on George IV Bridge, opposite the Central Library, was founded in 1682 and is one of the four largest libraries in Britain. As well as enjoying the right to claim a copy of every book published in the British Isles, the Library owns a wonderful collection of illuminated manuscripts and documents relating to Scottish history, including the original copy of the last letter Mary, Queen of Scots, wrote to her cousin Elizabeth on the eve of her execution. You can also see the written order that set in motion the Massacre of Glencoe in 1692.

Greyfriars Bobby, further on down George IV Bridge, opposite the entrance to Chambers Street, is the statue of an endearing Edinburgh character. Bobby was a Skye terrier who watched over his master's grave for 14 years, from 1858. He was fed by local people and granted Edinburgh citizenship in order to save him from being destroyed as a stray dog.

Set back beyond Greyfriars Bobby, across Candlemaker Row, **Greyfriars Kirk** is another of the Old Town antiquities. The adoption and signing of the National Covenant took place here in 1638—that 'great marriage day of this nation with God', as Lord Warriston called it. In fact it led to even greater bitterness, hatred and bloodshed than before. Ironically, 1400 Covenanters were imprisoned in the Kirkyard in 1679.

The Royal Museum of Scotland (open daily: free) is less than five minutes walk round the corner into Chambers Street, a splendid Victorian building with a great soaring glass interior and a range of exhibits that are so diverse you could wander happily for days. Collections include art, archaeology, ethnology, natural history, technology and social history, covering the whole world.

Greyfriars Bobby

171

The University Old College is in South Bridge, beyond the museum, and is of both aesthetic and morbid interest. It is Robert Adam's largest work in the city and, built in 1789, it contains good examples of his distinctive interiors. The upper library was designed in 1830 by William Playfair. The building stands partly on ground that belonged to Kirk o' Field, where Darnley met his nasty end.

The Talbot Rice Art Centre, also here (open daily except Sun: free), contains an old master gallery and an exhibition gallery where the collections change about every five weeks. The Torrie Collection, with important paintings and bronzes, some of which date from the 16th century, came to the Talbot Rice from Sir James Erskine of Torrie. The exhibitions are mainly of contemporary art.

The New Town

Princes Street is unique: where else in the world does a city's main street have shops on one side of the road only and gardens backed by a cliff-top castle on the other? When the town planners were busy building the New Town, they drained the stinking Nor' Loch, in the 19th century, and agreed to leave the south side of Princes Street open, with no buildings—the effect is breath-taking. Coming down any of the side streets into Princes Street from the north, you see the silhouette of the roofs and spires of the Royal Mile on the ridge above and beyond, a marvellous frieze of architecture leading dramatically up to the Castle. Seen at sunrise, this view is memorable.

The shops on the north side of the street are unfortunately mainly chain stores, catering for all tastes and purses, and the wide pavement is usually jammed with shoppers.

After a couple of hours of exhausting, ruinous shopping, it is nice to cross the road and relax in Princes Street Gardens—in the summer, anyway. Terraced lawns and flower-beds, shaded by old trees, make a perfect haven from the exhausting jostle of the shops. Tame grey squirrels beg for scraps and fat pigeons strut fearlessly at your feet. On the first day of spring, which can come any time from April till June in Edinburgh, a miraculous 'rebirth' occurs, at lunchtime, in the gardens. The city's workers erupt into the sunshine with their lunch packets, throw off their winter coats and lie around on the grass like holidaymakers on a Mediterranean beach. An open-air café in the piazza is serenaded by music from the bandstand nearby, at lunchtime in the summer. Also in the gardens is the **Floral Clock**, a horticultural showpiece.

The Scott Monument at the eastern end of the gardens, will be familiar from photographs. Its 287 steps (open weekdays: adm) lead to a panoramic view of the city. Somehow, this very Victorian monument, erected in 1840, seems entirely suitable and just the sort Sir Walter might have designed for himself. He and his dog Maida look out from under a great canopy, set with niches containing 64 of his characters. The stone, until recently blackened with city grime, has been cleaned, greatly improving this previously rather grimey memorial.

Waverley Market is beyond the Scott Monument, above Waverley Station, and contains the main Tourist Information Centre. Only recently created over the roofs of Waverley Station, it is an imaginatively designed indoor shopping precinct, on several levels, light and airy with a fountain and pool in the middle and bistro-style cafés around.

Apart from the shops and waggon-stalls, this is a colourful, cheerful place for a rest and a snack, often with live entertainment going on near the fountain in the summer.

Calton Hill rises beyond the east end of Princes Street; a well-known part of the Edinburgh skyline, with its semi-Parthenon at the top, built as a war memorial for the Napoleonic Wars and left unfinished when funds ran out. There are marvellous views from the 102 ft (31.1 m) high **Nelson Monument** at the top, erected 1815 (open daily except Sun: adm). The buildings of the old Royal Observatory are open, too, on application to the custodian. (The present observatory is on Blackford Hill, due south, where there is a visitor centre (open daily: adm) where you can learn about the work of astronomers all over the world.)

North of Princes Street, **George Street** runs parallel to it, along the ridge, with some of the city's best shops and wonderful vistas down the intersections towards the Firth of Forth and across to Fife.

St Andrew's Square lies at the east end of George Street, a mixture of old and new buildings, dignified but somehow lacking the character of other squares in the New Town. The coach station is in the northeast corner, with a taxi rank just outside.

Charlotte Square, at the west end of George Street, is a distillation of all the elegant charm of the New Town. Robert Adam designed it but died before it was finished: it is accepted as one of his masterpieces and renowned throughout Europe. The elegance of the buildings is outstanding, even when the square is full of cars. **The Georgian House** (open daily, April–Dec: adm) is on the north side of the square. Restored and furnished in its original, late 18th-century style, it gives a fascinating picture of the domestic and social conditions of a wealthy family in those days.

Beyond Charlotte Square to the north, there are a number of other fine crescents and squares, all part of James Craig's original Georgian design for the New Town: Moray Place, Ainslie Place, Randolph Crescent and many more, surrounding attractive gardens and linked by well-proportioned streets. Happily, most of the buildings are still private houses and flats.

Art Galleries and Museums in the New Town

Edinburgh's art galleries are magnificent and it would take weeks to explore them all thoroughly. If there is only time to explore one, it ought to be the National Gallery, described by the art historian Sir John Pope-Hennessy as 'the finest small gallery in the world'.

The National Gallery of Scotland (open daily: free) stands at the foot of the Mound, across an attractive piazza—a favourite haunt of buskers. The gallery, a beautiful neo-Grecian building designed by William Henry Playfair, was built in the middle of the 19th century. The first stone was laid by Prince Albert in 1850; a wing was added in 1978 and the end of the 1980s marked a complete refurbishment. The Director of Scottish Galleries, Timothy Clifford, has restored the gallery to Playfair's original conception, with the paintings crowded together (some say too much so) on walls whose colours are carefully chosen to fit the theme of each room. The result is stunning: burgundy walls in the main rooms are not only a striking foil for gilt frames but also intensify the colours of the paintings. Clifford follows his contention that the gallery should provide a variety of vistas, as in an 18th-century landscape garden: sublime, contemplative, unexpected, diverting and even witty. Picture hanging is an art form in itself and he has demonstrated this most effectively.

Among the gallery's Scottish paintings are works by that great painter of Scottish scenery, William McTaggart; portraits by Allan Ramsay, whose masterly portrayal of women makes them seem familiar; ebullient works by David Wilkie, whose 'social history' pictures sum up the life of ordinary people in Scotland in the 18th and 19th centuries, including the heart-rending picture *Distraining for Rent*, and bucolic *Pitlessie Fair*. There are several of Raeburn's magnificent portraits, including a self-portrait. Downstairs, there is a library, a print room and a prints and drawings gallery. Every January, 38 watercolours by Turner are displayed—the Vaughan Bequest—a lovely collection whose colours are so delicate that they are only allowed into the light for one month each year. (They can be seen for the rest of the year by request in advance.)

In the main part of the gallery, on two floors, there is a large collection of European and British paintings, many of which will be familiar from art books and magazines. For instance, to name but a few: *Madonna and Child*, attributed to Verrocchio and brought to Britain by John Ruskin. Raphael's *Holy Family with a Palm Tree* is memorable for the tender love on the face of St Joseph as he offers the Babe a handful of flowers, and the pensive sadness on Mary's face, as if she sees into the future. Titian's *Diana and Actaeon* is a rich study of flesh and cool stone, and his *Mars and Venus* depicts a surprisingly bashful Mars, who seems not quite sure how to cope with the beguiling armful of half-draped Venus on his lap. The temptress in his *Three Ages of Man* is quite different: a rather stodgy, fully clad damsel stares soulfully into the besotted eyes of a naked youth, with past childhood and future senility in the background. Rubens' *Feast of Herod*, sumptuously displayed against red walls that enhance the rich colours, is a masterly study of emotion: horror, avarice, evil, contempt; full of detail and frozen movement.

Rembrandt's *Woman in Bed* peers voluptuously out from behind the curtain. El Greco's *Saviour of the World* is a compelling study of the humanity and strength of Christ. Velasquez' *An Old Woman Cooking Eggs* is so real that the smell of slightly rancid oil, so integral to any Spanish scene, wafts across the room, accompanied by a mouthwatering sizzle from the pan. Claude's *Landscape with Apollo and the Muses* shows the artist at his most typical, with an ageing Apollo reclining in the foreground backed by a tableau of graceful Muses below a temple and one of those vistas of receding landscape that he painted so brilliantly. *A School for Boys and Girls* is a splendid example of Jan Steen's gift of painting scenes of the everyday life of ordinary people with perception and subtle humour. Each fresh look at this picture reveals a new detail. Boucher's famous *Madame de Pompadour* is a study of finery so elaborate it is hardly surprising the elegant lady has to recline so stiffly on her couch. Tiepolo's *Finding of Moses*, with the ladies in 17th-century costume, is an extraordinary demonstration of his imaginative power: some of the faces are nightmarish. Constable's *Dedham Vale* is one of his most tranquil landscapes, though artist's licence allowed him to move the church tower. Corot's *Ville d'Avray—Entrance to the Wood* beckons the traveller out of the hot sunlight into the cool, dappled shade of the wood.

Degas' dumpy *Diego Martelli* muses and hugs his plump stomach beside a littered table, while Van Gogh's *Head of a Peasant Woman* stares uncompromisingly out of the canvas, forbidding anyone to take liberties. Poussin's *Seven Sacraments* are on their own for silent contemplation, in room 5, off Room 4 where the rest of the Poussins hang, in a setting meant to be an evocation of the Poussin interiors. The marble floor is newly laid, the walls drab and dimly lit. The colours in the paintings are so rich and deep they are almost indigestible and the faces glow with life. One of the most spectacular vistas in the gallery is that from Room 8, down the enfilade of wine-red galleries, to the largest canvas in Scotland, *Alexander III King of Scots Saved from the Fury of a Stag by the Intrepid Intervention of Colin Fitzgerald,* by Benjamin West.

A poignant story is attached to the gallery's wellknown portrait, *The Hon Mrs Graham* by Gainsborough. In 1774, at the age of 17, Mary Cathcart married Thomas Graham. The couple adored each other, continuing to exchange passionate love letters until Mary died at the age of only 34. Thomas was so heartbroken that he could not bear to look at this portrait, painted within the first year of marriage, when she was still half a child. She glances uncertainly from beneath her plumed hat, dressed in a magnificent gown, giving the impression she wishes the artist would hurry up so she can change into something more comfortable and curl up with a book. Thomas hid the painting away and it was forgotten, until his heir inherited the property, found the portrait locked away in London and gave it to Scotland on the proviso that it should never leave the country again.

The Royal Scottish Academy of painting, sculpture and architecture (open daily during exhibitions: adm) is just beside the National Gallery, facing on to the Mound. It was founded in 1826 to promote Fine Arts in Scotland and it holds two main exhibitions a year: the Annual Exhibition, in the summer, and the Festival Exhibition. These vary enormously and cover all aspects of Fine Art.

The City Art Centre (open daily: free, except for special exhibitions) is tucked away behind Waverley Station. This gallery houses the city's art collection, including many Scottish works, and holds a number of first-class exhibitions from all over the world.

The National Portrait Gallery (open daily: free, except for special exhibitions) is at the east end of Queen Street, and includes the excellent Queen Street Café. From this splendid building, opened in 1899, statues of illustrious Scots stare down at the street from a series of Gothic niches in the outside walls, each carefully vetted for authenticity before erection between 1889 and 1906: John Knox, looking rather benign, Mary, Queen of Scots, William Wallace, Robert the Bruce and many more. Inside, a vast floor-to-roof hall of arches, with an upper gallery, is decorated with murals and friezes depicting Scottish history, and these alone deserve hours of study. Painted by William Hole, commissioned in 1897, they display a remarkable talent. A processional frieze of Scottish characters over the centuries, all dated and named, against a richly gilded background is astonishing. No one has been left out: Caledonia, Scotland personified, sits as the alpha and omega, with Stone Age Man on one side and Thomas Carlyle on the other. The procession is endless.

As for the portraits themselves, it has to be said that the Scots are good subjects for portraits: they seem to have particularly strong faces. The scope in this gallery is vast and presents a history lesson, sewn together by many of Scotland's most famous people, painted by the leading artists of their times. Darnley, aged nine, by Hans Eworth, looking as if butter wouldn't melt in his mouth. His wife Mary, by an unknown artist, carrying all the sadness of her life in her enigmatic face. James VI/I, her son, by John de Critz, weak faced and dour. The gruesome *Execution of Charles I*, artist unknown, with intricate detail and rich, gleaming colour. Paintings by Lely include Anne Hyde, Duchess of York, a decidedly come-hither look on her sensuous face, and one of John Maitland, Duke of

Lauderdale, brilliantly portraying the gross coarseness of an unprincipled Secretary of State who dominated Scotland after the Restoration. Lovely Mary of Modena, by Willem Wissing, mother of James, the Old Pretender, caresses a parrot, symbol of purity and religious salvation. Heroes and villains, kings and regents, tyrants and philanthropists—all are here.

There are also excellent temporary photographic exhibitions, some of which are as exciting as old master paintings.

Another branch of **The Royal Museum of Scotland (Antiquities)** (open daily: free except for special exhibitions) is incorporated in the Portrait Gallery. Relics from Scotland's history go right back to the first settlers: excavated artefacts from Stone Age man; early Christian carved stones and crosses; pagan carvings; implements; pottery, and many other artefacts. Perhaps the most fascinating exhibit in the museum is the treasure dug up from Traprain Law in 1919: 4th-century Christian and pagan silver-gilt bowls, goblets, jewellery, clasps, etc., possibly buried by pirates.

The Fine Art Society (open daily except Sun: free), 137 George Street, was established in London in 1876 and has been dealing in Edinburgh since 1969. They moved recently into this series of elegant Georgian rooms and display a comprehensive stock of British paintings and works of art of the period between 1800 and 1950. They combine their own works with loan exhibitions so there are always new things to see and they manage to combine the role of grand 19th-century picture dealers with that of 20th-century art consultants.

The Modern Art Gallery (open daily: free) in Belford Road, northwest of Princes Street, was opened in 1984. The best possible use has been made of a magnificent, neo-classical building, designed by William Burn in the 1820s as a hospital, later converting to John Watson's School for fatherless children. It stands back from a green sward dotted with trees and sculptures, some by Henry Moore. When the plan to form a separate gallery for modern art was finally executed, the trustees of the National Galleries of Scotland allocated a large proportion of their total purchase grant to the new gallery to allow it to catch up with the others. Thus significant examples of many of the great 20th-century movements were acquired before escalating prices made this prohibitive; they own paintings and sculpture by key English, Scottish and foreign artists. They have also gained a number of important works through bequests and gifts. Altogether the gallery owns some 3000 paintings, sculptures, drawings and prints, its greatest strengths being in its works of German Expressionism, Surrealism and French art. There are two floors of galleries, with an excellent, licensed café in the basement, staffed mostly by friendly, impecunious students.

There is far too much in this gallery to digest in one visit. Among the many fine works is that brilliant, if awkwardly posed, full-frontal nude, *Le Lever* (Getting up) by Balthus, 1908, who, almost unbelievably, taught himself to paint. *Mizpah*, by Scottish-born John Bellany, 1942, demands close attention and concentration. It is full of religious symbolism: Mizpah, painted across the boat's transom, is biblical Hebrew for beacon or watch tower. The jumble of sea-related images form a crucifixion, the cross being the mast and furled sail of the boat; a fish—symbol for Christ—hangs round the man's neck. Even greater attention is needed for *Le bougeoir (The candlestick)* by Georges Braque, 1911, a perfect example of Cubism, as developed by Braque and Picasso and almost impossible for the layman to 'read'. Described as a still life on a bedside table, the candlestick itself is the only instantly recognizable object, though closer inspection reveals a pipe, scissors, and a copy of L'Independant, costing five centimes. Very much easier on the eye is *The model* by Francis Campbell Boileau Cadell, 1883–1937, one of the Scottish Colourists, greatly influenced by French painting. The pale nude model stands in her boudoir, reflected in a mirror, like a pearl in an oyster. In contrast to the rich purity of Cadell's model, *Nude girl on a fur* by Otto Dix, 1932, is a startling depiction of corrupted sexuality—ugly and compelling. Another nude is *Dancing woman* by Roger Hilton, 1963, a primitive, child's drawing, crazy, humorous and exhilarating, full of movement and vitality. Quite different is *Collioure* by André Derain, 1880–1954, whose bold, flat brushstrokes of unmixed paint, straight from the tube, unsubtly portray the heat of the little Mediterranean village. In *Catterline in winter* by Joan Eardley, 1963, a cold January sun hangs over a row of fisherman's cottages which cling precariously to a snowy hillside, vividly portraying the artist's knowledge of the bleak beauty of her world. *Rocky Mountains and tired Indians* by David Hockney, 1965 is a marvellous composition, put together from a collection of almost random subjects—a bright, colourful cliché created from clichés. *Lake Thun and the Stockhorn Mountains* by Ferdinand Hodler, 1910, is splendidly clean and cool—very Swiss, in fact. Gwen John's *Young nun* painted in the early 20s is a masterpiece of quiet spiritual reflection, unlike *A reading of Ovid (Tyros)* by Percy Wyndham Lewis, 1920, which is a harsh ugly satire depicting Roger Fry and Clive Bell. L. S. Lowry's *Canal and factories*, 1955, is a splendid example of the artist's popular 'cityscapes', complete with his familiar matchstick people. *Poppies against the night sky* by William MacTaggart, (who was *the* William McTaggart's grandson,) is a vivid celebration of rich colour and bold form. *The painting lesson* by Henri Matisse, 1919, is a delightful composition, the apparent simplicity belied by Matisse's clever play on real and reflected light. *The Indian Rug or Red slippers* by Anne Redpath, 1942, is an excellent example of her fondness for pattern and forms of peasant art, as well as textures, shown in the motif of the rug. *Christ delivered to the people* by Stanley Spencer, 1950, is a typical example of Spencer's unorthodox interpretation of Christianity and whether you like it or not, it is undeniably food for thought. *If not, not* by R. B. Kitaj, 1975–6 is an intriguingly complex painting that draws one back time and again. The key, or one of them, to the meaning of the composition dominates it: the gatehouse to Auschwitz.

Other artists include: Picasso, Caulfield, Peploe, Sickert, Ben Nicholson, Paul Nash and many others. Among the sculptures is John De Andrea's *Model in repose*, 1941, which is so incredibly lifelike that one is almost embarrassed to be spying on a nude, and Duane Hanson's *Tourists*, 1925, which is a joke of brilliant cruelty.

Cathedrals

Among Edinburgh's many churches of all denominations, there are two cathedrals, not counting St Giles.

St Mary's Episcopal Cathedral, 1879, is in Palmerston Place, west of Princes Street, its central spire visible from all over the city. In the grounds the charming little late 17th-century house, Easter Coats House, is the cathedral's music school. As well as services, the cathedral holds public concerts throughout the year, with the programme posted up outside.

St Mary's Metropolitan Catholic Cathedral is round the corner from York Place at the east end of Queen Street. Its all-male choir has been acclaimed as being among the best in the land, 'because they sing not as trained professionals, but with their hearts'. At the start of a high mass, the choir, starting with the trebles, moves in procession into the church through a door from the vestry and the sound of their voices, swelling and deepening as they move forward, filling the entire building with glorious sound, is an experience not quickly forgotten.

The Environs of Edinburgh

Holyrood Park and Surrounds

Holyrood Park stretches away south and east of the Palace. The steep hill rising abruptly, south of the Palace car park is Arthur's Seat, less of a slog than it looks and the easiest way up is from Dunsappie Loch to the east. The name has no connection, alas, with legendary King Arthur: it might relate to Prince Arthur of Strathclyde, but it is more likely to be a corruption of *Ard Thor*—Gaelic for 'height of Thor'. Panoramic views from the top make the climb well worthwhile. On the eve of May Day, as darkness falls, crowds of people head up the slopes of Arthur's Seat, like colonies of ants. It is traditional to greet the dawn of May Day from the top, and most years there are well over 2000 people there, including pipers, morris dancers, ministers of the church and gents in evening dress.

Salisbury Crags, the rocky peaks west of Arthur's Seat, are part of the park. There are also three lochs, **Duddingston Loch** in the southeast being a bird sanctuary preserving a surprising variety of bird life so close to the city. The village of Duddingston, to the east of the Loch, was the encampment for Prince Charlie's army for six weeks in 1745, during which time he reigned in Holyrood Palace.

Meadowbank (open daily), northeast of Holyrood Park, is a huge leisure centre, internationally known as the venue for the Commonwealth Games. It has every sort of facility and hires out equipment.

Restalrig Church, just east of Meadowbank, was destroyed in 1560 by John Knox and his fanatical followers. They branded it 'a monument of idolatry' and pulled it apart. Later it was restored. The small hexagonal chapel beside it, with a lovely groined roof resting on a central pillar, was the chapel of a college founded by James III in 1478. When it was restored in the 20th century, the new floor was split open by a spring of water, believed to be a spring once used to cure eye diseases. The original chapel that stood over the spring was called St Triduana: there was in fact no saint of that name, which comes instead from a three-day fast practised by the old Celtic Church.

The Royal Botanic Gardens

The Botanic Gardens (open all year: free) north of the city between Inverleith Row and Inverleith Terrace, deserve almost daily visits from early spring till late autumn, to appreciate their ever-changing beauty. The herbaceous borders are spectacular, backed by a gigantic beech hedge. There are glasshouses and pavilions full of exotic vegetation, steamy-hot and lush as a tropical jungle. The rock garden is huge, full of rare alpine plants, rising in miniature mountains from the water garden and sweeping lawns. There is none of that prim 'keep-off-the-grass-don't-feed-the-birds' feeling in these gardens: they are beautifully kept but somehow informal. In the summer students lie around on the lawns, studying and relaxing.

Warriston Cemetery

Not many people would think to seek an hour or two of delightful peace among the dead, but this can be done in Warriston Cemetery. Just to the east of the Botanic Gardens, follow the Water of Leith northwards, across Inverleith Row and along Warriston Road towards the crematorium. The cemetery was bought by a property speculator who then found that some of the graves were too recent to allow excavation: it is now a public, secret garden, half-tended, just enough to clear the paths but not so much as to spoil its lovely wild character, with forgotten graves overhung by trailing creepers, shaded by fine trees. You wander in dappled sunlight, pausing to read the inscriptions, brushing aside a swathe of Old Man's Beard to examine a draped urn or a marble angel. There is no feeling of bereavement: it is all tranquillity and the ghosts are happy. Don't, however, go through the tunnel that leads under the road into an older part of the cemetery: there is an evil presence here, so tangible one almost receives a physical shock.

Leith

Leith, to the northeast, is the historic port of Edinburgh. Formerly an area of high unemployment and destitution, it is now becoming fashionable, as gentrification proceeds apace. A number of wine bars, bars and restaurants have opened up along the waterfront, some with outside tables from which to watch maritime activity within the port. The English used to batter Leith during their many campaigns against Edinburgh. Mary, Queen of Scots, landed here when she came back from France to take up her loaded crown in 1561. One can't help wondering what a mixture of feelings—of hope, excitement and anxiety—raced through her mind as she received her first Scottish hospitality. Two years before, her mother, Mary of Guise, used Leith as headquarters probably in Water Street during her struggles with the Lords of the Congregation.

Charles I played golf on **Leith Links** and it was while he was playing here in 1641 that he was stopped, mid-putt, and told the news of the Irish Rebellion. Cromwell built a fort in Leith which the Jacobites captured in 1715. George IV landed in the port in 1822 making his celebrated visit to Edinburgh, organized by Sir Walter Scott. It was at that time that he showed himself to his northern subjects in an astonishing tartan outfit, complete, some say, with tights.

Andrew Lamb's House, in Burgess Street, is owned by the National Trust. This four-storey building, with a projecting staircase tower, was built as a house and warehouse combined and is now an old people's day centre. It was here that Mary was entertained on arrival in 1561 by Andrew Lamb, one of the rich merchants of Leith.

Trinity House, in Kirkgate, Leith, was founded as an almshouse in 1555, rebuilt in Victorian times, and contains four portraits by Raeburn, which can be seen on request. The much-restored **Church of St Mary**, nearly opposite, was built in the 15th century.

Dean Village

The Dean Village

Northwest of the city centre, the main road north crosses the Dean Bridge, giving no hint of the attractive Dean Village in the valley below. There was a grain-milling community here for 800 years, straggling along the Water of Leith. The old buildings are now being restored and converted into comfortable flats and houses. It is possible to walk for miles along this waterway, a peaceful haven close to the heart of a busy city.

Lauriston Castle

Lauriston Castle (open daily except Fri, April–Oct, weekends, Nov–March: adm) is further to the northwest, off Cramond Road South, overlooking the river in the suburb of Davidson's Mains. The original 16th-century tower has been extended into the present beautiful house which contains good paintings, furniture, tapestry and 'Blue John Ware'.

Edinburgh Zoo

The zoo (open daily: adm) is at Corstorphine, going west out of Edinburgh on the A8. It is one of the biggest zoos in Britain, with a large collection of mammals, birds and reptiles. The perimeter fence of the zoo runs halfway up Corstorphine Hill: an eerie experience for insomniacs or early risers is to climb the hill in the early morning dawn to watch the sun flooding in over the Lothian Plain to drench the city. Suddenly, close by, the harsh roar of some African beast bellows out to greet the dawn.

Craigmillar Castle

Craigmillar Castle (open daily except Fri: adm) is three and a half miles southwest of the city centre on the A68—a route through open countryside in the days when Mary, Queen of Scots used to ride out with her court. The massive ruins of the castle stand high and proud above a straggle of modern buildings that threatens to encroach from all sides and yet fails to diminish its aloof splendour. These mellow, well-preserved walls, dating

180

from the 14th century, have witnessed some of the darker moments of Scotland's history. In 1475, James III imprisoned his brother, John, Earl of Mar, in the keep, accusing him of 'conspiracy'. Later, Mar died from 'overzealous bloodletting'.

Craigmillar was Mary's favourite country retreat: the village nearby became known as Little France, when the overflow from her court used to take lodgings there. It was here, in 1566, at the Craigmillar Conference, that Mary was urged by her lords (including Bothwell) to divorce Darnley. It is heartrending to picture her, young, passionate and impetuous as she was, torn by the conflict between her strict Catholic upbringing, her repugnance for her dissolute husband and her growing passion for Bothwell. She lay in her chamber, beating her pillow and sobbing: 'Would that I had died, that time in Jedburgh' (see p. 58).

The great banqueting hall on the first floor is served by four stairways and it is easy for the mind to furnish it with hanging tapestries, straw on the flagged floor, blazing logs in the vast open hearth and a minstrel in the gallery below the barrel-vaulted ceiling. There are lovely views from the roof across to Arthur's Seat, the Firth of Forth with the hills of Fife beyond, and the soft contours of the smoke-grey Pentlands on the southwestern horizon. The two ancient yew trees that still flourish in the courtyard are relics from the days when they were believed to ward off evil spirits (a more prosaic explanation for their presence being that their wood was needed for making bows).

ENTERTAINMENT
An Information Centre with ticket service is at 31/2 Waverley Bridge, just beside the station. They advise on theatre and concert ticket availability, information about events in Edinburgh and coach tours around the area, and sell tickets.

There are top-class concerts, opera, drama, ballet, variety shows, etc. in Edinburgh's theatres and the latest films in the cinemas.

Theatres
Queen's Hall, Clerk Street, tel 031 668 3456. Home of Scottish Chamber Orchestra and Scottish Ensemble and important Jazz Centre.
Playhouse, at the top of Leith Walk, tel 031 557 2590. Family entertainment, pop concerts and the main opera house.
Usher Hall, Lothian Road, tel 031 228 1155.
Kings Theatre, Leven Street. Recently done up and restored to its original Georgian splendour, tel 031 229 1201.
Royal Lyceum Theatre, Grindlay Street, near the Usher Hall, Scotland's largest repertory company, tel 031 229 9697.
Netherbow, High Street, a multi-arts centre with a large variety of shows and exhibitions, tel 031 556 9579.
Theatre Workshop, 34 Hamilton Place, tel 031 226 5425.
Traverse Theatre, West Bow, off the Grassmarket. A leading experimental theatre, tel 031 226 2633.

Cinemas
Edinburgh Filmhouse, Lothian Road. All the good films you ever missed, or longed to see again, tel 031 228 6382.

SCOTLAND

Cannon, Lothian Road. Several screens showing new films, tel 031229 3030.
Odeon Film Centre, Clerk Street. Same as above, tel 031 667 3805.
Dominion, Newbattle Terrace. Same as above, tel 031 447 2660.

SHOPPING IN EDINBURGH
Princes Street and George Street, together with their connecting streets and the whole area between them, are the main shopping areas in the city centre. Jenners, in Princes Street, is the 'Harrods' of Edinburgh: if you can't get what you want anywhere else, they usually have it. There are any number of tweed, tartan and wool shops, including The Tartan Gift Shop, 96 Princes Street.

Rose Street and its lanes, running parallel between Princes Street and George Street, are lively, humming with bars and restaurants, hot-food take aways and boutiques. Many of the shops here are 'fun' places, with gimmicky knick-knacks and craft work. Les Cadeaux, 121 Rose Street, sell a good range of china, crystal and gifts, and they run a tax-free mailing service to the USA.

The St James Centre, at the east end of Princes Street, is an indoor shopping complex, with a John Lewis ('never knowingly undersold') and many smaller shops.

Waverley Market, already mentioned, is most attractive to wander about in, with lots of specialist shops and representatives of larger stores elsewhere.

Hamilton and Inches, at 87 George Street, sell antique and modern silver and jewellery, Highland accessories, watches, clocks, crystal and china: an old-established shop of the class that high-born grandparents remember.

There are plenty of gift shops in and just off the Royal Mile, as well as antique shops, bars and restaurants.

The Grassmarket and the area around it is good shopping territory. There is a well-stocked print shop, already mentioned, in Victoria Street, with framed and un-framed prints of almost anywhere in Scotland at reasonable prices. There are second-hand bookshops here and several antique shops worth browsing in.

Droopy and Brown, 37–39 Frederick Street, have built up a reputation for their own design of clothes: 'classic fashion but not neat little navy blue suits'. It is well worth a visit for all ages from 18 to 80.

Campus, at 42 Grassmarket, pride themselves on stocking top design clothes as well as more ordinary fashions, so that they usually have something for all ages and tastes.

Stockbridge, down by the Water of Leith, in the New Town, has a village community atmosphere of its own and several good shops.

St Stephen Street, at the bottom of northwest Circus Place, is lined with antique and junk shops. Some are smart and expensive, some a delightful clutter of cast-offs: many of Edinburgh's students are dressed from head to foot with bargains from St Stephen Street. Buy a box of old 78 rpm records, or a glass jar full of buttons.

On the corner of St Stephen Street, Galloways is an antique shop that also does very high class interior decoration, with lots of tempting things on view.

Herbys, at 66 Raeburn Place, further down, is a licensed delicatessen and take-away with everything anyone could want for an impromptu picnic: mouth watering cheeses, pâtés, cold-cuts, bread, etc.

The James Pringle Woollen Mill, in Bangor Road, has a splendid range of tartans, tweeds and knitwear. They also have a 'trace your clan' computer, for Smiths and Jones who pine for a Mac.

WHERE TO STAY AND EAT
The choice is enormous and you should consult the Tourist Centre. Book well ahead during the summer and especially during the Festival. The following is a small selection of hotels in the city centre—an easy walk or short taxi ride from the station.

Expensive
Caledonian Hotel, west end of Princes Street, tel 031 225 2433. The Caledonian has a long established reputation for comfort and impeccable standards; there are several bars and restaurants, including the elegant Pompadour Restaurant.

Edinburgh Sheraton, at the bottom of Lothian Road, tel 031 229 9131, is only a few years old. It stands back behind fountains and a paved garden and is well up to the standard of all Sheraton hotels.

Roxburghe Hotel, Charlotte Square, tel 031 225 3921, is a comfortable, old-established hotel with excellent service and food, overlooking Edinburgh's loveliest square.

The George Hotel, east end of George Street, tel 031 225 1251, has long been one of Edinburgh's top hotels, with a 'high class' reputation and all possible comforts and amenities.

The Balmoral, at the east end of Princes Street, tel 031 556 2414, will be better known to many as The North British Hotel, from the days when it was the doyen of Edinburgh's hotels, stage for elegant balls and smart receptions attended by Scotland's aristocracy. It suffered a grim decline but a recent facelift has restored it to the top rank.

Howard Hotel, 32–36 Great King Street, tel 031 557 3500, is a completely refurbished hotel in Georgian New Town, highly commended.

Moderate
Scandic Crown Hotel 80 High Street, tel 031 557 9797, is a splendid, castle-like old building and very confortable.

The Carlton Highland Hotel on (literally) North Bridge, tel 031 556 7277, is a turreted baronial pile, very much at the hub of the city, with a sports and leisure centre underneath and very un-baronial decor.

Thistle Hotel, 59 Manor Place, tel 031 225 6144. A friendly establishment in the west end, not far from the centre.

Cheap
Osbourne Hotel, 53/9 York Place, tel 031 556 5746. A comfortable townhouse hotel within a few minutes' walk of Princes Street.

Maitland Hotel, 33 Shandwick Place, tel 031 229 1467. A Georgian house near the centre in the west end, once owned by the Earl of Maitland. It offers a variety of package holidays which include dinner, B&B, and visits to many parts of the city.

It has been written, perhaps unfairly, that Edinburgh rates only with Cardiff and Belfast for paucity of good city-centre eating. This may be so, but there are masses of restaurants, cafés and wine bars, tucked away down steps, in narrow wynds and courtyards or on the main streets where you can eat very well. When the sun shines you can even sit at tables in the street, though the licensing laws are such that it is not always possible to drink alcohol at pavement tables. The choice is endless and today's 'in' place may be old hat tomorrow. Ask around: the following are just a few suggestions—and it is always wise to book.

Expensive

Pompadour Restaurant, Caledonian Hotel, tel 031 225 2433. Remembering Scotland's Auld Alliance with France, this elegant restaurant is decorated in the style of Louis XV's famous mistress, Madame de Pompadour, its bar overlooking the castle. Somehow, the Pompadour embodies Edinburgh's golden age, with subtle colours and delicate murals to soothe the digestion. As long as you don't mind having to put on a jacket and tie, and don't mind music while you eat, you can't hope for a better meal anywhere.

Prestonfield House, Priestfield Road, tel 031 667 8000. A 17th-century house in attractive grounds where peacocks strut and highland cattle graze. Excellent food in a country house atmosphere.

L'Auberge, 56 St Mary Street, tel 031 556 5888. Elegant, stylish restaurant serves best Scottish produce imaginatively and skilfully Frenchified. Try terrine of venison.

Howard Hotel, 36 Great King Street, tel 031 557 3500. Classical Scottish dishes: try the kipper and whisky mousse, poacher's broth, and Flummery Drambuie. Original Georgian dining room.

Merchants Brasserie, Merchant Street, tel 031 225 4009. Small, friendly atmosphere in converted tartan warehouse.

Not for the timid, **The Witchery**, 352 Castlehill, tel 031 225 5613, has ghoulish decor to emphasize its original purpose as a haunt for witches, and good food. For those who like organized spookery, walking tours set out from the Witchery at various times, with costumed guides and simulated ghoulery.

Moderate

Martin's Restaurant, 72 Rose Street North Lane, tel 031 225 3106. This personally run, intimate restaurant, aptly described as 'a country restaurant in the city', is among the best in Edinburgh. First-class food. No smoking in the dining room and a cheese board that defies description for freshness and imagination. Martin will give the history of each cheese. Highly recommended.

Le Marché Noir, in Eyre Place, tel 031 558 1608, has splendid French provincial food and atmosphere: nouvelle cuisine but not precious. Excellent set menus, limited à la carte.

Tinelli Ristorante, 139 Easter Road, tel 031 653 1932 (opposite the entrance to Hib's stadium), is straight out of Italy. Highly recommended for food, bistro decor, service and atmosphere. Follow the advice of Paulo when choosing from the menu.

Another good Italian place is **Ristorante Ravello,** 86 Morningside Road, tel 031 449 9724, old-established with a first-class menu.

Restaurant Alphorn, 167 Rose Street, tel 031 225 4787. Genuine Swiss atmosphere, good service.

L'Etoile, 8a Grindlay Street (by Lyceum Theatre), tel 031 229 5405. Excellent French food, in friendly, casual atmosphere.

Café Royal Oyster Bar, Register Place, tel 031 556 4124. If you saw the film *Chariots of Fire*, you will recognize this 1830s restaurant with its dark gleaming wood and reflecting glass. Marvellous 'traditional' atmosphere.

On the waterfront at Leith there are several good seafood restaurants with a 'waterfront' atmosphere, tables outside and excellent fish dishes. Try **Skippers Bistro,** 1a Dock Place, tel 031 554 1018. A nice Bohemian atmosphere and friendly staff. The menu, chalked up on a blackboard, is changed twice a day: mouth-watering smoked salmon roulade and scallops.

Cheap

City Café, in Blair Street off High Street, tel 031 220 0125, is a newish, trendy bar-restaurant, full of modern haircuts and imaginative food.

Keepers Restaurant, 13b Dundas Street, tel 031 556 5707. Candlelit pre-theatre dinners in friendly 'bistro' atmosphere.

Bannermans, 212 Cowgate, tel 031 556 3254. Built in the 1770s as a shell-fish warehouse, then a dwelling, and later a tavern called 'The Bucket of Blood', Bannermans has managed to retain its original tavern atmosphere, with plenty of bare wooden surfaces: you almost expect to see rushes on the floor. Traditional Scottish folk music, live, on Sundays, Tuesdays and Wednesdays. Excellent soup and homely food. Highly recommended for atmosphere.

The Bungalow, 23 Brougham Place, tel 031 229 2537. Very good curries of all sorts and strengths. Far Eastern rattan decor.

Ferri's Pizzeria, 1 Antigua Street, tel 031 556 5592. Happy Italian atmosphere (genuine). Good for children and extremely reasonable.

Le Bouzy, 22 Brougham Place, tel 031 229 0869. Small, intimate, French atmosphere.

Madogs, 38 George Street, tel 031 225 3408. This American-inspired cocktail bar specializes in exotic cocktails that are sometimes more mouth-watering to behold than to consume. It is known for its hamburgers but there is a wide alternative choice.

The true gourmet should forget all the above and go out of town. There are three restaurants within easy motoring distance that have been classed among the top ten in Britain—some go further and rank them the top three.

La Potinière is 15 or so miles east along the coast at Gullane, tel 0620 843214 (see 'Lothian', p. 139).

The Peat Inn, tel 033484 206, is further away at Peat Inn, near Cupar, in Fife (see p. 305).

To complete this trio, **Champany Inn,** Champany Corner, Linlithgow, tel 050683 4532, is less than 15 miles from the city centre, a whisker off the M9, and surely the best steak house in Britain (see 'Lothian', p. 146).

Part VIII

STRATHCLYDE: EXCLUDING GLASGOW

Culzean Castle

Strath means 'broad valley' but Strathclyde is much more than just the valley of the Clyde. Glasgow lies at its heart, astride the river and surrounded by a straggle of satellite towns, not beautiful but vibrant with character. To the south, a string of glitzy seaside resorts line the sandy coast—Glasgow's playground—backed by farmland. The eastern boundary cuts through Loch Lomond, an over-popular beauty spot. Argyll, to the west, is completely different. Remote and wild, its serpentine sea lochs eat into the land to form long peninsulas and narrow isthmuses, like a misshapen lobster claw. Moor, hill and forest are fringed by miles of glorious beaches, with many islands lying off the coast, like stray pieces of a jig-saw.

The ancient Dalriada Scots from Ireland settled in Argyll and formed their powerful kingdom. Here, Columba landed to spread the Christianity Saint Ninian had introduced at Whithorn, more than one and a half centuries earlier. Welsh Celts moved up and occupied the land south of the Clyde. As well as dozens of pre-historic burial mounds, stones and cairns, Strathclyde's coast is punctuated by the remains of fortresses and watch-towers, built to defend the land from invasion by sea. South of the Clyde is rich in Covenanting history and there is a Covenanting Trail, with one of the many leaflets issued by Cumnock and Doon Valley Tourist Association, visiting a number of the places associated with those turbulent times.

Strathclyde's economy has risen and fallen with Glasgow's. Since the decline of shipbuilding and its related industries, diversification into electronics and the silicone

186

chip has brought a new prosperity to Clydeside towns. In rural Argyll fishing, farming and tourism are the main occupations.

Most of the towns have a Summer Festival or Civic Week, with gaily decorated streets and an excuse for plenty of light-hearted entertainment and music.

As Burns-lovers know, Ayrshire is Burns country. A nostalgic Burns Heritage Trail takes in all the landmarks in the poet's short life and is highly recommended. (For full details, write to Land o' Burns Centre, Alloway, Ayr.)

SPORT

Sailing. Strathclyde's coast is a sailor's paradise, with hundreds of interesting inlets and lochs, islands and promontories to explore and any number of havens from storm. Clyde Week is a regatta attracting yachtsmen from far and wide and the coast is well supplied with marinas. Boats can be hired but amateurs should be wary of setting to sea without an experienced hand on board: there are savage rocks, strong currents—the notorious Corryvreckan whirlpool is one of Strathclyde's parlour tricks—and capricious winds.

Windsurfing. Tiree is internationally renowned as an ideal windsurfing area. If beginners want to be inspired they should watch the championships there. For the less ambitious, the whole coast is good for windsurfing and most centres offer tuition and board hire.

There are a number of **water-skiing** centres, all with instruction. Other **water sports** available round the coast and on Loch Lomond include **canoeing, swimming and sub-aqua.**

Turnberry is internationally famous for its **golf** and there are plenty of other excellent golf courses. **Riding and pony trekking** can be found in most of the rural areas. In Argyll, and south to Ballantrae, you can find excellent **game fishing** and there is also reasonable trout fishing to be found in the rural area south of the Clyde between Kilmarnock and Lanark.

Climbing. In Argyll, Ben Vorlich, Beinn Ime, and Ben Cruachan are all 'Munros', mountains over 3000 ft offering testing climbing for experts and amateurs alike. There are dozens of other hills and because of the contrasts of land- and sea-scapes the views are staggering. Beginners contemplating the more challenging hills should follow the advice given on p. 16. There is also plenty of scope for hill-walking in south Ayrshire.

Walking. There are endless good walks, especially in Argyll, though the rural hinterland south of Glasgow and in south Ayrshire have some pleasant rambling country too, with surprisingly wild moorland so close to the urban sprawl.

TOURIST INFORMATION

Tourist Information Centre, 35–39 St Vincent Place, Glasgow, tel 041 227 4880.
Clyde Valley Tourist Board, Horsemarket, Ladyacre Road, Lanark, tel 0555 2544.
Tourist Information Centre, The Promenade, Largs, tel 0475 673765.
Ayrshire and Burns Country Tourist Board, 39 Sandgate, Ayr, tel 0292 284196. 24-hour answering service.
Ayrshire Valleys Tourist Board, 62 Bank Street, Kilmarnock, tel 0563 39090.
Mid-Argyll, Kintyre and Islay Tourist Board, The Pier, Campbeltown, Argyll, tel 0586 52056.

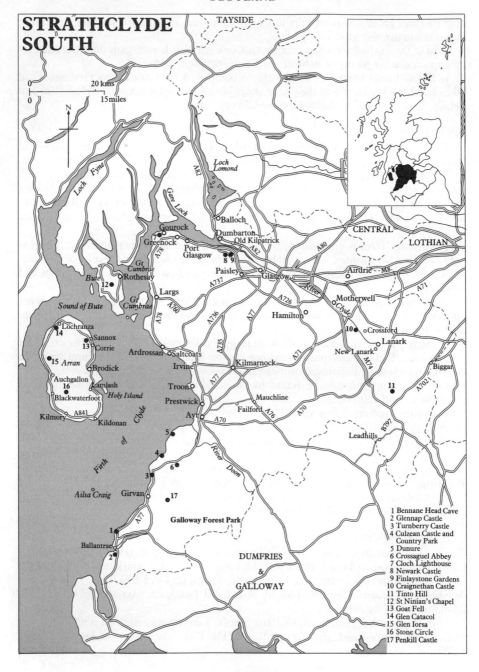

STRATHCLYDE SOUTH

TAYSIDE

Loch Lomond

Loch Fyne

Gare Loch

A82

Balloch

Gourock

Greenock

Dumbarton

Old Kilpatrick

Port Glasgow

A8

A82

CENTRAL

LOTHIAN

A80

Paisley

Glasgow

Airdrie — M8

River Clyde

A737

A71

Gt Cumbrae

Rothesay

Bute

12

Largs

Motherwell

A726

A760

Gt Cumbrae

Sound of Bute

A78

Hamilton

A7

A736

10

Crossford

Lanark

Lochranza

14

Sannox

Corrie

13

Ardrossan

Saltcoats

A78

New Lanark

M74

Biggar

15 Arran

Irvine

A735

Kilmarnock

A71

11

A702

Auchgallon

16

Brodick

Lamlash

Blackwaterfoot

Holy Island

Troon

Prestwick

A77

Mauchline

Failford

A76

A70

Leadhills

B197

Kilmory

A841

Kildonan

Firth

of

Clyde

Ayr

A70

River Doon

5

4

6

3

Ailsa Craig

Girvan

17

Galloway Forest Park

1

Ballantrae

2

DUMFRIES
&
GALLOWAY

1 Bennane Head Cave
2 Glennap Castle
3 Turnberry Castle
4 Culzean Castle and
  Country Park
5 Dunure
6 Crossaguel Abbey
7 Cloch Lighthouse
8 Newark Castle
9 Finlaystone Gardens
10 Craignethan Castle
11 Tinto Hill
12 St Ninian's Chapel
13 Goat Fell
14 Glen Catacol
15 Glen Iorsa
16 Stone Circle
17 Penkill Castle

0   20 kms
0   15 miles

N

Dunoon and Cowal Tourist Board, 7 Alexandra Parade, Dunoon, tel 0369 3785.
Garrison House, Millport, Isle of Cumbrae, tel 0475 530741.
Oban, Mull and District Tourist Board, Information Centre, Oban, tel 0631 63122.
Isle of Arran Tourist Board, Brodick, Isle of Arran, tel 0770 2140/2401.
Isle of Bute Tourist Board, Rothesay, Isle of Bute, tel 0700 2151.
There are also a number of seasonal Tourist Offices, usually open from April to October.
24-hour What's on for Tourists recorded information, tel 0475 686786.

South of the Clyde: Burns Country

All excursions south of the Clyde are an easy day-trip from Glasgow. The M8/A8 runs west from the city and hugs the south bank of the Clyde, at low tide a vast mud-flat, no longer the busy waterway it once was. It then becomes the A78 and runs down the coast, linking the seaside resort towns that are the playgrounds of Glasgow.

Finlaystone House and Gardens are about 20 minutes west of the city just past Langbank. (House open Sun afternoons, April–Aug, or by appointment: garden open all year: adm.) Dating from 14th century and extended in 1760, the house belonged to the Cunninghams, Earls of Glencairn, for five centuries. The 14th Earl befriended Robert Burns who spent some time here and wrote a stirring poem, 'Lament for James, Earl of Glencairn'. John Knox was another of Finlaystone's better known visitors. Owned and run by the Macmillan family, it is now a centre for the Clan Macmillan and home of its chief.

The house has exhibitions of Celtic art and Victoriana and a collection of dolls from all round the world, and is sometimes the stage for concerts and musical entertainment. The gardens are outstanding and as varied as rooms in a house, reflecting the owner's personality. A leaflet describes all the features, including a laurel hedge on a bank, cut once a year by a Flymo on water-skis. Landscaped in the 1830s and still being lovingly developed by the family today, its many 'rooms' open off sweeping lawns with magnificent views across the Firth of Clyde to the hills beyond. Look out for the ingenious Celtic Paving, near the bog garden and folly. This was laid in 1984 by the present chief's wife as an alternative to a maze. Its six circles and semi-circles form a continuous line, adapted from a one-inch design in the *Book of Kells*. The **John Knox Tree** behind the house (moved 40 yards from round the corner in 1900 because the lady of the house complained it made the drawing room too dark for her to sew in) is a yew, said to have been where Knox held the first reformed Communion in the West of Scotland in 1556. As well as the formal gardens there are woodland walks, a ranger service, pick-your-own strawberries and raspberries, a tea room and visitor centre, a play area and orienteering.

Port Glasgow, Greenock and Gourock form a more or less continuous urban sprawl along the south bank of the Clyde. Once the hub of the mighty Clydeside shipbuilding industry, these towns were hit hardest by the Depression and for many years were a gloomy spectacle of dying shipyards and dole queues. But the tenacious spirit that is part of the Clydeside character is revitalizing the area; buildings are being cleaned up, enterprising new developments are replacing the skeletons of the shipyards and a keen eye can pick out some fine architecture amongst the uncompromising Victorian red brick. Within a stone's throw inland, narrow lanes run through miles of unspoiled moor, dotted with gorse and heather, and charming small villages.

Port Glasgow was built in the 17th century, the nearest deep-water port to the city.

Newark Castle (open daily: adm), east of the town, dates from the 16th century, with a 15th-century tower, and is said to be one of the best examples of a Scottish mansion house of this period. A solid, fortified pile, on a green sward overlooking the river, it is still almost intact with courtyard, hall and a large number of chambers. In the days when it was a Maxwell stronghold, with none of the surrounding scars of industry, it was strategically well placed with commanding views of the river.

Also in Port Glasgow, there is a replica of the 25-ton *Comet*, the first commercial steamship in Europe, an elegant craft built by John Wood in 1812. It had a three horsepower engine and dashed along at about six knots.

Greenock, merging with Port Glasgow's western suburbs, boasts some splendid Victorian architecture including the Municipal Buildings with a 245-ft tower, and a Classical-style Custom House. The stained glass windows in Old West Kirk, on the Esplanade, include work by pre-Raphaelites Burne-Jones, Rossetti and Morris. This was the first church to be built after the Reformation, in 1591, and the first Presbyterian church to be acknowledged by Parliament. It was moved here from its original site in 1920 to make room for development.

The Maclean Museum and Art Gallery in Union Street, Greenock (open daily except Sun: free) has exhibits of local and natural history, including model ships and information about James Watt who was born and educated in the town. The Art Gallery has work by Guthrie, another native of Greenock.

Among Greenock's other famous sons was Captain William Kidd, born in 1645 to a Covenanting minister. He went to sea as a boy privateer and earned a reputation for bravery, for which he received a reward of £150 from New York City. In 1696 he was given a ship with 30 guns and sent off to fight the French and capture pirates. A year later he got to Madagascar, the pirates' main headquarters, and, finding plunder more lucrative than government service, became a pirate himself. He was hanged in England in 1701.

Burns fans should go up Nelson Street to the cemetery, to see **The Tomb of Highland Mary** (see 'Topics', p. 46), moved here when Old West Kirk was rebuilt. The original Burns Club was founded in Greenock in 1802.

On Lyle Hill, above Greenock, the huge granite **Cross of Lorraine**—with its two transversals rising from a gigantic anchor—is the Free French Memorial. During the Second World War, Greenock was a Free French Naval Base and this is the memorial to the sailors who died in the Battle of the Atlantic.

Gourock, merging with Greenock's western suburbs, is on the shoulder where the Clyde swings round from the east to flow out to sea. Half resort, half port, Gourock is the home of Caledonian MacBrayne who run most of the west coast ferries, several of which depart from here. It is also a thriving yachting centre. Gourock Highland Games are held in May.

Granny Kempock's Stone, on Kempock Point, beside the A78 overlooking the Firth, is a 6-ft-high block of grey stone, dating from pre-historic times, thought to have been part of a Druid temple. Superstitious fishermen believed Granny Kempock

190

commanded the sea. They used to bring her offerings which they laid before her while they walked round her seven times, begging for fair weather and good fishing. Newly married couples embraced her and asked for children. Today she is railed off, to prevent such familiarity.

Cloch Lighthouse, built in 1797, is an imposing white landmark, on rocky Cloch Point just west of the town, always greeted with relief by homecoming sailors during wartime and by fishermen after a stormy night at sea.

Inverkip, a couple of miles south on the A78, has one of the biggest marinas in these parts, well supplied with chandlers and shore facilities. Skippers of bigger yachts should beware of the narrow, shallow entrance at low tide. A small back road east out of Inverkip leads up to **Cornalees Bridge** in the open moorland of **Clyde-Muirshiel Regional Park**. A nature trail here follows the aqueducts that used to supply the coastal towns with drinking water and power for the mills.

Cunninghame is the area from Skelmorlie to south of Irvine, including Arran and the Cumbraes.

Wemyss Bay is so called from the caves here, where Stone Age nomads may have lived while making foraging expeditions from Ireland.

Largs is easily the nicest of the Clyde resorts, with a history that adds stature to its bustling streets. Tucked in on a shelf below rolling moorland, with views across the Firth to Great Cumbrae and Bute, Largs was the theatre for a crucial, though rather ineffectual battle in the 13th century. Old King Haakon of Norway, determined to dominate the Western Isles and worried that Alexander III had the same intention, launched his mighty fleet from Kirkwall in Orkney in July 1263. The weather was appalling. The fleet battled round Cape Wrath and down the Minch as far as Skye, suffering much damage. In Skye they were joined by Magnus, King of Man, and a few others. Into the teeth of southwesterly gales they struggled on, past the Inner Hebrides and down round the Mull of Kintyre. They were well into the Clyde by the end of September when they were caught by a post-equinoxial gale which tore Haakon's ships from their moorings and drove them on to the Ayrshire coast at Largs. The sailors waded ashore to meet Alexander's army. There was a chaotic confusion of arrows and horses and then the Scots withdrew and allowed the Vikings to wade back to their ships and sail away. History doesn't relate *how* they managed to get those cumbersome long-boats off a lee-shore, nor *why* the Scots, with such a strategic advantage allowed them to, but the outcome was conclusive. Haakon lost interest and died, and his successor, Erik, sold the Western Isles for less than £3000 in 1266 and married Alexander's daughter Margaret. A phallic obelisk, known as the Pencil, on Bowen Craig, south of the town, celebrates the battle, and every September hundreds of Scandinavians come to Largs to join in the Viking Festival.

The **Largs Historical Society Museum**, in Kirkgate House, Manse Court, (open June–Sept, afternoons daily: donation box) reconstructs the battle, and has exhibits of local history in general.

The **Christian Heritage Museum**, in a Benedictine Monastery at 5 Mackerston Place (open daily, Apr–Sept: adm). tells the history of Christian monasticism in Britain and southwest Scotland, with some fine vestments and displays as well as a café in the refectory, and a shop.

The town is packed with 'entertainment' for all ages. There are a couple of golf courses, a National Sports Training Centre, a big swimming pool—and the sea. Three times a week the last sea-going paddle steamer, *Waverley*, sails from the pier to other resorts on the Clyde. Largs is the port for Great Cumbrae Island (p. 222).

The Largs Yacht Haven south of the town has berths for over 500 yachts and offers all marina facilities including chandlers, sea-school, diving equipment, provisions, sales, charter and repairs.

Muirshiel Country Park covers nine miles of high roadless moorland northeast of Largs. At **Lochwinnoch** there is a boating and fishing loch, with signposted nature trails, picnic sites and four information centres.

Kelburn Country Centre, on A78 between Largs and Fairlie, offers a good day out for the family. Kelburn has been the home of the Boyle family, Earls of Glasgow since 1703, for 800 years and Kelburn Castle, dating from 13th century with many later additions, is the home of the present Earl. (Open for 5 weeks, Apr–May: adm. Booking advisable.) The grounds and gardens (open daily: adm), range from wild woodland, dramatic waterfalls and gorges, pools and grottos with wild flowers, ferns, rare trees and shrubs, to a walled garden called The Plaisance full of rare plants. There is a licensed café, a lampoon-type Cartoon Exhibition depicting the history of the Boyle family, and a Museum with New Zealand exhibitions. Other attractions include a Commando Assault Course built by the Royal Marines, for adults; an Adventure Course and Stockade, for younger Tarzans; and a Ranger Service offering advice, guided walks, talks and slide shows. There are also an Animals and Pets' Corner, a Riding Centre and Pony Trekking.

The A78 runs on down the coast through **Fairlie and West Kilbride**, to **Ardrossan and Saltcoats**, a string of unremarkable resort towns, some of which contain interesting museums and visitor centres. The little museum in West Kilbride, for instance, has costumes and a large collection of Aryshire lace and embroidery, (open Tue, and Thur–Sat: free). Ardrossan is the port for the island of Arran (p. 223). Saltcoats was an important producer of salt in the days of James V. **North Ayrshire Museum**, at Kirkgate, Saltcoats is in a late 18th-century church and gives various aspects of life in this area.

At **Kilwinning**, three miles east of Saltcoats, **Dalgarven Mill** is an early 17th-century flour mill, imaginatively restored to provide a working museum, with displays of the artifacts of the period and live models in authentic costume. At **Kilwinning Abbey**, founded in the mid 12th century, and now derelict, an annual archery competition for the Papingo Trophy has been taking place for 600 years and is the oldest such event in the world. Kilwinning claims to be the first centre in Scotland of freemasonry, that secret society for men, supposed to be based on brotherly love, faith and charity. It was introduced by the stonemasons working on the abbey.

Eglinton Country Park, just south of Kilwinning, is a landscaped park with gardens, picnic sites, a visitor centre and walks, centred on the ruins of **Eglington Castle**. Here, in 1839, below the 100 ft-high tower, built in 1796 and now derelict, a romantic attempt was made to re-establish ancient chivalric ceremonies. The Eglinton Tournament was a whimsical Victorian longing for 'the good old days': a jousting tournament, performed amidst much jovial back-slapping and frolicking. Napoleon III took part as one of the knights, practising, no doubt, for his next abortive attempt at the French throne the following year. In his novel, *Endymion*, published some time later, Disraeli borrows from this event.

192

Irvine, three miles south of Kilwinning, is Scotland's only coastal New Town. Under its modern façade, however, its history goes back a long way. William Wallace was deserted by his followers here in 1297, when they decided to sign a treaty with the English. Marymass is a week-long festival every August, which culminates with a procession past the castle and the crowning of a queen. At Marymass there is a horse race alleged to be the longest in the world. There is also a three-day Harbour Festival in July.

The Scottish Maritime Museum (open daily, April–Oct: adm) is in Irvine harbour, once one of Glasgow's main ports, and includes several floating vessels. Working boats, a puffer, sailing boats and lifeboats give an idea of what life was like for seamen in the past. There is a collection of documents, artifacts, photographs and small craft, all illustrating Scotland's sea-going heritage. There is also a reproduction of a tenement house, showing the 'room and kitchen' of a typical shipyard worker's dwelling at the turn of the century, very authentic, complete with range, utensils and drying laundry.

Glasgow Vennel is the historic core of Irvine. Vennel means lane and this was the main road to Glasgow until the end of the 17th Century. Derelict and facing demolition in the 1970s, the Vennel was rescued and designated a conservation area in 1974: its 18th- and 19th-century buildings are now restored and in use on an attractive cobbled street.

Glasgow Vennel Museum 4 and 10 Glasgow Vennel (open daily except Wed, June–Sept; Tues, and Thurs–Sat, Oct–May: free) includes Burn's Lodgings at No. 4 with a reconstruction of his attic room, and the thatched Heckling Shop where he worked. Heckling was a well paid but unpleasant job, involving separating the fibres of the flax plant from the stalk. It was backbreaking, dirty and stiflingly smelly and 22-year-old Burns loathed it, working from 10 to 12 hours a day, drawing the bundles of flax through the heckles. He suffered bad bouts of depression and it was during this time that he wrote 'Winter, A Dirge' and 'Prayer under the pressure of Violent Anguish':

> ... *Sure Thou, Almighty, canst not act*
> *From Cruelty or wrath!*
> *O, free my weary eyes from tears,*
> *Or close them fast in death!*

Fortunately for posterity, the Almighty chose an alternative escape: on New Year's Eve, 1781, during a drunken party in the Heckling Shop, Burns' aunt, Mrs Peacock, also drunk, knocked over a candle which ignited the bundles of dry flax and demolished the shop. Burns remarked with glee: 'The shop burnt to ashes and left me like a true poet, not worth a sixpence'.

There is also an art gallery in the the Vennel with local and international exhibitions.

James Galt, the 18th/19th-century writer and traveller who gave his name to Galt in Canada, was born in Irvine.

Although this is not the place for lovers of solitude and beauty, Irvine has splendid facilities for gregarious visitors, including a seaside park and a Magnum Leisure Centre, with swimming pools, water-chutes, an ice rink, squash courts, theatre, cinema, restaurants, bars and cafés.

Kilmarnock is about eight miles inland, east of Irvine, the centre of industry in this area with whisky as its most important product. The Johnnie Walker Distillery must be world famous—the contents of its bottles certainly are—and they run tours of the premises on weekdays from April to October. The company was founded in 1820 when an Ayrshire man, John Walker, gave up farming and bought a grocery, wine and spirit business in Kilmarnock. Other important industries include BMK, the carpet design and manufacturing company, whose clients include the Houses of Parliament in London and the Disneyland Hotel in California. There are tours of the mills by special arrangement only.

Kilmarnock holds a lively carnival in the last week in May. There is also a Festival of Leisure, in September.

The Burns Monument Museum, in Kay Park, is a tall, red-sandstone tower which has recently been renovated. Burns was closely associated with the town and his first collection of poems, *The Kilmarnock Poems,* was produced here by John Wilson in 1786, a slim, 35-page volume containing 44 poems. Its success was immediate, rescuing the impoverished poet from emigration to Jamaica.

Kay Park has a boating pond, children's play area, crazy golf and an assault course. The Kilmarnock Bowling Club, next door is the oldest in Britain having just celebrated its 250th anniversary. Robert Burns and his friends used to bowl here, pausing frequently to quench their 'drouth' at the Kay Park Tavern, still there today.

The Dick Institute (open daily except Sun: free), in Elmbank Avenue, has geological and archaeological exhibits and family archives for anyone interested in geneaology and local history, as well as an art gallery with frequent exhibitions. It is the finest library in Ayrshire and the headquarters for the International Burns Federation.

Dean Castle and Country Park (open daily: adm) is in a wooded hollow in Dean Road, off Glasgow Road. The massive 14th-century fortified keep with a 15th-century palace, contains collections of armour, weapons, old musical instruments and tapestries. There is a splendid banqueting hall, old kitchens, a minstrel's gallery, and a gloomy dungeon.

There are a number of different events held in the castle, including Ancient Warfare demonstrations, and a jazz festival.

The 200-acre Country Park is always open. As well as formal gardens, there are nature trails, a visitor centre, picnic sites, a Burns Garden, a riding centre and a ranger service. Special tours of the park cover such subjects as Bird Life, Ecology, Geology and Industrial Heritage. A garden is being cultivated by groups of disabled people. There is a children's corner and a deer park.

The Galleon Centre is an indoor leisure complex with swimming pools, ice rink, bowling hall, squash and badminton courts, a curling rink, sauna, fitness room, bar, crêche and lots more for health freaks.

Not far to the east of Kilmarnock, **Newmills** and **Darvel** are renowned for their lace and woollen industries, and in **Stewarton**, to the north, traditional Scottish bonnets are made. All the mills have shops and there are good bargains to be had.

Dunlop is three miles north of Stewarton. Dunlop cheese was first made here in the 17th century, from milk from Dunlop cows—now internationally famous as Ayrshires. When the Milk Marketing Board tried to export Dunlop Cheese to England their customers, influenced by the name, complained it tasted rubbery: it is now called Scottish Cheddar and sells well.

On the way back to the coast from Kilmarnock on the A759, the rugged ruin of 13th-century **Dundonald Castle** is about three miles southwest of the outskirts, not open to the public but viewable from the road. Dundonald was inhabited by the Fitzalans, Lord High Stewards, from whom the Stewart line descended. Robert II, the first Stewart king, died here in 1390, as did his son Robert III in 1406.

On the coast again, **Troon**, about five miles south of Irvine, is another seaside resort with sandy beaches and good golf courses. *Troone* means 'nose', referring to the craggy hook of land thrusting out into the sea with a lighthouse on the end. Lady Island, three miles off the point, is a bird sanctuary.

Prestwick was chosen as an International Airport because of its reputation for being fog-free. **Bruce's Well** is in a railed enclosure surrounded by lawn and flowers in a residential area behind St Ninian's Church, south of the town and signposted from the Ayr Road. Here, Robert Bruce, probably in the early stages of the skin disease that killed him, is said to have struck at the ground with his lance in desperation because he was exhausted and parched with thirst. Water gushed from the ground and he was revived.

Ayr and Alloway

Ayr, its northern suburbs merging with Prestwick's, is the main holiday centre on this coast and seems almost to sparkle with friendliness. It is a spacious town bordering a long sweep of sandy beach, with wide roads and villas set far apart in pleasant gardens. In spring it is a riot of pink and red blossom, carpeted with bluebells and daffodils. There is every sort of entertainment here: good shops, three golf courses, fishing, and a famous racecourse. There was a settlement here as far back as the 8th century. Early in his struggles for Scotland, Robert Bruce burnt down 'The Barns of Ayr' (a temporary barracks) with 500 of Edward I's troops inside.

For many, Ayr is of supreme importance as the capital of Burns country. Robert Burns was born on 25 January 1759, in the dear little village of Alloway, now a suburb of Ayr to the south. Although he only lived there for seven years, the atmosphere in Alloway is electric with his presence and it would be difficult to go there and not catch mild Burns fever. Straggling round the River Doon, a cluster of attractive buildings and monuments to the poet echo with his salty humour.

The Burns Heritage Trail, organized by the Scottish Tourist Board, visits all the places of importance relating to Burns' life and work. It is fun to follow the trail with a copy of his poems and a brief summary of his life: *Poems and Songs of Robert Burns*, edited and introduced by James Barke, Fontana, is excellent. You can get a copy at **The Land o' Burns Centre**, in Alloway, a first-class visitor centre and the best place from which to start this nostalgic pilgrimage. As well as an excellent book and gift shop, and café, they have an audio-visual show (adm) giving a good introduction to the poet's life. Burns is frequently misunderstood; many of his admirers tend to deify him and miss the full flavour of his personality (see 'Topics', pp. 45–7).

Burns Cottage and Museum (open daily, except closed Sun, Nov–March: adm) is a few minutes' walk to the right from the Land o' Burns Centre. The simple white thatched cottage is the 'auld clay biggin' built by his father, William, where the poet was born. Family and animals shared the same roof in this long, low building—a practice that helped to warm the living quarters in winter, if also to make them rather smelly. The museum, adjoining the cottage, contains a wealth of Burns memorabilia including the family bible and many original manuscripts. A recent addition is an imaginative Burns' Interpretation Gallery, with theme music.

> *...And, wow! Tam saw an unco sight!...*
> *Warlocks and witches in a dance:*
> *Nae cotillion, brent new frae France,*
> *But hornpipes, jigs, strathspeys, and reels,*
> *Put life and mettle in their heels.*

Alloway Kirk is across the road from the Land o' Burns Centre, scene of Tam o' Shanter's witches' orgy. Tam was making his way home after a monumental bender with his 'trusty, drouthy crony—Souter Johnnie'. Built in 1510, the kirk is a tiny shell now, but you can peep in and see the very *winnock-bunker* 'window seat' where Old Nick sat, in the guise of a shaggy dog 'black and grim and large' and the tombs from which the dead held up lights to illuminate the witches' wild dance. Perhaps the poet was somewhat inebriated himself, when he came here one moonlit night and let the setting work on his vivid imagination. The grave of William Burns, Robert's simple, devout father who died of overwork, lies in the shadow of the walls.

Burns Monument on the left past the kirk, overlooking the River Doon, is a fanciful Grecian-style temple on an Egyptian base, built in 1823. Fluted columns support a round, domed roof surmounted by an urn held up by three dolphins—symbols of Apollo, patron of the Muses. Inside, a simple chamber displays such treasures as Jean Armour's wedding ring, and Highland Mary's bible with a lock of her hair. Books, papers, pictures and documents, including a photocopy of an original manuscript, fill this small museum. An interesting selection of Burns' work includes translations into Russian, made as early as 1800, and Esperanto. The well-kept gardens around the monument are full of unusual shrubs and trees: tulip trees, rare heathers, cultivated thistles and many more. In a little pavilion—the Statue House—life-sized statues of such familiar characters as Tam o' Shanter and Souter Johnnie sit in perpetual companionship, brought in from their original site in the garden, where weather threatened erosion of their soft-stone bodies.

Brig o' Doon, down beyond the monument on the right, is a 13th-century, single arched bridge, soaring to a graceful peak, duplicated in reflection to form a frame for attractive river scenery. This is the bridge over which Tam o' Shanter escaped on his Maggie, leaving the witches to their 'hornpipes, jigs, strathspeys and reels' in the kirk.

The Auld Kirk in Ayr is down a wynd off the High Street, on the banks of the river Ayr, and is where Burns was baptized. Through Kirk Port, look for the rather morbid 'mort-safes' dating from 1655, which were put over freshly filled graves to discourage body-snatchers. Cromwell supplied the funds to build this church, having used the old one as part of a great fort he built in Ayr, of which little now remains.

The Auld Brig dates from the 13th century and was Ayr's only bridge until a new bridge was built in 1788 and replaced in 1877. Burns wrote a poem, in which he watched the pretentious construction of the new bridge being built, through the contemptuous eyes of the old bridge, prophesying, with uncanny prescience, that the new bridge would not stand the test of time. 'I'll be a brig when ye're a shapeless cairn'. Sure enough, the new bridge had to be replaced after a flood in the 19th century.

Loudoun Hall (open in the summer or by arrangement, tel 0292 282109: free) is in Boat Vennel, Ayr, one of the few places around here that has nothing to do with Burns.

Among the oldest surviving examples of townhouse architecture in the country, it was built for a rich merchant, in the late 15th century. It has been beautifully restored, having previously been condemned as a slum and threatened with a demolition order, and is now a Culture Centre.

Heading for Mauchline on the A758, turn off to **Tarbolton** after about six miles. Burns lived here between the ages of 18 and 24. He joined the local dancing class 'to brush up my manners'. He also helped form the Bachelors Club, a debating society, in a 17th-century thatched house now owned by the National Trust for Scotland (open daily 1 April–31 Oct). He was also initiated into freemasonry here in 1781.

A somewhat incongruous pillar with a ball on top, in a field in **Failford**, just outside Mauchline, is Highland Mary's Monument. Burns is said to have parted from Mary Campbell on this spot, for the last time before she died.

Mauchline, 11 miles northeast of Ayr on the A758, is an important step on the Burns Heritage Trail. A little cul-de-sac in the centre of this unremarkable main road town leads to **Burns House Museum** (open 11.30–12.30, and 1.30–3.30, Mon–Sat, and 2–5, Sun: adm). A room on the upper floor of this small, red stone cottage is where Burns installed his mistress Jean Armour and lived with her for a few months before and after their marriage in 1788. She gave birth to twins, for the second time, a week after they moved in. Furnished in the style of the period it contains many relics of the poet and his times. It was in the kirk above the cottage that Burns was forced to sit on the 'cutty stool' or stool of repentance, a humiliating punishment inflicted by the Elders of the Kirk because of his 'irregular marriage' with Jean. (It is said he refused to sit and stood defiantly beside the stool.) Four of his children are buried in the kirkyard and a board shows the graves of many of his contemporaries who feature in his poems: Poosie Nansie, Tootie and the Bleth'rin Bitch. **Poosie Nansie's Tavern**, an ale shop and lodging house in Burns' day, is opposite the kirk. The tower on the northern edge of the town is another Burns Monument, erected in his memory in 1895 and recently renovated. There is a Tourist Information Centre on the ground floor, an audio visual display 'Mauchline in the Time of Burns,' on the first floor, and 'Local Industries Past and Present' above. Good views from the roof are aided by telescopes.

Andrew Kay and Co, Victorian Works, is one of the only two curling stone factories in the world. Burns and his brother Gilbert farmed at **Mossgiel**, just to the northwest, without much success, from 1784–8.

It is only a short walk to **Ballochmyle Viaduct**, a unique structure over the River Ayr. In one great curving arch of massive sandstone blocks, it spans 181 ft across the river and is the largest masonry arch railway bridge in Britain: it is also the highest. A path along the north side of the river takes you through a red sandstone gorge. Bronze-Age cup-and-ring markings can be seen on the sandstone a few yards from the path, discovered in 1987.

While in this area, anyone interested in James Boswell, Dr Johnson's admirer and biographer, should go to **Auchinleck Boswell Museum**, five miles southeast of Mauchline on the A76. Formerly a Celtic cell and later a chapel, the museum adjoins the Boswell family mausoleum, and is the burial place of five generations of Boswells including James. Boswell and Johnson set off from here on their celebrated tour of the Highlands in 1773. (For entry and guided tour, ring 0292 20757 in advance: donations welcome.)

Dunure (always accessible: free) is a gaunt ruin on the edge of the cliff about four miles southwest of Alloway back on the coast road A719. Once one of the many strongholds of the powerful Kennedy family who ruled Ayrshire and considered themselves above the law, it has a conical dovecote, jagged walls, and a carpark in its precinct. Mary, Queen of Scots came here in 1563 during one of the lighter moments of her reign, when she toured her kingdom accompanied by a splendid cavalcade of courtiers. It is said that in 1570 the Earl of Cassillis, Chief of the Kennedys, 'roasted' Allan Stewart, Commendator of nearby Crossraguel, in an attempt to persuade him to hand over the abbey lands. This gruesome event took place in the black vault, and so that 'rost suld not burne, but that it might rost in soppe, they spared not flambing with oyle'.

Going south from Dunure on A719, watch out for **Electric Brae**, an optical illusion that makes your car appear to be going downhill when it is in fact going up.

Culzean Castle and Country Park (castle open daily, 1st April–31 Oct: park open all year: adm) overlooks Culzean Bay less than four miles south of Dunure. Pronounced 'Culain', the castle was built on top of the cliff in 1777 by Robert Adam, incorporating an ancient tower that was one of the many Kennedy strongholds guarding the coast. Built with an eye to grandeur rather than defence, this sumptuous mansion is full of architectural marvels that dazzle rather than soothe. There is the Round Drawing Room with a specially woven carpet, an Oval Staircase under a great glass dome, and a profusion of Adam mouldings that make you feel you are encased in Wedgwood china. When Culzean was given over to the National Trust for Scotland in 1945, it was with the condition that an apartment be set aside for anyone whom Scotland might wish to honour. The first tenant for life was General Eisenhower.

The Country Park was created in 1969, the first in Scotland, with a Visitor Centre in the Adam farm buildings. An audio-visual show gives information about Culzean and there are exhibitions, a shop and a restaurant. The terraced gardens, with castellated walls enclosing a sunken fountain, are crammed with rare shrubs, palm trees, swathes of riotous colour and wafts of heady scent. There is also a camellia house and orangery. Guided walks throughout the 565 acres of lovely grounds include a swan pond, aviary and deer park. Culzean is a day out in itself.

Crossraguel Abbey (open daily except closed Thurs and Fri, Oct–March: adm), remote, in sweeping fields, is a couple of miles back towards the coast on the A77. Founded in 1244, it resisted the dissolution of the monasteries until, in 1592, the Reformation took its toll. It is a scattered ruin, parts of it more intact than most, giving a good idea of monastic life in those days. The 16th-century turreted gatehouse is particularly well-preserved.

Kirkoswald is another step on the Burns Trail, two miles on towards the coast on the same road. Burns went to school here and bewailed 'a charming filette who lived next door to the school and overset my Trigonometry and set me off on a tangent from the sphere of my studies.' The poet learnt to drink here, with John Davidson, the village cobbler, immortalized as 'Souter Johnnie', in the poem 'Tam o' Shanter'. Tam was Douglas Graham of Shanter Farm, nearby. **Souter Johnnie's Cottage**, owned by the National Trust for Scotland (open daily except Fri, April–Sept: adm), was Davidson's home, a thatched cottage with a cobbler's workshop and Burns memorabilia. Life-sized statues of the Souter, Tam, the innkeeper and his wife are in the restored ale-house in the cottage garden. Both Davidson and Graham are buried in the churchyard.

Turnberry is about three miles south of Culzean on the coast road. The castle is a scrap of a ruin on a cliff-top by the lighthouse, which stands on what was the castle's court yard. There are some who claim that Turnberry, rather than Lochmaben, was the birth place of King Robert Bruce, and if this is so, he grew up with glorious views to inspire him. The castle was brought into the Bruce family by his mother, Margaret, and certainly Robert's supporters used to meet here, to plot his accession to the throne.

More recently, Turnberry is internationally known as a golf centre, with two excellent courses and a huge hotel. It is incredible, looking at the velvet sward today, to think that these golf courses were surfaced with tarmac and used as an airfield during the war, while the hotel was requisitioned as a hospital.

Girvan, about six miles south of Turnberry, is another typical Ayrshire seaside holiday resort, with good sandy beaches, golf courses, a harbour where pleasure-boats mingle with fishing trawlers, and easy access to the lovely Galloway Forest Park to the east and south (see 'Dumfries and Galloway', p. 125). They have a Folk Festival in May, a Civic Week in June, and an Easter Cycle Race. **Knockcushan** is an attractive public garden with an aviary, above the harbour. There used to be a hill fort here, and a stone commemorates the granting of a charter by Robert Bruce, who administered justice from this hill.

Penkill Castle, four miles east of Girvan on B734, an imposing 15th-century castle, was the home of the artist and poet, William Bell Scott, 1811–90, and a favourite haunt of his fellow pre-Raphaelites, including William Morris and Dante Rossetti, who wrote some of his poems here. There is fine 17th- and 18th-century furniture as well as tapestries and paintings. They do conducted tours and buffet lunches by arrangement, tel Old Dailly 261. (Ask about 'The Curse of Penkill'!)

Ailsa Craig

Boats run from Girvan to Ailsa Craig, the 1114 ft-high volcanic lump rearing from the sea, 10 miles due west and known as Paddy's Milestone because it lies half-way between Glasgow and Belfast. At low tide it is possible to walk the two-mile circumference of the rock. From the top there are lovely, if rather windy, views over to Arran and Kintyre, and back to the mainland. Ailsa Craig comes from the Gaelic for fairy rock, an incongruous name for the place where miscreant monks were once sent to cool off, and where persecuted Catholics took refuge during the Reformation. It is now a bird sanctuary, with gannets and puffins among its avian population: the guano smells quite powerful on a warm day. A special granite used for making curling stones was once quarried from Ailsa Craig.

Carleton Castle (always accessible: free), five miles south of Girvan, was one of the chain of watchtowers built by the powerful Kennedy family to defend this part of the coast. A ballad tells of Sir John Cathcart of Carleton, who lived in the castle and pushed seven rich wives, in turn, to their deaths over the cliff. When it came to Mary Cullean, his eighth wife, he noticed she was wearing a sumptuous dress. He ordered her to remove it; coyly, she asked him to hide his eyes. When he obliged she gave him a shove and over he went.

Bennane Head a few miles further south gives magnificent views as far as Turnberry, Ailsa Craig, the Mull of Kintyre and sometimes even Ireland. On the shore below lies ghastly **Sawney Bean's Cave**. Access is extremely difficult and only the very sure-footed should attempt to visit this macabre spot, the alleged hide-out of Sawney Bean. In the 16th century it is said that a number of wealthy travellers, known to have passed through this area, vanished without trace. Suspicion and local gossip led the authorities to this cave where they discovered Sawney Bean and his large, incestuously-bred family, with an enormous quantity of human bones. Sawney and his ghoulish tribe had been living off the flesh, and the gold, of their unfortunate victims for years. Some accounts of the discovery of the cave describe a gruesome array of 'joints' pickled in brine or hanging from the roof like hams in a farmhouse kitchen. Sawney Bean and his family were taken to Edinburgh and executed.

Ballantrae, three miles south, was immortalized by Robert Louis Stevenson and twice tricked by literature. Burns wrote a lovely song about the Stinchar valley, which carried the River Stinchar into the sea at Ballantrae, but fastidious editors changed it to: 'Beyond yon hill where Lugar flows', depriving Ballantrae of its rightful acclaim. Then Stevenson was attracted to the name of the place, and used it for his novel *The Master of Ballantrae*, but set the story further south in the Stewartry of Kirkcudbright.

Carrick Forest starts eight miles due east of Girvan. Wild, hilly, country, studded with lochs and forests, offers a welcome respite from holiday crowds and fruit machines. **Loch Doon**, on the eastern edge of the forest, marks the border with Dumfries and Galloway. The castle on the southwest shore once stood on an island in the loch. When the Hydroelectric Board raised the level of the water, the ruined castle was dismantled and re-built on its present site. It used to be called Balliol Castle and was owned by King John Balliol, the ineffectual 'Toom Tabard'.

Paisley

West of Glasgow on the A737, Paisley's suburbs merge with those of the city. This historic town gave its name to an internationally acclaimed design of shawl. Soldiers returning from India at the end of the 18th century brought with them the shawls they had bought in Kashmir. The people of the town adapted these and created the distinctive Paisley design, based on segments of pine cones, which were Kashmiri in origin. The town has its annual Festival in May.

Paisley Abbey was founded in 1171 for Cluniac monks and was almost completely destroyed by Edward I. Rebuilt after Bannockburn, its tower collapsed in 1553, wrecking the nave, and it remained in this state for many years. The present restoration, which includes work by Robert Lorimer, is the parish church, a dignified building, austere but serene. **The Barochan Cross** in the abbey is a weathered 10th-century Celtic cross that once stood on a hillock overlooking Port Glasgow. The tombs of several of the Bruces are in the choir, under a stone-vaulted ceiling, and there is a charming little chapel dedicated to St Mirin, a 6th-century saint who was adopted as Paisley's patron saint.

Paisley Museum and Art Gallery (open daily except Sun: free) has among its many interesting exhibits a fascinating display of at least 500 Paisley shawls with their looms and design patterns. The **Sma' Shot Cottages**, in George Place (open daily May–Sept: free), are traditional 19th-century millworkers' two-storey houses with iron stairways, displaying social conditions in Victorian times. **Coats Observatory** in Oakshaw Street (open daily except Sundays: free) has had a continuous tradition of astronomical observation and meteorological recording since it was built in 1882 and is one of the best in the country. The **Lagoon Leisure Centre** has all kinds of swimming attractions.

The Clyde Valley

The A724/72 south from Glasgow follows the Clyde Valley, once renowned for orchards cultivated by the Romans, now rather overshadowed by suburban developments.

Bothwell Castle, seven miles southeast of the city on the A74 (open daily except closed Thurs afternoons and Fri, Oct–March: adm), is an impressive red sandstone castle on the banks of the Clyde, once the largest and finest stone castle in Scotland. Dating from the 13th century and rebuilt in the 15th century, it was a stronghold of the powerful Black Douglases.

The David Livingstone Centre is just beyond Bothwell, at Blantyre (open daily: adm). Here, on the banks of the Clyde, was the birthplace of the famous explorer and missionary in 1813. (He died in 1873, looking for the source of the Nile.) The 'single-end' tenement where he was born, and the cotton mill where he worked, give fascinating details of his life and the social conditions of the day. There is an Africa Pavilion, built in the shape of a cluster of rural African huts, illustrating African life today.

Hamilton, the former county town of Lanarkshire, is a busy commercial and administrative centre. Originally called Cadzow, it was here that St Mungo converted King Rederech of Strathclyde to Christianity in 568. David I made the town a Royal Barony in the 12th century and this was superseded by a charter from James II, changing the name to Hamilton in recognition of the great landowning family in the area. In 1570 the town was sacked as reprisal for the Hamiltons' loyalty to Mary, Queen of Scots. Between 1770 and 1870 the population rose by 800 per cent, due to cotton and coal. By 1880, more than half Scotland's coal was produced in this area.

Hamilton Museum in Muir Street (open Mon–Sat: free), dates from the 17th century and was once the Hamilton Arms Coaching Inn. It houses a transport museum and the 18th-century Assembly Room complete with original plasterwork and musicians' gallery. There are history displays, a Victorian kitchen, a natural history section and displays of local industry. **The Cameronians Regimental Museum**, in Mote Hill off Muir Street (open daily except Thurs and Sun: free), displays uniforms, medals, banners and documents of this famous Covenanting regiment.

Alexander, 10th Duke of Hamilton, known as Il Magnifico, built the domed **Hamilton Mausoleum** in Strathclyde Park behind the Museum, very prominent from the A74. In 1852, he had his ancestors removed from the graveyard of the old Collegiate Church and placed in the Mausoleum. He installed an Egyptian sarcophagus on a marble pillar for himself but was worried that it would be too small to contain him. The story is told of his testy order, as he lay dying, to 'double me up; double me up', and it is even said that his feet had to be amputated to get him into the coffin. (The bodies were moved in 1921.) The chapel was never used as a place of worship, owing to a disconcerting echo, lasting 15 seconds. The Park has a 200-acre loch used for watersports, and nature trails and a Roman Bathhouse.

Chatelherault is just beyond the southern outskirts of Hamilton on the A74 (open daily: adm). This magnificent hunting lodge was built by William Adam in 1732 for the Duke of Hamilton, who had also the title Duke of Chatelherault. The buildings, recently restored, include gardeners' and keepers' bothies, stables, kennels, banqueting hall, the Duke's apartments and kitchens (the head keeper had the use of the Duke's apartments when he was away). The mansion and part of the 18th-century park around Hamilton Palace, now demolished, were sold to the Scottish Office to help pay death duties. The gardens are in the process of being restored to their former grandeur. It is said the the oaks in the park were planted by David I. The Visitor Centre illustrates the 18th-century characters who helped build Chatelherault. The Banqueting Hall and kitchens are available for hire for weddings, concerts, conferences, etc.

Craignethan Castle

Craignethan Castle (open daily: adm) is about nine miles southeast of Hamilton on the A72, at Crossford, reached across an unfenced green plateau where shaggy cattle roam free among grotesquely gnarled old thorn trees. The castle materializes abruptly, on a spur between the deeply eroded beds of the Water of Nethan and the Craignethan Burn. This 16th-century stronghold was destroyed after Mary, Queen of Scots, was hounded from her throne, because the Hamilton family who owned it had been loyal supporters of her cause. The well-preserved ruin has a keep, passages, basement and well, round an open courtyard. In 1962, excavations unearthed a rare 'caponier'. Buried for nearly 400 years, this dank, stone-roofed vault was built across the floor of a dry moat to protect and conceal 'handgunners' defending the castle. It still contained bones of cattle, sheep, rabbits and chickens from the hasty meals of those 16th-century gunners.

Although he himself denied it, Craignethan is believed to have been the inspiration for Tillietudlem Castle, in Walter Scott's stirring Covenanter novel, *Old Mortality*, home of the heroine Edith. A nearby halt on the long-disused branch railway was called Tillie-tudlem, in its honour.

Lanark

Lanark is less than 14 miles southeast of Hamilton, just after the junction of the A72/73, on a plateau high above the upper reaches of the Clyde. The agricultural market centre for the area, it could be just another main-road town, with the busy A72 carrying heavy traffic right through its centre. A closer look reveals a strong individual character inviting further exploration.

The main street is so broad that a long central flower bed, studded with chain-linked pillars, divides it into a dual carriageway. It slopes down between cheerfully painted houses and shop fronts, apparently oblivious of the ceaseless flow of traffic, to the 18th-century parish church standing like a bulwark at the bottom. Don't let the person in the car behind prevent you from stopping here to inspect the statue of William Wallace in a canopied niche in the face of the tall, colour-washed church tower. It is an endearing statue: a huge, genial, Father Christmas-like figure who seems to be embarrassed by his bare, fat knees. He certainly doesn't look like the man who roused the Scots to rebellion and helped them to struggle free from despair in 1297. The statue was presented to the town in 1822 by its sculptor, Robert Forrest, who, it is said, was self-taught. This is easy to believe. William Wallace lived in Lanark and, when the English murdered his wife (or mistress) Marion Bradfute, it was here that he struck the first blow for Scottish independence. Every June Lanark celebrates Lanimer Day, which coincides with the Riding of the Marches.

New Lanark

It would be easy to dash through Lanark and miss New Lanark, a delightful backwater a mile to the south. Stop at the top, as the narrow road takes a final hairpin bend before descending into New Lanark. The view down over the village to the distant Falls of Clyde belongs to a painting by Turner. A mist of spray rises from the trees above a glint of foaming water and if the sun is shining and it happens to be autumn, there are few more breath-catching views in this part of Scotland. New Lanark was built in 1784 as a model cotton manufacturing village by a rich industrialist, David Dale and his partner Richard Arkwright. Dale's son-in-law, Robert Owen became manager of the estate in 1800 and instituted some very radical innovations, including the founding of the first infant school in Britain. Owen's reforms for better working conditions and 'villages of unity' were the forerunners of today's cooperative societies.

Today, New Lanark is a monument to those days of reform. (Visitors Centre open daily: adm.) The old buildings have been brought back to life, austere but not ugly, uncluttered by architectural adornment, rising tall and plain from the street, some with outside stairways, overlooking the river. The old bell that summoned the people to work or to pray still hangs high in its belfry. There are exhibitions illustrating the social history of this classic industrial village.

Falls of Clyde Nature Reserve can be reached on foot from the far end of New Lanark. A fenced path follows the Clyde a couple of miles upstream past the Falls of Corra Linn to those of Bonnington Linn. The river tumbles over treacherous black slabs of granite, overhung by pines, oaks and birches, spray rising like smoke. This stretch of the river, known as the Falls of Clyde and beloved of many romantic artists, runs through Corehouse Nature Reserve. On the way is **Wallace's Tower**, or Corra Castle, far too dangerous to enter but stirring to the imagination. It clings to a rock pinnacle high above Corra Linn, its walls rising directly from the edge of the sheer cliff. Although this reach of the Clyde is harnessed to serve the hydro-electric power stations and is thus robbed of much of its full splendour, enough water remains to provide salmon with access to their spawning grounds up-river and to give dramatic effects as it pours over gigantic layered slabs of granite. Corra Linn drops 86 ft in a series of steps, to a dark still lagoon below, set in an amphitheatre of rock, and hung with damp vegetation and precariously rooted trees. **Bonnington Linn** is about a mile further on, with two branches of the river descending round a rock island.

Leadhills

Leadhills is 18 miles due south of Lanark as the crow flies. A pink road straggles over humpbacked bridges between dry-stone walls with views across farmland and smooth-turfed hills. Forest and pasture create a patchwork on the hillsides, all shades of green and brown and sepia, dotted with rural cottages, rising to desolate moor and peat bogs where the farms are linked by single telephone wires. High on this lonely moorland, Leadhills is second only to nearby Wanlockhead (p. 122), as Scotland's highest village. In the small, windswept cemetery above the tiny village lie the remains of John Taylor who died at the age of 137, having worked for more than 100 years in the lead mills, which doesn't say much for the toxic effects of lead, proclaimed by doom-merchants today.

Allan Ramsay, the 17th-century poet, was born here, surrounded by hills alive with the ghosts of Covenanters who used their shelter for holding conventicles.

Biggar

Biggar, 10 miles southeast of Lanark on the A72, close to the Borders Region, is a typical lowland market town, the main road running through its centre widening to form a market place. **Cadgers Brig** at the bottom of the town is the bridge where William Wallace is said to have crossed the burn dressed as a *cadger* (pedlar), on a spying mission. The bridge is more likely to have been named after the cadgers who crossed it on market days. Biggar has several good museums.

Moat Park Heritage Centre, in the town centre (open daily: adm), is in a former church, adapted to show the history of the Upper Clyde and Tweed Valleys, from the days of volcanoes and glaciers 6000 years ago, to the present. Among a collection of embroidery is the largest known patchwork quilt from the mid-19th century.

The Gladstone Court Museum (open daily, Easter–31 Oct: adm) is a reproduction of a Victorian Street complete with grocer, photographer, dressmaker, bank, school, library, ironmonger, chemist, china merchant, etc. It is an imaginative museum to enchant anyone who once enjoyed 'playing shop'.

Greenhill Covenanters House at Burn Braes (open Easter, and daily, mid-May–mid-Oct: adm), is a 17th-century farmhouse with strong Covenanting connections. It contains furniture and relics from those times, as well as a collection of dolls, rare breeds of animals and poultry and an audio-visual programme.

Biggar also has the oldest surviving rural gasworks in Britain, built in 1839 and now a museum, only open in July and August. **Biggar Puppet Theatre** (open daily except Tues, March–mid-Jan: adm) is a complete Victorian puppet theatre in miniature. As well as puppet plays, there are guided tours, an exhibition, tearoom and outdoor Victorian games.

Tinto Hill, 2220 ft, is six miles southwest of Biggar, west of the A73 and dominates the landscape for miles. It is a long but not too arduous climb through scrée and heather and the views from the top are terrific. Keen eyes on a clear day will see 18 counties plus peaks in Cumberland, the tip of Ireland, the Bass Rock, Ailsa Craig, Arran and Jura. Tinto is wrapped in legend: William Wallace camped on the hill with his army in the 13th century, and there is a depression in a boulder at the top called, somewhat doubtfully, **Wallace's Thumbmark**. Tinto is derived from the Gaelic *teinteach* (place of fire) hinting that it may have been one of the sites for the ancient Beltane fire rites, sometimes connected with human sacrifice.

WHERE TO STAY AND EAT

For anyone wishing to stay south of the Clyde, there is a vast choice. The whole region is within easy reach of Glasgow. They all serve meals but the small ones usually close their dining rooms early; it is wise to book in by 6 pm.

Gleddoch House Hotel, Langbank, tel 047 554 711, is a converted family mansion in 250 acres overlooking the Clyde and Loch Lomond Hills and, though expensive, is without doubt the pick of the bunch. It contains many of the original furnishings and pictures which give it the atmosphere of a private country house. Guests automatically become members of The Gleddoch Club, with free use of the 18-hole golf course, squash courts, snooker room and sauna. There is also riding. The food is renowned, the service excellent, and dogs are allowed in the bedrooms. Also expensive, **Manor Park Hotel**, Skelmorlie, tel 0475 520832 stands on a hill overlooking magnificent views of gardens, hills and sea lochs on the Clyde coast. It is very comfortable, the food and service are good and there are even peacocks in the grounds. Slightly cheaper, **Chapeltoun House Hotel** at Stewarton, three miles off the A77 on B769, tel 0560 82696, was built in 1900 as a family house and has a nice rambling feeling. There are 20 acres of garden with views across Ayrshire countryside. Friendly, efficient staff and excellent food and wine. Golfers have to say a prayer to their bank manager and go to **Turnberry Hotel**, tel 0655 31000. (Single B&B a mere £145). This vast golfing mecca on the coast, has everything the punter could possibly ask for. Modest in comparison, but not cheap, **Montgreenan Mansion House Hotel**, Kilwinning, tel 0294 57733, is a country house in 45 acres near a championship golf course. For those who like to know exactly what they are going to, the **Hospitality Inn** at Irvine, tel 0294 74272, is predictable, and expensive. Ultra modern outside, the interior has arches and rattan, palms and bold carpets and a stifling heating system. Some of the suites open on to an amazing tropical lagoon with lush jungle, rocks, waterfalls, bridges and hot air.

Elderslie Hotel, John Street, Largs, tel 0475 086460, looks across to Cumbrae and Arran, is cheap and nicely old fashioned. Also cheap with a good atmosphere, **Burns Monument Hotel**, Alloway, tel 0292 42466, is by the river Doon, opposite Burns Monument, its floodlit garden running back to the Brig o' Doon. Another cheap one is **Finlayson Arms Hotel**, Coylton, tel 0292 570298, a cosy country pub/hotel. **Kings Arms Hotel**, Dalrymple Street, in the middle of Girvan, tel 0465 3322, has nothing much to recommend it except that it is cheap and John Keats wrote 'A Tribute to Ailsa Craig' here, in the summer of 1818, three years before his death. Other bargains include **Jolly Shepherd Hotel**, Barr, near Girvan, tel 0465 86 233, a friendly little place with only five bedrooms. **Kings Arms**, also in Barr, tel 046 586 230, is much the same, a small, unpretentious, whitewashed inn. Burns fans should go to **Poosie Nansies Inn,** in Mauchline, tel 0290 50316. Echoing with memories, if not with mod cons, it is dirt cheap. Also in Mauchline, **Loudoun Arms**, tel 0290 51011, is another bargain and you get a generous breakfast served by an easy-going Irish host in an upstairs room full of Burns murals.

There are literally hundreds more, most of which feature in the relevant tourist brochures with details and pictures.

North of the Clyde

There is nothing much to detain you in Strathkelvin, just across the Clyde. Apart from the Campsie Fells, a few parks and gardens, a scrap of the Antonine Wall on Bar Hill at Twechar, and the Forth Clyde Canal, there are mainly uninspiring dormitory towns. Take the Erskine Toll Bridge over the river, off the M8, a magnificent sweep of modern engineering replacing a tiny cable-ferry.

The Heatherbank Museum of Social Work (open all year by appointment, tel 041 956 2687: free) is about four miles northeast of the bridge on the A809. It is the only museum of its kind in the world, with over 2500 slides of life in the 19th and early 20th centuries and a 5000-volume reference library.

Some say St Patrick was born at **Kilpatrick** a couple of miles west of the Erskine Bridge—a claim made by many other places on this coast and down as far as Cumbria. Certainly he was captured near here in the 4th century and deported to Ireland as a slave. *Kil* means burial place, and Patrick was buried in Ireland. True or false, the Kilpatrick Hills to the north are attractive moorland with rivers and reservoirs.

Dumbarton

Dumbarton is a large industrial town, about three miles west of the Erskine Bridge. Whisky has taken over in importance from the shipbuilding that once flourished on the water-front. The famous clipper, *Cutty Sark*, was built in Dumbarton in 1869, named after the 'short shirts' seen by Tam o' Shanter when he watched the witches' orgy.

Dumbarton Castle (open daily: adm) stands high in a cleft in Dumbarton Rock overlooking the Clyde, a lump of volcanic basalt shaped like Gibraltar, site of a fortress since pre-historic times. The name is derived from Dun Bretane (Hill of the Britons). From about the 5th century, this fortress rock was the centre of the kingdom of Strathclyde. It was a royal castle in the Middle Ages, later a barracks and now a museum. Mary, Queen of Scots sailed to France from here in 1548, aged five, going to what was possibly the only happy period in her tragic life.

A wall protects the front, shaped like the prow of a ship, with turret and guns. Up the steps, Wallace's Gatehouse is where William Wallace was imprisoned before being taken to his trial and barbaric execution in London in 1305. It was Sir John Monteith, Governor of Dumbarton Castle at the time, who finally betrayed Wallace, that brave rebel who struck such a memorable blow for Scottish independence.

The town of Dumbarton is modern, but there are a few old buildings in it, particularly 'Greit House', built in 1623, once the home of the Duke of Argyll and the tower arch of the collegiate church of St Mary, founded by the Duchess of Albany in 1454.

The Scottish Maritime Museum's **Denny Experiment Tank** is in Castle Street (open all year, Mon–Fri: adm), the oldest surviving experimental tank in the world, showing how wax and wooden scale models were used to test for such things as stability and resistance. The first tank of its kind, it was built in 1882 by William Denny and used for over 100 years.

Loch Lomond

Oh, ye'll take the high road,
An' I'll take the low road,
An' I'll be in Scotland afore ye,
But me an' my true love will never meeet again
On the bonnie, bonnie banks o' Loch Lomond.

There is a choice of two routes north from Dumbarton, one being West Loch Lomond-side on the A82. (The boundary with Central Region goes up the middle of the loch.) A fast new road gives good views across the loch with its islands and anchorages, to the hills on the far side. This is particularly beautiful in the early morning when there is no other traffic and mist clings to the glassy water as the sun rises over Ben Lomond. Bluebells carpet the ground under oak woods, serenaded by bird song. The loch is 24 miles from north to south, its southern end as much as five miles wide, narrowing to a long, thin neck in the north. The largest inland loch in Scotland, Loch Lomond is one of the most beautiful, though being so accessible it is also one of the most popular.

The song, 'Loch Lomond' was composed in Carlisle jail by Donald MacDonald of Keppoch, a Jacobite awaiting a trial that ended in brutal death after Culloden. The English were capricious in their distribution of justice: some prisoners were arbitrarily sent to the gallows, others were set free and told to walk home. MacDonald, fairly sure of his fate, wrote that his spirit would get back to Scotland on the low road of death faster than his living companions on the high road.

Balloch, at the south end of the loch, is a popular holiday resort, not for those in search of peace and solitude.

A number of cruise boats operate on the loch. *Countess Fiona* sails from Balloch to Inversnaid, calling at Balmaha, Luss, Rowardennan and Tarbet, from Easter to October. The route passes the islands scattered over the south end of the loch. Small and serene-looking, these are steeped in history. **Inch Cailleach** (Island of the Old Women) was the burial place of the fierce MacGregor clan. It belongs to the Nature Conservancy Council and has trails and woodland paths. Ruined **Lennox Castle**, on Inch Murrin (Isle of Spears) was where the Duchess of Albany retired, after James I had slaughtered her husband, sons and father in 1425 (not without cause, see History, p. 56). No doubt the Duchess turns in her grave when she looks down, or up, and sees the hotel, restaurant and bar complex that has been built on her sanctuary.

For those who prefer to be at the helm there are plenty of places to launch small boats There are also a number of boats for hire from the many marinas, holiday parks and water-sport centres lining the shore.

Drymen is an attractive little village about eight miles north east of Balloch.

Helensburgh

The other route north from Dumbarton is the A814 via Helensburgh and Loch Long. This route is narrow and twisting in some parts, clinging to the water most of the way and keeping company with the railway.

Helensburgh, at the mouth of the Gare Loch, eight miles northwest of Dumbarton, is a residential resort built on a grid of wide, peaceful streets, the town sloping up from the Clyde with an air of dignified respectability. Ferries cross the river to Gourock and this is sailing territory, the water usually speckled with craft of all sizes. There are good shops, plenty of places to stay and lovely views across the Clyde. Helensburgh was the birthplace of John Logie Baird who invented television.

Hill House, in Upper Colquhoun Street (open daily: adm), was designed by Charles Rennie Mackintosh (see pp. 252–3) for the publisher, W. W. Blackie, in 1902 and is his finest domestic work demonstrating his flair for simplicity of line. Owned by the National Trust for Scotland, in a lovely position overlooking the Clyde, its gardens are being restored to Mackintosh's original design. There is an audio-visual programme on the life of the architect.

Glen Fruin, within easy walking distance of Helensburgh is a wonderful place to roam on a good day, surrounded by grand beauty and solitude, serenaded by the clatter of many streams flowing down from the hills into the valley. Climb **Ben Chaorach** and look back down into the glen. Perhaps you will hear the echo of war cries and sad pleadings for mercy. In 1603 there was an horrific battle between the Colquhouns (pronounced Ka'hoon) and the MacGregors, arising from boundary disputes and accusations of cattle pilfering. The MacGregors slew not only the Colquhoun men, and their families who had been shut away in a barn for safety, but also a party of schoolboys who had been taken along to watch the fun. The clan was proscribed, in punishment.

The less bloodthirsty visitor may prefer to go a little further on to **Rhu**, a mile west of Helensburgh and another boating mecca, and enjoy the woodland and lovely shrubs at **Glenarn Gardens** (open in the summer: adm).

The two routes meet at Tarbet where the A82 goes north past the massive hulk of **Ben Vorlich** into Central Region. The Strathclyde route goes west to the Cowal Peninsula, through Glen Croe on the A83.

WHERE TO STAY AND EAT

Ardlui Hotel, tel 03014 243, is a small country hotel on the northern tip of Loch Lomond, with its own mooring facilites. It is a delightful place, very friendly, and moderately priced. **The Inverbeg Inn** at Luss, tel 0436 86678, also overlooks Loch Lomond and runs a fleet of self-drive motor cruisers, with sleeping accommodation for from two to 12 people. Prices on request. **Rosslea Hall Hotel**, Rhu, tel 0436 820684, is in pleasant grounds overlooking the Gare Loch and the Firth of Clyde. Moderately priced, it has good food and wine, pony trekking from the hotel and a free dram on arrival. **Tarbet Hotel**, tel 03012 228, is a Scottish baronial-style mansion overlooking Loch Lomond, with a comfortable modern interior, friendly staff and reasonable food. It is cheap, and what is lacking in elegance is made up for by the position. **Duck Bay Hotel and Marina** on Loch Lomond, tel 0389 52789 is a lively spot for boating people and extroverts, not too expensive. **Buchanan Highland Hotel** in Drymen, tel 0360 60588, is an excellent, expensive-ish place with good food. Also in Drymen and much cheaper, **Salmon Leap Inn**, dating from 1759, is a lively, friendly place with good bar meals.

The Cowal Peninsula

The Cowal Peninsula is very beautiful, attracting climbers, sailors and holidaymakers in large numbers in the summer. The drive west from Tarbet through Glen Croe on the A83 is spectacular. The distinctive shape of **The Cobbler**, 2891 ft, looms threateningly to the north of the road as it twists and climbs up the shoulder of **Beinn Ime** to the **Rest and Be Thankful**—which speaks for itself. The views from the car park here are worth stopping for. A stone commemorates the completion of this military road in 1750, part of the network constructed to try to keep order in the Highlands after the Jacobite risings. Known as the **Arrochar Alps**, the hills round here offer excellent climbing for experts. Apart from The Cobbler and Beinn Ime, there are Beinn Narnain, Ben Vane and Ben Vorlich, marching away to the northeast, all 'Munros' over 3000 ft. Amateurs should read the advice to climbers on p. 16.

The Cowal Peninsula stretches to the south, part of Argyll's misshapen lobster claw, washed on either side by Loch Long and Loch Fyne. **Carrick Castle** is a 14th-century ruin on a promontory in fjord-like Loch Goil. The Glen Mhoir approach down the B828 from the Rest and be Thankful is dramatic, the road dropping from 1000 ft to sea level in only three miles. This was where the Argylls kept their documents and their prisoners. A remote enough place in those days, the great shell of the keep is still impressive, even with its rash of water-sport enthusiasts. The road ends here but you can just see where the loch joins up with Loch Long, to the southeast. The area within the triangle formed by Rest and be Thankful, Loch Long and Loch Goil is known as **Argyll's Bowling Green**. A more unlikely name would be hard to find: measuring eight miles by four, it includes 10 major summits. Wild and beautiful, it is only accessible on foot. Fantastic views can be had from the top of any of the hills: a glorious jigsaw of moor and hill, each irregular piece linked by a gleaming slither of water. Time is the only barrier to exploring this peninsula properly—on foot.

The motorist must retrack to where the road branches, three miles north of Lochgoilhead.

The award-winning **European Sheep and Wool Centre**, at Lochgoilhead, (open daily, Apr–Oct: adm), is the first of its kind in Europe. There are 19 different breeds of sheep, and you can watch live demonstrations of shearing and a shepherd and his dog working the sheep (three shows daily, at 11 am, 1 and 3 pm: Sat by prior arrangement only). A shop sells masses of woollen products and there is a coffee shop. Adjacent, is **Drimsynie Leisure Complex**, with a heated swimming pool, jacuzzi, sauna, 9-hole golf course and a restaurant. In the winter (Nov–Mar), Drimsynie is converted into a 4-lane **Curling Rink**.

The B839 then runs northwest through **Hell's Glen**, a steep hanging valley with a marvellous view over Loch Fyne at the far end.

Loch Fyne is renowned for its sea fishing and the Loch Fyne oyster. A string of delightful villages line the loch: Cairndow, St Catherines and Strachur. This whole area, much of which is covered by the Argyll Forest Park, is a kaleidoscope of indescribable scenery.

From Strachur, the A815 runs south down forest-fringed Loch Eck. Branch left at the Whistlefield Hotel and take the long way round, down Glen Finart—more lovely views—to **Ardentinny**, a picturesque village with a sandy beach washed by Loch Long. The road hugs the shore to Strone Point and back northwest along Holy Loch. Now home of a naval base, the loch is said to have been so named when a ship, carrying earth from the Holy Land intended as suitably sacred foundations for Glasgow Cathedral, foundered in a storm as it tried to get round the corner into the sheltered Clyde and finished up in this appendix of the mighty river.

Younger Botanic Garden (open daily, April–Oct: adm) is barely two miles north of the head of the loch. In May and June the gardens blaze with yellow, orange, flame and crimson azaleas, and rhododendrons ranging from white to deep maroon. There is a splendid avenue of sequoias (Giant Californian Wellingtonias).

Dunoon

Dunoon is five miles south of the junction with the A815 and is the chief resort on the Cowal Peninsula. It was just a village until early in the 19th century, when rich merchants built villas and developed it into a resort. The long, low sprawl of the town, washed by the Firth of Clyde, is backed by a crescent of blue-green tree-covered hills. Two ferry companies operate a service across the Clyde between Gourock and Dunoon—a 20-minute crossing. Dunoon is an ideal family holiday centre with any amount of places to stay, to suit all pockets, with a huge choice of things to do, on the threshold of some of the finest walking and climbing country that anyone could hope for. It is also at the heart of idyllic sailing water. For those who prefer to let someone else take the helm, there are cruises on the Firth of Clyde in the summer.

The Cowal Highland Gathering is one of the town's highlights of the year, on the last Friday and Saturday in August. More than 150 pipe bands compete, drawing huge, appreciative crowds. It also stages World Highland Dancing Championships.

Dunoon Castle, of which you can now see only a trace, dates from the 13th century. It was built on the site of an earlier fort, with a colourful history that kept it bouncing back and forth between English and Scottish hands like so many of the strongholds of Scotland. Edward I took it; Robert Bruce re-took it; then Edward Balliol, who was ousted by Robert II. In 1471 the Earls of Argyll were made Honorary Keepers by James III, on condition that they paid the crown a fee of a red rose, whenever demanded. When Queen Elizabeth II visited Dunoon in 1958 she was presented with a red rose without having to demand it.

An attractive drive south from Dunoon goes down to Toward Point with a lighthouse on the tip. The track beyond goes only halfway up the east side of Loch Striven and then stops.

Lazaretto Point, north of Dunoon on the A815, beyond Hunter's Quay, was the quarantine station for servicemen fighting in the Napoleonic Wars. It is hard to feel sorry for these men if you look out at the views they had as they waited for the development of some rare foreign disease.

To explore the rest of the peninsula, the B836 runs west from the head of Holy Loch to the head of Loch Striven, through more lovely scenery to the A886. Here turn left and take the new road down the east side of Loch Riddon to Colintraive, with spectacular views across to Tighnaburaich and the Kyles of Bute. A car ferry runs from Colintraive to Bute (see Islands of Strathclyde, pp. 226–8). The new road then peters out but it is possible to get on down to Strone Point and some way up the west shore of Loch Striven.

Back up to the head of Loch Riddon on the A886, take the A8003 down the west side, a staggering new road, high above the Kyles of Bute with panoramic views in all directions. **Tighnabruaich** (house on the hill) and **Kames** are two popular resorts in a splendid position looking across the Kyles to Bute. A B road runs on down to Ardlamont Point, the most southern tip of the Cowal Peninsula, rising to 205 ft. The waters of Loch Fyne, Kyles of Bute, Sound of Bute and Kilbrannan Sound meet at the foot of the headland.

From Ardlamont, go north about four miles to Millhouse and then west (left), a couple of miles to **Portavadie**. With deep water off-shore, this area was chosen as an oil-platform construction site and £14 million was spent on ground preparation. An enormous dry dock was built. But no one seemed to want any oil-platforms and the place stood unused. Eventually, the sea-wall was breached, the dock flooded and the £14 million washed away.

Back to Millhouse, take the B8000 north, through Kilfinan, a dear little hamlet where the hotel has 16th-century vaults and the church stands on a Celtic site. **Otter Ferry**, 3 miles to the north, takes its name from the Gaelic *oiter* (sandbank): yachtsmen beware. The sandbank sticks out more than a mile into Loch Fyne, prominent at low tide but easy to trip up on when submerged by the flood tide. The Norsemen who fought in the Battle of Glendaruel in 1100 beached their long-ships side by side on the sand bar, clambered ashore and marched over the pass into Glendaruel five miles to the east. They were slaughtered by the Scots, who threw their bodies into the river: *ruel* is a corruption of the Gaelic for 'blood flowed'.

The B8000 hugs Loch Fyne, and joins the A886, back up to the head of the Loch.

WHERE TO STAY AND EAT

The choice is unlimited, the standard mainly good and with so much coast line, many of the hotels command glorious views.

Dunoon has a wide choice, all typical resort hotels. **Esplanade Hotel**, tel 0369 4070, overlooks the traffic-free West Bay Promenade, a few minutes' walk from the pier. This is a cheap, friendly, jovial hotel for the gregarious with a Victor Sylvester atmosphere. **Ardfillayne Hotel**, West Bay, tel 0369 2267, looks over the Firth of Clyde, is moderately priced and has an excellent reputation for service, comfort and food. **Abbeyhill Hotel,** Dhailling Road, tel 0369 2204, has a good view overlooking East Bay Promenade, is cheap, comfortable and well run. Also cheap, **Rosscairn Hotel**, Hunter Street, tel 0369 4344, is in a quiet, residential area next to the 18-hole Cowal Golf Club, and offers free golf in March, April and October. **Hafton Country Club, Hotel and Lodges**, Hunter's Quay, tel 0369 6205, is an excellent base for a moderately priced family holiday, with both baronial-style hotel accommodation and self-catering chalets. Prices include club membership for all the facilities of this lochside complex: swimming pool, snooker and games room, video cinema and video games, table tennis, tennis, putting. For an extra fee, golfers get unlimited play over Cowal Golf Course.

Moderately priced, with special packages, **Ardentinny Hotel**, tel 0369 81 209/275, is in an idyllic position, right on the clear blue-green waters of Loch Long, surrounded by rhododendrons and glorious scenery. Boats can be hired from the hotel and package holidays include free ferry tickets, and entry to the Younger Botanic Garden and Inveraray Castle. The food is first class. **Drimsynie House Hotel and Leisure Complex**, Lochgoilhead, tel 03013 247/284, is a mock castellated mansion, with cardboard-fort battlements and turrets and it's cheap. It stands in wooded grounds overlooking fjord-like Loch Goil and has a 9-hole golf course around the head of the loch. Heated swimming pool and jacuzzi, good food and a pool room.

Kilfinan Hotel is a moderately priced, old coaching inn in a rural hamlet near Loch Fyne. Whitewashed and olde worlde, with 16th-century vaults, it has excellent food and blazing log fires. Among the many hotels overlooking the scenic Kyles of Bute, try moderately priced **Kames Hotel,** tel 0700 811489, on the seafront in Kames. Comfortable, reasonable food and friendly atmosphere.

Mid-Argyll:
Knapdale and Kintyre

This is walking country where spectacular views unfold at every turn of the road and along every path and mountain track, and the best places are often inaccessible except on foot.

Loch Fyne, a long narrow arm of sea, washes the western shore of the Cowal Peninsula. It seems to be eating its way into the Highland scenery—a mixture of hill and forest, in some parts rising steeply from the water, in others rolling back in great sweeps of farmland. At the head of the loch, near Cairndow, look out for the long, white-washed 'Oyster Bar'—a really excellent restaurant with a shop selling a mouth-watering selection of fresh and smoked sea food including oysters from the local oyster beds, mussels, salmon and scampi; also fresh and smoked venison.

At the head of Loch Shira, an appendix off the northwest corner of Loch Fyne, a track leads north up remote Glen Shira to a ruined cottage where Rob Roy hid for some time during one of his adventures. It is eerie to think of the Robin Hood-like outlaw, peering up and down the valley for sight of his enemies, or climbing one of the surrounding hills for a better all-round view.

Inveraray

Inveraray stands on the northwest shore of Loch Fyne, a small, 18th-century town with an air of slightly privileged graciousness. It is a pretty place, curiously un-Scottish, built in a T-shape with the road north passing through an archway and the parish church on a mound, dividing the Main Street. Inveraray was once a small fishing village, always a Campbell of Argyll domain. It was sacked by Montrose in 1644. The present town was the creation of the third Duke of Argyll, in 1743, employing Roger Morris and William Adam. Both of these men died before the work was finished. John Adam, son of William, completed the job with the help of Robert Mylne. Between the lot of them they created an extremely attractive town.

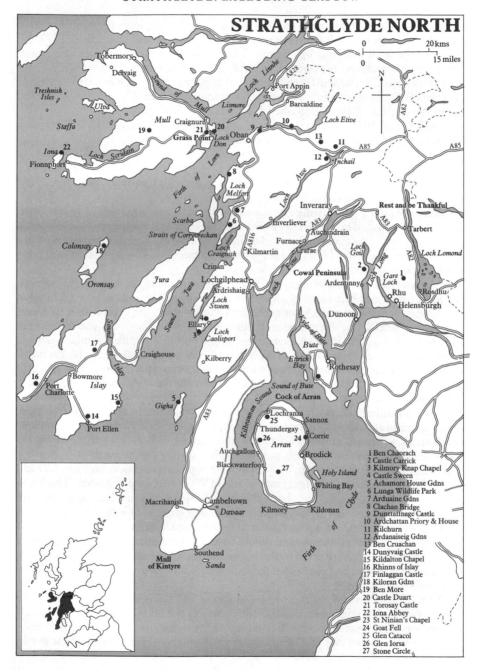

STRATHCLYDE NORTH

0   20 kms
0   15 miles

N

Tobermory
Dervaig
Treshnish
Isles
Ulva
Staffa
Mull
Iona 22
Fionnphort
Craignure
21 20
Grass Point
19
Loch Scridain
Loch Don
Oban
9
Sound of Mull
Loch Linnhe
Port Appin
Barcaldine
Lismore
Loch Etive
10
13
11
12 *Inchail*
Inchail
A828
A82
A85
A85

8
Loch
Melfort
7
Scarba
6
Straits of Corryvreckan
Colonsay
18
Oronsay
Jura
17
Craighouse
Sound of Jura
4
Ellary 3
Loch
Caolisport
Kilberry
16
Port
Charlotte
Bowmore
Islay
15
14
Port Ellen
Gigha
5
A83
Kilbrannan Sound

Firth of Lorn
Loch Awe
Aros
Loch
Craignish
Kilmartin
Crinan
Lochgilphead
Ardrishaig
Loch
Sween
Inverliever
Auchindrain
Furnace
Crarae
A816
A83
Loch Fyne
Inveraray
Rest and be Thankful
Tarbert
Loch
Goil
Loch Long
A82
Loch Lomond
Cowal Peninsula
Ardentinny
2
Gare 1
Loch
Rhu
Rosdhu
Helensburgh
Dunoon
Kyles of Bute
Bute
Ettrick
Bay
Rothesay
Sound of Bute
Cock of Arran
Lochranza
25
Sannox
Thundergay
26
24 Corrie
Arran
Auchgallon
Blackwaterfoot
Brodick
27
Holy Island
Whiting Bay
Macrihanish
Campbeltown
Davaar
Kilmory
Kildonan
Clyde
Firth
of
Mull
of Kintyre
Southend
Sanda

1 Ben Chaorach
2 Castle Carrick
3 Kilmory Knap Chapel
4 Castle Sween
5 Achamore House Gdns
6 Lunga Wildlife Park
7 Arduaine Gdns
8 Clachan Bridge
9 Dunstaffnage Castle
10 Ardchattan Priory & House
11 Kilchurn
12 Ardanaiseig Gdns
13 Ben Cruachan
14 Dunyvaig Castle
15 Kildalton Chapel
16 Rhinns of Islay
17 Finlaggan Castle
18 Kiloran Gdns
19 Ben More
20 Castle Duart
21 Torosay Castle
22 Iona Abbey
23 St Ninian's Chapel
24 Goat Fell
25 Glen Catacol
26 Glen Iorsa
27 Stone Circle

213

Inveraray Castle (open daily except Fri, Easter–mid-Oct, open Fri also, July/Aug: adm) is on the site of a 15th-century fortress, but the present castle dates from 1770, the time that the town itself was being built. The castle is a great square pile with round towers topped by dunce-hat cones. Designed by Roger Morris, with help from William Morris who was Clerk of Works, and decorated by Robert Mylne, it may have been based on a sketch by Vanbrugh and is imposing rather than beautiful. The grounds are on the site of the original village, demolished when the castle was built.

A bad fire in 1975 destroyed the roof and top floor but these have been rebuilt. Magnificently decorated rooms provide perfect settings for paintings, tapestries, Oriental and European porcelain, 18th-century furniture and many other treasures. Among the paintings are portraits by Kneller, Raeburn, Hoppner, Gainsborough, Batoni, and Ramsay. The grounds, with lovely old trees framing vistas out over Loch Fyne, are reminiscent of an 18th-century painting.

Inveraray Bell Tower, in the Episcopalian church (open daily, early May–late Sept: adm), was established in this century by the 10th Duke of Argyll, its peal of 10 bells being rung in memory of the Campbells who died in the First World War. When there is no live bell ringing in progress, visitors can listen to recordings. The 126-ft granite tower gives splendid views over Loch Fyne and Inveraray.

Inveraray Jail (open daily: adm) in Church Square at the top of the wide main street, is a must for anyone interested in social history. This Jail Museum has the Old Prison with ghastly cells where men, women children and lunatics were crammed, with sound effects and smells; the New Prison (19th-century), with improved conditions; the courtroom as it was in 1825 when men were deported to Australia for minor crimes; many fascinating exhibitions, especially one on Crime and Punishment with details of medieval punishment—hanging, branding, tongue-boring and burning. You can also see the awful open-air cages called airing yards where the prisoners took exercise. There is a souvenir shop.

Argyll Wildlife Park, two miles south of Inveraray (open daily: adm), is a 60-acre site with a splendid selection of European wildfowl, a large owl collection and such unlikely residents as wallabies, who hop about the forest tracks. Wildcats, badgers, Highland foxes, deer, wild goats, soay sheep and many other species can be seen.

Auchindrain Museum (open daily Easter–30 Sept, except closed Sat June, July and Aug: adm), six miles south of Inveraray, is an old West-Highland township. The 18th- and 19th-century cottages and outbuildings have been imaginatively restored and furnished in their original styles, giving a fascinating glimpse of what life was like for Highlanders in the old days. On display are parlours, kitchens with box beds, byres, barns, a smiddy, and all the old utensils. There are demonstrations of the run-rig or strip-farming methods prevalent in the Highlands until the end of the 18th century, in the days when villages had communal tenancy of farmland, and paid their rent jointly, in this case to the Argylls.

The name of **Furnace**, a couple of miles further on, is an unhappy reminder of the troubled times that reigned during the 18th century. It is so called from the charcoal-burning smelting furnace, established here to utilize trees felled by order of the Hanoverian government, so that rebel Highlanders still clinging to the Jacobite cause would have less cover in which to hide.

Crarae Woodland Garden (open daily: adm), three miles south, has lovely azaleas and rhododendrons in season. Attractive walks cross and re-cross a burn as it cascades over falls and through a gorge among a variety of conifers, hardwoods and shrubs.

Lochgilphead

Lochgilphead, 24 miles southwest of Inveraray, at the head of Loch Gilp and another appendix off Loch Fyne, is a jolly, bustling holiday resort as well as the shopping centre for the area. It is prim, elegant Inveraray's jovial country cousin. There is an excellent choice of good shops around the wide main street that was the market place. The Mid Argyll Show takes place in Lochgilphead in August.

The **Crinan Canal** cuts through from Ardrishaig in Loch Gilp to Crinan on the west coast. It was built at the end of the 18th century, and stretches for nine miles, with no less than 15 locks, through the top of the Kintyre Peninsula. It was designed to cut out the treacherous waters around the Mull of Kintyre that inhibited trade between the west coast and Glasgow, and was much used at first by commercial puffers, fishing boats and passenger craft. With the decline of the herring industry and the introduction of rail and road networks, it lost most of its commercial traffic and is now mainly used by pleasure boats, saving the sailor 130 miles of often rough passage. Going down the canal in a small boat is a delightfully peaceful way of passing a fine day, though you have to work the lock gates yourself, straining at the handles that wind up the sluices in the massive wooden gates, and leaning on the great timber arms that swing them open when the water either side is level. In 1847, Queen Victoria sailed down the canal in a magnificently decorated barge drawn by horses ridden by postilions dressed in scarlet, on her way to the Western Isles.

Crinan is a hamlet round a sheltered harbour, with the tidal gate between the canal and the open sea. The Crinan Hotel is one of the best in Scotland if you want a memorable break in lovely surroundings, overlooking the island-speckled Sound of Jura.

Knapdale

Knapdale is nearly an island. It runs south from Lochgilphead like a clenched fist, just managing to hang on to the long arm of Kintyre. autumn here is glorious; a wonderful range of colours shades the hills. So too is spring, when the rhododendrons and azaleas are in full bloom against the soft new green and the sparkle of water. Perhaps the best time of all, though, is November, when a light dusting of snow covers the last autumn leaves, and the water shows steel-grey against the hills etched in white. It is possible to drive right round the coast from Lochgilphead and across the middle from Inverneil to Achahoish. Along the coast each mile opens up a fresh view to the islands of Jura and Islay in the west, or down through layers of hills to distant lochs and the sea.

Going clockwise from Lochgilphead, **Kilberry**, in the southwest corner of Knapdale on the B8024, has a collection of 9th- and 10th-century stones and some from the Middle Ages, gathered up from the surrounding area and housed under cover in a steading, just north of the hamlet, signposted **Kilberry Stones**, from the road.

St Columba's Cave, 12 miles northwest of Kilberry on the western shore of Loch Caolisport (pronounced Killisport) near Ellary, is an enchanted spot, almost tangibly

215

spiritual. There is an altar on the right with two crosses carved above, a smaller cave, reached by steps, traces of dwellings outside the cave and the ruin of a chapel. As its name indicates, tradition associates this cave with the saint's mission in Scotland: in such a peaceful setting, unchanged over the centuries, it is easy to believe the folklore. Excavations in the 19th century unearthed evidence that there was a settlement here as far back as 8000 BC, making St Columba comparatively modern.

Unfortunately, due to a private road with a locked gate, it is not possible to go on round the peninsular and you must back-track via Lochgilphead to explore Loch Sween.

Castle Sween, on the eastern shore of the loch, in a splendid position guarding the entrance to Loch Sween, now alas surrounded by a caravan site, could be the oldest stone castle on the Scottish mainland. It dates from the 11th century and is a great sprawl of a ruin, rather overwhelmingly restored, Norman in style, with buttresses. The old ovens can still be seen, and the well, and the original drain and rubbish-chute in the wall of the round tower, down which everything, including sewage, was indiscriminately cast.

The castle was a stronghold of MacSweens in the 12th and 13th centuries but they lost their lands when they sided with the English in the 14th century. Robert Bruce besieged it and installed the McNeills of Argyll to maintain it, one of whom married a MacMillan. Thus, Knapdale became MacMillan territory. The castle was destroyed in 1647 by Royalists, fighting the cause of Charles I.

13th-century **Kilmory Knap Chapel**, on the southern tip of the peninsula, north of Loch Caolisport, contains a collection of sculpted stones and **MacMillan's Cross**. This cross was elaborately carved in the 15th century, possibly by monks from the monastery at Kilberry.

Kintyre

An isthmus between East and West Loch Tarbert, straddled by the attractive village of Tarbert, joins Kintyre to Knapdale. Here, in the 11th century, Malcolm Canmore struck a bargain with the Norwegian King Magnus Barelegs who was harrassing him. He told Magnus he could claim any western island he could get to by boat with his rudder down. Magnus had his Vikings tow him across the isthmus— and claimed Kintyre as his.

A road circles most of the coast of the peninsula, passing through delightful villages and hamlets, most of which cater for summer visitors. The landscape is similar to that of Knapdale, cut by wooded valleys rising to hilly moorland. The east and west routes meet at **Campbeltown** at the head of Campbeltown Loch, a haven for boats in a westerly gale, and subject of that hopeful song: 'O Campbeltown Loch I wish you were whisky'. It is a sturdy holiday town and boating centre, and was once an important herring port, with 33 distilleries, of which 2 remain open.

Flora Macdonald sailed to North Carolina from Campbeltown in 1774, emigrating with her family nearly 30 years after her brave actions helped save the life of Prince Charlie. William McTaggart, that great painter of Scottish life and scenery, was born in the town in 1835. He was no doubt inspired by the local land and seascapes.

Campbeltown Museum (open daily except Wed and Sun: free) in Hall Street has a fascinating demonstration of how vitrified forts were formed.

Davaar Island, at the mouth of the loch, accessible at low tide along a shingle spit on the southern shore, is a lump of rock with a cave in it. Here, in 1887, a man called Archibald Mackinnon, inspired by a dream, secretly painted a picture of the Crucifixion on the rock. It is a moving picture, after the style of El Greco, lit by a shaft of light that streams into the large cave through an aperture. When the artist was 80, in 1934, he returned to the cave and restored the painting.

Machrihanish, six miles west of Campbeltown, and fully exposed to the fury of Atlantic gales, is a popular holiday village, with a hotel, golf course, camp site and glorious sandy beaches, as well as the airport.

Mull of Kintyre

Southend, tucked round the corner to the east of the Mull of Kintyre, is another holiday village. There is a golf course and wonderful sandy beaches with dunes, covered in marram grass, which offer shelter from the wind. Nothing remains today of **Dunaverty Castle** which once stood above vicious rocks here, shrouded in uncomfortable memories; 300 of Montrose's men, fighting the cause of Charles I, were besieged there by the merciless Covenanting General, David Leslie. Forced by thirst to surrender, the Royalists, mostly Irish mercenaries, were shamelessly massacred.

Keil, just west of Southend, has a flat rock which is traditionally regarded as the place where St Columba first landed in Scotland. Keen eyes will see the two footprints burnt into the rock where he stood, turning his back on the land that had outlawed him.

From Southend you can hire a boat and go out to **Sanda Island**, about two miles to the south, where Robert Bruce hid in 1306, while making his way back from Rathlin Island.

The Mull of Kintyre, the southern tip of the peninsula, is a dramatic rocky extremity, with a lighthouse and sheer cliffs. You must walk the final one and a half miles or so. Only 13 miles from Ireland, it is impressive in a westerly gale. This was the subject of the song by Paul McCartney, who bought a house close by, which sent a number of confused fans off to the island of Mull in search.

WHERE TO STAY AND EAT
Inveraray is a good centre. **The Great Inn**, tel 0499 2466, overlooks Loch Shira and Loch Fyne, close to the castle entrance. Open April to October, this is a respectable, moderately priced, family hotel without too many frills. **Stag Hotel** on a 'bold corner site' in the town centre, is a little cheaper and one of the rooms has its own jacuzzi. Cheaper still and also in the middle of the town, **George Hotel**, tel 0499 2111, is solid and dependable, but not wildly imaginative.

Crinan Hotel, tel 054683 261, already mentioned, is expensive but worth it. Supplied daily by fishing boats that unload a short distance from the kitchen, the food is renowned. The views out across the water to the islands are marvellous, especially during a good sunset. Open mid-March to end October. **Stag Hotel**, Lochgilphead, tel 0546 2496, is on a corner in the middle of the town, with friendly, easy-going staff and cheap, comfortable rooms.

217

Stonefield Castle Hotel, Tarbert, tel 08802 207, is a large, white castellated hotel overlooking Loch Fyne, which gets very booked up during the Loch Tarbert regatta. Good food and service, moderately priced. **Tarbert Hotel**, tel 08802 264, is right on the harbour in this popular sailing centre, cheap and popular for *après* sailing.

Campbeltown has quite a few hotels. Most of them are unexciting but dependable. **Royal Hotel**, Main Street, tel 0586 52017, overlooks Cambeltown Loch from the harbour. It is cheap and quite lively. **White Hart Hotel**, tel 0586 52440/53356, is family hotel, cheap on a busy corner in the Main Street.

Lorne and Oban

The new A816 runs up the west coast from Lochgilphead to Oban. It flirts with the sea, dipping and rising, pulling away and swooping back again with magnificent views.

This part of Argyll is drenched in ancient history. Four miles northwest of Lochgilphead is all that is left of **Dunadd Fort**, capital of the kingdom of Dalriada from the 6th to the 9th centuries. This was a great and powerful political centre, all those years ago, headquarters of the early missionaries, including St Columba, until Kenneth MacAlpine decided it would be sensible to move the capital to Pictland. A rocky hillock above a meandering river is all that remains, with marvellous views all round, and, if you search carefully, a rock with carvings of a boar, some Ogham inscriptions . . . and a footprint. Historians believe this was the place where kings were crowned and that St Columba crowned Aidan here in 574, using the disputed Stone of Destiny as the throne (see 'Topics', p. 42). The footprint is indisputable and only the most prosaic could resist the urge to stand in it and imagine those ancient ceremonies on this lofty site.

From Dunadd to **Kilmartin** is a distance of only about three miles, but the area is packed with pre-historic standing stones and burial cairns dating from the Stone Age and Bronze Age. They have been well labelled. If there are not too many people about the imagination can reel, trying to picture those ancient people performing their mysterious rites here. Some of the cists have been reconstructed and visitors can go inside and see the carvings on the walls.

Carnasserie Castle, nine miles north of Lochgilphead, is the ruined home of John Carswell, first Protestant Bishop of the Isles, who in 1597 translated Knox's liturgy into Gaelic. It was the first Gaelic book ever to be published.

Lunga Wildlife Park, on the Ardfern Peninsula, north of Loch Craignish, has indigenous animals in beautiful surroundings, and there is experimental white fish-farming in the loch.

Arduaine Gardens, just north on Loch Melfort (open daily: adm) have a wonderful display of sub-tropical plants. There are magnolias, rhododendrons and azaleas, a water garden and rock garden and many rare trees and shrubs.

Seil is a hook of land west of Loch Melfort—an island joined to the mainland by the much-photographed, hump-backed Clachan Bridge, celebrated as, 'The only bridge over the Atlantic'. From this bridge a narrow road twists down to Easdale, which is scarred by old slate-quarry workings. Part of the original film of *Whisky Galore* was made here, many years ago, transforming the little township into a stage set.

Oban

Oban is 37 miles north of Lochgilphead and is unmistakeably a seaside resort. It is a hive of activity in the summer, when the streets seethe with visitors and traffic. The town rises steeply from a crescent-shaped bay, and its main street fronts on to the harbour. High above stands **McCaig's Tower**, a large circular temple with pillars, built in 1897 by the banker, McCaig. His intention was to give work to the unemployed and to create a museum and observation tower as a memorial to his family. However, it was never finished.

The Catholic See of Argyll and the Western Isles has its cathedral, St Columba's, in Oban, overlooking the harbour and well attended. Although this area is predominantly Protestant, there are still communities which were left untouched by the Reformation.

The harbour is a busy boat terminal. MacBrayne's steamers ply between Mull and the Inner and Outer Hebrides, and smaller ferries, fishing boats and pleasure craft create an ever-changing scene. The quays are thronged with cars, people and freight. The town is fringed by respectable hotels and neat villas offering bed and breakfast. Cafés and restaurants are packed and there is a fairly lively night life offering a choice between discos, public *ceilidhs*, or family fun shows.

Oban Distillery in Stafford Street, tel 0631 62110, is open to visitors on weekdays: ring for an appointment.

World in Miniature, on North Pier, (open daily: adm) is a delightful display of miniature rooms, furniture, dioramas etc, all scaled at one inch to one foot.

Among the many entertainments, the Argyllshire Gathering in August is a great Highland occasion, with lots of piping and dancing and traditional games. In September the Oban Gala Day and Street Fair is a colourful carnival, especially when the sun shines.

Oban Rare Breeds Animal Park is a couple of miles on past the Golf Course, with unusual breeds of sheep, cattle, goats, pigs, poultry, ducks, deer, etc. There are also: a Pets' Corner, nature trails, tea-room and shop.

Ganavan Sands, just north of Oban, is a good place to relax if you enjoy company—it tends to become densely populated in good weather. It has a restaurant, bar, coffee shop, car park, play area, putting, donkey rides, watersports and a launching slip. The bathing is safe.

Oban is an excellent base for sub-aqua divers, with good air supplies in the town and marvellous underwater terrain. The Sound of Mull is littered with wrecks and the waters all round offer a wealth of marine life and cliff scenery. It is also ideal for sailing, with some fairly challenging, breathtakingly beautiful stretches, especially south through the Firth of Lorne to the Sound of Jura, past the infamous Corryvreckan whirlpool (see p. 231).

Lismore Island

From Oban, a car ferry (taking an hour) runs six miles north to Lismore Island in Loch Linnhe. There is also a passenger ferry from Port Appin. This long slither of rock, overlaid with loam and heather, was the seat of the diocese of Argyll from 1200 to 1507, in the days before Luther stirred up the beginnings of the Reformation. Traces of the miniature cathedral that was here in those early times are incorporated into the parish church, which was built in 1749. The bishop's dwelling, the 13th-century **Achadun Castle**, is at the southwest end of the island, but is now a ruin. The overgrown, jagged ruin of **Coeffin Castle**, in the northwest, also dates from the 13th century. The remains of **Broch of Tirefour** stands on the northeast coast, overlooking the mainland.

Bachuil House (open by arrangement, tel Lismore 256: free) is on the island and contains the Bachuil Mor, or pastoral staff of St Moluag, the man who converted the island to Christianity in the 6th century. Moluag and Columba are said to have been rivals, the one being a Pict, the other a Celt.

Dunstaffnage Castle (open daily except closed Thurs afternoon and Fri, Oct–March: adm) is four miles north of Oban on a rocky promontory guarding the entrance to Loch Etive. A splendid ruin, it seems to grow out of the rock. Parts of it stand over 60 ft high, its massive walls more than 10 ft thick. Flora Macdonald was held prisoner here for a few days after helping Prince Charlie in 1746. Tradition holds that the Stone of Destiny came here from Dunadd, staying until Kenneth Macalpine moved it to Scone in an attempt to draw together his kingdom of Picts and Scots (see 'Topics', p. 42).

The coast road north from Oban and Dunstaffnage crosses the crooked finger of Loch Etive at Connel, where sea and loch are in constant turmoil trying to pour in and out through a bottleneck. It loops round Loch Creran, clinging to the coast in places with more good views. This northern tip of Strathclyde is rugged, mountainous hinterland laced with rivers and cascading burns, cut by Loch Etive.

About a mile north of the Connel Bridge, a minor road to the right (east) runs five miles out to the northern shore of Loch Etive and **Ardchattan Priory** (always accessible: free) founded in 1230. This was the meeting place of Robert Bruce's Parliament, in 1308, one of the last to be held in Gaelic. Among the remains of the priory, burned by Cromwell's soldiers, some carved stones can still be seen. The gardens of **Ardchattan House** (open April–November: free) are next door.

Castle Stalker, recently restored (open by appointment, March–Sept: adm, tel Upper Warlingham 2768), dates from 1500 and was the home of the Stewarts of Appin. It has a magnificent setting, on a tiny islet off Port Appin. Keep a sharp eye out for seals round here; they bask on the rocks in large numbers, flopping down into the water if disturbed, to pop up and stare balefully at intruders with great velvety eyes (see 'Ballachulish', p. 401, for the Appin Murder.)

The A828 goes on north up Loch Linnhe and crosses into the Highland Region.

The A85 east from Connel to Loch Awe is an attractive drive with views of Loch Etive, through the Pass of Brander below the looming bulk of **Ben Cruachan** (3695 ft). **The Hollow Mountain**, six miles beyond Taynuilt, is a great cavern hewn out of Ben Cruachan to accommodate an underground power house (open daily March–Oct: adm). Electric buses run through the tunnel and there is a visitor centre. This glistening subterranean empire is not for the claustrophobic.

Anyone with the time and energy to climb Ben Cruachan will get some of the best views in Scotland from its lofty summit on a clear day, often held upright by the wind.

Loch Awe is a 23-mile long serpent of water with thickly wooded shores, many islands, and more than its share of midges clinging to the dense vegetation.

Kilchurn Castle lies on a commanding site at the north end of the loch. Dating from 1440, it belonged to the Campbells of Breadalbane who occupied it until it was taken over by Hanoverian troops in 1746, with the consent of the Campbells who were anti-Jacobite. The gale that destroyed the Tay Rail Bridge also demolished one of Kilchurn's turrets.

When the level of the loch is low, traces of several *crannogs* can be seen—man-made islands where early settlers built dwellings for greater protection against attack. Some of the islands were used as clan burial grounds, especially **Inchail**, where there is a ruined chapel dating from the 13th century and several graves of the Macarthur Clan.

There are good walks either side of the loch. On the west side there is an information centre at **Inverliever**, with useful advice and directions for the best trails to take.

Ardanaiseig Gardens (open 31 March–31 Oct: adm) are at the north end of the loch, east of the B845. They contain rhododendrons, azaleas, rare shrubs and trees, and some of the best views across the loch to Ben Cruachan. There is a hotel with a restaurant, open for coffee, lunch and tea.

White Corries Chairlift (open daily in summer and weekends, Jan–April: adm) is north of Tyndrum on the A82, almost on the border with the Highland Region. The lift climbs 2100 ft into the hills with glorious views over Rannoch Moor and into Glencoe.

WHERE TO STAY AND EAT

Oban is crammed with hotels, guest houses and bed and breakfasts. **The Manor House**, Gallanach Road, tel 0631 63053, on Oban Bay, was built by the Duke of Argyll in 1780 as his Oban pad and later used as a Dower House. Moderately priced with marvellous views, it is comfortable and serves good Scottish and French food, expecially seafood. The following four are all very similar: comfortable, old-fashioned seaside-resort hotels. They all overlook the harbour and give good value for money if you aren't looking for excitement. They all serve wholesome, predictable food. Moderately priced are **Alexandra Hotel**, tel 0631 62381; **Columba Hotel**, tel 0631 62183 and, slightly more lively, **Great Western Hotel**, tel 0631 63101.

Cheaper are the **Caledonian Hotel**, tel 0631 63133 and **Argyll Hotel**, tel 0631 62353, which is less maiden-auntish. There are dozens more.

South of Oban, **Knipoch Hotel**, Kilninver, near Oban, tel 08526 251, is open all year except January and expensive. It looks across Loch Feochan to a sunset behind the Hills of Lorne. Knipoch stands on the burial route along which the Kings of the Scots (including Macbeth and Duncan) were carried from Scone Palace to Iona. With award-winning food, it caters for 'the more discriminating traveller'. **Loch Melfort Hotel**, Arduaine, tel 08522 233, moderately priced and only open April–Oct, has established a reputation for good service, comfort and excellent food. Cruisin' yachtsmen of the yellow-boot, Captain O. M. Watt-sailing-outfit category tend to stop off here for a civilized evening out, swappin' Force Nine stories in the Chart Room Bar. The main house, built in 1900, gazes out across an island-speckled sea. The six bedrooms are done up like guest rooms in a country house. An adjoining Cedar Wing, long and low, has 20 rooms, each with its own bathroom, balcony and picture window, facing south across the water. **Galley of Lorn Inn,** at Ardfern, further south, tel 08525 284, is an unpretentious, family-run inn, cheap and not over-endowed with mod cons.

North of Oban, **Falls of Lora Hotel** at Connel, tel 063171, overlooks Loch Etive, five miles from Oban. Another of the old-fashioned style hotels, they give good, dependable service and are cheap. Moderately priced **Isle of Eriska** at Ledaig, tel 063172 371, is a splendid Scottish baronial pile, built in 1884, connected to the mainland by a bridge. Its proprietors, Robin and Sheena Buchanan-Smith, have created a comfortable private-house atmosphere, with blazing log fires and an excellent kitchen. Also moderately priced, **Invercreran Country House Hotel**, Glen Creran, near Appin, tel 063173 414/456, in a sheltered glen surrounded by hills, is a well-run, comfortable hotel, with an excellent dining room. **Ardsheal House**, Kentallen of Appin, Appin, tel 063174 227, stands high on a peninsula with lovely views over Loch Linnhe to the Morvern hills. Also moderately priced and only open from April to November, Ardsheal was built in 1760 in 900 acres of woods, meadows and beach. Oak panelling, open fires and antiques give it a country house atmosphere and the food is excellent. Another moderately priced one, **Airds Hotel**, Port Appin, tel 063173 236, overlooking Loch Linnhe, Lismore and Shuna and Morvern hills, is a charming place, very comfortable, with good food and friendly staff. The proprietor, Eric Allen, recently made a complete recovery from falling off his roof. Open from March to January with special winter reductions.

Moderately priced **Ardanaiseig**, Kilchrenan, tel 08663 333, stands beneath Ben Cruachan on the shores of Loch Awe, in a gorgous garden of rhododendrons and azaleas. It was built in 1834 to designs by William Burn and has a 'country house' atmosphere, and has been the family home of the proprietors since 1964. The food is excellent, and the accommodation very comfortable.

Strathclyde Islands

CUMBRAE

Great Cumbrae is so close to the Ayrshire mainland that it hardly counts as an island, and takes just seven minutes to reach in the roll-on, roll-off ferry that runs every 15 minutes from Largs.

TOURIST INFORMATION
All year, Largs: tel 0475 673765.
Tourist Information Centre, Millport, tel 0475 530753, April–Oct.

Less than four miles in length and two in width, the island has a 12-mile coastal road round it and is ideal for bicycling.

Millport straggles around a wide bay looking south across the Tan to Little Cumbrae. A great many people go to Cumbrae in the summer so don't expect to 'get away from it all'. The beaches are packed on a fine day.

There is a National Water Sports Centre on the island and these waters are excellent for sub-aqua diving.

Although Cumbrae is not ideal for the recluse, it has some interesting rock formations and the plant and animal life are good. The earliest village was at **Kirkton** about half a mile from the old pier in Millport, where the chapel was dedicated to St Columba in 1330 and replaced in 1612. The 'Cathedral of the Isles', in Millport, is the smallest cathedral in Britain.

The **Museum** (open Tues and Sat in season: free) shows the history of Millport and Cumbrae over the centuries. Boats run from Millport to Little Cumbrae. The ruined castle there was a residence of Robert II in the 14th century.

WHERE TO STAY AND EAT
There are a few hotels, guest houses and bed and breakfasts in Millport, but the standard is not high. The **Royal George Hotel**, tel 0475 530301, overlooking the bay, is probably the best bet. Or **Millerston Hotel** West Bay Road, tel 0475 530480, only open April to October. Prices for both these on application.

ARRAN

The miracle of Arran is that it has clung on to its character despite the thousands of holiday makers attracted every year by its beauty. It is slightly larger than the Isle of Wight, about 20 miles from north to south, nine miles across and 56 miles in circumference. Although hotels, guest houses and chalet settlements ring the island, it is possible to roam inland for miles, and feel totally remote.

Arran was inhabited way back before the dawn of recorded history, as its ancient stones and burial cairns prove. Since then its lovely landscape and mild climate have been put to use by many a marauding culture. The Irish Scots came over and settled in the early 6th century, making Arran part of the Kingdom of Dalriada. The Vikings held it for a time, until they were ousted by Somerled, Lord of the Isles, who was possibly of Norse descent himself. In the 18th century sportsmen established deer here, overrunning the crofts and driving out many of the tenant farmers.

There is so much to do here it would be easier to list what is not available. Sea sports include: swimming, sailing, windsurfing, water skiing, sub-aqua diving and fishing. Land sports include: golf, riding, pony trekking, tennis, squash, bowling, and of course, walking and climbing. It would be possible to walk and climb for an entire holiday and never cover the same ground twice.

Arran is a treasure trove for nature lovers. Time spent birdwatching here will reward you with sightings of rare species, and the flora and fauna of the island are diverse and fascinating.

A holiday atmosphere prevails on the ferry from Ardrossan to Brodick on Arran. For an hour, crowds jostle for tables in the bar and lounges; knapsacks are piled everywhere and the uniform is jeans and fluorescent kagools. If it is raining at Brodick don't worry; Arran usually manages to show a smiling face for at least some of the day.

GETTING THERE
The car ferry from Ardrossan, with train link from Glasgow, takes about an hour. April–Oct: Claonaig, Kintyre–Lochranza takes half an hour. Further information: Caledonian MacBrayne Ltd, Ferry Terminal, Gourock, Renfrewshire, tel 0475 33755 (enquiries)/34531 (reservations).

TOURIST INFORMATION
The Pier, Brodick, tel 0770 2140/2401.

Brodick

Brodick is a large resort-village with plenty of hotels, guest houses, and bed and breakfast places. It has spread around Brodick Bay, and is overlooked by Brodick Castle.

Brodick Castle (open Mon, Wed, Sat, April and first half Oct, daily May–Sept: grounds open all year: adm) belongs to the National Trust for Scotland. It was built in the 13th century on the site of a Viking fortress. This splendid, rather grim, fortress was the home of the Dukes of Hamilton. There is some magnificent treasure on display here, much of which was brought to the castle by Susan Euphemia Beckford, who married the 10th duke in 1810. She inherited it from her father, William Beckford, the reclusive, eccentric collector of fine art, who built Fonthill Abbey in Wiltshire, and wrote *Vathek*. The guide book to the castle gives details of all the silver, porcelain, paintings and furnishings. The castle is a tall, stately building of red sandstone, backed by the sea and surrounded by a range of hills dominated by Goat Fell. The gardens are a surprise—the fabulous colours and pungent scents are exotic enough to to have been part of the rich oriental settings in *Vathek* itself.

Isle of Arran Heritage Museum (open Easter–Oct, Mon–Sat: adm) is in an 18th-century croft-farm on the edge of Brodick. The smithy, cottage and stable block illustrate changing conditions from the far past to the turn of the century. Delightful rooms in the cottage show nostalgic Victoriana, complete with black kettle on the hob and iron bedstead under the eaves.

The road round the island only loses the sea in a couple of places, and the String Road cuts through the middle from Brodick to Blackwaterfoot. Another road cuts through Glen Scorrodale from Lamlash to Lagg Inn.

Goat Fell, 2866 ft, north of Brodick, dominates Arran. It is best attacked on a clear day and is not for the unfit. It takes at least 3 hours to reach the top; there are several ways up, and the last bit is fairly strenuous. The views from the top make it all worth while. There won't be any goats— 'Goatfell' comes from *Gaoth Bheinn* windy mountain, but you could well see golden eagles gliding on air currents in a corrie below.

Corrie is a chocolate-box village about six miles north of Brodick. Its white cottages, trim colourful gardens, harbour, quay and beach, have made it a favourite with artists.

Walk up into the glens that cut into the hinterland like spokes of a wheel. There are two at **Sannox**—delightful, secret places away from the road, with heather, lichens, mosses and alpine willow, and many rare wild flowers such as purple and starry saxifrage. The Fallen Rocks, beyond Sannox, are thought to be the relics of a landslip in the Palaeozoic Age, which sent these massive boulders, some as big as houses, tumbling to the beach. This is a popular place for rock climbers. Sannox has a 9-hole golf course.

Lochranza, possibly from Loch of the *chaoruinn* (rowan), lies two miles southwest from the northern headland, Cock of Arran. 13th/14th-century Lochranza Castle (open daily: free) is a romantic ruin on the tidal flats, backed by rugged mountains. The castle is L-plan, three storeys high with a pit prison in the vaulted basement. It is said to have been a staging post for Robert the Bruce in 1307, when he returned from the famous goading by the spider of Rathlin Island. Seen against a flaming sunset, this roofless shell is stunning. Lochranza has a 9-hole golf course.

Going south from Lochranza down the west side of the island the road clings to the sea with hills tumbling down almost on to the beach. Steep-sided **Glen Catacol** runs inland up into the hills, through beech, oak and larch, chestnut and fir, and vivid green ferns. **Thundergay**, five miles south of Lochranza, gets its strange name from Tor-na-Gaoith (hill-of-the-wind). Two miles further south, **Pirnmill** is derived from the bobbin mill that was here in the days when linen was an important industry in the island. The mill has now been converted into holiday flats. **Glen Iorsa** runs northeast through marshy bog land, and is hemmed in by barren hills. It is a great tract of lonely, waterlogged moor, which lies below frowning crags, and is cut by steep ravines and lochans.

The southwest quarter of Arran is rich in pre-historic remains. These include **Auchagallon Stone Circle**, 15 red sandstone blocks which once encircled a cairn; the **Farm Road Stone Circle**, close by (within range of the 9-hole Machrie golf course), the **Machrie Standing Stones**, slim, primeval monoliths whose mysterious purpose baffles man today, and the **Kilmory Cairns**, at Lagg Inn.

King's Caves at Drumadoon, Blackwaterfoot, are where Robert the Bruce is said to have sheltered when returning to free Scotland from the stranglehold of English domination. Legend brings Fingal, or Fionn, MacCumhail here, the 3rd-century warrior-poet, father of Ossian and leader of the Feinn, who feature in the old sagas. There are rock carvings in the caves, of typical Pictish hunting scenes and animals.

There is a lovely 10-mile walk up **Glen Scorrodale**, from **Sliddery**, along Sliddery Water to Lamlash Bay.

Kildonan, six miles east of Sliddery, is a sprawling farming village with two hotels and a fine sandy beach. There are good views from here of Pladda Island Lighthouse and Ailsa Craig, which rises like an iceberg 13 miles out to sea. Look out for a large colony of grey Atlantic seals along the shore towards Bennan Head to the west. Unafraid and curious, they come quite close to the shore to inspect passers-by. The mysterious carcass of a large sea-creature was once discovered here, baffling the world of science and unidentified to this day. Before the headland a winding path used by smugglers in the 18th century, hugs the cliffs, and leads to the road above.

Whiting Bay, five miles north of Kildonan, is a popular holiday village. Here, shops and hotels jostle with holiday cottages all along the wide bay. There are also craft shops which specialize in leather, pottery and wood carving. A Jewellery Workshop, signposted at the north end of the village, sells locally made silver and gold jewellery. For evening entertainment, **Nags Bistro** has live music and a disco in the summer. There is an 18-hole golf course with fine views across the Firth of Clyde to the Ayrshire hills. **Glen Ashdale Falls** are signposted from the south end of the village, up a steep, wooded glen to where crystal water cascades down on to glistening rocks. **The Giant's Graves** (signposted) are a stone circle traditionally associated with Fionn MacCumhail.

Lamlash completes the circular tour of the island. It is three miles south of Brodick on Lamlash Bay, which is almost blocked at the mouth by Holy Island. This wonderfully safe anchorage, now a yachtsman's haven, has given shelter to many an important traveller. King Haakon and his fleet took refuge here after they had been defeated in the Battle of Largs in 1263, and, in 1548, the ship carrying five-year-old Mary, Queen of

Scots, to France from Dumbarton, sheltered here. Lamlash has annual sea angling competitions, renowned throughout Scotland.

Holy Island, with St Molio's Cave, is not at present open to the public.

Take home one of Arran's unique blends of mustard, locally made and sold at **Arran Provisions**, The Old Mill, Lamlash. The range is enormous. They also do delicious jams, jellies, sauces, and chutneys. Another local speciality is Arran cheese, a Dunlop cheese, made at The Creamery, in Kilmory.

WHERE TO STAY AND EAT

There are hotels and guest houses all over the island, as well as a large number of self-catering places, static caravans and camp sites.

Moderately priced **Auchrannie Hotel**, Brodick, tel 0770 2234/5, is a 19th-century mansion, five minutes from beach and golf course. The excellent food is served in a conservatory-style restaurant. **Douglas Hotel**, Brodick, tel 0770 2155, is on the sea front, with lovely views. Also moderately priced it offers live entertainment, dancing, sauna and a beauty salon. **Arran Hotel**, also on the sea front in Brodick, tel 0770 2265, is cheap, welcomes children at reduced prices and has a nice garden. Open March to October. Also cheap, **Invercloy Hotel**, Brodick, tel 0770 2225, is opposite a safe sandy beach and has balconies in front and a friendly atmosphere.

Kinloch Hotel, overlooking the sea at Blackwaterfoot, tel 077086 444, is a moderately priced, comfortable modern eyesore with good food, indoor swimming pool, solarium, sauna and squash court. Not for the recluse. **Lagg Hotel**, Kilmory, tel 077087 255, is an 18th-century coaching inn set in 10 acres of attractive woodland by the Lagg Burn. It's cheap and the food is first rate.

For an evening out, try **Wishing Well Restaurant**, Lagg, tel 0770 87255, in converted stables. Seafood is a speciality, with lobster when available.

BUTE

Bute is a popular holiday island, attracting a great many people in the summer. Rothesay is a town of bright lights and tourist traps, but it is possible to find a few hidden corners, if you are prepared to walk to some of the less accessible beaches and coves. Sailors exploring the coast will find a number of secret little bays populated only by seals and sea birds.

In August, the island has an 11-day Highland Festival. This culminates in a Highland Games, which is a tartan bonanza of caber tossing, weight putting, piping and dancing. As well as the traditional games, there are many other competitions, from bowling to angling, and sailing to golf, to watch, or even enter. The Banqueting Hall of Rothesay Castle houses dancing, ceilidhs, poetry readings and variety shows. There are also art exhibitions and a flower festival. For these 11 days, the whole island reverberates with Scottish music from accordions, folk groups and pipes. The atmosphere is distinctly 'holiday camp': good, clean fun.

There is plenty to do on Bute. For the sporting, there are three golf courses, tennis, riding, good fishing and every sort of water sport in wonderfully clear water. Nature lovers will appreciate the walking, and birdwatching. There is plenty of organized jollity to while away the evenings, in the way of ceilidhs and shows. A variety of pleasure cruises run in the summer, round the island and adjacent waters.

GETTING THERE
There is a roll-on, roll-off car ferry from Wemyss Bay, which is an hour's drive or train journey from Glasgow. There are frequent sailings daily, lasting half an hour. The roll-on, roll-off car ferry from Colintraive, Argyll, also has frequent sailings daily; the crossing takes 5 minutes. For further information, contact Caledonian MacBrayne, The Ferry Terminal, Gourock, Renfrewshire, tel 0475 33755.

TOURIST INFORMATION
15 Victoria Street, Rothesay, tel 0700 502151. It is open all year.

Rothesay is the thriving hub of Bute, a town humming with activity and tourist attractions for gregarious visitors.

Rothesay Castle (open daily except Thurs mornings and Fri, Oct–March: adm) was built in 1098, in the days when Norsemen dominated the islands. It reverted to Scottish hands after the Battle of Largs, in 1263. Added to over the centuries, it is an impressive fortress with high curtain walls and drum towers enclosing a circular courtyard. King Robert Bruce captured it in 1313 and it was his great-great-grandson who was first created Duke of Rothesay, a title still held by Prince Charles. The castle was used as a headquarters when both James IV and James V tried, with little success, to subdue the arrogant rule of the Lords of the Isles. Cromwell battered it badly during the Civil War and it was burned by Argyll in 1685 during the Monmouth Rebellion; it then lay in ruins until restoration in the 19th century.

Bute Museum is behind the castle (open every day except Sun during April and May; daily from June–Sept, and Tues–Sat afternoons, Oct–March: adm). There are displays of Bute's geology, ancient history, maritime traditions, culture and natural history.

Winter Garden Visitors' Centre in Victoria Street, in a restored 1920s seaside theatre, contains a Heritage Centre, cinema and Bistro.

Kyles of Bute are the very beautiful narrow straits separating the island from the mainland in the northwest and northeast. The northwest corner of the island is reasonably remote, being only accessible on foot, and the views are glorious.

Ardencraig Gardens (open daily May–Sept: free) south of Rothesay, supply plants for the whole island. As well as demonstration gardens and fish ponds, there are aviaries with exotic foreign birds. Fuchsias add a vivid splash of colour.

Canada Hill, above Loch Fad, in the lower middle of the island, is an easy climb, and gives panoramic views of the Firth of Clyde, Argyll and Arran.

St Blane's Chapel, on the southern toe of Bute, is a 12th-century ruin with a Norman arch, built on the site of a monastery founded by St Blane in the 6th century.

St Ninian's Chapel, halfway up the west coast, was another early settlement, on a point by a glorious sandy bay.

Ettrick Bay, further north, has a good sandy beach.

WHERE TO STAY AND EAT
The choice isn't wildly attractive but the following are all cheap. **Guildford Court,** Watergate, Rothesay, tel 0700 3770, is a listed building overlooking the harbour with

both hotel accommodation and self-catering suites. **Kingarth Hotel**, at the south end of the island, tel 070083 662, is comfortable and friendly with a bowling green, near a golf course. **Bayview Hotel**, 22 Mountstuart Road, Rothesay, tel 0700 2339, is a Victorian house on Craigmore Shore, 10 minutes from the pier with lovely views of Rothesay Bay. **Royal Hotel**, Albert Place, Rothesay, tel 0700 3044, overlooks the yacht marina, a short distance from the ferry terminus. Cabaret every night during the season. Private loch fishing arranged and special terms for golfers. **Glenburn Hotel**, Glenburn Road, Rothesay, tel 0700 2500, stands in 6 acres overlooking the water. It's rather a busy place, next door to a heated swimming pool and a golf course, and the food isn't too bad.

Ardencraig, tel 0700 4550, has seven cheap self-catering chalets in lovely grounds high above the Firth of Clyde. Each chalet has one public room and two bedrooms which sleep six.

GIGHA

(Pronounced with hard g and without the gh: *Ge'er*).

Gigha is Norse for god, and indeed this is an earthly Garden of Eden, six miles long, never more than one and a half wide, warmed by the Gulf Stream, with frost almost unknown.

GETTING THERE
Six ferries a day (four on Sundays) run to Gigha, from Tayinloan, halfway up the west side of Kintyre. (Fewer in winter.)
For further information contact Caledonian MacBrayne, tel 0475 33755.

TOURIST INFORMATION
Mid Argyll Tourist Board, The Pier, Campbeltown, tel 0586 25056.

The island was recently put up for sale. The asking price £2–3 million—included 39 estate cottages, six tenanted farms and more than 1300 acres of farm and woodland, together with a baronial title and a very tight-knit community. Perhaps the most celebrated of Gigha's residents is Seumas McSporran, a sturdy figure, just past his half century, with a genial smile almost as wide as his face. He has lived on the island for all but two years of his life and holds some 14 or 15 jobs. 'I have to consult a list to get up to date with them.' His jobs include: sub-postmaster, postman, registrar, Pearl Assurance agent, special constable, fireman, ambulance driver, taxi driver, and undertaker. He and his wife run the general store and he has a uniform or outfit to go with each job.

Achamore House Gardens (open daily Apr–Oct, 10am–6pm: adm) are a riot of sub-tropical plants and shrubs, all thriving in this mild westerly climate. The gardens were developed by Sir James Horlick, who bought the island in 1944. A lucky combination of the acidic soil, the warm air of the Gulf Stream and Sir James' milk-drink-derived fortune created this paradise of rhododendrons, camellias, and azaleas. There are carpets of bulbs and many exotic blooms to give a vivid foreground to lovely views.

The ruined church at Kilchattan dates from the 13th century. There is a golf course, a visitor centre, a hotel and a Boathouse Bar.

WHERE TO STAY AND EAT

Gigha Hotel, tel 05835 275, would be a perfect honeymoon retreat on this paradise island. Almost ranch-style, moderately priced, not a bit grand, it has good local food and lovely views. Down the scale a bit, cheap and also full of character, **Post Office House**, tel 05835 251, has four bedrooms, one public bathroom and a great atmosphere.

For those who like freedom, **Gigha Enterprises** have a house and two cottages, self-catering, tel 05835 254; quite pricey.

ISLAY

(Pronounced *Iler*).

Islay, the most southerly of the Hebrides, is some 14 miles off Kintyre, about 25 miles from north to south and 20 across at the widest point. It is a land of contrasts: peaceful farmland rises to wild moor cut by burns; and rugged coastline gives way to great open sweeps of beach. It is a favourite holiday island for birdwatchers, naturalists, photographers and artists. There are many remains to interest archaeologists, as the island has been inhabited since Neolithic times.

Excellent trout and salmon fishing can be found on the rivers Duich and Sorn, and on well-stocked lochs such as Gorm, Torrabus and Ballygrant. Boats can be hired locally for sea-angling, too. Warmed by the Gulf Stream, or so they say, miles of sandy beaches offer swimming and sunbathing. The surf is sometimes good. Machrie 18-hole golf course is well known for excellence.

Perhaps best known for its distinctive, smokey malt whisky, Islay has eight distilleries which scent the air with the pungent smell of smouldering peat. Now and then, islanders tangle with conservationists who insist that the special Duich Moss peat, essential for the flavour of Islay whisky, should be preserved for rare Greenland white-fronted geese. At a stormy meeting not so long ago, the islanders, furious at Green interference, argued that whisky was more vital to their survival than 'any bloody goose'. The distilleries welcome visitors.

GETTING THERE

Ferries run to Port Ellen and Askaig, from Kennacraig, in northwest Kintyre, taking just over two hours.

Loganair fly from Glasgow or Campbeltown, to the island's airport at Glenegadale. Flights take half an hour.

A local bus service links most of the island communities with extra runs in the summer. There are day tours of beauty spots and places of interest.

TOURIST INFORMATION

Mid Argyll, Kintyre and Islay Tourist Board, The Pier, Campbeltown, tel 0586 52056.
Tourist Information Centre, Bowmore, tel 049681 254.

Port Ellen is the ferry arrival point at the south of the island. Port Ellen Distillery, built 1815, dominates the skyline overlooking Leodamus Bay. Closed during the slump of the

1930s, it was then modernized. It was closed briefly again in 1983, due to a 'Whisky Lake', and makes Port Ellen Single Malt.

Ruined 14th-century **Dunyvaig Castle**, three and a half miles east of Port Ellen, was once the stronghold of the Macdonalds of Islay in the days when the Lords of the Isles considered themselves to be separate from the authority of the Crown. Ruined **Kildalton Chapel and Cross**, seven miles further north along this road, is presently undergoing restoration. Look out for the 9th-century Celtic cross carved from a single block of blue stone and inscribed with early Christian symbols. It is similar to one in Iona Cathedral, and is one of the finest in the country. There is a hotel here and the views are glorious. **Claggain Bay**, beyond the chapel, is a lovely sandy bay with rocky pools, backed by Beinn Bheigeir (1609 ft), the highest hill in Islay.

Rugged **Oa Peninsula**, five miles southwest of Port Ellen, was once a haunt of smugglers and illicit whisky distillers, who made cunning use of the sheer cliffs honeycombed with caves. One road runs across it but most of the peninsula is only accessible on foot.

Machrie, north of Oa, has an 18-hole golf course on the machair, and borders the sandy crescent of Laggan Bay.

Bowmore, 14 miles or so north of Port Ellen, was the old capital and administrative centre of the island. It was seat of Islay Parliament, a sort of feudal court, between 1718 and 1843. The intriguing, round church of Kilarrow was built in 1767, by a Campbell Lord of Islay. Italian in design, its shape deprives the devil of any corners in which to lurk. Bowmore Distillery, established in 1779, claims to be the oldest legal distillery on Islay and is still privately owned.

Brigend is a hamlet among woods at the head of Loch Indaal with good beaches and a hotel.

The Rhinns of Islay sticks out from the west side of the island like a great hammer-head. Here there are more wonderful walks and views out to sea. Bruichladdich Distillery overlooks Loch Indaal and brews an excellent 10-year-old single malt.

Award-winning **Museum of Islay Life** is in a converted church in **Port Charlotte**, on the southeast shore of the Rhinns (open daily Easter–Oct, Sun afternoons, Nov, Jan–March, closed Dec: adm). Exhibits cover the history of the island from prehistoric times to the present, with traditional craft work and tools, a maritime section, domestic artifacts, and a good selection of publications. A Lapidarium, below the museum, displays an important collection of carved stones dating from the 16th century. There is a Wildfowl Sanctuary at **Ellister** south of Port Charlotte, and an RSPB Reserve at **Loch Gruinart** to the north. **Portnahaven** is the southwest tip of Islay, with the green shores of Ireland only spitting distance away. The seas can be wild in westerly gales.

Finlaggan Castle is a ruin on an islet in Loch Finlaggan, just off the road from Bowmore to Port Askaig. This was the main stronghold of the Macdonalds, Lords of the Isles. The 14 chiefs of the Lordship were summoned to council meetings here, to confer with their overlord. They came from all over the Kingdom of the Isles, in coracles, accompanied by members of their clans. They were proud men, who settled their disputes and problems independently of the Scottish Parliament, often with great wisdom and justice.

Port Askaig is the other ferry terminal, and boats run from here to Jura. The views across the narrow Sound of Islay to the Paps of Jura are glorious. There is a hotel and a roadless hinterland to the north for idyllic walks.

WHERE TO STAY

Port Askaig Hotel, tel 049684 245, looks over the harbour is cheap and open all year, an attractive, cosy place, with three public bathrooms between nine bedrooms. **Lochside Hotel**, Bowmore, tel 049681 265/244, also cheap, overlooks Loch Indaal, and is an old-fashioned, friendly hotel, ideal for birdwatching. Open all year. (Two public bathrooms to seven bedrooms.) **Bridgend Hotel**, tel 049681 212, has not only 10 private bathrooms for its 10 bedrooms, but three extra, public ones as well. Moderately priced, it has a pretty garden, good food and is open all year.

JURA

Just off the northeast coast of Islay, Jura has very little tourist accommodation so is far less frequented. Wild and rugged, it is famous for its deer, which are keenly stalked by sportsmen. Over 20 miles long and sparsely populated, it has a small village, Craighouse, a distillery and a hotel. Silver and white sandy beaches give way to rugged shingle which teems with wildfowl. Loch Tarbert almost cuts the island in two from the west. Three forest-covered Paps of Jura rear up at the south end of the island; the highest (2571 ft) gives wonderful views. A single track road runs south from the ferry, and then some way up the east coast. Most of the island is only accessible on foot.

GETTING THERE

A car ferry runs frequently from Port Askaig in Islay to Feolin. It is a 10-minute crossing (there are fewer ferries on Sundays).

TOURIST INFORMATION

Mid Argyll, Kintyre and Islay Tourist Board, The Pier, Campbeltown, tel 0586 52056.

Craighouse, the only village, has the island's single hotel, **The Jura**. They will arrange riding, fishing, sea-angling, boating, shooting and water skiing.

The **Corryvreckan Whirlpool** in the strait between Jura and Scarba, is one of the features of the island. Notorious to west-coast sailors, the Corryvreckan is both lion and lamb. In the right conditions of tide and weather its mighty maw has been known to suck down whole boats, roaring like an express train. But at slack tide, it can be approached by sea, its satin-smooth water ruffled by tiny eddies that pull gently at the boat without harm.

Seven miles beyond Ardlussa, on a rough track, lies **Barnhill**, the white farmhouse where George Orwell lived, and wrote *1984*, struggling against the consumption that killed him.

WHERE TO STAY

Jura Hotel, Craighouse, tel 049682 243, has a relaxed, friendly atmosphere in a lovely setting, with good food. It's cheap and the 17 bedrooms share four public bathrooms.

There is a self-catering house at Craighouse, sleeping five: c/o Mrs Mary Keith, Keills, Craighouse, Isle of Jura, Argyll PA60 7XG, tel 049682 214. Open April–Oct, and cheap. And another, a bit more expensive, sleeping six, c/o Mr Renwick, 5 Kelvin Drive Glasgow tel 041 946 4361. Another, at Ardfarnal, sleeping nine, c/o Mr A. Fairman, 83 James Street, Helensburgh Dunbartonshire, tel 0436 75760.

COLONSAY AND ORONSAY

These two tiny islands, joined at low tide, lie 10 miles west of Jura, 25 miles from the mainland. To the west, the only thing between them and Canada is **Du Hirteach Lighthouse**. The landscape is made up of craggy hills, woods and a rocky coastline broken by wonderful silver sands. Their names are derived from the Saints Columba and Oran who landed here on their way to Scotland from Ireland. Legend holds that when Columba discovered he could still see the shore of the land from which he had been exiled, he pressed on to Iona; whether from repugnance or sadness is not related. It is also said he banished snakes from the two islands, as he did on Iona, presumably to make himself feel more at home. Both islands are paradise for botanists, archaeologists and ornithologists, as well as for people looking for peace and quiet. They have a high average of sunshine. Over 500 species of wild flowers can be found, including rare purple orchids, sea samphire and marsh helleborine. Bluebells and primroses bloom in the woods, wild irises flower in damp corners, harebells nod on the sand dunes and purple thrift clings to the rocks. Eucalyptus, palm trees and rare, tender shrubs flourish in the mild climate. There are also over 150 different birds.

GETTING THERE
The car ferry from Oban, three times a week, takes two and a half hours.

TOURIST INFORMATION
Tourist Information Centre, Oban, Argyll, tel 0631 63122.

Colonsay House Gardens (open daily: free) have a wealth of sub-tropical shrubs and plants, rhododendrons, embothriums, magnolias and palm trees.

Wild goats roam the island, reputedly descended from survivors of a Spanish Armada wreck in 1588. Otters can be seen occasionally, and lots of grey seals. **Balnahard** is a beautiful beach with hundreds of cowrie shells in the coves. **Kiloran Bay** in the northwest is spectacular, and when the wind is in the west there is excellent safe surfing in huge Atlantic rollers. **The Strand** is a beach a mile wide in the south of the island festooned with mussels on the rocks, and prawns in the pools. At low tide, the Strand is the causeway, accessible for about three hours, to Oronsay, an enchanted island populated by sheep and serenaded by skylarks.

St Oran's Chapel, on Oronsay, is a ruined 14th-century priory, named after St Columba's faithful companion. Although the cloisters have fallen this is a splendid ruin with gravestones carved with boats and warriors and hunting scenes. A tall, beautifully carved Celtic cross stands at the entrance. Excavations, of which there are no trace now, revealed that Oronsay was inhabited in the Middle Stone Age. Certainly Norsemen lived here, long before the present chapel was built by Columban monks.

WHERE TO STAY

You are not spoilt for choice. **Isle of Colonsay Hotel**, tel 09512 316, is moderately priced, comfortable and informal, highly recommended and serves good food. The hotel also has three self-catering chalets, each with two bedrooms and one public room. There are three bed and breakfast places, all quite cheap: **Baleromindobh Farm**, tel 09512 305, a farm house, with three bedrooms; **Seaview**, tel 09512 315, a working croft with three bedrooms; and **Garvard**, tel 09512 343, a farmhouse with three bedrooms. There are also a number of cottages to let on Colonsay and flats in Colonsay House.

MULL

Mull, 'isle-of-the-cool-high-bends' is the largest of the Inner Hebrides and deserves a whole book to itself. Shaped like a caricature of the British Isles, its southwestern peninsula kicking frivolously upwards, it is encircled by 300 miles of rugged coastline, deeply cut by lochs. It is an island of contrasts, with many wooded hillsides and marvellous secret corners, easily reached by coastal roads. The western seaboard is sprinkled with spectacular islands: **Inch Kenneth, Ulva, Staffa** and, further west, the **Treshnish Isles** with **Coll** and **Tiree** beyond. There are plenty of boat trips to the islands and some of the hotels charter their own boats. In addition, there are always local men who will take you out fishing or sightseeing. The whole coast is a sailor's paradise. Around the head of Loch Na Keal, in the middle of the west coast there are staggering steep cliffs fringed by sandy inlets. Sunsets are as romantic and memorable as you can ever hope to find. The hinterland is a mass of hills, dominated by **Ben More**, 3169 ft, in the west.

Johnson and Boswell came to Mull during their tour of the Hebrides. Johnson lamented the lack of trees, attributing it to idleness, but applauded the excellent French wine he was given.

There are more red deer on Mull than people: over 3000 roam the island and the smaller fallow deer can be seen in the woods around Gruline and Salen. There are also polecats, weasels, stoats, escaped mink, feral ferrets and, for the patient observer, otters. Wild white goats can be seen from Grass Point down to the Ross of Mull.

Unlike some other islands, the depopulation of 150 years has been reversed in Mull. With fishing, farming, tourism and building to employ them, fewer young people are seeking the bright lights of the mainland and there are a number of incomers who prefer insular peace and beauty to the materialistic scramble of the cities.

There is a Drama Festival in March, a Music Festival in April, Tobermory Highland Games in July, and also Children's Highland Games. West Highland Yachting Week takes place in early August, Salen Show, which includes a dogshow, is in August and there is a Car Rally in October.

GETTING THERE

Car ferries run quite frequently from Oban–Craignure in just under an hour; Oban–Tobermory takes about 2 hours and Lochaline–Fishnish, a quarter of an hour.

There is also a car ferry from Mingary (Kilchoan) to Tobermory, taking half an hour. You can get 'Multi-stop' ferry tickets, much cheaper, if you want to visit several places. Further information: Caledonian MacBrayne, tel 0475 34531, or 0631 62285. There is an airfield on the island to which charter flights can be arranged from Glasgow. Virtually all the roads are single-track with passing places.

TOURIST INFORMATION
Tourist Information Centre, Tobermory, Isle of Mull, tel 0688 2182.
Oban, Mull and District Tourist Board, Oban, Argyll PA34 4AN, tel 0631 63122.

Island cruises
Inter island cruises in high-speed charter boats, to Staffa, Treshnish, Coll, Eigg, Muck, can be booked from Richard and Judy Fairbairns, Dervaig, tel 06884 223, and if you are lucky you might see whales and dolphins. Or try Turus Mara, tel 06884 242/0631/63122. You need to go prepared: take a good picnic, plenty of weatherproof clothing as conditions can change quickly, and seasick pills—the slow Atlantic swell can be disastrous for uneasy stomachs.

The boat from Oban passes **Lady Rock**, a tiny islet off Lismore Lighthouse at the head of Loch Linnhe. In the 16th century, a Maclean of Lochbuie, disenchanted by his wife, tethered her to this rock. Passing fishermen took pity and released her and she fled to her father, Campbell of Inveraray. This irate chief invited Maclean to stay on the pretext of commiserating with him at the death of his wife. At the end of dinner, the 'deceased' wife confronted her husband, and her relatives set on him with broadswords.

Fishing
Wet- or dry-fly trout fishing is available in Mishnish Lochs, Loch Tor and Loch Frisa. Licences, tackle and bait can be obtained from Brown's Ironmongers in Tobermory High Street or the National Forestry Commission's office at the south end of Loch Frisa. You can also hire rods and boats.

Tobermory
Having stopped off at Craignure, the ferry sails up the Sound of Mull to Tobermory —meaning Well of St Mary—the 'capital' of Mull. Founded as a fishing village in 1789 on the site of an earlier Christian settlement, it has one of the most sheltered harbours in Scotland, tucked round behind a headland. The village clusters round the anchorage. Terraced houses, colour-washed in strong reds, pinks, yellows, blues, ochres, rise from the harbour up a steep, wooded bank. Yachtsmen and fishermen jostle cheerfully for mooring space. At the end of the day, the calm is shattered by jovial voices as sailors hail each other across the water, having last met up in some other west coast anchorage, maybe years before. *Ceilidh*s erupt spontaneously in the bars and hotels that line the waterfront; lights twinkle from cabin portholes and everywhere is the sound of laughter; dinghies come and go between the boats during long summer evenings. Tobermory is fun.

Mull and Iona Museum (open weekdays, May–Sept, adm) is in a converted church in the Main Street, with exibitions of the island's history. In the bay beyond the harbour lies the wreck of a galleon, the *Florencia*, part of the Spanish Armada, which is still a focus of attention for treasure seekers today. The ship sought shelter here in a storm in 1588. Always hospitable, the islanders treated the Spaniards with courtesy, restocking their stores and entertaining them in grand style. But Scotsmen are thrifty, as well as hospitable, and when rumour came that the *Florencia* was about to depart, without having paid its dues, a local man, Donald Maclean, went aboard to remonstrate. He was locked up in the ship's cell, but managed to escape. In retaliation he blew up the ship, together with the vast hoard of gold and treasure it was alleged to have been carrying. So far, only a few coins and cannon have been discovered, but the search continues. Divers should note, however, that the wreck is protected and it is forbidden to dive in its area.

Tobermory has a 9-hole golf course, on the northern tip of the island, owned by the Western Isles Hotel. Spectacular views down the sound of Mull are apt to distract the players.

Going west on the B8073, look out for three small, linked lochs where there is trout fishing. Snake Pass, beyond the last loch, is said to be the home of many adders. This is also the start of a good walk to Loch Frisa.

On the steep hill down into **Dervaig** there is a cemetery at Kilmore, with some of the oldest gravestones on Mull. Film goers may recognise this as one of the sets for *Where Eight Bells Toll*. **Mull Little Theatre**, in Dervaig, six miles from Tobermory, is in the Guiness Book of Records as the smallest professional theatre in Britain, with 37 seats. Six times a week in the summer, two or more actors from visiting professional companies stage really excellent productions, which should be booked well in advance: tel 06884 245. In the winter there are amateur productions. A restaurant and guest house has just opened, serving dinner before and after the show. Lunch is also served before matinées. Meals should be bookcd, tel 06884 345.

The Old Byre Heritage Centre, a mile beyond Dervaig (open daily, Easter–mid-Oct: adm) is a crofting museum with fascinating tableaux showing life at the time of the Highland Clearances, most cleverly done in every detail, with the family and animals round the central fire, busy about their daily lives. A half-hour audio-visual programme illustrates further what life was like. Well worth a visit.

The west coast road gives glorious views out to the scattering of islands that create such wonderful seascapes, especially when seen against a setting sun. There are a

Staffa, Fingal's Cave

number of good sandy beaches and it is usually possible to find shelter on one of them.

Boats run from Dervaig or Ulva to the **Treshnish Isles** and to **Staffa**, when the weather is fair. A new landing stage on Staffa makes access considerably easier in rough weather and some cruises allow you an hour ashore. The organ-pipe rock formation inspired Mendelssohn in 1829 to write *The Hebridean Overture*.

Cruises which include **Lunga** in the Treshnish Isles, are especially good during the nesting season. You are advised not to linger too long over the puffins at the start of your tour because they are so bewitching you may never see the rest of the island. They sit scratching, chatting and popping in and out of their burrows just an arm's length from you. There are also kittiwakes, razorbills, shags and guillemots and lots of black rabbits.

The island of Ulva will be familiar to anyone who had to learn the poem 'Lord Ullin's Daughter' at school. It tells the sad tale of 'The Chief of Ulva's Isle' and his lover, fleeing her father's wrath and drowning in the ferry, crossing to the island. Lord Ullin stood helpless on the shore, while:

> *The waters wild went o'er his child,*
> *And he was left lamenting.*

A couple of miles before the Ulva Ferry, look out for the Eas Forss, a waterfall that cascades over the cliff into a pool and then under a rock, arching into the sea.

The walks and views all down the west coast are memorable. Much of the coastline is columned basalt with sandy bays and rock coves, with seals, guillemots, oystercatchers and herons in the rock pools. Wild flowers are abundant: wild orchids, bright pink thrift, yellow irises.

Where the road turns south, before cutting back inland across the Ardmeanach peninsular, you can look out across the entrance to Loch na Keal, to Inch Kenneth. This was the burial place of many Scottish kings, visited by Johnson and Boswell in 1773, as guests of Sir Allan Maclean and his two daughters. Unity Mitford took refuge here after her unfortunate association with Hitler and the Nazis. To the right, **Tragedy Rock** is a huge boulder which crashed onto the cottage of a young local couple on the first night of their married life, 200 years ago, killing them both.

The Ardmeanach Peninsula, owned by the National Trust for Scotland, has a treasure, at the end of a 12-mile walk. At Burgh on the southern tip, aptly named The Wilderness, there is a fossilized tree, 50 million years old, embedded in the shore.

The Ross of Mull is the southwest headland, with softer scenery. **Erraid**, the tidal islet off the southwest tip of the Ross, was once home of Robert Louis Stevenson, and it was here David Balfour swam ashore from the wreck of the brig *Covenant*, in *Kidnapped*. **Uisken** on the south side, reached by a road from Bunessan, is a lovely beach with lonely crofts, mostly ruined—another village abandoned in the Clearances.

Isle of Mull Wine Co at Bunessan welcomes visitors and will arrange tastings by appointment, tel 06817 403. They make the Isle of Mull Vermouth, and The Mull Riveter, a blend of their own vermouth and bitters with vodka. Children will enjoy a visit to the **Angora Rabbit Farm** at Ardtun near Bunessan, where they can see how their clipped coats are made into wool. Further east, at Pennyghael, take the road south to Carsaig, a lovely spot where salmon fishermen still work. The amazing Carcaig Arches is a famous geological freak—a natural, jagged archway through the rock.

The A849 goes inland back towards the east coast from the head of Loch Scridain. At Ardura a road turns south to Loch Buie, a lovely drive down past Loch Spelve and Loch

Uisg. Moy Castle, at the end, now a ruin, was the ancestral home of the MacLaines of Lochbuie. If you take the track on round the coast for three miles you come to Lord Lovat's Cave.

Duart Castle (winner of the Castle of the Year award in 1988: open daily, May–Sept: adm), is 15 miles east of the head of Loch Scridain across great tracts of moor and hill. It is an impressive fortress on a headland guarding the approach to the Sound of Mull. It dates from the 13th century, and was the home of the Chiefs of Maclean, until it was confiscated after the Jacobite rising in 1745. It was bought back and restored in 1912 by Sir Fitzroy Maclean, who was then the chief. He was a gallant Hussar Colonel who had ridden with the Light Brigade in the Crimea and died at the age of 100, affectionately known as Old Man A Hundred. The widow of the last Lord Maclean, who died in 1990, still lives at Duart for most of the year.

As well as the keep, visitors can see the cell where prisoners were held from the Spanish galleon, *Florencia*, after it had been sunk in Tobermory, in 1588, by Donald Maclean. There are relics of the Maclean family in the main hall, with many of the gifts presented to the late Chief—who was among many other things, Chief Scout—during his world tours. There is also an Exhibition of Scouting throughout the Commonwealth, in the old staff rooms at the top of the castle.

Just south of Duart, the road to **Grass Point**, on Lochdon, was the old drovers' road for cattle and sheep from the outer isles, bound for mainland markets. It was also the landing point for pilgrims going to Iona. The seals on the rocks round the bay are rather a different species to those living in the waters round Mull. These seals are the handiwork of the eminent sculptor, poet and writer, the late Lionel Leslie. First cousin of Winston Churchill, he and his wife Barbara came to live in the old Drover's Inn, after the last war, building it up with their own hands. Boatloads of visitors used to come over from Oban in the summer, to have tea, buy local crafts and listen to the sculptor's stories. Even in his mid-eighties, his wit was a sharp as the stone he could no longer see to carve. There are also bas reliefs of a deer, an eagle, fighting swans and horses on the rocks, in lasting memory of a great artist. Sadly, the house is now decayed.

Torosay Castle (open daily, late April–mid-Oct: adm) is a mile south of Craignure near Duart. This splendid 19th-century Scottish baronial building, with all the embellishments so beloved by the Victorians, was designed by David Bryce. The 11 acres of terraced Italian-style gardens with a statue walk and water garden were laid out by Robert Lorimer. Among the things to see in the house are some magnificent paintings of wild life by Thorburn, Landseer and Peter Scott, and family portraits by Poynter, de Lazlo, Sargent and Carlos Sancha. There are also hunting trophies, a library and an archive room with photographs and scrapbooks going back over 100 years. In the high season boats run from Oban direct to Torosay. A **miniature railway** runs from Craignure Pier, a mile and a half, to the castle, the only passenger train service in the Hebrides.

The roofless, ruined church, by the cemetery at **Salen** is unlikely to be restored. A very wicked Maclean of Duart was buried here many years ago and the consequence was the roof blew off. Three times they put it back and three times it blew away, unable to settle over the remains of such a villain. Sadly, the first-century statue of the Virgin Mary that used to be in this church has been stolen.

IONA

No one can visit Mull without making a pilgrimage to the 'cradle of Christianity', though, in fact, St Ninian was spreading the word for nearly 150 years before St Columba founded his church on Iona in 563. The island is beautiful; white cockle-shell sand and vivid green slopes, slashed with rust-red granite and painted with wild flowers.

The powerful Irish saint, of royal descent, outlawed from his own land, came here with a few followers and set about converting the heathen Picts of Scotland to the Celtic Christianity of his homeland. Many Scots, Irish and Norse kings were buried on Iona including Macbeth and Duncan.

GETTING THERE
The passenger ferry from Fionnphort, on Mull, to Iona, takes five minutes. There is also a Sacred Isles Cruise, on certain days in the summer, sailing from Oban, via Staffa, to Iona. They allow two and a half hours on Iona before the return journey.

In 1938, George Macleod, a saintly Presbyterian Socialist, who renounced an inherited title but accepted one bestowed by the State, settled a new community on the island. Its purpose was to restore the ancient stones and create the present abbey and its domestic building. When Johnson and Boswell came here in 1773, before Iona was restored and the abbey was a complete ruin, Johnson was deeply moved by the atmosphere: 'That man is little to be envied ... whose piety would not grow warmer among the ruins of Iona.' Today he may not have been so impressed. Opinions differ about this historic abbey: for some, the sanctity of the stark, unadorned interior has been erased by stalls selling postcards, souvenirs and booklets. They complain that the sightseers, slung about with cameras and macintoshes, are seldom inspired to kneel and say a prayer, and unfriendly ferrymen have been known to ram visiting boats which innocently trespass on ferry berths. But even if it does not, at first sight, feel like the house of God, Iona is electric: St Columba was here, all those years ago. If you scratch below the rather worldly exterior, you will find informal services, taken by the warden and his wife, at which visitors are welcomed to share in the community worship. Visiting preachers and members of the Community take part and everyone is encouraged to meet up afterwards for tea and coffee. There is a well stocked bookshop.

Anyone feeling a tug of disappointment at the 'pay-at-the-door museum' feeling of this sacred spot should climb the small hill, **Dun I**, to the north of the abbey. Look down on the buildings, the boats around the pier, the trails of people in bright anoraks and strap-hung impedimenta; chattering, munching and scattering litter. Stay very quiet and listen: you may catch a faint echo of ironic laughter, and feel a gentle Celtic presence beside you. St Columba was known to have a well developed sense of humour.

WHERE TO STAY
Western Isles Hotel, Tobermory, tel 0688 2012, stands high above the harbour, with magnificent views, open March to October. It is a good, old-fashioned hotel, cheap and comfortable with friendly staff. **Tobermory Hotel**, tel 0688 2091, is right on the waterfront, also cheap and full of character. **Ardfenaig House**, Bunessan, tel 06817 210, is a small, moderately priced country house hotel, peaceful and remote, open May to September, with very good food. **Craignure Inn**, tel 06802 305, is the original

drovers' inn, once scene of pungent activity, now more genteel with cars rather than beasts parked outside. Four bedrooms and one public bathroom—which was more than the drovers got), and it's cheap. **Isle of Mull Hotel**, Craignure, tel 06802 351, was certainly not there in the drovers' day: a Benidorm-style monstrosity whose moderately priced 60 bedrooms *all* have private bathrooms. **Druimnacroish Country House Hotel** Dervaig, tel 06884 274/212, has what its name implies: a country house atmosphere and excellent service, expensive by Mull standards, but worth it for the *ceilidhs* that errupt when locals visit the bar. Run in conjuction with the Muk Little Theatre, they serve excellent dinners, by arrangement, before the plays begin. **Quinish House** is a guesthouse in Dervaig, tel 06884 223, cheap, family run and comfortable. **Tiroran House** tel 06815 232, is another of the more expensive places, specializing in a small country-house atmosphere and candlelit dinners.

Mull has dozens of self-catering places, most of which are in the Tourist Board Brochure, ranging from one-bedroom cottages to large country houses. Artists should head for **Inniemore**, at Pennyghael, tel 06814 201, a guesthouse-painting-school for promising amateurs, with first-class tuition. Prices on application. **Glenforsa Hotel** near the airport at Salen, tel 06803 377, is a cheap, log-cabin hotel with an easy, relaxed atmosphere.

On Iona, **The Abbey**, tel 06817 404, offers full board from March to December and visitors are expected to take part in the day to day activities of the Community. There are also week-long courses: details from the joint wardens, Philip and Alison Newall. It's very cheap and pretty spartan, with 23 rooms, four bathrooms and monkish food (no licence). **Argyll Hotel**, tel 06817 334, on the shore looking back towards Mull, is cheap, open April to October. Or **St Columba Hotel**, tel 06817 304, also cheap; a modern, rather utilitarian place with 27 bedrooms and not much soul.

For an evening out, try **The Puffer Aground**, in Salen, tel Aros 389. The food is good and you should book.

COLL AND TIREE

Coll and Tiree, less than 11 miles off the northwest tip of Mull, are low islands which look barren from the sea but are charming, with soft green fields surrounded by an almost continuous string of deserted white beaches—mile upon mile of solitude, where you will see many sea birds, seals and even otters. Sturdy cottages have rounded, tar-felted roofs to withstand the winter gales.

You can hire cars which meet you at the ferry, very reasonably.

Coll

Coll is fish-shaped, about 13 miles long and three wide. Beaches of clean sand, crystal-clear azure water, rocky coves, backed by machair strewn with wild flowers in spring make this another away-from-it-all paradise. The record of sunshine is good (usually tempered by a persistent wind).

Coll's history goes back a long way. Two standing stones at Totronald, called *Na Sgeulachan* (the Tellers of Tales), are thought to be part of a pagan temple, and traces of pre-historic forts and duns scatter the island. Adamnan, Saint Columba's biographer, mentions it in his *Vita Sancti Columbae*. During the Norse occupation of the islands, Coll was the headquarters of Earl Gilli, brother-in-law of Sigurd, Ruler of the Orkneys and Hebrides in 1000. By the end of 13th century it belonged to the MacDougalls of Lorne from whom it was taken by Robert the Bruce—because they opposed him. It passed to a second son of the Macleans of Duart in the early 1400s and remained in their keeping until 1856, when Hugh Maclean, last laird of Coll, was forced to sell his estates to pay for his extravagant way of life. John Stewart of Glenbuckie, factor to the Duke of Argyll, bought it and his ruthlessly efficient farming methods resulted in mass emigration to Canada and Australia by the unfortunate crofters who could no longer afford inflated rents (see 'Topics: Highland Clearances'). Traces of their abandoned croft houses can still be seen at the northern end of the island. The resident population is now about 130, with quite a few incomers and holiday-home owners. Coll has attracted a number of *literati* and features now and then in glossy magazines. Over a dram, these foreigners tell of the distinction between Old Odds and New Odds. In the parlance of the local shop, the 'Odds' were the summer residents with a credit book separate from that of the locals. When a new book was opened, kudos was gained from being in the Old Odds' book.

Coll is known for its trout-filled lochs. Sea fishing is also good and local fishermen will take visitors out in their boats. Walking, bicycling, swimming, birdwatching, botany and relaxation are the chief occupations for visitors. There is a recently made 9-hole golf course at Arinagour. This village is the main concentration of population, a trim little place with twee cottages and gardens which lies round the western shore of Loch Eatharna.

The economy depends mainly on farming, commercial fishing and tourism. A recent innovation is a small factory in Arinagour where a range of herbal skin-care products are made.

Breachachadh Castle, recently restored and private, dates from the 15th-century, tel 08793 444/353.

GETTING THERE
Boats run from Oban, four times a week in summer and three times in winter, and take three hours. Boats also run from Tobermory, taking two hours. For details, contact Caledonian MacBrayne, tel 0631 62285.

TOURIST INFORMATION
Tourist Information Centre, Oban, tel 0631 63122.

WHERE TO STAY AND EAT
Isle of Coll Hotel, tel 08793 334, at the head of Arinagour Bay overlooking the Treshnish Islands, is cheap and has six bedrooms and a lovely Hebridean atmosphere. Also in Arinagour, and cheap, with a restricted drink licence, **Tigh-na-Mara Guest House**, tel 08793 354, is a modern house overlooking the bay with eight bedrooms and an equally friendly atmosphere. Self-catering places aren't too expensive and include: one chalet and three flats in Arinagour, c/o Janet Driver, Arinagour, Isle of Coll, tel 08793 373; and a house, a bungalow and a bothy, c/o Mrs Stewart, Estate Office, Isle of Coll, tel 08793 339.

Tiree

Tiree, just southwest of Coll, is about 12 miles long, seven at its widest, dwindling to less than one. Its name comes from *Tir Eth* (Land of Corn), dating from the days when it supplied corn to Iona, and it is so low and flat it has the Gaelic nickname *Tir fo Thuinn* (Land Below the Waves). It used to be famous for its snipe before much of the ground was drained. The highest hill, **Ben Hynish**, is a 480 ft pimple. It shares with Coll a reputation for glorious beaches, abundant wild flowers and birds, as well as a high average of sunshine. This, with its magnificent Atlantic rollers, has earned it the title 'Hawaii of the North'. Windsurfers come from all over Britain to compete in Tiree where conditions are first rate. During championship weeks, world-class windsurfing can be watched. Tiree also has a phenomenal population of hares.

A standing stone near **Balinoe** is thought to have been part of a Druid temple. Many of the island names are Norse in origin, dating from the 400 years of Norse occupation from about 890–1266. Among the many ancient remains scattered over Tiree is **Dun Mor Broch**, on lovely **Vaul Bay**, on the north coast, a well-preserved ruin of one of the tall, hollow towers probably built for refuge from Norse and other invaders. It is 30 ft in diameter, its walls as much as 13 ft thick. **Gott Bay** is a three and a half-mile crescent of sand, backed by rich machair carpeted with wild flowers. **Hynish** is very interesting: it has a small dry dock, flooded by an elaborate system of fresh water from springs. There is a young people's outdoor training centre, based in the lighthousemen's houses. On the north shore of **Balephetrish** another good beach, *Clac á Choire* (Stone of the Corrie) is a large granite boulder perched on a rocky base, a relic from the Ice Age. Decorated with intriguing pre-historic carvings it is known locally as the Ringing Stone because of the metallic note it produces when struck. It is said that when Clac á Choire shatters, Tiree will sink below the waves.

Views are marvellous all round the coast, especially those to the Treshnish Islands to the east with the distinctive aircraft-carrier-shaped *Bac Mor* (The Dutchman's Cap). One of the best places to see the bird-life is under the sheer cliffs below Carnan Mor in the south. Look out for the distinctive 'Greenstone' on the beaches, found also in Iona. Tiree has a 9-hole golf course.

Skerryvore Museum in the old signal tower at Hynish tells the story of the construction of the Skerryvore Lighthouse, visible at the end of a telescope, built by the father of Robert Louis Stevenson.

GETTING THERE
Loganair fly twice daily from Glasgow to Tiree, tel 041 889 3181.

The car ferry from Oban to Tiree usually calls at Coll on the way, a four-hour journey in all. Boats also run from Tobermory. Further information: Caledonian MacBrayne, tel 0631 62285.

TOURIST INFORMATION
Tourist Information Centre, Oban, tel 0631 63122.

WHERE TO STAY AND EAT
Scarinish Hotel, tel 08792 308, stands on the sea, with 11 rooms, one with private bathroom and two public bathrooms between the other 10. It's cheap, with good

Highland hospitality. **Tiree Lodge Hotel**, tel 08792 353/368, also overlooking the sea and cheap, has 12 bedrooms, seven with private bathrooms plus two public ones, and the same lovely easy atmosphere. **Balephetrish Guest House**, tel 08792 549, is a pebble-dash croft house, overlooking Balephetrish Bay, cheap, with four bedrooms and one bathroom. **The Glassery Guest House**, with a restaurant, is at Sandaig on the west coast, tel 08792 684 and also cheap.

Part IX

GLASGOW

Crow Steeple

Beautiful city of Glasgow, with your streets so neat and clean,
Your stately mansions, and beautiful Green!
Likewise your beautiful bridges across the River Clyde,
And on your bonnie banks I would like to reside...

—from Scotland's worst poet, William McGonagall

Glasgow was once the ugly, boisterous, working-class hub of redundant industrial Scotland. Because of the flourishing Clydeside shipyards and all the associated heavy industry that grew up after the Industrial Revolution, Glasgow was particularly badly hit by the great Depression of the 1930s. Unemployment brought terrible hardship to seething warrens of slum tenements. But now, the 'Gorbals Image' (brilliantly encapsulated in *No Mean City*, by Λ. McArthur, written in the 1950s) has disappeared. Glasgow is a punchy, 20th-century city, humming with enterprise and vitality.

Edinburgh, with its International Festival, its gracious Georgian buildings, its historic past and its genteel Morningside ladies, was for many years lulled into a complacent acceptance of its role as cultural centre of Scotland. That complacency has been brutally exploded: Glasgow celebrated its reign as Cultural Capital of Europe in 1990, only the sixth city to be nominated, succeeding Athens, Florence, Amsterdam, Berlin and Paris. Poor Edinburgh: quietly, almost stealthily, that dirty, slum-infested tramp that was 'Glasgie', had moved up and surged into the lead. Only Glaswegians themselves are unsurprised.

243

History

It is amusing to reflect that when Edinburgh consisted of just a cluster of huts round a wooden fort, St Mungo was busy in Glasgow, establishing a church from which the present cathedral grew, on a site that had already been consecrated by St Ninian, two centuries before in the 4th century. So, although it cannot boast a saga of glittering royal dramas, its recorded history goes right back to the dawn of Christianity and relates to the fortunes of the church from that time.

Assuming that legend is born from fragments of fact, a Pictish princess, possibly the daughter of King Loth, was banished from her father's court at Traprain Law in Lothian in the 6th century because of her liaison with an undesirable suitor. She was cast adrift in a coracle on the Firth of Forth, and landed at Culross in Fife. St Serf (or Servanus) took her in and cherished her during the birth of her son, Kentigern. St Serf baptized mother and babe and brought the child up, giving him the affectionate nickname of Mungo (or Munchu) the Latin-Welsh endearment for 'dearest friend'. Mungo became a missionary: in fulfilment of a prophecy, he took the bones of a holy man, Fergus, and carried them until God told him to stop. Glasgow Cathedral now stands on that spot, and the bones of Fergus are interred there. The town that grew up around the church was called *Glas Cau* (Gaelic for 'the dear green place') and in the mild, dampish climate that prevails the land would certainly have been very green and fertile. Indeed, aerial photographs show a surprising amount of grass even now—over 70 parks in all.

Glasgow's coat of arms incorporates a salmon, a ring, a tree, a bird and a bell, all of which are related to the patron saint. Mungo saved the honour, and the life, of a queen by arranging for a ring that she had given her lover to be found in a salmon in the river, and returned to her to be shown to her suspicious husband. The tree is a branch that burned miraculously, enabling Mungo to rekindle the monastery fire that he had been entrusted to keep alight. The bird was a robin, a favourite of St Serf's, killed by accident and brought back to life by Mungo. The bell was one given to Mungo on his ordination and taken everywhere with him.

Glasgow's wonderfully self-confident motto, 'Let Glasgow Flourish', stems from the rather more cautious invocation that was inscribed on the 16th-century bell on the Tron Church: 'Let Glasgow Flourish Through the Preaching of the Word and Praising Thy Name'.

The city saw some moments of secular history: William Wallace defeated the English in a battle in 1300, over what is now the upper end of the High Street. The university was founded in 1451 by Bishop Turnbull, only 40 years after St Andrews. Mary, Queen of Scots', final bid for power after her escape from Leven Castle, in 1568, took place at Langside, near Queen's Park. She watched the battle from her horse, at Castle Knowe, riding forward into the mêlée to encourage her loyal troops, who were, even so, soon defeated. Cromwell came to Glasgow in 1650, and heard himself denounced as a 'sectary and blasphemer' by the Rector of the University, Zachary Boyd, in a two-hour sermon. Cromwell appears to have taken this public humiliation with rare humour, inviting Boyd to dinner and making him sit through three hours of prayer. Bonnie Prince Charlie lodged in the town on his way to Culloden, in 1745.

Separated from America by only the Atlantic, Glasgow merchants grew rich on the import of tobacco and sugar, after the Union of Parliaments in 1707. The Clyde, once a shallow salmon river, was deepened by dredgers and the city flourished as a major port, developing into the world's leading shipbuilding centre. Times of recession always hit hardest at areas of heavy industry, however, and Glasgow's docks are no longer the hives of activity that they used to be: Clydeside no longer reverberates to the ceaseless clang and clatter and fizzle of thriving shipyards. The Clyde is no longer the busy waterway it once was. But Glasgow has shaken itself free of dependence on heavy industry and diversified its economy so successfully that it is now a centre of modern technology that covers almost every form of manufacture.

Modern Glasgow: Renaissance

Glasgow offers as much top-class entertainment as anywhere in the country. Home of the Scottish Opera, one of Scotland's most prestigious possessions, as well as the Scottish National Orchestra and Scottish Ballet, Glasgow owns the Burrell Collection, attracting art lovers from all over the world. The three-week Mayfest, only a few years old, is the second-largest arts festival in the UK, next to Edinburgh. There are Folk and Jazz Festivals in June and July and the World Pipe Band Championships, in August, all attracting huge crowds. The Third Eye Arts Centre is the best in Scotland, stimulating great interest from people all over Britain and abroad. It mounts major art seasons with international themes—Polish, 1988, Soviet, 1989. Glasgow was recently said to rival Milan and Barcelona as one of the design capitals of the world.

Because the river flows through the heart of Glasgow it is very much the main artery of the city, flanked by greens and quays, spanned by a network of bridges. A huge redevelopment programme has transformed the old docklands so that it is now possible to take a 'scenic' walk from Glasgow Green to Finnieston without danger of being hoisted on a crane. Glasgow Green, the oldest public park in Britain, used to be the common grazing ground for the medieval city.

From any elevation on a clear day, the horizon is smudged by distant hills: to the north, beyond the modest Kilpatrick Hills and Campsie Fells, the great humps of Ben Lomond, Ben Venue and Ben Ledi; the hills of Strathclyde in the west; the Lowther Hills to the south and the Pentlands to the east.

Architecturally, Glasgow is a curate's egg. Some of Britain's finest Victorian buildings are jostled by some of the 20th-century's worst acts of architectural sacrilege, mostly high-rise. The highly efficient motorway network, taking traffic through the heart of the city at 50 mph, has improved communications beyond belief but heartrending acts of vandalism were committed to build it. Many of the older buildings have been cleaned recently: streets that used to be grimly blackened by pollution have been restored to the warm glow of biscuit and red sandstone. On the whole, the suburbs are a nightmare: an almost surreal jungle of shoddy, ugly monsters marching away in all directions, built in a misguided attempt to depopulate the slums. In time, as people move back into the now tenable inner city, these travesties of architecture may be replaced.

All this is somehow incidental to Glasgow's magic: the history, the monuments, the blossoming culture in every field of Fine Art are mere facets in a glittering diamond. In the earlier chapter on Edinburgh, there are long lists of things to see; a great parade of attractions and amusements as glossy as mink: compared with that, this chapter may seem disappointingly bare and lacking in specific descriptions. Glasgow is not easily revealed on paper: its magic lies not in its tangible, visible, material assets, but in its soul. It is an elusive magic: a will o' the wisp vitality; a vibrant atmosphere; a bewitching character only discovered by experience.

This magic is to be found in the streets of the city; in the bars and cafés; down on the waterfront; in the markets and shops. It is found in conversation with the man on the news-stand; the ticket-collector; the out-of-work dosser; the sharp-faced, sharp-tongued housewife with henna-ed hair in rollers under a pink chiffon scarf. It is found among the stall-holders, the taxi-drivers, the students and the old-age pensioners.

If comparisons must be made, and perhaps this is inevitable with two major cities so close to each other, Glasgow is to Edinburgh what New York is to Washington. The Glaswegian is to the Scottish music hall what the Cockney is to the English, and as in all parodies, there is some truth in these images but only in self-mocking overstatement. The Glaswegian is unique: a blend of the Irish who came over in their starving hundreds during the potato famine, and the deposed Highlanders, driven from their crofts by sheep farmers. He has the lyrical, romantic charm of the former and the gentle courtesy of the latter, combined with the Celtic wit and sensitivity of both. He adds to this endearing mixture a shrewd, worldly cockiness that stems from his independent spirit and courage.

Glasgow is like any strong personality: on first acquaintance one feels daunted and nervous and perhaps a little shy. But perseverance will uncover the warm character under the awe-inspiring façade and it soon becomes a 'dear, familiar friend'. Walk down to the river and stand on one of the bridges at night: the lights and reflections transform the work-a-day city into a fairystory kingdom of ethereal beauty.

It has to be said that Glasgow's climate, mild and moist, includes a higher than average rainfall that makes possession of an umbrella almost mandatory.

The logo that announced the city's explosive re-birth in the early 1980s, was a beaming yellow 'Mr Happy', with the words: 'Glasgow's miles better'. If this is a *double entendre*, it sums up the ebullient spirit of Scotland's most warm-hearted of cities.

Festivals

In 1990, Glasgow surpassed the Edinburgh Festival and Fringe, and it will be interesting to see whether it will continue to hold its own without its Cultural Capital status. It has more than its share of annual festivals and it would not be surprising to find that some of these have moved into the front line over the next few years, given the enthusiasm and enterprise mushrooming in the city's cultural pastures.

In February there is a **Festival of Music, Speech and Dance,** at Pollok, providing a launching-pad for plenty of new talent.

The Mayfest, now well established, and second only to Edinburgh as an Arts Festival, attracts international companies with first-class reputations. Drama, music, ballet, opera and art; all flood the theatres and halls and galleries for three weeks in May, incorporating various side-shoots of a 'fringe' character. A German beer company erects a beer tent in George Square for the duration of the festival, providing musical entertainment as well as liquid refreshment throughout the day.

SNO Proms are performed for two weeks in June, at Kelvin Hall.

The **Flower Festival** in Glasgow Cathedral is at the beginning of June—a spectacular celebration of nature in an ideal setting.

During the **Folk Festival** and **Jazz Festival**, in June and July, the city hums and vibrates with folk music and jazz, indoors and out, played by groups from all over the world, especially Scandinavia and northern Europe. Ceilidhs and musical gatherings go on far into the night.

Streetbiz is an annual festival of Street Theatre and entertainment in August.

The Easterhouse Festival, also in August, is an enterprising parade of drama, music, ballet and opera at Easterhouse.

For sailors, the **World Yachting Grand Prix** at Inverclyde in August is an essential entry in the diary.

TOURIST INFORMATION

Greater Glasgow Tourist Board and Convention Bureau. 35/39 St Vincent Place (off George Square), tel 041 204 4400. As well as an information centre, this is a Bureau de Change, with booking facilities for accommodation—both local and national, theatres, concerts, etc., as well as coach and tour tickets.

Scottish Tourist Guides Association, 3 Myrtle Avenue, Lenzie, tel 041 776 1052, for information on guided tours throughout the country.

British Telecom: Dial-a-what's-on-service, tel 041 248 4000. A resumé of what's on in Greater Glasgow each week, from theatre to festival, baby show to marathon, carnival to pop concert.

Treasures of Scotland Tours, 3 Silk Street, Paisley, tel 041 667 1143. Good specialized tours of Scotland.

Mayfest Central Office, 18 Albion Street, Glasgow, tel 041 552 8000.

GETTING TO GLASGOW

By air: Glasgow Airport, in Renfrew, tel 041 887 1111, is 15 minutes from the city centre. Regular scheduled flights are operated by Northwest Airlines from Boston, American Airlines from Chicago, Air Canada from Toronto and Halifax, and British Airways from New York. There are also regular flights from London and other UK cities, and cities throughout Europe. Prestwick Airport, tel 0292 79822, with transatlantic and international flights, is only an hour away.

By rail: there is a high-speed rail link with London, taking five hours with overnight sleeping cars available, as well as direct or connected links with all other major towns in UK. British Rail do a number of special packages, frequently changing and well worth asking about. Central and Queen Street Stations, tel 041 204 2844: 24-hour service.

By road: there are direct motorway links with all major UK cities. A number of inter-city coaches operate between Glasgow, London and other main towns. This is far the cheapest form of public transport and not uncomfortable. A mid-week return to London costs from £22. Anderston Bus Station, tel 041 248 7432. Buchanan Bus Station, tel 041 332 9191.

GETTING AROUND GLASGOW

Buses run frequently in and around the city as well as a large number of taxis. There is also an underground railway, 'The Subway', circling the city from Hillhead, north of

GLASGOW

0 ————— ½ km
0 ————— ¼ mile

N

Botanic

Gardens

VICTORIA PARK

GREAT WESTERN

CROW RD.

DUMBARTON RD.

BYRES RD.

19

Kelvingrove

2

3

1

CLYDESIDE

ARGYLE

EXPRESSWAY

17

River

GOVAN RD.

PAISLEY RD. WEST

M8

DUMBRECK RD.

1   Art Gallery and Museum
2   Glasgow University
3   Kelvin Hall Musuem of Transport
4   People's Palace
5   Citizens Theatre
6   City Halls
7   Henry Wood Hall
8   Kings Theatre
9   Pavilion Theatre
10 Theatre Royal
11 Ticket Centre
12 Glasgow School of Art
13 Glasgow Cathedral
14 Greater Glasgow Tourist Board
15 Police HQ
16 Provand's Lordship
17 Scottish Exhibition and Conference Centre
18 Anderston Quay
19 Hunterian Museum and Art Gallery
20 Tenement House
21 The Barrows (Barras)
22 Tron Theatre
23 Third Eye Centre
24 Glasgow Royal Concert Hall

*To Pollok Park
and Burrell Collection*

Kelvingrove Park, round as far as Buchanan Street to the east, across the river to Shields and Kinning Park in the south and back round to Govan in the west before re-crossing the river to Partick. Because of the excellent motorway network, it is possible to get from the city centre to, for instance, the Burrell, way out in the suburbs, in a matter of minutes. A one-way system makes driving in the heart of the city remarkably un-fraught. The Tourist Office will give information about a number of guided coach tours in the city and to other parts of Scotland.

There are also Clyde Cruises in river boats, including the paddle steamer *Waverley*.

Discovering Glasgow

Don't try and cram all Glasgow into one day: if that is all the time you have, take a guided coach tour to orientate yourself in the morning, spend the afternoon at the Burrell Collection and Pollok and sample one of the dozens of entertainments in the evening. Or if history and culture are paramount, go to the cathedral and Provand's Lordship in the morning, or to the Museum and Art Gallery, and Hunterian Museum, at Kelvingrove Park.

Two days would allow you to do all the above things and in three days you could take in a cruise on the Clyde, and find time to wander through the older parts of the city.

Glasgow Cathedral

Glasgow Cathedral (open daily: free) is on the site of the church built by St Mungo, and Glasgow grew up around it. It is the city's parish church, less than a mile east of the centre. There are still traces of the original stone building, dedicated in the presence of King David I in 1136 and rebuilt after a fire in 1197 in the lower church. The crypt, choir and tower were built in 1233, the rest being added at various stages in the succeeding years. During the appalling destruction of church embellishment, in the Reformation, the last Catholic Archbishop, James Beaton, stripped Glasgow Cathedral of its finery and carried the treasures off to France, together with the archives, for safe-keeping. Tragically, in the later turmoil of the French Revolution, these were lost and have never been found. In 1578, when the iconoclasts of the Reformation threatened to destroy the cathedral entirely, the city's trade guilds intervened, and, miraculously, managed to prevent them: thus, today the cathedral is one of the finest examples of pre-Reformation Gothic architecture in Scotland. Austere, as most Scottish churches seem to be, it is still very impressive.

St Mungo was buried here in 603. His tomb stands under a fan-vaulted ceiling among a forest of pillars in the Lower Church. In 1451, the Pope decreed that it was as meritorious to make a pilgrimage to Glasgow Cathedral as to Rome, and many thousands of pilgrims made their way here in medieval times. Look out for the rood-screen with fire-and-brimstone carvings of the Seven Deadly Sins on its corbels.

The cathedral stands on a grassy slope embedded with horizontal gravestones, backed by the Necropolis, on a hill behind. This gives a splendid sky-line of elaborate monuments, overshadowed by a Doric column from which John Knox keeps a stern eye on the city.

Provand's Lordship

Provand's Lordship (open daily: free), in Castle Street, opposite the cathedral, dates from 1471 and is Glasgow's only other pre-Reformation building of interest. Built as a priest's house and well preserved, it is now a museum. Among its exhibits are 17th- and 18th-century furniture, tapestry and pictures, as well as the key of Leven Castle in Tayside, where Mary was imprisoned. She may have stayed in this house when she came to Glasgow in 1567 to visit her husband Darnley, who was sick with some disfiguring disease diagnosed as anything from smallpox to syphilis. Whatever it was, she took him back to Edinburgh—and murder. Provand's Lordship is the oldest house in the city, visited by both James II and James IV during their reigns in the 15th and 16th centuries. Mysteriously, among its exhibits is an early 20th-century sweetie shop.

George Square

George Square is at the heart of the city, barely a quarter of an hour's stroll from the cathedral, along Castle Street and George Street. There is something pleasantly continental about the square on a sunny day, like the main piazza of a Mediterranean town, where crowds gather to pass the time: visitors in shirt sleeves, slung about with cameras, linger among the trees and statues. Parades are sometimes held here, for anyone to watch, with the pipes and drums and military bands of various Scottish regiments, beating the retreat on summer evenings. The square is dominated by a statue of Sir Walter Scott on an 80 ft (244 m) high column (a column that was first intended for a statue of George III). This mighty monument was the first to be set up in honour of Sir Walter, in 1837, although he was barely 10 years old when the square was laid out in 1781. He towers over Queen Victoria, Prince Albert, Robert Burns, James Watt, and many others, wearing his plaid across the wrong shoulder as was his custom.

The amazing Italian Renaissance City Chambers, topped by a wedding cake concoction of cupolas and a soaring tower, forms the eastern side of the square. A free guided tour of its sumptuous interior (tel 041 221 9600) includes a loggia, a great staircase, marble columns, soaring vaulted ceilings and a banqueting hall. It only lacks a gilded potentate, attended by bowing courtiers, stepping out from behind one of the columns to hold an audience in the Council Chamber.

Museums and galleries

The Museum and Art Gallery (open daily: free) occupies a vast red-sandstone building on the western side of Kelvingrove Park about one and a half miles west of the city centre. Ranking among Britain's best, this place needs several leisurely visits to be properly appreciated. Built as recently as 1901, it has a splendidly solid, Victorian feeling about it. An enormous central hall soars to the full height of the building, used sometimes for organ recitals and special exhibitions.

The museum has fascinating archaeological collections, including a reconstruction of the Antonine Wall, and some Bronze Age cists with their contents. There are also displays of armour, ethnological exhibits, natural history and social history. The engineering collection is so big that it is not possible to display everything: people with a special interest must ask at the enquiry desk.

The art gallery claims to have one of the finest collections owned by any city, beautifully displayed in upper galleries leading off the balcony that encircles the central hall. On the balcony there are sculptures (including works by Rodin and Epstein), ceramics, silver, jewellery, and furniture displays (including work by Charles Rennie Mackintosh, the Glasgow-born architect who had a considerable influence on European design in the late 19th and early 20th centuries).

Among the art gallery's many treasures are Giorgione's *The Adulteress Brought Before Christ*, Rubens' *Nature Adorned by the Graces*, Rembrandt's familiar *Man in Armour* and Ribera's *St Peter*. Other artists include Delacroix, Corot, Millet, Manet, Degas, Raeburn, Allan Ramsay, Reynolds, Hogarth, Whistler and Turner. There are lots of Impressionists and post-Impressionists; a Glasgow gallery, and a gallery for recent and contemporary paintings.

Perhaps the best known painting in the gallery is Salvador Dali's *Christ of St John of the Cross*. Dramatically hung at the end of a corridor, approached as if down a long avenue, the rich colour and the almost three-dimensional perspective are stunning. As if from heaven above, the viewer looks down on the bowed head and shoulders of Christ, slumped forward on the cross, face hidden, suspended in a limbo of black sky above a bright, sunlit sea. A comprehensive description of its conception is displayed beside it, with illustrations. Dali was inspired by a 16th-century drawing of the Crucifixion by a Spanish Carmelite friar who became known as St John of the Cross. He painted the picture in 1951, saying that he wanted to create a Christ who would be 'as beautiful as the God that He is'. He succeeded.

Kelvingrove Park is an ideal setting for the Museum and Art Gallery. It has a peaceful, academic atmosphere, with the River Kelvin flowing through its 85 acres. It was twice used for international exhibitions at the turn of the century as well as for the Scottish National Exhibition in 1911. Concerts are performed several times a week in the summer, in the amphitheatre on the river bank. Strolling among the trees, lying on the grass, listening to the music—it is hard to believe one is close to the pulsating heart of this vibrant city. In winter, at dawn, the frost sharpens the skeleton trees and breath hits the cold air like smoke. The sun comes up over the roof tops, painting the walls of the university on its hill a glorious fiery pink and you want to fling out your arms and shout with joy. Usually, however, you don't, because by that time the first joggers are emerging, as well as the man with his road-sweeping equipment.

Glasgow University was founded in 1451, as just a few classes in the cathedral crypt. It then moved to the High Street, south of the Cathedral Square, and was finally moved to Kelvingrove in 1870 where it expands continually to cater for more than 10,000 students.

The Hunterian Museum and Art Gallery (open daily except Sundays: free) is in Hillhead Street, running north from the university and part of it. William Hunter was a student at Glasgow University in the 1730s. Having risen to fame and fortune as a physician he left his collections of coins, paintings, prints, books, manuscripts, zoological, mineral and medical specimens to the university. The Hunterian Museum opened in 1807, Scotland's first public museum, and since 1980 the Hunterian Art Gallery has been housed in a separate building.

The Museum has, as well as the world-famous Hunter Coin Cabinet, excellent geological, archaeological and ethnographical collections among its many exhibits. The Art Gallery's collection of work by Whistler, the contents of his studio at his death in 1903, is rivalled only by the collection in Washington's Freer Gallery. These paintings were inherited by Rosalind Birnie Philip, his sister-in-law, in whom he had instilled a determination that the English should not get their hands on work by a man who's genius they had failed to acknowledge. Rosalind gave a number of the paintings during her lifetime, on condition they should never leave the university. She bequeathed the remainder on her death in 1958. The present collection is made up of 80 paintings, over 100 pastels and several hundred watercolours, drawings and prints. Many of the works are unfinished.

The Hunterian houses the largest and most comprehensive print collection in Scotland, as well as paintings by Rembrandt, Chardin, Stubbs, Pissarro, Ramsay, Reynolds, Sisley and many more; and sculptures, including work by Rodin, in the courtyard.

The Hunterian also boasts a comprehensive collection of work by Charles Rennie Mackintosh (1868–1928). One of Glasgow's talented sons, this architect and designer was a leading exponent of Art Nouveau, highly influential throughout Europe though less so in Britain. There is a splendid reconstruction of No. 6 Florentine Terrace nearby, now demolished, where he lived from 1906–14. The rooms show all the decorations, alterations and improvements done to the original house by Mackintosh, together with some from his previous home at 120 Mains Street. For anyone who admires his austere approach to architecture and design, his clean, stark lines and manipulation of space and light, this must be among the finest existing example of his innovative flair and brilliance.

Glasgow is proud of her son Charles Rennie Mackintosh and he has left his stamp all over the city:

The Glasgow School of Art, for instance (open weekdays when the school is open and by arrangement, tel 041 332 9797), in Renfrew Street, is said to be one of Mackintosh's most outstanding creations. He designed it in 1896 and each façade of the building reflects a different facet of his imaginative style. Members of staff will conduct tours whenever they are free.

The Willow Tea Room, 217 Sauchiehall Street, is another memorial to Charles Rennie Mackintosh. Restored to his original design, it is furnished with chairs and tables of his design and they serve light lunches and tea, between 9.30 and 5.

The Headquarters of the Charles Rennie Mackintosh Society (open Tues, Thurs, Fri and Sat: free) is in the former Queen's Cross Church, at 870 Garscube Road, north of the Willow Tea Room. Built in 1897 Art Nouveau-Gothic style, the only church Mackintosh designed, it has an information centre, reference library and book stall.

The Art Lover's House, Bellahouston Park, tel 041 427 1000, is a new building based on Mackintosh's original 1901 drawings. It has exhibition, studio and office space and is open on weekday afternoons and at weekends.

The Third Eye Centre (open daily except Mon: free) is at 350 Sauchiehall Street, in a Grecian building that caused a stir when it was designed by Alexander Thomson in 1865. This is Scotland's largest, liveliest contemporary arts centre; a dynamic example of how the city has exploded into the forefront of the arts scene. Founded in 1975, it contains galleries, a studio theatre, a bookshop, café and bar. It holds an average of 30 exhibitions a year, usually accompanied by a descriptive publication, and these exhibitions tour internationally as well as nationally. Programmes include drama, dance, music, readings, talks, films and festivals. The Third Eye Centre demonstrates effectively just how much Glasgow has reinterpreted its sobriquet of 'no mean city'.

McLellan Galleries 270 Sauchiehall Street, tel 041 331 1854, has recently been done up and has exciting visiting exhibitions.

The Regimental Museum of the Royal Highland Fusiliers (open weekdays: free) is in 518 Sauchiehall Street, with uniforms, pictures, medals, documents, photographs, trophies, and memorabilia, going back over the 300 years of the regiment's history.

The Tenement House (open daily 1 April–31 Oct, and otherwise at weekends: adm) at 145 Buccleuch Street, a few blocks north of Sauchiehall Street, is a first-floor apartment in a red-sandstone tenement built in 1892, restored to give an insight into the living conditions of the working-class family who lived here for half a century. There are two rooms, as well as kitchen and bathroom, with the original kitchen range, period furniture and fittings. Although authentic, it is perhaps a little too clean and neat. It is not difficult to visualize what was more likely the reality—the overworked mother, standing over her 'jaw-box' sink, admonishing her brood of children, anxiously awaiting the tipsy return of her man, on payday.

The People's Palace (open daily: free) is on the eastern side of Glasgow Green, half an hour's easy walk southeast of George Square, so called because it was built in 1898 as a cultural centre for the people in the east end of Glasgow. It is a splendid museum, devoted to the story of the city from 1175 to the present, including the growth of trades and industry, trade unions, labour movements, women's suffrage, entertainment and sport. Among its many exhibits are a purse and a ring belonging to Mary, Queen of Scots; a bible that belonged to the notorious Archbishop Beaton, an organ built by James Watt and portraits of many famous Glaswegians. There is a café, shop and an exotic winter Garden, with tropical plants and birds.

Glasgow has a number of museums of specialist interest. From the People's Palace, cross the river and go southwest to Albert Drive.

The Museum of Transport (open daily: free) is in the Kelvin Hall, in Argyle Street, across from Kelvingrove Park, and is one of the most renowned of its kind. Most forms of transport are represented, from bicycles and motor cycles and a delightful painted and carved caravan, to six railway engines, some of which are 100 years old. There are trams, horse-drawn vehicles, commercial vehicles and cars. The Clyde room is a shipping gallery with splendid models. Old photographs show many of the exhibits in use. Incorporated into the museum is an imaginative reconstruction of a 1930s street, with shops, a cinema, cars and delivery bikes and an underground station.

Haggs Castle (open daily: free) is at 100 St Andrew's Drive, a mile to the west of the Museum of Transport. Built in 1585, and much restored, Haggs Castle was opened in 1976 as a museum for children, although only the snootiest of adults could fail to be fascinated by some of the very imaginative exhibits. There is a reconstructed Victorian nursery; an 18th-century cottage interior, and period gardens. Children are encouraged to use the workshops for museum-based activities such as spinning, weaving, candle-making and other crafts.

The **Museum of Education** (open weekdays, free conducted tours) is in Scotland Street, a short walk north of Haggs Castle. Housed in a Charles Rennie Mackintosh building, the museum has a display of school furniture and equipment over a span of 80 years. Recent complaints that cuts in the education budget will hamper the chances of modern schoolchildren are reduced to laughable proportions when you see the facilities and equipment that were responsible for the education of some of Scotland's leading industrialists, economists, doctors, historians, artists, writers, and academics.

The Burrell Collection

Open daily, free, the Burrell Collection is three miles southwest of the city, in Pollok Country Park, well signposted off the main roads and motorways, served by a good bus service. Buses 21, 23, 45, 48A and 57 run from the centre, and 34, 89 and 90 across the south of the city.

Opened in 1983, the Burrell is Glasgow's greatest treasure attracting many thousands of visitors from all over the world. The fabulous collection was given to Glasgow by the wealthy industrialist, Sir William Burrell (1861–1958) in 1944. Sir William joined his father's shipbuilding firm at the age of 15 and even then he had begun to collect paintings, against the wishes of his father who would have preferred him to spend his money on more 'manly' pursuits. By the time he was 96, he had some 8000 objects, an average of two acquisitions a week. He was a careful collector, canny in his haggling, sometimes missing an important piece because he refused to pay inflated prices.

In 1971, a two-stage architectural competition was staged, with the almost impossible brief: to design, not an institution, but a home in scale and in sympathy with the Collection and the environment of the park. Had there not been a postal strike, causing the entry deadline to be extended, the winning design by Barry Gasson would not have been submitted in time. The building has now won prestigious architectural awards. From the big car park it is all sharp angles, glass, red-sandstone and wood, designed to give the best possible light and perspective to the treasures inside, making full use of the trees and grounds of Pollok beyond the windows. Opulent courtyards and arcades create the illusion of being out of doors.

The scale and breadth of Burrell's taste is astonishing. He was a traditionalist, with no time for the avant-garde, but within that scope his eye was caught by anything: pre-historic artifacts, oriental art, stained-glass, porcelain, silver, paintings, sculpture, carpets, crystal, and tapestries. The beauty and sheer diversity of the collection, gathered by one man, dazzles the senses. Ideally, it should be taken in several bites to avoid aesthetic indigestion.

Reconstructions of the dining room, hall and drawing room of Hutton Castle, the Burrell's home on the Whiteadder near Berwick-on-Tweed, are incorporated into the building. Medieval stone and oak fireplaces and chimneypieces, antique furniture, tapestries, Eastern carpets, stained glass and the original soft furnishings, are all displayed with splendid effect.

From ancient civilizations, there are objects from Egypt, Iraq and Iran, Greece, the eastern Mediterranean and Italy. Among these can be seen: stone reliefs, bronzes, alabaster figures, an almost life sized terracotta lion's head, amphora, Greek earthenware vases, mosaics.

Almost a quarter of the collection is Oriental. Chinese ceramics include marvellous polychrome figures from the Tang Dynasty (AD 618–907); porcelain from 14th-century Yuan and 15th-century Ming dynasties; every sort of domestic ware and bright ceramic roof tiles with elaborate figures on them, to ward off evil spirits. Chinese bronzes include a 'champion vase': two cylinders joined by an eagle with outspread wings standing on a bear's head, probably awarded in archery contests. Chinese jades include jewellery, vessels, animals, fruit, and figures. There are Japanese prints, ceramics from the Near East, and wonderful Near Eastern carpets.

From medieval Europe, there is a 12th-century limestone portal from a church in Montron, in France, looking entirely right in its ultra-modern setting, as does the magnificent 16th-century sandstone portal from Hornby Castle. Medieval church art and sculpture are also well represented.

Burrell looked on his medieval tapestries as being the most valuable part of his collection. Most were originally woven for churches and private houses and displayed as status symbols by ecclesiastics and nobles alike. The colours of some are still so rich it is hard to believe they were stitched over 500 years ago. Look out for the 15th century *Ferret Hunt*, and *Hercules Initiating the Olympic Games*, also 15th-century.

Another relic of the Middle Ages is stained glass, and not all of it comes from churches. There are some delightful vignettes of everyday life including a jolly man warming his bare toes before a roaring fire and an industrious Dutchman making roof tiles.

In the field of Decorative Arts, the Burrell Collection includes exquisite porcelain, silver, gilt, glass, 'treen' (made of wood), needlework, furniture, armour and weapons.

Sir William Burrell started his collection with paintings and was still buying them two years before he died, 80 years later. As with the rest of his treasures, he seems to have had an astonishingly catholic taste, ranging from Degas and Cézanne to Bellini and Hans Memling, whose *Annunciation* is so rich in colour and yet so simple in conception. Some of the paintings are disappointingly hung and lit and not easy to appreciate. There are a number of good Impressionists and an assortment of prints and drawings including Rembrandt's etching: *Abraham Francen: Apothecary* with the feeling of strong sunlight streaming into a dusty room, and Daumier's satirical *Bons Confrères*, with two leering, hypocritical lawyers greeting each other outside court, totally unconcerned about the tragic woman emerging behind them.

Among the sculpture in the collection is Rodin's *The Thinker*, a bronze from one of the many casts of this best known of his works, in the original size. (The Thinker was meant to be Dante, pondering the fate of mankind, crowning Rodin's magnum opus, *The Gates of Hell*.)

Pollok House (open daily: free) is in the same grounds as the Burrell Collection—a much older-established show-piece now often neglected in favour of its magnificent neighbour. This is a pity. It was built in 1750 and given to Glasgow in 1966 by the Maxwell Macdonald family, including the 361 acres of garden and parkland, and it contains one of the finest collections of Spanish paintings to be found anywhere in Britain. These were acquired by Sir William Stirling Maxwell when Spanish art was neglected and underrated and range from 16th-century Cosida, across the whole field of Spanish painting, including El Greco, Murillo and Goya. There are also many works by other European masters, 18th- and 19th-century furniture, silver, ceramics and crystal.

Look out for the unusual astronomical clock, looking just like a standard grandfather clock until closer inspection reveals a face set with complicated dials. It is a lovely house in a fine setting and should certainly not be missed.

Pollok Park includes a **Demonstration Garden**, laid out to inspire amateur and professionals alike, displaying all aspects of landscape gardening.

Outdoor attractions

Glasgow Zoo (open daily: adm) is in Calderpark, six miles southeast of the city, on the A74. Here are lions, polar bears, leopards, monkeys, camels, deer, elephants, wallabies, porcupines and a lot more besides, making a good outing when the children have grown tired of sightseeing.

The Fossil Grove (open daily: free) in Victoria Park west of Kelvingrove, is an unusual place. In 1887, when this park was being laid out, workmen, cutting a path across an old quarry, revealed this fragment of a 230-million-year-old forest. The weird stumps and roots were formed by the setting of mud, within the bark of the trees: trees which, compressed for millions of years, became the coal that fired the Clydeside furnaces in the 20th century. The stresses and worries of yesterday and tomorrow suddenly seem rather trivial, seen in the perspective of this remarkable relic of antiquity.

The Botanic Gardens (open daily: free) are in Great Western Road, north of Kelvingrove. The gardens cover 42 acres with flowers, trees and shrubs and a famous collection of orchids. **The Kibble Palace**, a splendid Victorian glass pavilion, houses a luscious collection of tree ferns, and plants from the temperate zones of the world.

'The Barras', (Barrows) (open every weekend) at Gallowgate, north of Glasgow Green, is Glasgow's flea-market—internationally renowned. With over 800 traders, selling anything you want from the mass of stalls, barrows and shops all along Gallowgate, the market is a shopper's delight. But it isn't just for shoppers: it is a light-hearted, festive place to idle away a sunny day. A good-humoured, jostling crowd fingers the bargains: beaten copper pots, leatherwork, straw mats, wicker baskets, silks and batiks, cottons and man-made fibres, polished wood and plastic urns. Stalls, like still-life paintings, are piled with fruit and vegetables, health-foods, cheese booths, fish and meat. One is quite likely to be serenaded by a busker; touched for a fiver by a conscience-stabbing down-and-out, or have one's wallet slid dexterously from a pocket or bag as one haggles over the price of a strip of foam rubber. For more information, go to 244 Gallowgate, or tel 041 552 7258.

ENTERTAINMENT
Top-class drama, music, ballet, variety shows, etc. can be found in Glasgow's theatres and cinemas.

Glasgow Royal Concert Hall, tel 041 332 3123, specially designed by Sir Leslie Martin and opened by The Princess Royal in 1990, has a 2500-seat hall, two good restaurants, conference and exhibition facilities. Leading international orchestras perform classical music and jazz here, as well as the Glasgow-based Scottish National Orchestra, BBC Scottish Symphony Orchestra and City of Glasgow Philharmonic.

Theatre Royal, Hope Street, tel 041 331 1234. Home of Scottish Opera and frequent host to the Scottish Ballet, Scottish Theatre Company, National Theatre, Ballet Rambert and other international companies.

Kings Theatre, Bath Street, tel 041 552 5961. Drama, family entertainment, shows, musical and amateur shows.

Citizens Theatre, Gorbals Street, tel 041 429 0022/8177. Glasgow's repertory theatre, opened in 1878 as a music hall.

Mitchell Theatre, Granville Street, tel 041 221 3198. Meetings, lectures and amateur dramatics.

Glasgow Theatre Club, Tron Theatre, 38 Parnie Street, tel 041 552 5961. Actors and musicians meet in a club atmosphere.

City Hall, Candleriggs, tel 041 552 5961. A versatile stage where you can see anything from the Scottish National Orchestra to pop and folk concerts.

Henry Wood Hall, Claremont Street, tel 041 221 4952. In what was Trinity Church, this classical concert hall is the home of the Scottish National Orchestra.

Pavilion Theatre, Renfield Street, tel 041 332 1846. Family entertainment, variety, pop, rock, and pantomimes.

Odeon Film Centre, Renfield Street, tel 041 332 8701. Three screens.

ABC Cinema, Sauchiehall Street, tel 041 332 9513. Five screens.

Glasgow Film Centre, Rose Street, tel 041 332 6535. One screen.

Tramway Theatre, Albert Drive, tel 041 423 7527.

SHOPPING
Glasgow's main shopping area radiates out from George Square with branches of most leading chain stores. Don't miss a visit to the 'Barras' market, in Gallowgate, every weekend.

Princes Square, 48 Buchanan Street, is a luxury specialist shopping area, and the St Enoch Centre, 55 St Enoch Square, has over 50 stores under one huge glass roof.

For tweeds, tartans and woollen things, try The Edinburgh Woollen Mill, 72 St George's Place, or Loch Lomond Mill, 61 King Street, or Pitlochry Knitwear Company, 130 Buchanan Street, or The Scotch House, 87 Buchanan Street.

For stylish new collections of fashionable clothes, people are talking about Warehouse, 61–65 Glassford Street. For trendy clothes, try Graffiti, 63 Queen Street. For hand-knitted originals, go to Cruise Clothes in Renfield Street. For shoes and handbags try Sarti, in the Mews Arcade. Bambolini, 165 Hyndland Road, is the shop for fashion-conscious babies. Flip, in Queen Street, specialize in American-style clothes. For leather and suede fashions, go to Vous, 425 Great Western Road.

WHERE TO STAY
There is a large choice of hotels, guest houses and bed and breakfast places in Glasgow, to suit all tastes and pockets. Most are listed in the Greater Glasgow *Where to Stay Guide*. The following is a small selection within an easy walk or short taxi ride from the main stations.

Expensive
Albany Hotel, Bothwell Street, tel 041 248 2656. A large (248 rooms en suite), ultra-modern but friendly 4-star hotel that won the 1986 Hotel of the Year Award. Good food and very central.

Copthorne Hotel, George Square (formerly The Diplomat), tel 041 332 6711, is an elegant, listed, 18th-century hotel; recently refurbished, incorporating the house in which Sir William Burrell grew up. International cuisine with a reasonable table d'hôte dinner or à la carte, eaten either in the conservatory or in The Window on the Square Restaurant.

Crest Hotel, 377–83 Argyle Street, tel 041 248 2355, is another 4-star, modern building in the city centre with all comforts and a friendly staff.

Buchanan Hotel, 185 Buchanan Street, tel 041 332 7284. An old-fashioned Victorian hotel with friendly personal service. The Buonasera is their Italian restaurant, serving Italian and continental food.

Kelvin Park Lorne Hotel, 923 Sauchiehall Street, tel 041 334 4891, recently renovated, with a friendly relaxed atmosphere. Their Butlers Restaurant has been designed in manor-house style and the food is good at a reasonable price. Newbery's Bar is decorated in the style of Charles Rennie Mackintosh and honeymoon couples get a special deal.

Also in the expensive range there are: a **Holiday Inn,** Argyle Street, tel 041 226 5577, **Hospitality Inn and Convention Centre,** 36 Cambridge Street, tel 041 332 3311, and a number of **Stakis Hotels.** These may all be predictable, but on the whole they maintain top quality.

Moderate

Beacons Hotel, 7 Park Terrace, tel 041 332 9438, overlooking Kelvingrove Park, dates from 1865. The food is good and reasonably priced.

Babbity Bowster Hotel, Blackfriars Street, tel 041 552 5055, is small and friendly with an old-style tavern atmosphere.

Kirklee Hotel, 11 Kensington Gate, tel 041 334 5555/339 3828, is in Glasgow West, quieter and comfortable.

Central Hotel, Gordon Street, tel 041 221 9680, is a massive Victorian building in the city centre, with a warm friendly welcome. Food very reasonable; there is a carvery buffet and you can 'eat Scottish'.

Cheap

Burnbank Hotel, 67–85 West Princes Street, tel 041 332 4400. All modern conveniences in splendidly Victorian surroundings. The staff are friendly, the food reasonable, with a full Scottish breakfast.

Arfon Hotel, 969 Sauchiehall Street, tel 041 334 7802, is in an attractive terrace in the centre and good value.

Coach House Hotel, 14 Hyndland Road, tel 041 357 2186/339 6153, is also good value.

EATING OUT

It is worth remembering that the quality of a restaurant usually depends on its chef and manager, both of whom are liable to move on at any moment. It is worth asking around for the current 'in' place. The larger hotels mostly have good restaurants with set menus, à la carte, and bar meals. It is always wise to book ahead.

Expensive

The Buttery, 652 Argyle Street, tel 041 221 8188, serves good food in the style and enviroment of a Victorian gentleman's club.

Poachers Restaurant, Ruthven Lane, Byres Road, tel 041 339 0932. Small, privately owned restaurant in 1870 farmhouse, with fresh Scottish produce cooked when ordered: prime meat, fish, shellfish and game.

Rogano, 11 Exchange Place, tel 041 248 4050. Dating from 1876, the Rogano was remodelled in 1935, when the *Queen Mary* was being built on the Clyde, in classic Art-Déco style and is now renowned for its atmosphere and excellent seafood. (It has a cheaper **Café Rogano** downstairs where the food is just as good.)

Moderate

See Café Rogano, above.

The Colonial Restaurant, 25 High Street, tel 041 552 1923. In the merchant part of old Glasgow, the Colonial uses only fresh ingredients, mostly local: fillet of beef, shellfish, chanterelles from Fort William.

Hospitality Inn, 36 Cambridge Street, tel 041 332 3311. Garden café restaurant in American style, or elegant Prince of Wales cocktail bar and restaurant.

Kensington's Restaurant, 164 Darnley Street, tel 041 424 3662. Small intimate restaurant tucked away in a quiet backwater on the south side of the city. West-coast seafood, venison, game, Scottish beef and lamb. Speciality: Scottish puddings.

Albany Hotel see above. Good Scottish food in the Four Seasons Restaurant, and a self-service carvery.

Butlers Restaurant Kelvin Park Lorne Hotel, see above. Traditional manor-house decor and excellent food.

Ubiquitous Chip, 12 Ashton Lane, tel 041 334 5007. Plants, a waterfall, batiks and murals, in a lively cobbled courtyard restaurant. Original and traditional recipes using best Scottish ingredients.

Cheap

Baby Grand, 3 Elm Bank Gardens, Charing Cross, tel 041 248 4942. Likened to a New York café, Baby Grand specializes in fish dishes, accompanied by the Baby Grand, whose mood varies depending on the pianist: jazz, soul, blues, requests.

Entresol Restaurant, Central Hotel, see above. In an olde worlde setting, the menu includes haggis and trimmings, fillet of sole Bressay, whisky cream crowdie.

Ewington Hotel, 132 Queens Drive, tel 041 423 1152. West-coast fresh seafood, Aberdeen Angus beef and home-made soups such as delicious Cullen Skink.

Part X

CENTRAL

Stirling Castle

The heart of Scotland. Coming into the Central region on the M9 or the M80 you meet a densely populated industrial sprawl, flat and dreary with Stirling rearing up like a sentinel on its crag ahead; but the long view is of hills all round and the promise of Highland scenery beyond. Small and compact, this area offers an astonishing variety of scenery, some of it very beautiful, but because it is so close to Edinburgh and Glasgow its attractions are often smothered by hordes of holidaymakers. The Trossachs, a subtle combination of loch, wooded slopes and crag, backed by green and russet hills, are especially beautiful and an irresistible magnet to tourists.

Within the protection of these hills and with no sea coast, the climate is gentle and often hot. Lush vegetation carpets the glens, vivid green ferns and mosses, with great slabs of forest, hardwood and conifer, climbing the shoulders of the hills and giving a glorious display in autumn. Further north is wild, rugged moorland.

This was Pictland, home to those mysterious aboriginal settlers, indigenous long before the Irish Scots, the Angles and the Welsh began to push north, followed by the Romans, who built the Antonine Wall in AD 140. Hadrian's Wall, further south, had been built ten years previously but was not proving to be strong enough to deter the ferocious northerners. This new wall was built by Roman legionaries in a somewhat futile attempt to push the barbarians back and cut them off. It stretched 37 miles, from Old Kilpatrick on the Clyde to Bridgeness on the Forth and you can see some of its best-preserved sections around Falkirk. If possible, go first to the Royal Museum of Scotland in Edinburgh, or the Hunterian Museum in Glasgow where there are excellent descriptions of how it was constructed as well as many relics. In spite of the enormous

261

1 Rough Castle
2 Watling Lodge
3 Airth Castle
4 Castle Campbell
5 Bannockburn
   Heritage Centre
6 Wallace Monument
7 Stirling Castle
8 Finlarig Castle
9 Blair Drummond
   Safari Park
10 Falls of Dochart
11 Culcreuch Castle
12 Loup of Fintry
13 Doune Castle and
   Motor Museum
14 Inchmahome

CENTRAL

0   10 kms

0   10 miles

N

Loch Tay

T A Y S I D E

A9

A85   St Fillans   A85   Perth

Loch Earn

M90

Callander

A81   *Allan Water*   O   c   h   i   l   s

River Teith   **13**   A9   **Hillfoots**

A873   Doune   Dunblane   Rumbling

9   **4**   Bridge

Bridge   Dollar   Powmill

River Forth   of Allan   Menstrie   Tillicoultry

6   A91   Alva

A811   Blairlogie

Kippen   **7**   A907

M9   Stirling   Alloa   **FIFE**

5

Dunfermline

11   *Loch*   M90

Walton

Fintry   **12**   **3**   KINCARDINE

Carron Valley   BRIDGE

Reservoir   *River Carron*   *Firth   of   Forth*

Campsie Fells   **Carron Valley**   M80

Forest   Bonnybridge

A803   **1**   **2**   Falkirk

LOTHIAN

M8

effort that went into the building of it, the wall was abandoned by the Romans after less than 25 years, and the Picts were left to their own devices.

Christianity crept in from the west, spread first by St Ninian's missionaries in the 4th century and then by those of St Columba in the 6th. The Picts were canny about change: you will find sacred stones carved with a combination of Christian and pagan symbols to appease any of their old gods who might be jealous. In the 9th century, when Kenneth Macalpine drew the Picts and Scots together, the Picts began to lose their identity as a dominant race and gradually faded from existence before their history could be recorded.

Stirling reflects the subsequent history of this central hub of Scotland: in 1297 William Wallace kindled the fire of rebellion against English suppression at Stirling Bridge, and Robert Bruce refuelled the blaze in 1307 by defeating Edward II at Bannockburn. Stirling became a favourite royal residence as well as an important fortress, guarding one of the gateways to the highlands. Bonnie Prince Charlie wasted valuable time and resources laying siege to the castle in January 1746 but failed to capture it.

Today, the region draws its wealth from the pulsing industrial belt in the southeast, from a thriving tourist trade, from agriculture on the flat lands below the hills, and from sheep on the moors.

While you aren't likely to get the nose-to-tail traffic so familiar near popular resorts in England, you can expect frustration on twisting single-carriageway roads, when dozens of impatient drivers get trapped behind slow-moving, impassable caravans.

SPORT
Once you get out of the industrial belt, you can **walk** for ever in the hills or through the lovely wooded glens. The landscape is surprisingly varied for such a small region, with every sort of walk from a gentle saunter to a challenging climb. There is plenty of **golf**, some good **fishing** on the lochs and rivers, and a number of **riding** and **pony-trekking** centres. Lochearnhead has a big **Water Sports** Centre with sailing, windsurfing, canoeing, and waterskiing.

TOURIST INFORMATION
The head office is at Tourist Information Centre, Dumbarton Road, Stirling, tel 0786 75019, open all year round. The smaller centres, usually open April or May–Sept, are at Falkirk: The Steeple, High Street, tel 0324 20244, open all year, and Pine 'n Oak, Kincardine Bridge Road, Airth, tel 0324 83422; Tillicoultry: Clock Mill, tel 0259 52176; Stirling: 41 Dumbarton Road, tel 0786 75019; Dublane: Stirling Road, tel 0786 824428; Callander: Leny Road, tel 0877 30342; Aberfoyle: tel 08772 352; Killin: Main Street, tel 05672 254; Tyndrum: Car Park, tel 08384 246.

Falkirk, the Hillfoots, and Stirling

The southern corner around Falkirk is dominated by Stirling on its cone of volcanic rock, and though parts of it are not attractive for the sightseer, it contains unexpected treasures and a wealth of history. Beyond, where the Ochils guard the way north, fringed by the Hillfoots towns and villages, lie beautiful glens, whose fast-flowing rivers once powered woollen mills for processing the fleeces of the sheep of the hill slopes. In spite of its proximity to the bustle of the industrial belt, this area has a peaceful, unspoilt charm.

Falkirk

Falkirk, deep in the heart of industrial Scotland, does not, on first acquaintance, tempt one to linger; but there is a mass of history packed in behind its modern face and it should not be passed by too quickly. Plans to create a pedestrian precinct within the High Street will make the town centre very much more attractive, and an enterprising council has plans for a number of other schemes that should revitalize the whole place. This is where the best preserved sections of the Antonine Wall can be seen.

Falkirk was once one of the cattle drovers' main trysting places—hard to picture the scene now in the busy streets: those tough nomads, wrapped against the cold, surrounded by their herds and flocks, pausing to exchange news with others of their kind, seen always in transit. Two battles were fought here; one in 1298, when William Wallace was defeated by Edward I, and one in 1746, when Prince Charles Edward Stuart, retreating north, turned to defeat the government forces who pursued him. His victory was partly due to the cowardice of the Hanoverian troops, many of whom, when confronted by the ferocity of the charging Highlanders, threw down their arms and fled!

Falkirk Museum in Orchard Street, behind the main car park, is small but extremely interesting (open daily, except Sun: free). Here you will find the history of the area, including a good section on the Antonine Wall, and details of the two battles. Prince Charlie lodged in **Callendar House**, which you can see in Callendar Park surrounded by attractive woodland. The house is not at present open to the public, though publicly owned, but it makes a good centrepiece for the park, where you can walk and play golf.

The **Marina Leisure Centre** is one of Falkirk's new projects, at Camelon. It boasts a pool with tropical decor and wave machine, a chute (down an elephant's trunk), saunas, solarium, squash courts, multi gym and restaurants.

The Antonine Wall

The Antonine Wall was an earth rampart consisting of a ditch, with a military road running along its south side and the displaced earth thrown up to create a wall on the north side. Forts were built about two miles apart along its entire 37-mile length. A part of it can be seen in Callendar Park Housing Estate, to the east, and another at Watling Lodge, on the western outskirts of the town by the canal. Here, just by the road, you can see clearly how the wall must have been and there is a description board. But to get the best idea of it, go to **Rough Castle**, well signposted, one and a half miles from Bonnybridge, west of Falkirk and accessible at all times. Even the slag heaps that overshadow the plateau fail to detract from the queer feeling that you get, standing there thinking of those unfortunate legionaries, accustomed to gentler postings, condemned to this bleak place, menaced by a wild race of men who appeared from nowhere with blood-curdling war cries and primitive but lethal weapons, and equally easily vanished again. There are information boards to help the imagination, explaining where there was a fort, barracks, commander's house, granary, headquarters and a bathhouse.

North of Falkirk, and now closed, are the famous **Carron Ironworks**, a massive place founded in 1759, where Britain's cannons were once made. Robert Burns paid a visit to the works and was so horrified that he dashed off a quick verse to express his feelings:

We came na' here to view your works
In hopes to be mair wise,
But only lest we gang to hell
It may be no surprise!

The Carron Valley

Before you head for Stirling, the Carron Valley is surprisingly rural, even though it lies so close to the industrial belt, and offers some nice walking country.

Five miles west of Falkirk, at Dunipace, the B818 takes you westwards along the River Carron for six miles to the reservoir. Just before this, a bridge reaches an island picnic spot, surrounded by the white tumult of the river.

Less than a mile further on beyond the reservoir, just past Loch Walton, you can leave your car and walk across the bracken to the left to the Loup of Fintry. Here, the Endrick Water tumbles in long creaming falls to the valley below, filling the air with its noise and spray. **The Campsie Fells** guard the southwest of the Carron Valley, offering easy climbs with fine views.

Culcreuch Castle

Culcreuch, at Fintry, three miles west of the falls, was built by the Galbraith clan in 1296. The Galbraiths lived here until their chief, Robert, had to flee to Ireland after a scandal in 1630. The castle has had various owners since then and is now a remarkably well-preserved mansion run as an hotel, with the old keep incorporated. There is lovely parkland, a walled garden and pinetum and loch.

The Pineapple

Instead of going straight up to Stirling on the motorway take the A905 four miles north of Falkirk, past the road to **Kincardine Bridge**. Past the Airth Castle Hotel turn off left on B9124. Not far along the road, a clear sign directs you to **The Pineapple** (always accessible on the outside: free), an amazing garden folly, built as a retreat on the Dunmore estate in 1761 and now owned by the National Trust for Scotland. This is a splendid relic of the days when the privileged classes could indulge their fancies with the help of a large labour force. A double wall surrounds a 14-acre garden, the space between the walls being for the circulation of hot air from furnaces. On top of the north wall you will see a vast stone pineapple, 45ft high, whose interior forms the domed roof of a circular chamber below. Pineapples were grown here in 1761, under hothouse conditions in the buildings flanking this centrepiece, with an army of stokers beavering away to feed the fires that provided the necessary heat. The buildings are now converted to a holiday home which you can rent through the Landmark Trust (tel 0628 825920).

Rumbling Bridge

Go back past Airth Castle Hotel to the roundabout and cross Kincardine Bridge, taking the A977 north for nine miles. Turn off left after Powmill to Rumbling Bridge. It would be all too easy to cross the River Devon at Rumbling Bridge and completely miss the significance of its name, so narrow and steep is the gorge as you cross the bridge by car. There is a car park just beyond the hotel on the right. A gate by the bridge gives access to steps, from where you can see this breathtaking chasm, 120 ft deep and so narrow in places that you could shake hands with someone on the far side, if you were both acrobats.

The gorge was formed from the fast-moving water from melting ice sheets at the end of the last Ice Age, about 10,000 years ago. From an observation point, well fenced, you can see how the present bridge, built in 1816, spans the older one, built in 1713, with a queer, leap-frog effect. The lower bridge is an alarmingly narrow stone span lacking any sort of parapet, and this was once the main highway.

A path, recently built by sappers of the British Army, winds along the river from the bridge, securely fenced, much to the relief of most people. Trees cling tenaciously to the steep limestone rock face of the gorge, as well as vivid green ferns, mosses, liverworts and trailing vines, with the river rumbling over the rocks far below.

A short distance up from the bridge is **Maceachin's Cave**, a truly romantic spot where an escaping Jacobite, Hector Maceachin, hid after Culloden in 1746, having escaped from Castle Campbell (see below). He was hidden by the daughter of the local Laird, Hannah Haig. How could they not have fallen in love in this wonderful setting? They did: and were married. You can walk a short distance up to Devil's Mill, where the thumping of the water on the boulders sounds like a mill grinding; it is so called because it didn't even stop for the Sabbath! Downstream from the bridge you get to **Cauldron Linn**, a double waterfall that is impressive after rain.

Castle Campbell

Castle Campbell (open daily except closed Thurs afternoons and Fri, Oct–March: adm) is three miles west of Rumbling Bridge and a mile north of Dollar. Visitors should use a map and look out for the Historic Scotland signs, for the castle is not well advertised. Everyone has a favourite place, to be revisited and revealed to favourite people: Castle Campbell must be such a place for some.

Try to go there on a fine day, preferably in autumn. The reasonably agile can park at the bottom, instead of driving up the rough track to the car park, and take the footpath up the burn, through steep, mossy, wooded banks; a secret place overhung with ferns where you must watch where you walk. The path crosses narrow foot bridges, offering sudden glimpses of cascading water through rocky ravines. Suddenly, ahead, high up and apparently inaccessible, is the castle, soaring in lofty isolation on a narrow spur above the rocky, wooded ravines of the Burn of Care and the Burn of Sorrow, backed by a dramatic crescent of bracken-covered hills, which are copper-coloured in autumn.

Enigmatically, the castle was once called *The Gloume* (Gloom), yet even with the dismal names of the two burns, it is the least gloomy of any place in the world. Seen in sunlight, with the trees at their fullest autumnal best, it is much more a castle of enchantment.

The present castle dates from the 15th century, built on the site of an earlier fortress and acquired in marriage by the Campbells of Argyll, who changed its forbidding name by Act of Parliament in 1489. John Knox preached here in 1556, on the grassy slope now called Knox's Pulpit. Montrose's army tried (and failed) to take the castle in 1645. (Some of his troops, of the Maclean Clan, having a private feud with the Campbells, wanted an excuse to burn it.) General Monk was also here, 9 years later, and his troops made a better job of destruction.

You walk through a vaulted 'pend' into the courtyard and there is a substantial amount of the ruin intact. In the tower there is the great hall where you can see the entrance to the pit prison, on the right of the fireplace. From the roof there are glorious views down across Dollar Glen and up into the hills.

The Hillfoots

The Hillfoots villages, strung out westwards from Rumbling Bridge under the smooth slopes of the Ochils, provide a fascinating and extremely scenic **Mill Heritage Trail**, tracing the history of the development of wool production in this area. The villages of **Dollar, Tillicoultry, Alva** and **Menstrie** grew up at the foot of the Ochils, above the marshy bog of the plain, in the 16th century. The good grazing of the hills and the pure, soft water of the burns that ran down to feed the River Devon, were ideal for the foundation of what was to become a world-famous woollen industry, with easy access to the markets in Stirling, Edinburgh, Glasgow and Perth. As you follow the Mill Heritage Trail westwards from Dollar to Stirling, take time off to walk up any of the glorious glens that run north into the Ochils, where the burns that used to drive the mills cascade downwards, filling the air with their chattering. If you stay very still, you may even see a kelpie, one of the elusive river horses that bewitch these secret corners. The hills beyond are haunted by the ghosts of Covenanters who took refuge here.

Dollar is best known for its Academy, one of Scotland's leading schools, once called MacNabb's School. John MacNabb, who died at the beginning of the 19th century, was a local boy who made a fortune at sea and returned to his native land to share his wealth. The village straddles the tree-lined River Devon, with attractive stone cottages whose gardens shout with colour in the summer. You can see Castle Campbell, high on its crag, floodlit at night—a most impressive sight. Dollar's milling tradition was the least developed in the Hillfoots villages, possibly because the local landowners were reluctant to encourage industry so close to the prestigious MacNabb's School. **Brunt Mill**, by the burn above the village, was built in 1820 and now belongs to the Academy.

Tillicoultry, less than three miles to the west, at the heart of the Mill Trail, has the **Clock Mill Heritage Centre** with all the information you could want: looms, workshops and an audio-visual show. There is also a Tourist Information Centre. This village was producing cloth in Mary, Queen of Scots' day and their coarse, hand-woven cloth became known nationally as Tillicoultry Serge. Don't miss a visit to **Paton's Mill** in Lower Mill Street, where you can buy Glen Gordon knitwear from the mill shop. **Sterling Mill**, built in 1846 and used as a barracks in the First World War, was later a paper mill. Now a furniture warehouse, it has a picture gallery, gift shop, garden centre and restaurant.

Alva, a couple of miles or so further west, is dominated by the massive six-storey Strude Mill, now empty, built in 1827 when the cottage-based woollen industry was being taken over by factories. If you walk up Alva Glen you see traces of a complex water system of pipes, weirs and overflow channels, once used to feed the waterwheel of the mill. There are several mill shops to visit in Alva. **Inverallan Hand Knitters** in Shavelhaugh Loan are the largest hand-knitting company in Europe, employing about 2000 knitters who work in their own homes. Their patterns go back to AD 830 and are found in the Book of Kells.

Menstrie is a couple of miles west of Alva; another of the Hillfoots villages with a milling tradition. **Menstrie Castle** (open by appointment with the NTS Perth Office, tel 0738 31296: adm) is a 16th-century tower house. It has been rather over-enthusiastically restored and rises from the middle of a housing development like a toy fort on the nursery floor among a clutter that should have been tidied away. It contains a Nova Scotia Exhibition Room, run by the National Trust for Scotland in honour of Sir William Alexander, who was born here. He was sent off to found a Scots colony in Canada, in 1621, as a reward for his services to the Crown. He was an indifferent poet and an unpopular Secretary of State for Scotland, and one thing he would never have permitted is the building of a modern housing estate on his doorstep.

Still going west towards Stirling on the A91, about one and a half miles beyond Menstrie, look out for a concealed entrance signed 'The Square'. This leads to the tiny village of **Blairlogie,** a delightful huddle of pretty old houses and a whitewashed church, built along narrow, winding streets on a ledge below the Ochils among orchards and colourful gardens. Blairlogie is one of the first of the Hillfoots communities. It grew up around the castle, a sturdy little fortress on a shelf above the village, not open to the public.

Stirling

Stirling beckons to you from whichever way you approach. It rises abruptly from the flat plains: a fortress-crowned rock with a grey town clinging to its steep sides—a colourful but blood-stained history book. Because of its strategic position, guarding the route north, this was a fortress town since earliest times; bitterly fought over, bravely defended. Seven battlefields, including Bannockburn, lie within its shadow. Stuart monarchs held court here. In 1746, Prince Charlie tried to capture it, wasting precious time and equipment besieging it. The history of the town is encapsulated in the castle.

Stirling has flung itself into tourism with wholehearted gusto. It is the ideal centre for a family holiday, if you like plenty of organized fun. For the entire summer the town is ablaze with colour and excitement, humming with every sort of entertainment, exhibition and event, decorated with flowers and banners. There is **Stirling Tartan Week** in July, a celebration of all things Scottish, with dancing, ceilidhs, concerts and guided walks. This is followed by **Stirling Festival**, spanning a couple of weeks at the beginning of August: an international programme of dance, jazz, drama and folk, interspersed with Scottish events like fiddlers' concerts and piping. **The Top of the Town**, centred on Broad Street, the heart of the Old Town and former market place, is vibrant with medieval street stalls, period costumes and buskers. There is an **Orientation Centre** opposite the **Tolbooth** where you can find out exactly what is on offer. During the summer, an antique open-topped bus links the Old Town with the commercial centre.

Stirling Castle

Stirling Castle (open daily: adm) stands aloof above all the summer frivolity at its feet. Run by the National Trust for Scotland, the castle has a Visitor Centre in the car park where there is an excellent short film of introduction.

Legend credits King Arthur with having taken the castle from the Saxons, adding a touch of romance to a stronghold that seems otherwise too solid for the chivalric wisps of Arthurian tales. What is certain is that Alexander I died there; Henry II took it as part-payment for the release of William the Lion after the Battle of Alnwick; and that same William died there in 1214. In those days it would have been built of timber, superseded by masonry in the 13th century. Continual alteration and restoration have resulted in the castle seen today, most of it 15th- and 16th-century with some splendid Renaissance architecture added by James IV and James V.

Every inch seems drenched in history and interest. Perhaps the most intriguing is the **Douglas Room** where, in 1452, James II summoned the eighth Earl of Douglas, whom he suspected of disloyalty, stabbed him to death and threw his body out of the window at the end of the passage. Tradition held that a skeleton, found in the garden below in 1797, was that of Douglas. You can't help feeling sorry for the frantic king, trying to heave the gory remains through the window: particularly if you remember that when he was only eight years old, he had been forced to witness the murder of a previous Earl of Douglas, at the notorious Black Dinner in Edinburgh Castle in 1440.

In **The Chapel Royal**, 9-month-old Mary was crowned Queen of Scots, surrounded by scheming nobles and a miasma of conflicting loyalties and ambitions. Mary lived in the castle until she was taken to France at the age of five. The chapel was rebuilt by her son, James VI/I, and is now the Memorial Hall for the Argyll and Sutherland Highlanders, whose headquarters are in the castle. In the recently expanded **Argyll and Sutherland Highlanders Museum** you can see a good collection of regimental memorabilia with some 15 Victoria Crosses won by members of this famous regiment.

In the **Lions' Den,** outside the palace, James III and James IV both kept lions. Catching and shipping them must have presented a terrible problem for whoever had the job of supplying them.

There are marvellous views from the castle on a fine day, and several hours should be allowed to take in all the things there are to see up here. Floodlit at night, it is transformed into a fairytale castle, visible from miles away. A number of stirring events take place periodically on the castle esplanade: Beating the Retreat, solo piping, massed pipe bands, all enhanced by the historic setting.

The Old Town

The old part of Stirling town is clustered up the hill to the castle: Spittal Street leading up to St John's Street and Broad Street, which converge at the top to form Castlewynd. A number of historic buildings line the steep, narrow streets, including the **Church of the Holy Rude**, built uphill with the choir elevated, where Mary of Guise was made Regent for Mary. **Mar's Wark**, at the top of Broad Street, is the remains of a palace that was started in 1570 by the Regent, the Earl of Mar, but never finished and mostly destroyed during the Jacobite rising in 1746.

Below the Old Town, the **Thistle Centre** is a covered precinct for those more interested in modern shops than history. **Rainbow Slides Leisure Centre** (open daily: adm), in Goosecroft Road, has over 200 metres of translucent water tubes, filled with lighting and sound effects, down which you swoosh, in breathtaking spirals. There is also a pool, solarium, sauna, steam room and café.

Smith Art Gallery and Museum in Dumbarton Road (open daily except Mon: free) was founded in 1874. Extensive redevelopment recently won it the Scottish Museum of the Year Award. Not only is there an excellent introduction to the history of Stirling, but also a constantly changing programme of exhibitions, demonstrations and lectures.

Bannockburn Heritage Centre

Sir Robert the Bruce at Bannockburn
Beat the English in every wheel and turn,
And made them fly in great dismay
From off the field without delay...

—from *The Battle of Bannockburn*,
by William McGonagall

A visit to Bannockburn is more of an historical pilgrimage than a search for scenic beauty. From Stirling follow the signs for Bannockburn Heritage Centre (open daily, April–Oct: adm), not for Bannockburn. The Battle of Bannockburn actually took place over an area that is now mostly mining country, less than two miles from Stirling, and dominated by slagheaps and pithead constructions, which are the modern developments of the liberated Scotland that Robert Bruce fought for, and won, in 1314.

The Heritage Centre is on higher ground, to the southwest, at Borestone Brae where Bruce is said to have set up his standard on the evening before the battle. You can see fragments of the 'bored-stone' with its socket hole, in the visitor centre where an audio-visual theatre gives an excellent history of the battle.

If you walk through the hedge from the car park you come to the imposing **Robert Bruce Memorial Statue**. Bruce was that great general who won his battle mounted on a pony, a golden circlet on his helmet to identify himself, armed only with a battle-axe. He instructed his men to dig man-traps all over the plain, disguised with branches, and to scatter iron spikes, or calthrops, over the field. Before the battle, Bruce's army knelt to receive a blessing from a friar who walked among them with a crucifix in his hands. Edward mistook the situation and thought they were begging for mercy.

271

'They are,' he was told, 'but from God, my liege, not from us. Yonder men will win the day or die upon the field.'

The Wallace Monument

A visit to Stirling is not complete without going to see the Wallace Monument (open daily, except closed Wed and Thurs, Oct, Feb and March: adm). Almost as much of a landmark as the castle, one and a half miles northeast of the town on top of 300-ft-tall Abbey Craig, it is a Victorian monster of a tower, 220 ft (66 m) high with a mighty bronze statue of Wallace set in its wall above the door.

It is quite a steep, zig-zagging climb from the car park but there are plenty of seats where you can rest. Inside, in a hall at the base of the tower, William Wallace's two-handled sword hangs dramatically in a corner, a long steel blade glinting above a tartan plaid. There are two audio-visual programmes in this hall: one is a guide to the scenery, wildlife and history of the Forth Valley and the other a history of William Wallace and the Battle of Stirling Bridge in 1297, which he is said to have directed from the top of Abbey Craig. There is a Hall of Arms above, and then another flight of stairs takes you to the Hall of Heroes where you will find yourself surrounded by the marble busts of some of Scotland's heroes. Don't be daunted if you can't recognize them all: there is an audio-visual presentation which leads you round and fills you in on each of them. This display won a British Tourist Authority Award recently. You can climb to a parapet below the crown of the monument for dizzying views across the Carse of Forth to the castle on its rocky eminence above Stirling town. From here you can see seven battlefields, each of which played an important part in Scotland's history: Cambuskeneth, Stirling Bridge, Falkirk (two battles), Bannockburn, Sauchieburn and Sheriffmuir. There are woodland walks, a picnic area, a tea room and gift shop.

Bridge of Allan

A couple of miles north of Stirling, Bridge of Allan was a spa town in Victorian times, visited by fashionable people from near and far. There are some pleasant riverside walks, to remind you of Burns' 'Banks of Allan Water'. The University of Stirling is southeast of the town. The Strathallan Highland Games take place here in August.

Dunblane

Dunblane, four miles north of Stirling and by-passed by the A9, is a small town built around its ancient cathedral in the valley of the Allan Water. A narrow main street leads up to the cathedral close, with some fine old buildings around it.

The imposing **Queen Victoria School**, on the northern outskirts of the town, is a state-endowed bording school for the sons of servicemen, run on military lines, where the boys receive both a good education and a firm discipline not always found in the fee-paying public schools of today.

The Doune and Dunblane Agricultural Show is in July.

Dunblane Cathedral (open daily, free) was founded in 600 by St Blane of Bute, grandson of King Aidan of Dalriada, and still has parts of the old Celtic church in its red sandstone walls. Most of the present cathedral was commissioned by Bishop Clement in the mid-13th century. The roof was stripped after the Reformation but it was restored in 1892 and is now the parish church. This lovely Gothic building has an oval window that you can only see from outside, decorated with carved leaves and flowers and called the Ruskin Window because John Ruskin praised it. After a visit to the cathedral, he said: 'I know not anything so perfect in its simplicity, and so beautiful, as far as it reaches, in all the Gothic with which I am acquainted.'

Stand for a moment in the cathedral by the three poignant stone slabs in memory of Margaret Drummond and her two sisters, all poisoned in 1502 by scheming nobles. James IV was in love with Margaret. (Some go further and say he was secretly married to her.) Politicians desired a union with England, and Margaret Drummond was a threat to this plan. Why her luckless sisters had to be eliminated as well remains a mystery—perhaps they all ate from the same dish. Within a year of this awful crime, James married 14-year-old Margaret Tudor and found himself the brother-in-law of bellicose Henry VIII.

The Cathedral Museum and **Library** (open daily in the summer except Sun, with a donation box) is in the cathedral close. The museum was the Dean's House, built 1624, now home to displays of local history.

Blair Drummond Safari Park

Blair Drummond Safari Park (open daily, mid-March–Oct: adm) is on the River Teith seven miles to the southwest. This is one of Scotland's more enthusiastic attempts to cater for whole families on holiday. Here you can see lions, giraffes, tigers, hippopotami, etc., or take a boat-trip on the lake and see a chimp island, or take a 'Flying Fox' cable slide across the lake. This is definitely a bonanza for children, with aquatic mammal shows, a pets' corner, adventure playground, a 3D 'Cinema 180', an 'Astraglide', picnic areas, shops, amusement arcades, restaurants and a bar for exhausted parents. The house, which is a school for handicapped children, is not open to the public.

Doune

Doune, three miles west of Dunblane, is a small, winding village with wooded hills rising in folds to the north. In the 17th and 18th centuries, this was an important pistol-making town, with three factories to support the industry, and the drove road linking Highlands and Lowlands for carrying the pistols to market. The coat of arms has crossed pistols on it.

Stand in the attractive, triangular market square and try to picture the scene when it was a 17th-century sheep and cattle market, to which people flocked from miles away. There would have been ramshackle stalls selling broth and ale; a press of wild-looking men from the hills, herding their beasts; smoke from fires and the smell of animals and the unwashed. It was a living, seething scene, full of bawdy jokes and raucous laughter, with underlying tension and sharp eyes on the watch for trouble between Covenanters and soldiers.

Doune Castle

Doune Castle (open daily, except closed Fri and alternate Sat, Oct–March: adm) is one of Scotland's best preserved medieval castle ruins. Built in the 14th century by Robert, Duke of Albany, and his son Murdoch, it was annexed by the crown after the wholesale execution of the Albany family by James I. James IV gave it to his Queen, Tudor Margaret, who in turn passed it to her second husband, Henry Stuart, Lord Methven. Later it passed to the Earls of Moray who still own it; the Bonnie Earl of Moray, in the ballad, who came 'soondin' through the toon', lived here. The gatehouse of this splendid ruin is a self-contained complex complete with its own water supply in case of siege. Built round a large courtyard, it is protected by two rivers and a deep moat. A long, vaulted passage leads into the courtyard with a vaulted chamber on the right where Prince Charlie put the prisoners he took at the Battle of Falkirk, having captured the castle.

You can climb up to the Lords Hall, on the first floor of the main tower, and picture it when it was filled with smoke from the blazing fire, rushes on the floor, dogs squabbling over bones, a great throng of people jostling for attention from the nobles at the high table. The castle contains a host of domestic details that are fascinating to the modern eye, making it easier to see those distant people living their daily lives, eating and sleeping and loving like anyone today. The gardens were created in the early 19th century by the tenth Earl of Moray. They have a walled garden, a pinetum, lovely shrubs and plants and woodland walks through the attractive glen.

The Bridge in Doune was apparently built by Robert Spittal, in 1535. Spittal was tailor to the wife of James IV. (He also founded Spittal's Hospital in Stirling, so the queen must have paid him well!) Spittal is said to have come to the ferry that preceded the bridge and been refused passage because he had no money on him. He built the bridge to spite the unfortunate ferryman.

Doune Motor Museum

The Doune Motor Museum (open daily, April–Oct: adm) contains Lord Moray's collection of vintage cars and is a must for the enthusiast. Most of the cars are in working order and the collection includes such makes as Hispano Suiza, Bentley, Jaguar, Aston Martin, Lagonda, and the second oldest Rolls Royce in the world. There is a tarmac track, about a mile long, for Racing Hill Climbs, and during Hill Climb Weekends the Motor Museum and café are only open to people attending the Climb. As well as these Climbs, a number of motoring events take place here throughout the summer including car rallies, and radio-controlled aeroplane rallies.

WHERE TO STAY AND EAT

There is an enormous choice of hotels in this area, ranging from converted castles to simple farmhouses, as well as a mass of self-catering establishments. **Culcreuch Castle** at Fintry, tel 036086 228, will satisfy anyone looking for antiquity and history (see above). This 14th-century castle is moderately priced, log-fire cosy, without too many frills, and if the ghosts keep you awake you can wander through 1600 acres of parkland. A very different sort of atmosphere greets you at **Airth Castle Hotel** near Kincardine, tel 0324 83411, also moderately priced. The castle's history goes back to the early 14th century, but conversion to hotel has somehow robbed it of any feeling of history, and though it is extremely comfortable, it is too restored and mod-connish to keep you on the watch for ghosts. Even in the Dungeon Bar and restaurant you are too aware of the self-conscious decor to pick up any echoes of the screams and moans of the wretched prisoners.

In Stirling, there are dozens of hotels. **Golden Lion** in King Street, tel 0786 75351, won't let you down if it's moderately priced comfort and dependability you are after. The decor is a bit glitzy but the food is good. Also in the moderate range, **Park Lodge Hotel**, 32 Park Terrace, tel 0786 74862, is a treat. Partly Victorian, partly Georgian, this charming town mansion overlooks the park and castle, in nice gardens. Some of the rooms are wonderful replicas of period rooms, with antique furniture and drapes, old paintings, and ornaments. There is a four-poster bed, haute cuisine and a good wine cellar.

North of Stirling, **Cromlix House**, Dunblane, tel 0786 822125 is a typical Victorian country house, exuding an air of self-satisfaction that might have something to do with an impressive collection of awards and stars. It is very expensive, undeniably comfortable, and the food, like the curate's egg, is good in parts. For less than one third of the price, you could have a much jollier time at the **Stirling Arms Hotel**, Dunblane, tel 0786 822156, a 17th-century coaching inn on the banks of the Allan Water. Its Oak Room Restaurant will give you a good meal. Not much more expensive, **Stakis Dunblane Hydro Hotel**, tel 0786 822551, is large, modern, comfortable and convenient. It has an indoor swimming pool, a whirlpool spa and sauna, all-weather tennis, crazy golf, an adventure playground and a gymnasium.

The Trossachs

Callander

Once beyond Doune, you begin to feel the lure of the Highlands. Callander, eight miles from Doune and a good holiday centre for this area, is a sturdy, friendly little town to the east of the Trossachs, overshadowed by Ben Ledi. The town was rebuilt to its present wide design by military architects in the wake of Prince Charlie, perhaps because it is easier for rebels to hold a town if the streets are narrow and houses close together. Telly addicts might experience a sense of *déjà vu* here, for this is Dr Finlay's *Tannochbrae*. It also features in *The Country Diary of an Edwardian Lady*. From here you are within easy reach not only of the Trossachs but also of lots of invigorating walks up through wooded glens into the moors, with streams and rivers rushing down to fill Loch Lubnaig and the River Teith. Walk up to the Bracklinn Falls and remind yourself that Sir Walter Scott once rode his horse across here for a bet: or to the Falls of Leny and watch out for the water sprites, dancing in the spray-mist. In the summer, Callander is the stage for a variety of entertainments such as organized ceilidhs, open-air pipe-band concerts and Highland dancing, as well as wild-life slide shows.

There is no one particular thing to see in and around **The Trossachs**. The scenery is attractive if you have not already been spoiled by the Highlands. Because it is easily accessible from the densely populated industrial towns to the south, it has become popular and perhaps a little over-rated. Preferably explored outside the tourist season, this area is best appreciated on foot. Even in the high season, most sightseers prefer to stay within sight of their cars and few are on the prowl before ten o'clock in the morning. You have only to make an early start and get away from the roads to shake off the feeling of claustrophobia that can attack when there are too many people. autumn and early spring are the best time in this land of forested ravines and gullies.

Although people tend to refer to the whole of the area between Callander and Lochearnhead, on the east, and Loch Lomond on the west, as the Trossachs, in fact the Trossachs proper is only the gorge that runs from Loch Achray to Loch Katrine, a rugged pass barely a mile long. Locals will give you two meanings for this strange name: 'bristly country' or 'the crossing place'; no one is sure which is correct. Thick woods often obscure the view, but now and then you get a hint of the magic that enchanted Sir Walter Scott. The road twists and climbs through gorse and bracken and very green moor, past rhododendrons, with plenty of signed footpaths leading off.

Loch Katrine

Loch Katrine, nine miles west of Callander, is the setting for Walter Scott's 'Lady of the Lake'. Ellen's Isle is named after the heroine of the poem. From 1 May to 28 September you can take a 45-minute trip in the Victorian steamer, *Sir Walter Scott* and cruise along the nine-mile length of the loch from Trossachs Pier to Stronachlachar. As you watch the passing shore, picture fair Ellen being wooed by the mysterious James FitzJames, who bore a remarkable resemblance to King James V, that monarch who enjoyed roaming the countryside disguised as the Goodman of Ballengiech. A prosaic guide will tell you that this lovely loch is also Glasgow's water supply. Because of this, there is a large notice at the pier forbidding you to swim, paddle, picnic, fish, camp, light fires, or throw coins in the loch: in fact, forbidding fun, though why anyone should feel the urge to throw their money into a loch is a mystery.

There is a café at the pier, and gift and souvenir shops.

Aberfoyle

Aberfoyle guards the southern approach to the Trossachs and is a lively holiday centre. As well as walking and touring from here you can go ponytrekking. The road north, 'Duke's Pass', is too densely wooded to let you have more than a glimpse of the lochs below. Walter Scott made his first notes for *Rob Roy* in the dining-room of the village manse.

David Marshall Lodge is a modern stone visitor centre just before you come down into Aberfoyle, with good views, an ornamental lake and signposts telling you where to walk and how long it will take you. In the lodge, displays illustrate the wild-life and vegetation of **Queen Elizabeth Forest Park** and there is a shop and café.

Energetic people can walk right through the park to the eastern side of Loch Lomond. A single track road runs south from Rowardennan and you can climb Ben Lomond from here (3192 ft, 958 m), for a glorious bird's-eye view. For those who like organized sightseeing, the 45,000-acre park includes a forest car trail, and a cycle-way that takes you to all the best places in the area.

The Trossachs Highland Games are held in **Kinlochard** on Loch Ard.

Inchmahome Priory

Before going on north from Callander, take the A81 six miles southwest to Lake of Menteith and take the ferry to Inchmahome Priory, a semi-roofed ruin on the largest island of three on the lake. (The weather dictates the running of the ferry, for which you pay and the priory is open daily April–Sept: free.)

Founded for Augustinians in 1238, the priory was a refuge for Mary, Queen of Scots, for a short while before she was sent off to France to grow up out of range of Henry VIII's 'Rough Wooing'. It is nice to think of the little girl, in the garden now called Queen Mary's Bower, happily playing hide-and-seek, perhaps, with the indulgent monks.

A surprising number of pilgrims come here to see the grave of Robert Cunninghame Graham, the 'rebel laird' of the estate, who died in Buenos Aires in 1936 aged 84. This flamboyant character travelled extensively in South America, Spain and Morocco; married a Chilian poetess; was imprisoned for 'illegal assembly' in 1887 (a Socialist demo in Trafalgar Square); was elected first president of the Scottish Labour Party in 1888 and wrote many travel books, essays and short stories. He was a close friend of both Conrad and W. H. Hudson.

Balquhidder

> *A famous man is Robin Hood,*
> *The English ballad-singer's joy!*
> *And Scotland has a thief as good,*
> *An outlaw of as daring mood;*
> *She has her brave Rob Roy . . .*
>
> —from *Rob Roy's Grave*, by William Wordsworth

Another popular literary association in this area is at Balquhidder, on Loch Voil, north of the Trossachs, 10 miles or so north of Callander, and just west of the A84. (Turn off opposite the Rob Roy Tryst and Clan Gregor Centre.) This is where Rob Roy lived, died and is buried. This colourful, Robin Hood-ish character, much romanticized by Scott, lived between 1671 and 1734, son of Macgregor of Glengyle. **Rob Roy** (Gaelic for Red Robert) started life peacefully enough as a herdsman. But the Macgregors had been outlawed for their bloodthirsty habits and life was hard. He took to cattle rustling and smuggling, robbing the rich to pay the poor, and legends of his daring escapades and narrow escapes around Loch Katrine make good reading, even if, in reality, he was no doubt a rogue and a menace to his neighbours. He died uncharacteristically in his bed and you can pay homage to him in Balquhidder churchyard. You can't miss the grave: the Clan Gregor have been unable to resist the temptation to 'do it up' with monstrous results.

Lochearnhead

14 miles north of Callander on the A84, you come to Lochearnhead, an attractive little village on the western corner of Loch Earn. There are several good hotels here and a

boating and water-skiing centre. The loch runs seven miles east to St Fillans (see 'Tayside', p. 337), a beautiful ribbon of water sheltered by hills and an ideal place for a holiday.

WHERE TO STAY AND EAT

Once again, the choice in this tourist-oriented area is vast. Refurbished and under new management, **The Lake Hotel**, Port of Menteith, tel 08775 258, stands right on Scotland's only lake, looking across to Inchmahome. Moderately priced, with good food, they've retained much of the Art-Deco furniture and decor. The **Stronvar Country Hotel** in Balquhidder, tel 08774 688, will give you four-poster beds in a laird's mansion with crow-stepped gables overlooking Loch Voil. With only five bedrooms, this hotel is peaceful, and moderately priced. **Bridgend House Hotel**, in Bridge Street, Callander, tel 0877 30130, is cheaper. It faces the road with a coy, olde worlde, mock-Tudor face but it also has good views, four-poster beds and tries hard with its garden. Victorian **Brook Linn**, in Callander, tel 0877 30103, is cheaper still, and has a marvellous position with spectacular views from a two-acre garden. It is only open from March to November and the food isn't bad.

Probably your best bet is **Roman Camp Hotel** in Callander, tel 0877 30003. In 20 acres of garden beside the River Teith, on which you can fish, this hotel dates from 1625 and was a hunting lodge of the Dukes of Perth. It's only open from mid-March to mid-November, and is expensive, but the food is good, the rooms comfortable and the atmosphere relaxed. **Forest Hills Hotel** in Kinlochard, near Aberfoyle, tel 08777 277, is a big country-house hotel with a multi-million-pound leisure centre in 20 acres of informal gardens overlooking Loch Ard. With a swimming pool in the garden and attractive surroundings, this is ideal if you have a family who like to be entertained. Moderately priced, they also have luxury self-catering apartments. In Lochearnhead, **Clachan Cottage Hotel**, tel 05673 229, is a charming old white cottagey building overlooking Loch Earn, with lovely views. It's cheap, and what it may lack in sophistication is made up for in atmosphere.

Breadalbane

Called after the Earls of Breadalbane (emphasis on the middle syllable) who used to own most of it, the land north of the Trossachs is your overture to the Highlands. In the days before the clan system was abolished, many bitter battles were fought for supremacy over these lonely hills and moors. Campbells, MacNabs, Macgregors and MacLarens contested every inch, committing ghastly atrocities to wreak revenge on each other. You are likely to find a different sort of tourist here: more energetic, striding out with knapsack and climbing boots. It is a wild, rugged territory, where you may see roe deer and golden eagles, tumbling rivers, spectacular falls, and deep, dark lochs. For botanists there are masses of wild flowers and unusual plants. Cut by the glens of the Rivers Dochart and Lochay, and veined by the network of burns that pour down out of the hills to feed them, this is glorious walking and climbing country, backed by the massive hills of Strathclyde to the northwest.

Killin

Killin is about seven miles north of Lochearnhead, a couple of miles off the A85, on the A827. This attractive village with hotels, shops and eating places has an almost alpine feel to it, especially when there is snow on the hills. It sits astride an old bridge, under which the Falls of Dochart carry the River Dochart in a rushing tumble of falls and rapids, swirling down through the village into Loch Tay, long and deep between two massive ranges of hills (see p. 335 for the Ben Lawers Visitor Centre, on the north side of Loch Tay).

On **Inchbuie**, the lower of two islets below the old bridge in Killin, you can see the burial ground of the MacNabs, an aggressive clan who ruled the district until they emigrated to Canada in the 19th century, forever at loggerheads with the neighbouring clans of Neish and Gregor. The Tourist Information Centre has the key to the burial ground.

Finlarig Castle,hidden among trees on a primrose carpeted mound, half a mile north of Killin past the cemetery, is a dangerous ruin now. It was the seat of the sinister sounding Black Duncan of the Cowl, a fierce Campbell chief. All that remains is a stark keep and a separate building with a coat of arms on it, possible a chapel. Close to the tower, you can still see a gruesome 'beheading-pit'. It is said that it was the privilege of the gentry to be beheaded, while the common people were hanged from a tree. Beyond the ruin are two 20th-century graves with simple Celtic crosses: Sir Gavin Campbell, Marquess of Breadalbane, and his wife of 50 years, Lady Alma.

Crianlarich

From Killin the A85 takes you about 11 miles west to Crianlarich, a tiny village, tucked in among the moors, about 13 miles southwest of Killin. Isolated but by no means deserted—it has the somewhat incongruously urban-sounding title of 'railway-junction'. This is where the railway lines from Oban and Fort William join up on their progress south. (The West Highland Line, from Glasgow to Mallaig, takes you through such glorious scenery that it is worth travelling on it for the journey itself.) If you want to be spared changing trains and stations in Glasgow at crack of dawn, and are in no hurry to catch your steamer from Oban to the Outer Isles, you can get out of the night train from the south, on to the tiny platform at Crianlarich, and while away two delightful hours before your connection comes along. Eating hot bacon baps in the early morning in the station buffet, after a night sitting up in the train, is an experience you don't forget, especially if the weather is kind and you can wander off into the hills, leaving your luggage perfectly safely on the platform, keeping an ear open for the approach of your train.

There are usually a number of people striding around Crianlarich in climbing boots and knapsacks: the 90-mile West Highland Way passes by on its way from Milngavie (pronounced Milngi) to Fort William, and this is a favourite staging post.

Three road-routes also meet in Crianlarich: south to Loch Lomond, northwest to Oban and Fort William, or northeast to Pitlochry.

Tyndrum

Five miles north, on the A82, brings you to Tyndrum, nestling in a glacial valley, gateway
to the Highlands. This is another junction of three roads: south, north and west, where
the cattle drovers used to meet meet up on their way to markets at Falkirk and Crieff.
These days Tyndrum is gaining a 'gold rush' status: extensive gold mining in the area has
led to the speculation that this is about to become an important gold centre in Britain.
Tyndrum has several hotels and gives the feeling of being a holiday stepping-off place,
exuding energy, with marvellous walks in all directions, and several hills rising to heights
above 3000 ft (900 m).

WHERE TO STAY AND EAT

Ardeonaig Hotel, Ardeonaig, Killin, tel 05672 400, is a drovers' inn, dating from
1680, on the south side of Loch Tay. It's moderately priced and standards have
improved since the drovers used to come here. **Clachaig Hotel**, Killin, tel 05672 270,
overlooking the bridge, is cheap and good value. The bedrooms are all en-suite, and
there's a cosy bar-restaurant, the Salmon Lie, in a converted smithy, with stone walls, big
log stove and reasonable food. **Morenish Lodge Hotel** near Killin, tel 05672 258, is a
former shooting lodge with panoramic views over Loch Tay, and private fishing rights.
Moderately priced, open from April to October, this is a friendly, cosy place.

There are a number of hotels in Crianlarich. Try **Portnellan House**, tel 08383 284, a
19th-century shooting lodge overlooking Loch Dochart. As well as the hotel, which is
cheap but only has three bedrooms, there are also 17 rooms in chalets on the surrounding hillside. Clay-pigeon shooting and free fishing.

Part XI

FIFE

The Study, Culross

Tiny little Fife sticks out between the Firth of Forth and the Firth of Tay, thrusting its nose into the North Sea like the head of an aggressive Scottie dog, with the M90 as its collar, Dunfermline as its silver name-tag and St Andrews as its beady eyes. Bordered thus on three sides by water it has a disproportionate ration of coastline for its size. Industrial towns in the south give way to attractive fishing villages around the East Neuk, strung out along miles of sandy beaches. Filmgoers may recognize the golden strands around St Andrews as those used for the running scenes in *Chariots of Fire*. Apart from a few small humps like Largo Law, and the Lomond Hills on the western boundary with Tayside, Fife is flattish, so the slightest elevation gives you a wonderful feeling of open spaces, and vast skies with sweeping views inland over a landscape of rich farmland broken by clumps of trees. A network of rivers, lochs and reservoirs provides agricultural irrigation and some fishing. Because of the lack of height, you won't find staggeringly dramatic scenery, but Fife has an elusive charm of its own, tied up in its history and its coast: watch the sunrise from Crail harbour wall and you will understand.

With the sea so close, Fife takes its share of battering when the wind is in the east, but it has a higher average of sunshine and less rainfall than most of the rest of Britain. Seaside holidays are bracing.

A surprising amount of history has soaked into this tiny corner of Scotland. Abernethy, just over the border in Tayside, was once a Pictish capital, whose overspill left many pre-historic sites to be excavated in the whole area. Once known as the Kingdom of Fife, two of its towns go back to the dawn of history: Dunfermline was the capital in the 11th century, and some say St Andrews received the shipwrecked remains of that saint in the 4th century. Geographically isolated, Fife used to be a place people went to, but not

FIFE

10 kms
10 miles

1 Falkland Palace
2 Earlshall
3 Tay Bridges
4 Balmerino
5 Lindores
6 Scotstarvit Tower
7 Kellie Castle

through, until the Tay Road Bridge was opened in 1966. When the new regional divisions were planned in 1975, the tiny Kingdom of Fife was to be split horizontally, one half to become part of Tayside and the other, part of Lothian. But the planners reckoned without the people of Fife, who had no intention of being annihilated and who protested so violently that Fife was allowed to remain intact.

Coal mining and heavy and light industry in the southwest corner give way to agriculture in the fertile hinterland. Fishing is still a way of life for some. Tourism, especially round the coast plays an important part in the economy, including, as everyone knows, golf.

SPORTS

Golf, of course: St Andrews is universally known and there are many other courses, some excellent. Green fees are modest, restrictions are few and apart from the Old Course at St Andrews, membership is not necessary. Lots of hotels and guest houses will arrange golf for you, or if you prefer to have it all taken out of your hands in advance—play, tuition, events and accommodation—you can book a spring Golf Week from the St Andrews Tourist Centre.

With so much coast, all **water sports** are available, and **sand yachting** on the West Sands at St Andrews is one of the most exhilarating and challenging of sports. Good **trout fishing** can be had on Cameron Reservoir, Carhurlie Reservoir, Clatto Loch, Lindors Loch, and on stretches of the Eden River and Ceres Burn. **Sea angling** for cod, plaice, mackerel, wrasse and saithe can be arranged from many of the coastal villages. **Riding and pony trekking** are available from a large number of riding centres.**Gliding** enthusiasts are catered for at Portmoak, near Glenrothes. With some of the best high-altitude airwaves in Britain, the Scottish Gliding Union operates a fleet of single- and double-seater gliders with holiday gliding courses.

There are a number of **Sports Centres** in Fife who lay on activity holidays covering everything from archery and abseiling to bird-watching and historic tours.

TOURIST INFORMATION

The following are open all year: St Andrews and North-East Fife Tourist Board, 78 South Street, St Andrews, tel 0334 72021; Forth Road Bridge, Inverkeithing, tel 0383 417759; Information Centre, Esplanade, Kirkaldy, tel 0592 267775; Glenrothes Tourist Association, Glenrothes, tel 0592 756684; 4 Kirkgate, Burntisland, tel 0592 872667; South Street. Leven, tel 033 29464. The Centre at Dunfermline, tel 0383 417759, is open Easter–end Sept, and there is also an Information Centre at the Museum and Heritage Centre, Crail, tel 0333 50869.

South Coast

The south coast of Fife is the northern shore of the Firth of Forth: an unpretentious string of industrial towns and villages whose people have toiled in coal mines and dockyards, factories and fishing boats. (The holiday resorts that serve these towns are popular in the summer; on a hot day their beaches can become as overcrowded as those of the Costa Brava.) Among the sprawl of utility buildings that must support such communities, there lurk hidden gems.

Culross

Going anti-clockwise round the coast, the first stop will be at Culross (pronounced Coeros). This miniature town on the shore of the Firth of Forth has been restored by the National Trust for Scotland over the past 50 years. A showpiece Royal Burgh of the 16th and 17th centuries, it looks almost exactly as it must have done in those days though, like most museums, it can never restore the smell and teeming, boisterous splurge of real life as it was. But, like good museums, it gives the imagination an accurate framework on which to build.

Culross was once one of the largest ports in Scotland, comparable in importance to Liverpool. It traded in coal, iron, fish, hand-loom weaving, and salt, extracted from sea water in salt pans heated by local coal. The combination of the Industrial Revolution and a bad storm that silted up the port severely damaged the economy, and the little town became a backwater until the National Trust moved in, in 1932.

Historically, Culross was the site of a 5th- or 6th-century religious foundation presided over by St Serf (or Servanus), and St Kentigern was born here (see 'Glasgow', p. 244). Leave your car on the outskirts of the old part and explore the steep, narrow, cobbled streets on foot.

The Palace (open daily: adm) was built in 1597 by a prosperous merchant, Sir George Bruce, overlooking the river which in those days came much closer to the town. Standing within a walled court, with crow-stepped gables, decorated dormer windows, and pantiled roofs, its garden rising steeply behind with terraced walks, the whole complex is most attractive. Bruce, trading local salt for valuable glass, cheated James VI of window tax by incorporating half-shutters of wood into the windows. You won't find a better example of a Scottish laird's house anywhere else, with Bruce's private counting house through an iron door. It is stone-vaulted, fireproof and has safes sunk into the walls. The painted ceiling, with allegorical figures, Latin texts and 'improving' admonishments, is on the second floor and is one of the best in Scotland. The curator has a fund of fascinating stories and manages to bring the place to life by pointing out a mass of small domestic details that might easily be missed.

The Town House, or Tolbooth (open daily, 1 May–30 Sept or by arrangement, tel 0383 880359: adm) built in 1626, is on the right of the palace. It has a double outside stair and was restored, with the tower being added, in 1783. The National Trust for Scotland have their headquarters here and you can see an excellent audio-visual show in the visitor centre, telling the history of the town and showing how it was rescued from decay. You can see the iron house, or prison, on the ground floor, the council room with a painted ceiling and the debtors' room. The 'high tolbooth' or turret was apparently used for witch-spotting. The tron, or public weighing scales, stood outside the tolbooth, where traders' measures could be checked against the standard weights to curb cheating.

The Study (open all year by arrangement and weekends in April, June, July, Aug and Oct, tel Newmills 880359, adm) is an L-plan, late 16th-century house with a turnpike stair and a small room at the top of its tower, which gave it its name. It is reached by climbing steep, narrow streets, cobbled and paved, behind the Town House until you get to a tiny asymmetrical market place with a reconstructed mercat cross. Inside the house is a small museum with furniture, pottery, pewter of the period and maps illustrating the early town.

The Little Houses of Culross, which are privately occupied, can all be enjoyed from the outside. They represent wonderful examples of the domestic architecture of the relatively humble working-class people of those days, in apparently random positions against each other, straggling up the narrow streets.

Culross Abbey (open daily: free) was founded in 1215 for Cistercian monks on the site of St Serf's church. The present parish church, dating from 1300, was rebuilt in 1633 from the original choir and central tower. Inside is a spectacular alabaster monument in memory of Sir George Bruce who built the Palace.

East from Culross, just along the shore, is the ruin of **St Mungo's Chapel** (always accessible, free). Built in 1513, it commemorated the spot where a Pictish princess, after escaping the wrath of her family, landed and gave birth to St Kentigern, affectionately known as Mungo (see 'Glasgow', p. 244). You get lovely views across the Forth from here. The flaming stacks of the Grangemouth Refinery on the far shore are strangely ethereal when seen through the haze they create, or in the half-light, against a darkening sky, reflected in the water.

Undulating farmland reaches inland, with narrow lanes and sudden splendid views. Along the shore you pass through picturesque little harbours and villages such as **Charlestown,** six miles east of Culross. This 18th-century village surrounds a green on a wooded plateau above the Forth. Charlestown Harbour, now a tiny haven that dries out at low tide, was built by the 18th-century Laird, the 5th Earl of Elgin, for sailing ships bringing iron ore and carrying away locally quarried lime. This is Bruce country, for the Earls of Elgin trace their descent from King Robert. It was the 7th earl who 'acquired' the ancient Greek marble sculptures, mostly a frieze from the Parthenon (now called the Elgin Marbles), and sold them to the British Museum in 1816 for £35,000. (The Parthenon was being used by the Turks, who were then occupying Athens, for target practice.) These marbles continue to be a bone of contention between Britain and Greece. Just before the Second World War they were cleaned, emerging so pristine from this laundering that the public were outraged and the Assistant Keeper in the Department of Greek and Roman Antiquities was most unfairly forced to resign.

Limekilns, a mile east of Charlestown, is an old-world village whose pretty cottages were lived in by the seamen who worked the ships out of Charlestown. Although those days are gone now, there is a great feel of community here in the riverside settlement.

Oakley, a few miles inland, northwest of Limekilns, is a mining village built to house workers in the Comrie Colliery. Many of the miners came from declining areas in the west to create a strongly Catholic community. The church, endowed by the Catholic Laird, Captain Smith-Sligo, in 1958, has some beautiful stained glass, and woodwork carved by a local craftsman.

Dunfermline

Dunfermline is two miles inland, about seven miles east of Culross, and was once the capital of Scotland. Hub of the southwest corner of Fife, it is dominated by the Abbey and Palace that stand above the town like sentinels. The town falls away from this crowning glory, an endearing mixture of Scottish Baronial, Modern Industrial and ancient ruins. Dunfermline means 'fort-by-the-crooked-pool' after a fort that stood in what is now Pittencrief Park, sloping down from the abbey to the southwest.

King Malcolm Canmore lived in Dunfermline in the middle of the 11th century. He was an unremarkable, blood-thirsty, perhaps rather boorish man, until along came saintly Margaret, an English princess, fleeing with her brother from the Norman Conquest. She married Malcolm in 1067 and set about Anglicizing Scotland, both culturally and ecclesiastically. Edward I held court here during his campaigns against the Scots at the end of the 13th century; Charles II agreed to accept the Covenant while staying in Dunfermline in 1651.

The town is probably best known today as the birth place of Andrew Carnegie (1835–1919), the son of a humble linen weaver, who went to America and made a fortune in steel. One of the best known philanthropists of the modern world, he used his millions for the benefit of mankind in numerous ways, including giving to his home town: Pittencrief Park, public baths, a library and an annual Festival of Music and Art. Dunfermline has a Civic Week in June, an excuse for all sorts of festivities, parades and entertainment.

Dunfermline must be firmly lodged in many minds as the subject for the ballad about Sir Patrick Spens. Sir Patrick was dispatched on a mission by his king who 'sat in Dumfermline toune, drinking the blude-reid wine'. Poor Sir Patrick put out in a storm, against his better judgement, and drowned, 'half owre, half owre to Aberdour, wi' the Scots lords at his feit'. According to Sir Walter Scott, Spens' voyage was to collect the Maid of Norway in 1290, but that cannot have been so because the maid was not collected until the king was dead.

The Abbey (open daily: free) is reached by steps from a terraced car park. The church, much restored, stands adjacent to the ruined monastery buildings and palace, which are linked to each other by a pend. It is hard to believe, when you look at these remains, that in the 13th century they were said to be 'big enough to hold two sovereigns with their retinues, at the same time, without inconvenience to one another'. There was a Culdee Chapel on the site where Malcolm Canmore, a widower, married Margaret. Two years later, the queen, horrified by the lax ways of the Celtic Church, began to build a new church to be administered in the English manner to which she was accustomed. When she endowed the Benedictine priory, she set up a shrine, with a relic of the True Cross, and encouraged pilgrims to come from miles away to venerate it.

The present church stands on the foundations of Margaret's church, some of which you can see through iron grilles in the floor. Frequently sacked and burned over the centuries, today's building is a jigsaw of different tastes and styles, the nave dating from 1128 and the massive buttresses from the 16th century. In 1818, workmen unearthed a vault with a stone coffin in it, containing a skeleton wrapped in thin sheets of lead. Shreds of cloth-of-gold clung to the bones and the breastbone had been sawn through, almost conclusively proving that this was the coffin of King Robert Bruce. Bruce died in 1329 having begged Sir James Douglas to carry his heart to Palestine and bury it in Jerusalem. (He had always intended to make a pilgrimage to the Holy Land in atonement for murdering his rival for the throne, Red Comyn.) Douglas set off with the heart but was killed in Spain in battle with the Moors. The heart was retrieved from the battle-field, returned to Scotland and buried in Melrose Abbey where it is today. Bruce's remains were reinterred and you will see a brass plate, set in Italian porphyry, under the pulpit, marking the spot. To celebrate this historic find, an over-enthusiastic architect designed the vast inscription that you cannot fail to notice, written in stone-fretwork round the top of the square tower: 'King Robert the Bruce'.

Malcolm Canmore and Queen Margaret died within a few days of each other in 1093, and their shrine is against the outside wall of the present abbey, where the Lady Chapel once stood. The abbey succeeded Iona as the burial place for Scottish kings.

The ruined **Palace** (open daily: free), still magnificent against an evening sky, was built when Margaret and Malcolm married. You can imagine the queen, walking up each day from Malcolm's Tower, now a ruin in Pittencrief Park below, to inspect the progress of her new home. Although she would have chosen to have been a nun rather than a queen, Margaret loved fine clothes, and exotic furnishings and no doubt her palace was very splendid. It provided an admirable setting for her task of 'refining' the rough, Celtic ways of her husband's court.

Pittencrieff Glen is reached through a gate opposite the west door of the abbey. When Andrew Carnegie was a boy, before he emigrated to Pennsylvania to make his fortune, he was forbidden entrance to the privately-owned park. He never forgot this and when he returned with his millions, he bought it and gave it to the people of Dunfermline so that 'no wee child should ever feel locked oot of it, as I was'. So now you can roam at will among lovely shrubs and flowers and trees, along the steep-sided, wooded glen, where birds sing and a burn tumbles down over its rocky bed and no child is ever 'locked oot'. It is a beautiful place, and Queen Margaret, known for her generosity to the poor, would have heartily approved.

Pittencrieff House (open daily except Tues, May–Oct: free) was built in 1610. It, too, was bought by Carnegie and makes a good focal point in the park. Inside there are displays of local history, costumes and an art gallery.

The Carnegie Museum (open daily: free) is in Moodie Street. This small cottage was Carnegie's birthplace. The rooms are furnished as they were in his lifetime, and the millionaire himself, remarkably life-like in waxen effigy, sits at his desk in his study, looking rather stern, perhaps planning where to bestow his next gift.

Dunfermline Museum (open daily except Sun: free) is at Viewfield. This Victorian villa has displays concentrating on the local history, including the weaving and the linen industies, both of which enriched the town in the past.

Rosyth

Rosyth is three miles south of Dunfermline, on the shore of the Forth. Its dockyard, now privatized, has played an important part in British naval history over the years. At one time it was the only naval dockyard where the entire fleet could anchor at any state of the tide. More recently, it was the only place that specialized in the refitting of nuclear and Polaris submarines.

St Margaret's Hope is east of the dockyard, near the foot of the Forth Road Bridge. Tradition has it that it was at this rocky promontory that saintly Queen Margaret landed for the first time in Scotland. Perched on a terrace on the point is the house of the admiral who commands the navy in Scotland. In the recent past, another admiral lived on

Castland Hill, across the marsh opposite, and the two old salts communicated by hoisting witty signal flags on their respective flagpoles—an essential part of any naval establishment.

North Queensferry

North Queensferry, a mile southeast of Rosyth, was originally the northern terminal of the ferry established by Queen Margaret to carry pilgrims to Dunfermline. It remained a ferry terminal until the road bridge was opened in 1964, and is now an attractive backwater with a big yacht marina.

Inverkeithing

It is worth stopping off in Inverkeithing, a stone's throw north of Queensferry. It is an older place than you might think at first glance— granted a Royal Charter in 1165.

Behind the busy central square in the High Street the 14th-century **Greyfriars Hospice**, restored as a community centre, has a small museum (open all the year round from Wed–Sun: free). Not only is the museum crammed with items of local interest—religious, military, industrial and domestic history—but it is presided over by a curator who will tell you everything you want to know about the area.

Dalgety Bay

Keeping to the shore road, a couple of miles east of Inverkeithing, you come to Dalgety Bay, now fringed by a sprawling residential development, but haunted by ghosts.

Donibristle House, stands on the site of the house where, in 1592, 'the Bonnie Earl of Moray' was murdered by an avenging Huntly on the order of the king. There are many versions of the murder story, one being that there was a tunnel from the house down which the unfortunate earl tried to flee, but because his hair had been set alight by his enemies he acted as a living torch for his pursuers. Whatever the story, it is a gloomy enough place now, its once lovely terraces overgrown with weeds.

St Bridget's Church is further along the shore of Dalgety Bay. This charming ruin is an unexpected little place right beside the water, its mossy banks dotted with tumbled headstones. It was dedicated in 1244; the eastern part of the church is the oldest. It was a two-storey kirk with a burial vault and laird's loft.

Aberdour

Aberdour, only five miles east of the Forth Road Bridge, is a popular resort, known for its silver sands. There is plenty here for a family holiday: golf, water sports, a sailing centre and a little harbour. The picturesque town has a cluster of medieval buildings above it, overlooking the sea. These include St Fillan's Church, the castle and dovecote.

St Fillan's Church is part Norman, part 16th-century, like a tiny cathedral, with a leper-squint in the west wall and an atmosphere of peace and timelessness that fills the soul with contentment.

Aberdour Castle (open daily except Thurs mornings and Fri: adm) stands close by on 14th-century foundations and still has its original tower. It was added to in succeeding

288

centuries, and is now an imposing, rather gloomy place, but it adds majesty to the overall scene. The circular **Dovecote** is part of the castle complex.

Inchcolm

A boat runs from Hawkcraig Point, in Aberdour, tel 0383 830665, to the tiny island of Inchcolm, across Mortimer's Deep, the watery grave of poor Sir Patrick Spens (under Dunfermline, p. 286), or a boat runs from the pier at South Queensferry.

Inchcolm is a perfect place to visit on a fine day, the boat trip making it more special. There are usually a few private boats at anchor in the tiny harbour, with much good-natured 'giving-way' to the official cruise boats. On calm days the water is often ruffled by the wakes of powerboats and waterskiers.

The Abbey of St Columba (open daily, weather permitting, except Wed afternoon and Thurs in winter: adm) is just next door to the landing jetty, overlooking a small rocky bay. It was founded in 1123 for Augustinian monks by Alexander I. A Columban monk, a hermit, who lived on the island, saved the king when his boat foundered on the rocky shore, and building the abbey was the king's act of gratitude. There is a very rough cell at the northwest corner which could have been the hermit's. Although it was often sacked by the English and desecrated during the Reformation, the abbey has been restored and looks a little too new, but the monastic buildings are the best you will find in Scotland. You can see the 13th-century octagonal chapter house with stone roof, and a 14th-century cloister with chambers above.

Burntisland

Burntisland, three miles east of Aberdour, once famous for shipbuilding, is now more popular as a holiday resort, its boatyards closed down. The town climbs up from the water and on a fine day in the summer the beach resembles that of any Mediterranean resort, with scant room to lay a lilo!

The octagonal **Church of St Columba** was the first to be built in Scotland after the Reformation. It was copied from a church in Amsterdam and has a central pulpit and galleries reached by outside stairs. The tower, added in 1749, is joined to the corners of the church by great flying arches. The General Assembly of the Kirk of Scotland was held here in 1601, when, in the presence of James VI, it was proposed that there should be a new translation of the Bible, the Authorized Version, published in 1611.

Agricola is said to have used the natural harbour for his fleet in about AD 83—strange to think of those Roman galleys at anchor where fibre-glass pleasure boats are now moored.

Rossend Castle is a 15th-century tower house that was saved from demolition and recently restored. Now it is one of Burntisland's treasures. It is used as offices but can be seen from the outside. It was here that an ardent French poet, Chastelard, hid himself in Mary, Queen of Scots', bedroom in 1563, a crazy escapade that cost him his life. He was executed in St Andrews and died reciting poetry and crying 'adieu, thou most beautiful and most cruel Princess in the world'. It is tempting to speculate whether perhaps the lively, 21-year-old widow had led him on, lonely for the French manners she had grown up with.

Kinghorn

At Kinghorn, a couple of miles further along the coast, you will see a Victorian monument beside the road in the shape of a Celtic cross. This is where Alexander III was thrown from his horse and killed, an event which completely altered the course of Scottish history. The king had been sitting in council with his lords in Edinburgh. They had eaten well and washed down their meal with plenty of wine. He set off to return to his new wife, Jolande, married only six months earlier in a desperate attempt to get himself an heir. There was a violent storm but he insisted on being taken across the Forth, at Queensferry. On the far side, he refused to shelter till daybreak but set off, galloping eastwards towards Pettycur where his still barren queen awaited him. His horse stumbled on the edge of the cliff at Kinghorn and that was the end of the King, thus fulfilling the prophecy made at his wedding feast in Jedburgh. The country was plunged into many years of bitter conflict and power struggles. Kinghorn is now a thriving holiday resort, with a sandy beach, good hotels, a golf course and campsites.

Inchkeith

You need to hire a boat to go out to the island of Inchkeith, southeast of Burntisland. Its strategic position in the Firth of Forth has made it an important defensive stronghold over many centuries, ever since Mary of Lorraine (Queen Regent for the infant Mary, Queen of Scots, in the 16th century) invited her French compatriots to fortify and occupy the island to defend Scotland's shores from English invasion. The island was used in the last two World Wars, to defend Rosyth dockyard and the rail bridge. It is now occupied only by the lighthouse keepers and by thousands of seagulls whose colony has been infected by virulent botulism from one of their scavenging grounds, so that the ground and shore are littered with their dead and dying bodies.

The story is told of an experiment that was tried by James IV. He wanted to see what language a child would speak if it had no example to follow. He sent two infants to the island with a totally dumb woman as their nurse. Some say that the children grew up speaking excellent Hebrew, others, that they emerged from the experiment speaking fluent Gaelic.

Kirkcaldy

Once known as 'the Lang Toun', Kirkcaldy (pronounced Kirkoddy) stretches along the coast three miles north of Kinghorn. It is a busy seaport, thriving industrial centre, holiday resort, and Fife's main shopping town, with four miles of seafront and an esplanade whose retaining wall was built in the early 1920s in an effort to relieve unemployment as much as to hold back the pounding sea.

Linen, weaving and textiles were the town's first occupations, until a weaver of sail cloth, Michael Nairn, turned his talents to the invention of linoleum, which quickly erupted into a major industry. It is said that, at the height of the linoleum boom, you could smell Kirkcaldy from many miles away. With the development of man-made fibres and more sophisticated floor coverings, the town's industry has diversified tremendously. Furniture manufacture is now an important part of the economy. Among

Kirkcaldy's famous sons are the architects Robert and James Adam, and Adam Smith, a brilliant scholar and philosopher who wrote, among other learned works, *Inquiry into the Nature and Causes of the Wealth of Nations* in 1776.

Every April, the Esplanade is closed for five days for **The Links Market,** the largest and oldest fair in Britain. A great gala of events is presented with plenty of music, colour, pomp and ceremony. The Esplanade also boasts a modern indoor swimming centre with sauna and fitness rooms to help you sweat off an over-indulgent holiday.

If you explore the heart of Kirkcaldy you will find that it is not just a modern town full of good shops and busy streets. You can wander into the older parts and come upon delightful little wynds and courtyards and old houses with pantiled roofs and crow-stepped gables, as for example in the eastern suburb of **Dysart.**

This quaint little quarter is full of character, and has its own picturesque harbour below the ancient battlement tower of St Serf's Church. In the old days, Dutch traders in tall-masted sailing ships came here to barter, exchanging cart-wheels, kegs and pipes for local coal, salt, beer and cured fish.

Kirkcaldy Museum and Art Gallery (open daily: free) is in the War Memorial Gardens, next to the station. They have a good archaeological collection with 300-million-year-old fossils, and you can also learn about local social history, natural history and industry. The art gallery, though small, has a splendid collection including work by many Scottish artists. A whole room has been devoted to William McTaggart, that great master who captured simple everyday life and familiar scenes so well. Other artists include Peploe, Lowry, Sickert and Raeburn. There are also displays of the local Wemyss Ware pottery.

The McDouall Stuart Museum (open every afternoon, June–Aug: free) is an award-winning museum in Fitzroy Street, Dysart, in a building restored by the National Trust for Scotland. The house, which has a lintel dated 1575, was the birthplace of John McDouall Stuart, the first man to cross Australia from south to north through the central desert in 1866. The museum tells you all about Stuart and his fascinating, and often hair-raising, expeditions, including his encounters with Aborigines and Australian wildlife.

The town has several parks: **Beveridge Park** with flower gardens and a boating lake; **Dunniker Park,** to the northwest, with a nature trail and golf course, shaded by cedar trees; and **Ravenscraig Park**, along the shore beyond Dysart.

Ravenscraig Castle

Ravenscraig (open daily: adm) towers dramatically above Ravenscraig Park, on a rocky promontory overlooking the river. This substantial ruin dates from 1460 when James II intended it as a dower house for his wife. He lost interest in it when she died. James III gave it to the Earl of Orkney in exchange for Kirkwall Castle which he had long coveted, and it was finally demolished for Cromwell in 1651 by General Monk. It was the first castle in Britain to be designed for defence by and against cannon shot and you can still see the wide gun loops in the massively thick walls. The views out over the Forth are lovely and in the days when such things were important, it was a splendid vantage point against invasion. Walter Scott called it Ravenshough, in his poem 'Rosabelle'. Near the castle, the steps that lead from the high-rise flats in Nether Road down to the beach should number 39, and are said to have inspired John Buchan to write that gripping book, though he moved his 39 steps several hundred miles south.

West and East Wemyss

West Wemyss is one and a half, and East Wemyss three miles east of Dysart. They are so called from the many 'weems', or caves, that honeycomb this bit of the coast. People have sheltered in these caves for many thousands of years and the graffiti they have left behind them is fascinating, dating back possibly to the Bronze Age (2500 BC). Due to erosion the caves are not at the moment safe to explore, but a campaign to Save Wemyss' Caves is under way.

The ruin just east of East Wemyss is called **Macduff's Castle,** and was once the stronghold of the Thanes of Fife.

Leven

Leven, three miles up the coast from the castle, on Largo Bay, is another holiday centre with a good beach and plenty of holiday facilities, including golf and fishing. It is hard to believe that the harbour was once a busy port, used to ship in provisions to the Royal Palace of Falkland. It silted up and is now a car park and, from the end of 1989, a swimming pool complex.

In **Silverburn Estate**, east of Leven near the beach, you can walk in the woods and gardens and observe the wildlife, including, if you are lucky, red squirrels. There are paddocks where the Silverburn Shetland ponies graze if they are not pulling carts in the park, and in spring there are usually foals to see, as well as pygmy goats from Africa and pot-bellied pigs from Vietnam.

Lethem Glen, on the northern outskirts of Leven, is another Nature Centre, with displays and information about wildlife, with a 45-minute Nature Trail and a Pets' Corner for young children.

Lundin Links, also on Largo Bay, is yet another family holiday resort. It has a sandy beach, sea fishing and golf. The standing stones just to the west are thought to have been part of a Druid temple.

Glenrothes

Five miles inland from either Kirkcaldy or Leven, Glenrothes is for the gregarious holidaymaker who enjoys masses of organized, modern entertainment. It is the sort of place you would not be surprised to find in America. The town is new and unbeautiful: the entertainments cover all tastes from indoor swimming, bowling, snooker, skating and curling, to outdoor gliding, parachuting, hang-gliding and golf. Glenrothes is not for the recluse.

WHERE TO STAY AND EAT
The choice is huge, the standard patchy. **The Old Toll Tavern** in St Leonards Street, Dunfermline, tel 0383 721489, was once what its name implies, so if you like antiquity you might do worse, and it's cheap. If you prefer modern comfort and convenience to

292

antiquity, however, the brand-new, moderately priced **Queensferry Lodge Hotel** in North Queensferry, tel 0383 413685, is undoubtedly the place for you. With panoramic views of the River Forth, not only will you get all the mod cons you'd expect in a new hotel, but also a Tourist Information, Craft and Interpretation Centre. For cosiness rather than glitz, try **Grey Craig House** at Saline near Dunfermline, tel 0383 852334. The house is old and attractive, more like a home than a hotel. It's cheap and only has three bedrooms.

Hawkcraig House, Aberdour, tel 0383 860335, is a gem and very cheap: the old ferryman's house at Hawkcraig Point, on the water's edge overlooking the harbour and Inchcolm Island. Open from February to mid-December, it only has two bedrooms so book well in advance. You can lean out of the window and watch the seals and birds, or eat the excellent home-cooked food. They don't have a licence but you are encouraged to bring your own wine. No credit cards. Another cheap one is **Forth View Hotel**, also on the water at Hawkcraig Point, Aberdour, tel 0380 860478, with gorgeous views near Silver Sands Beach and the golf course. It is only open from April to October and the food isn't at all bad.

Inchview Hotel in Kinghorn, tel 0592 872239, is a listed Georgian building overlooking Pettycur Bay. Not wildly exciting but cheap, and they do golf packages. Probably the most elegant of the hotels in this area is **Rescobie House** at Leslie, north of Glenrothes, tel 0592 742143. Secluded and creeper-clad, in four acres of lovely garden and grounds, this is a peaceful place to stay and moderately priced. It feels like a home, with sporting prints on the walls, antique furniture and log fires. A good base for golfing. Most of the rest are exactly what you would expect to find in any coastal holiday resort.

East Neuk

Neuk is a Scots word meaning 'corner', and that is exactly what this small wedge of land is, jutting off the eastern edge of Fife from Largo Bay to St Andrews, coming to a point at Fife Ness. This is a genteel holiday centre, where you are more likely to stumble on quaint pantiled cottages with neat, bright gardens than on fun-parks and theme-schemes. On a nice day, tour the fishing villages that ring the East Neuk, each with its own individual charm and character. In medieval Scotland there was much sea-trade with Europe and Scandinavia. Scottish wool, coal, leather and cured fish were exchanged for timber and manufactured goods. As well as goods, however, fashions were exchanged: crow-stepped gables, for instance, are of Flemish origin. When trade declined, fishing took over, particularly for herring, and was at its height in the last century. Now these little ports are less busy: built round picturesque harbours, crow-stepped houses rise in steep terraces, joined by twisting cobbled streets. The very names of these villages suggest stoic Scots dependability with no frills and flounces: Pitten-weem, Anstruther, Crail, names to be reckoned with. The beaches are gorgeous and less populated than those further south, the hinterland is pleasant farmland, and St Andrews provides history and culture.

Largo

Largo, at the head of Largo Bay, three miles northeast of Leven, was once an important fishing centre. It is now mainly residential and very popular in summer with its golden crescent of sand. Look out for the statue of Alexander Selkirk, who was born in Lower Largo in 1676. Selkirk was a wild young man who ran away to sea, quarrelled with his captain and was dumped, at his own request, on an uninhabited island, Juan Fernandez, where he existed for five years until he was rescued. He and his story were immortalized by Daniel Defoe, in his novel *Robinson Crusoe*.

While you are here, climb the volcanic cone of Largo Law, where an ancient chief is said to have been buried, dressed in silver armour. There are good views of Fife from the top.

Colinsburgh

Colinsburgh, inland, four miles east of Largo, was built by Colin, third Earl of Balcarres, in the 18th century. He was an ardent Jacobite and he built the village for his soldiers when he realized that the Stuart cause was hopeless.

Elie and Earlsferry

Elie and Earlsferry, at the eastern end of Largo Bay, six miles from Largo, are more or less one place. Both are popular resorts with lovely sandy beaches where, if you look carefully, you may find garnets in the sand. Earlsferry is the place where Macduff, Earl of Fife, is believed to have hidden from Macbeth in the 11th century in a cave at Kincraig Point, before being ferried to Dunbar. **The Elie Fair** is in July.

St Monans

St Monans, three miles northeast, has a charming cluster of old houses reaching down to the sea. When the wind is in the southeast the spray rises over the churchyard wall to wash the gravestones in the cemetery of a dear little fishermen's church that stands on the edge of the water. The foundations of this church date from 1362 when David II dedicated it to St Monans, or Mirren, an Irish missionary, in gratitude for a miraculous recovery from an arrow wound. The unusual T shape of the church is because the nave was never built.

The town rises steeply from a double harbour, an attractive network of narrow, twisting streets and restored old houses. **Miller's Yard**, close to the harbour, is one of the oldest surviving boatbuilders in Scotland, established in 1747 and still building traditional fishing boats.

Pittenweem

Pittenweem, meaning 'place-of-the-cave', a mile up the coast, is the home port of the fishing-fleets of the East Neuk, with a thriving fish market and an Arts Festival in August. It is an attractive, cheerful town, its old harbour often crammed with fishing boats, its quays stacked with fish boxes and gear. It is well worth getting up early in the morning to see the fish market in full fling—a seething mass of activity, sound, smell and vitality.

The National Trust for Scotland has done tremendous work on several of the buildings in the town. These include **Kellie Lodging**, a tower that juts into the High Street, and **The Gyles**, an attractive group of 16th and 17th-century houses by the harbour. You can see the remains of a priory in the grounds of the Episcopal Church, founded in 1114, whose Augustinian monks established a shrine in St Fillans Cave, where services are still occasionally held.

Kellie Castle

Kellie Castle (open Easter weekend and daily, 1 May–30 Sept and weekends, April and Oct; grounds open daily all year: adm) is three miles inland on the B9171. Kellie dates from the 14th century, an impressive great pile of mainly 16th- and 17th-century domestic architecture, in an attractive setting of landscaped gardens. It was rescued from decay in 1875 by Professor James Lorimer, and his grandson, the sculptor Hew Lorimer, is the resident custodian. It has some splendid plaster work and painted panelling.

Anstruther

Anstruther, a mile up the coast from Pittenweem and contracted to 'Anster' by locals, was once an important fishing centre but is now better known as a holiday resort. It has, however, hung on to its link with its fishing past.

The Scottish Fisheries Museum and Aquarium (open daily: adm), at the head of the harbour, gives a unique insight into the life and work of a fishing community, with marvellous interiors of a typical fisherman's home—complete with wife, baby and cradle. You come away filled with admiration for the men who put the haddock on your plate, determined that you will never take a fish supper for granted again.

You can also see over the **North Carr Lightship**, in the harbour, which did 43 years service off Fife Ness. This is a magnet for young boys. Try to picture what life must have been like for the seven-man crew in those cramped quarters for weeks on end, particularly in bad weather. There is also a Fife fishing boat you can go round.

East Neuk Outdoors, in Anstruther, runs activity holidays with abseiling, archery, boardsailing, canoeing, climbing, coastal walks, cycling, bird-watching, historic tours and special activities for children. They have a playgroup for 2–5 year olds (tel 0333 311929).

There are guided historical walks round Anstruther from the end of June to the end of September, and there is a Holiday Fair week in July. Boats run from here to the Isle of May, weather permitting: tel 0333 310103.

The Isle of May

Boats run from Anstruther and Crail to the Isle of May, the largest of the four islands that command the entrance to the Firth of Forth, and once of vital strategic importance. The island, one mile long and about a quarter of a mile in width, has an intriguing history stretching back into the dark ages and embroidered with legend, all told in *The Story of the May Island*, published by Largo Field Studies Society, in Upper Largo. 'The May' became a National Nature Reserve in 1956 since when the seabird population has increased dramatically. Look out especially for puffins with their unreal-looking striped beaks, living in burrows in the turf, and the incredible camouflage of nesting eider ducks who manage to stay totally motionless within only a few feet of the path. Other birds include guillemots, razorbills and kittiwakes. You are more than likely to see seals here, too.

The remains of a beacon in the middle of the island are from the first Scottish lighthouse, built in 1636. The tower was at least twice the height of today's and it had a huge brazier on top that burned coal at the rate of between one to four tons a night, depending on the wind. It needed stoking every 20 minutes, was invisible upwind and was easily confused with the lights of the saltpans along the mainland shores. In a storm in 1792, sulphurous fumes from the cinders of the beacon killed the lighthouse keeper and his family—seven in all, as they slept. The present lighthouse was built by Robert Louis Stevenson's grandfather, also called Robert, in 1816.

Crail

Crail, three miles beyond Anstruther, is another well-restored little fishing town with one of the prettiest harbours in Fife. (The Harbourmaster, Roger Banks, is an acclaimed artist and paints exquisite cameos of natural history. He has several books to his name.) Crail was a Royal Burgh in 1310 and was granted the right to trade on the Sabbath. (This can't have pleased John Knox when he came preaching here some 200 years later.) Picturesque colour-washed houses and cobbled streets lead down to the harbour and its crow-stepped customs house: a lovely place to sit on the harbour wall, a glass of beer in your hand, the sun on your face, and listen to the sounds of the water slapping at the stones. Crail Festival Week is in July.

The Church of St Mary is a 12th-century church. The large blue stone at its gate is said to have been hurled there by the Devil, from the Isle of May, five miles out to sea. You can see an 8th-century Pictish cross slab in the church, and in Victoria Gardens the early Christian **Sauchope Stone**. The restored **Tolbooth** dates from the early 16th century, and at 62 Marketgate you can explore the **Crail Museum and Heritage Centre** (open for two weeks around Easter and daily, June–Sept: adm) and learn much of the history of this ancient town. There is a Tourist Information Centre in the Museum, too, tel 0333 50869.

Kingsbarns

From Crail, the coast road turns northwest towards St Andrews and you lose the sea for a while. You come first to Kingsbarns, three miles from Crail, whose name will tell you that this is good farmland. There is a nice story attached to the original owners of **Pitmillie**, just north of the village. In the 11th century, before Malcolm Canmore was King, he asked a stranger for the loan of 'a few pennies'. 'Not a few: mony pennies' (sic), came the munificent reply. King Malcolm did not forget. When he came into power he granted his benefactor the lands at Kingsbarns and the family became known as 'Moneypenny'.

While you are here, visit **Cambo Country Park**, signposted from the main road. Sloping down to the sea, this attractive estate has converted its farm buildings into a visitor centre with a licensed café and shop and a play area. You can walk in the grounds and there are tame farm animals for the children.

St Andrews

St Andrews, 10 miles beyond Crail, unfolds below you: its ghosts beckon irresistably. Many of the stones used to build the older houses came from the ruined cathedral on the eastern edge of the town, towards which the three main streets lead. Scotland's oldest university, founded in 1411, is now the living heart of the town whose medieval spirit is kept young in many ways. For instance, you might be lucky and see the Sunday parade of students processing from the chapel in the scarlet medieval gowns that were introduced so that they could be spotted easily when entering brothels. (Divinity students wear black gowns: presumably they were above suspicion.)

Andrew, brother of Simon Peter and the first disciple to be called by Our Lord, was 'the most gentle of the Apostles'. Among his many converts was the wife of the Roman Governor of Patrae. The governor was so furious and jealous of his wife's conversion that he had Andrew crucified. (Andrew asked to be tied to an X-shaped cross so that he should not appear to be emulating Christ.) According to legend, St Rule, who was custodian of the Saint's remains in Patrae, some time between the 4th and 8th centuries, had a vision of an angel who ordered him to take five of Andrew's bones, sail to the western edge of the world and build a city in his honour. Rule set off and was shipwrecked on the rocks just to the west of today's harbour. He hurried ashore and enshrined the sacred relics on the headland where the ruins of the 12th-century cathedral now stand. The shrine became a place of worship for Christian pilgrims from far and wide and a special ferry was kept on the River Forth to transport them. St Andrew became Scotland's patron saint and the city where his sacred relics lay enshrined became the ecclesiastical capital of Scotland.

In spring, the **Kate Kennedy Pageant** takes over, with 60 to 70 students parading the streets in costume. Kate, the niece of one of the founders of the university, was so beautiful that all the students were in love with her. The pageant is all-male, with Kate played by a first-year student.

The Lammas Fair, in August, is Scotland's oldest surviving medieval market, with showmen from all over Britain setting up stalls and booths in the streets—a bright, colourful carnival that lasts for two days. There are also the bi-annual St Andrews Festival, the Festival of Food and Wine in March, St Andrews Highland Games in July, and great celebrations for St Andrews Day on 30 November. On top of all this there are the golf championships: the Annual Golf Week in April and the Dunhill Nations Cup in September.

St Andrew's Cathedral (open daily: adm), founded in 1160, was once the largest cathedral in Scotland. Medieval pilgrims came in their thousands to pray at one of its 31 altars. It is strange to stand in front of the remains of the high altar and recall that Robert Bruce stood here at the consecration of the cathedral in 1318, 160 years after the building began. Here too stood James V and Mary of Guise at the ceremony of their marriage. In 1559 that zealous reformer, John Knox, preached some stirring sermons on the 'cleansing of the temple' and so roused his congregations to hysteria that they stripped the cathedral of its glorious embellishments and riches, leaving it to decay into ruin. Even as a ruin it is magnificent. A great twin-towered façade soars towards the sky, surrounded by neat green turf, graves, the foundations of the priory, a few massive walls and a Norman arch.

The **Cathedral Museum** is full of interesting relics including a unique sarcophagus. **St Rule's Tower** is also within the precinct: a stern, gaunt chaperone. Here the holy relics were kept until the cathedral was completed. If you feel energetic you can climb the 158 steps inside the tower and see wonderful views of the town and out to sea. **The Pends**, now roofless, was the vaulted gatehouse entrance to the cathedral precinct. Dating from the 14th century, it is said that it will collapse when the wisest man in Christendom walks through the arch. Fortunately, the prophecy doesn't include women so the Pends still stands.

St Andrew's Castle (open daily: adm) is northwest of the cathedral on a rocky headland overhanging the sea beyond a deep moat. Now a ruin, it was built as the Bishop's Palace at the end of the 12th century and it witnessed some extremely nasty incidents in the bloodstained history of the Scottish Church. George Wishart, the ardent Protestant reformer, was burned at the stake in front of the castle in 1545 and tradition tells of the notorious Catholic Cardinal Beaton, lying on velvet cushions inside the castle, watching his death throes. Whether this is true or not, Beaton paid for Wishart's life with his own. A worldly, immoral man, the Cardinal did not hesitate to plead for mercy on account of his priestly status two months later, when he was brutally stabbed to death by a party of avenging Reformers. His body was hung over the battlements and then slung into the 'bottle dungeon', a fearsome rock pit, where it was preserved in salt until its discovery more than a year later. After the murder, the Reformers held the castle against a siege, having been joined by John Knox and others, before they were all captured and sent off to serve time as galley slaves. Knox was a close friend of Wishart: it was to be 14 years before he returned to stir the reforming pot again.

The castle fell into ruin in the 17th century but you can still see the bottle dungeon. A large number of the Reformers were imprisoned in this hell-hole: it is hard to believe that many can have survived. Beaton's apartments are thought to have been in the tower to the southwest.

One of the features of the castle is the mine and counter mine, tunnelled through the rock during the siege that followed Beaton's murder in 1546–47. The besiegers started their tunnel but were frustrated by the defenders who tried to intercept them. Uncertainty about who was where led to abandonment. The galleries were later useful as secret tunnels in those days of intrigue.

The Church of St Salvator is among St Andrews' many fine university buildings. In North Street, it was founded as the University Chapel by Bishop Kennedy in 1450, uncle of the beautiful Kate who is fêted in the April pageant. The Bishop's tomb is in the church, along with a magnificent mace from his time which is still carried on ceremonial occasions. The pulpit was the one John Knox preached from, carried here from the parish church. It is exciting to imagine him standing there, thumping out his message on that very wood.

Patrick Hamilton, the proto-martyr of the Reformation, was burned for his Lutheran heresy in front of St Salvator's College in 1528. Archbishop James Beaton, uncle of the notorious Cardinal, was mainly responsible for his persecution.

The Royal and Ancient Golf Club makes history pale into insignificance for golfers. Known to the cognoscenti as the R and A, this world-famous establishment determines the rules of the game, although it is by no means Scotland's oldest club. The club house is open to members only. The autumn Golf Meeting, at the end of September, is the main event of the year and when you see the preparations beforehand (the tents and booths and marquees) you would imagine an army was preparing for a major battle. It is at this meeting that the Captain for the Year plays himself into office, watched by thousands of anxious eyes, in case he should miss that important ball. Of the four courses, 'The Old' is the most famous.

St Leonard's College, founded in 1512 and no longer extant, was on the present site of St Leonard's Girls' School, beyond Abbey Street (known to its inmates as The Prison). Many ardent reformers, including John Knox it is thought, studied at the college, and the term 'to have drunk at St Leonard's Well' was coined from those times, meaning to have listened to the Protestant doctrine. The library of St Leonard's School is in Queen Mary's House, in South Street, where Mary is believed to have stayed, in 1563, taking a holiday with her ladies from the burdens of State affairs. While she was there she planted a thorn tree that still flourishes in the quadrangle of St Mary's College.

The Byre Theatre, which you get to through the attractive South Court, stages an excellent range of productions throughout the year and began its life in a cowshed of the Old Abbey Street Dairy Farm, hence its name. Another place to visit is the **Crawford Centre for the Arts,** which has a changing programme of art exhibitions, professional theatre and music performances in its drama studio and galleries.

West Port at the end of South Street, built in 1589, was the main entrance to the old city. It gives a good idea of what it must have been like in the days when a town could literally shut its gates and defend itself from within.

In North Street, there is the **St Andrews Preservation Trust** in a 17th-century building, where you can learn more about all the treasures in this ancient city.

Don't miss the picturesque **Harbour**. The main pier was rebuilt in the 17th century with stones from the ruined cathedral and castle.

Craigtoun Country Park

Craigtoun Country Park, two miles south of St Andrews, is 50 acres of parkland surrounding Mount Melville House, now a hospital, and open to the public all year. The park has an Italian garden, a Dutch village surrounded by an ornamental lake built in 1918, a Rio Grande Miniature Railway, putting, bowling, trampolines, shops, a licensed restaurant and a picnic area. There are Nature Walks and a Ranger Service, too. They run a Country Fair in May.

Leuchars

The railway line to St Andrews was closed some years ago and Leuchars, five and a half miles northwest, is now the station that serves the town. In the village of Leuchars you could easily miss one of the best relics of Norman architecture in Scotland. Only an apse and chancel remain, incorporated into the parish church, with an arcaded exterior to the apse. If you look carefully you can see the axe-marks of the ancient masons on the blind arches and pilasters. It is a pity that the modern church is so plain, but perhaps its dullness offsets the triumph of the Norman part.

Earlshall Castle

A mile east of Leuchars, Earlshall Castle (open Easter and June–3rd Sunday in Sept: adm) was built in 1546 by Sir William Bruce, ancestor of the present owners. It is a massive fortress, with thick walls and musket loops, set somewhat incongruously among fanciful topiary—the yews are supposed to be chess men—and beautiful, peaceful gardens. Mary, Queen of Scots, stayed here only 15 years after it was built, and you can see her bedroom. In the long gallery the ceiling is painted with the arms of Scotland's leading families interspersed with mythological beasts. Hanging from the walls are over 100 broadswords. Lots of historic memorabilia to see here, and guides bursting to tell you strange tales of mysterious red shoes and the footsteps of The Bloody Bruce who can be heard on the stairs now and then. They stage special exhibitions in the Rod and Gun Room, and in the Museum Room you can see letters dating back 200 years and bagpipes that were played at Waterloo.

WHERE TO STAY AND EAT

The East Neuk has plenty of hotels and guest houses. **The Craw's Nest** in Anstruther, tel 0333 310691, was built as a manse in 1703 and has been extended considerably since those days. The extra size makes it a bit impersonal but it is comfortable and moderately priced. **The Smuggler's Inn,** also in Anstruther, tel 0333 310505, is a bit cheaper, overlooks the harbour and is full of atmosphere. You eat well here, in great comfort with cosy log fires, and as you lie awake you hear the tramp of the excisemen outside your window and the whisper of the smugglers as they hastily hide their booty.

Golfers could do worse than **Lundin Links Hotel**, tel 0333 320207, a mock-Tudor house with an air of solemn respectability. Surrounded by golf courses and close to the beach, it is cheap and offers special golfing breaks. Or try the moderately priced **Old Manor Hotel**, also at Lundin Links, tel 0333 320368. From your window you can look over the golf course to the sea, and the food is excellent.

St Andrews has a huge choice. The most expensive, **St Andrews Old Course Hotel**, tel 0334 74371, is very swish, with free use of Spa facilities. Quite a bit cheaper and much better value, **Rufflets Country House Hotel** in Strathkinness Low Road, tel 0334 72594, is a real treat, set in 10 acres of glorious award-winning gardens, with superb food, and quiet, friendly service. It has been owned and personally managed by the same family for more than 35 years which probably accounts for its high standards. **Rusacks,** at 16 Pilmour Links, tel 0334 74321, is a little cheaper: very luxurious and prestigious. If you want to be flexible and self-supporting, **Kincaple Lodges,** St Andrews, tel 0334 85217, are nine pinewood chalets, built among trees along the beach three miles west of St Andrews. They provide everything you could ask for, including linen, electric blankets and televisions and are not expensive. There are tennis courts, play areas and a babysitting service.

South of the Tay

The north coast of Fife is less developed than that of the East Neuk and has more of an estuary feeling, with lovely views of the river over the mudflats and a rich bird life. Inland is all farms and sturdy little towns and villages with uncompromising names like Auchtermuchty, and Strathmiglo. Falkland, with its splendid Palace, lies at the heart of this area which has several other interesting ruins as well.

Tentsmuir Forest

Going north towards the Tay you come to the Tentsmuir Forest a couple of miles northeast of Leuchars. Pines grow right down to the broad, sandy beach, providing shade for picnics on summer outings. Keep your eyes skinned for deer and families of seals, sunning themselves on the sands, as well as lots of different birds.

Tayport and Newport-on-Tay

Tayport and Newport-on-Tay, five and a half miles north of Leuchars, are holiday resorts on the southern shores of the Firth of Tay. Both claim to have had the oldest ferry in Scotland and it seems likely that boats might have run from both places since earliest times when they were crude settlements. Neolithic remains have been excavated on this northeastern corner of Fife.

The Tay Rail Bridge

The southern approach to the Tay Rail Bridge is a short distance west of the one that collapsed in a gale on 28 December 1879, sending a train and about 100 passengers into the water, a disaster that shocked the world and still brings a shiver of horror to hearts today. Anyone who has not read the account of the disaster as told by that astonishing poet, William McGonagall, should do so at the first possible opportunity.

> So the train mov'd slowly along the Bridge of Tay,
> Until it was about midway,
> Then the central girders with a crash gave way,
> And down went the train and passengers into the Tay!
> The storm Fiend did loudly bray,
> Because ninety lives had been taken away,
> On the last Sabbath day of 1879,
> Which will be remember'd for a very long time.

The new rail bridge, built only a few years later, is a graceful construction curving across the river like a two-mile memorial to the disaster. The road bridge, two miles downstream, is a toll bridge.

McGonagall was fascinated by the Tay and wrote several other of his epic verses in its honour. There was one about a monster whale that came to 'devour the small fishes in the silvery Tay' and one to the railway bridge before it collapsed, and even an address to the New Tay Bridge. In fact, no traveller in Scotland should set out without a copy of the poetic gems of William McGonagall, poet and tragedian.

Balmerino Abbey

Balmerino Abbey (always accessible: free) is a ruin three miles west of the rail bridge, on a hill overlooking the river. It was founded for Cistercians in the 13th century, by Alexander II, whose mother is buried here. It was mostly destroyed by the English in 1547, during the 'Rough Wooing' and a later attempt to restore it was foiled by the Reformation. The last Lord Balmerino was a brave old man, beheaded as a Jacobite in 1746. Seen against a stormy sky, it is a sad, poignant shell, with just the entrance to the chapter house and the roofless sacristy standing among farm buildings.

Lindores Abbey

The scattered remains of Lindores Abbey (always accessible: free) are eight miles southwest, just before Newburgh, and also overlooking the Firth of Tay. This abbey was an important religious community until it was secularized in 1600. The main entrance arch and part of the west tower still stand in jagged isolation, all that remain of a place that witnessed the savage burning of exquisitely illuminated mass books and manuscripts by John Knox. Lindores was founded in the 12th century for Benedictines and numbered among its many pilgrims several Scottish monarchs.

Newburgh

Newburgh, 13 miles southwest of Newport, almost on the border with Tayside, is a Royal Burgh with a pretty little harbour. In June, it holds a fair, called the Haggis Market, which includes a race for salmon cobles on the river. On the hill to the south of the town you can see the remains of Macduff's Cross, the legendary place of sanctuary for any Macduff who had committed a murder in hot blood. To achieve pardon, the murderer had to touch the cross, wash himself nine times at Ninewells nearby, and forfeit nine cows, each to be tied to the cross.

Laing Museum (open daily, 16 March–15 Oct, and Wed, Thurs and Sun for the rest of the year, adm) has recently reopened. Here you can see excellent exhibitions, including fossil fish discovered in Dura Den, a feature on Scottish emigration, and Victorian displays including a reconstructed Victorian study.

Falkland

Falkland, nine miles south of Newburgh, is one of the jewels of Fife. This ancient, beautiful town clings to the lower slopes of the Lomond Hills, looking across the Howe of Fife. The rich farmland that you see now was once a forest full of deer and wild boar. Many of the 17th- to 19th-century buildings have been restored, making it a delightful place to wander about in, especially on a fine day when the sun plays tricks with the old stones, dappled with light and shade.

Falkland Palace (open daily Easter–30 Sept and weekends in Oct: adm) was built in the 15th and 16th centuries as a hunting lodge for the Stuarts. Much of it has been carefully restored, giving a wonderful example of early Renaissance architecture— compact and ornate, its massive walls and barred windows a reminder that even hunting lodges had to be fortified. The south wing is the best preserved, with an elaborate façade, mullioned windows and gate house flanked by round towers.

It was in an earlier castle on this site, in 1402, that the heir to the throne, the Duke of Rothesay, was starved to death by the ambitious and greedy Duke of Albany. Falkland was annexed by the crown when James I eliminated the powerful Albany family by the simple, if somewhat drastic, method of murdering all their menfolk. The elegance of the architecture was enhanced by French masons employed by James IV and then by his son James V. James V came to Falkland in 1542, after his defeat at Solway Moss. He died here, a broken man, having just heard of the birth of his daughter, Mary. He prophesied on his death bed that his infant daughter would be the last of the Stuarts to rule Scotland.

The palace was restored from complete ruin by the Hereditary Keeper, the third Marquess of Bute, in 1887 and he also rescued the gardens and many of the houses in the town. The original Royal Tennis Court, 1539, is still in use as one of Britain's few 'royal' or 'real' tennis courts. Perhaps Queen Mary had a game here. She certainly played golf and is known to have come often to Falkland on hunting expeditions.

Wander along the High Street, beyond the palace gates, through the Market Square, and up the Maspie Burn on to East Lomond Law. From here, the landscape is all rolling hills and rounded hillocks, and attractive little villages with stone cottages and pantiled roofs. This is the Howe of Fife, 'howe' meaning sheltered place.

Cupar

Cupar, 10 miles northeast of Falkland, heading back to St Andrews, was once the administrative centre of Fife. It is a cheerful, friendly little town with elegant 18th-century houses built of mellow, honey-coloured stone. In 1276, Alexander III held an Assembly of the Three Estates in Cupar, made up of the Church, the burghers, and the aristocracy. It was this that inspired Sir David Lindsay, who lived nearby, to write 'Ane Satire of the Thrie Estates', holding them up to ridicule. The play has recently been revived and is aired now and then during the Edinburgh Festival. Cupar has a Gala Week in June.

The Scottish Deer Centre (open daily, adm) is three miles west of Cupar on the A91. Children will enjoy seeing deer at close quarters and even touching them, and there is lots to see and do in the Visitor Centre in the Georgian courtyard, which has a restaurant. Outside there is a Farm Walk and Nature Trail.

Hill of Tarvit

Hill of Tarvit (open Easter; weekends only April and Oct; afternoons daily 28 April–30 Sept: adm) is a mansion two miles south of Cupar. Dating from 1696 and splendidly remodelled by Robert Lorimer in 1906, the house has a nice lived-in feeling. The collection of treasures inside includes: tapestries, porcelain and paintings, and 18th-century English and French furniture. There is also an Edwardian laundry where you can almost see steam from the boiling sheets in the copper and feel the ache of the women's tired muscles at the end of the day. The gardens are laid out in French style, with box hedges and yews: there is a woodland walk and a hilltop 'toposcope'. The view of the house from the garden, with a double flight of steps leading up to the terrace, is lovely.

303

Scotstarvit Tower opposite Hill of Tarvit (open daily: free) is a five-storey, 16th-century tower house with battlements and turrets. It was the home of John Scott, a 16th- and 17th-century scholar and mapmaker in the days when new routes were opening up all round the globe.

Pitlessie

Pitlessie, four miles southwest of Cupar, will be familiar to fans of David Wilkie, from his famous painting 'Pitlessie Fair'. The artist was born at Cults Manse nearby in 1785 and many of his wonderful paintings of ordinary everyday life were set locally, so that you find yourself looking round for one of his jovial, bucolic peasants. Very sadly, the manse was destroyed by fire in 1926, together with a wealth of wall paintings done by Wilkie in his youth.

Ceres

Ceres is an attractive village four miles east of Pitlessie. Pantiled cottages surround a green on which annual games are still held, dating from victory celebrations after Bannockburn in 1314.

The Fife Folk Museum (open afternoons daily except Tues, April–Oct: adm) is spread between a restored 17th-century Tolbooth Weigh House, two cottages and out of doors. This award-winning museum has collections of the domestic and agricultural tools and equipment in daily use before the invention of electricity and the petrol engine. Don't miss the dungeons in the tolbooth. There are also two nature trails from the village, planned by the Scottish Wildlife Trust, of botanical and geological interest.

Peat Inn, three miles to the southeast, is a hamlet that takes its name from its inn. It is well worth a detour to this inn, where you can eat as good a meal as you could hope for anywhere in the country.

Magus Muir is three miles north of Peat Inn and just south of Strathkinness. This grizzly spot is where a party of Covenanters butchered Archbishop Sharp in 1679, in the presence of his daughter. Sharp's attempts to restore Episcopacy to Scotland had not been entirely straightforward and he had won for himself universal detestation. Hardly surprising, when you remember that he went, as a Presbyterian, to plead the Covenanters' cause with Charles II and returned as the consecrated Bishop of St Andrews.

Old Dairsie, about three west of Magus Muir, has a bridge over the River Eden that was built by Archbishop Beaton in 1522. **Dairsie Castle** (always open: free) lies above the river, where David II spent part of his youth. Dura Den is a wooded gorge south of the bridge, where a large number of fossils have been found. These fossils gave vital clues to the formation of land and life here, over many millions of years. Beside the Ceres Burn that cuts the gorge, you can see the ruins of several linen and jute mills, once an important part of Fife economy.

WHERE TO STAY AND EAT

Fernie Castle Hotel, near Letham, tel 033 781381, is a must for the castle addict. Built in 1510 in 30 acres of park and woods, this is a prince among castles, with a round tower and a prize-winning French chef. Well placed for golfers, it's quite expensive and well worth it. **Sandford Hill Hotel** near Wormit, Newport-on-Tay, tel 0382 54180, is built round three sides of an attractive courtyard garden with quaint narrow passages leading to comfortable bedrooms. It's moderately priced with special golf packages and the food is good.

In Falkland, **Covenanter Hotel,** tel 0337 57224, with only three bedrooms, is moderately priced with a quaint charm that makes it attractive. Cheap and a little different is **Redlands Country Lodge** near Ladybank, tel 0337 31091: a country lodge in lovely gardens surrounded by open country, with separate pine log-cabin bedrooms, self-contained and comfortable. The food is excellent and they'll arrange golf, fishing, shooting, wildfowling and pony-trekking. If you prefer self-catering, you could do a lot worse than **The Weaver's House**, Auchtermuchty, tel 0337 28496, a sweet little cottage, very well set up for six people, but expensive.

People travel a long way to eat in the 18th-century **Peat Inn**, tel 033 484206, at the junction of B940/941 in the village of that name. This is a true French auberge, complete with Michelin star, modelled on the proprietors' favourite establishment in Vonnas, France, with decor and ambience to match. The food is accurately aimed at discerning taste buds, the wine list is excellent and the service unbeatable.

Part XII

TAYSIDE

Glamis

The sun shines kindly on Tayside and the east wind hones its coast. In winter the peaks glisten with snow; in summer the hills and moors are bruised with purple heather. Birch, conifer and hardwood trees shade the glens, giving a blaze of metallic colours in autumn: bronze, gold, copper, rust.

Once the centre of the Pictish kingdom, Tayside's hill forts and mysterious stone circles are haunted by the ghosts of the Picts. The Romans came and went in the first and second centuries. They built sophisticated fortifications but failed to subdue the Picts, who reigned supreme, with their own kings and culture. They gradually absorbed Christianity as it crept in from the west and left carved stones to prove it. The Vikings swooped in from the sea, but were beaten off. In the middle of the ninth century, Kenneth Macalpine united Dalriada in the west with Pictland, and Scone, just north of Perth, became the capital until the middle of the 15th century, with nearby Dunkeld an important ecclesiastical centre. In the turbulent 17th century, many battles—political, religious and territorial—were fought in the narrow passes that linked north and south. The Battle of Killiecrankie, in 1689, was perhaps the best known, when the Highlanders almost annihilated the Government's army. Control of several of Tayside's castles was hotly disputed half a century later, during the final Jacobite rebellion.

Agriculture and fishing have been the main sources of income for these rural people, with little industrialization except around Dundee. Whisky distilling plays an important part in the economy and tourism is growing fast, backed up by the revival of old crafts.

Among the many local events to look out for are the Bull Sales in Perth, in February and October. Whether you are interested in cattle farming or not, this wonderful assembly of bucolics has faces as rich in character as any in a David Wilkie painting. Farmers come from far and wide and pay astronomic prices for the finest bulls in the land. Highland Games are held in a number of places, including Blair Atholl in May; Dundee and Arbroath in July, Perth and Birnam in August and Pitlochry in September. In May, the renowned Perth Festival of Arts is held and Pitlochry's Annual Summer Festival runs from May to October with a tremendous choice of plays, concerts and Fringe events. A traditional Scottish Folk Festival is held for three days every April in Glenfarg, drawing artists from all over the country. International Fly Fishing Championships are often held on Loch Leven in autumn.

Many people hurry through Tayside, blind to its attractions in their rush to get to the Highlands proper. They miss a great deal. Approaching through Kinross in the south, the main routes into Perthshire and Angus radiate from Perth, following the river valleys like the wavering legs of a giant spider. That is how this guide will cover the region.

SPORT

Walking is, as always, one of the best ways of exploring, and Tayside has some glorious treks to offer. You can stroll through the beautiful wooded glens or you can get into your climbing boots and tackle any number of the challenging hills that surround you, including Ben Lawers, 3987 ft, Schiehallion, 3554 ft, and Ben Vrackie, 2757 ft.

Skiing, at Glenshee, is quite an experience for those accustomed to cushy Alpine resorts. It's tough—and exhilarating. There is a network of 24 tows and chairlifts, directly accessible from the A93, and quite a few nursery slopes, as well as the terrifying Tiger Run. The weather is unpredictable and beginners should avoid attacking the daunting slopes when visibility is bad: rocks jump out at you when you least expect them. For skiing information, ring Glenshee Information Officer, tel 0250 5509. There is also *langlauf* skiing and Glen Isla boasts the longest cross-country track in Scotland.

Gliding is available from **Portmoak Airfield** in Scotlandwell, tel: 059 284 243. The surrounding hills are said to create ideal air currents for gliders.

Fishing for salmon and trout on the Tay is one of the region's five-star activities and not necessarily prohibitive. Loch Leven's pink trout are unique and there is good fishing on most other rivers and lochs. Coarse fishing is also available. The Perthshire Tourist Board's *Fishing in Perthshire* is a good investment.

Golf. Among the many good courses at your disposal is the internationally acclaimed golfing mecca at Gleneagles, but their courses are now only open to residents. The Perthshire Tourist Board have a *Golf in Perthshire* leaflet.

Riding is available for visitors throughout the region, both trekking and at riding schools, and the forest and hill tracks offer lovely rides.

Water sports. There are water sports centres on Lochs Rannoch, Tay and Earn, with sailing, windsurfing, waterskiing (on Loch Earn) and canoeing. All these can also be done around the coast and in the sheltered Firth of Tay.

Hang-gliding, for the intrepid, can be found at Cairnwell, where the Glenshee Chairlift Company operates Britain's longest established Hang-Gliding School, with instruction available from mid-May to the end of September, tel 033 83 320.

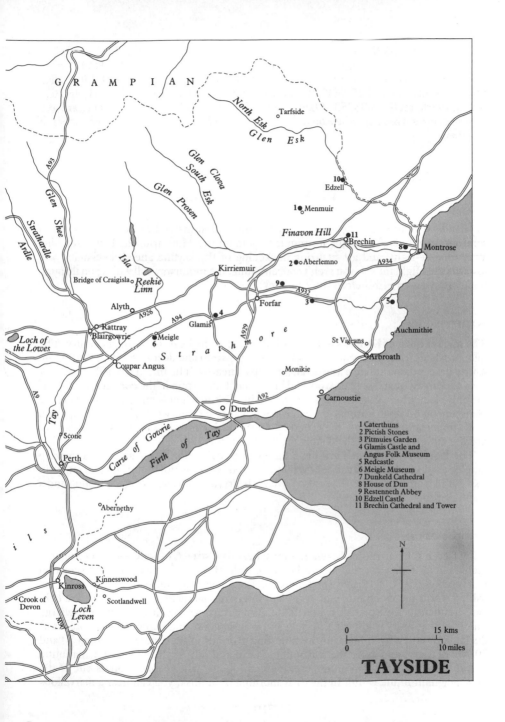

GRAMPIAN

North Esk

Tarfside

Glen Esk

Glen Clova

South Esk

Glen Prosen

A93

Glen Shee

Strathardle Ardle

10● Edzell

1●○ Menmuir

Finavon Hill

●○11 Brechin

Isla

Reekie Linn

Bridge of Craigisla

Kirriemuir

2●○ Aberlemno

8●○ Montrose

A934

Alyth○ A926

○ Rattray
Blairgowrie ○

A94

6● Meigle

4●

Glamis ○

9●○ A932

Forfar ○

3●○

A929

5●

Loch of the Lowes

S t r a t h m o r e

St Vigeans ○

Auchmithie

Coupar Angus ○

Monikie ●

Arbroath ○

A92

Carnoustie ●

Tay

A9

Scone ○

Carse of Gowrie

Firth of Tay

Perth ○

1 Caterthuns
2 Pictish Stones
3 Pitmuies Garden
4 Glamis Castle and
   Angus Folk Museum
5 Redcastle
6 Meigle Museum
7 Dunkeld Cathedral
8 House of Dun
9 Restenneth Abbey
10 Edzell Castle
11 Brechin Cathedral and Tower

Abernethy ○

N

i l s

Kinnesswood

Kinross ○

Scotlandwell ○

Crook of
Devon ○

M90

Loch Leven

0   15 kms
0   10 miles

TAYSIDE

TOURIST INFORMATION
The following Tourist Information Centres are open all the year: 90 High Street, Auchterarder, tel 0764 63450; 26 Wellmeadow, Blairgowrie, tel 0250 2960/3701; High Street, Crieff, tel 0764 2578; 27 Atholl Road, Pitlochry, tel 0796 2215/2751; 45 High Street, Perth, tel 0738 38353; 4 City Square, Dundee, tel 0382 27723. There are also several centres which open seasonally, generally from Easter to the end of September or October.

Kinross-shire

Scotland's second smallest county, Kinross-shire, is dominated by Loch Leven within a semi-circle of hills. You come in from the south on the M90, with the loch stretching away to your right, and a tantalizing thickening of the skyline ahead, beckoning you towards the Highlands. If you aren't concentrating, the motorway will whisk you through it and away past Perth before you can blink.

Kinross

The market town of **Kinross** is a sturdy little place at the heart of farming country. The tolbooth dates from the early 17th century, later repaired and decorated by Robert Adam whose descendants still live at Blairadam House, nearby. The thriving woollen industry goes back many years to when wool and linen were hand-spun in the cottages. Kinross is the only place where cashmere is spun in Britain. The goat hair is imported, but there are plans among Scottish farmers to establish Scottish goat farms which, it is thought, could be an important addition to the economy. In the 17th century, Kinross was famous for making cutlery, until Sheffield stole the market in the 19th century.

The Butterfly Farm at Turfhills, Kinross (open daily, April–Oct: adm) is an amazing jungle paradise where you can see literally hundreds of colourful butterflies and moths in a splendid tropical setting. They also have an aviary, a childrens' farm, a gift shop and a tea house.

Loch Leven

Loch Leven is by no means Scotland's most beautiful stretch of water—in fact from the scenic point of view it could almost be called dull. But it has an irresistible fascination that lures one back. To dispose of its most prosaic aspect first, the loch is renowned in the fishing world for its unique pink trout and international fishing competitions are held here frequently. Less prosaic is its wildlife. As a nature reserve, it gives refuge to a large variety of migratory wildfowl: pink-foot and greylag geese and many different breeds of duck. They come from their northern nesting grounds in the autumn, between 10 and 20,000 of them, and graze the surrounding farmland during the winter. The haunting sound of them, coming in on the evening flight in arrowhead formation, is one of the most poignant in the world. In the early morning or at dusk, you can hear a marvellous low symphony of chattering birds: little runs and rills of sound; murmurs and mutterings and an occasional squawk as a fussy mother calls her family to order.

When the level of the loch dropped by more than four feet in a 19th-century drought, the remains of a crannog emerged—a prehistoric lake-dwelling built on wooden piles driven into the bed of the loch. Unfortunately the elements quickly demolished it: it was just off the pier where the ferry leaves for Castle Island.

The largest island on the loch is **St Serf's Inch,** where Culdee (Servants of God) monks lived in the now ruined priory, in the 8th century.

The true cause of the mysterious charm of Loch Leven, however, is **Loch Leven Castle** on **Castle Island**. Anyone with a drop of romance in their veins will be compelled to make this pilgrimage, crossing the olive green water in the wake of Mary, Queen of Scots. A ferry leaves Kinross Pier when the castle is open.

The solid-looking ruin (open daily, Easter–end Sept: adm), with forbidding tower and curtain wall, against a backdrop of trees, dates from the 14th century. As you step ashore, let your mind go back to when Mary arrived here as a prisoner, over 400 years ago. It was a June day in 1567. Mary was in ragged clothes, her hair shorn, from her days as a fugitive. She was wretched from her defeat at Carberry Hill, already pregnant from her all-too-short marriage with Bothwell; exhausted, sick and utterly despairing. How must she have felt, as she landed at the little jetty into the custody of unsympathetic Lady Douglas? Not long after her arrival she suffered a devastating haemorrhage and mis-carriage of—it is said—twins. She stayed in the castle for 11 months, during which time she so charmed an 18 year-old youth, William Douglas, that he helped her to escape. He rowed her ashore, throwing the keys of the locked castle into the loch (whence they were recovered, 300 years later). Mary's elusive spirit haunts this castle more than almost any other of the places she visited.

On the southern shore of the Loch, **Vane Farm** is the RSPB's Visitor Centre where you can learn a bit more about the birds on the loch. There are panoramic views from **Benarty Hill**, behind.

Kinnesswood is a tiny hamlet tucked into the foot of West Lomond, four miles from Kinross on the eastern side of Loch Leven. In the old days, the villagers used to make vellum from calf skin, and parchment from sheep skin—an art they learnt from monks in the 8th century. Walk up Puddin Wynd to the humble cottage where Michael Bruce, 'the Poet of Loch Leven', was born in 1746. This little memorial museum contains letters and books of the poet who died at the age of 21, could read the Bible at the age of four, and who wrote many paraphrases familiar to Scottish kirkgoers, including 'O God of Bethel'. If you want to stretch your legs, park in the car park by the kirk and walk up Bishop Hill. The views are good.

The well at **Scotlandwell**, about a mile to the southeast, is fed by a spring of very clear, pure water that bubbles up through the sand and is reputed to cure leprosy.

Burleigh Castle (open, you get the key from the farm opposite: free) is a mile north of the loch and dates from 1500. It was the seat of the Balfours of Burleigh who were visited here several times by James VI.

At **Crook of Devon**, six miles west of Kinross on the A977, there is a fish farm where you can feed the fish with pelleted food or try to fish them out of the tanks. They sell delicious fresh and smoked trout. The pub in this tiny hamlet has excellent food.

Abernethy

Strictly speaking, Abernethy is in Perthshire, not Kinross, but it is en route to Perth from the south. Take exit 9 from the motorway, 11 miles north of Kinross, and go four miles east on the A913.

It would be easy to dismiss Abernethy as 'just another village' but that would be a mistake. The Romans certainly sailed up the Tay this far and left the remains of a fort just to the south. More important, however, Abernethy was once a mighty Pictish kingdom. The 74 ft (22 m) high, slender tapering tower, whose lower part dates from the 9th century, is one of only two such on the mainland of Scotland, the other being in Brechin. When Abernethy was the centre of the Celtic Church, this tower provided the clergy with an almost impregnable refuge, as well as an excellent look-out in times of threatened invasion. The upper part dates from the 11th century and you can see a 7th-century stone, set into the base, carved with mysterious Pictish symbols. Also set into the wall is the 'jougs', an iron neck collar by which malefactors were chained for punishment. The design of these elegant towers came over from Ireland with the missionary priests.

It was here in Abernethy, below the Ochil Hills, that Malcolm Canmore was forced to kneel and pay token homage to William the Conqueror in 1071. William had come north, conducting such a brilliant campaign against Scotland that Malcolm's humiliating capitulation seemed the only way to prevent the country being devastated. Perhaps he only intended to acknowledge William as his overlord in connection with his English estates. Whatever his motive, he allowed his son by his first marriage, Duncan, to be taken as a hostage to England, and his submission was to create centuries of unrest in both countries.

WHERE TO STAY AND EAT

If you don't want to push on north, you've a good choice of places to stay and eat around here. In Cleish, at the foot of the hills, there is **Nivingston House Country Hotel** and Restaurant, tel 05775216, a Victorian mansion in 12 acres of landscaped gardens with terrific views. Log fires and candle-lit dinners cooked by a gold-medallist chef make this a nice place to stay, at the top end of the moderate price bracket. The food is delicious, especially if you go for unusual sauces. **Duchally House Hotel**, Auchterarder, tel 0764 63071, in 28 acres of landscaped gardens and woodland is moderately priced, with good food and sporting packages. If it's atmosphere and history you want, try **Lomond Country Inn** in Kinnesswood, tel 0592 84 253. It's cheap and the food isn't bad. Lovely view across Loch Leven from the dining room and fishing permits available. Also cheap, **Bein Inn** in Glenfarg, tel 057 73216, is an old country inn, with public rooms full of character and a reasonable restaurant. **Kirklands Hotel** in Kinross, tel 0577 63313, is another old coaching inn, recently done up, and cheap.

Gourmets should try **Croftbank House Hotel and Restaurant** in Station Road, Kinross, tel 0577 63819. People come a long way to eat the food prepared by the chef-patron, who recently won the Scottish 'Chef of the Year' award. There are four bedrooms only in this Victorian house, so it is more of a restaurant than a hotel. Bed and breakfast is cheap so you can afford to splash out on dinner. Although recently opened,

The Grouse and Claret, at Heatheryford, junction 6, M90, tel 0577 64212, is rapidly gaining a reputation for good game and fish dishes and the dining room overlooks the loch.

Perth

Anyone visiting Perth for the first time should have Walter Scott's *The Fair Maid of Perth* as a companion. The city is 17 miles north of Kinross and as you come down into it from the motorway, you get a fine view of the town, spread out below you round the Tay. This view, 'new' since the building of the motorway, is in fact the old one, extolled by Scott in the first few pages of introduction to *The Fair Maid*. Two wide green parks, North and South Inch, unfold on either side, with a collage of spires reaching for the sky.

Perth was the first place where it was easy to bridge the river. It was a thriving port in the old days and is now an important livestock market at the centre of a productive agricultural area. Its fine setting earned Perth the title 'The Fair City' in the past, and a recent transformation has done much to restore it to that status. In the days before conservation became fashionable, many of its old buildings were replaced by utilitarian monsters that are little short of architectural vandalism, but now, with traffic-free shopping streets and award-winning floral displays, Perth is once again an attractive town. If you poke around you will find traces of the town's past and there are some very fine late-Georgian terraces, especially round the Inches, and nice vistas of the river. When a new Marks and Spencer store was being built in the High Street some time ago, the remains of a medieval market were unearthed, resulting in a valuable stay of execution. A new by-pass has considerably eased traffic congestion in the town centre.

Perth's history goes back a long way. Traces of an old city wall indicate that there was a Roman camp here, although the town doesn't appear in the records until the 12th century. A devastating flood destroyed Old Perth in 1210 and William the Lion granted a Royal Charter to the town that was built in its place the same year. It was the capital of Scotland for a while, until the middle of the 15th century.

Among the more colourful of the historical events that touched the city was the Battle of the Clans, so graphically woven by Scott into the convoluted plot of *The Fair Maid*. This was a contest between the Clans Chattan and Quhele (pronounced Kay), to establish who should take precedence in battle—a hotly disputed honour in those swashbuckling days. 30 men from each side were to fight in a tournament on the North Inch, watched by King Robert III, his wife and court. One of the Clan Chattan lost his nerve at the last moment and fled. The rule was that the two sides must be matched man-for-man, so a blacksmith, small and bandylegged, offered to stand in for the price of half a French crown. All but one of the Quhele Clan were slaughtered. Among the survivors of the Chattans was the blacksmith, who had done more than anyone else to secure victory (he is Scott's Henry, who wins the hand of virginal Catharine).

The highly dubious drama of the Gowrie Conspiracy took place in 1600, in the now demolished Gowrie House in Perth. According to James VI, the Earl of Gowrie and his brother, Alexander Ruthven, lured him to an upstairs room in the house and tried to tie him up. He shouted for his lords through an open window, was rescued, and Gowrie and

Ruthven were killed in the flurry. The whole affair was shrouded in mystery and speculation, with hints of homosexual motives mingled with hints that the king set the thing up in order to get rid of the brothers, whose ruthless political ambition was notorious.

Perth Art Gallery and Museum (open daily except Sundays: free), in George Street, has local history displays and an exhibition showing the growth of the whisky industry which plays an important part in the economy of the area.

St John's Church (open daily) was restored in 1923, with a War Memorial Chapel designed by Robert Lorimer. It dates from the 15th century and is on the site of a church built in the 12th century. Edward III is said to have killed his brother, the Earl of Cornwall, in that earlier church in 1335. It was in St John's that John Knox preached one of his iconoclastic sermons in 1559, urging his followers to purge the churches of idolatry; a sermon that led to the destruction of a great many of the churches and monasteries in the area and helped to fuel the Reformation. This church alone had at least 40 richly decorated altars, dedicated to saints. A few of the sacred treasures rescued from the purgers include the 16th-century German Cellini Cup, given to Mary of Guise by the Pope, 17th-century chalices and a 16th-century baptismal basin.

The Fair Maid's House (open daily except Sun: free, Gallery shut in Jan) is behind Charlotte Street, in North Port, and was the home of virtuous Catharine Glover, The Fair Maid of Perth. One of the oldest buildings in the town, it holds a series of month-long exhibitions of contemporary Scottish crafts and paintings. Perhaps a little over-restored, it is nevertheless an intriguing place. There is a craft shop.

Blackfriars Street, nearby, was the site of long vanished Blackfriars Monastery, where James I was murdered in 1437. Brave Catherine Douglas tried to bar the door to the murderers by thrusting her arm through a staple, in place of a missing iron bar. She survived the mutilation of her arm and went down in history as Catherine 'Barlass'.

Balhousie Castle, a 15th-century castle beyond Rose Terrace on the west side of North Inch, has been restored in imposing Scottish Baronial style. It contains the **Regimental Museum of The Black Watch** (open weekdays, and Sun in summer: free), which was raised in 1739 to help the government pacify the restless, rebellious Highlanders. There is a comprehensive display of the history of this brave, famous regiment, with uniforms, weapons, pictures, documents, photographs and trophies, all recording its many honours and triumphs.

Dewars Whisky Plant dominates the western suburbs of Perth. Free conducted tours during the week enable you to see how Scotland's most popular export finds its way into the bottles.

The Perth Leisure Pool has the reputation of being the best in Scotland, with more than 700,000 visitors a year.

Kinnoull Hill rises 729 ft (218 m) above the town, barely a mile to the east. An easy climb gives you a bird's eye view of the geological 'Highland Line' that divides the Highlands from the Lowlands.

Fairways Heavy Horse Centre is at Kinfauns, about two miles east of Perth on the A85. Here, in an attractive setting between the Tay and Kinnoull Hill, you can see the magnificent great Clydesdales and shire horses and their foals, ride in waggons, or watch video shows of horses and farriers at work.

314

Scone Palace

Scone Palace (open daily, Easter–Oct, or by arrangement, tel 0738 52300: adm) is two miles north of Perth on the A93. Pronounced 'Scoon', the palace is a 19th-century restoration of 16th-century and earlier buildings, with battlements, a toy fort façade and the original gateway. In 1297, Edward I stole the Stone of Scone, and took it to London (see 'Topics', pp. 42).

The abbey and palace that stood here in the 16th century were destroyed by John Knox's followers, after he had denounced 'idolatry' in his sermon from St John's in 1559.

The palace contains French furniture, including Marie Antoinette's writing desk; 16th-century needlework, including bed hangings embroidered by Mary, Queen of Scots; porcelain; 17th and 18th-century ivories; 18th-century clocks. The walls are lined with Lyons silk. There is a coffee shop with home baked food, a gift shop and gardens with a playground and pinetum.

WHERE TO STAY AND EAT

There are dozens of hotels to choose from. **Ballathie House Hotel** at Kinclaven, 10 miles north of Perth, tel 025 083 268, is an overgrown shooting lodge in its own estate overlooking the Tay; open from early March to mid-January. If you have delusions of grandeur this baronial pile will satisfy you. Four-poster or canopied beds, ancestral furniture and paintings, haute cuisine, croquet, tennis, putting, trout and salmon fishing, shooting and all mod cons. (The shooting and fishing must be booked ahead.) It even has its own helipad for tycoons. Prices vary seasonally from cheap to expensive. If it's history you want and you don't mind being in the town, **Salutation Hotel**, 34 South Street, Perth, tel 0738 30066, should please you. Established in 1699, this hotel was Bonnie Prince Charlie's headquarters for a while and you can still hear echoes of his stormy encounters with Lord George Murray, newly recruited and impervious to advice. In those days the Salutation was an inn kept by a vintner called John Hickson, and it was in one of the rooms that the prince yanked his Quartermaster General out of bed at crack of dawn to settle some problem. Cheap and considerably more comfortable today, the hotel has the largest Adam-style window in Scotland in its dining room. Modernization has obliterated all trace of the past, but you can see the Prince's ops room, now a meeting room. Also in Perth, **The Royal George**, in Tay Street, tel 0738 24455, got its Royal appendage from a visit paid by Queen Victoria in 1848. It is a Trust House of the good old-fashioned style, in the moderate to expensive price bracket, right on the river.

If you are an outward-bounder and like a cheap, organized holiday, try **Kinfauns Castle,** a couple of miles east of Perth on the A85, tel 0738 20777, but don't expect to be pampered. Another baronial pile with battlements, in 40 acres of woodland, Kinfauns is owned by the Countrywide Holiday Association. They lay on walking and outdoor holidays, with group-leaders and a host and hostess who arrange your evening entertainment. But if luxury is more to your taste, particularly if you are a golfer, and you can afford it, **The Murrayshall Hotel** at Scone, tel 0738 51171, will suit you. This attractive country-house hotel stands in 300 acres of parkland with an 18-hole, par 73 golf course. There is a multiple-award-winning chef; tennis, croquet and bowls and, if you book ahead, shooting, fishing and riding. What more could you ask?

If you don't want to eat in your hotel—or can't afford to—try one of the plethora of restaurants of all types which have sprung up in Perth recently. **Timothy's**, 24 St John's Street, Perth, tel 0738 26641, for instance. This is cheap, informal and relaxed, half Scottish and half Danish, and you'll eat well. Another is **Patrick's Wine Bar**, in Speygate, Perth, tel 0738 20539, in the old wine cellars, all stone and wood: very atmospheric with nice cheap food—burgers, salads, etc. There are dozens more.

Angus and Perthshire: east of the A9

Angus covers most of that part of Tayside that lies to the east of the A9, north of the Firth of Tay. The coastal plain consists of gently rolling farmland in the Carse of Gowrie, running back up into the Sidlaw Hills where winter can linger into spring, and from whose southern slopes you get magnificent views across the Firth of Tay to northern Fife. The coast is rugged red sandstone with sandy bays. The rest of the land east of the A9 is Perthshire, and here you are in the Highlands with all the wonderful range of scenery they contain. Perth is the hub from which all the following routes lead.

Dundee

> *'Twas in the month of December, and in the year 1883,*
> *That a monster whale came to Dundee,*
> *Resolved for a few days to sport and play,*
> *And devour the small fishes in the silvery Tay . . .*

—from *The Famous Tay Whale*, by William McGonagall

Dundee, fourth-largest town in Scotland and administrative headquarters for Tayside, is 22 miles northeast of Perth on the Firth of Tay.

Although the history of the town goes way back, there is little to show for it architecturally: what was not destroyed by the English and by the Reformation, the Dundonians replaced, in the name of modernization and progress. The architectural vandalism of the 1950s and 1960s, however, is now being substituted by more dignified modern developments.

Traces of Bronze Age settlements have been found locally, and a number of Pictish stones underline the importance of this area in the Dark Ages. 'The Law', with the remains of a Roman hill fort on top, is the highest point of the city, just north of the centre—an excellent place from which to get a bird's-eye view of the area.

Kenneth Macalpine used it as his headquarters in 834, when he was campaigning for the union of Picts and Scots. William the Lion granted it a Royal Charter in 1190. William Wallace went to school in Dundee (the town, in competition with Lanark, that it was here he tangled with authority and was outlawed). It was the first town in Scotland to adopt the reformed religion and it took George Wishart as its paragon, suffering badly as a result, when he was burned at the stake in 1546. Hereford pounded the town for Henry

316

VIII, during the 'Rough Wooing'; Montrose stormed it in 1645 during the Civil War and General Monk occupied it in 1651. In 1689, James VII raised his standard on The Law, after William and Mary had been declared King and Queen of Scotland. Fickle in their loyalties, the Dundonians swung between the Jacobite and the Hanoverian causes, conferring the Freedom of the Burgh on Butcher Cumberland after his victory at Culloden.

In 1889 Queen Victoria granted Dundee a charter confirming all previous charters given since the 12th century, one of which, from Charles I, allowed rights over revenues earned from the river—including salmon fishing. She also made it a city and a county in its own right so that, strictly speaking, it is not in Angus.

As part of the great surge of energy that swept through Scotland during the Scottish Enlightenment period, Dundee earned its popular alliteration as the town of **Jam, Jute and Journalism**. Towards the end of the 18th century, Mr Keiller, a local grocer, bought a bargain crate of oranges, down at the docks. They proved too bitter to sell, so frugal Mrs Keiller boiled them up with sugar and water and made delicious orange jam. This caught on and in 1797 the Keillers opened their famous jam business. There are various explanations for the name marmalade. One is that it comes from *marmelo* (quince); another, accepting that Mrs Keiller was not the first to make orange jam, that when it was made for Mary, Queen of Scots, she announced that it was good for *ma malade*. The original white stone jars in which Keiller's Marmalade was sold are collectors' pieces.

The jute industry, helped by whale oil from a flourishing whaling fleet, blossomed in the early 19th-century, introduced by people from Angus who settled in Calcutta. Dundee became a 'boom-town', with factories and tenements shooting up like mushrooms. This prosperity lasted for 100 years until India learnt to develop her raw jute and materials became scarce. Until as late as the 1950s, up to 7000 people were employed at the jute mills and there are many who remember the flood of people, pouring out of the mill gates at five o'clock. Some of the old mills have been nicely restored: one, opposite the Police Station, a handsome, mid-19th-century building, has been converted into a number of small workshops. A little jute is still worked but industry has diversified in recent years and includes oil-related enterprises. Whaling remained an important industry for many years, with large numbers of boats going out from Dundee, as far as the Arctic.

One of the by-products of the jute boom was the arrival in Dundee of many hundreds of Catholic Highlanders and Irish, dispossessed by the potato famine and land clearance, flocking to find work in the jute mills. As a result, the city today is about one-third Catholic, an unusually high proportion for the east of Scotland.

Journalism, the third of Dundee's Js, is the great Thomson and Legg empire. This autocratic publishing firm, who have no truck with unions or Catholics, are renowned for their wholesome, unsalacious publications, which include: *The Sunday Post, People's Friend, The Dandy* and *The Beano* and dozens more. *The Dundee Courier* is the last reputable daily newspaper to have no news on the front page.

Dundee cake, that rich dark fruit cake with sliced almonds on top, finds its way on to tea tables all over the world.

Dundee University was founded in 1883 and incorporated with that of St Andrews in 1889, but became independent again in 1967.

In spite of its ancient history, Dundee is a modern city catering for modern tastes, bursting with young enterprise rather than inherited culture. Among the city's imaginative innovations is their Public Art. In 1982, artists, sponsored by the Manpower Services Commission and the Scottish Development Agency, went on to the streets with their paints and tools and got to work. The result is a stimulating trail of open-air sculpture, ceramics, murals, mosaics and every sort of graphic and plastic art. Start at the corner of Nethergate and Marketgait, outside the Angus Thistle Hotel, and wander. You'll trip over examples wherever you go. It is a remarkable achievement.

There is enough amusement laid on to please any gregarious holidaymaker. The Dundee Highland Games are in July. Other summer entertainments include Dundee Water Festival which encompasses a number of events both on and off the water, and Jazz and Folk Festivals which spill out of the theatres into the city's pubs and clubs.

Dundee has three city churches under one roof, just west of City Square, forming a large, cruciform building surrounded on three sides by a pedestrian shopping precinct. **The Old Steeple**, or St Mary's Tower, Dundee's oldest surviving building, is 15th-century, the only part that remains of the pre-Reformation church that stood here since the 12th century.

The Howf (burial ground or meeting-place) is northwest of the square. It was once the orchard of the Greyfriars Monastery, founded in the 13th century. Mary, Queen of Scots, gave the land to the city and it became a cemetery. You can still see a number of quaint old gravestones with curious inscriptions.

McManus Galleries (open daily, except Sun: free), a Victorian Gothic building in Albert Square, north of City Square, is the Central Museum and Art Gallery. Exhibitions cover local history, archaeology, and a guide to the development of the town. The art gallery contains work by Flemish, Dutch, French and British artists with some lovely Scottish paintings and frequent modern exhibitions.

The Barrack Street Museum (open daily, except Sun: free) lies further west, along Meadowside. This museum concentrates on natural history and is in the process of developing themes such as the relationship between nature and art. There are displays of exotic wildlife and geology and the skeleton of the Tay Whale.

If you have salt in your veins, HM Frigate *Unicorn* and Captain Scott's Royal Research Ship *Discovery* lie in **Victoria Dock**. *Unicorn* (open daily: adm) is a 46-gun wooden warship, launched at Chatham in 1824. She is the oldest British-built ship still afloat and the fourth-oldest ship afloat in the world, a unique survivor from the transitional period between wooden sailing ships and iron steamships. She was never fully rigged and never engaged in enemy action: for some years she was a prison hulk. You can go aboard and see what life was like for sailors in the early 19th century: it is easy to understand why Bligh of the *Bounty* had such a tricky time, only three decades before this ship was built.

Discovery (open 1 April–9 Oct: adm) is the ship that Captain Scott used for the first of his two expeditions to the Antarctic at the beginning of the century. Built in Dundee and now returned home, it has been enthusiastically equipped to jog sluggish imaginations, with smells and sounds and life-sized models and gives a graphic impression of what it must have been like to be a sailor in those days.

On top of **Balgay Hill** northwest of City Square, **Mills Observatory** (open daily except Sun: free) has telescopes, displays on astronomy and space exploration, a lecture room and a small planetarium. There is an audio-visual programme, and an astronomer in residence. Even without the telescopes, the view from up here is good.

Camperdown Park further northwest, one of Dundee's 28 parks and gardens, was opened by the Queen in 1946, when she was still Princess Elizabeth. It consists of about 400 acres of wooded parkland and garden with some rare trees, a golf course, tennis courts, and a children's zoo. Camperdown House, the mansion in the middle, was designed by William Burn in 1828 and contains a restaurant. **Clatto Country Park** in Dalmahoy Drive off the A972 is a reservoir area with 24 acres of water sheltered by woods; popular for windsurfing and sailing, and you can hire equipment. **Dundee University Botanic Gardens**, (open daily except Sun: adm) off Riverside Drive, has an award-winning visitor centre and landscaped gardens with native and exotic plants, both outside and in tropical and temperate pavilions.

Claypotts Castle (open daily 1 April–30 Sept, adm) jumps out at you from a nightmare housing development just off the busy junction of the A92 and B978. One of the few castles in Scotland to remain unaltered since it was built in the 16th century, Claypotts is a four-storied Z-plan tower house with two round towers, crow-stepped gables, tiny windows, massive stonework and parapet walks. Incongruous as the setting now is, the castle somehow manages to retain a certain dignity, shrugging off the clutter of modern suburbia that sprawls at its feet. It belonged to the Grahams of Claverhouse and was given to the Douglas family after the famous 'Bonnie Dundee', Earl of Claverhouse, was killed at the Battle of Killiecrankie. Keep an eye out for the ghost that haunts its chambers, the vengeful spirit of a favoured maid servant who was unfairly deposed by a jealous rival.

Broughty Ferry, dominated by its castle, is on the coast road four miles to the east. Although the fishing fleet has long vanished, a number of fisher cottages remain, in the narrow wynds and courtyards off Fisher Street, steeped in the seafaring history of the community. It is easy to imagine the old fishermen, mending their nets on the shore by their boats, drawn up above the tide. The village still mourns the tragic loss of its lifeboat *Mona* in 1959, with her crew of eight brave men, stranded and capsized on nearby Budden Sands in one of the ferocious gales that sweep this coast. The beach stretches away to the east in a long, sandy crescent.

> *Ancient Castle of Broughty Ferry*
> *With walls as strong as Londonderry;*
> *Near by the sea-shore,*
> *Where oft is heard and has been heard the cannon's roar*
> *In the present day and days of yore,*
> *Loudlu echoing from shore to shore...*

—from *Broughty Ferry*, by William McGonegall

Broughty Castle (open daily except Fri and Sun all year, and including Sun, July–Sept: free) stands on a rocky promontory, towering over the tiny harbour that dries out at low tide. Built in the 15th century on the site of a Pictish fort, it had a commanding position guarding the entrance to the firth, from which to levy tolls from ships wanting to come up the river. The Gray family who owned the castle also controlled the ferry linking Broughty with Fife. The fourth Lord Gray sided with the English during the 'Rough

319

Wooing' and allowed English troops to occupy this strategic stronghold for three years until the French managed to recapture it for the Scots in 1550. Extensively restored in 1860, it is now a museum devoted mainly to the whaling industry that once flourished along this coast and to the ecology of the Tay.

Anyone interested in archaeology should make a two-mile detour inland from Broughty Ferry, to **Ardestie**, on the A92, and **Carlungie**, a mile to the north. Historic Scotland signs lead to two very well preserved 'souterrains'. These underground earth-houses, once covered by stone roofs, have chambers and passages which were the byres and silos of Pictish farmers in the first and second centuries. It is thought they did not live in these souterrains, but nothing is certain about the Picts and they probably used them as places of refuge. Think of those enigmatic people, busy about their fields and their cattle around these ancient ruins, just as their descendants are today.

At **Monikie,** five miles north of Broughty Ferry on the archaeological detour, there is a country park round the reservoir, with attractive walks, boating and picnic sites. You get splendid views from up here, down over fertile farmland to the distant coast where the constantly shifting sandbanks have claimed many ships over the centuries. The trees on the ridge above are sculpted into curious wedge shapes by the strong prevailing wind.

WHERE TO STAY AND EAT
You are spoilt for choice: on the whole, the names and prices of the hotels in and around Dundee reflect their quality.

The Angus Thistle Hotel, 101 Marketgait, Dundee, tel 0382 26874, for instance, is modern, soul-less and antiseptic, but it is comfortable and convenient and the food won't choke you. If you want to indulge yourself, you can have an expensive 'executive' suite with four-poster bed and whirlpool bath. But you can also get a moderately priced bed and breakfast. **The Stakis Earl Grey Hotel** on the waterfront in Earl Grey Place, tel 0382 29271, is, again, just what you would expect, with every possible convenience including a Leisure Club with swimming pool, sauna and whirlpool. It's expensive, but they do packages. A very different atmosphere awaits you at **The Old Mansion House Hotel** at Auchterhouse, seven miles north of Dundee, tel 082 626 366/7. This is a 16th-century baronial home in 10 acres of lovely gardens and woodland. There is an outdoor heated swimming pool, squash court, croquet and tennis. It's expensive and the food is worth travelling for.

If you want to eat out, **Mains Castle** at Caird Park, Dundee, tel 0382 456797, gives 'Jacobite Nights' with a four-course banquet in 15th-century trappings, with jolly Scottish entertainment all evening and dancing. (Hermits, stick to your cells.) **Raffles,** 18 Perth Road, tel 0382 26344, is a popular restaurant near the university with reasonable food. Or what about **Fat Sam's Night Club, Discotheque Diner** at 31 South Ward Road, Dundee, tel 0382 26836 where they run all sorts of special events such as Fat Sam's Cocktail Night with half-price drinks all night? Take your ear-plugs.

Carnoustie

Back on the coast road, Carnoustie, 10 miles east of Dundee, is a holiday resort and golf centre, with a championship course. Right on the sea, the town is a popular place in summer with its own musical society, plenty of holiday activities and a conference centre which seats 500 people. Campers will find an attractive caravan site among trees in the grounds of Carnoustie House.

Arbroath

Arbroath is 17 miles northeast of Dundee. The massive ruin of the red sandstone abbey rises up from the heart of the town, surrounded by lawns and flower-beds, the hub of a thriving holiday resort and fishing centre. The Declaration of Independence was signed in the abbey in 1320 after Robert Bruce's victory at Bannockburn, establishing Scotland's independence from England.

Perhaps Arbroath is best known now as the home of the 'smokie'—haddock, smoked over wood-chip fires in the backyards of the fishertown between the harbour and the abbey. Many of the cottages display signs, indicating that they sell the freshly smoked fish, and anyone who has not tried an Arbroath smokie should do so. One of the nicest ways to eat them is cold, with brown bread and butter, and plenty of lemon juice and black pepper.

Arbroath Highland Games are in July and there is also a Donkey Derby that month. The Flower Show is a colourful event in August and there is a Festival of Highland Dancing in September.

Arbroath Abbey (open daily: adm) was founded by William the Lion in 1178 and dedicated to Thomas à Becket who had recently been murdered in Canterbury Cathedral. You can see William's tomb in the sacristy. The abbey managed to survive the Reformation until 1606, when it was made a temporal lordship. Its final decay was due to neglect rather than vandalism or deliberate destruction. Parts of the ruin date from the 13th century, including the gable of the south transept and the west façade with its tower and entrance. They used to put lamps in the round window high above the south transept, as a landmark for ships at sea. The abbot's house is now the **Museum** with displays illustrating the domestic life of the religious community and a collection of Scottish medieval art.

Signal Tower (open daily except Sundays: free) is a museum with exhibitions of local interest. It was originally built in 1813 as the signalling station for the Bell Rock Lighthouse and its displays include fishing, the flax industry, archaeology and natural history. There is an **Art Gallery** in the library, which has works by Breughel as well as a good variety of Scottish paintings.

Whiting Ness, north of the wide promenade, is worth a visit on a fine day. From here you can walk for miles along the cliff top, with the sea pounding restlessly at the redstone rocks below, honeycombed with caves and deep inlets. Wild flowers cling to the steep slopes: thrift, vetch and sea grasses. The lonely cry of curlews with long, curved beaks and the shrill 'kubik-kubik' of black and white oystercatchers with vivid orange beaks can be heard over the booming sea. From the narrow path you get marvellous views over the water, dotted with trawlers, tankers, coasters and small boats. If the visibility is good you should be able to see the **Bell Rock Lighthouse**, 12 miles out to the east and familiar to anyone who learnt Southey's 'Ballad of the Inchcape Rock' at school. The Abbot of Arbroath fixed a warning bell on the hazardous rock to warn off mariners. Sir Ralph the Rover, a notorious pirate with a grudge against the abbot, cut the bell adrift. Later, sailing home in a fog, the pirate was wrecked on the rock.

321

The cliff path takes you to **Auchmithie**, three miles to the north. It is referred to as Musselcraig, in Walter Scott's *The Antiquary* and is an ancient, picturesque village believed to have been the fishing centre in the old days. In the 18th century fishermen carried on a flourishing lobster trade with London and it was here that the smokie industry was born. It is built on a rocky ridge above a tiny harbour with a flat chequer-board of farmland stretching away inland. The caves along this coast were much used by smugglers in the 18th century.

St Vigeans

As you come out of Arbroath going north on the A92, take the road signposted to St Vigeans, on the left. It is less than a mile and you have to park at the railway bridge and cross the Brothock Burn by footbridge to discover this little gem of a hamlet, nestling out of sight below modern housing developments. A small red sandstone church is perched on top of a steep mound, 40 ft high, like an upturned basin, neatly kept and studded with gravestones. Extensive restoration conceals the 12th-century origins of the kirk, but you can find traces inside.

A row of pretty red sandstone cottages with stone-slabbed roofs forms a semi-circle at the foot of the mound and in one of these is the fascinating **St Vigeans Museum** (open daily: free). The museum contains a well-displayed and comprehensively explained collection of Pictish and Celtic stones. The **Drosten Stone** has an inscription in the Pictish language, suggesting that the Picts were more literate than is often supposed. Even if archaeology bores you stiff, you will find that you become more and more intrigued as you examine the intricate carvings on these ancient stones, and read the descriptions: they quickly become more than 'just a few more old stones'.

Redcastle (always accessible) is seven miles up the coast. A 15th-century ruin jutting out on a cliff high above the sea, it dominates the sandy crescent of Lunan Bay below. To reach it you have to climb up a short, steepish path through trees and whins. The castle was built on the site of an old fort, to protect the coast from Danish pirates, and William the Lion lived here while he was building Arbroath Abbey. It witnessed several battles and was partly demolished during one that sprang from a feud between its occupant and her divorced husband.

Montrose

Beautiful town of Montrose, I will now commence my lay,
And I will write in praise of thee without dismay,
And in spite of all your foes,
I will venture to call thee Bonnie Montrose...

—from *Montrose*, by William McGonagall

Montrose is 14 miles north of Arbroath, not far from the Grampian border and is almost on an island. It has sea to the east, the River South Esk to the south, and a wide tidal basin to the west. There is an airy, spacious feeling about the town, the middle section of its High Street being as wide as a market square. You can still see a few of the houses that were built gable-end on to the street, leading through to narrow closes and secret courtyards. Records tell of a Danish invasion of Montrose in 980.

The castle that once guarded the town was taken over by Edward I in 1296 and destroyed by William Wallace a year later. It was from here that Sir James Douglas embarked, carrying the heart of Robert the Bruce, on its abortive pilgrimage to the Holy Land. James Graham, the brave, tragic Marquis of Montrose, was born in Old Montrose on the south side of the tidal basin in 1612. In 1715, the first of the Jacobite Rebellions ended ignominiously in Montrose when the Old Pretender set sail back to France from here.

A tenth of the world's population of pink-footed geese migrate to Montrose's tidal basin every November, from their Arctic breeding grounds. This great wildfowl sanctuary is a marvellous place in winter when you can hear the ceaseless grumble and chatter of the birds as they feed on the mud flats, and the sound of their cries haunting the air as they circle in from the sky. It is remarkable to find such a wild haven so close to the bustling town with its docks and shipping, its sturdy buildings and oil-related prosperity.

A profitable slave trade flourished briefly in Montrose, and smuggling was a thriving activity in the 18th century. Because of its out-of-the-way situation, and a shortage of customs officers, the strongly Jacobite population had no conscience about defrauding a Hanoverian government of its income from excise duty. The words *Mare Ditat* (the sea enriches) are aptly inscribed on the Montrose coat of arms. The undulating countryside has several good golf courses. In July the town holds its Rose Queen Ceremony and in August, a flower show and a Highland Games.

The House of Dun, three miles west of Montrose (open daily in summer: adm) is a recently opened modest-sized Palladian house overlooking Montrose Basin. Owned by the National Trust for Scotland, it was designed by William Adam in 1730 for David Erskine, Lord Dun. One of his descendants married Augusta, the natural daughter of William IV and Mrs Jordan, who created the lovely garden. It has magnificent flamboyant plasterwork in the saloon and much of the original furniture, found hidden away when the house was resurrected. Outside, there are woodland walks and exhibitions in the courtyard including bothies containing a keeper's room and a gardener's potting shed and weaving displays.

WHERE TO STAY AND EAT
Although there are a number of places to choose from, there is no hotel worthy of particular mention. The moderately priced **Park Hotel** in John Street, Montrose, tel 0674 73415, is probably your best bet.

Brechin

Returning to Perth on the inland route, Brechin is an attractive town nine miles west of Montrose, sprawled up a steep bank above the South Esk in fertile Strathmore.

You can get a good picture of the local history in a small museum in the library.

The Cathedral and Tower (always open: free) are the focal points of this ancient town. These red sandstone buildings are perched above the town's twisting wynds, little courtyards and houses built gable-end on to the road. The tapering tower, restored in 1960, is one of only two such towers in mainland Scotland, the other being in Abernethy. (It is a curious coincidence that Malcolm Canmore was forced to acknowledge the sovereignty of William the Conqueror at Abernethy, in 1072, and the weak John Balliol was forced to renounce his crown to Edward I in 1296, near Brechin, as if the two round towers have survived as monuments to two unhappy events.) Dating from 990, the tower's door is 6 ft (18 m) above the ground, giving the inhabitants greater security. The feet of the crucified Christ, carved on the lintel, are uncrossed, indicating an Irish influence in the design. (There are 76 of these towers in Ireland today.)

Now a parish church, the cathedral dates from the 13th century and was restored in 1900. The Pictish stones inside have interesting carvings on them and you can also see a 16th-century font and 17th century pewter and silver.

Maison Dieu, off Market Street, is a single wall with a pointed, arched door, three narrow windows and a piscina—all that remains of an almshouse, hospice and chapel that were founded in 1256.

Edzell

Six miles north of Brechin on the B966, Edzell, in the attractive valley of the North Esk, is one of the places visited by Queen Victoria, with a memorial arch to show for it.

Edzell Castle (open daily: adm). The 16th-century ruin forms a splendid red backdrop to the Pleasance, a walled garden designed by David Lindsay, Lord Edzell, in 1604. Even if your taste runs to gardens that overflow and burgeon, all soft lines and merging shapes, you cannot but be impressed by this immaculate formal garden. It is modelled on the gardens at Nuremburg and the flower-filled recesses in the walls are intricate heraldic emblems, concealing gun loops. A beautifully kept box hedge, bordering rose beds, has been clipped to spell out the somewhat phlegmatic Lindsay family motto: *dum spiro spero* (while I breathe I hope). The foundations of a bath house were excavated in the corner of the garden in 1855, revealing a bath and a dressing and reclining room with a fireplace.

Mary, Queen of Scots, held a council in the castle in 1562 and it was garrisoned by Cromwell's troops in 1651. A grisly story is told of a curse put on the Earl's family at Edzell by a gypsy after they had caused the hanging of her two dumb sons, for poaching. Lady Crawford died the same day and her husband was torn apart by wolves a year later.

The Caterthuns are six miles southwest of Edzell, at **Menmuir**. These are two Iron Age hill forts on a ridge, the higher one having spilled its masonry down the hill to mix with the lower. The original enclosing wall must have been as much as 40 ft (12 m) thick. If you follow the wooded valley of West Water from here up into the hills towards Loch Lee, you are following in the footsteps of Macbeth, as he fled from his defeat at Dunsinane.

Before you go on towards Forfar, you should explore **Glen Esk** running north into the Grampians, carved by the North Esk and its tributaries. **Glenesk Folk Museum** (open Easter weekend, and daily, June–Sept: adm) is 10 miles northwest of Edzell at Tarfside. Once a shooting lodge, it contains a collection of exhibits that give you a fascinating picture of what life was like in this area from about 1800 onwards.

Finavon Castle (always open: free) is six miles southwest of Brechin on the A94. This jagged ruin is overgrown by nettles and scrub. It doesn't look much of a place now, until you look up at the 86 ft (26 m) tower and think of the day when the notorious Earl Beardie Crawford hanged his minstrel from a hook somewhere at the top. This he did because the wretched minstrel had foretold Earl Beardie's defeat at the Battle of Brechin in 1452. The history of the Lindsay family is full of bloodcurdling stories, and it is for these that the ruin is memorable, rather than for its appearance.

Finavon Hill

Take the little back road that climbs and twists two miles southeast from Finavon, up over the hills through rugged scenery of dry stone walls and moorland, where black-faced sheep graze the turf between patches of bracken and gorse. As you come down the far side of the ridge, Finavon Hill is on your left. It is a short climb to one of the finest vitrified Iron Age hill forts in the land, in a shallow depression at the top. Its shape and turf-covered ramparts are easily seen, and there is a central spring, or well. Excavations in the 1930s revealed evidence of metal working, pot making, and weaving on this lofty summit with its glorious views up Strathmore to the Mearns and west to Blairgowrie. It is strange to think of those tough Picts busy up here, striving to exist on the hill top, keen-eyed and ever alert for danger.

Aberlemno

If you are interested in the early settlers, go on down the back road from Finavon to the B9134 and turn left (north) a few hundred yards to **Aberlemno**. This tiny hamlet has four remarkable Pictish stones. Three stand beside the road. The finest, however, is in the kirkyard. The carvings on this stone, 7 ft (2 m) high, are amazingly clear: a Celtic cross on one side, flanked by intertwined creatures, and a stirring battle scene on the other, all with intricate detail. This stone is believed to mark the grave of a Pictish King, Feradach. The little kirk is simple and charming. Inside you will find an 18th-century Bible which has dates printed at the top of each page, the date of Genesis being set at 4004 BC.

Pitmuies Garden, off the A932 to Forfar (open all year: adm) is an outstanding garden, round an 18th-century house, with masses of spring bulbs, roses, herbaceous borders and many shrubs. There is an attractive waterside walk and fine old trees. Look out for Guthrie Castle (private), close by on the main road. The entrance was built about 150 years ago to disguise a bridge on the old railway.

Restenneth Priory

Restenneth Priory (always open: free) is five miles southwest of Aberlemno, just before you get to Forfar on the B9134. It stands surrounded by gently sloping meadows and scattered trees, rising from a bowl of marshy ground. It was once on a peninsula jutting into a loch which was drained in the 18th century.

In AD 710, Nechan, High King of the Picts, was baptized here by St Boniface. Nechan used Northumbrian masons to build a church in Romanesque style, possibly to celebrate his victory over the King of Northumbria at the Battle of Nechtansmere. In the 13th century, Augustinian monks built a priory on the same site, incorporating the original tower. It is a tranquil place, the mellow old stones rising from green sward. You can almost hear the voices of those far off monks, chanting plainsong, as you stand in the ruined choir. An infant son of Robert Bruce is believed to have been buried here.

Forfar

Just southwest of Restenneth, the busy town of Forfar has little left to see of its history. Once a thriving jute and linen milling centre it now produces man-made textiles, as well as tartans and tweeds. The Town and County Hall is early 19th century, designed by William Playfair, with a splendid Council Chamber in which you can see paintings by Raeburn, Romney, Hoppner and Opie. The town centre is attractive, with cobbled streets and warm sandstone buildings swirling round an island on which the Town Hall stands. Just round the corner in West High Street is the Meffan Institute (open daily except Sun: free) which houses, as well as the library, a small museum of local interest, in which you can see the dreadful **Forfar Bridle**. This is a metal collar, hinged to clip round the neck, with a prong in front to gag the unfortunate women who wore it while being burned at the stake as witches in the 17th century. Forfar Loch, west of the town, is a so-called pleasure park, with picnic areas around an uninspiring small stretch of water.

From Forfar, you have a choice of two main routes back to Perth.

Glamis

The southern route, on the A94, takes you first to Glamis (pronounced *Glarms*), about six miles southwest. This tiny hamlet in a wooded hollow lies just off the main road, where you could easily pass a whole summer's day and not be bored.

Glamis Castle (open every afternoon except Sat, 1 May–1 Oct or by appointment, tel 030784 242: adm) is approached down a wide tree-lined avenue and is so familiar from photographs that the reality is almost an anti-climax. From the top of the avenue it is a splendid spectacle: the pink-grey castle stands out against the distant hills, all angles, towers, wings, turrets and heraldic embellishments. It is grand rather than beautiful.

Queen Elizabeth, the Queen Mother, spent much of her childhood at Glamis and her daughter, Princess Margaret, was born here. Don't rush a visit to this history-steeped castle; take it slowly and absorb the atmosphere under the tourist-wooing gloss. It's well worth getting the excellent guide book.

The land was granted to the Lyon family, Earls of Strathmore, by King Robert II in 1372, and it was their descendants who became Earls of Glamis, Kinghorne and Strathmore. Glamis has the reputation for being the most haunted castle in Scotland and many are the spine-chilling tales that have been born from its stones. No one dares to enter the sealed crypt where huge red-bearded Beardie Crawford played cards with the Devil on the Sabbath; no one can account for the window that looks out from a chamber that does not exist on an upper floor.

The present castle dates mostly from the 17th century, with bits of the older buildings incorporated, including King Malcolm's room, where Malcolm II is said to have died. The oldest part is Duncan's hall, traditionally the setting for Shakespeare's Macbeth.

There are formal 19th-century Italian gardens and extensive parkland. A licensed restaurant sells light lunches and teas and there is a superior gift shop, a gallery shop selling paintings by Scottish artists, a garden shop and a playground.

The Angus Folk Museum (open Easter weekend and daily, 1 May–30 Sept: adm) is in Kirkwynd in the little village beyond the castle, past the Strathmore Arms and a thatched cottage that is a rare sight among the pantiles and slates in this area. In the care of the National Trust for Scotland, the museum is in a terrace of picturesque early 19th-century cottages, meticulously restored in 1957, with stone-slabbed roofs and flagged floors. There are over 1000 things to see, including a kitchen from 1807 with all the original fittings and furnishings, and a collection of agricultural tools and equipment. The museum gives a fascinating picture of how country people lived, up to 200 years ago. There is even a Victorian manse parlour.

The Glamis Stone is in the garden of today's manse, opposite the museum, visible from the road. This 9 ft (3 m) high stone has intricate Pictish carvings. It is also called King Malcolm's Stone, from the belief that Malcolm II was buried here in 1034, having died in the castle. In fact, the stone is of an earlier date, possibly 9th century.

If ancient stones are what you enjoy, you will find plenty more nearby including **St Orland's**, or the **Crossans Stone**, standing 7 ft (2 m) tall in a field by the railway two miles to the north. This slender, repaired stone has carvings showing men in a boat.

Meigle

Meigle, nearly seven miles southwest of Glamis, is the legendary burial place for poor faithless Guinevere. It also has the most remarkable collection of early Christian Pictish stones in Scotland. **Meigle Museum** (open daily except Sun: adm) in the old school contains about 30 stones, from the 6th to the 10th centuries, almost all found in or near the old churchyard. The amazing carvings disprove any idea that the Picts were half-naked savages loping around like ape men. Instead, they show elaborate clothing, weapons and equipment and an unquestionable civilized culture. The large stone in the centre is thought to be Queen Guinevere's grave stone and portrays *Daniel in the Lion's Den*, possibly symbolizing Guinevere being torn apart by wild beasts. Beautifully displayed, with a descriptive leaflet, these stones stir the imagination.

Coupar Angus

Coupar Angus, about five miles southwest of Meigle, is in the Tay valley. It makes a good centre from which to tour this area, lying, as it does, on the edge of lovely Highland scenery. It is a pleasant little market town, very typical of the area and so called to distinguish it from Cupar Fife.

Only the gatehouse remains of a once flourishing Cistercian abbey, beside the Dundee Road. It was built about 1164 by Malcolm IV and destroyed in 1559. The parish church stands on the site of the old monks' chapel and you can still see the remains of the original piers from the nave. From Coupar Angus it is about 12 miles back to Perth, passing Perth Aerodrome.

Kirriemuir

If you take the northern route back to Perth from Forfar on the A926, Kirriemuir is six miles to the west, an attractive place on a hillside with a straggle of narrow streets lined by picturesque houses. This jute manufacturing town is where J. M. Barrie was born. He renamed it 'Thrums' in the series of novels he wrote based on small town life in Scotland. The house where Barrie was born, 9 Brechin Road, is now maintained by the National Trust for Scotland as a museum called **Barrie's Birthplace** (open Easter weekend and daily, 1 May–30 Sept: adm). It contains a nostalgic collection of manuscripts, letters, personal possessions and mementoes of the writer who belonged to that group known as 'The Kailyard School' at the end of the 19th century. These Kailyard writers exploited a sentimental, romantic image of small town life in Scotland that brought them a certain amount of contempt from their critics. Their naivety was blown by George Douglas, in *The House with Green Shutters* which, according to Priestley, 'let the east wind into this cosy chamber of fiction'. However much people may despise whimsicality, no one can deny the talent of a man who, among the many things he wrote, created Peter Pan, Mary Rose, Dear Brutus and the Admirable Crichton. James Barrie was made a Freeman of Kirriemuir and was buried in the churchyard in 1937.

A **Camera Obscura** in the Barrie Pavilion, above the town, gives a panoramic view of Strathmore by an ingenious method of reflection.

You should make time to go north from Kirriemuir to explore some of the lovely glens that stretch back into the Grampians—Glen Clova, Glen Prosen, Glen Isla; each with a mass of tributary glens like the veins of a feather, with tumbling rivers and tranquil lochs, hidden away among the hills.

Reekie Linn

It is worth making a detour from Kirriemuir to see Reekie Linn. It is about nine miles due west and if you've got a good map, the back roads are very attractive. Park at the Bridge of Craigisla and take the footpath through the wood. Reekie Linn is a dramatic waterfall haunted by water sprites and kelpies. The River Isla, constricted by narrow rock cliffs, pours down into a deep gorge in a single cascade, the spray rising like smoke, stirring the dark waters of the river into tumult. The path takes you to a spur jutting out level with the top of the falls. If you suffer from vertigo you should go along to the right and see them from further off.

Barry Hill is beside the road about three miles south of the falls, just short of Alyth. It is a short, steep climb through whins and bracken, over turf honeycombed by rabbits. On top are the ruins of a large Pictish fort in a shallow depression. The oblong shape is very clear with round turrets and ramparts. Romance clings to these stones. If you believe the Scottish versions of the Arthurian legends, Queen Guinevere was imprisoned in this fort by King Arthur, because of her love affair with a Pictish prince. If this was true, the captive queen had some glorious views for miles around to comfort her.

Alyth, below the hill, is a pleasant little milling town bisected by the Alyth Burn.

Blairgowrie

Blairgowrie, five miles southwest of Alyth, beside fast-flowing Ericht Water, is a popular tourist centre all the year round, much favoured by golfers. In summer there are the Highlands to explore and in winter you can ski at Glenshee. The extremely fertile soil produces abundant raspberry crops. This is magic walking country: fast-flowing rivers slice through steep mountain glens, with sudden glimpses of snow-capped peaks, massing on the horizon.

While you are in this area, visit Mrs MacDonald in Rattray. You can't miss the shop, which flies a Swiss flag outside. Switzerland means cheese and chocolate, and Mrs MacDonald can sell you the very best of both.

Glenshee

Glenshee runs north from Blairgowrie into the Grampian region and is one of Scotland's main skiing centres, its challenging pistes are often icy and demanding. Weather conditions can be extreme, roads sometimes becoming impassable in snow (see 'Sport', p. 15). For skiing information ring the Glenshee Information Officer, Blairgowrie, tel 0250 5509.

From spring to autumn, the A93 to Braemar—Britain's highest main road—is a spectacular route and in the summer you can take the chairlift up to the top of Cairnwell mountain for panoramic views and invigorating walks. **Strathardle** forks off west of Glen Shee from the **Bridge of Cally** where the River Ardle and Black Water converge: another good launching pad for climbers and walkers.

From Blairgowrie, it is about 16 miles back to Perth on the A93.

Birnam

> Be lion-mettled, proud, and take no care
> Who chafes, who frets, or where conspirers are:
> Macbeth shall never vanquish'd be, until
> Great Birnam wood to high Dunsinane hill
> Shall come against him.
>
> —witches' prophecy

Birnam, about 14 miles north of Perth, by-passed by the A9 is a village familiar to all students of Shakespeare. From Birnam Hill you can see Dunsinnan, or Dunsinane, 12 miles to the southeast—opinions and tastes dictate the spelling. Macbeth, in his castle on 'Dunsinane Hill', confidently believed the witches' prophecy that he was immortal until 'Birnam Forest come to Dunsinane'. Meanwhile, Malcolm was busy instructing his soldiers to camouflage themselves with branches from the trees in Birnam Wood and march on Dunsinane. There are remains of a fort on Dunsinnan Hill, thought to be Macbeth's. Some of the trees in Birnam Wood are thought to date from the original forest.

Dunkeld

15 miles north of Perth, just off the A9 route, Dunkeld is a charming old cathedral town on the banks of the Tay, sheltered by wooded hills and much favoured by fishermen. Its

history goes back to early times when it was a refuge for Pictish kings. Being close to the ancient capital of Scone, Dunkeld became a stronghold of Columban monks who founded an abbey here in 729, having been driven from Iona by Norsemen. They enshrined holy relics of St Columba in their abbey. The Saint himself is believed to have come to Dunkeld in the 6th century, and to have founded some sort of religious establishment with the help of St Mungo. There is a St Colms Well nearby.

Dunkeld suffered badly during the bitter Covenanting Wars and it was here that the Cameronians, extreme Covenanters, held the town against a troop of Highlanders in 1689. Triumphant after Killiecrankie, the Highlanders stormed the town, whereupon the Cameronians set fire to most of its buildings, driving the Highlanders out and securing eventual supremacy for William and Mary.

Dunkeld Cathedral (open daily: free) is a substantial ruin in a beautiful setting beside the River Tay. The choir has been restored and is the parish church. The nave and great northwest tower date from the 15th century and the original medieval cathedral, which took two centuries to build, was only entire for about 60 years before the Reformers reduced it to a roofless ruin. Ironically, it contains the rather splendid tomb and effigy of the Wolf of Badenoch, who was a keen destroyer of churches, including Elgin Cathedral.

The Little Houses, lining Cathedral Street, were built after the destruction of the town in 1689, and were saved from demolition by the National Trust for Scotland in 1950. Well restored and privately occupied, they form a delightful approach to the cathedral and give the old part of the town a unique character.

Loch of the Lowes

A couple of miles northeast of Dunkeld, Loch of the Lowes is a nature reserve, where you can watch ospreys from a hide. These large brown and white sea-eagles, cousins to the falcon, are common in America, where they nest on every navigation mark in the estuaries. Here, they are a rare, protected species though their numbers are increasing slightly now that their nesting sites are so fiercely protected.

Pitlochry

Pitlochry, 13 miles north of Dunkeld on the A9, is in the middle of Scotland, cradled by hills, with Ben Vrackie (2759 ft) looming to the north. With above-average hours of sunshine and below-average rainfall, this has been a popular holiday town since Queen Victoria, staying at Blair Atholl, declared it to be one of the finest resorts in Europe. This royal stamp of approval resulted in many fine houses and mansions being built in the area, with spas that are now hotels. Today, it is hard to believe it was once a remote hamlet. There were no roads north of Dunkeld until General Wade built his network of military roads, after the Jacobite uprisings, linking up the trouble-spots in the Highlands. Now, in spite of its popularity, it manages to retain a leisurely, strolling atmosphere, a perfect centre from which to explore the Highlands. The rivers Tummel and Garry converge from their beautiful valleys into Loch Faskally, two miles to the north, and hurry through the town to join the Tay at Ballinluig to the south. The main street is cheerful with its bright façades, hotels and shops, distilleries and hydroelectric development. Pitlochry runs a summer school in July with a host of activities ranging from pottery to clay pigeon shooting. There is also a Gala Day in July.

The Pitlochry Festival Theatre was founded in 1951. Its lively summer programme includes drama, concerts and foyer events and you can also see exhibitions of Scottish art.

The Hydroelectric Dam and Fish Ladder which is open all year round has an observation chamber where you can see its ingenious method of ensuring that the salmon cycle is not broken. Thousands of salmon are 'lifted' annually and you can watch them through glass walls. If you look carefully you can often see the sealice clinging to the fish, showing that they have come fresh from the sea. There is also a **Visitor Centre and Exhibition**, with an excellent description of all the activities throughout the country and in the Loch Tummel group in particular. Few purists can deny that the hydroelectric schemes often enhance rather than spoil the Highland scenery.

Blair Atholl Distillery on the southern edge of Pitlochry has a beautifully presented Visitor Centre where you can learn all you want to know about whisky (open daily, Easter–Oct, and daily except Sun for the rest of the year, free). Conducted tours, audio-visual shows and a free dram at the end make this a splendid outing and there is a coffee shop and bar where you can get snacks, as well as a shop selling—whisky.

Edradour Distillery (open daily, Easter–31 Oct: free) is the smallest in Scotland, hidden in the hills, less than three miles east of Pitlochry. This little gem was founded in 1825 by a group of local farmers, a tiny complex of white-washed buildings under neat grey slate roofs, tucked into a hollow beside the rushing Edradour Burn. Here, after a conducted tour of the distillery, virtually unchanged since Victorian times, you get your free dram in a cosy barn before a peat and log fire.

Walking in this area is endlessly rewarding; every path you choose reveals fresh beauty and unexpected views. There are waterfalls and gorges, festooned with lush ferns; woods and hills; rivers running fast over shallow rocky beds.

Pass of Killiecrankie

> *Six thousand veterans practised in war's game,*
> *Tried men, at Killicrandy were arrayed*
> *Against an equal host that wore the plaid,*
> *Shepherds and herdsmen. Like a whirlwind came*
> *The Highlanders, the slaughter spread like flame...*

> —from a sonnet by William Wordsworth

The road north from Pitlochry climbs along the upper slope of the Pass of Killiecrankie, a recently opened section of road that cost a great deal of money and took considerable skill to engineer. It clings precariously to the densely wooded gorge where, far below, the River Garry cuts its way through to join up with the Tummel. At the far end of the pass about three miles from Pitlochry, there is a National Trust for Scotland **Visitor Centre** (open daily from 1 May to 31 Oct: free) where you can see a pictorial description of the history of the Battle of Killiecrankie. Graham of Claverhouse, 'Bonnie Dundee' and his brave Jacobite Highlanders charged the British army under General Mackay in 1689, in

331

an attempt to depose William of Orange and restore James VII/II to the throne. The British were almost annihilated by the wild Highlanders, but Claverhouse was mortally wounded and his death, leaving his army without a leader, ensured the subsequent victory of the government troops three weeks later at Dunkeld.

You can walk down to the river from the visitor centre, past the terrifying **Soldier's Leap**, an 18 ft (54 m) jump across the gorge, said to have been made by one of Mackay's soldiers, escaping from the Highlanders. Queen Victoria walked along this path and noted its great beauty in her diary in 1844.

Blair Atholl

Three miles north of Killiecrankie, the new road by-passes the village of Blair Atholl and gives you a very good view of **Blair Castle** from across the river. This white, turreted baronial castle (open daily, Easter–Mid-Oct: adm) is the home of the Duke of Atholl, dating from 1269. It has seen many royal visitors: Mary, Queen of Scots, stayed here; Prince Charlie accepted hospitality here on his march south in 1745; Cumberland garrisoned his troops here the following year, during which time the Duke of Atholl's brother, Lord George Murray, inflicted severe damage on the castle in his attempts to win it back; Claverhouse stayed here before the Battle of Killiecrankie and it was here that his body lay after the battle.

Queen Victoria visited the castle in 1844 and granted the Duke of Atholl the privilege of being the only British subject allowed to retain a private army, the Atholl Highlanders.

The interior gives you a good idea of what castle life was like in the old days. The rooms are numbered and there is a guide book. Look out for the Tapestry Room, hung with rich tapestries and containing a sumptuous four-poster bed topped by two vases of ostrich feathers. The Old Scots Room is furnished in the style of a simple cottage living room, complete with box bed, cradle, and spinning wheel. There is a vast collection of valuable and interesting things to see, ranging from arms and armour, to Jacobite relics, china, toys, furniture, lace and marvellous paintings (including portraits by Lely, Ramsay and Raeburn). There is even a natural history museum. There is a licensed self-service restaurant and if you want to impress your friends, there is a separate dining room for private parties of up to 50 people. If you really want to splash out, you can also use the ballroom for up to 200 people, a truly noble setting for a knees-up, its panelled walls hung with a forest of antlers under a timber-ribbed roof with plenty of ancestral portraits to add distinction. In the grounds there is a large caravan park.

Beyond Blair Atholl is good walking and climbing country, over moor and scree, with lovely views. A nice walk is that to **The Bruar Falls**, well-signposted about three miles to the west and you can park by the road. A short walk takes you up to the falls, where the River Bruar cascades down through rocky chasms and over great gleaming slabs of granite. Robert Burns came up here when he was a guest of the Duke of Atholl. He was so disgusted by the treeless moorland that then surrounded the falls that he dashed off a poem: 'The Humble Petition of Bruar Water', and dispatched it to the Duke.

Wad then my noble master please,
To grant my highest wishes,
He'd shade the bank wi' towering trees,
And bonnie spreading bushes.

This plea, as you can see, found its mark and inspired the fourth Duke of Atholl to plant the trees that now grow there. Walk on beyond the falls up the path for another mile or so, through birches and rhododendrons. A bridge then takes you over the stream and down the other side, making a round trip of about two and a half miles. In autumn, when the sun is shining and the sky is clear, this is a glorious walk.

WHERE TO STAY AND EAT
Almost certainly one of your best bets is **Kinloch House Hotel**, near Blairgowrie, tel 025084 237. This is a typical Scottish country house with oak-panelled hall and magnificent gallery, antique furniture and paintings, in 20 acres of wooded grounds. The food is first-class and has won an award. Moderately priced, its rates vary seasonally; it would be silly not to dine here. They will arrange shooting, fishing and golf. **Altamount House** is a moderately priced guest house in Coupar Angus Road, Blairgowrie, tel 0250 3512; a very nice Georgian manor house in 6 acres of ground. It shuts from early January to mid-February. **Castleton House Hotel** by Glamis, tel 030 784 340, in 11 acres of garden and woodland, was built in 1902 within a 13th-century moat. It's moderately priced and the food is good. If you want expensive modern comfort, **Stakis Dunkeld House**, tel 03502 771, won't let you down. It stands in 280 acres on the Tay and provides just about everything you could ask for except simplicity. Indoors there are a swimming pool, sauna, spa bath, steam room, solarium and multi-gym. If you've any energy left, there are tennis courts, croquet, salmon and trout fishing and mixed game shooting. Hermits and stoics, beware.

Pitlochry offers a vast choice. There's the moderately priced **Pitlochry Hydro**, tel 0796 2666, a great stone building above the town overlooking the Tummel Valley. It has an indoor swimming pool, jacuzzi, sauna, solarium and gymnasium. Also moderately priced, **Killiecrankie Hotel and Restaurant**, tel 0796 3220, was once a dower house and is now an attractive, whitewashed house with very Laura Ashley bedrooms if you like that sort of thing, in pleasant grounds close to the Soldier's Leap. The staff spring around in kilts which is all very jolly and the food is excellent. It's only open from February to November. **Dalmunzie House Hotel**, Glenshee, tel 025 085 224, is known as 'the Hotel in the Hills' and is cheap. It is a vast great mansion in 6000 acres of lovely Highland scenery, with a 9-hole golf course, tennis courts and fishing. Shooting and stalking can be arranged. Very comfortable with roaring log fires and good Scottish cooking, and only five miles from the ski slopes.

Perthshire: west of the A9

There are a number of glens running westwards from the A9 through breathtaking scenery to the Central Region.

Lochs Tummel and Rannoch

If you take the B8019 west from Pitlochry you should start humming Harry Lauder's famous song *The Road to the Isles*: 'by Tummel and Loch Rannoch and Lochaber I will go ...' The drive out to Rannoch Station on the northern side of lochs Tummel and Rannoch to where the road ends, and back along the south side is a round trip of about 65 miles. The scenery is beautiful all the way, dominated by the great cone of **Schiehallion** in the south, with a kaleidoscope of vistas out through the trees and the lonely wasteland of Rannoch Moor stretching away to the west. Loch Tummel is less dramatic than Loch Rannoch, its gentler scenery re-shaped by the hydroelectric development.

Queen's View, two miles up from the dam, was so called before Queen Victoria visited it in 1866. Perhaps Mary, Queen of Scots, also stood on the promontory and looked down to the water, glinting in the sunlight, far below.

The Loch Tummel Forest Centre (open daily April–Sept: donation box) is at the southeast corner of the loch. Here you can learn about the geography and ecology of the area and how to find the Black Wood, south of Loch Rannoch, with part of the remains of the old Caledonian Forest.

Harry Lauder must have taken to the moors, when he was 'walking with his crummock to the isles' because the road ends at Rannoch Station, appropriately on the border with the Highland Region.

Five miles south of Pitlochry, the A827 takes you 10 miles west to Aberfeldy, and then out through Strath Tay to Loch Tay.

Aberfeldy

> Let Fortune's gifts at random flee,
> They ne'er shall draw a wish frae me,
> Supremely blest wi' love and thee
> In the birks of Aberfeldie.

> —from *The Birks of Aberfeldie*, by Robert Burns

Aberfeldy is another good centre from which to explore the Highlands—a pleasant little town on the Urlar Burn at its confluence with the River Tay. Robert Burns' poem refers to the silver birches beside the burn. The bridge over the Tay was built by General Wade in 1733 and is said to be the best of the many he was responsible for during his arduous task of trying to link up all the remote trouble-spots in the Highlands during the Jacobite uprisings. The dramatic **Falls of Moness** are just a few hundred yards' stroll south of the town.

The **Black Watch Monument** is at the south end of the bridge: a kilted soldier, erected in 1887 to commemorate the raising of the Black Watch by General Wade in 1739.

The **Oatmeal Mill** (open Mon–Fri: adm) in Mill Street demonstrates the process of milling raw grain into oatmeal, and you can buy the finished products. **Aberfeldy Distillery** runs free tours and tastings from April to October.

Castle Menzies (pronounced Mingies) (open daily, 1 April–30 Sept: adm), a mile west of Aberfeldy, is a 16th-century, Z-plan fortified tower house, with carved gables over its dormers. In the process of restoration after centuries of neglect, it belongs to the Clan Menzies Society and houses their Clan Museum.

Loch Tay is five miles west of Aberfeldy. This long, dark snake of water, bordered by several private estates, has many moods, under the brooding hulk of Ben Lawers, at 3984 ft Perthshire's highest hill. All types of water sports take place on the loch, though keen fishermen might wish otherwise.

Ben Lawers is well worth climbing on a clear day, if you are fit and it could take you as much as three hours. At the top you can see from the Atlantic to the North Sea. There are masses of mountain flowers and birds. Look out for the great brown buzzard, sailing lazily on broad wings, or the kestrel, hovering on pointed wings, long tail fanned out. Listen for the distinctive whirring of red grouse, and their 'go-bak, go-bak-bak-bak-bak', the mournful, liquid song of the golden plover, the lonely cry of the curlew and silly cuckoo call. Needless to say, there is a Visitor Centre, for those who like their wildlife in consumer packages, off the A827 six miles northeast of Killin. Run by the National Trust for Scotland, who care for the southern slopes of the hill, it is a particularly dismal place where they dish up the inevitable booklets, information sheets and audio-visual programmes together with nannyish instructions about what to wear and take if you climb the hill. (For which they can be forgiven: the Mountain Rescue people are frequently called out to risk their lives rescuing idiots who would be better to confine their outdoor activities to Hyde Park.) You are even commanded to keep your dog on the lead.

Kenmore, at the head of the loch, was built for estate workers in 1760, by the fourth Earl of Breadalbane and is now a conservation village. You can hire boats here for fishing on the loch.

If you can't climb Ben Lawers, you can drive round it—about 25 miles in all. Leave the A827 at Fearnan on Loch Tay and take the little back road along Glen Lyon, Scotland's longest glen, to **Bridge of Balgie**, and then drive through the hills, south back to the loch past the NTS Visitor Centre. You can complete the circle on the main road along the loch back to Fearnan, but the nicest way to see Loch Tay by car is on the minor road that hugs the southern shore.

At **Fortingall**, two miles to the northwest as the crow flies, the yew tree in the churchyard is said to be over 3000 years old. This delightful little village has a single street of cottages, some thatched, and an intriguing legend. Some say that Pontius Pilate was born here, son of a Roman officer who had been sent on a peace mission to the Picts in Dun Geal, a fort on the steep, rocky hill behind the village. True or not, it adds romance to an already enchanted spot. You should try to abandon your car in this area: it is marvellous walking and climbing territory.

From Kenmore, take the narrow back road down through **Glen Quaich** to **Amulree**, nine miles south of Aberfeldy. This was an important junction of the old drove roads, where drovers broke their lonely journeys to exchange news and banter, their flocks and herds filling the air with noise.

The Sma' Glen

The Sma' Glen is the moorland valley, through which the A822 descends from Amulree to Crieff. It follows the River Almond as it thunders down over rapids and falls, with hills rising steeply to about 2000 ft on either side. You can see salmon leaping in September and October; the best place for this is the Buchanty Spout, in Glenalmond on B8063, just off the A822.

After Newton, look out on the left of the road for **Ossian's Stone**, said to mark the grave of Ossian, the legendary Gaelic hero and bard who spent many years in fairyland until he was baptized by St Patrick. The stone was in fact moved to its present position by General Wade's road-builders, when it blocked the path of one of their roads. Traces of a pre-historic burial, found when they lifted the stone, were given a re-burial in a secret place by local Highlanders who were convinced that they were indeed the remains of the poet. Wordsworth thought so too:

> *In this still place, remote from men,*
> *Sleeps Ossian, in the narrow glen.*

Crieff

Crieff, about 12 miles south of Amulree, is a Highland holiday town, built on a steep hill, bustling and cheerful. Facing south over the valley of the River Earn, the town is dominated by the Knock of Crieff, 911 ft (277 m) high in the north, a woodland area with footpaths and good views from the top.

Nothing much is old in the town today. It was sacked and destroyed by Highlanders during the Jacobite rebellion. Later, a bleaching and tanning industry brought prosperity to its people. It became a spa town in the 19th century and you get echoes of Victorian splendour as you look at the Crieff Hydro Hotel, above the town, with its glass domes and pavilions. Crieff is an excellent centre from which to explore the Highlands.

Glenturret Distillery (open all year, Mon–Sat: adm) is the oldest in Scotland. Conducted tours show all stages of whisky distilling. The tour includes a taste, and a visit to the award-winning **Visitors' Heritage Centre** with an audio-visual show, exhibitions, a whisky museum and retail shop.

Stuart Crystal (open daily: free), in Muthill Road, is a crystal factory where you can see the whole process of glass-making, and buy the products.

Crieff Visitor Centre (open daily) has factory tours showing Thistle Pottery and Perthshire Paperweights being made. There is a video presentation, showroom, restaurant and Plant Centre.

Weavers House and Highland Tryst Museum (open daily: adm) is in a restored weaver's house, with handloom weaving demonstrations and a local heritage museum telling the story of Crieff.

Bookworms should slip off to **Innerpeffray Library**, four miles southeast of the town (closed Thurs: adm). This is the oldest public library in Scotland, founded in 1690 by Archbishop Hay Drummond, in the attic of the chapel next door, and moved here in the middle of the 18th century. Among the collection of old and antiquarian books, mostly religious or classical, is the Bible printed in 1508 and carried by Montrose when he was finally defeated at the Battle of Carbisdale in 1650. If you are good on scripture, look out for the *Treacle Bible*, so called because 'Is there no balm in Gilead?' is translated as 'Is there no treacle..?'

Comrie

Comrie, six miles west of Crieff along the River Earn, is an attractive conservation village. At midnight on Hogmanay, the unique Flambeaux Procession takes place, with villagers parading round in a torchlit procession, followed by much revelry that lasts well into the New Year. This custom has its roots in the ancient pagan fire-festivals, held to drive off evil spirits for the coming year.

Because it lies on the Highland Line—the geological fault that divides Highland and Lowland Scotland—more seismological tremors have been recorded here than anywhere else in Britain. Shocks were especially common during the 19th century: in recent years tremors never do more than rattle the village teacups.

Earthquake House was built in 1874 to house one of the earliest seismometers in the world. They have a model of the original instrument as well as a modern one, in use, and a chart recorder.

The Scottish Tartan Museum (open daily: adm) is the world headquarters of The Scottish Tartans Society, the leading authority on tartan and Highland dress. They have over 1300 tartans on display as well as comprehensive information, a library, weaving demonstrations and a fascinating garden that shows which plants produce what dyes. You can look up your own name and discover which tartan you are entitled to wear.

Drummond Fish Farm (open daily: adm) is a working fish farm where you can catch your own supper.

Just north of Comrie, and a pleasant walk, **Deil's Cauldron** is an impressive waterfall carrying the River Lednock down to meet the River Earn.

Fowlis Wester is a dear little hamlet, five miles east of Crieff. Here, 13th-century St Beans Church has a leper squint, an 8th-century Pictish stone and a fine lych gate—the roofed gateway to the churchyard where coffins could await the arrival of the priest sheltered from the elements.

St Fillans, on Loch Earn six miles further west, is a popular holiday resort for anyone who enjoys sailing, waterskiing and windsurfing. It is also a good centre for walking and climbing.

Drummond Castle Gardens

Two miles south of Crieff, Drummond Castle Gardens (open afternoons daily, May–Aug, and Wed and Sun only, Sept: adm) are approached down a mile-long avenue. The sundial is dated 1630 and there are lovely flowers and shrubs in a formal Italian setting, against the backdrop of the castle. Founded in 1491, this was the setting for a terrible murder in 1502. Margaret Drummond and her sisters were poisoned, to prevent James IV from making Margaret his queen. Cromwell did his best to destroy the castle and it was deliberately damaged in 1745 by its owner, the Duchess of Perth, to prevent Hanoverian troops from capturing it.

Muthill

Muthill is a conservation village three miles south of Crieff, with late 18th- and early 19th-century houses delightfully unspoiled. Muthill—pronounced Mew-thill—is derived from Moot-Hill (hill of meeting). **Muthill Folk Museum** (open April–Sept: adm)

337

is a quaint little museum with exhibits illustrating past domestic life in the village. Also in Muthill are the ruins of a once important 15th-century church with its 12th-century Norman tower.

A couple of miles to the east of Muthill, **Tullibardine Chapel** is one of the very few of its kind that has not been altered. It was founded as a collegiate church in 1445 by Sir David Murray, whose arms and those of his wife can be seen on the inside west wall. Since the Reformation, this cruciform red sandstone gem has been used as a burial vault for the Drummond Earls of Perth.

Gleneagles Hotel

About six miles south of Muthill and a mile or so west of the village and station, Gleneagles Hotel is Scotland's premier golfing mecca, whose internationally famous courses lie along the edge of the Muir of Ochill, looking towards the Ochil Hills and Glen Devon.

Braco

Ardoch Roman Camp is at Braco, about four miles west of Gleneagles Hotel. Grass-covered earthworks are all that remain of a Roman fort, dating from the 2nd century. It was once big enough to house as many as 40,000 men. You can still see the shape of it—a great rectangle with ditches and ramparts. Here, in wooden dwellings, the Romans tried to subdue the barbaric tribes who swooped down on them from the hills and glens and forests, in an unsuccessful attempt to protect the Antonine Wall further south. The old Roman road runs north of Muthill and then east towards Perth, and an overgrown arch beside the bridge over the River Knaik is all that remains of the Roman bridge.

Auchterarder is eight to 10 miles southeast of Crieff depending which road you take, tucked in under the northern slopes of the Ochil Hills. This is another good holiday centre, with a golf course, good fishing and walks.

WHERE TO STAY AND EAT
Once more, the choice is large. **Gleneagles Hotel**, Auchterarder, tel 076 46 2231, is Scotland's only 5 (red) star hotel. Prices and details on application (comfort doesn't come cheap). If you get fed up with the sauna, the solarium, the jacuzzi, the gymnasium, the shooting, the fishing, the snooker, the swimming, the squash, the bowling, the croquet and the tennis, you can always fall back on a round of golf. The 5-star rating embraces the chef as well as everything else. Don't look at the right-hand side of the menu: who wants to toy with an omelette in a place like this? In contrast, **Achray House Hotel** in peaceful St Fillans, tel 0764 85231, is cheap and cosy, right on Loch Earn, with excellent food. Their high reputation is endorsed by the fact people go back. The following four are all moderately priced. **Drummond Arms Hotel**, also on Loch Earn in St Fillans, tel 076485 212, is quiet and unspoiled, with a friendly staff and relaxed atmosphere. **Kenmore Hotel**, tel 08873 205, is Scotland's oldest inn, established in 1572, with its own salmon fishing and rights over all Loch Tay. It has a good atmosphere and a golf course on the estate. **Loch Rannoch Hotel**, tel 088 22 201, in 250 acres of lovely grounds beside the loch, has pretty well every sort of facility to offer: indoor pool,

jacuzzi, sauna, solarium, steam bath, squash, tennis, sailing, windsurfing, canoeing, dry-ski slope, snooker, bicycles, fishing plus live entertainment and Highland Evenings. **Crieff Hydro**, tel 0764 2401, beams down on the town from the hill, with its splendid glass pavilion in front like a very respectable dowager. Available are: an indoor swimming pool, riding, tennis, free golf, sailing, windsurfing and waterskiing. In the evenings activities include dancing, films, discos and competitions, if you are the sort of person who likes to be organized.

Part XIII

GRAMPIAN

Craigievar

Grampian, better known as the shires of Kincardine, Aberdeen, Banff and Moray, is that shoulder of Scotland that juts out into the North Sea below the neck of Caithness and Sutherland. The name Grampian has a forbidding and stark ring to it, but in fact the region is lovely. It is a fertile land veined with rivers, half-girt by sea and backed by splendid mountains. Routes, along the coast and inland following the straths and glens of famous rivers, radiate from Aberdeen like the ribs of an outspread fan. From the Cairngorms and Grampians in the west, a series of ravines and waterfalls, wooded glens and heathery straths carry the River Dee through forest and moorland to the east coast. Further north the River Don makes more gentle progress to the sea. Moors give way to undulating farmland that forms a wide coastal plain, patchworked with neat fields. The coast road links a chain of unpretentious fishing towns and villages with sheltered harbours offering refuge from the wild North Sea. The coastline is both rugged and gentle—gaunt rock cliffs interspersed with long sweeps of clean sand.

Many pre-historic remains tell of early settlement on the fertile plains, but the region doesn't feature much in history books until Kenneth Macalpine united its Picts with the Dalriada Scots in the 9th century. One of the Comyns, who came over with William the Conqueror, made his way north, married the daughter of a local chief and rapidly gained supremacy in the area. The Comyns, Earls of Buchan, were as much of a threat to Robert the Bruce's ambition to rule Scotland as the English. In 1307 he came north and crushed them in a couple of decisive battles.

With the Comyns effectively subdued, the Gordon family clambered to power. They ruled the land like despots for about 250 years, becoming Earls of Huntly and too big for

340

their boots. Being so far from the seat of government their dominance didn't seem threatening until Mary, Queen of Scots, came to the throne in 1561. Sir John Gordon, third son of the 4th Earl of Huntly, was then rash enough to boast of his aspirations to be consort to the widowed queen. Mary tossed her head, stamped her foot and raged north with an army to curb such impertinence. Having hung the Huntly Governor of Inverness Castle for refusing to admit her, she stormed into Aberdeen and disposed of the 4th Earl and Sir John (see p. 345). From then on, except for an occasional rumble of rebelion, the city of Aberdeen was loyal to the Crown and disinclined to rally to the Jacobite standard.

In the middle of the 19th century, Prince Albert and Queen Victoria discovered Scotland and bought Balmoral. From then on, a stampede of tartan-clad southerners over-ran Deeside and its environs, oo-ing and ah-ing over the scenic splendours. They tiptoed after the deer, slaughtered the game and hooked the fish, integrating with the landed families. They built or refurbished a series of baronial mansions and castles to enhance their status. Balmoral is still the holiday home of the British Royal Family and even today the struggle for royal recognition goes on.

The oil boom of the seventies brought great prosperity to Grampian, whose wealth had relied previously on farming, fishing, granite, textiles and paper. Land prices soared; property speculators thrived. But now that the oil in the established offshore oilfields is past its peak, many of the jobs that went with its exploitation are gone. A number of upwardly mobile outsiders have taken advantage of plummeting land prices and Grampian is gradually changing hands, though a number of the old landed families remain. To wring a living from vast estates, some are forced to supplement farming revenues by opening their castles and stately homes to the public and also by squeezing fortunes out of trigger-happy sportsmen and fishermen.

Grampian is the home of the Gordon Highlanders, raised in 1794 by the Duke of Gordon to fight the Napoleonic Wars. They wear the Gordon tartan and it is said that the Duchess of Gordon helped in a recruiting drive by giving a kiss to each volunteer.

From June to September the tartan-tinged air vibrates with the skirl of pipes and the thud of the caber, as towns stage exuberant Highland Games. These unique Scottish gatherings, dating from the 11th century when Malcolm Canmore held contests to find the best soldiers for his struggles against the Normans, are usually well supplied with beer tents and sideshows. The most popular are probably the Braemar Highland Games in September because of the presence of the Royal Family: others include Aberdeen, Drumtochty, Grange, and Burghead in June; Forres, Elgin, Dufftown and Tomintoul and Strathavon in July; Aboyne, Aberlour and Strathspey and Ballater, in August. A large number of other entertainments take place throughout the region during the summer months.

One of Grampian's attractions is the 70-mile Malt Whisky Trail that takes in conducted tours of eight distilleries where some of the best known malts are produced. It would be churlish to say 'if you've seen one, you've seen the lot': it is an attractive drive and you don't have to go over them all. (But each one beckons with a free dram.)

There is also a castle trail, taking you on attractive tours of some of the many castles in the region.

SPORT
Fishing, mainly for salmon and trout, not only on the Dee and the Don, but on many of the lesser-known rivers such as the Ythan, the Bogie, the Ugie, is as good as you'll get

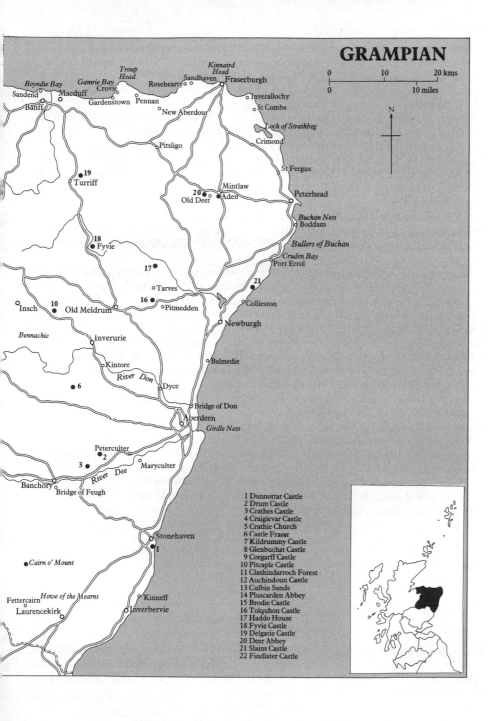

GRAMPIAN

0   10   20 kms

0   10 miles

N

Troup Head
Kinnaird Head
Boyndie Bay *Gamrie Bay* Crovie Rosehearty Sandhaven Fraserburgh
Sandend Macduff
Banff Gardenstown Pennan
New Aberdour Inverallochy
St Combs
Loch of Strathbeg
Pitsligo Crimond
● 19 St Fergus
Turriff
Mintlaw Peterhead
20 ● Aden
Old Deer *Buchan Ness*
Boddam
18 ●
Fyvie *Bullers of Buchan*
17 ● *Cruden Bay*
Port Errol
Tarves
21
16 ● Pitmedden Collieston
Insch 10 ●
Old Meldrum Newburgh
Bennachie
Inverurie
Balmedie
Kintore
River Don
● 6 Dyce
Bridge of Don
Aberdeen
Girdle Ness
Peterculter
● 2
3 ● Maryculter
Banchory *River Dee*
Bridge of Feugh
Stonehaven
● 1
● *Cairn o' Mount*
Fettercairn *Howe of the Mearns* Kinneff
Laurencekirk Inverbervie

1 Dunnottar Castle
2 Drum Castle
3 Crathes Castle
4 Craigievar Castle
5 Crathie Church
6 Castle Fraser
7 Kildrummy Castle
8 Glenbuchat Castle
9 Corgarff Castle
10 Pitcaple Castle
11 Clashindarroch Forest
12 Auchindoun Castle
13 Culbin Sands
14 Pluscarden Abbey
15 Brodie Castle
16 Tolquhon Castle
17 Haddo House
18 Fyvie Castle
19 Delgatie Castle
20 Deer Abbey
21 Slains Castle
22 Findlater Castle

anywhere in the world. Though it could cost you an arm and a leg to fish a small stretch of the Dee, you can fish humbler waters for a reasonable sum. Most hotels will arrange fishing for you and provide permits. Sea angling is also available from the coastal towns and villages but beware: that stretch of ocean can cook up a particularly long, slow swell that is disastrous to an uneasy stomach.

Shooting is one of Grampian's sports and if you enjoy slaughtering game, and aren't a tycoon able to hire one of the hunting lodges for the season, some of the hotels will arrange shooting. The following companies will all arrange sporting packages for you: Game International Ltd, near Turriff, tel 0888 68618; Howie Irvine Sporting Factors, in Aberdeen, tel 0224 580913; MacSport Ltd, in Aboyne, tel 03398 86896; Mortlach Sporting, in Huntly, tel 0466 2716; and Scotia Sporting Agency in Ballater, tel 03397 55034/03398 86891.

Golf. Golfers aren't likely to get bored in Grampian: it is possible to play on a different course each week of the year, both inland and coastal, and most have a professional coach. Golf Holidays Scotland, in Aberdeen, tel 0224 211770, will arrange golf packages for you.

Water sports including sailing, windsurfing and waterskiing are all available along the coast. It isn't ideal for small-boat sailing, the only shelter being the harbours, with long stretches of open coast that can be unfriendly in bad weather.

Skiing facilities are rapidly expanding on the border between Grampian and Tayside and when the weather is right you'll get as good skiing as you could ever wish for (see previous chapter). There are any amount of ski packages to be had and the Tourist Information Centres have all the brochures and leaflets with details. Glenmulliach Nordic Ski Centre, at Tomintoul, tel 08074 356 is a good base. Ski Holidays Scotland Hi-Line, in Dingwall, tel 0349 65000 arrange packages.

Hang-gliding at Cairnwell in the Grampians might tempt some. You can go on courses from two to ten days from £65 to £225. Book through Gustav Fischnaller, Cairnwell Hang-gliding, Braemar, Aberdeenshire, tel 03383 331.

Walking is less demanding and usually considerably less hazardous. There is everything from bracing cliff-top walks and gentle woodland strolls, through invigorating hikes over moors and hills to grappling with ice-axe and crampons hitched on to a sheer rock face by a piece of thin rope. The **Speyside Way** goes from Spey Bay to Ballindalloch, 30 miles, through varied and lovely scenery, with a spur from Ballindalloch to Tomintoul, 15 miles, which is even better.

TOURIST INFORMATION
There are a number of tourist information centres throughout Grampian.
The following are open all year: St Nicholas House, Aberdeen, tel 0224 632727; 17 High Street, Elgin, tel 0343 542666/543388.

ABERDEEN

Aberdeen is the obvious place from which to begin to explore the Grampian Region. It is an ever-changing city, the third largest in Scotland, hiding its true nature under a brittle, cosmopolitan exterior. Always a great port as well as a fish and cattle market, exporting granite, textiles and paper, Aberdeen suddenly found itself in the centre of an oil boom in the 1970s. Country and Western music emanated from dignified old buildings; bars and restaurants changed their characters overnight; American accents were two-a-penny and the opening ceremony of the American Club was like a visit to Texas. Property prices soared: entrepreneurs flourished.

Somehow, through all this, Aberdeen managed to retain its character. The Granite City, they call it, and it softens this austere title by decking its streets and parks with what must be some of the most spectacular displays of roses in the British Isles. (Aberdeen has won the Beautiful Britain in Bloom Contest no less than ten times.) No oil boom could change the silvery-granite splendour of the Georgian part of the city, with gracious terraces, squares and crescents; nor the solid Victorian buildings that accompanied the 19th-century prosperity brought to the city by astute merchants; nor the long, wide sweep of Union Street; nor even, for all the smart new buildings, the waterfront. Expensive oil-rig supply vessels can never spoil the character of the harbour—a salty old reprobate smelling of fish.

Frequently touched by history the city was never a slave to it, as Edinburgh was. Aberdeen was granted a Royal Charter by William the Lion in 1179, now preserved in the Town House in Union Street, endorsing an earlier one granted by David I. William Wallace is said to have burned 100 ships in the harbour in the 13th century. Robert Bruce held a council here in 1308. As a reward for the loyal support of the citizens, who forced the English to surrender their hold on the castle, he gave the city its coat of arms and the motto *Bon Accord*. Edward III burned down Aberdeen in 1336.

The Gordon clan, incomers from Berwickshire and Lothian, who had dominated this northeastern corner for 250 years, over-reached themselves in their ambition for power and began to eye the throne. Mary, Queen of Scots, was forced by her Protestant half-brother, Moray, to come north in an attempt to quell them. The Countess of Huntly, however, had been promised by a local witch that the Earl would be in the Tolbooth in Aberdeen, entirely unwounded after any battle he cared to fight. She begged her husband to stand up to Mary so he summoned his army and fought. He was defeated and he and his son were captured. The shock brought on a massive heart attack which killed him. His unwounded body was taken to the Tolbooth. Mary executed Sir John Gordon and ordered the posthumous trial of the embalmed body of his father, for treason.

Montrose sacked the city in 1644, fighting for the cause of Charles I. General Monk occupied it during in the mid-17th century when he was Governor of Scotland for Cromwell. Although nominally Jacobite, the citizens of Aberdeen were not enthusiastic supporters of the cause.

Old Aberdeen

This area, north of the city centre, is best explored on foot. Start at the little **Brig o' Balgownie,** a Gothic gem spanning the River Don near its mouth. This is the oldest medieval bridge in Scotland, built by Richard the Mason on the orders of Robert Bruce and affectionately known as Dick the Cement. There was a time, some years ago, when the unrestricted discharge of effluent from mills and factories up the river so polluted the water that you had to hold your nose here, looking down into thick green water. Stricter

1 Marischal College
2 St Andrew's Cathedral
3 Town House and Tolbooth
4 Provost Skene's House
5 Kirk of St Nicholas
6 Art Gallery
7 James Dun's House
8 Maritime Museum & Provost Ross' House
9 Fish Market
10 Lighthouse
11 Brig o' Balgownie
12 Satrosphere

ABERDEEN

control and conservation have had their effect and the Don flows cleaner now, the salmon once again making their way upstream to spawn. On the north side of the bridge you can see a terrace of quaint old stone cottages with pretty, colourful gardens: the one nearest to the bridge was once an ale-house on the drove road. Walk away from the bridge and look back at the simple pointed arch, reflected in the water.

Stroll through **Seaton Park,** Old Aberdeen, to twin-spired, fortified **St Machar's Cathedral** (open daily: free) in Chanonry. It is the oldest granite building in Aberdeen and the only granite cathedral in the world. Founded in 1157, St Machar's stands on a promontory overlooking the Don, taking its name from the Saint who founded a Celtic church here in the 6th century. A 14th-century red sandstone arch is all that remains of an older building, in contrast to the simple dignity of the later granite. Look out for the oak heraldic ceiling, added in 1520, with 48 heraldic shields.

Old Aberdeen grew up round the cathedral, an independent burgh with its own council and charter. Today, cobbled streets and charming old houses, some of which date back to 1500, give an air of tranquillity undisturbed by the roar of the modern city beyond. Opposite the cathedral, **Cruickshank Botanic Gardens** (open daily May–Sept and weekdays in winter, free) belong to the University, with extensive collections of shrubs, herbaceous and Alpine plants, and a rock and water garden.

King's College, in the High Street (open daily except Sun: free), stands on a green sward with a distinctive 'crowned' tower and buttressed walls. This was Aberdeen's first university, founded in 1495, in the reign of James IV. Its chapel, first Catholic, then Protestant, is now interdenominational. The tomb of its founder, Bishop William Elphinstone, is a magnificent sarcophagus outside the chapel, supported by figures of the Seven Virtues.

Marischal College (pronounced Marshal), Broad Street, in the city centre, was founded in 1593 as a Protestant rival to King's, the two colleges being united to form Aberdeen University in 1860. The present building is a great edifice of soaring pinnacles; a neo-Gothic granite fantasy, glittering with mica, its roots in the 19th century with some of the older parts incorporated. The granite façade was added in 1906. Award-winning **Marischal Museum** (open daily except Sat: free) has local, classical, Egyptian and Chinese antiquities and illustrates evolving cultures of the world.

Provost Skene's House (open daily except Sun: free) is opposite the college. Now a museum, this well-restored building dates from 1545. It was named after one of its owners, Sir George Skene, who was Provost of Aberdeen in 1676 and responsible for extensive renovation of the house. Butcher Cumberland lodged here from February until April 1746, on his way to defeat Prince Charlie at Culloden. In those days the house formed two dwellings, both of which suffered considerable losses from the misbehaviour of the Duke and his officers. They made free with the stocks of provisions: coals, candles, ales and other liquors in the cellars. They milked the cow, spoiled the bed and table linen and robbed their landlady of her hoard of precious sugar. It is a fascinating museum with some of the original decoration. The Painted Gallery, known as the Chapel, on the second floor of the west wing, revealed traces of religious paintings in 17th-century style, showing that medieval ideas and imagery persisted in this northeastern corner of Scotland far into the Reformation period. On the top floor, exhibits illustrate the history and domestic life of Aberdeen over the ages. There is a coffee shop in the original kitchen.

The Tolbooth, on the corner of Broad Street and Castle Street, was built in 1627. Its ancient town jail with original cells was the stage for the death of the 4th Earl of Huntly after his wife's witch had misleadingly promised him immunity from battle scars.

From the Tolbooth, go up Union Street to **Kirk of St Nicholas**, beyond the shopping precinct a few blocks along on the right. The old parish church (open daily) stands among trees in a peaceful churchyard, bordered by Upperkirk and Back Wynd. Its 48 bell carillon rings out across the roar of the city. Founded in the 12th century and split into two at the Reformation, the present building dates from 1752. In the east part of the church you can see a little stone-vaulted crypt-chapel, St Mary's, dating from the 14th century. Witches were imprisoned down here in the 17th century, and you can see the rings to which they were chained. More prosaically, the chapel has also been used as a plumber's workshop and an early Victorian soup-kitchen. The Oil Industry Chapel is in the church.

Aberdeen Art Gallery and Museum (open daily: free) is also in Schoolhill. Among the many things to see, there are: 20th-century British paintings and sculptures, Raeburn portraits, works by Zoffany, Romney, Reynolds, Augustus John and Ben Nicholson, and an important collection of Scottish domestic silver and glass. There are also regular exhibitions, music, dance, poetry readings and films, a reference library, gallery shop, print room and café.

James Dun's House (open daily except Sun: free) is almost opposite, in what was the Georgian home of James Dun, former master and rector of Aberdeen Grammar School. There are a variety of exhibitions and audio-visual shows.

His Majesty's Theatre, a little further on in Rosemount Viaduct, was built in 1906. Recently refurbished, it is the town's main theatre: a splendid building seating 1500 people. Its varied programmes include ballet, opera and concerts.

The Maritime Museum (open daily except Sun: free) is in Provost Ross's House, Shiprow, north of Trinity Quay and the Upper Dock. Overlooking the harbour, it is one of the oldest houses in the town and a fine example of early Scottish domestic architecture. Displays include Aberdeen's maritime heritage of fishing, shipbuilding and trade and models of offshore oil installations.

Aberdeen Harbour is a conglomeration of seafaring life: fine old buildings line the waterfront where fishing boats are packed tightly into the inner basins, some old and rusty, some so sophisticated that they need an electronic genius to understand them. If you want to see another face of Aberdeen, get up early one weekday morning and visit the **Fish Market** before the sales start at 7.30 am. Action starts at around 4.30 am and the earlier you go, the more impressive it is. As one of Britain's major fishing ports, Aberdeen exports hundreds of tons of fish daily. The boats dock in the cold pre-dawn and unload box after box of fish, stacking them in open-sided warehouses. Fat gulls squabble over the fish. Fishermen with faces as resilient as the granite of the city, toil at the final stages of their demanding job, their rich, salty humour warming the often bitterly cold air. Then the auction begins, in an unintelligible language of grunts, yells, mutterings and gestures.

The Satrosphere (open daily except Tue: adm) is a marvellous Science and Technology centre where you can find out about such subjects as prisms, light, lasers etc, and you are encouraged to take part in do-it-yourself experiments. This is a Discovery Playground for all ages, whether science is your thing or not.

GRAMPIAN

The **Gordon Highlanders Regimental Museum** in Viewfield Road, southwest of the city centre, is about to reopen after extensive renovation. On display will be the uniforms, pictures, medals, letters and documents, weapons and memorabilia of this famous, locally recruited regiment which has fought with distinction all over the world.

Duthie Park Winter Gardens, south of the city on the banks of the Dee, were recently hailed as Scotland's top tourist attraction. The newly opened glasshouse extension makes them the largest glassed gardens in Europe. They include a Japanese Garden, the biggest collection of cacti in Britain, birds, fish, and turtles. Sit under a palm tree in mid-winter and picture yourself in some tropical paradise. Outside, in **Duthie Park**, there is a play area, boating pond, Victorian bandstand and the incredible Rose Mound, which brings on a severe attack of gardener's elbow, as you contemplate the pruning season.

Footdee known locally in the inimitable Aberdonian accent as 'Fittie', is a charming fishing village at the mouth of the Dee. The early 19th-century houses were designed by the fisherfolk themselves. Come here in an easterly gale and watch the sea breaking high over the harbour walls.

Another place from which to watch the changing moods of the sea, is **Girdleness Lighthouse** in Walker Park, the grassy headland that juts out eastwards from the other side of the harbour. You get a splendid bird's-eye view of the harbour and the city from here.

A sandy beach stretches two miles northwards from the harbour, backed by dunes matted with marram grass and fringed by golf courses, an amusement park, and the Beach Leisure Centre, with everything from wave machines, water cannons and jet streams to aerobics, keep-fit training and ball games. It is open daily from 8.30 to 10.30 and has a crêche, café and bar. Bathing in the North Sea is only for the hardy: watch out for undercurrents.

Festivals

Scottish Connection—a festival celebrating all things Scottish, in March/April; Scottish Fiddle Orchestra Concert and Granite City Car Rally, in April; a Marathon Road Race, in May; Aberdeen Highland Games, and the Aberdeen Festival, in June; Aberdeen Arts Carnival and an International Football Festival, in July; Clydesdale Horse Show, Summer Flower Show, the Fish Festival, the Rose Festival and the International Youth Festival, in August; a Drama Festival in September; Aberdeen Alternative Music Festival,in October; Christmas Shopping Festival in November/December and finally, St Nicholas Festival in December.

WHERE TO STAY AND EAT
There is plenty of accommodation in and around Aberdeen, ranging from luxury hotels to simple little bed and breakfasts, with an equivalent price range. You should look at the tourist brochure which gives full descriptions and pictures. The following are merely examples of what's on offer. **Altens Skean Dhu Hotel**, Souter Head Road, tel 0224 877000, is expensive, comfortable and has a heated outdoor swimming pool. **Atholl Hotel** in Kings Gate, tel 0224 323505, is a typical Aberdeen granite town house in the west end; moderately priced, no frills but respectable. They have an interchange dining

349

agreement with three other west end hotels, and a private box at Aberdeen FC. Golfing, fishing and shooting can be arranged, and also distillery tours. You can even have secretarial services if you need them.

Caledonian Thistle Hotel overlooking Union Terrace Gardens in the city centre, tel 0224 640233, is moderate to expensive. It is more or less what you'd expect from the name—with modern fittings, good food and not much character. There are in-house movies, tea/coffee-making facilities in the bedrooms, sun-beds and a sauna room. **Copthorne Hotel**, Huntly Street, tel 0224 630404, is an expensive city-centre hotel off Union Street and near the Catholic Cathedral. The decor is fanciful, with fluted columns and dribbling fountains, and they have a good restaurant called **Poachers**. **Swallow Imperial Hotel**, Stirling Street, tel 0224 589101, is also central and has an imposing frontage that makes you think of top hats and carriages. They give good service, the food's not bad and moderately priced.

If you want something less overpowering, **Palm Court Hotel**, 81 Seafield Road, tel 0224 310351, is in a quiet residential area, cosy, friendly and moderately priced. **Stakis Tree Tops Hotel** in springfield Road, tel 0224 313377, is in wooded landscaped grounds, 10 minutes from the city centre; moderate to expensive depending on what sort of room you take. The hotel has all the Stakis extras, like a swimming pool and leisure complex, and excellent food in a split-level Regency-style restaurant.

Ardoe House, South Deeside Road, Blairs, tel 0224 867355, on the outskirts of Aberdeen, is a baronial-style mansion overlooking the Dee Valley. It's expensive, elegant and comfortable and the food is excellent.

The more expensive hotels have good restaurants, but if you want to eat out try **Mr G's**, 74 Chapel Street, tel 0224 242112. This is a wine bar and restaurant where the food is excellent and there is a nice friendly atmosphere. **Gerards**, 50 Chapel Street, tel 0224 639500, has an outstanding chef and you eat in a garden room with a glass roof. **Atlantis Seafood**, 16 Bon Accord Crescent, tel 0224 591403, do good, fresh sea-food and **Poldinos**, 7 Little Belmont Street, tel 0224 647777, do excellent pizzas. Otherwise, ask around for the current 'in' eating place: fashions change fast.

The Coast, south of Aberdeen

The A92 south from Aberdeen takes you along the coast with the North Sea stretching away to the horizon, always busy with shipping. When the wind is in the east, big seas pound the beaches and cliffs, sending up great plumes of spray.

Stonehaven

Stonehaven is a holiday resort town, as sturdy as its name implies, 14 miles south of Aberdeen, crouched around a bay below massive red sandstone cliffs. The sheltered harbour is used mainly by pleasure boats now. Ideal centre for a family holiday, Stonehaven has a heated open-air swimming pool, a golf course, boating and wind-surfing, fishing and sea-angling, pony trekking, and a new indoor leisure centre.

Tolbooth Museum (open daily except Tues June–Sept: free) is a 16th-century building on the quay by the north pier. Here you can get a good idea of the local history and archaeology, with a special emphasis on fishing. The building was a storehouse of the Earls Marischal, later used as a prison. In 1748–9, three Episcopal priests were imprisoned here, for their insistence in following the old religion. During their incarceration, women came from all over the county, smuggling babies in creels on their backs, to hold them up to the barred windows so that the priests could baptize them.

Every New Year's Eve the town celebrates a 'Swinging the Fireballs' ceremony, going back to pagan times when fireballs were swung through the streets to ward off evil spirits.

Dunnottar Castle (open daily except closed Fri, Oct–April: adm) is about two miles south of Stonehaven, just off the A92. This spectacular ruined fortress stands high on a rocky promontory towering 160 ft (48 m) above the boiling sea, protected to landward by a deep natural cleft. It has been written: 'Dunnottar speaks with an audible voice; every cave has a record every turret a tongue.' A Pictish fort stood here in the Dark Ages, and one of the earliest Christian chapels. The fort was replaced by a primitive castle in the 13th century. William Wallace stormed the English garrison in 1297, burning down the church where they had taken refuge, but failing to take the castle. Dunnottar was a stronghold of the Earls Marischal of Scotland from the 14th century. The extensive ruins include a great square tower and the chapel, built by Sir William Keith in 1392, and a gatehouse, built in 1575, said to be the strongest in Scotland. In 1645, the 7th Earl Marischal, a stubborn Covenanter, withstood a siege by Montrose, who took his revenge by laying waste to Stonehaven and all the surrounding lands. His actions are recorded by a chronicler as having left the country 'utterlie spoilzeit plunderit and undone'.

During the Civil War, the Scottish Regalia were brought to Dunnottar for safety. The castle was besieged in 1652, but the governor refused to surrender until the Regalia had been smuggled out in the apron of the local minister's wife, Mrs Grainger, and in a bundle of flax carried by her servant. They were hidden in the kirk at Kinneff and kept safe until the Restoration of the Monarchy.

Dunnottar Castle

351

In 1685, 167 Covenanters were imprisoned at Dunnottar in such awful conditions that you can almost sense the horror now, looking at the 'Whigs Vault' where many of them were confined 'ankle deep in mire, with one window to the sea, they had not the least accommodation for sitting, leaning or lying and were perfectly stifled for want of air and no access to ease nature'. Some tried to escape through the window that overlooks the sea, but were re-captured and cruelly tortured. Many died. It was a chapter in the history of the castle that seems to overshadow it, even now adding a gloomy touch to the very well preserved ruins.

Dunnottar's history is further commemorated in the 18th-century kirk at **Kinneff** (usually open). Kinneff is seven miles to the south, just off the A92. Parts of the old kirk are incorporated into the current building and include those parts in which the Scottish Regalia were hidden for nine years by the Rev. James Grainger. The hiding place was under the flagstone below the pulpit. You can see memorials to Grainger, his wife, and to Sir George Ogilvy, Governor of Dunnottar Castle at the time.

Inverbervie is a little milling town two miles further south on the banks of Bervie Water. Here, at Craig David on the north shore, David II and his wife, Johanna, were driven ashore by a storm while returning from 9 years' exile in France in 1341. King's Step is the rock where David is said to have stepped ashore. He granted the town a Royal Charter the following year. There is also a memorial to Hercules Linton, the man who designed the famous clipper *Cutty Sark*.

This wild, rugged coastline offers little refuge from the ferocious storms that often rage in from the North Sea. The villagers take what shelter they can from harbours built into the cliffs.

Arbuthnott House and Gardens are three miles inland from Inverbervie (open by arrangement, tel Inverbervie 226: adm). The house has a 17th-century Renaissance façade, with 18th-century additions, and there is an extensive 17th-century formal garden, attractively terraced with a pretty 18th-century stone bridge. A tower on the site of the house was the home of the Arbuthnott family in 1206. The chancel of the village church dates from 1242.

The sheltered area to the west of here is called Howe of The Mearns and contains several good forest trails and picnic sites. (Howe is a wide plain, surrounded by hills, or a shallow depression.)

Glenbervie, just off the A94, is six miles southwest of Stonehaven. It was the home of the ancestors of Robert Burns and you can see the family tombstone and a cairn in memory of the poet, whose father it was that emigrated west to Ayr.

Anyone who has read the trilogy *A Scot's Quair* by Lewis Grassic Gibbon (James Leslie Mitchell) will recognize in this area much of the setting of the three novels. Mitchell's powerful Scottish lyrical prose brings to life the red clay of the Mearns, the land of his childhood, as it was at the beginning of the 20th century.

From here, you can make a quick detour inland, a scant 10 miles on the B9102, through Laurencekirk to Fettercairn and Fasque. There is a gem here, almost on the border with Tayside, often missed by tourists hurrying north on the main road.

Fasque

Just to the north of **Fettercairn,** with its turreted arch into the village, commemorating a visit by Queen Victoria and Prince Albert in 1861, Fasque is down a side road to the left.

This delightfully rambling mansion is a nugget of gold for Victoriana addicts. (Open every afternoon except Fri, May–Sept: adm). The house, built in 1809, was the home of the Gladstones, including one of Britain's best known Prime Ministers, W. E. Gladstone—he who chewed each mouthful a hundred times to aid digestion. He spent his honeymoon here before moving to Wales. Fasque, still owned by the family, has managed to preserve all the marvellous relics of Victorian times without becoming like a museum. Nothing seems to have changed for a hundred years. The kitchens are pure joy and you can see portraits of all the family servants. A slightly ramshackle air hangs over the whole, fascinating place.

While you are here go a few miles north on the B974 and climb Cairn o' Mounth for a panoramic view of the area.

WHERE TO STAY AND EAT
On the whole, the standard in this area tends to be a bit 'basic seaside', but you shouldn't go far wrong at **Heugh Hotel,** Westfield Road, Stonehaven, tel 0569 62379. A turreted granite baronial mansion, with lots of oak panelling and nice grounds, it won't raise your blood pressure with excitement but you'll eat well and be comfortable and it's moderately priced. The best thing about the **Marine Hotel,** Shorehead, Stonehaven, tel 0569 62155, is that it is right on the waterfront in the harbour and it's cheap. The staff are friendly and they cater for children. Or if you want something a bit different but aren't much good at planning, what about **Hiking and Biking Scotland**, Bogfur, Inveruric, tel 0467 21312. From April to November, they lay on walking and cycling holidays, using guest-house accommodation or country hotels, guided or independent, with comprehensive information packs. Their routes take in the Castle Trail and the Whisky Trail, as well as mountain and island tours. Prices vary.

Royal Deeside

The River Dee is born high in the Cairngorms, to the west. It boils down through steep-sided ravines, thunders over precipices gathering myriad tributaries from corries in the surrounding hills, foams through the deer forests of Mar, ripples at a suitably majestic pace past Balmoral Castle and finally meets the North Sea in Aberdeen.

You can enjoy Deeside all through the year: perhaps best of all in autumn when the rich blaze of colour is unforgettable. In winter the landscape becomes a dramatic sweep of snow-covered hills and torrents of ice: a skier's delight, with the Glenshee Ski Centre, to the south. In summer, with a good map and sensible equipment, you could spend a whole holiday exploring the hills and valleys of the Cairngorms and Grampians.

Peterculter and Maryculter

Leaving Aberdeen on the A93, to follow the Dee west, you pass Peterculter and Maryculter (pronounced kooter), seven miles from the city and once a Roman camp. William the Lion granted the lands to the Knight's Templar—the powerful soldier-monks of the Crusades—who built a chapel to St Mary, in the late 12th century. Its ruins can still be seen in Templars' Park on the south bank of the river. The highly coloured statue of Rob Roy standing above the Leuchar's Burn has no historic significance. It was originally a ship's figurehead and has been replaced twice since it was erected.

Not only children will enjoy **Story Book Glen**, off South Deeside Road in Maryculter (open daily, 1 March–31 Oct and at weekends for the rest of the year: adm). A host of familiar characters await introduction, ingeniously arranged among flowers, streams and waterfalls.

Drum Castle (open daily 1 May–30 Sept: adm, grounds open all year) is about three miles to the west, signposted off the A93, and is one of the three oldest tower houses in Scotland. A massive granite tower, built towards the end of the 13th century, adjoins a mansion built in 1619. Robert Bruce gave Drum to his standard bearer, William de Irwin, in 1324, and it remained in the possession of the family until the late Mr H. Q. Forbes Irvine left it to the National Trust for Scotland in 1975. It contains antique furniture, silver, portraits, family treasures and relics. The grounds are lovely, with an oak wood, rare trees and shrubs, sweeping lawns, woodland nature trails, and a café.

Crathes Castle and Gardens

Crathes is five miles beyond Drum, signposted off the A93. (The castle, visitor centre, shop and restaurant are open at Easter, at weekends in April and Oct and daily from 1 May–30 Sept: the grounds are open all year: adm). Although Crathes is familiar to many people from picture books, postcards, calendars and chocolate boxes, it still gives a nudge of pleasure when seen in reality. The Burnett family had been granted lands north of the Dee by Robert Bruce early in the 14th century, and it was Alexander Burnett, in 1552, who decided to move from his stronghold on an island in the Loch of Leys nearby, and build a modern house, in keeping with his status as laird. The castle took many years to complete and the result is one of the best examples of Scottish domestic architecture as it developed from the previously necessary fortified dwellings. It was a style that was to die out within 60 years. When a Victorian extension, overlooking the upper garden, was burnt down in 1966, it was agreed to restore the castle to its present, original proportions. The interior is just as it was, with painted decorations on the beams and woodwork, allegorical designs, proverbs and biblical texts. You can see some of the original furnishings, too, among the many treasures that are on show. The little ivory hunting horn in the main hall symbolizes the Burnetts' right of tenure over part of the Royal Forest, given them by Robert Bruce.

Crathes has its ghosts, notably The Green Lady, who haunts certain rooms, dressed in green and carrying a baby in her arms. A baby's skeleton was unearthed under the hearthstone in The Green Lady's room during the 19th century, and the story is told of a young girl, under the laird's protection, giving birth to a baby, fathered by one of the servants. Mother and infant died, under mysterious circumstances.

The gardens are a delight in every season of the year and you could happily pass days enjoying them. They consist of a series of small, interlinked gardens, each with its own motif and character, a profusion of glorious colours, scents and blended textures. There are also nature trails laid out in the grounds.

354

Banchory

Banchory, about three miles beyond Crathes, is a pleasant, sheltered town on the Dee. It rises in layers of terraced streets, backed by the **Hill o' Fare,** 1545 ft (464 m), to the north, and rolling hills to the south. You catch an air of genteel respectability as you stroll among its antique shops and high-class boutiques.

Banchory Museum (open on Wed, Fri, Sat and Sun afternoons in summer: free) is in the old Council Chambers in the High Street and tells the history of the area.

In the 5th century, St Ternan, a local man and follower of St Ninian, established a monastery where the churchyard now is, and you can still see traces of its medieval successor. Incorporated into the walls of the manse, delicately carved wheel-crosses date from this early Christian period. Palaeolithic flints, excavated nearby, suggest a very early settlement. There is a golf course by the river and the salmon fishing is renowned. **Ingasetter Lavender Distillery** is open on weekdays, in North Deeside Road. The five-acre field of lavender is a memorable sight and smell in July and August before harvest.

Walk to the south of the town, where the Dee is joined by the Feugh, at **Bridge of Feugh**. The footbridge above the rapids is a good place from which to watch the salmon leaping up the ledges to get to their spawning grounds. There are forest and riverside walks as well as energetic hill climbs.

Aboyne

Aboyne, 13 miles to the west, is famous for its annual Games. This Highland Gathering takes place every September on the large green, with all the traditional activities such as tossing the caber, putting the weight, piping and dancing. Aboyne is a good base from which to explore this part of Deeside and there are some excellent walks in the area. Follow the Water of Tanar, southwest of the town, through Glen Tanar, in whose woods you can see remnants of the old Caledonian Forest. Tanar oak was much used in the building of ships, being floated down the Dee to Aberdeen, in the 19th century. **The Braeloine Visitor Centre** (open daily April–Sept: donation box) is five miles up the glen, with all the usual educational information on local wildlife, farming, and forestry, as well as advice on where to walk. There are several tracks leading south, over the hills, one of which, Fir Mounth, is thought to be the route taken by Macbeth as he fled from the castle at Dunsinane to his death at Lumphanan.

Lumphanan is five miles northeast of Aboyne. The **Peel Ring** is a medieval motte with wall, earthworks and ditches and is believed to be where Macbeth fought his final battle, against Malcolm Canmore in 1057. Macbeth's Cairn, in a circle of trees on the hillside, marks the spot where he is said to have died, crying: 'Lay on Macduff; and damn'd be him that first cries "Hold enough!"' (Actually, Shakespeare sets the death scene at Dunsinane.)

Tarland

Tarland, less than five miles northwest of Aboyne, is an old-world village set round a square and is the centre of the MacRobert Trust—a huge and complicated complex of farming and charitable foundations. Walk a short way to the east, beyond the golf course to the well-preserved souterrain, **Culsh Earth House** (open daily: free), by Culsh Farmhouse. Its roofing slabs are intact over a large chamber. Another pre-historic remain is **Tomnaverie Stone Circle**, on a rocky hillock a mile to the southeast, unexcavated and recumbent, probably dating from 1800 BC.

From Tarland, drive round Scar Hill on the B9119 and back to the A93 at **Dinnet**. The **National Nature Reserve** here covers heathland, scrub and birchwood, with old oaks and fenland.

Ballater

Ballater, 11 miles west of Aboyne on the A93, used to be the end of the line for the Royal Train, before the railway was closed. It's a very popular holiday centre in the summer, in beautiful wooded moorland where you can roam for miles in all directions, discovering fresh enchantment at every turn.

The town developed in the late 18th century after an old woman discovered the healing powers of the bog at the foot of Pannanich Hill. Her discovery was exploited by an ex-Jacobite, Francis Farquharson of Monaltrie, 20 years after his exile and near-execution, following Culloden. This enterprising entrepreneur built an inn at the hamlet of Cobbletown of Dalmuchie and developed it into a spa, which quickly became fashionable. After Queen Victoria fell in love with Scotland and came to Balmoral, the whole area developed into the prosperous place it is today.

The views from **Ballater Golf Course**, sweeping away to the hills, must be distracting enough to kill concentration on the game. Ballater Highland Games are in August in Monaltrie Park, with all the traditional events, both athletic and musical, and a Hill Race to Craig Cailleach, south of the bridge.

There are some sizeable hills to climb, with panoramic views, and always the sound of rushing water and the song of skylarks and linnets.

Balmoral

Balmoral (grounds and paintings in ballroom open daily except Sun, in May, June and July unless members of the Royal Family are at home: adm), seven miles west, is another of those places so familiar from photographs that its reality is almost an anti-climax. Queen Victoria lost her heart to 'this dear Paradise', and she and Prince Albert bought the estate and the old castle in 1852, for £31,000. The old building, however, was too small for the royal household, and Prince Albert commissioned the building of the present white granite mansion in 1853, a Scottish Baronial edifice designed by William Smith of Aberdeen. It is still the Royal Family's holiday home and it holds a place of great affection in most British hearts as being the place where their much-loved 'First Family' relax and enjoy the same sort of country pursuits as ordinary people.

Crathie Church, just north of the castle, was built in 1895 to replace a series of previous churches whose origins went back to the 9th century. It is attended by members of the Royal Family when they are on holiday.

Lochnagar towers over the Balmoral area among 11 peaks over 3000 ft (900 m) high: massive sentinels, reflected in the waters of Loch Muick to the south. This scenery inspired Byron to write:

> *England! thy beauties are tame and domestic*
> *To one who has roved o'er the mountains afar:*
> *Oh, for the crags that are wild and majestic!*
> *The steep frowning glories of dark Lochnagar.*

More recently, Lochnagar inspired another writer, Prince Charles, to write a delightful story, *The Old Man of Lochnagar*, to amuse his brothers during a cruise in the royal yacht.

A good eight-mile walk starts at **Spittal of Glenmuick** northeast of Loch Muick and goes round the loch anti-clockwise to the southwest corner and then across to the Dubh (black) Loch, deep in a corrie among brooding cliffs. You are about 2000 ft up here, and ice lingers on the water well into summer. Watch out for golden eagles, soaring overhead on long, splay-tipped wings. Less rare than they used to be, they are still a protected species, hated by sheep farmers. Another bird of prey you might see up here, and also protected, is the sinister peregrine falcon, plummeting to earth, its long pointed wings and tail streamlined, diving on its unfortunate victim at speeds of up to 180 miles per hour. In autumn you might hear the roaring of rutting stags.

Braemar

Braemar, nine miles southwest of Balmoral, is a very popular holiday centre. It lies at the heart of some of Scotland's most beautiful scenery, almost indigestibly spectacular.

Braemar Castle (open daily except Fri, from May–early Oct: adm) is a massive turreted fortress, built by the Earl of Mar in 1628. It was burnt by the Farquharsons in 1689 and garrisoned by the English after the Jacobite risings in both 1715 and 1745, to protect the military road from Perth. The castle has great barrel vaulted ceilings, a sinister pit prison, spiral stairways and gun loops. Look out for the carved graffiti on the internal woodwork, left by off-duty soldiers in the 18th century. There is a good *Son et Lumière* (Sound and Light Show) in August and September.

The Invercauld Arms stands on the spot where the Earl of Mar raised the Jacobite standard in 1715, and there is a plaque in the hotel commemorating the occasion.

Braemar Royal Highland Gathering is held every year on the first Saturday in September, drawing upwards of 50,000 people. It includes all the traditional events both athletic and musical, together with plenty of stalls and sideshows. The Royal Family attend the games, which might be why it is one of the biggest events of its kind in Scotland. The origins of these Highland Games are said to date from the 11th century when Malcolm Canmore held contests to find the best soldiers for his struggles against the Normans.

Linn of Dee

There is a circular tour of about 12 miles that takes you west from Braemar through the wooded Dee Valley to the Linn of Dee. It is an attractive drive which means it is also popular. The traffic can be tedious as the narrow road winds up through birches, with splendid views up the valley to the Cairngorms. Park at **Inverey** and walk the couple of miles on to the Linn of Dee. The narrow, rocky gorge is about 150 yards long and the river boils through this bottleneck in a tumultuous frenzy, filling the air with noise and a haze of spray. A lovely place, best appreciated by hermits early or late in the day.

Experienced walkers should try the famous **Lairig Ghru**, a testing walk from Linn of Dee over the Cairngorms to Aviemore.

Another walk from Inverey is south up the Ey Burn to **The Colonel's Bed**. The Colonel was John Farquharson of Inverey, a legendary character known as the Black Colonel, who used to ride his horse up sheer rock slopes and summon his servants by firing at a shield on the wall which rang like a bell when hit by a bullet. The Colonel's Bed is a ledge of rock in a gorge through which the Ey runs, where the Black Colonel hid after his castle had been burnt down by government troops following the Battle of Killiecrankie in 1689.

WHERE TO STAY AND EAT

It depends what you are looking for: hotels can be overwhelmingly classy to match the daunting noblesse of this district, and their brochures burgeon with rosettes and stars and awards, all well deserved. But there are plenty of simpler places to stay, where you don't feel obliged to hush your voice and glance over your shoulder and apologize if you cough. Up-market, there is **Invery House**, Banchory, tel 03302 4782, a luxury country-house mansion by the River Feugh, where you could be forgiven for trying to remember who has invited you so you can thank them for having you to stay—until you get the bill—it's expensive. They'll arrange golf and salmon fishing for you and you'll eat like a king. A little cheaper, **Raemoir House Hotel**, at Raemoir, near Banchory, tel 03302 4884, is an 18th-century mansion, converted from a private house in 1943. A number of rooms have tapestried walls and antique furniture as well as all mod cons. They will arrange shooting, game fishing and stalking in season, and there is a tennis court and a mini 9-hole golf course in the grounds. There are also four self-catering apartments in the coachhouse and the food is first class. Moderately priced **Banchory Lodge Hotel**, Banchory, tel 03302 2545, is a Georgian house in a lovely position where the Water of Feugh flows into the Dee. Nice old-world hospitality and decent food makes this popular with the fishing fraternity. Closed in January. The views alone make moderately priced **Darroch Learg Hotel**, Ballater, tel 0338 55443, worth a visit. This granite country house is in five acres of nice gardens with views across the golf course to Lochnagar. Closed in January, it has a friendly atmosphere.

Craigendarroch Hotel and Country Club, Ballater, tel 0338 55858, prides itself on its leisure facilities and is expensive. It is comfortable, if a little soul-less, standing in 29 acres of wooded hillside, overlooking the River Dee and Lochnagar. They have a 55 ft (165 m) indoor swimming pool, a whirlpool bath, two saunas, two squash courts, snooker, games room, gymnasium, health and beauty treatment, and a dry ski slope. When you've worked up an appetite there are three restaurants to choose from.

Invercauld Arms Hotel, Ballater, tel 0338 55417, is a Victorian pile overlooking the Dee. It stands on the spot where the Earl of Mar raised the Jacobite standard in 1715 and displays a plaque commemorating the event. Some rooms overlook the river, it's cheap to moderate and the food isn't bad. Further down the scale, **Hazelhurst Lodge**, Aboyne, tel 0339 2921/2, is a really friendly little place, cheap, with only four bedrooms, and excellent candlelit dinners. For really good value, try **Netherley Guest House**, Ballater, tel 0338 55792. This pretty little house overlooks the green in the centre of the town and is cheap.

Aberdeen to Tomintoul

The A944 takes you west from Aberdeen through farm and moorland towards the hills. Less spectacular than Deeside, it is nevertheless attractive country with several prosperous private estates.

Castle Fraser

Castle Fraser (open every afternoon 1 May–30 Sept: adm; gardens and grounds open daily all year by donation) is about 15 miles from Aberdeen, to the north of the road. It is one of the most spectacular of the Castles of Mar, Z-plan, dating from the 16th century and incorporating an earlier castle. The Great Hall conjures dreams of feudal lairds: look for the eavesdropping device known as the 'Laird's Lug'. If you look closely at the great heraldic panel on the north side, you can see the inscription 'I Bel', left by one of the Bel family, who were important master masons, very active in Aberdeenshire. They may also have helped to build both Crathes and Craigievar. An exhibition, off the courtyard, tells the story of the Castles of Mar.

Alford

Montrose fought one of his victorious battles against the Covenanters in 1645 near Alford, 10 miles further west, on the ground between the village and the bridge over the Don. A sad story hangs over the scant ruin of Terpersie Castle, four miles northwest of Alford, and dating from 1561. The last owner, George Gordon, fought for Prince Charlie at Culloden. He fled to the castle after the battle, to lie low until the worst of the reprisals were over. His young children, unaware of the threat, revealed that 'papa was at home' to his pursuers. He was captured in the castle and later executed.

Craigievar Castle

Make a detour, six miles south of Alford on the A980 to Craigievar (open every afternoon 1 May to 30 Sept: adm; grounds open all year). Craigievar is one of the finest 17th-century tower-house castles you will find anywhere. It stands among trees, almost as if it, too, had grown from the ground in a single great trunk, its smooth sides rising to a cluster of turrets, crow-stepped gables, balustrades and corbels.

Built between 1600 and 1626 by a rich merchant, William Forbes—known as Willie the Merchant or Danzig Willie—Craigievar is a picture-book castle with a gorgeously elaborate interior, representing that short period of Renaissance sunshine that preceded the gloom of the Civil War. The painted decorations common at that time were being set aside in favour of the moulded plasterwork just coming into fashion. There are good examples on the ceilings, particularly in the hall. Fortunately, the castle was left unscathed during the vandalism of the Civil Wars and later, the Victorians refrained

359

from adding any of their favourite billiard room wings. Thus, Craigievar is almost exactly as it was when it was built.

Kildrummy Castle

Kildrummy (open daily, April–Sept: adm) is a ruined courtyard castle 10 miles west of Alford, on the A97. Founded in the early 13th century,it is one of the most impressive and historic of the castles in this area. Edward I captured it and altered its design. Robert Bruce sent his wife and children here when he went into exile on Rathlin Island in 1306. The story is told of a treacherous blacksmith who betrayed the fugitives to the English in return for their promise of 'as much gold as he could carry'. He set fire to the castle, whose inhabitants surrendered, receiving as his reward the molten gold, poured down his throat. The English executed Nigel Bruce, Robert's brother; the garrison was 'hangyt and drawyn' but Robert's intrepid wife, Elizabeth, escaped with her children and fled north to Tain. In 1404, Alexander Stewart, son of the Wolf of Badenoch, kidnapped the Countess of Mar, having killed her husband in order to widow her, and forcibly married her, to gain the title of Mar. The castle was destroyed because of the part it played in the 1715 rebellion.

It is an extensive ruin, with a broad ditch and curtain wall, round towers, a keep and gatehouse. The gardens are lovely, with a Japanese rock and water garden built in the quarry from which stone was taken for the castle, and a replica of Old Aberdeen's Brig o' Balgownie, spanning the stream among shrubs and alpines.

Two miles to the south, at **Glenkindie**, you can see a well-preserved earth house in a clump of trees, its short entrance passage leading to two chambers, under massive roof slabs. You need a torch for the inner chamber.

From Glenkindie, follow the course of the Don through the valley of Strathdon and up into the hills to the west for less than three miles. **Glenbuchat Castle** stands by the road at Bridge of Buchat, and dates from the 16th century. It was the seat of 'Old Glenbucket' (sic), a staunch Jacobite, who died in exile in France after Culloden.

Corgarff Castle

About a mile south, go right (west) on the B973 for eight miles, through Strathdon to A939: turn right for about a mile to Corgarff Castle (open daily, April–Sept: adm; contact key keeper in winter, tel 097 54 206). It is a stark, 16th-century tower house, within a star-shaped wall with gun loops. One terrible day, in 1571, the family of the Laird, Alexander Forbes, was besieged here by supporters of the deposed Mary, Queen of Scots. In her husband's absence, Forbes' wife refused to surrender. Edom o' Gordon ordered that the castle be burned, and she died in the flames, with her entire family and household, 24 in all. Corgarff was used by Jacobites in both 1715 and 1745. In 1748, as one of the aftermaths of Culloden, the Hanoverians converted it into a garrison post and barracks to guard the military road from Perth to Fort George. In the 19th century the castle was used by Redcoats in their unpopular campaign against whisky smuggling.

This is skiing country, for hardy skiers who don't need too many sophisticated lifts and resorts. **The Lecht Road**, from Corgarff to Tomintoul, is part of the military road built by the Hanoverians after Culloden. It rises steeply from 1330 ft (399 m) to 2100 ft

(630 m) within a distance of about three miles. The wild moorland is frequently cut off by snow in winter, when fierce winds cause high drifts: remote farms and communities can be isolated for days.

Lecht Ski Centre is at the summit of the road, with several ski tows, ski school, ski hire and a café and crêche. A little further on is the **Glenmulliach Nordic Ski Centre** for *langlaufers*, with ski hire and tuition and miles of trails.

Lecht Mine in the hills north of the Lecht Road near Well of Lecht is where lead was mined between 1730 and 1737. The ore was taken on pack horses over the hills to Nethy Bridge where there was timber for smelting. Later it became a manganese ore mine but fell into disrepair when the price of ore fell.

Tomintoul

Tomintoul, on the border with Highland region, eight miles northwest of Corgarff, is second only to Dalwhinnie as the highest village in the Highlands, at 1150 ft (345 m). Pronounced Tom-in-Towel, the name comes from the Gaelic *Tom-an-t-sabhal*, meaning 'hill of the barn'. The village lies along a gentle ridge, flanked on one side by the River Avon, famous for the clarity of its water and on the other by Conglass Water. It is easy to drive through in a hurry and miss the attractions of this lofty, wild territory. Walkers will discover valleys, hidden in folds of the hills, with tumbling burns and tiny lochans, rich in bird, animal and plant life. The Tomintoul and Strathavon Highland Games are held every July.

Tomintoul Museum (open daily from Easter to the end of Oct: free) is in an old baker's shop in the square and incorporates a Tourist Information Centre. Displays include a reconstructed farm kitchen with all the old implements, a blacksmith's shop, a peat-cutting exhibition and information on wildlife, climate, landscape and geology.

Glenlivet, running north to the Spey is not only at the heart of whisky country but is also a settled farming area. In 1594, 1500 local men routed 10,000 Highlanders at the Battle of Glenlivet, and after the 1745 Rebellion army units were garrisoned in Glenlivet to maintain order and to try to stamp out the illicit distilling of whisky. Catholicism has remained strong here, especially in the secluded Braes of Glenlivet where the Seminary of Scalan was the only place in Scotland for young men to train for the priesthood. The tiny college survived several attacks by Hanoverian soldiers and was finally moved to become Blairs College, near Aberdeen.

Tamnavulin Distillery (open daily except Sun, mid-March–end Oct: free) is about five miles north of Tomintoul on the B9008 and is one of the eight on the Malt Whisky Trail. In an old carding mill on the banks of the Livet, it gives you the usual tour, audio-visual show and free dram, and claims to be the most attractive and friendliest of them all. Opinions may differ on this, depending on how many free drams have already been tucked away, if you are doing the whole 70-mile binge.

The Glenlivet Distillery Visitor Centre (open daily except Sun from Easter–end Oct: free) is a couple of miles north and also on the Trail. It was founded as an illicit still in 1746 by a fugitive Jacobite after Culloden. (He changed his name from Gow to Smith because Gow, being the anglicised spelling of the Gaelic word meaning Smith, was liable to arouse suspicion.) The distillery was subsequently made legal by his grandson. They offer the usual tours and a 10-minute audio-visual show called The Ballad of The

Glenlivet. There is a coffee shop and salad bar and a souvenir shop. You get your free dram and children under eight aren't allowed on the tours: either for safety or perhaps to protect them from the evils of the demon drink.

WHERE TO STAY AND EAT
If you like a touch of class, **Kildrummy Castle Hotel**, by Alford, tel 09756 71288, will suit you well and is moderately priced. With all the style of a country mansion and the comforts of a modern first-class hotel, it stands in gardens and woods overlooking the castle from which it takes its name. There is a good restaurant and they offer skiing, fishing and shooting packages. For impoverished skiers, **Allargue Arms Hotel**, Corgarff, by Strathdon, tel 09754 210, is cheap and close to the Lecht slopes in gorgeous scenery. It is very friendly and relaxed. **Blairfindy Lodge Hotel**, Glenlivet, tel 08073 376, a former shooting lodge in 5 acres overlooking Glenlivet, has log fires, a friendly, country house atmosphere and is cheap. In an elegant dining room you'll eat as well as anywhere in Scotland; leave room for the pudding trolley. They have their own fishing and will arrange shooting. For skiers, the Lecht is only 20 minutes' drive and Aviemore an hour away. If you want something different, try **Glenavon Hotel**, Tomintoul, tel 08074 218. They do Adventure Activity Holidays, including hill-walking, rock-climbing, abseiling, canoeing, pony-trekking, gorge-walking and mountain-biking, all with instruction. Prices vary and they will tailor-make courses for you if you prefer.

Aberdeen to Elgin

The A96 is the main road from Aberdeen to Inverness, flanked by rich farmland and studded with ancient castles. Along the minor roads lie quiet farming communities in pleasant, undulating scenery.

Kintore

About 10 miles from Aberdeen is the little village of Kintore, a Royal Burgh since 1506. Its quaint town hall, with outside stairs, was built in 1737. The church has a 16th-century tabernacle decorated with painted angels on a panel. A Pictish stone in the graveyard has both Christian and Pictish carvings—a good example of how confused those early Christians were and how they were careful not to offend any pagan gods that just might exist in spite of what the missionaries said. (The more prosaic explanation is that the converted Picts recycled their pagan stones after their conversion.)

Inverurie

Inverurie, 16 miles from Aberdeen, is surrounded by Pictish remains. The **Museum** (open daily except Wed and Sun: free) has an interesting permanent archaeological exhibition. It also stages three 'thematic' exhibitions each year. The **Bass** is a 60 ft (18 m) high motte, just outside the town, the site of a 12th-century castle. Mary, Queen of Scots, visited a castle on this site in 1562. You can see Pictish stones in the cemetery, with some clear carvings on them. There is a Tourist Information Centre in the Town Hall in the Market Place, open from May to September.

Brandsbutt Stone is two miles north of Inverurie, with clear Pictish symbols and Ogham inscriptions, dating from the 8th century. The **Harlaw Monument**, on the B9001 less than five miles north of Inverurie, is a red granite obelisk marking the site of a particularly bloody clan battle in 1411. The cause of this carnage was the Countess of Ross. She renounced her inheritance to become a nun, leaving two uncles to fight for it: Donald, Lord of the Isles and Buchan, son of Regent Albany. Donald was beaten and not only lost his claim to the title but was also forced to swear allegiance to the Crown at a time when the Lords of the Isles considered themselves to be kings. Not much further along the road you can see the **Loanhead Stone Circle**, a burial cairn marked by a ring of standing stones surrounding a mass of smaller ones.

Pitcaple Castle

Pitcaple Castle (open if convenient: tel 04676 204) is on the A96, south of Loanhead, a 15th- to 16th-century Z-plan tower house with 19th-century additions including two round towers. It is still a family home. Mary, Queen of Scots, came here in 1562 and danced on the lawn, as did her great grandson, Charles II, in 1650. The tree under which these two monarchs danced was replaced with a red maple by Queen Mary in 1923. On a tragic day, also in 1650, Montrose was brought here, a prisoner, renounced by the king for whom he had fought, on his way to execution in Edinburgh.

A mile south of Pitcaple, antiquity lovers should inspect the 9th-century **Maiden Stone**, thought to be one of the finest early Christian monuments. It is 10 ft (3 m) high and has a Celtic cross and Pictish symbols.

Bennachie (pronounced Ben-a-hee) is the long, wooded ridge rising to 1733 ft (520 m) to the south, with an Iron Age hill fort on **Mither Tap**, one of the peaks. Many claim Bennachie to be the site of the Battle of Mons Graupius, where Agricola penetrated the northeast and defeated the tribes in AD 83. The Forestry Commission has developed signposted walks in this area, for those who like to be regimented.

The Picardy Stone, dating from the 7th or 8th century, is about 13 miles northwest of Inverurie on the B9002. Its Pictish symbols include a serpent, mirror and the mysterious 'spectacles' that are featured so often in those ancient carvings.

Leith Hall

Leith Hall (open every afternoon 1 May–30 Sept: adm, garden and grounds open all year by donation) is four miles west of the Picardy Stone, down a splendid avenue. The earliest part of the house dates from 1650, a tower house with turrets and gables, with further wings added during the 18th and 19th centuries, around a central courtyard. In the exhibition room, you can see a writing case presented to Andrew Hay, the Laird, by Prince Charlie on the eve of Culloden, and the official pardon given to Andrew Hay after he had fought for the prince. The grounds include a splendid zigzag herbaceous border, a rock garden, pond walk with observation hide, picnic area and a flock of Soay sheep. The 18th-century stables are fun and there is an ice house from before the days of refrigeration.

Eight miles north of Leith Hall, you pass through **Strath Bogie**, with **Clashindar-roch Forest** to the west, cut by picturesque valleys.

Huntly

Huntly, 38 miles northwest of Aberdeen, is a pleasant 18th-century town on the plain, surrounded by hills, lapped by the Rivers Deveron and Bogie.

Huntly Castle, once Strathbogie Castle (open daily: adm), is the ruin of a stately 17th-century palace in a wooded park above Deveron Water. It was the seat of the Marquesses of Huntly (the Gay Gordons), the most powerful family in this part of Scotland until the middle of the 16th century. The 12th-century fortress on the motte was owned by the Earl of Fife, a Gaelic Norman. Robert Bruce convalesced here in 1307 after an illness, but just before the Battle of Bannockburn, the laird turned against Bruce. After the battle, his lands were forfeited and given to Sir Adam Gordon of Huntly, who had supported Bruce.

In those days the fortress was made of wood, gradually being replaced by stone and finally destroyed during the Civil War of 1452, in the reign of James II. James IV was a frequent visitor, during an era when the Gordon Earls of Huntly were at the zenith of their power, and it was here that he witnessed the marriage between Catherine Gordon and Perkin Warbeck in 1496. Warbeck was a Flemish impostor, Pretender to the English throne, claiming to be Richard, Duke of York, the younger of the two 'princes in the tower'. It suited the Scottish King to encourage his claims, but Warbeck met his come-uppance in the Tower of London and was executed in 1499.

The rise and fall of the Gordons was reflected in the rise and fall of Huntly Castle, until the second Marquis of Huntly lost his head for supporting Charles I, having first been imprisoned in the castle. Don't miss the awful dungeons and the basement passage walls marked by the graffiti of the dungeon guards. The carved fireplaces and heraldic doorway are splendid.

Huntly Museum (open Tues–Sat: free) in the library in Main Square, gives a good grounding in local history, with temporary 'thematic' exhibitions throughout the year.

Dufftown

Dufftown, 10 miles west of Huntly, was founded in 1817 by James Duff, 4th Earl of Fife, to give employment after the Napoleonic Wars. The clock on the battlemented tower at the junction of the four main streets is known as 'the clock that hanged MacPherson'. MacPherson was an infamous freebooter who was condemned to death in Banff, to the north, in 1700 for robbing the rich and giving to the poor. A local petition for his reprieve was successful, but Lord Braco, the Sheriff of Banff, who loathed MacPherson, advanced the clock by an hour and hanged him before the reprieve arrived. The clock was subsequently removed from Banff and installed in this tower.

Dufftown is known as the capital of Scotland's malt whisky distilling, giving rise to an old couplet:

> *Rome was built on seven hills*
> *Dufftown stands on seven stills.*

Good barley, peat and the right sort of water are the three essential ingredients for whisky making and this area has all three. Whisky is more than just an industry in Scotland, it is part of its social history, with romantic tales of smugglers and illicit stills. The **Glenfiddich Distillery** is part of the Malt Whisky Trail (open weekdays all year and also at weekends May–mid-Oct, closed from Sat before Christmas to Sunday after New Year: free). It was founded by William Grant who bought second hand equipment at a knock-down price in Cardhu, and produced the first brew on Christmas Day 1887. This is one of only two distilleries to have its own bottling plant. Their audio-visual show is in six languages and you get your free dram at the end.

Dufftown Museum in the Clock Tower (open daily except Sun, May–Sept, and including Sun in July and Aug: free) has a collection of local photographs and information about Lord Mount Stephen who founded the Canadian Pacific Railway. The Tourist Information Centre is here too.

Auchindoun Castle (plainly visible on a steep hill above the River Fiddich but unsafe and not open to the public), two miles southeast of Dufftown, is a massive three-storey keep, enclosed by pre-historic earthworks. It was built by Robert Cochran, who was one of the favourites of James III and was hanged by enraged barons in 1482. In 1689, a party of Jacobites gathered within these walls to hold a council of war after the death of their gallant leader, Graham of Claverhouse (Bonnie Dundee) at Killiecrankie.

Balvenie Castle

Some of the stones from Auchindoun were removed and used in the building of Balvenie Castle (open daily April–Sept: adm), a mile north of Dufftown. Now a picturesque ruin, this was a 14th-century stronghold owned by the Comyns. Edward I was a visitor in 1304; Mary, Queen of Scots, spent two nights in 1562 while campaigning against the powerful Gordons; Montrose took refuge here in 1644; victorious Jacobites occupied the castle in 1689 after Killiecrankie and Cumberland's troops occupied it in 1746.

Mortlach Parish Church (check opening times, tel 0340 20380), on the southern edge of the town, is one of the oldest places of Christian worship in Scotland, believed to have been founded in 566 by St Moluag, a contemporary of Columba. There are monsters, beasts and a horseman carved on the weathered Pictish cross in the graveyard and an earlier Pictish stone in the porch. Substantially reconstructed in 1876 and again in 1931, it still has traces of an earlier building. There is a leper squint in the north wall and the lancet windows date from the 13th century. The watchtower in the graveyard, now used as a power house, was originally used to keep watch for body-snatchers.

Keith

Keith is 11 miles northwest of Huntly, on the Isla, the hub of an area of rich farmland. The present town was developed in the late 18th and early 19th centuries but its history goes back to at least 700 when St Maelrubha of Applecross converted the inhabitants to Christianity. Scotland's first post-Reformation saint, St John Ogilvie, was born in 1580 at Drumnakeith. He studied in Europe and returned to preach to his own people. He was hanged in 1615 for refusing to take the anti-Catholic oath of loyalty to the Crown. Beatified in 1929, he was then canonized in 1976. There is a statue of him in the Roman

Doric style Catholic church. This building, partly copied from Santa Maria degli Angeli in Rome, comes as a surprise in an area that is not given to ornamentation of churches. It was built in 1830, helped by a donation from King Charles X of France, who took refuge in Scotland after he was exiled. He also gave the picture over the altar, *The Incredulity of St Thomas* by François Dubois. The stained glass windows are by Father Ninian Sloane of Pluscarden Abbey. The imposing copper dome was added in 1915.

Keith has a Festival of Traditional Music and Song in the second weekend in June.

The **Strathisla Distillery** (open on weekdays, mid-May–mid-Sept: free) is nearby, on the Malt Whisky Trail, giving you another chance to watch the processes that produce Scotland's most popular export and to sample the result.

Fochabers

Fochabers, eight miles northwest of Keith, on the Spey, is a good base from which to explore this area with its attractive riverside walks, excellent fishing and proximity to the Whisky Trail. The village grew in the shadow of the walls of Gordon Castle which provided employment for most of the people in the old days. It was moved to its present site in the 18th century to make room for extension of the castle. Part of the High Street is conserved and the buildings are much as they were when first built.

The Spey, with only three miles left in its race to the sea, runs slower now through shingle banks that threaten to close the mouth which has had to be dredged—four times in this century, the most recent being in 1989. Salmon netting has been carried out for centuries from the spit at Tugnet, just down the river at Spey Bay, and this estuary region is rich in birds: toy-seagull kittiwakes, torpedo-shaped fulmars, black cormorants, trilling sandpipers swooping low over the water, curlews with their long curved beaks, tan-headed teal and black-collared ringed plovers.

The northern section of the **Speyside Way**, goes south from Spey Bay for 30 miles to Ballindalloch and then, if you are still feeling energetic, it's only another 15 miles to Tomintoul. The walk begins at **Tugnet Ice House** built in 1830 to store ice for packing the netted salmon and now a visitor centre with an exhibition on the salmon fishing industry, as well as information about local wildlife, (open daily, June–Sept: free).

Fochabers Folk Museum in the High Street, (open daily: adm) has the largest collection of horse-drawn vehicles in the north of Scotland and a mass of memorabilia from the days of service to the castle. There is a reconstructed village shop from the turn of the century, before the days of plastic wrappings and prepacked food.

Baxters Visitor Centre, a mile west of Fochabers, is well worth a visit (open weekdays, early March–Dec, weekends during summer; check for tour days, tel 0343 820393: free). George Baxter was a gardener at Gordon Castle 120 years ago. He opened a grocery shop in Fochabers and sold jam made by his wife Margaret. From this simple beginning evolved a business that has been handed down through the family to the present, producing a wide range of food that can be bought all over the world. The Duke of Richmond and Gordon, Baxter's old boss, took a keen interest and personally measured out the site for the factory one Sunday on his way home from church. You can see a Victorian kitchen similar to the one where the first Mrs Baxter tried out new receipes, and the modern kitchen where they are still experimenting to create new products. There are guided tours, an audio-visual show, shops, and a restaurant. Outside there are landscaped gardens by the river.

Elgin

Elgin, 17 miles northwest of Keith on the banks of the River Lossie, is the administrative and commercial capital of Moray, a busy market for the prosperous farms of the region and a popular holiday centre. The ruined cathedral is one of Scotland's jewels. The town, at first sight sturdy and austerely granite, invites closer inspection. Wander through it and you will discover a number of very fine, old buildings, excellently proportioned with delightful embellishments and intriguing glimpses into wynds and closes. Elgin is drenched in history and is an excellent centre for exploring the northwest corner of Grampian.

First mentioned in history books in 1190, Elgin was the northern limit of English King Edward I's progress through the country. The town was partly burned by the Wolf of Badenoch in 1390, and again in a struggle for power between the Douglases and Huntlys in 1452. James II of Scotland used Elgin as a royal residence in the 15th century and Bonnie Prince Charlie lodged at Thunderton House for 11 days before Culloden.

The town's Highland Games are held in July and a Fiddlers' Rally in September.

Elgin Cathedral (open daily: adm) stands on grass beside the river, a soaring symphony of arches, towers and windows, fretted against the sky. It was founded in 1224 and damaged by fire in 1270. In 1390, the Wolf of Badenoch, the wild and vicious natural son of Robert II, having been excommunicated by the bishop, burned down both town and cathedral, which contained treasures and valuable documents and manuscripts, with his 'wyld, wykked Helandmen'. After many ups and downs, the cathedral was stripped of its lead in 1567, by order of the Privy Council, in order to raise funds for defence. This act of authorized sacrilege was rewarded by the sinking of the ship that carried the lead. In 1650, Cromwell's troops did their worst to what remained, tearing down a beautiful rood screen and smashing the tracery of the west window. Peace and sanctity still cling to this mellow ruin.

Bishop's House is just northwest of the cathedral. Here you can see a wing of the Precentor's Manse, with a 16th-century coat of arms on the wall.

Elgin Cathedral

367

Elgin Museum (open Tues–Sat, June–Sept and by appointment in winter: adm) is newly renovated in an Italian-style building in the High Street, and won the 1990 Scottish Museum of the Year award. There is a collection of old red sandstone, Permian and Triassic fossils. Other exhibits include Bronze Age relics and natural history displays.

Little Cross in the High Street, dating from 1733, replaced an earlier one erected in 1402. In the old days, this was the place of public punishment, with stocks and jougs.

Lady Hill, opposite the post office in the High Street bears only scant remains of the castle that once stood here, occupied by Edward I in 1296. The column, 1839, and statue, 1855, were put up in memory of the 5th and last Duke of Gordon.

Moray Motor Museum (open daily, April–Oct: adm) is in an old converted mill in Bridge Street. The small collection of vintage cars and motorbikes includes: a stately 1929 Rolls Royce Phantom I, a 1913 Douglas motorbike and a macho 1939 SS100, gleaming red.

Oldmills (open daily except Mon, May–Sept: adm), west of the town on the Lossie, is a working meal mill dating from 1793. You can watch the milling in progress and learn what it's all about in the Old Mills Visitor Centre.

Spynie Palace is a couple of miles north of Elgin— access to small car park from the Elgin–Lossiemouth Road. This is the ruined castle of the Bishops of Moray in the 13th to 17th centuries. It is strange to think that at one time the sea reached as far as the hillock on which the palace stands, with a good harbour and town. The sea then threw up a bar of sand and shingle across the mouth of the estuary, cutting off Spynie and turning the area into a loch surrounded by marshland. A canal was built by Thomas Telford in 1808, to drain the loch into the sea five miles north at Lossiemouth. Great floods in 1829 destroyed all the works and the loch grew again until the 1860s. The old palace saw much history. Mary, Queen of Scots, stayed there in 1562 during her tour of the north, and it became a refuge for Covenanters in 1654, during Montrose's campaigns. James Ramsay MacDonald, Britain's first Labour Prime Minister, was buried in Spynie Churchyard in 1937. (The church was moved to New Spynie, four miles to the west.)

Pluscarden Abbey

Pluscarden Abbey (always open: free) is signposted off the A96, about five miles southwest of Elgin, and is one of Grampian's jewels. Lying in a sheltered valley below a ridge of wooded hills, Pluscarden represents an act of faith that must be an inspiration to believer and non-believer alike. You can hardly fail to come away without feeling spiritually uplifted. The original abbey was founded by Alexander II in 1230, for an order of white-habited monks, the Valliscaulians, whose mother house was in France. It suffered damage from Edward I of England in 1303, and far worse damage from the Wolf of Badenoch, during his revenge on the Bishop of Elgin in 1390. In 1454 it took in Benedictines from Urquhart Priory, probably for economic as well as political reasons. Just before the Reformation took off, a greedy, scheming prior, Alexander Dunbar, anticipating what was to come, managed to 'redistribute' priory funds and lands in favour of his family. He died in 1560 and by the end of that century the priory had passed into the authority of a lay commendator. The estate passed through various hands, gradually falling into disrepair and ruin.

In 1943 the Pluscarden lands were given to the Benedictine community of Prinknash Abbey, near Gloucester, a breakaway community from an Anglican order, whose proposals of doctrinal reform had caused some of its monks to rebel and become Catholic. This order of converted Benedictines started rebuilding Pluscarden in 1948 and today you can see what they have achieved: a truly remarkable feat.

The choir and transepts are entire, as are the domestic buildings. The interior is a haven of timeless tranquillity, lit by a rich glow of colour from the modern stained glass windows and overlaid by a lingering smell of incense. If you are lucky, you may hear, filtering through the walls from the Lady Chapel, the sound of the monks, singing their daily office. You can go into the transept aisles, now a public chapel, and kneel at the south end and look through a wide squint into the Lady Chapel.

Monks, dressed in coarse white habits, busy about their work on the land, add a medieval touch to Pluscarden.

Coastal towns and villages beyond Elgin are mentioned in the final section of this chapter.

WHERE TO STAY AND EAT

The pick of the bunch on this route has to be **Leslie Castle** near Insch, tel 0464 20869, especially if you fancy a touch of class and don't mind paying for it. This nicely restored 17th-century castle, with corner turrets and a truly ancestral feeling, will fill you with illusions of grandeur and you'll eat well. Alternatively, and a bit more expensive, **Pittodrie House Hotel,** at Pitcaple, is a 15th-century pile overlooking farmland, furnished with antiques, tapestries and fine paintings. The food is Cordon Bleu and they have two squash courts, tennis court, billiards, croquet and clay pigeon shooting.

Rothes Glen Hotel, Rothes, tel 03403 254, is a castle-style Victorian mansion designed by William Smith who designed Balmoral, in 40 acres of attractive parkland grazed by Highland cattle. It's moderately priced and the food is good, especially the local beef and fish. **The Old Manse** at Bridge of Marnoch, near Huntly, tel 04665 873, is an attractive Georgian country guest-house in peaceful surroundings in the Deveron Valley, and cheap. Moderately priced **Thainstone House Hotel** in Inverurie, tel 0467 21643, is an attractive country house surrounded by meadows and woods, with a comfortable, easy-going atmosphere. There are only eight bedrooms and the food isn't at all bad.

Strathisla Hotel in Church Road, Keith, tel 05422 235 2150, is cheap, unpretentious and dependable. **Gordon Arms Hotel**, in Fochabers High Street, tel 0343 820508/9, is a moderately priced old coaching inn on the A96 to Inverness, full of old world atmosphere and an ideal stopping-off place for excellent food. **Mansion House Hotel**, The Haugh, Elgin, tel 0343 48811, is a moderately priced, comfortable mock castle by the river where you will eat and sleep well and not feel cheated.

Aberdeen to Turriff

The northeast shoulder of Grampian, well clear of the dramatic hills and spectacular glens further west, is mainly flattish farmland, studded with clumps of trees and a maze of burns and small rivers.

Pitmedden Garden and Museum

Pitmedden is best reached along the rural lanes to the east of the A947, 14 miles north of Aberdeen off the B999. The garden (open all year, daily: adm) was created by Sir Alexander Seton who inherited Pitmedden in 1667: it was restored by the National Trust for Scotland in 1952. July and August are the best months to see this re-creation of a formal 17th-century garden, split-level with an upper garden and terraces overlooking the Great Garden. Sir Alexander modelled three out of the four symmetrical parterres, bordered by box hedges, on floral designs first used in Holyrood in 1647, in honour of Charles I. The fourth depicts the Seton coat of arms. Pillared gates lead into the great garden, down a graceful twin stairway, with two ogee-roofed pavilions. There is a fountain in each garden and no less than 27 sundials, none of which is more than ten minutes off true time. Whether you admire formal gardens or not, you cannot fail to appreciate the splendour of this one. You can see Sir Alexander's bathhouse, in one of the two-storied pavilions, and a key to all the flowers in the garden. (The two 'thunder houses', are rare in Scotland.) In the other pavilion is an exhibition on the evolution of formal gardens.

The Museum of Farming Life (open daily 1 May–30 Sept: adm) has a collection of agricultural and domestic implements. You can walk around the 100-acre estate, through attractive woods and farmland and there is the usual adventure playground, picnic area and visitor centre.

Tolquhon Castle

Tolquhon Castle (open daily: adm) is a roofless ruin, a mile northwest of Pitmedden. Once the seat of the Forbes family, a 16th-century quadrangular mansion was built on to an early 15th-century rectangular tower. The forbidding fortress exterior hides a domestic residential inner court. You can still see the kitchen, cellars and stairways, with the hall and Laird's Room (which has a private stair to the kitchen) on the first floor. An inscription on the gatehouse is an endearing trumpet blast from the laird who did so much to enlarge the original castle: 'Al this wark, excep the auld tour, was begun be William Forbes 15 Aprile 1584, and endit be him 20 October 1589'.

William Forbes' master mason was Thomas Leiper, of a renowned family of masons, and it was he who designed the elaborate Gothic tomb of William and his wife Elizabeth Gordon, in the church at **Tarves** a couple of miles north. It is rich in Renaissance detail, with statuettes of the couple standing on either side.

Haddo House

Haddo (open daily 1 May–30 Sept: adm) is less than four miles north of Tarves. This fine Georgian mansion was built in 1732 by William Adam on the site of a former house, House of Kellie, home of the Gordons of Haddo, Lords of Aberdeen, for over 500 years and burned down by Covenanters. The present house stands in a park surrounded by lovely gardens, showing all William Adam's mastery of symmetrical design. It has a wealth of antique furniture, pictures and treasures in its elegant rooms. The stained glass window in the chapel is by Burne-Jones.

Haddo has developed its own choral society, with a theatre, beside the house. This is one of Scotland's leading musical bodies with productions of opera and concerts starring international artists. (If you are interested, write to the Choral Secretary, Haddo House, Grampian. Seating is limited.)

Fyvie Castle

Fyvie is about six miles northwest of Haddo, off the A947. The castle (open daily 1 May–30 Sept: adm) dates from the 13th century and was opened to the public for the first time in 1986. Once described as the 'crowning glory of Scottish Baronial architecture', Fyvie stands on a mound above a bend in the River Ythan, approached up a long drive that skirts the lake among trees and rhododendrons. In the days when kings moved from house to house, William the Lion used to visit Fyvie. It passed through many hands over the centuries and its five towers represent its five dynasties of lairds: Prestons, Meldrums, Setons, Gordons and Leiths. The National Trust for Scotland acquired it from Sir Andrew Forbes-Leith in 1984. The splendid edifice incorporates substantial remains of the medieval Fyvie. The square and round towers soar to a mass of corner turrets, conical roofs and corbels and inside there is an impressive wheel stair.

Alexander Forbes-Leith bought the estate in 1889. He used the fortune that he had made in the American steel industry to restore the castle, sweeping away much of the ugly additions that had been added over the years, and filling it with treasures that can still be seen there today. The paintings include some of the finest portraits you could ever hope to see, by Gainsborough, Romney, Opie, and Raeburn. The *pièce de résistance*, perhaps, is the 18th-century portrait of Colonel William Gordon, by Pompeo Batoni; a deliciously romantic study of a patrician colonel, standing in rich silken tartan, gazing somewhat disdainfully at a statue of Roma. Fyvie is a stately home not to be missed.

Gight Castle is an ivy-clad ruin to the east of Fyvie, in a gorgeous setting by the River Ythan, reached by a footpath off the B9005. There isn't a signpost but look for a turning by the scrapyard near Cottown. It dates from about 1560 and is associated with a particularly wild branch of the Gordon family infamous for murders and suspiciously sudden deaths. Watch out for the Hagberry Pot, close to the castle—a bottomless pit reputed to be a direct route to Hell. The 13th Laird of Gight was Catherine Gordon who married 'Mad' Jack Byron. Their son was George Gordon, Lord Byron. Mad Jack, alas, was a compulsive gambler and gambled the castle away long before the birth of his talented son.

Towie Barclay Castle (open by appointment, tel 088 84 347), three miles north of Fyvie, is an ancient stronghold of the Barclays dating from 1136, recently restored and the winner of a number of major European restoration awards. There is a formal walled garden in the grounds.

Turriff

Turriff, eight miles north of Fyvie on the A947, stands at the confluence of the River Deveron and the Water of Idoch. It is a small red sandstone town, first mentioned in the 6th century when the Gaelic poet Ossian described it as the capital of a Pictish prince,

Lathmon. It is believed that St Congan founded a monastery near the village in the 8th century. The old church, now a ruin, at the end of Castle Street existed in the 11th century, and in 1179 Knights Templar—soldier monks of the crusades—were given land in Turriff to found their second Scottish base. The 20 ft (6 m) high restored mercat cross in Castle Street is 16th-century. The town is still remembered for 'The Trot of Turriff', when a party of Royalists defeated the Covenanters in the first skirmish of the Civil War, in 1639.

More recently and within living memory of a few, Turriff hit the national news in 1913, when a local farmer, Robert Paterson, refused to join Lloyd George's National Health Insurance Scheme. One of his cows was impounded and the Sheriff Officers tried to sell it in the town, to cover the National Insurance payments Paterson owed. There was a riot; the officers were chased out of town. Attempts to sell the cow in Aberdeen were also unsuccessful and finally Paterson's neighbours bought it and gave it back to him. The 'Turra Coo' was front-page news. The two-day annual Turriff Show in August is one of the largest agricultural events in Europe, attracting over 50,000 people each year.

Delgatie Castle (open by appointment only: tel 0888 63479: adm) is two miles east of Turriff. This L-plan tower house, home of the Clan Hay, dates back to the 12th century, with later additions. Inside there are pictures, weapons, the widest turnpike stair in Scotland and fine 16th-century painted ceilings which are believed to caricature people who lived in the castle at the time. Mary, Queen of Scots, stayed here for three days in 1562 and there is a portrait of her in the room she used. Part of the castle and stables have been converted into self-catering holiday flats.

Eden Castle, seven miles north of Turriff, not open to the public but visible from the outside, is a ruin with a grizzly legend attached to its 17th-century stones. The wife of a tenant on the estate asked the laird to control her wild son. He did so, by drowning the boy in the river, and the mother's subsequent curse caused the castle to fall down. All that remains now is the tower, inhabited by animals from a nearby farm.

WHERE TO STAY AND EAT
The hotels mentioned in the previous section, Aberdeen to Elgin, and those in the following, coastal route section, are the best ones to go for, unless you want to sample one of the self-catering flats mentioned under Delgatie Castle, above. The prices vary: tel 0888 63479.

The Coast: Aberdeen to Forres

Going north from Aberdeen on the coast road you see another face of Grampian: miles of sandy beaches interspersed with towering rock cliffs, bordering an endless stretch of ocean to the east and north. Sturdy fishing towns and villages are strung out along the way, each with its legends of seafaring adventures and smuggling. *The Fringe of Gold* by Charles Maclean is a delightful collection of anecdotes and illustrations about these places. Inland lie prosperous farms and good fishing rivers. Golfers will find a number of courses, both coastal and inland.

Leaving Aberdeen on the A92, you go through **Bridge of Don**, past the barracks that were once the home of the Gordon Highlanders. Long, dune-backed beaches fringed by brambly golf courses, and an army firing range, stretch north for six miles to **Balmedie Country Park**. Further up, **Ythan Estuary** cuts into the dunes at **Newburgh** and from here to **Collieston** a vast nature reserve comprises heath, dunes, pasture and cliff: a haven for both ornithologist and botanist.

The sandy sweep of **Cruden Bay**, about five miles north of Collieston, is where the pipeline comes in from the Forties Oil Field, over 100 miles out in the North Sea. The name Cruden comes from *croju-dane*, meaning slaughter of the Danes. This refers to a bloody battle between Malcolm II and the Danes in 1012, led by Canute, later King of England. The Scots won and the Danes withdrew, undertaking to leave Scotland alone. Canute then turned his attention to England which he conquered four years later. Once a tiny fishing hamlet, Cruden Bay was to be a luxurious holiday resort at the end of the last century. The Great North of Scotland Railway built a huge 55-bedroom hotel with tennis courts, croquet lawns, bowling greens and a championship golf course. It was too isolated, however. The project failed and the hotel was demolished after the war.

Whinnyfold, the tiny cliff-top village at the south of Cruden Bay, once had 24 fishing boats, despite not having a harbour. The boats were drawn up on the shingle beach and the fish laid out on the stones to dry. The jagged rocks off here—The Scours of Cruden—have claimed many wrecks. It is said that at a certain time of year the bodies of those who have perished during the previous 12 months come out of the sea to join their spirits in heaven or hell. (This legend inspired Bram Stoker to write *Mystery of the Sea*. It is said that Stoker was inspired by Slains when he wrote *Dracula* and used Cruden Bay for the setting when the vampire comes ashore to vampirize the unfortunate Lucy. He used to holiday in the area and finally retired to Whinnyfold.)

Slains Castle

Walk north from Cruden Bay, a couple of miles along the cliffs till you get to Slains Castle (always accessible: free). This extensive ruin stands high above the sea, which rages at its feet in rough weather. It was built by the 9th Earl of Errol in 1598 to replace Old Slains Castle, further south, of which only a fragment remains. Old Slains was destroyed by James VI to punish Erroll for taking part in a revolt of Catholic nobles. 'New' Slains is a splendid, awe-inspiring ruin and its extremely dangerous situation makes it unsuitable for children to visit unaccompanied. It is amusing to walk among its massive, rather gloomy walls and recall Johnson and Boswell's visit in 1773. Johnson was most impressed by its position, writing: 'when the winds beat with violence it must enjoy all the terrifick grandeur of the the tempestuous ocean . . . the walls of one of the towers seem only a continuation of the perpendicular rock, the foot of which is beaten by the waves.' Boswell, always fastidious about his comforts, wrote: 'I had a most elegant room: but there was a fire in it which blazed; and the sea, to which my windows looked, roared; and the pillows were made of the feathers of some sea-fowl which had to me a disagreeable smell: so that by all these causes I was kept awake a good while.' Slains reached its zenith at the turn of the century when the 19th Earl, a philanthropic man, created what has been described as a mini welfare state in the district and played host to many writers, actors, musicians and singers of the day. As a result of crippling death duties, taxation and the 19th Earl's generosity, his heir was forced to sell the castle to an absentee landlord who allowed it to fall into disrepair.

Johnson and Boswell also visited the **Bullers of Buchan,** just north of Slains Castle. Here the sea has eroded a sheer 200 ft (60 m) rock chasm, into which the water pounds through a natural archway. Bullers means 'boilers'. Johnson wrote of this: 'which no man can see with indifference, who has either sense of danger or delight in rarity'. Much to the horror of Boswell, Johnson insisted on exploring the cavern by boat, writing later: 'If I had any malice against a walking spirit, instead of laying him in the Red Sea, I would condemn him to reside in the Buller of Buchan.'

Buchan means 'the land at the bend in the ocean' and was the name of Scotland's most northeasterly corner where the North Sea meets the Moray Firth. **Boddam,** about three miles north of Slains, is an old fishing village on Buchan Ness, the most easterly point on the mainland. There is a pleasant 19th-century character in the older parts of Boddam, though it is hard to believe they once boasted 85 herring drifters and 13 curing yards. All the fishing is now operated out of Peterhead.

Peterhead

Peterhead, originally called Peterugie, is a couple of miles north near the mouth of the River Ugie and is known locally as the 'Blue Toon'. It is the most easterly town on the Scottish mainland. The first harbour was built in 1593 and the town has always been linked with fishing, from early times when the first fishermen used lines to catch cod and ling. Whaling began in 1788 and Peterhead quickly became the leading whaling port in Britain, until herring fishing took over in 1818. By 1836, 260 boats fished out of Peterhead, rising to over 400 by the middle of the century. During this time extensive, deep water harbours were built, so that when fishing boats grew larger and could no longer use the smaller ports, Peterhead flourished. Although herring fishing is dying fast, the town continues to prosper, with white fish as its main catch. It is now the largest white fish port in Europe with over 400 highly sophisticated boats. It was also ideally placed to cope with the influx of sea traffic during the oil-boom of the 1970s.

Peterhead was a popular spa town in the 17th, 18th and 19th centuries and the remains of a mineral well and some baths can still be seen by the lifeboat shed. Burns was one of the many people who took the waters here. Surrounded by sandy beaches, golf courses and dunes, it is the largest town in the northeast, after Aberdeen. Many of the houses are built of local pink granite.

The Harbour with its three main basins is a marvellously energetic place, with boats coming and going; vessels being refitted, repaired, repainted; chandlers and all the clutter of a seafaring port. The **Fishmarket**, as in Aberdeen, is a splendid place to visit early in the morning when the boats are landing their catches in up to 14,000 boxes. Business starts at 8.30 am except on Sundays, but you are best to go well before this to get the full flavour of this salty industry. Catches include whiting, haddock, sole, cod, mackerel and herring.

Town House, built in 1788, has a spire 125 ft high. The statue in front is of Field Marshal Keith, born in Peterhead, who became Frederick the Great of Prussia's most trusted general, killed in battle in 1758.

The Arbuthnot Museum and Art Gallery (open except on Sundays: free) is in Arbuthnot House. Displays include interesting information about fishing and whaling as well as local history.

Deer Abbey (officially open Thurs–Sun, but the caretaker is usually there and will let people in) is nine miles west of Peterhead. This insubstantial ruin was a Cistercian monastery founded in 1219 by Comyn, Earl of Buchan. It thrived until the late 16th century and you can see the ground plan quite clearly, though most of the masonry was taken away for other uses.

Aden Heritage Centre is a mile west of Mintlaw, near Deer Abbey (open daily May–Sept and at weekends in April and Oct: adm). The charming semi-circular farm steading, recently restored from almost total dereliction, was inspired by the French wife of a former laird. (Aden is pronounced Adden.) Excellent reconstructions of many aspects of past and present farming life in this agricultural area provide brilliant aids to sluggish imaginations. You can almost smell the oatcakes, cooking on the griddle. Audio-visual shows and frequently changing exhibitions give further information on the life of estate staff at the turn of the century. There is a shop, a café, a picnic area and separate camp site. Aden stands in a country park around the ruin of the old mansion with nature trails and all the trimmings, open all year.

Back to the coast, the little villages along this northeast corner are unspoiled and soaked in seafaring history, their deserted sands a hermit's dream. Many of the original fisher cottages remain, sturdy and low, their gable-ends to the sea, to take the full force of the wild winter storms. In some of the villages, the old tradition of painting the houses with oil paint to protect them from the weather has become a competitive attempt to produce the most striking colour.

Rattray is a wild, unfrequented area south of Loch of Strathbeg, about six miles north of Peterhead. Once a thriving fishing port and Royal Burgh, its records go back to the 12th century, to the days when the loch was open to the sea. In 1720, a great storm caused the dunes to shift, cutting off the loch and silting up the harbour. Today, all that remains is a ruined chapel, said to have been built in the 13th century in memory of the son of the Earl of Buchan who drowned in a well there, and the remains of a Comyn fortress in the process of excavation by Aberdeen University.

You will find no trace today of **Cox Haven**, or Cockshafen, a tiny hamlet that existed in the 18th century round the Strathbeg Burn, somewhere north of Rattray. Thought to have been refugees from religious persecution in Holland, the people are believed to have held curious ritualistic ceremonies connected with 'fresh water' dolphins that were stranded in Loch of Strathbeg during the storm that cut it off from the sea. The community was completely wiped out during a cholera epidemic in the 19th century.

Loch of Strathbeg Nature Reserve covers 2300 acres including the loch, with over 180 different birds recorded, including such rarities as the Caspian tern with its black crown and heavy orange-red bill, the pied-billed grebe from North America—so rare that only five have been seen since 1963—and the red-footed falcon with bright red patches round its eyes as well as its legs. There are two hides and entry to the reserve is by written permission only; write to The Warden, Loch of Strathbeg Nature Reserve, Crimonmogate, Fraserburgh.

Crimond, just west of the loch on the main road, has two claims to fame. Its clock shows 61 minutes to the hour—a slip of the clockmaker's hand—and the Crimond version of the 23rd Psalm was composed by Jessie Seymour Irvine, daughter of the local manse.

On the southern slopes of **Mormond**, the hill to the west of the main road and the highest point in this area, at 768 ft (230 m), the glittering white quartzite horse and stag were cut out of the hill in the 18th century by a Captain Fraser, possibly as memorials. Fraser built the now ruined hunting lodge above the horse.

Cairnbulg and Inverallochy, one either side of the B9107 about three miles north of Loch of Strathbeg, are among the oldest coastal settlements in the area with their original fisher cottages. One of these, known as 'Maggie's Hoosie', is in the process of restoration and will be fitted out to show life in a 19th-century fishing community.

Fraserburgh

Across Fraserburgh Bay from Cairnbulg Point, Fraserburgh stands on the shoulder of Grampian at Kinnaird Head, a great slate rock thrusting into the North Sea and the Moray Firth. It is not a beautiful town but an unmistakable tang of the sea lurks in its bones, giving it great character, and its three miles of dune-backed beach has won international awards for cleanliness. Known locally as the Broch—Scots word for burgh—the town began as a village called Faithlie. The Frasers bought the lands of Faithlie in 1504 and began developing the town. The first harbour was built in 1546 and in the 1570s Sir Alexander Fraser built a castle on Kinnaird Head. At the peak of the herring boom during the last 30 years of the 19th century, more than 1000 drifters would land their fish during the season which ran from July to September. Today the town is a major white fish port and the harbour is an increasingly busy commercial port.

Kinnaird Head Lighthouse is the oldest in Scotland and the original was built on to the castle in 1787. Admission by appointment: tel 0346 28175. **The Wine Tower**, overlooking the cove beside the lighthouse, is thought to have originally been a chapel dating from the 16th century and then perhaps a watch tower. It is a strange building with three floors which have no connecting stairs. Six carved pendants attached to the arched room have been acclaimed as the finest examples of late 16th-century three-dimensional heraldry in Scotland. Access by arrangement with the Tourist Board.

The **Mercat Cross** in Saltoun Square is dated 1736 but thought to have been carved around 1603, as it is the only one in Scotland to show the royal arms of both the old Kingdom of Scotland and the new United Kingdom. The carved **Moses Stone** inside the South Church, dated 1613, is all that remains of the University of Fraserburgh, a short-lived establishment that attracted many students for a brief time when there was a cholera epidemic in Aberdeen.

Rosehearty about four miles west of Fraserburgh, is one of the oldest ports in Scotland. A party of Danes are said to have been shipwrecked here early in the 14th century. They were absorbed by the crofting community whom they taught to fish, an industry that was to swell to vast proportions along this coast. In the mid 19th century, Rosehearty rivalled Fraserburgh as a fishing port but when the herring fishing declined, Fraserburgh's railway link and larger harbour drew the new steam drifters and Rosehearty's industry dwindled.

Pitsligo Castle (always accessible: free), half a mile to the south, was built by the Frasers in 1424 and is now a large and impressive ruin with 9 foot thick walls. Originally the square keep had three rooms, one on top of the other: a vaulted kitchen, a vaulted banqueting hall and at the top, a sleeping apartment with 24 beds. It was extended into a courtyard castle in the 1570s.

The last laird was Alexander Forbes, 4th and last Lord Pitsligo, a fervent Jacobite who was forced into hiding when his lands were forfeited after Culloden in 1746. He dressed in rags and hid in caves or in the houses of his tenants for 46 years until he died at the age of 84. He is remembered for his generosity to the poor. The castle has recently been bought by one of his descendents, an American multi-millionaire, Malcolm Forbes (publisher of *Forbes Magazine*), who is said to have plans for turning it into the inevitable heritage centre.

New Aberdour, a mile inland from Aberdour Bay, west of Rosehearty, was built in 1798 to succeed an earlier village on the bay. Saints Columba and Drostan are said to have landed here around AD 597 and founded a Celtic monastery at **Old Deer**, some 10 miles southeast as the crow flies. *The Book of Deer* came from here—one of the most precious literary relics of the Celtic church—a 9th-century Latin manuscript of parts of the New Testament, with Gaelic notes in the margin. (Now in the Fitzwilliam Library in Cambridge.) Ruined **Old Aberdour Church** stands above the Dour Burn on the road down to the bay. It was founded by the two saints and part of it is Norman. The old font is said to have held the miracle-working bones of St Drostan and the oldest readable gravestone is dated 1440.

The broad sweep of Aberdour Bay is popular with holidaymakers, with rock pools and caves. At low tide you can get away from the crowds by walking round the headlands to more deserted stretches of clean sand. Everyone has heard of Grace Darling; not so many of Jane Whyte whose memorial can be seen on the ruin of a woollen mill where she lived, on the bay. In 1884, this brave lass saved the lives of 15 men, shipwrecked when their steamer ran aground during a storm. She struggled through raging seas to carry a line out to the ship along which the seamen could escape.

Dundarag Castle is a spectacular ruin on the cliffs above Aberdour Bay to the northeast. Dun Dearg—Red Fort—was probably Pictish before it was turned into a monastery by St Drostan. It later became a Comyn stronghold and was destroyed by Robert the Bruce in 1308. Quickly re-fortified, it was as quickly re-demolished, this time in the 16th century by the English. It is now privately owned and can be visited with permission from the owner who lives in the gatehouse.

Rocky **Ceard's Cove**, west of Aberdour Bay, has a Hermit's Cave, where an anti-social retired sailor lived in the 1920s and 1930s.

Pennan, on the western side of Aberdour Bay, is a picturesque village on a ledge below high red sandstone cliffs with a pebbly beach running down to the sea. You have to be practically on top of the village before you see it. If it seems familiar to film-goers, it was the setting for *Local Hero*, including the public telephone box from which the central character made his reports to his American boss. The smuggling of liquor and silk ran a close second to fishing as the main industry here with lots of secret coves and caves in which to evade the exciseman.

Bronze Age **Fort Fiddes**, on a promontory above sandy **Cullykhan Bay**, west of Pennan, is said to be the earliest industrial site in Europe. Beads from the Rhine region are among the artefacts excavated from the ruins by archaeologists, suggesting that the inhabitants traded with the continent as far back as 700 BC. It's an impressive site, overlooking the sheer face of Lion Head and the deep gash in the cliff called Hell's Lum.

Troup Head is a massive red sandstone headland beyond the bay, separating Pennan from **Crovie**, which is reached either by a narrow footpath along the bottom of the cliff or by a steep, zigzag road with a 1 in 5 gradient. It's a dear little place, clinging to the foot of the cliffs, its cottages with one gable-end practically in the sea and the other tucked into the cliff. There is only a narrow footpath between the cottages and the sea. This tiny village once had nearly 100 fishermen and over 60 boats. A tremendous gale in 1953 drove many of the villagers to seek a more sheltered home and Crovie was temporarily deserted.

Gardenstown, a mile to the west, is larger, built on the cliff that rises from Gamrie Bay in a series of narrow terraces. The road through the village descends steeply in a series of hair-raising bends dropping from roof level behind a house to run level with the door in front. The original Seatown is at the bottom with narrow footpaths and huddled, whitewashed cottages. This lower bit, severely threatened by the gale that depopulated Crovie, was saved by the newly built seawall.

There were no inland villages in Buchan before the 18th century. Between 1750 and 1850 local landowners built a succession of 'planned' villages, to house and employ displaced tenants during a period of 'enclosures' for estate improvement. These little inland villages have down-to-earth names: **Auchnagatt, Longside, Maud, Mintlaw, Stuartfield, Cuminestown, Fetterangus, New Blyth, New Leeds, New Pitsligo, Strichen**. Dotted over the hinterland, each of them retains a strong community spirit and many of the traditional trades continue to flourish.

Macduff

Macduff is a plain, unpretentious fishing town about six miles west of Gardenstown, at the foot of the Hill of Doune beside the Deveron estuary. It developed as a spa when **The Well of Tarlair**, a mineral spring just east of the town, was found in 1770 to have healing properties. Health fanatics used to flock to drink the waters until the well dried up. (It was blown up by a mine in the last war and is now a derelict swimming-pool.) Macduff stands around a four-basin harbour, with a thriving fish market and a customs house. Next to the Doune Church there is an anchor, 13 ft long, weighing more than three tons. It is believed to be from an 18th-century sailing ship and was dragged up in a fishing net. It was placed here by the Town Cross to symbolize the town's long association with the sea. If you climb the hill to the 70-ft (21 m) high octagonal War Memorial Tower, you get splendid views of the rugged coastline.

Banff

Banff, less than two miles west of Macduff, is a beautiful old county town looking across the Deveron Estuary and Banff Bay. From the 16th to the 18th century, the landed gentry built themselves elegant town houses in Banff, to retreat to during the winter months, when their castles became too cold and draughty. The town's history goes back to 1120 when it was one of the Hanseatic trading towns sending ships as far afield as the

Mediterranean and the Baltic carrying hides, wool, sheepskin and salted salmon. Smuggling was rife. Banff was an important herring fishing port, with 90 boats and an annual export of 30,000 barrels of herring, until the harbour silted up after a storm and caused the Deveron to change course. The fleet then moved across the bay to Macduff.

Duff House (open daily, April–Sept: adm) is beside the golf course. Although incomplete, this house (designed by William Adam for the first Earl of Fife) is among the finest works of Georgian Baroque architecture in Britain and could accurately be described as unique. Inside there is an exhibition that interprets the motif. In its time, Duff House has been a hotel, a hospital and a prisoner of war camp.

Banff Castle, now a municipal building, was also designed by William Adam, built on the site of a medieval fortress of which the moat remains.

Banff Museum (open daily except Thurs, June–Sept: free) has a collection of armour, costumes, burial urns, silver and local natural history.

Plaques have been put up on many of Banff's finest old buildings and you can get a *Royal and Ancient Banff* booklet from the Tourist Information Centre, giving details of a town walk.

Every July there is a yacht race to or from (alternate years) Stavanger in Norway. Banff Golf Week is in September.

A two-mile walk south along the river from Duff House takes you to **Bridge of Alvah**, a single-arched bridge built high across a spectacular gorge of the Deveron: not for vertigo sufferers.

Whitehills, just west of Banff, is the smallest village to retain its own fishing fleet and daily fishmarket. It is another place where the 19th-century cottages, built gable-end to the sea for protection from storms, are unchanged. In the New Statistical Account of 1845, the Rev A. Anderson wrote of a prosperous fishing village whose villagers were 'cleanly in their habits,' so that 'fish cured by them has a superior reputation'. He also noted that the women of Whitehills were dominant over the men, claimed the entire proceeds of the white fish market, and were of a 'superior comeliness'.

Whitehills is built round **Knock Head**, said to be where grey rats first came ashore in Scotland, from a wreck. There is a good sandy beach to the east, at Boyndie Bay. **The Red Well**, near the shore past the caravan park, is a beehive shaped house built by the Romans to protect a spring with a high iron content. At the spring and autumn equinox, the first rays of the sun, rising over Troup Head 10 miles away, illuminate the interior of the well while the surrounding area is still in complete darkness. This phenomenon only occurs at the equinox and it is thought the well must have been some sort of calendar.

Boyne Castle is a crumbling ruin in a pretty wooded valley above the Burn of Boyne, not far to the west. It was built by the Ogilvy family in 1580 and in those days was a great complex with four corner towers, four storeys high. The Ogilvys lost their estate after Culloden and the castle eventually fell into ruin.

Portsoy is a fishing town, less than five miles west of Whitehills, built round a 17th-century harbour. Many of the 17th- and 18th-century buildings were restored in the 1960s, and a large part of the town is preserved as a conservation area. Among the buildings to look out for are **The Old Star Inn** dating from 1727, and **Soy House**, possibly built in 1690 and the oldest house in the town. Green and pink Portsoy marble was cut from a seam of serpentine which runs across the hills west of the harbour, and provided two chimney pieces for Louis XIV's Palace of Versailles. The **Portsoy Marble**

Workshop and Pottery (open daily except Sun: free) continues to make things out of the local marble and you can buy small samples in the form of paperweights and knick-knacks.

Fordyce, three miles southwest of Portsoy, is a picturesque village nestling under Durn Hill. This cluster of cottages, among narrow streets, with a small late 16th-century tower and quaint church, has won many conservation awards.

Sandend, a couple of miles north on the coast is a 19th-century fishing village much painted by artists and said to have the smallest harbour in Scotland. It stands on the western arm of Sandend Bay, one of the most popular beaches in the area.

Findlater Castle is a spectacular three-storey ruin built into a rock face beyond Sandend, its windows overlooking a sheer drop of 50 ft to the sea. Built as a fortress by the Ogilvys in 1455, it was unsuccessfully besieged by Mary, Queen of Scots, when she was trying to subdue the powerful Gordons in 1562. Although easy to get to, the castle is highly dangerous and adults should keep a firm hand on their children.

Cullen, about three miles further west, is tucked in under a steep hill overlooking Cullen Bay with a wonderful sweep of white sand on which are curious red sandstone rocks called the 'Three Kings of Cullen'. The small harbour, once busy with herring boats, is now mainly used for pleasure craft. One of the things you notice here is the series of railway viaducts which divide the Sea town from the Upper town. They were built in 1886 because the Countess of Seafield refused to allow the railway line to cross the grounds of Cullen House. The village specialized in smoked haddock and the local delicacy, 'Cullen Skink', is a fish stew based on smoked haddock. George Macdonald, a 19th-century Congregationalist Minister who was rejected by his congregation and had to support his family of 11 by writing, set two of his novels in Cullen, *Malcolm*, and *The Marquis of Lossie*. He is better known, however, for being the author of *The Princess and the Goblin*.

Portknockie, three miles west of Cullen, had to be built on the clifftop because there was no room between the water and the foot of the cliff, and has wonderful views across the firth to the hills of Sutherland and Caithness. Its harbour is the only one in the area that is accessible at lowest tides. An archaeological dig revealed the remains of an Iron Age fort on the promontory.

Findochty, a couple of miles further west, is a striking example of villages that paint their houses in brightly coloured oil paints, vying with each other for effect. Red and blue shout at pink and green. The old smugglers' route to Buckie runs along the edge of the Strathlene Golf Course and beach. In the old days, the pack ponies of the nightriders, with their hoofs muffled, would not have had the footbridges and steps.

Buckie

Buckie is another two miles on, taking the A942 round the coast, overlooking **Spey Bay**. This long town is an important fishing base with all the attendant maritime establishments: chandlers, boat builders, ice works, fish market and the largest scampi-processing factory in Scotland. It's a solid, unpretentious town with fisher houses typical of the area, some restored, with external stone steps going up to what used to be the net loft on the upper floor.

Buckie Maritime Museum (open daily except Sun: free), in Cluny Place, has a comprehensive display of fishing methods, coopering, lifeboats, navigation and all aspects of local maritime history. You should also see the **Peter Anson Gallery**, beside the museum, with water colours of the east-coast villages and the development of the fishing industry in Scotland. There is a Heritage Room, with documents and photographs relating to the history of Buckie.

The mouth of the River Spey is about three miles to the west. A footbridge crosses the river on the old railway viaduct and you can walk an invigorating eight miles along the beach to Lossiemouth. Spey Bay is also the beginning—or end— of the Speyside Way, which goes south to Ballindalloch and Tomintoul, via Tugnet.

Lossiemouth

Lossiemouth is a popular resort with a pretty harbour and two good beaches. It is also a busy fishing port. It developed as the port for Elgin, five miles to the south, after sand and shingle silted up the previous port at Spynie. Ramsay MacDonald, Britain's first Labour Prime Minister, was born here in 1866 and his house is marked with a plaque. There is a reconstruction of his study in the **Lossiemouth Fisheries and Community Museum** (open daily except Sun, May–Sept: free), as well as exhibits relating to the fishing industry of the area.

This stretch of coast is wild and windswept, with great sweeps of sand, rich in wild fowl.

Burghead

At Burghead, seven miles west of Lossiemouth, there are traces of both Iron Age and Norse forts. In the Iron Age fort you can go down steps to what is called the 'Roman Well', probably an early Christian baptistry, fed by a natural spring. In common with many communities, Burghead re-enacts ancient ceremonies that were performed to scare away evil spirits. In a ceremony called 'Burning the Clavie', a lighted tar barrel is carried through the streets every 11 January—the old-style New Year's Eve—unless it falls on a Sunday when the ceremony takes place on the tenth.

Findhorn Bay

Findhorn is a small, pretty village, seven miles on along the coast, on the eastern arm of Findhorn Bay, a large expanse of tidal flats which dry out at low tide. If the name is familiar it may be because of the local sailing club's recent challenge for the America's Cup in 1991.

In the huge caravan park at Findhorn, there is the Findhorn Foundation, an international community of some 200 members, founded in 1962, as a centre for 'spiritual and holistic education'. The inhabitants stroll about, smiling politely and somewhat vacantly, and you will need determination to get through their apparent unwillingness to communicate with strangers. (If holistic stems from holism, it's not surprising the inhabitants seem bemused—the dictionary definition is: the tendency in nature to produce wholes that are more than the sum of the parts by creative evolution.)

In the little village of **Kinloss**, on the southern edge of Findhorn Bay, the small overgrown ruin of Kinloss Abbey was once an important Cistercian centre. It was founded by David I who was led there by a dove after he had lost his way in the forest.

Much of this coastline has changed dramatically over the years, as a result of the storms that batter it. **The Culbin Sands**, stretching away to the west of Findhorn Bay were built up over the years by wind-blown sand until 1694, when a mighty storm finished the job. They now cover 3600 acres of dunes and marram grass.

Forres

Forres, a scant three miles southwest of Kinloss, has a long history going back to before the legendary day when Macbeth and Banquo met the witches on the blasted heath, on their way to the town to attend the court of King Duncan. The location of the heath is fairly flexible, including Macbeth's Hillock, five miles west, and Knock of Alves, eight miles east. The town preserves its medieval layout with the main street widening to form the market place, linked to parallel streets by a series of narrow lanes. Forres has very well kept parks, especially Grant Park, at the foot of Cluny Hill, which is a riot of colour in summer, with amazing floral sculptures. The town won a certificate of commendation in the European 'Entente Florale', in 1990. **Nelson Tower**, on top of the hill, is a landmark for miles.

The Crimean Memorial Obelisk, at the west end of the High Street, stands on the site of Forres Castle, where King Duncan held his court. **The Falconer Museum** (opening times under review: free), also in the High Street, gives you an idea of the town's history. It has displays of natural and social history, fossils and archaeology and temporary exhibitions. **Witch's Stone** in Victoria Road is thought to date from Pictish times and to have been used as an altar to the Sun God. It marks the site where one of three barrels, containing three condemned witches, came to rest, having been rolled down Cluny Hill.

Sueno's Stone, on the northeastern outskirts of the town, is an outstanding example of a Pictish sculpted stone. It stands over 20 ft (6 m) high, a slender sandstone shaft dating from the 9th or 10th century. It is clearly carved with a battle scene on one side, full of bodies and heads and weapons, round a broch, with a cross on the reverse side (probably a cenotaph commemorating a victory). Its once splendid setting, overlooking the Moray Firth, is about to be vandalised by encasing the stone in a protective building.

Brodie Castle

Brodie (open daily, Easter–30 Sept, and at weekends in Oct: adm) is about five miles west of Forres. It was built on land given to the Brodies by Malcolm IV in 1160 and owned by them until the present day. Part of the existing building dates from 17th century, rebuilt after the castle was destroyed in 1645. There are also 18th- and 19th-century additions. It is a pale cream-coloured building, with conical turrets and coats of arms on the outer walls, approached down a beech avenue. The castle contains French furniture, English, Continental and Chinese porcelain and a wonderful collection of paintings. There are woodland walks by a 4-acre loch, a picnic area, adventure playground, car park and shop.

Darnaway Farm Visitor Centre (open daily, May–Sept, but check, tel 03094 469: adm) offers the opportunity to see a working dairy farm on a large modern estate. Attractions include an exhibition, audio-visual show, guided walks and estate tours, including a visit to **Darnaway Castle**. Seat of the Earls of Moray, this has a magnificent 15th-century oak hammer beam roof. Among the Stuart portraits there is one of the murdered 'Bonnie Earl'.

Randolph's Leap at Logie, seven and a half miles south of Forres on the B9007, should be called Cumming's Leap. Robert the Bruce gave land belonging to the Cummings to Thomas Randolph, Earl of Moray. The Cummings raided Darnaway Castle in retaliation but were forced to flee. Alistair Cumming leapt across the narrow gap above this impressive gorge to evade pursuit.

WHERE TO STAY AND EAT
Crown and Anchor Inn, in picturesque Findhorn, tel 03093 30243, is an 18th-century coaching inn on the Bay. Friendly, lively atmosphere, cheap, with free boats. **Royal Hotel**, Tytler Street, Forres, tel 0309 72617, also cheap, is a comfortable Victorian town house retaining many of its original features, but plenty of mod cons as well. **Skerrybrae Hotel**, Lossiemouth, tel 034381, is a typical seaside hotel, on the edge of the golf course, yards from the sea, cheap, with splendid views. **Saplinbrae House Hotel**, Old Deer, tel 0771 23515, is a nice old country house in 400 acres, with shooting, fishing and pony trekking. It's moderately priced and the food is good. **The County Hotel**, High Street, Banff, tel 02612 5353, is an elegant Georgian mansion overlooking Banff Bay and cheap. Also in Banff **Fife Lodge Hotel**, tel 02612 2436, is an historic building overlooking River Deveron and Duff House Gardens. Moderately priced, the Lodge specializes in traditional cooking. It is hardly necessary to recommend **Pennan Inn**. People book far ahead and travel across oceans to stay in one of the six simple bedrooms here (though, actually, it is not *the* inn that featured in the film *Local Hero*, set in Pennan). The seafood is good and it's cheap.

Part XIV

HIGHLAND

Highland cow

Behold her, single in the field,
Yon solitary Highland Lass!
Reaping and singing by herself;
Stop here, or gently pass!
Alone she cuts and binds the grain,
And sings a melancholy strain;
O listen! for the Vale profound
Is overflowing with the sound...

—from *The Solitary Reaper*, by William Wordsworth

When the new regional boundaries were drawn in 1975, Highland Region encompassed the northern two-thirds of Scotland but excluded Perthshire and Argyllshire, both of which belong to 'the Highlands' in their true sense.

Until relatively recently, when Jacobites made a bid for the English throne, the Highlands were so isolated, geographically, that very few outsiders ventured into them. Communication between remote communities, cut off by impassable mountain ranges and huge tracts of water, was arduous. It was only after 1715 and the first Jacobite rebellion that General Wade's planned road system evolved and people like Dr Johnson were able to travel about and 'discover' this untapped source of purple prose.

The Battle of Culloden sparked off the death of the clan system and contributed to the mass exodus that took place over the succeeding century or so. All that remains are tumbled stones, where villages of crofters once squeezed a living from the poor soil, subsisting under the protection of their chief.

Agriculture, fishing and tourism are the main occupation of Highlanders. Main roads are excellent but it is often necessary to drive long distances to get round mountains and sea lochs. Many of the minor roads are single track, with passing bays; infuriating in the caravan season.

In the remoter parts, not much has changed in the last hundred years or so. There may be new hotels with picture windows, pile carpets and bathrooms-en-suite, but the people who staff them are not very impressed by these modern trappings. Round the back there are probably a dozen derelict vehicles, discarded over the last 20 years. The surrounding countryside is littered with rusting beer cans and empty whisky bottles, and it would not be surprising to find a live sheep among the inhabitants of a kitchen.

It is in the Highlands, particularly in the west, that you will find, if you are lucky, the old bards and tellers of folk tales that have been handed down orally over the centuries. And in those parts of the Highlands that were untouched by the Reformation, and by the banning of fun and gaiety by the stern Calvinists, you will find the best fiddlers and pipers.

Highland Games are a popular summer diversion throughout the region, usually less showy than the smart dress parades of Grampian. A lone piper practises a pibroch behind a shed, pacing with precise steps, while his rival faces a row of intent judges in the ring. Two little girls, in full Highland costume, perform the intricate steps of a sword dance on a wooden platform. A huge man with bulging biceps, totters under the weight of a gigantic caber; another heaves a cannon-ball weight across the grass, another a javelin. Young men hurl themselves up and over a high jump. There are side shows and stalls, hot dog stands, fish and chips, and always a well attended beer tent. Sometimes these games were fairs, organized by clan chiefs but they usually had a serious purpose: the chief would be talent-spotting for fit men for his army.

Look out for **Sheep Dog Trials**, where these intelligent animals are put through their paces. There can be few things more stirring than to see a first-class pair of dogs working a flock of sheep, controlled by a minimum of monosyllabic or whistled commands. The Great Glen Sheepdog trials, in Fort William, in July, are one of the best of these, and there are often smaller trials at agricultural shows.

SPORT
Walking is an endless pleasure, with undiscovered beauty spots round every corner: secret glens, remote lochs, waterfalls, and a million different seascapes. Good bird and wild flower books and Ordnance Survey maps are essential equipment, together with comfortable, sturdy footwear and waterproof clothing.

Climbing is challenging even for the experienced. Amateurs should read the advice given on p. 16. It may seem over-cautious, but statistics prove there are many who put their own lives, and those of the Mountain Rescue teams, at risk.

There is plenty of **shooting**: mainly for grouse, pheasant and wildfowl, and **stalking**. Both these can be expensive unless you have landowning friends. There is excellent **fishing** in rivers, lochs and the sea. **Pony trekking** is a nice way to explore and there are dozens of centres. **Golf** courses are mostly on the coast, The Royal Dornoch being internationally renowned.

Sailing, particularly off the west coast, is idyllic, but capricious weather, lethal currents and dramatic rise and fall of tides make it essential to have an experienced

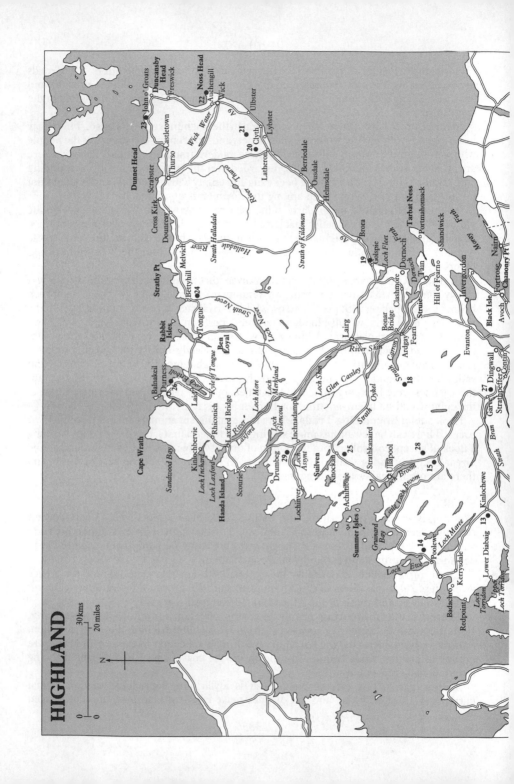

HIGHLAND

30kms
20 miles

N

John o' Groats
Duncansby Head
Freswick
23 Castletown
Noss Head 22 Auchengill
Wick
Dunnet Head
Scrabster
Thurso
Ubster
Ulbster
Lybster
21
20 Clyth
Cross Kirk
Dounreay
Latheron
Berriedale
Ousdale
Helmsdale
Strathy Pt
Melvich
Bettyhill 24
Brora
Golspie
19
Loch Fleet
Tarbat Ness
Portmahomack
Dornoch
Clashmore
Shandwick
Rabbit Isles
Tongue
Ben Loyal
Lairg
Bonar Bridge
Pain
Hill of Fearn
Balnakeil
Durness 26
Laid
Kyle of Tongue
Rhiconich
Laxford Bridge
Loch More
Loch Shin
River Shin
Ardgay
Fearn
Strue
Evanton
Invergordon
Black Isle
Avoch
Fortrose
Chanory Pt
Nairn
Cape Wrath
Sandwood Bay
Kinlochbervie
Loch Inchard
Handa Island
Scourie
Loch Laxford
Glen Cassley
Strath Carron
18
27 Dingwall
Garve
Strathpeffer
Conon
Drumbeg
29
Loch Assynt
Sulven
Knockan
25
Strathkanaird
28
15
Lochinver
Achiltibue
Ullapool
Loch Broom
Summer Isles
Grainard Bay
Little Loch Broom
14
Poolewe
Loch Ewe
Kinlochewe 13
Lower Diabaig
Badachro
Redpoint
Kerrysdale
Loch Torridon
Upper Loch Torridon

1 Culloden Battlefield
2 Clava Cairns
3 Kincraig Highland Wildlife Park
4 Ruthven Barracks
5 Corran Ferry
6 Ardtornish Castle
7 Castle Urquhart
8 Fort Bernera
9 Morvich National Trust
  Visitors Centre
10 Kintail Estate
11 Falls of Glomach
12 Eilean Donan Castle
13 Beinn Eighe National
   Nature Reserve
14 Inverewe Garden
15 Corrieshalloch Gorge
16 Moniak Castle
17 Kessock Bridge
18 Croik Church
19 Dunrobin Castle
20 Rangag Broch
21 Grey Cairns of Camster
22 Sinclair Castle
23 Castle of Mey
24 Invernaver National Nature Reserve
25 Inverpolly National Nature Reserve
26 Smoo Cave
27 Rogie Falls
28 Lael Forest
29 Ardvreck Castle

GRAMPIAN

STRATHCLYDE

skipper. All other **water sports**, including **wind-surfing** and **sub-aqua diving** can be found, but whatever they say about the Gulf Stream, the sea is icy and wet-suits are advised. There is challenging **skiing** in the Cairngorms, from Aviemore, and in Glen Coe.

TOURIST INFORMATION
Open all year:
Inverness, Loch Ness and Nairn Tourist Office, 23 Church Street, Inverness, tel 0463 234353.
Aviemore and Spey Valley Tourist Office, Main Road, Aviemore, Inverness-shire, tel 0479 810363.
Ross and Cromarty Tourist Office, North Kessock, Black Isle, Ross-shire, tel 046373 505.
Ross and Cromarty Tourist Office, Gairloch, Ross-shire, tel 0445 2130.
Sutherland Tourist Board, The Square, Dornoch, Sutherland, tel 0682 810 400.
Caithness Tourist Board, Whitechapel Road, Wick, Caithness, tel 0955 2596.
Fort William and Lochaber Tourist Board, Cameron Centre, Cameron Square, Fort William, tel 0397 3781.
Hi-Line, Dingwall, tel 0349 63434.
There are also a number of seasonal Information Offices, usually open from Easter to the end of September or October.

Inverness

As the capital of the Highlands and the junction of many routes, Inverness is a good place from which to explore the Highland area. The River Ness flows through the heart of the town, converging with the northern end of the Caledonian Canal. Although not out-standingly beautiful, parts of Inverness have a certain sturdy charm and the riverside is most attractive. Perhaps the best view is from the bridge below Bridge Street. Fishermen stand thigh-deep in the fast flowing River Ness, flanked by well-proportioned houses and churches. When the sun shines, it is a curiously continental picture.

Its sheltered position beside the sea made Inverness a natural place for trade to develop and it has been an important centre from earliest times. In the Middle Ages it developed as a port and ship-building centre, with trade links with Europe. It was often the focal point of clashes between Highland and Island Chiefs who ruled their lands like kings, and the Scottish Crown, ever trying to subdue them. It is now the communications and administrative centre for the north of Scotland.

St Columba is recorded by his biographer, St Adamnan, as having visited the Pictish King Brude in a castle somewhere near the River Ness in AD 565 and converted him and his people to Christianity. This could have been on Craig Phadrig, the small hill just west of the town which still has the remains of a 4th-century vitrified fort. It is more likely, however, that Brude's stronghold stood on the site of Macbeth's castle on Auld Castle Hill, east of today's Castle Hill.

Historical fact and poetic fiction have become so inextricably interwoven around the story of Macbeth and his bloodstained journey to the throne that there are several different claims for the true setting for King Duncan's murder. The most reliable sources say the deed was done in a house near Elgin, in 1039, not in Macbeth's castle in Inverness, but it is believed that Malcolm Canmore destroyed the Inverness castle in revenge for Duncan's death. A new castle was built in the 12th century on the site of the present one, and was much abused in subsequent years. The English occupied it in the War of Independence and Robert Bruce destroyed it. Its successor became the hub of conflict between Highlanders and those trying to subdue their wild ways. Mary, Queen of Scots, hanged its rebellious governor from the ramparts, when he refused her entry in 1562. Jacobites occupied it in 1715 and 1745, after which they blew it up, to keep it from government hands. The present castle was built in the 19th century and looks brand new, its pinkish walls rising from the small hill exactly like a toy fort. It houses the law courts and local government offices. There is a small exhibition (open Easter–Oct: free) telling the history of the castle.

The centre of the town is compact, with the Station Square right in the middle, dominated by a war memorial statue of a Cameron Highlander. The Camerons, now amalgamated with the Seaforths to become The Queen's Own Highlanders, were the local regiment. There are some excellent shops in a hideous new indoor shopping complex.

Inverness stages a Folk Festival in March, Highland Games in July, a Festival Week and Cadet Tattoo in August. The Northern Meeting Piping Competition is in September, when the finest pipers of the day compete for prestigious awards.

Inverness Museum (open weekdays: free) in Castle Wynd, between the castle and the town hall, has excellent displays of social and natural history, archaeology, and the culture of the Highlands and Jacobite relics. There are often special exhibitions, as well as interesting talks and slide shows.

St Andrew's Episcopal Cathedral is to the south. An imposing, pinkish building on the banks of the river, it was built less than 100 years ago, with an octagonal chapter house and a very elaborate interior.

Eden Court is beyond the cathedral. This great glass edifice, built in 1976, incorporates the 19th-century house of Bishop Eden. It is an 800-seat multipurpose theatre, conference centre and art gallery, with an excellent restaurant. Ambitious programmes are laid on throughout the year: concerts, ballet, drama, the latest films and many good exhibitions of art.

Ness Islands, up-river away from Eden Court, form a public park spread over a series of small islands in the River Ness. They are linked by foot-bridges, with good views back down the river towards the town.

Tomnahurich—Hill of the Yews, sometimes called Hill of the Fairies—is the small, boat-shaped hillock to the southwest. Two wandering fiddlers, Thomas and Farquhar, were lured to Tomnahurich by the Fairy Queen, to play for a night's dancing. In the morning they found the town and its people strangely altered and everyone laughing at them. The 'night' had lasted a hundred years. They crept into a church for refuge—and crumbled into dust. Tomnahurich is now the town's cemetery, with many elaborate monuments clinging to the steep, wooded sides and a splendid viewing point from the top. Below lie the environs of Inverness, with neat, sturdy villas, well-kept gardens and an air of dependable respectability.

The northern entrance to the **Caledonian Canal** is in the western suburbs. It was constructed in the 19th century by Thomas Telford, and much used in the old days by boats wishing to avoid the long and often hazardous slog round the north coast. Still used by fishing boats, it now offers a perfect way for sailors to explore the Great Glen. Cabin cruisers can be hired from the marinas just down from the entrance, and passenger cruises operate in the summer.

The **Mill Shop** of Holm Woollen Mills (James Pringle), in the western suburbs of Inverness, is a good place to stock up on woollens, tweeds, kilts, rugs, etc. They also do factory tours.

19th-century **Cameron Barracks** stands on a ridge high above Millburn Road on the eastern edge of Inverness—a wise old sentinel guarding the town. From here, many a brave young Cameron Highlander walked out, newly trained, to give his life so that his Highland home should remain free.

Inverness to Nairn

The south side of the Moray Firth is flattish open farmland with sweeping views across to the Black Isle and the hills of Easter Ross.

Culloden

Taking the back roads, east of the A96, Culloden is about five miles east of Inverness. Start at the first-class new Visitor Centre on the edge of the battlefield (open daily, Easter–end Oct: adm for audio-visual show and cottage). The audio-visual show gives details of the tragic battle, on 16 April 1746, when Prince Charles Edward Stuart and his 5000 exhausted, starving and ill-equipped Highlanders were defeated by the Duke of Cumberland, son of George II, and his 9000 well-trained and equipped army. During that battle 1200 Highlanders fell; many more were butchered by order of the Duke as they lay wounded. Accounts of the Prince's reaction to the failure of his dreams vary: some say he tried to rally his Highlanders; some that he had to be held back from galloping forward to a hero's death; others are less starry-eyed. Whatever is true, one thing is sure: he was led away and hidden by loyal Highlanders for five months, with a price of £30,000 on his head, until he returned to the Continent in a French frigate, to live out the rest of his life in wretched, debauched exile.

As well as exhibitions and displays, the visitor centre has a study room for school parties, with a library and Jacobite relics. In addition there is a coffee shop and restaurant and a very good bookshop with a comprehensive range of Scottish publications.

The old cottage, outside, is the only building that survived the battle. It was still inhabited at the beginning of the 20th century and is now a Folk Museum. It still has its old furnishings and domestic equipment; taped music and Gaelic add an authentic touch.

On the battlefield (always open: free), wooden plaques tell which clan fought where, and how the battle progressed. There are clan graves: communal burial sites with headstones bearing clan names, and a great memorial cairn, erected in 1881. On the edge of the bleak battle site is the Well of the Dead where wounded Highlanders were slain as they drank water to revive themselves. A single stone bears the inscription 'The English were buried here'. The flat stone beyond the visitor centre is called the Cumberland Stone, thought to have been the vantage point from which the Duke viewed the battle.

The Clava Cairns are well signposted, a mile east of Culloden. These are a remarkable Stone and Bronze Age burial site, possibly dating from 2000 BC. Three large burial cairns in a peaceful glade of beech trees take you back in time to the pre-historic rituals that would have accompanied the internment of those farmers and herdsmen so many years ago. Two of the cairns have passages leading into them; the third has curious stone strips radiating from it like spokes of a wheel. Each is surrounded by a circle of standing stones, some inscribed with cup and ring symbols. Excavations revealed traces of cremated human bones, pottery and other remains: poignant memorials of people who were alive nearly 4000 years ago.

Kilravock Castle (pronounced Kilrawk) is five miles northeast of Culloden, still keeping to the back roads (open Wed afternoons, April–Sept, or by appointment, tel 06678 258: grounds open daily except Sun: adm). Dating from 15th century, this castle has been preserved almost intact because the owners never had enough money to mess about with its original design. In 1190, a Norman called Rose came north, married into a local family and settled on these lands. Kilravock has been the home of the Rose chiefs ever since. Among its relics are two reminders of Culloden—a punch bowl and a pair of leather thigh boots. Rose of Kilravock entertained Prince Charlie to lunch, the day before the battle, and offered punch from this bowl. He was not a Jacobite, but the Prince had ridden over to call on him and no true Highlander refuses hospitality. Shortly afterwards, Cumberland came blustering up, flushed with celebration of his 25th birthday: 'I hear, Sir, you've been entertaining my cousin!' Rose explained and was excused. Cumberland, for some inexplicable reason, left his boots behind. These two relics are an ironic reflection of the two people associated with them: Prince Charlie, merry and charismatic, who later drowned his failure in alcohol. Butcher Cumberland, brash, gross and cruel—very much a Jack-boot image. The gardens and grounds are lovely, especially in spring. Prince Charlie walked here with his host and watched young trees being planted. He remarked on the contrast between this peaceful scene and the commotion that was going on all round, preparing for the battle. Some of the beautiful old trees today must be the ones that were being planted. (Kilravock is now a hotel: see Where to Stay and Eat, below.)

Cawdor

Cawdor, pronounced Cawder, eight miles northeast of Culloden, is familiar to anyone who has read Shakespeare's *Macbeth*. Within moments of having been told by the witches he was to become Thane of Cawdor, Macbeth is told the king has indeed bestowed the title on him. The fulfilment of this prophecy encouraged him to bring about the final one, that he would be king, by murdering King Duncan.

Cawdor Castle (open daily 1 May–1 Oct: adm) dates from 1372, when the central tower was built. Domestic buildings were added in the 16th century and later re-modelled. Protected by a gully on one side and a dry moat on the other, the castle has a lovely walled garden, ablaze with colour in the summer. Floodlit at night, it is a real gem. Entry is over a drawbridge and the castle feels like a living home, rather than a museum, probably because it is indeed the home of the Cawdor family. The almost cosy, domestic atmosphere makes it easy to imagine it in medieval times, with its winding stairways and massive walls. Among the things to see are: Flemish tapestries, paintings, weapons, old domestic equipment and family heirlooms. Carbon dating has confirmed that the scrap of an ancient tree, railed off in the basement, is older than the castle, thus authenticating an old story. The original founder, Thane William, was granted a licence to build himself a fortress. He was told in a dream to load a donkey with panniers of gold and build a castle wherever it stopped. He obeyed and the donkey stopped for a rest in the shade of a thorn tree round which Thane William built his castle.

Outside there are nature trails, a nine-hole mini-golf course, putting green and picnic spots, as well as a licensed restaurant and souvenir shop.

In a conservation area, Cawdor village, straggling round the castle grounds, is not at all typical of Scotland: its peaceful cosiness matches that of the castle. The church is 17th-century, built in thanksgiving by the twelfth Lord Cawdor after he was saved from a shipwreck.

Cawdor Tavern is in the heart of the village. This delightful inn has a dark wood and velvet interior and is decorated by ornamental plates and hunting scenes, its atmosphere being almost that of an English pub. A bust of Shakespeare gazes benignly over the saloon where they serve quite good food.

Just northwest of Cawdor, across the River Nairn, **Nairnside Farm Sheep Dairy** is fascinating (shop and farm open daily except Dec and Jan: sheep-milking open Easter–Oct: adm). Sheep's milk was used to make cheese many centuries ago but the process almost died out after the 17th century. This enterprising revival, using the rich full-cream milk of ewes grazed on organically grown pasture, was started in 1985 with six sheep. There is now a flock of over 100 Friesland ewes whose milk is used to make delicious cheese, yogurt and yogurt ice-cream. Visitors can watch the sheep being milked at 3.45 pm from April to October. The farm shop sells all the dairy products, home-made jams and chutneys and local craftware. There is a miniature animal farm, pony and cart rides, a children's adventure play area, a tea room, and BBQ lunches—barbequed Highland beef and lamb steaks.

Fort George

Fort George (open daily: adm) is about eight miles northwest of Cawdor on the B9006, on a windswept promontory jutting out into the Moray Firth. It is the most unspoilt example of an artillery fort in Europe. Built between 1748 and 1769, to replace 'Old' Fort George in Inverness, destroyed by Prince Charlie in 1746, it is a classic 18th-century fortress. The defences include the traditional outer works: ravelin, ditch, bastion and rampart, designed by William Skinnor who was in his day the leading expert on artillery fortification. The government contractor who built it was John Adam, oldest son of architect William Adam, and brother of Robert.

Passing through the forbidding fortifications, one is brought to a delighted standstill by the mellow pink sandstone garrison buildings, their impeccable 18th-century proportions mercifully unscarred by Victorian or later 'improvement'.

The fort was built to house a garrison large enough to overawe Jacobite support in the Highlands, but by the time it was completed the Jacobite threat was finally dead, so it has never had a history of conflict. It became a base where a long series of regiments were mustered and equipped and whence they embarked for service in America, the West Indies, the Middle East, India and South Africa. In 1881, when each British infantry regiment was allocated its own territorial recruiting area and home base, Fort George became the depot of the Seaforth Highlanders. Generations of Highland soldiers trained there for colonial service, for two World Wars and for modern Cold War campaigns.

The regiments of the garrison change over every two years, and they have the privilege to live in barracks that are the oldest in the world still occupied by a battalion of British infantry.

The **Regimental Museum of the Queens Own Highlanders** (open daily except some Sat, April–Sept; weekdays, Oct–March: free, donations welcome) is in the fort. Formed in 1961 by the amalgamation of the Seaforth Highlanders and the Queen's Own Cameron Highlanders, they are the present-day descendants of the two historic regiments of the northern Highlands. In the building formerly used by the Lieutenant Governor, the Queen's Own Highlanders preserve a superb collection of uniforms, pictures, medals, weapons, colours, artifacts and treasures, representing nearly every major campaign fought by the British army over the past 200 years. The splendour of red coat and tartan, the glitter of gilt plate and dirk, the glint of steel broadsword and bayonet, cannot fail to stir the imagination and make hearts beat a little faster. With its history, its atmosphere and its garrison, Fort George is unique as a 20th-century military base where the 18th century lives on.

Nairn

Nairn, not quite nine miles east of Fort George, is a seaside holiday town, sometimes called the Brighton of the North. On the mouth of the River Nairn, it has wonderful sandy beaches along the Moray Firth, several golf courses and a reputation for a high average of sunshine. Imposing houses built by retired Victorian Empire-builders, and trim villas with neat gardens give it an aura of old-fashioned gentility. The Nairn Highland Games are in August. There is a Holiday Week and a Vintage Car Rally in July. The Fairground Fortnight and the Farmers Show are also in August.

Originally called Invernairn, the old fishertown is a picturesque collection of restored cottages. **Nairn Fishertown Museum** (open afternoons except Sun, May–Sept: adm) is in Laing Hall, King Street. Here you can see photographs and articles relating to the Moray Firth and the herring fisheries during the steam drifter era. There are also good displays of domestic life in a fishing community. **The Little Theatre**, also in Fishertown, is a small theatre with a repertory company who perform twice weekly in the summer.

See Grampian for Brodie Castle and Pluscarden Abbey, nearby, both well worth a visit during this tour from Inverness.

WHERE TO STAY AND EAT

Inverness has dozens of hotels and guest houses. **Caledonian Hotel**, Church Street, Inverness, tel 0463 235181, is convenient, right in the middle of town backing on to the river, but expensive, huge and soul-less with cabaret most nights. Another big one is **Drumossie Hotel**, on the A9 to Perth, three miles out of town, tel 0463 236451. Very modern, with glorious views over the Moray Firth, they are moderately priced and the food isn't too bad. **Bunchrew House Hotel**, Bunchrew, tel 0463 234917, is a much better bet, though bordering on expensive. A 16th-century mansion in 15 acres of gardens on the shores of the Beauly Firth about five miles west of Inverness, it has turrets and towers and a tremendous atmosphere. They only have six bedrooms. **Culloden House Hotel**, four miles east of Inverness, tel 0463 790461, is a lovely Georgian mansion built round a Jacobean castle. Prince Charlie made it his headquarters for two months before the Battle of Culloden, when it was the home of Duncan Forbes, the Lord President. (He and his officers managed to get through 60 hogsheads of the Lord President's claret—3150 imperial gallons—so perhaps the outcome of the battle was inevitable.) The hotel is expensive and luxurious, with an Adam dining room, four-poster and curtain-framed beds, ornate plasterwork and attractive grounds. The food is worth staying in for. **Dunain Park** , Inverness, tel 0463 230512, is a country house on the western outskirts, in six acres of lovely grounds. Comfortable and well-run, but bordering on the expensive. **Glendruidh House**, Old Edinburgh Road, Inverness, tel 0463 226499, is a delightful, family-run hotel in attractive grounds overlooking the Moray Firth and the town—and cheap.

Kilravock Castle, Croy, tel 06678 258, (see above for description) is a great experience for anyone who is an abstemious Christian. Pronounced 'Kilrawk' this historic old castle is where Prince Charlie lunched before Culloden. It stands in lovely, peaceful grounds near the river and the emphasis is very much on God: grace before meals, Bible readings and comment at breakfast and dinner; no drink—though naughty guests have been known to smuggle bottles into their cells and smoke up the chimney). There is a Wing, which is cheap, with country-house bedrooms, and historic rooms in the castle for a few pounds more.

Carnach Country House Hotel, Inverness Road, Nairn, tel 0667 52094, is at the lower end of the moderate price bracket, comfortable and peaceful, in eight acres overlooking the Moray Firth. Also overlooking the Firth, close to the Golf Course, at the top end of the moderate bracket, **Golf View Hotel**, Nairn, tel 0667 52301, is a family hotel with tennis courts, outdoor swimming pool, sauna, games room and regular entertainment.

All these hotels have their own restaurants: for a night out go to Culloden House, tel 0463 790461, and don't look at the prices. (An Adam dining room adds to the occasion.)

Inverness to Kingussie

The Spey, Scotland's second longest river, is born high in the hills above Loch Laggan, 40 miles south of Inverness and cuts across the southeast corner of the Highland region. Beginning as a tiny stream, it gathers momentum as it flows east and then north to the sea near Buckie in Grampian region, fed by many burns that drain from the hills on either side, turning it into a rushing tumult of water. Running between the great Cairngorms in the east and the Monadhliath Mountains to the west, the Spey is famous for astonishing natural beauty. In spring, fresh green shows through winter brown and snow still caps the mountains; in summer it is a patchwork of mulberry heather, emerald bracken, sparkling water and grey granite, enhanced by birdsong; in autumn, snow already dusts the hills making a backdrop to the splendour of the turning leaves; in winter, a white Alpine world dazzles and enchants. Get off the main roads and explore any of the minor roads and tracks: most of them reveal beautiful surprises.

Grantown-on-Spey

About 26 miles down the A9 from Inverness, branch left at Carrbridge on the A938. Grantown-on-Spey, 10 miles east and six miles south of the Grampian border, is one of Speyside's tourist centres. A pleasant Georgian town at the junction of several routes, it is well situated as a base for exploring the area. Standing by the river among trees, the town was founded in 1776 by Sir James Grant, one of the Highland's 'improving lairds'. With the development of skiing in the hills, this area is popular all the year round for holidays that offer a large variety of things to do, for all ages and all incomes. The Grantown-on-Spey Highland Games are held in June.

The Loch Garten Nature Reserve, eight miles south of Grantown-on-Spey, is well known for its breeding ospreys. Americans, accustomed to seeing these 'fish-hawks' in countless numbers nesting in their rivers and estuaries, are amused by the tight security that surrounds Scotland's few pairs, but it must be remembered that before the mid-1950s (when one pair set up their nest in a tree at Loch Garten) these birds had not been seen in Britain for almost 50 years. When an over-enthusiastic egg thief robbed this precious nest in 1958 precautions had to be taken. Now, it is not so unusual to look up and see the slow, flapping flight of one of these brown and white birds, or hear its shrill, cheeping cry. The nature reserve has a lot more than just ospreys for any one who is prepared to stand still and observe. Its rich bird life includes blackcock, capercailzie and crossbills, and among the animals are red squirrels and deer. In winter the haunting cry of geese and the eerie honk of whooper swans float across the dark waters of Loch Garten.

Boat of Garten, west of the loch, is so called after the ferry that operated here until a bridge was built in 1898. It is the home of the **Strathspey Steam Railway Association**, which has its own station and some remnants of the old Highland railway (closed in 1965). It was opened again in 1978 and enthusiasts can travel to Aviemore in a steam train. There is a small museum of railway memorabilia.

Aviemore

Aviemore, about 14 miles southwest of Grantown-on-Spey, is a thriving tourist centre and ski resort, teeming with energetic holiday makers. Dominated by the Cairngorms, with several peaks over 4000 feet, this area has some of Scotland's grandest scenery.

For some, the chocolate-boxy **Loch-an Eilean**, just south of Aviemore, with its pines, hills and castle, is a gem.

Aviemore has every sort of accommodation, cafés and restaurants, bistros and bars, gift shops, craft shops, souvenir stalls, amusement arcades and discos. It is just the place for gregarious people looking for action. Throughout the year the surrounding country-side is a kaleidoscope of anoraks and knapsacks, or psychedelic skiing clothes, or shorts and tee-shirts.

Within spitting distance of this seething hub of sporting activity lie remote, heather-clad moors, craggy mountains, wooded valleys, cool, tumbling burns and deep, mysteri-ous lochs.

The Aviemore Centre (open daily: adm for various attractions) offers a bewildering choice of activity. There is an ice rink and curling rink, swimming pool, theatre, cinema, ballroom, artificial ski slope, games room, sauna, solarium, squash courts, go-kart track, craft village and children's outdoor amusements.

Loch Morlich, five miles to the east, has developed as a water-sports centre for gregarious aquarians—camping and caravanning included, not for the recluse. **Kincraig Highland Wildlife Park** (open daily, March–Nov: adm) is six miles south-west of Aviemore. Animals that used to roam free over the Highlands live here in a natural setting: boar, wolves, bears, bison and many more. You drive through the park and must leave any pets in the kennels provided. There are also aviaries with indigenous birds such as capercailzie, eagles and hawks, and an exhibition on man and fauna in the Highlands.

Loch Inch, a mile southeast of Kincraig, is formed by a widening of the river and is surrounded by blue hills and trees. **Loch Inch Watersports and Skiing Centre** offers courses in canoeing, wind surfing, sailing, swimming and skiing; an excellent action holiday.

The tiny white 18th-century church on a rocky point at the northern end of the loch was built on a site said to have been used by Druids, and used continually for Christian worship since the 6th century. Inside there is an 8th-century hand bell that was shaken to call the faithful to worship, before the days of bells in steeples. The Rock Wood Ponds, southeast of the loch are rich in wild life.

The gaunt shell of **Ruthven Barracks** (pronounced Rivven) stands on a hillock east of the A9, five miles southwest of Kincraig, dramatically floodlit at night. On the site of a stronghold of the Wolf of Badenoch (notorious son of Robert II) it was built after the 1715 Jacobite uprising to discourage further rebellion, and further extended by General Wade in 1734. Prince Charlie captured it from government troops during his ascend-ancy, and it was here, after Culloden, that some 1500 surviving Jacobites assembled, awaiting their Prince. They waited in vain, until they received the message that the cause was dead and they must now fend for themselves. On the day after the battle, Lord George Murray sat down in the Barracks and wrote a long, bitter letter to the Prince, resentfully listing all the blunders that had contributed to their defeat. Prince Charlie never forgave him. Before disbanding to return to the homes they had so eagerly left, the loyal Highlanders, abandoned by their leader, blew Ruthven up to save it from the enemy.

Kingussie

Kingussie, a mile to the west and now by-passed by the A9, is another popular holiday resort all the year round. Pronounced Kinusie, it is a pleasant little town with one main street, backed by lovely Highland scenery. The Badenoch and Strathspey Music Festival is held here in March.

The Highland Folk Museum (open daily, April–Oct, and on weekdays, Nov–March: adm) is a 'must' for anyone interested in Highland life and folklore. It was founded in Iona in the 1930s and later moved here under the control of the universities of Glasgow, Edinburgh, St Andrews and Aberdeen. Beautifully arranged, both indoors and outside, it includes an 18th-century shooting lodge, a black-house from Lewis, a clack mill (named from its 'clacking' noise), a turf-walled house from the central Highlands and many fascinating exhibits of farming and domestic life. Don't miss the exhibition of Highland tinkers.

From Kingussie, south to the Tayside Border, the A9 goes through magnificent scenery, backed by hills, forest and moor, through Glen Truim to Dalwhinnie, crossing the border through the Pass of Drumochter. Very isolated and unpopulated, this is not an area for running out of petrol on a winter's night.

The A86, west from Kingussie to Glen Roy and Spean Bridge, runs through glens flanked by steep hills, the road dipping and climbing beside Loch Laggan, alive with the clatter of falling burns. Cars should be abandoned for some of the glorious walks up valleys into the hills, past secret lochans and hidden glens.

WHERE TO STAY AND EAT

See also previous section. Moderately priced **Carrbridge Hotel**, tel 047984 202, is an old-established, rambling, easy-going establishment. **Struan House** also in Carrbridge, is an extremely nice friendly place in the middle of the village. It's cheap, with log fires, tennis and a small dry ski-slope and putting green. There are lots of hotels and guest houses in Grantown-on-Spey. **Grant Arms** in the town centre, tel 0479 2526, is a moderately priced, respectable, old-fashioned grey pile. A bit cheaper, **Garth Hotel** in Castle Road, tel 0479 2836, is a pleasant white and black building just off the square, dating from the 17th century, in four acres of landscaped garden, very comfortable with good service. Cheaper still, **Seafield Lodge Hotel,** in Woodside Avenue, tel 0479 2152, is a fishing hotel and runs fishing courses. Moderately priced **Boat Hotel** Boat of Garten, tel 047983 258, is a country house near the loch with 6 miles of fishing on the Spey, and a good reputation for food.

In Aviemore there is a big choice. **Stakis Badenoch**, which also has chalets, tel 0479 810261, and **Stakis Four Seasons**, tel 0479 810681, are both at Aviemore Centre and look more like something in Benidorm than the Highlands. Both also give moderately priced, soul-less comfort and all mod cons. **Stakis Coylumbridge Resort Hotel**, three miles out of Aviemore, is much the same. **Freedom Inn** in Aviemore Centre, tel 0479 810781, is a modern monstrosity, but moderately priced with a cheerful staff. Also moderately priced, **Red McGregor Hotel**, tel 0479 810256, on the main road in the village, is attractive, olde worlde and comfortable.

In Kingussie, **Columba House Hotel**, Manse Road, tel 0540 661402, and **The Osprey Hotel**, tel 0540 661510, are both cheap, good value with no frills. Moderately priced **Muckrach Lodge Hotel**, Dulnain Bridge, tel 047985 257, is an old family home with a good reputation for comfort and food in attractive grounds.

Inverness to Glencoe via the Great Glen

400 million years ago, Scotland split apart along what is now the Great Glen, the fissure being eroded by glaciers in the Ice Age until the final retreat of the ice as recently as 10 million years ago. The Caledonian Canal, a waterway through the glen, was surveyed by James Watt in 1773. Thomas Telford started work on construction in 1803, and finally completed it in 1847. 22 miles of its 60-mile length is true canal, the rest taking advantage of the natural lochs and rivers in the rift. The Great Glen, starting with Loch Ness, is spectacular and the best way to enjoy it is by boat. Caley Cruisers, Canal Road Inverness, tel 0463 236328, hire boats sleeping from four to eight. Passenger cruises include: Jacobite Cruises, tel 0463 233999 and Loch Ness Cruises (Drumnadrochit), tel 04562 395.

Loch Ness is world famous, thanks to Nessie: it is also extremely beautiful. Long and narrow, its steep wooded banks form a wind-funnel, causing surprisingly rough seas at times. Depths of 900 ft have been recorded, deeper than much of the North Sea.

Feelings run high over Nessie—the Loch Ness Monster—known to the *cognoscente* as Nessiterras Rhombopteryx. Sceptics may scoff, but St Adamnan, not given to telling fibs, records a sighting of her in his biography of St Columba, when they were sailing up the loch to convert Inverness. Columba, it seems, had a calming effect on her when she threatened one of his monks, and she has never been troublesome again. Setting aside whisky-induced hallucinations, and wishful-thinking sightings, many eye-witness accounts of Nessie come from people whose honesty and integrity are beyond doubt. A 16th-century chronicle describes 'a terrible beast issuing out of the water early one morning about midsummer, knocking down trees and killing three men with its tail.' A monk who was organist in Westminster Cathedral saw her in 1973, and several of the monks at Fort Augustus Abbey have seen her. Thirty hotel guests saw two humps appear in an explosion of surf which cruised half a mile before sinking, in 1961. Bertram Mills was sufficiently convinced to offer £20,000 to have Nessie delivered alive to his circus. However logical one is, it is impossible to drive down Loch Ness without hopefully scanning the dark waters. Anyone who spends a night at anchor in a boat on the loch will find themselves starting up in the darkness, every time a ripple slaps the hull.

There are two roads down Loch Ness from Inverness: the A82 is the main road down the west side, with excellent views of the loch and quite a lot of traffic in the summer. The B862/852 is much less frequented, very attractive, but with not so many views of the loch, some sections of it being inland.

The Loch Ness Monster Exhibition Centre is at **Drumnadrochit**, 15 miles down from Inverness on the A82, west-side route. (Open daily: adm.) Here, in a monstrous modern building, is all the information known about Nessie: documents, photographs, possible explanations, models, a sonar room, etc., presented objectively. A fascinating study for sceptic and credulous alike. In the summer there is also a tartan shop and a House of Heraldry, where people can check up on their origins. There is a glass blower, too, and a Hollywood model of Nessie for family photographs.

Urquhart Castle (open daily: adm) is just beyond Drumnadrochit on the southern tip of Urquhart Bay, overlooking Loch Ness with free off-road parking, from where there is an excellent overview of the whole layout before walking down to explore. A jagged keep rises from crumbling walls against a lovely backdrop of loch and hills beyond. This was once one of the largest castles in Scotland, dating from the 14th century. Built on the site of a vitrified fort, it was given to John Grant of Freuchie in 1509 by James IV. In 1692 it was blown up to save it from Jacobite hands. Romantics say that Nessie lives in a subterranean cave below the castle.

At **Balbeg**, about four miles on, is the memorial cairn to John Cobb who was killed in 1952, trying to break the world water speed record on Loch Ness's measured mile. The memorial is inscribed in Gaelic: 'Honour to the brave and to the humble'.

Fort Augustus, on the southern end of Loch Ness, is the halfway halt down the Great Glen; a popular tourist centre with an ancient history. There is a pre-Christian crannog, Cherry Island, just to the north in Loch Ness.

The town's original name was Kilcumein (burial place of Cumein who was one of St Columba's followers). After the Jacobite rising in 1715, barracks were built in the town to quell further rebellion and there are still traces of the old buildings behind the Lovat Arms Hotel. General Wade made his headquarters here in 1724, and in 1729 began the building of the fort, beside the loch. It was named Augustus after William Augustus, Duke of Cumberland, at that time the fat, eight-year-old schoolboy son of George II, who was to go down in history as Butcher Cumberland. Jacobites took the fort in 1745 and held it until after Culloden. Lord Lovat bought the ruins and presented them to a Benedictine community in 1876, for the founding of an abbey, now a public school. Much of the old fort was incorporated into the ground floor. The Great Glen Gala is a lively occasion in Fort Augustus in July.

To complete a circular tour of Loch Ness, rather than go on down the Great Glen, take the B862 from Fort Augustus back up the east side, which is prettier and quieter, with several good walks and lovely views. Part of the way is one of General Wade's military roads, built in anticipation of further Jacobite uprisings.

Just after Whitebridge, 10 miles from Fort Augustus, the road forks. Five miles to the right, at Aberchalder, there is an alpine garden nestling in a glen in the hills, its ornamental rockeries overlaid by the sweet scent of pines. The left fork goes to **Foyers**, where there are lovely signposted woodland walks and a spectacular waterfall. From Inverfarigaig, about three miles northeast of Foyers, back to Inverness, there are a large number of excavated remains of burial chambers, forts and cairns, some in good condition, including a vitrified Iron Age fort, at **Ashie Moor**, west of Loch Duntelchaig.

Going on down the Great Glen from Fort Augustus, **Tobar nan Ceann** is the 'Well of the Heads' monument beside the road on the western shore of Loch Oich. An obelisk supports the bronze heads of seven men, held together by a dirk through their hair. Beyond, steps lead through a damp tunnel to a sinister well underneath. This is where Iain Lom MacDonell, poet of his clan, washed the severed heads of the murderers of his chief, Alasdair MacDonell, 12th Chief of Keppoch, in 1663. He presented the washed heads to MacDonell of Glengarry, who had refused to help him avenge the murder. It was the 15th Chief MacDonell of Glengarry who erected the monument in the 19th century. Inscribed in English, Gaelic, French and Latin are the words: 'this ample and summary vengeance'.

Nearby, three days before the raising of the standard at Glenfinnan, two companies of government troops surrendered to a handful of Jacobite Macdonalds. They had heard a great din of pipes and noise and believed themselves to be in the midst of a mighty army.

A little further down, at **Laggan** between Loch Lochy and Loch Oich, there was a ferocious clan battle between the Frasers and the Macdonalds in 1544. It was called the Battle of the Shirts, because it was so hot they all threw off their cumbersome plaids and fought in their shirts.

Several routes meet at **Spean Bridge**, about 12 miles south down Loch Lochy. Just short of the village is the much-photographed **Commando Memorial** by Scott Sutherland, erected in 1952. A bronze group of commandos stand on a high promontory looking out over the magnificent view towards Ben Nevis and Lochaber, surrounded by the wild, harsh terrain where they trained during the Second World War. The stark simplicity of the statue is dramatic.

Spean Bridge Woollen Mill is worth a visit for anyone who wants to buy traditional Scottish tweeds and woollens.

Glen Roy is a slight detour from Roy Bridge, three miles east of Spean Bridge on the A86. At first it seems just another wild glen, with the River Roy tumbling down through wooded gorges to flatten out and meander at a more stately pace across the valley floor, bare hills rising on either side. Stop at the large observation car park some way along and look down the valley. A number of horizontal lines run across the hillside, quite high up, each line exactly matched by one on the opposite side of the valley. These 'parallel roads' are terraces left by the receding water-line of the ice lake that once filled the valley. They are geologically famous because of their clarity, and date from a late Ice Age build-up about 11,000 years ago.

Several secret glens lie beyond the end of the track. Tucked away up in the hills the source of the Roy, about six miles from the end of the road, is very close to the source of the Spey, gathering courage for its long trek to the sea.

Glen Loy is another detour from Spean Bridge, six miles west on the B8004, through Kilmonivaig. This was the route taken by Prince Charlie, marching at the head of his army just after raising his father's standard at Glenfinnan—a proud, ill-equipped, untrained column of men, fired with the heady fuel of loyalty and hope for a better future.

Continuing on down the Great Glen from Spean Bridge on the A82, **Inverlochy Castle** stands by the road about eight miles to the southwest. The 15-foot wire fence round it is because of the state of its stonework. This crumbling ruin dates from the 13th century. It has a walled courtyard and round corner towers, one of which was the keep, and a water gate. The castle was once a stronghold of the Comyns and scene of several battles, including one in 1645, in which Montrose defeated a Covenanting army under Argyll with a loss of 1500 men. Legend tells of a Pictish settlement on this site, where King Archaius signed a treaty with Charlemagne in 790.

Fort William

Fort William is 10 miles southwest of Spean Bridge and is the southern gateway to the Caledonian Canal. It is a busy little tourist resort, the epitome of a west Highland town, shopping centre for the whole of this area and the hub of several routes. It lies in the lee of Ben Nevis, Britain's highest mountain, 4406 ft—a rather ugly lump, with several ways to the top depending on expertise and physical fitness.

The fort from which the town was named was demolished in the 19th century to make way for the railway. It was first built by General Monk in 1655, an earth construction that proved to be of insufficient strength when put to the test by rebellious Highlanders later in the century. It was then re-built in stone and named Maryburgh after the wife of King William III, before being named in honour of the king himself. It withstood Jacobite attacks in 1715 and 1746. The town which grew up around the railway is Victorian and sturdy, with a cheerful holiday atmosphere.

Steam trains run from Fort William to Mallaig from May to October, past many historic sites, through glorious scenery. Special trips linked with a visit to Skye are arranged every Sunday from the end of June to mid September. It is essential to book in advance: tel 0397 703791.

Don't miss the **Great Glen Sheepdog Trials** at the end of June or beginning of July. The Highland Games are also in July and the Lochaber Agricultural Show is in August.

The West Highland Museum (open daily except Sun: adm), in Cameron Square, is crammed with interesting historical, natural history and folk exhibits. There is a crofter's kitchen, just as it was in the old days with all the original equipment, as well as agricultural implements. Montrose's helmet and many Jacobite relics are displayed. The most fascinating exhibit is the 'secret' portrait of the prince, used in the days when loyal Jacobites toasted 'the king across the water', a meaningless blur of paint until you view it from the right angle through a cylinder, when it is transformed into a recognizable portrait.

It is fun to pass a sunny hour or so leaning over the rails beside the long ladder of locks that bring the Caledonian Canal down to the level of the sea. The locks are used by fishing boats and pleasure craft and the gates are hydraulically operated, the water boiling through sluices until the level is equal either side. Eight of the 11 locks that link Loch Linnhe with the canal are called **Neptune's Staircase**, a rise of 80 ft which presented Telford with an enormous problem when he built the canal.

There is a new skiing complex four miles north of Fort William on **Aonach Mor**, close to Ben Nevis. Nevis Range, the operators, anticipate more people using the Gondola System lifts in the summer than in the winter.

A fast road runs along the east side of Loch Linnhe to the new Ballachulish Bridge, 13 miles to the south (pronounced Balla-hoolish). The bridge spans a narrow constriction between Loch Linnhe and Leven, where not so long ago a small car ferry used to slither and slide on the fast current. Look out for the stark, stone memorial to James Stewart, with its bitter inscription, beside the road. Stewart was falsely hanged for the 'Appin Murder' in 1752, on which R. L. Stevenson based *Kidnapped* and its sequel, *Catriona*. The staunchly Jacobite Stewarts of Appin had to forfeit their lands after Culloden. The Crown factor, Colin Campbell of Glenure, known as The Red Fox, took delight in evicting Stewarts in favour of Campbells. He was assassinated during one of his forays and James Stewart was unjustly used as a scapegoat, tried before the Duke of Argyll at Inverary by a jury of 11 Campbells, found guilty and hanged. The rough stone on top of the monument came from his farm.

Loch Linnhe is always busy with pleasure boats in the summer.

Glencoe

Glencoe is four miles to the east. This dramatic pass with raw peaks reaching up on either side is slashed by white scars of cascading water. In good weather, away from the road, Glencoe is staggeringly beautiful, with creaming burns and falls, glistening rocks and hidden lochs and glens. But when the weather closes in, there is an unmistakable aura of doom, enhanced by its well-known history. *Glen Coe* means 'Glen of Weeping', and many tears were shed on 13 February 1692. Macdonald of Glencoe, late with his oath of allegiance to King William III, provided the government with an excuse to get rid of his powerful clan. It was an affair of the greatest possible dishonour. Campbell of Glenlyon billeted himself and 128 soldiers with the Macdonalds for several days, living as guests and accepting the generous hospitality that was such an integral part of Highland life. The Campbells, acting on higher authority, rose one dawn and massacred their hosts as they slept. No one can drive through the glen now, 300 years later, and not glance up into the hills and remember that bitter morning and hear the cries of the women and children, and see the bloodstains in the snow. The Massacre Memorial, in the village of Glencoe, is a tall, slender cross—a poignant reminder of senseless slaughter.

Glencoe and North Lorne Folk Museum (open daily except Sun: May–Sept: adm) is in Glencoe village. It contains many Jacobite and historic exhibits, domestic implements, weapons, costumes, photographs, dolls and dolls' houses, tools, and much else, all housed in a group of thatched houses.

The National Trust for Scotland has a Visitor Centre, two miles east of the village. Already efficient and full of information, a refurbishment is planned to coincide with the tercentenary of the Massacre. Meanwhile, the existing one is more than adequate.

Clachaig, two miles east of Glencoe village, is a rather run-down hotel/hostel which always seems to be peopled by cold, wet climbers sitting about looking miserable. Here a resident warden will advise about good walks and climbing in the glen. This is a centre for some of the most challenging mountaineering in the country, much of which is not suitable for amateurs. There is a chair lift and T-bars for skiers at the head of the glen, and good skiing on Meall a Bhuridh, when conditions are right.

Loch Ossian is about 17 miles northeast of Glencoe as the crow flies, tucked into a valley surrounded by hills and inaccessible by road. There is a youth hostel and the train stops at Currour Station, but the energetic should get out the map and attack it on foot. It is a lovely 10-mile tramp from Black Corries Lodge, over the shoulder of Stob na Cruaiche, round the eastern end of Blackwater Reservoir and along the course of the railway.

Beyond Glencoe, Rannoch Moor stretches away to the east, a vast swampy wasteland, unpopulated except by birds, bleak even in summer.

WHERE TO STAY AND EAT

The grandest is the Victorian mansion, **Inverlochy Castle Hotel**, at Torlundy three miles north of Fort William, tel 0397 702177. Like certain high-class jewellers, it is so exclusive it doesn't publish its prices. When you enquire, in a discreet whisper, the answer is equally hushed. Check with your bank manager; if he sounds foxy, try **Croit**

Anna Hotel Fort William, tel 0397 702268. It's cheapish, ugly, and modern. Fort William has dozens of other hotels and guest houses. **Alexandra Hotel**, tel 0397 702241, in Old Fort Parade, is old-fashioned, moderately priced, not wildly exciting but dependable. **Ballachulish Hotel**, tel 08552 606, has a marvellous position overlooking the water and the food is excellent.

Kings House Hotel in Glencoe, tel 08556 259, claims to be Scotland's oldest inn. Whether it is or not, it is cheap and cosy, in dramatic surroundings.

Corriegour Lodge Hotel, Loch Lochy, near Spean Bridge, tel 039781 685, is a lot more fun, with the sort of easy-going atmosphere money can't buy, good views over the loch and reasonable food, moderately priced. Slightly more expensive, **Spean Bridge Hotel**, tel 039781 250, is old-fashioned, comfortable and jolly. **Roy Bridge Hotel**, tel 039781 201, is at the entrance to Glen Roy, a cheap, pleasant, well-run hotel with passable food. **Glengarry Castle Hotel**, at Invergarry, tel 08093 254, is a rather grim-looking pile but should suit those who hanker for ghosts. Not historic itself, it has in its grounds the ruins of Invergarry Castle, where the seven severed heads were presented to the chief of the MacDonells of Glengarry (see Tobar nan Ceann, p. 399). The hotel is moderately priced, quite comfortable, in a lovely position overlooking Loch Oich, only open from April to October. **Invergarry Hotel**, tel 08093 206, is nice, cheap, and recently completely refurbished.

For Monster-spotters, **Loch Ness Lodge Hotel** at Drumnadrochit, tel 04562 342, has a lot to offer. Moderately priced, perched above Loch Ness, the hotel is comfortable and friendly and includes a Visitor Centre with interesting exhibits of local history and culture and a 200-seat cinema with simultaneous translations in six languages. Another one for Monster-spotters is **Drumnadrochit Hotel** at the Exhibition Centre, tel 04562 218. Surrounded by monsterabilia, this is cheap and slightly tawdry. **Lewiston Arms Hotel**, near Drumnadrochit, tel 04562 225, is a charming, 200-year-old inn in a pretty garden and very cheap. **Glenmoriston Arms Hotel**, tel 0320 51206, is a traditional Highland inn, also cheap, with comfortable rooms, good food and a choice of 170 malt whiskies.

Lovat Arms Hotel, Fort Augustus, tel 0320 6206, is moderately priced and comfortable, overlooking Loch Ness and the abbey. Good food. **Knockie Lodge Hotel**, Whitebridge, tel 04563 276, in a old family house, in wild, remote scenery high above Loch Ness, is expensive and comfortable, with fishing.

West of the Great Glen to Kyle of Lochalsh

There is a lovely detour from Invermoriston or from Invergarry, 13 miles to the south, off the A82. The two roads join up and go west of the Great Glen to Kyle of Lochalsh, the stepping stone to the Isle of Skye. The A887 from Invermoriston goes 16 miles through lovely Glen Moriston to meet the A87 from Invergarry. 12 miles from Invermoriston, look out for the cairn beside the road beyond Achlain. It is in memory of a brave man,

Roderick Mackenzie, an Edinburgh lawyer, who had the dubious honour of being a Bonnie Prince Charlie look-alike. Hoping to deflect government troops from their quest for the Prince's head after Culloden, Mackenzie allowed himself to be captured. He lost his life for his gallantry and his head was presented to Butcher Cumberland in triumph at Fort Augustus.

The A87 is an excellent new road through impressive Highland scenery, along the north side of Loch Garry, over high wild moorland with sweeping views. Five miles west of Invergarry, a narrow single-track road goes out to **Kinloch Hourn**, Loch of Hell. This, despite its name, is another glorious sea loch, snaking out towards the western isles, steep sided and treacherous for sailors in certain winds. The Glengarry Highland Games are held in July.

After the two roads join, the A87 runs north of Loch Cluanie, through mountain passes that are a patchwork of heather and scree, with rich wooded glens where the many rivers and burns cascade down from the surrounding hills. The Five Sisters of Kintail dominate Glen Shiel.

At **Shiel Bridge** on Loch Duich, 10 miles west of Cluanie, a narrow, twisting road branches left and climbs over the **Mam Ratagan Pass**. This was the route taken by the drovers bringing cattle and sheep from Skye, down to trysts at Falkirk and Crieff. It follows the course of the military road out to **Fort Bernera**, eight miles west of Shiel Bridge. Johnson and Boswell travelled along this road in 1772, when soldiers were still working on it. The ruins of the Bernera Barracks are north of Glenelg, just before the ferry across to Kylerhea in Skye. They were built in 1722 and used until after 1790. Boswell eyed them as he shepherded an ill-humoured Dr Johnson towards what proved to be very poor lodgings: 'I looked at them wishfully, as soldiers have always everything in the best order.'

Glen Beg runs east off a narrow road two miles south of Glenelg. Here are two of the most splendid examples of the Iron Age brochs built to provide shelter and refuge for the chiefs and their people: **Dun Telve** and **Dun Troddan**. Their double walls are honeycombed with galleries, and pierced by a single small entrance, easily defended. At the end of the road a track leads to Dun Grugaig, an earlier fort, on the brink of a steep gorge.

Not far south of Glen Beg is Sandaig. The house where Gavin Maxwell lived with his otters was on the beach below Upper Sandaig—it was burnt to the ground. In his books, *Ring of Bright Water*, *The Rocks Remain*, etc, Maxwell miscalls the place Camusfeàrna (bay of the alders), in order to preserve its remoteness and isolation. There are many other, genuine Camusfeàrnas in Scotland, causing some confusion.

This rough road goes right on down to Arnisdale and Glen Corran on Loch Hourn, 10 miles or so to the south, with more glorious views.

Back on the main road round Loch Duich, stop at Morvich, two miles beyond Shiel Bridge at the head of the loch. There is a National Trust for Scotland visitor centre here, with an audio-visual exhibition giving an excellent picture of the surrounding Kintail estate, with its many walks and climbs. They have details of the route out to the spectacular Falls of Glomach, three miles further on by road to the northeast and then about a 4-mile walk and climb. The 370ft falls are among the highest in Britain, falling in two spectacular cascades over a projecting rock, into a breathtakingly deep chasm. The

Eilean Donan Castle

air is full of the sound of water and the sides of the gorge are hung with lush green ferns and foliage. Keep a wary eye out for water-sprites.

Eilean Donan Castle (open daily, Easter–Sept: adm) is 10 miles northwest of Shiel Bridge, one of the most photographed castles in Scotland. Standing on a rocky island reached by a causeway, on the edge of Loch Duich, it was built in 1230, on the site of an ancient fort, and was the seat of the MacKenzies, Earls of Seaforth. It was garrisoned by Spanish troops in 1719, supporting one of the Jacobite attempts to regain the throne for the Stuarts: in reprisal it was bombarded by English warships. Now most splendidly restored, it is open to the public and dedicated as a war memorial to the Clan Macrae, who held the castle as Constables to the Earls of Seaforth. Among other things are interesting Jacobite relics.

Kyle of Lochalsh is seven miles west, terminus for the railway from Inverness and the ferry to Skye. This busy little holiday resort has several shops and is usually full of a cheerful crowd of holiday makers. Cars queue up, waiting to catch the ferry to Kyleakin, a frequent service that takes only a few minutes. There are plenty of good walks round here.

WHERE TO STAY AND EAT
See also previous and following sections.

Lochalsh Hotel, tel 0599 4204, stands right on the water at Kyle of Lochalsh, a huge, expensive hotel, worth every penny for position alone, but also for comfort and good food. A lot cheaper and just as nice in a different way, **Balmacara Hotel** nearby, tel 059986 283, looks across Loch Alsh. **The Castle Inn,** Dornie, tel 059985 205, moderately priced, has a reputation for being particularly kind and hospitable to weary travellers. The food is good, they offer trout fishing and you can hire their motor launch.

The Southwest Corner

The southwestern corner of the Highland Region is Jacobite country. It is also yet another enchanted land, full of beauty as well as history. Cars should be abandoned whenever possible and sailors should put to sea.

The **Corran Ferry**, nine miles southwest of Fort William, crosses Loch Linnhe at the Corran Narrows, a frequent service taking 5 minutes. Several districts occupy the peninsula to the west and south: Ardgour, Moidart, Sunart, Ardnamurchan, Morvern and Kingairloch. Rugged, mountainous and beautiful, deeply cut by lochs and glens, with endless staggering vistas, this is one of the most magical corners of Scotland.

The road south from Corran goes down Loch Linnhe, branching left after seven miles to become the B8043. Keep on southwest through Morvern, cut by lush green glens alive with the sound of water and bird song. **Lochaline**, on the southern shore of the peninsula, means 'the beautiful loch'. It faces across the Sound of Mull to Fishnish Point, linked by a fairly frequent car ferry taking 15 minutes. Silica sand is mined at Lochaline, used for making optical glass.

There is no road to **Ardtornish Castle** on a point a couple of miles east of Lochaline. Built in 1340, it was for many years a stronghold of the Lords of the Isles. The ruined keep and ramparts are custodians of a stirring past when proud, independent chiefs ruled over this territory with a total disregard for the authority of the Crown.

Fiunary is five miles west of Lochaline along the coast, once home of the Macleods. George Macleod, the left-wing Presbyterian who re-established a community on Iona in 1938, took the name Lord Macleod of Fiunary when he was 'elevated' from cleric to life peer in 1967. There are lovely views across the sound from this road, which peters out after eight or nine miles.

Strontian, north of Lochaline on the A884, is at the head of Loch Sunart. From Strontian Lead Mines, opened in 1722, came the discovery of strontianite. (Strontium 90, the isotope, is produced in nuclear fall-out.) These mines, manned by French prisoners of war, provided bullets for the Napoleonic Wars. There is a well-stocked yacht chandler here and an inn where groups of holiday makers often create their own spontaneous ceilidhs in the summer months. It was just off Strontian, in Loch Sunart, that the 'Floating Church' was anchored, in 1843, during the 'Disruption', when the Free Church broke away from the Church of Scotland. The local laird refused members of the breakaway church land on which to build their kirk, so they bought an old ship on the Clyde, fitted it up as a church and towed it to Loch Sunart; the congregation rowed out to worship in it.

Loch Sunart is a perfect, safe anchorage for boats. For sailors, there can be few more enjoyable experiences than to sail out of Loch Sunart early on a fine morning, the wind on your quarter, the sun on your back, watching the whole of the island-studded Minch open up ahead.

Half-way along the north shore of Loch Sunart, the B8007 is a cul-de-sac branching west to **Ardnamurchan**, a rugged, windlashed peninsula, familiar to west coast yachtsmen as the most westerly point on the mainland of the British Isles. The ruin of **Mingary Castle**, about 16 miles along, was once the stronghold of the MacIans of

406

Ardnamurchan. The castle stood on a rock cliff guarding the entrance to Loch Sunart and to the Sound of Mull. James VI came to Mingary to receive the homage of the Lords of the Isles, and was disappointed by their lack of enthusiasm for his sovereignty. The castle was taken by Montrose's men in 1644 and garrisoned in 1745 by government soldiers, who built a barracks within the walls.

Ardnamurchan Point, about 22 miles from Salen, is wild, heather-clad bed-rock with a lighthouse at its tip, at present closed to the public. This dramatic headland takes the full force of westerly gales and can present quite a challenge to small boats, even in lighter winds.

Moidart, north from Salen, has a Jacobite legend in every glen, hill and loch. **Acharacle** (difficult to pronounce: the 'ch' is guttural) is a sheltered little village at the western end of **Loch Sheil**, three miles north of Salen. From here, **Ardtoe** is another three miles west on **Kentra Bay**. This sheltered, sandy haven has been turned into a vast seawater reserve for white fish farming. Ardtoe is a delightful little hamlet, very popular with artists.

Castle Tioram

Just north of Acharacle, an unmarked lane to the left twists and turns out to the South Channel of Loch Moidart, and one of the most stirring, romantic ruins in Scotland. Castle Tioram, pronounced Chiram, more or less, stands high on a rocky promontory, reached on foot by causeway at low tide. This 13th- to 14th-century castle was the seat of Macdonalds of Clanranald. It was burnt in 1715 by the staunchly Jacobite chief, to prevent it from falling into government hands while he was away fighting at Sheriffmuir. The tower dates from 1600; the walls enclose an inner courtyard, with several chambers. The castle has witnessed much of Scotland's history.

In 1984 these ancient walls became the fine setting for a gathering of Clanranald Macdonalds from all over the world. They were entertained by their chief, in the roofless banqueting hall, roasting whole lambs in the old hearth, and for a few hours the castle lived again. The darkness was vibrant with pipe music and laughter. The next day an open-air Mass was celebrated in the courtyard to re-dedicate the Clanranald banner, said to have survived from Culloden.

It was at **Kinlochmoidart**, five miles north of Acharacle, that Prince Charlie waited while the clans were rallied to his cause, and it was here that his charm won over the chiefs who were reluctant to take part in his rebellion.

The road twists up through Moidart and follows the zigzag of **Loch Ailort** to its head. Here turn left on the A830 (another cul-de-sac) for about six miles to **Loch nan Uamh** (Loch of the Caves). Here, on 25 July 1745, Prince Charlie landed from Eriskay, with only seven companions, at the start of his campaign to restore the crown to the Stuarts. A cairn, on a crag overlooking the loch beside the road, commemorates the event. A year later, broken and defeated, the Prince embarked from this same place, to return to France, effectively ending what became known as *Bliadna Thearlaich* (Charlie's Year). The nobbly hills of South Morar, to the northeast, mottled sepia-greyish, are rather gloomy.

Arisaig, about seven miles west of the cairn, has a sheltered anchorage and is a peaceful holiday village from which boat cruises run to the islands. Around the bay, where trawlers lie at anchor, attractive houses cling to the hillside. The prominent tower of the Catholic church was erected in memory of Alasdair MacMhaigstir Alasdair, one of the greatest of the Gaelic poets, who took the Jacobite side in 1745. The tower is a landmark for boats. Arisaig has its Highland Games in July.

Morar, about seven miles north of Arisaig, stands on a sheltered bay with the most glorious silver sands. **Loch Morar** runs nine miles eastwards, the deepest inland loch in Europe at over 1000 ft. North Morar, on its far shore, and Knoydart, beyond Loch Nevis to the north, are wild and roadless, accessible only by boat or on foot. Knoydart is in the process of being developed for holiday makers, but time moves slowly in these parts.

Mallaig

Mallaig, about 10 or 11 miles north of Arisaig, on the western tip of North Morar, is the road, rail and ferry terminus. This bustling little fishing port is unspoilt, in spite of being a favourite for holiday makers. The quays are a jumble of fish-curing sheds and all the clutter of fishing: stacks of creels and fish boxes, piles of netting and gear. If you want to take a box of kippers home with you, this is the place to buy them. Cruises run to many of the islands, and there is a steam train to Fort William. The Mallaig and Morar Highland Games are held in August.

Glenfinnan

From Mallaig it is necessary to back-track. Glenfinnan is 14 miles east of Lochailort. The road twists and is very steep, with lovely views, between banks of rhododendrons, until it drops into Glenfinnan. A column, topped by a Highlander, rises from a marshy plain at the head of Loch Shiel, where three glens meet against a backdrop of layers of blue-grey hills. The Glenfinnan Monument, another milestone in *Bliadna Thearlaich*, was erected in 1815 to commemorate the raising of Prince Charlie's standard on 19 August 1745.

It is easier to recall the past if you turn your back on this Victorian folly, and look down the loch and up into the hills. This was where the prince stood on that summer's day, so full of hope, surrounded by those of the clans who had already committed themselves to his cause, waiting to see if Cameron of Lochiel would join them, a man whose great influence would sway the decisions of other clans. This powerful chief had not been enthusiastic about the rebellion, but he was a brave man and a loyal one. 'I'll share the fate of my Prince', he had said, and now, in the still afternoon, the waiting clans heard the skirl of pipes. They turned to watch Lochiel, at the head of 700 clansmen, marching down from the hills to join Prince Charlie's cause.

The excitement must have mounted to fever-pitch, for Lochiel's action quickly brought in other clans and later in the afternoon the great red and white silken banner was unfurled: the Prince's father was proclaimed King James III of Britain, with Prince Charles Edward his Regent.

Whatever misguided folly may have influenced this final Jacobite rising, no one with a shred of romance in their veins can stand here, remembering that day, and not feel staunchly Jacobite. However, many wise, clear-sighted chiefs remained neutral, without dishonour, and it was those men, ruled by their heads rather than their hearts, who did more for Scotland's subsequent survival than the impetuous Jacobites.

Apart from the monument, there is a **National Trust for Scotland Visitor Centre** (open daily, April–Oct: adm) across the road. It provides excellent maps showing the progress of the prince's army, and traces his wanderings after Culloden out to the islands and finally back to Loch-nan-Uamh.

There is another monument to the Prince in the Catholic church nearby. The Glenfinnan Games are held every August on the nearest Saturday to 19th.

The old station at Glenfinnan has a new railway interpretive centre, which, no doubt, will be wildly interesting for some.

WHERE TO STAY AND EAT
What hotels lack in mod cons and sophistication in this area, they make up for in hospitality and courtesy. **Ardgour Hotel**, tel 08555 225, is very good, cheap and right on the water at Ardgour with glorious views. **Clanranald Hotel**, Acharacle, tel 096785 662, is a homely little hotel with not too many frills and masses of character. Open from Easter to October, it's cheap and the six bedrooms share two bathrooms. **Kilchoan House Hotel**, near Ardnamurchan, tel 09723 200, is an attractive Highland lodge with one bathroom between eight bedrooms. It's cheap and the food is good. **Glenborrodale Castle**, also near Ardnamurchan, tel 09724 266, is a restored Victorian pile in 850 acres overlooking Mull and Loch Sunart. Open from May to October, it's expensive and has a quirky Highland character; unreliable plumbing in beautifully fitted-out bathrooms, and a half-size billiard table. **The Arisaig Hotel**, is much less overwhelming, a delightfully warm, friendly coaching inn, moderately priced, with glorious sea views, and reasonable food. Another nice one is **Arisaig House**, highly recommended, with terraced gardens and views to sea; also moderately priced with good food and wine. **Glenfinnan House Hotel**, Glenfinnan, tel 039783 235, is a splendid old mansion overlooking the Glenfinnan Monument, with glorious views of Loch Shiel. Open April to October, it's cheap and you might get pipe music if you are lucky. **Stage House Inn**, Glenfinnan, tel 039783 246, is less imposing but more sophisticated, also on Loch Shiel. Open April to October, it's moderately priced and has good food. **West Highland Hotel**, Mallaig, tel 0687 2210, is a splendid family-owned hotel, overlooking the islands, oozing with hospitality. Open April to October and moderately priced. **Morar Hotel**, tel 0687 2346, is a good, cheap, family hotel in a lovely position overlooking the Silver Sands of Morar. Very friendly staff, open April to October. **Glenuig Inn**, near Lochailort, tel 06877 219, is a dear little inn on a secluded bay with sandy beach and freshwater trout lochs nearby. It's also cheap, and the food is first class, especially the seafood. Open April to October.

Kyle of Lochalsh to Inverness via the West Coast

The coastal route back to Inverness opens up more wonderful scenery. Take the narrow road to the left in Kyle of Lochalsh and follow the coast (and the railway) round about seven miles to **Plockton**. The views are across to Applecross and Torridon in the north and west to Skye. Plockton is an unexpected little holiday village, its neat stone cottages all painted and trim, with velvet lawns and palm trees, lush shrubs, birches and pines, all grouped most attractively round a sheltered bay. Built in the 18th century as a fishing village, it is now unashamedly given over to up-market holiday makers, with craft shops and pleasure boats, surrounded by picture-postcard scenery. This is an artist's haven. From Plockton the road follows the southern shore of lovely Loch Carron, to the narrows at Stromeferry (no ferry now), and up to Strathcarron at the head of the loch.

It is interesting to reflect that there were virtually no roads in this area until General Wade's military roads were constructed in the first half of the 18th century. When the Highlands were so devastated by the potato famine in the middle of the 19th century, Destitution Committees were set up to send supplies of meal and provisions to the starving Highlanders. Some of the 'Destitution Funds' collected were used to build access roads to remote communities, making it easier to send help and providing work for the people. Some of these roads became known as 'Destitution Roads.'

Applecross Peninsula, round the head of Loch Carron and west from Lochcarron village, is another area of striking Highland scenery. Spectacular *Bealach-nam-Bo*, Pass of the Cattle, is a steep, narrow road across the southern end of the peninsula with hair-pin bends that make the adrenalin flow. The scenery is almost alpine, fringed by cliffs and rock spurs, dotted with glinting lochans and burns, with the distant hills of Skye ever present to the west. Cattle were driven over this pass from Applecross en route for the lucrative markets on the east coast. Records in 1794 tell of 3000 cattle leaving the district.

There is a sandy beach at Applecross, on the west coast of the peninsula, in a sheltered bay. An Irish monk, Maelrubha, founded a monastery north of the village, in 673. It became an important centre of Christianity until it was destroyed by Norsemen. A cul-de-sac runs to the south of the peninsula, wild and remote. It is possible to drive right round the north coast from Applecross beach, along the southern shore of Loch Torridon, Loch Shieldaig and Upper Loch Torridon to Torridon village.

The 26,000 acre **Torridon** Estate was acquired by the National Trust for Scotland in 1967. There is a visitor centre at the road junction at the head of Upper Loch Torridon, with an audio-visual presentation, telling about the area. There is a deer museum and enclosures, a programme of guided walks and advice on where to go. The 750-million-year-old red sandstone mountains dominate the whole of this part of the region with their distinctive white quartzite peaks.

The Beinn Eighe National Nature Reserve, is northeast of Torridon, reached on the A896, and was the first in Britain established for the preservation and study of the remains of the Caledonian Forest. The wildlife in the area includes deer, wild mountain goat, wild cat, pine marten, and eagles. For those who like leaflets and posters and illustrated information there is a visitor centre at **Aultroy Cottage,** just northwest of **Kinlochewe**, with advice on nature trails (the modern name for walks), an illuminated model of the district and details about the work done on the Reserve.

The drive west along the northern shore of Loch Torridon goes through scattered crofting townships, with sea views, backed by massive hills, as far as Lower Diabaig, about eight miles. A track goes further round the coast to a youth hostel. From here it is a lovely walk up the rocky coast to Redpoint.

The A832 goes northwest from Kinlochewe along the south shore of beautiful **Loch Maree**, dominated by **Slioch** on the opposite side. Loch Maree is 12 miles long, its name derived from St Maelrubha, the monk who founded the monastery at Applecross. He spent some time as a hermit on one of the islands on the loch and is, according to tradition, buried there.

About eight miles along is the **Loch Maree Hotel** with an atmosphere that is pure Victorian. Nothing seems to have changed here since Queen Victoria visited in it 1877 and stayed for six days. A rock on a bank in front of the hotel, inscribed in Gaelic, commemorates the queen's visit. It is difficult not to whisper when asking for the tariff. This is a fishing hotel, with an impressive log of catches on the hall table. Some locals can still remember the day, in the mid 1920s, when a fishing party from the hotel ate sandwiches made from paste that had seen better days. Several of them died from botulism—others were dreadfully ill.

The A832 leaves Loch Maree soon after the hotel and goes west towards Gairloch. At **Kerrysdale**, about 10 miles beyond the hotel, the River Kerry dashes towards the sea, through mossy glades and silver birches, with a few gnarled oaks and feathery rowans. Carpeting the dappled turf are a profusion of wild flowers: lousewort, milkwort, primroses, bluebells, wood anemones, orchids, and many more.

Take the very minor cul-de-sac left from Kerrysdale, past the sheltered anchorage of **Shieldaig**, and the attractive bay at **Badachro**. This was once a large fishing station where curers bought herring, cod, ling, etc., from local fishermen. Now the community life is centred on a tiny, friendly shop-cum-post office. The road, which was built with money from the Destitution Fund, goes on to **Redpoint**. This is magic country. Heather carpeted moorland runs down to rocky cliffs and crescents of red-gold sand. The views are across to South Rona and Raasay, with the island of Skye beyond. An otter swims in the sea and builds its cone of fish-remains on the turf. Wheatears, ringed plovers, linnets and skylarks fill the air with song. Colonies of sea birds mass on the rocks: cormorants, shags, gulls, terns, fulmars, gannets. An old man with piercing blue eyes sits on a rock, sucking his pipe: 'You could never be bored, here', he says: 'If you run out of things to do you can just watch the weather.'

Back at Kerrysdale, turn left to **Gairloch**, a well-developed holiday resort with excellent sandy beaches and several hotels. The hub of this community seems to be the Wild Cat Stores, purveyors of fresh milk, fresh baps and local chat. Opposite, is the award-winning **Gairloch Heritage Museum** (open daily: adm), very easy to miss but well worth a visit. In only a few rooms one can learn a great deal about life in the western Highlands. The exhibits range from Pictish stones and relics to Victoriana. There is a portable pulpit for outdoor preachers of the Free Church; an old ice-making machine; stuffed birds and wild animals; an illicit still; spinning wheels with the various wools and natural dyes; a wash house; a school room, with Gaelic on the blackboard; a village store; and a fisherman and his gear. The highlight is the replica of the inside of a croft house. This is most beautifully set up with press buttons to illuminate it, set the spinning wheel in motion, and animate the old woman in front of the peat fire. She sings a haunting Gaelic lullaby to the baby, rocking in a cradle. An annex contains interesting history displays and old photographs of the area.

Poolewe is seven or eight miles northeast of Gairloch. Stop on the bridge to watch the mighty force of water from Loch Maree, thrusting its way out into Loch Ewe, forming the pool that gave the place its name.

Inverewe Garden (open daily: adm) at Inverewe, half a mile from Poolewe, is famous to horticulturists all over the world. It was created by Osgood MacKenzie, a Victorian who had spent much of his early life on the continent. Son of the Laird of Gairloch, he was given the estate at the head of Loch Ewe in 1862: a peninsula of red Torridonian sandstone, pocked by peat-hags and bare of vegetation except for heather, crowberry and dwarf willows. It is hard to believe, now, what this enterprising man achieved from such unpromising beginnings in an era when there were few roads and soil was carried in wicker creels. He planted an outer windbreak of Corsican and Scots pine, behind deer- and rabbit-proof fences. Plants were introduced from all over the world. Now, there are some 2500 species, in 50 acres of woodland, covering a steep hillside that juts into the loch, sheltered by hills behind. This exotic, sub-tropical paradise lies only a little to the south of the latitude that runs through Cape Farewell, in Greenland. The proximity of the Gulf Stream is responsible for making this garden so fertile. Palm trees, rock gardens, peat-banks, ornamental ponds, all display a profusion of blooms from Japan, Chile, South Africa, the Pacific, and many other places.

An attractive cul-de-sac drive down the west side of Loch Ewe goes as far as **Cove**. Cove Cave is so deep and sheltered it was once used as a place of worship.

Gruinard Bay, about 11 miles north of Poolewe, has sandy beaches surrounded by hills, and views out to the Summer Isles. It is a magnificent spot, with a campsite right on the beach at **Mellon Udrigle**. Gruinard Island, in the bay, was infected with anthrax during the last war and was forbidden territory for years. It is now decontaminated, and has been restored to its original owner.

Sand

A small sign beside the road not far east of **Laide** on the bay, points the way down a cliff path to two caves. The largest was a meeting place for hundreds of years and was used as a church for Presbyterians, as late as 1843. The smaller cave was lived in by an old woman and her girl companion in 1885. Families evicted from their crofts during the Clearances used to take shelter here. It is a magic place: at the entrance to the larger cave, with its protective wall in front, it is intriguing to picture how it was with perhaps several families huddled together inside, with what they had saved of their possessions and livestock. The fire would be burning, children and dogs playing, and people making do with whatever fish and game they had managed to catch. Picture it when the wind blew in from the north, rolling the great boulders on the shore. Picture it too, in summer, with thrift and honeysuckle growing down the rocks, and the sea as calm and clear as a Pacific lagoon.

The A832 skirts Little Loch Broom (stop and look at the spectacular **Ardessie Falls** about two-thirds of the way along), and cuts across the moors. The part of the road from Dundonnell, by Feithean, to Braemore Junction, was another built with funds raised during the potato famine and so is called the 'Destitution Road'. The name is misleading: it's lovely.

Braemore Junction is where the A832 meets the A835 to Ullapool about 28 miles from Gruinard. It is also the confluence of the **Rivers Broom, Cuileig and Droma**, known locally as 'The Valley of The Broom'. Stop at the large observation car park just before the A835. It is a staggering view down into the junction of the three valleys, the steep wooded banks ablaze with colour in the autumn. Less than a mile further on, a sign on the left marks the Corrieshalloch Gorge and the Falls of Measach. It is only a short walk from the road and there is an alternative approach from round the corner, where there is another car park and signs, on the A835.

Corrieshalloch

Corrieshalloch is unforgettable: a mile-long box canyon, 200 ft deep, its sheer rock sides festooned with ferns and mosses, saxifrage, sorrel, tufts of grasses and wood-millet. Miraculously rooted wych elm, birch, hazel, sycamore, Norway maple and beech trees cling to the sides, with goat-willow, bird-cherry and guelder-rose. There is an observation platform from which to look back at the Falls of Measach, a single cascade of 150 ft that seems to hang in the air like smoke. There is an even better view from the suspension bridge that spans the gorge, but this is not for vertigo sufferers. The deep pools below are rich in trout, and, above the roar of the falls, the angry 'pruk' of the ravens can be heard, as they nest on a ledge opposite the viewing platform.

The drive back to Inverness from here is attractive, through open moor, past lochs and glens. See the Inverness to Durness section for things to look at on the way.

WHERE TO STAY AND EAT

There is a reasonable choice of hotels, guest houses and self-catering establishments and the standard is varied. It's worth remembering that people often book a year ahead for favourite places.

Aultbea Hotel, tel 044582 201, is a small, cheapish hotel on the eastern shore of Loch Ewe, quiet and comfortable with good food. **Drumchork Lodge Hotel** close by, tel 044582 242, is slightly bigger, slightly more expensive, with the same stunning views. **Badachro Inn**, tel 044583 255, is a whitewashed inn with a small garden on the edge of the bay. Two bedrooms only, and one bathroom. Unpretentious food, and very cheap. The following are all moderately priced. **Gairloch Hotel**, tel 0445 2001, is a huge Victorian pile overlooking the sea, open from April to October. You expect to see pitchers and bowls in the bedrooms but actually it is reasonably modern and comfortable and, rare in this part of the world, all 66 bedrooms are en suite. **Shieldaig Lodge Hotel**, near Gairloch, tel 044583 250, is a Victorian country house, right by the water, backed by trees with good food. **Kinlochewe Hotel**, tel 044584, open April to November, is cheaper and reasonably comfortable. **The Haven Hotel** in Plockton, tel 059984 223, is a well-converted Victorian house with all 13 bedrooms en suite; open February to December. **Pool House Hotel**, at Poolewe, tel 044586 272, is a small family-run hotel by the bridge where Loch Maree pours out into Loch Ewe, within walking distance of Inverewe Garden, open from April to October. **Loch Torridon Hotel**, tel 044587 242, is a Victorian mansion with lovely views in 56 acres, open April to October. **Ocean View Hotel** at Sand, tel 044582 385, has a marvellously friendly, holiday atmosphere.

Inverness to Durness

The first part of the drive to Durness goes through gentle farmland backed by hills, rapidly turning to wild moor and rugged mountain as the road crosses to the west. Loch Broom opens up more glorious west coast scenery, and from there north is all mountains and vistas of loch, mountain and sea.

Beauly is 10 miles west of Inverness at the head of the Beauly Firth. This is Lovat country. The Lovat family came to Britain with the Normans and it was their French influence that inspired the name Beauly, *Beau Lieu*. (Romantics prefer to attribute the name to Mary, Queen of Scots, fresh from her French chateaux, exclaiming 'Ah, quelle beau lieu!')

The centre of Beauly is a widening of the main road, making an attractive rectangular market place with the ruin of Beauly Priory (open daily: free) at the north end, beyond the old cross. Founded in 1230 for Valliscaulian monks, the priory is now a roofless shell. In the south wall are three fine triangular windows embellished with trefoils dating from the original building. It fell into ruin after the Reformation.

The monument in the Square is in memory of the 16th Lord Lovat, who raised the Lovat Scouts during the South African War. Perhaps the most colourful member of the family was Simon, Lord Lovat, born in about 1667. His many notorious escapades included the attempted abduction of a nine-year-old heiress and his subsequent marriage by force to her mother, a deed that left him convicted of high treason and outlawed. Having come into the title, by devious means, he became a Jacobite agent, involved in conveying false information to the enemy. Outlawed once more, he turned government man and received a full pardon. Swearing loyalty to the Crown, he sent his son to fight for Prince Charlie in 1745. He was beheaded, finally, in London, meeting his end with humorous dignity. 'You'll get that nasty head of yours chopped off, you ugly old Scotch dog,' taunted a Cockney woman in the crowd. 'I believe I shall, you ugly old English bitch,' he replied. Hogarth painted a portrait of him in hideous old age, just before he was helped up the steps to the scaffold; bloated, villainous, with satanic eyebrows and a cruel mouth, wracked by gout. Known as 'The Old Fox of the '45', he was indisputably a rogue, traitor and hypocrite. Alternative, more kindly, reports also credit him with intelligence, charm and Celtic wit.

Internationally known, **Campbells of Beauly** faces on to the Square. This shop is a treasure-trove of tweeds, woollens, tartans and all possible Highland accessories, ready made or custom built. Visitors return, year after year, tempted by the remarkable range and quality of the products, efficiently served by the Campbell family.

Moniack Castle Winery and Wine Bar (open on weekdays) is an excellent staging post a few miles southeast of Beauly. They serve their own home-produced country wines, meads and a variety of delicious jellies, in converted out-buildings in an ancestral setting. The food is excellent and the wine is for sale.

In 1990, a number of idealists organised a sponsored 'Poethon' to raise money to establish a Writers Centre, Moniack Mhor, in outbuildings on the Moniack estate. For 24 hours, at various venues in London, 144 people recited contemporary poetry from memory, with the help of such celebrated poets as James Fenton and Wendy Cope. They raised a lot of money, but not enough: so the appeal is still open.

Before continuing north, it is worth making a detour to visit the **Glens of Farrar, Glass, Beauly, Cannich and Affric**. From Beauly, take the A831 southwest down Strathglass to Glen Affric, a beautiful tour through wooded glens following the River Beauly and then the River Glass. The remains of two Iron Age forts lie off to the right from **Kilmorack**, two miles from Beauly. Here, and at **Aigas**, three miles further on, are hydroelectric dams where visitors can watch salmon being 'lifted' on their way upstream to breed.

There are some lovely walks in this area where the three glens of the Farrar, Glass and Beauly meet; gentler scenery than that of the western Highlands but just as magnificent, enhanced rather than spoiled by the hydroelectric developments that have changed the landscape. Steep, pine-clad rocks rise from peaty lochs in broad, green valleys.

At **Glassburn**, look out for the **Holy Well of St Ignatius**, beside the road: an intriguing old headstone in a modern cairn, with ingravings that include references to: saints Columba 563, Bean 1015, and Margaret 1070, as well as Pope Leo XIII. There is also a poem which could be the marching song of the Temperance League:

> *'Water bright water, pure water for me,*
> *the drink of the wise, the wine of the free...'*

and a lot more in that vein.

Stop off at the chapel of St Mary's, in **Eskadale**, a mile beyond Aigas. This pretty, early Victorian church was once the main Catholic centre for this area. In the graveyard is a memorial to an almost-forgotten episode in Scotland's history: the graves of the 'Sobieski Stuarts'. These two brothers, John Sobieski Stolberg Stuart, 1795–1872, and Charles Edward Stuart, 1799–1880, conned Victorian society into accepting them as grandsons of Prince Charles Edward Stuart. They claimed that their father, Lieutenant Thomas Allen, Royal Navy, was Prince Charlie's son. They called themselves Counts d'Albanie and there is a splendid book, *The Sobieski Stuarts*, by H. Beveridge, about them. They lived at Eskadale House, further down the valley, and at Eilan Aigas House, where they kept deer hounds and invented several tartans with which further to impress their gullible friends.

More lovely scenery at Cannich, 17 miles southwest of Beauly, where the River Glass meets up with the Rivers Affric and Cannich. There is a youth hostel here. About three miles southeast, the Corrimony Cairn is a Stone and Bronze Age burial cairn, its passage still roofed and surrounded by a stone circle.

Although it is far nicer to walk, it is possible to drive the 12 miles up Glen Farrar to Loch Monar; it is a private road so permission must first be asked. A road runs eight miles up Glen Cannich to Cozac Lodge, and another up Glen Affric to a car park, two miles short of Affric Lodge (one of the most beautiful glens in Scotland). Each glen has its own charm, with tumbling burns, lichen-hung trees, glinting sheets of water, all sheltered by hills. From Affric Lodge there is a good hike, 10 miles west, to the youth hostel at Alltbeath. Another 10 miles or so reaches Loch Duich. It cannot be emphasized too often that anyone walking and climbing here, and anywhere else in the Highlands, should be fit, sensibly equipped, and should carry and know how to use a map and compass (see p. 16).

Contin, 11 miles north of Beauly, has an old coaching inn, on the west side of the River Blackwater, from which passengers used to depart on the tortuous journey west to

Poolewe and Ullapool, after the roads were built in the 18th century. Telford built the first bridge here, later swept away by flood water. Dealers used to come up from England to the Contin Horse Fair, to buy sturdy Highland ponies for work in the coal mines. Fair days were festive occasions, drawing people in from far afield, to jostle and gossip over the braziers, among the peddlers' stalls and animal pens.

Strathpeffer

Strathpeffer, a couple of miles northeast of Contin, was a famous spa town until the First World War. People came from overseas, including foreign royalty, to the sulphur and chalybeate springs. The springs were used as early as 1770, but it was not until the first pump room was built in 1820 that Strathpeffer's fame spread over the border. Lying in a sheltered hollow among wooded hills, the little town is a popular holiday centre, with plenty for the visitor to do, including climbing Ben Wyvis, the great bulk a few miles to the north. Houses and hotels rise in neat terraces from the heart of the town, whose gently refined atmosphere has won it the title 'Harrogate-of-the-North'.

Strathpeffer Highland Games are held in the grounds of Castle Leod in early August, with all the traditional events such as tossing the caber, putting the shot, piping and dancing.

The **Eagle Stone** stands 3 ft high on a hillock to the east of Strathpeffer, reached by a lane near Eaglestone House. It is a Pictish symbol stone with an engraved angel and a horseshoe and was the subject of one of the Brahan Seer's prophecies. If the stone should fall three times, he said, then ships would tie up to it. Setting aside a tidal wave this seems improbable, but the seer had an uncanny eye and it is said that the stone has already fallen twice (hence its having been cemented into place and surrounded by wire) and that on the second occasion the Cromarty Firth flooded up to the old county buildings in Dingwall.

Strathpeffer Craft and Visitor Centre (open in the summer: free) has craftsmen and women at work in what was the Victorian station.

At the **Water Sampling Pavilion** in The Square (open daily, Easter–Oct: adm), you can hold your nose and sample the sulphur waters that made Strathpeffer famous as a Victorian spa.

To the south, on a ridge called **Druim Chat**, meaning 'cat's back', there is a well-preserved vitrified fort, **Knockfarrel**, one in a line of three great Pictish defence sites, the other two being at Craig Phadrig in Inverness and Ord Hill in Kessock. You can see the foundations clearly—a vast place, extending to some 270 yds. This is believed to have been a stronghold of Fingal and his warriors, and many are the legends told about it.

A terrible clan battle took place to the southwest, at **Kinellan**, between the Macdonalds and the Mackenzies, in the 16th century. The Macdonalds, seeking vengeance after an alleged insult, lost the fight and were later punished by James IV who deposed them as Lords of the Isles.

Rogie Falls are just over two miles northeast of Contin, well signposted and only a short walk from the car park. It is a delightful picnic spot among birches, rowans and gnarled old oaks, carpeted in heather, bracken and mossy crags. It is possible to watch salmon leaping up a series of falls, from a suspension bridge over the river. They often achieve astonishing heights.

Five miles on, the road divides, beyond **Garve**. The A890 to the left goes southwest along attractive Strath Bran, past Loch Luichart and out to Achnasheen, a lonely, scattered hamlet where the railway widens to provide a passing place for trains. Here the road divides again, southwest to Loch Carron and Applecross (see p. 410) or northwest to Loch Maree (see p. 411).

Ullapool

Ullapool is 32 miles northwest of Garve, a pleasant drive through moorland and river-filled glens, backed by hills including massive Beinn Dearg, 3547 ft, to the north. The **Lael Forest Garden Trail** is further on, with over 150 different species of trees and shrubs, all labelled. There are good views across Loch Broom, fringed with beaches and nice picnic spots. The town is a popular holiday resort as well as an important fishing port and the ferry terminus for boats to Stornoway in Lewis. Freshly painted houses line the sea front, their upper windows sharply gabled, looking down on the jumble of quays and slipways, cluttered with small boats and fishing gear, creels, spars, nets and fish boxes. The town was developed as a fishing port by the British Fishery Society in 1788, Loch Broom providing an excellent deep-water anchorage for the boats. There are often east European and Russian fishing boats at anchor in the bay in the anchorage, usually scruffy looking tubs, bringing a gabble of foreign languages to the streets. It is not unknown to find a female skipper in Soviet boats. Locals will tell intriguing tales of shady people coming and going from the boats with very little interference: splendid material for a spy thriller. The town has a good range of shops, boutiques, restaurants and cafés, bars and every sort of accommodation. Some of the street names are written in Gaelic: the somewhat surprising *Shit phuirth* is in fact Seaforth Street.

The Loch Broom Highland Museum (open daily except Sun, April–Oct: free) gives a good insight into the history of Wester Ross, the life of a fishing village and the story of the Clearances. It also has displays of geology, wild life, military and farming history.

The Tourist Information Office will give information on sea fishing, boating, pony trekking and cruises. There is a youth hostel and the surrounding countryside is perfect for walking.

Drumrunie is about eight miles beyond Ullapool on the A835. Turn left here on to a minor road that skirts the **Coigach** peninsula, winding through land and sea-lochs in some of Scotland's loveliest and wildest scenery. **Achiltibuie**, about 13 miles round, well signposted, is a honeymooners' paradise and a perfect holiday base. Boats run to the Summer Isles, scattered a few miles off the Coigach Peninsula.

Horticulturists should visit the **Hydroponicum**, at the **Summer Isles Hotel**, in Achiltibuie (open daily, March–Oct: adm). Created by Robert Irvine, it has 'hi-tec soil-less growing houses'—an amazing place, with three distinct climates: Hampshire, Bordeaux and the Canaries. Strawberries are picked fresh every day from April to October and bananas flourish. Figs, lemons, passion fruit, vines, vegetables, flowers and herbs all grow luxuriantly without soil. One-hour lecture tours are given in the summer; these include information on the use of solar energy. It is often featured on television. For details tel 085482 202.

Achiltibuie Smokehouse (open weekdays, Oct–April, daily except Sun May–Sept: free): the process of curing and smoking of meat, fish and game can be watched and there is a retail shop. For details tel 085482 253.

Back on the A835, the road runs northwards through the Inverpolly National Nature Reserve, a remote, lonely stretch of moorland dotted with lochs, burns and great jagged red sandstone peaks. These include Stac Polly, 2009 ft , Cul Beag, 2523 ft and Sul Mor, 2786 ft, all very popular with climbers. There is a Nature Conservancy Council Visitor Centre at Knockan, less than five miles up the road with full information about this area.

Ledmore is less than eight miles beyond Drumrunie. Here, an alternative route southeast, runs 30 miles through Strath Oykel to Bonar Bridge, leaving the mountains and running through moorland and attractive wooded valleys.

Ardvreck Castle

Ardvreck Castle (always accessible: free) about six miles north of Ledmore, is a jagged fang of a ruin, three storeys high, on lovely **Loch Assynt**. Dating from 1490, it was one of the few castles to be built in this area where lack of roads in the old days made it difficult to maintain large establishments. It was a Macleod stronghold, and carries in its stones a poignant echo of the last days of Montrose. There are several conflicting stories but it is certain that the gallant, tragic hero, Montrose, fighting for Charles II, fled to Assynt in 1650 after his final defeat at Carbisdale, near Bonar Bridge. Some say he threw himself on the mercy of the Macleod laird of the time, who responded by selling him to the government for £25,000. Others say Macleod found him and took him prisoner honourably. Whatever the story, Montrose was imprisoned in this grim fortress, on its rocky peninsula jutting into the loch. From here he was taken ignominiously to Edinburgh, tied, back-to-front, on his horse, and abandoned by the king to whom he had given his loyalty.

Inchnadamph Caves, two miles south of Ardvreck, yielded evidence of occupation by early man and also bones of late Pleistocene animals, going back at least 10,000 years.

Lochinver is 10 miles to the west on the A837, along the north shore of Loch Assynt, a large-ish village and the only place of any size between Scourie and Ullapool. It is a delightful place on one of the most beautiful stretches of coastline in Scotland, with heart-stopping views all round. Two-hour wildlife cruises run from Lochinver, in the summer, with a chance to see some of the many birds and the colonies of seals basking on the rocks.

Dramatic sugar-loaf **Suilven**, 2399 ft, is five miles to the south in **Glencanisp Forest**, with **Canisp**, 2779 ft, two miles beyond to the east. Both are well worth climbing on a clear day. The coast road on round from Lochinver is another stunner, about 35 miles in all, back to join the A894 near **Kylestrome**, where a recently built bridge replaces the small ferry that used to hold up traffic for hours in the holiday season. Boats run from Unapool, down Loch Glencoul to the southeast, to see Britain's highest waterfall, Eas-Coul-Aulin, a fantastic sight, 658 ft high in a wild, melancholy setting that seems appropriate for such a giddy cascade.

Yet another beautiful drive of nearly 10 miles reaches **Scourie**, a popular holiday village in a sheltered bay with a sandy beach and rocky pools. Several varieties of orchid thrive in the mild climate here; boats run to the Nature Reserve on **Handa Island**, a mile off the sandy beach north of Scourie. Here you will see a great variety of sea birds, including razorbills, guillemots, puffins, kittiwakes and skua.

The road north goes inland a few miles to **Laxford Bridge**. An alternative route goes southeast from here to **Lairg** (see p. 427), an impressive drive through massive rocky mountains that tower threateningly over the road, with sharp turns and terrifying blind summits. On a sunny day, with the sparkling waters of Loch More, Loch Merkland, and Loch Shin, it can be beautiful, but on a grey, sullen day of mist and rain, it is an awe-inspiring route.

Four miles north of Laxford Bridge, at **Rhiconich**, a good new road goes four miles west to **Kinlochbervie**, on **Loch Inchard**, an important west-coast fishing port. Strong currents around the northern headland make swimming very dangerous here. For the most beautiful beach in Scotland, drive five miles on past Kinlochbervie to the end of the road and then walk on round the coast, about four miles over abandoned crofts, to **Sandwood Bay**. Entirely remote, it is outstandingly beautiful, with sand, cliffs and a columns of rock rising from the sea.

The drive north from Rhiconich is through a bleak wilderness of rock-strewn glens, forbidding mountains and dark, sombre lochs.

Durness

Durness is a sturdy village about 15 miles northeast of Rhiconich, perched on the north coast, built to withstand the fury of the elements. It is a good base for exploring this northwestern corner and has plenty of places to stay. Durness Highland gathering is in July.

Durness Old Church, on the bay and dating from 1619, is a roofless shell on the site of an older church. Look for the skull and crossbone carving on the wall; this is thought to mark the site of the grave of a notorious highwayman, Donald MacMurchov, who hoped to buy his way into the afterlife by making substantial contributions to the building of the church. The previous church on this site appears in records in the Vatican as having contributed to one of the Crusades in the 12th century. There was a summer palace for the Bishops of Caithness, where the farmhouse now stands, opposite the church.

Smoo Cave is signposted from the road, about a mile to the east. This vast limestone cavern has three compartments, two of which are difficult to get to. The main chamber is 200 ft long and 120 ft high, with holes in the roof. Consult the Durness Information Centre for advice on how to reach the inner sections and the 80 ft waterfall, where the Alt Smoo River pours down from the cliffs into the caves: very dramatic.

Balnakeil Craft Village, in a former MOD Early Warning Station camp, just along the track that runs west from Durness, stands on a lovely white sand bay. Sixteen or so non-local hippy-type craftsmen and women display and sell their astonishingly over-priced handiwork. The crafts include weaving, jewels, candles, rag dolls, bookbinding, painting, woodwork, pottery: most of it no better than 6th-form hobbies. In 1981 the Regional Council sold the buildings to the craftsmen and they then formed a Community Co-operative, which also runs the Visitor Centre. If Joan Baez strolled through, barefooted, singing 'We Shall Overcome' she wouldn't be out of place.

Cape Wrath

A passenger boat runs across the Kyle of Durness in the summer to link up with a minibus that goes out to the Cape 10 miles northwest. It is well worth walking one way, with binoculars and a good bird book: the promontory is an ornithologist's paradise.

Cape Wrath, pronounced Raath, got its name from the Viking word *hvarf* meaning 'turning place'. It was not named after the furious sea which pounds at the 523-ft-high cliffs. These cliffs have veins of rich pink pegmatite running through the gneiss. The views from this top left-hand corner of Scotland are astonishing. On a clear day you can see the Orkney Islands to the east, some 60 miles away, 45 miles west to the Butt of Lewis, and 80 miles southwest to Harris.

To the north lies the island of North Rona, with Stack Skerry and Skule Skerry further east. Turn your back on the great fort-like lighthouse and look across the bleak moor, **The Parbh**, that stretches away to the south. Wolves once roamed here in great numbers—an eerie thought as the mist comes creeping in across the desolate wasteland and you look around to make sure that the minibus hasn't left without you.

WHERE TO STAY AND EAT
See also Inverness. The following are all moderately priced: **Aigas Field Centre**, Beauly, tel 0463 782443, is a Victorian-Gothic mansion on a working estate in a magnificent setting. Guests are offered optional Field Study programmes—wildlife, etc. Very friendly and ancestral, open April to October. **Contin House**, tel 0997 21920, is a Highland fishing lodge, on a 35-acre island in the River Blackwater, in idyllic scenery surrounded by hills. Built in 1794, they cater for parties of from six to ten, and it is like going to stay with very special old friends, only you don't do the washing up. **Coul House Hotel**, Contin, tel 0997 21487, is a splendid 19th-century pile looking across to the Strathconon hills, with an excellent reputation for good food. **Cozac Lodge**, Cannich, tel 04565 263, is an Edwardian shooting lodge in rugged Glen Cannich, furnished like a country house, warm and friendly with excellent food. They are open March to October and over Christmas and New Year. **Ledgowan Hotel**, Achnasheen, tel 044588 252, originally built as a private shooting lodge, now converted into a comfortable country-house type hotel. Open Easter to November. **Inchbae Lodge**, Garve, is a small country-house hotel with good food, quite comfortable. **Ben Wyvis Hotel**, Strathpeffer, tel 0997 21323, is a huge, rather daunting Victorian pile in six acres of attractive gardens, open from March to November, and the food is patchy.

Ullapool has got lots of hotels and guest houses but nothing to compare with **Altnaharrie Hotel**, tel 085483 230, an old drovers' inn on the shores of Loch Broom, reached by private launch from Ullapool. Small, expensive and very select, its bedrooms are pretty, and the food is sublime. In Ullapool, **Royal Hotel** in Garve Road, right on the shore of Loch Broom, is probably the most sophisticated. It's quite big, moderately priced and has reasonable food. At the other end of the scale, **The Ceilidh Place**, in West Argyle Street, Ullapool, tel 0854 2103, is a cheap, mildly eccentric, rather hearty, and fun (if you like that sort of thing) establishment comprising: hotel, clubhouse, restaurant, coffee shop, bookshop, live shows of jazz, classical and folk music, and all sorts of other jollifications. You could do a lot worse, as long as you are gregarious. **Ferry Boat Inn** on Shore Street, tel 0854 2366, is a cheap, cosy, family-run inn looking across Loch Broom; rather noisy. **Four Seasons Hotel**, in Garve Road, tel 0854 2905, is a modern monster on the shores of Loch Broom; moderately priced, very friendly with good seafood.

Unquestionably, the next two are the pick of the bunch. **Summer Isles Hotel** Achiltibuie, tel 085482 282, open Easter to October, run by Mark and Geraldine Irvine and in the family since the 60s. Wonderfully remote, in a spectacular setting overlooking the Summer Isles and beyond to the Hebrides, it is almost entirely self-sufficient. It has: its own smokehouse; the Hydroponicum (see above) provides fresh fruit and vegetables; its own dairy, veal, quails, duck, fish, etc. There is everything here for lovers of solitude and beauty and it is exactly like going to stay with friends in a special place. In fact, once you've been there, that's what it becomes, except that you get a bill. It's not cheap but every penny is worth it. The other top choice is **Inchnadamph Hotel**, Loch Assynt, tel 05712 202, known as the 'Anglers' Retreat', and a bit cheaper. This is another genuine Highland establishment where homely comfort is more important than double glazing, trouser presses and 'hospitality trays' in the bedroom. In the most glorious surroundings at the head of the loch, this hotel has been in the hands of the Morrison family for 71 years, which is probably why you feel completely at home the moment you arrive. Free fishing for salmon, grilse and brown trout, excellent home-cooking, moderately priced. **Kylesku Hotel**, tel 0971 2231, is a delightful little place on the loch at Kylesku in lovely scenery, with good seafood caught in their own boat. Open April to October and cheap. **Culag Hotel**, Lochinver, tel 05714 270, is on the shore of Loch Inver with glorious views; an excellent place, and also cheap. **Eddrachilles Hotel** Badcall Bay, Scourie, tel 0971 2080, is in a beautiful position overlooking the bay and islands, with good-ish food. Open March to October, moderately priced. **Scourie Hotel**, tel 0971 2396, is comfortable with good home-cooking, and very friendly. Open March to October. Prices on application. **Kinlochbervie Hotel**, tel 097182 275, is highly recommended as a family hotel, with excellent food, overlooking Kinlochbervie harbour and Loch Clash. Moderately priced, comfortable and friendly. **Cape Wrath Hotel**, Durness, tel 097181 274, is an easy going, comfortable hotel on this far northern coast, open March to January, prices on application. Watch out for the very good-looking boatman with blue eyes, in the bar: he specializes in tall stories for tourists in exchange for a dram or two. **Parkhill Hotel**, Durness, tel 097181 209, is a temperance hotel—and cheap.

Inverness to John o' Groats

The A9 north from Inverness crosses the elegant Kessock Bridge, where the Beauly Firth meets the Moray Firth, in the lee of the Black Isle. Until 1982 this narrow neck of water was crossed in a small car ferry, known to side-slip in violent currents. The bridge, opened by the Queen Mother, won a design award. This east coast route to the top right-hand corner of Scotland crosses the gentle, fertile Black Isle and then hugs a fairly inhospitable coast almost all the way. The worst of the Highland Clearances took place in Sutherland and Caithness, and the scattered ruins of abandoned crofts can be found in deserted glens. Long straths run inland through vast tracts of moor and fen, linking the east with the north and west coasts. This is the Flow Country, the biggest blanket bog in the world, coveted by forestry kings. Conservationists are struggling to stem the huge plantations already eating up this amazing concentration of wild life. It is a fragile living surface of floating peat, with heather and sedges over a carpet of spagnum mosses. Among the threatened victims are 55 species of birds related to Arctic tundra, including 70 per cent of Britain's greenshanks, meadow pipits, red-throated divers with their primitive whale-like cries, peregrines and merlins. Among the many plants threatened is the rare insect-eating sundew. Dubh lochans, black from peat, speckle the land.

The Black Isle

The Black Isle is joined to the mainland between Beauly and Dingwall and has its own unique soft, sing-song dialect. It is made up of gentle, rolling farmland, wild-fowl beaches and pretty little fishing villages. The new main road seems to rip through it in a few moments, showing little of its charms. It would be a pity to dash through it without noticing. Take the first turning right after the bridge to explore it properly—a hidden turning, easy to miss.

Munlochy Bay, about three miles up this twisting minor road, is vibrant with the cackle of geese in winter, targets for sportsmen who like to see their wildfowl at the end of a gun. **Avoch** (pronounced 'Auch'—the *au* as in Australia with a guttural *ch*) about four miles further on is a picturesque little fishing village with an attractive harbour. There are miles of bracing walks on the tidal sandflats, with good views across the Firth.

Fortrose, a couple of miles on, is a pleasant, no-nonsense little resort town, sheltered by Chanonry Point and excellent for small boat sailing. **Fortrose Cathedral** (open daily: free) is a mere fragment of the great church founded by King David I in the 12th century. All that remains is the south aisle of the nave and the sacristy. In 1880, a hoard of silver coins was dug up from the green, dating from the reign of Robert III. Cromwell recycled much of the fabric of the cathedral for building a fort in Inverness. Look out for the memorial stone on **Chanonry Point** east of Fortrose. It marks the site where the legendary Brahan Seer was burned in a barrel of tar (see 'Topics', p. 41).

Rosemarkie, a mile beyond the town on the northern side of Chanonry Point, is a popular beach in summer, with golden sand and rock pools. St Moluag founded a school and a church here in the 6th century, and tradition holds that he is buried below the Pictish stone in the churchyard.

Groam House Museum (open daily, June–Sept: adm) in Rosemarkie has local and archaeological exhibits. This tiny museum has a wealth of treasure for antiquarians: fascinating carved stones found in the vicinity of the church, indicating the importance of Rosemarkie in early Christian times. Fragments of cross-slabs, and grave stones and a fine Pictish slab, all well displayed and explained. There is an audio-visual show and the curator is extremely knowledgeable.

Golf enthusiasts can enjoy an invigorating game within spitting distance of the sea on the 18-hole Fortrose and Rosemarkie golf course.

Cromarty

Cromarty, on the northeastern tip of the Black Isle about 23 miles northeast of the Kessock Bridge, is a delightful old 18th-century fishing town and port; a royal burgh for seven centuries. Sheltered by the great headland of the South Sutor at the mouth of the

Cromarty Firth, its rows of terraced cottages stand gable-end-on to the street, hunched against the wind, forming rope walks where the fisherwomen used to stretch out the new ropes from the rope factory. The town was bought in 1772 by George Ross, some of whose descendants still live there. He built the harbour, founded a cloth factory, a nail and spade factory, a brewery, and a lace industry and built a Gaelic chapel for the Highlanders who came flocking to the town for employment. Cromarty has been skilfully and imaginatively restored. The sheltered bay was used as an anchorage for destroyer flotillas in the First World War.

Cromarty Courthouse is a Visitor Centre and museum, with video, animated figures, a reconstructed trial, cells, shop and displays. (Open Apr–Sept: adm).

Hugh Miller's Cottage (open daily, Easter–Sept, excluding Sun until June: adm) in Church Street, offers a nostalgic journey into the past. This long, low, thatched cottage with crow-stepped gables, its tiny upper windows half buried in the eaves, was built in 1711 by the great-grandfather of Hugh Miller (1802–56). He rose from simple beginnings to become a famous geologist, stonemason, naturalist, theologian and writer. (Among other things, he wrote about the Brahan Seer in *Scenes and Legends of the North of Scotland*.) Restored by the National Trust for Scotland, the cottage contains a museum devoted to collections of his writings, personal belongings, geological specimens, and such endearing memorabilia as the wooden chair in which his mother sat to nurse him.

In four restored cottages near the seafront, the work of resident craftsmen and women are displayed and sold: pottery, silver, printed hangings, jewellery, etc. There is also a small art gallery with exhibitions of local paintings.

North and South Sutors guard the entrance to the Firth like two massive sentinels: the view north, to the oil installations at Nigg, is rather marred these days, but there are foreshore walks and long expanses of sand, lining Cromarty Bay. Charles II landed here on his way to be crowned at Scone in 1650. A car ferry runs between Cromarty and Nigg, one way of getting on north.

Continuing round the Black Isle, the B9163 runs down the coastal plain south of the firth 17 miles to **Conon Bridge** and across the neck of land that joins the Black Isle to the mainland, about four miles to **Muir of Ord**. The Black Isle Show is held just outside Muir of Ord in August.

To complete a circular tour of this attractive peninsula, a one-track road skirts the northern shore of the Beauly Firth, 10 miles back to the Kessock Bridge. It hugs the shore for the last stretch, where the tidal flats are rich in wildfowl, backed by blue-grey hills to the north. The ruined castle (private) behind a wall at the western end of the Firth is Redcastle, originally built by William the Lion in 1178. The original castle, Edradour, claimed to be the oldest inhabited house in Scotland and passed through several hands before it was annexed by the Crown after the fall from power of the notorious Douglas family. The Mackenzies held it for 200 years from 1570. According to stories they resorted to sorcery and human sacrifices in an attempt to save the land from a cattle plague. This illicit activity backfired, and the family was henceforth under a curse.

The Anchor and Chain is an extremely good restaurant on the shore a couple of miles further on, with well cooked, imaginative food.

North Kessock, an attractive village straggling along the shore of the Beauly Firth, used to be the ferry terminal. Surnames such as Patience and Skinner are said to date from when Cromwell's soldiers were here. You get good bar lunches in the listed pub.

Dingwall

Dingwall, at the southwestern corner of the Cromarty Firth, is at the junction of several main routes. It is a very busy little market town, its curious name being derived from the Norse words *Thing* (parliament or council) and *Volle* (place). Macbeth was born here, presumably in the castle that once stood in Castle Street. It is hard to believe that Dingwall was a thriving port, before the waterway at the mouth of the River Peffery became silted up. The canal at the end of Ferry Road was built by Telford, in an attempt to cut through the encroaching mud-flats. Dingwall has always been an important cattle and livestock market, and even today it is just possible to hear a few exchanges in Gaelic, around the market square any Wednesday. The Dingwall Highland Gathering is in July.

The Town House (open Easter–Sept: adm), dating from 1730, is a newly restored museum. A special exhibition relates to General Sir Hector Macdonald (1853–1903), a local man who rose from the ranks to become a distinguished soldier. He served in the Second Afghan War, the Egyptian Police and the Egyptian Army and was given command of troops in Ceylon in 1902. He surpassed himself at the Battle of Omdurman. There is an impressive monument to him on Mitchell Hill, the local cemetery, a battlemented tower that serves as a landmark for miles around.

A few old stones are all that remain of the castle. Robert the Bruce's wife was held prisoner here, during part of his exile.

The surprising **Indian temple**, on the hill above Evanton, known as Fyrish Monument, was a folly erected by General Sir Hector Munro (1726–1805), as a philanthropic gesture, giving work to the unemployed in the area. It is modelled on the gateway of Seringapatam, an Indian town captured by Sir Hector in 1781. It is clearly seen from the road, but much more fun close to and not an exacting climb.

The Tain Peninsula

Although the exploitation of North Sea oil fields has inevitably changed the character of the hammer-head peninsula jutting eastwards between Nigg Bay and Tain in the north, there are plenty of attractions to tempt the traveller to make a detour from the journey north.

Invergordon

Invergordon, 14 miles northeast of Dingwall, is a busy industrial centre on the western tip of Nigg Bay, dominated by all the surrealistic constructions built for the oil industry. The Cromarty Firth is one of the finest deep-water anchorages in the world and is now one of the most important European centres for the repair and maintenance of the exploration rigs. There is something curiously beautiful about some of these giant skeletons whose fragile-looking girders are built to withstand the full force of a North Sea gale. Inland, here and there, a lane or wood or farm is as peaceful as it was before the oil men came.

Fearn

Fearn, 11 miles northeast of Invergordon, is the hub of the peninsula, with cottages and pretty gardens grouped round a green. In restored 13th-century **Fearn Abbey**, the nave and choir are still used as the parish church. Fearn Abbey was the seat of the first martyr of the Scottish Reformation, Abbot Patrick Hamilton, who was burned at St Andrews for heresy, in 1528 (see St Andrews, p. 298). The Reformation was responsible for the decay of the original abbey. In 1742, after it had been partly rebuilt to accommodate the parish church, the soaring voices of the parishioners had a disastrous effect on the stone-vaulted roof, which crashed down and killed 44 of them.

Tarbat Ness, about nine miles beyond Fearn, on the northern tip of the peninsula, has one of the highest lighthouses in Britain, warning ships of the dangerous sandbanks threatening the entrance to the Dornoch Firth. The Norsemen called them Gizzen Briggs and were no doubt among their earliest victims. The views are stupendous and there are sometimes seals basking on the rocks below.

Portmahomack is a popular resort with a 9-hole golf course, a couple of miles south of the lighthouse. The small harbour once supported a fishing fleet.

Shandwick is half-way down the east coast, eight miles south of the lighthouse. Fossil hunters may be rewarded if they search below the red sandstone cliffs and in the caves here. The 9-ft-tall stone cross slab above the village was erected in memory of one of three Norse princes who were shipwrecked on one of the reefs.

Tain

Tain, derived from the Norse word *thing*—meaning parliament, council or meeting place—is a sturdy little town on the south side of the Dornoch Firth, 11 miles north of Invergordon. It is a holiday resort and market centre for the surrounding area and has an aura of proud antiquity.

St Duthus was born in Tain, in about 1000 and his bones were brought back here after his death in Ireland. **St Duthus Chapel** (always accessible) is an overgrown ruin in the cemetery between the town and the 18-hole golf course. It was built in the 11th century on the saint's birth place and is the repository for his bones. It was built as a 'prayer cell' with the resident hermit guarding the sacred relics. Elizabeth de Burgh, wife of Robert Bruce, and her children, took refuge here when fleeing to Orkney, relying on its status as a 'sanctuary' for fugitives. This was violated by the Earl of Ross, who ignored the safety zone and captured her in 1307—an act Scotland did not forget. The chapel was burnt down by a smuggler, McNeill of Creich, in 1427, to destroy an enemy he had chased inside.

St Duthus Collegiate Church was built in 1360 on the site of an earlier church, traces of which can be seen in the chapter house. It is now a show place and memorial, no longer used for worship. When the chapel was burnt down, the relics of St Duthus were transferred to this church: they disappeared in 1560. James IV came on an annual pilgrimage for 20 years but not entirely out of religious fervour. He liked to keep in touch with his subjects all over Scotland and he had established his favourite mistress, Flaming Janet Kennedy, in Darnaway Castle in Moray, giving him an excellent stopping off place on the way. Don't miss the stained glass windows, showing Malcolm Canmore and

Queen Margaret bestowing a royal charter on the town, and an assembly of the Scottish parliament in 1560, adopting John Knox's Confessions of Faith.

Tain and District Museum (open Easter–Sept, Mon–Sat: donation box) in Castle Brae, off the High Street, is well worth a visit. It is full of a large variety of items: relics, manuscripts, photographs, archaeological remains, etc. The museum was founded as an exhibition for the visit of the Queen Mother, in 1966, and became permanent. Details of St Duthus and of the patronage of James IV—though not of Flaming Janet—and good displays showing what life was like in 18th and 19th centuries in a thriving market town. This is also the Clan Ross Centre.

The Tolbooth is a lovely example of many others built in the 16th and 17th centuries, a tall, castellated keep with angle turrets and the original curfew bell of 1616.

The Highland Fine Cheeses Factory (open weekdays: free) shows how cheeses are made and allows sampling (tel 0862 2034/2734). North of the town is the Glen Morangie Distillery, founded in 1843, where Highland Queen whisky is produced, using water from the burn.

The drive along the southern shore of the **Dornoch Firth** to **Struie** is attractive but far the best approach from the south is on the A836 due north, three miles beyond Evanton. This road goes up over the moors and down to the Dornoch Firth. Stop at Struie, at the **Stone Viewpoint**, about 10 miles up the road, for panoramic views over the **Kyles of Sutherland**. There is a view indicator, and an interesting board explaining about the glacial action that created this beautiful spot. Windswept heather and pines fringe a road that zig-zags down through dramatic ravines.

Croick Church

Turn left at Ardgay—pronounced Ardguy as in Guy Fawkes—14 miles west of Tain, at the head of the Firth. Drive 10 miles up Strath Carron, along a tumbling burn bordered by lichen, bracken and birches. Little **Croick Church** lies in a walled churchyard, surrounded by a few wind-bent trees in a pocket of desolate moorland. This is one of the most poignant places in Scotland. In the spring of 1845, families who had been evicted from their crofts in Glencalvie and who had nowhere to go camped here in an improvised shelter made of tarpaulin, rugs and plaids stretched over poles. They scratched memorials on the diamond panes of this simple kirk, which can still be read today: 'Glencalvie people was in the church here May 24 1845 . . . Glencalvie people the wicked generation . . .' and one rather tart comment . . . 'this place needs cleaning'. Inside, it is plain with unadorned walls, an iron stove, benches and table and a big pulpit. There is an interesting display board with contemporary newspaper cuttings from *The Times*.

Bonar Bridge

Bonar Bridge, a mile north of Ardgay, is so called after the bridge that spans the Kyle of Sutherland. It is a good base from which to explore Sutherland and has excellent fishing, walking and boating. Aspiring politicians and diplomats should visit MacKenzie Harris, where top quality leather brief-cases and luggage are made. They supply Margaret Thatcher and countless European diplomats: not cheap. **Carbisdale Castle Youth Hostel**, high above the river at **Invershin**, a couple of miles northwest, is near the site of the final disastrous battle of Montrose, from which he fled to Assynt. This is a pleasant detour, up the River Shin, to Lairg. The **Falls of Shin**, on the way, are a popular beauty spot, complete with attendant café, gift shop, carpark and people.

Lairg, at the southern end of Loch Shin, is a fisherman's haven and a good base from which to explore the wild, rugged hinterland of Sutherland. For those who don't want to spend their holiday on the end of a fishing rod, there are lovely walks.

Returning to the A9, the wooded road to the east, along the northern shore of the Dornoch Firth passes several pre-historic remains: Dun Creich, a vitrified fort, on the promontory three miles out of Bonar Bridge; traces of a chambered cairn at Clashmore, west of the school; another cairn at Everlix; and a standing stone on the outskirts of Dornoch, 10 miles east of Bonar Bridge. These remains indicate what a large number of Pictish and Norse settlers populated this area.

Dornoch

Dornoch, isolated enough to retain its old world dignity, remains unspoiled by its popularity as a holiday resort, a charming, higgledy-piggledy town, full of character. Long famous as a golfing centre, its links have been played on since at least 1616. On the same latitude as Hudson Bay and Alaska, it is the most northerly first-class golf course in the world. Excavations have dated settlements here at least as far back as 1000 BC.

Dornoch Cathedral (always open: free) dates from 1224 when the town became a bishopric. It must be the cosiest cathedral in the country: small and cruciform with colourful windows illuminating its warm, mellow walls. It was burnt in a clan dispute between Murrays and Mackays in 1570, when only the tower and spire survived. Restored in 1616, it was then further, and tastelessly, restored in Victorian times. Mercifully, in 1924, it was again restored to celebrate its 700th anniversary. Much of the awful Victorian work was stripped away to reveal the original 13th-century stonework. It is now the parish church.

Dornoch Craft Centre and Town Jail (open daily, except winter weekends: free) is worth a visit. The restored jail gives a graphic example of what it would have been like to be imprisoned in the last century, and the crafts include the weaving of tartan on power looms, and kilt making. There is a book shop and coffee shop.

Dornoch is flanked by miles of glorious sand, ideal for holiday makers but not so good for the evicted crofters who, during the Highland Clearances, were expected to settle here and farm the infertile dune land. Small wonder so many of them emigrated.

Embo, about three miles walk north along the sands, has the remains of two Stone Age burial chambers dating from 2000 BC, at the entrance to the caravan site. When these were excavated it was discovered that two later cist tombs had been built into the original ones.

On the shore of **Loch Fleet**, a couple of miles further north, there is the scant ruin of 14th-century **Skelbo Castle** on a grassy mound. It was here, in an earlier, wooden castle, in 1290, that emissaries of Edward I waited to greet the little Princess Margaret, Maid of Norway, whose marriage to Edward's son was to solve the problem of sovereignty in Scotland. Whether it would have done so or not was never to be known for it was here that they heard of the child's death caused by sea sickness on the voyage. This triggered off the Scottish Wars of Independence and Edward's ruthless hammering of the Scots.

Golspie, nine miles north of Dornoch, is the farming centre for the area. There is an 18-hole golf course. 17th-century St Andrew's Church has a splendid old canopied pulpit, some fine panelled walls and carvings. The great statue on Ben Vraggie, behind Golspie, is to the first Duke of Sutherland, a man who was, on the one hand, blamed for his harshness to crofters during the Clearances, and on the other, praised for sponsoring many social improvements in the area.

Dunrobin Castle

Dunrobin Castle (open daily, June–mid Sept: adm) stands high on a natural terrace overlooking the sea, a mile north of Golspie. Built in the 13th century on the site of an ancient broch, this seat of the Dukes of Sutherland was considerably restored in Victorian times. The huge white extravaganza, standing on a massive plinth, is more like a château than a castle. Its towers and turrets are a flamboyant pastiche of French and Scottish architecture. Formal gardens, bordering a long terrace, are a riot of colour in summer. The castle contains some fine paintings, including two Canalettos, as well as magnificent furniture, tapestries, and family heirlooms. There is also a museum in a summerhouse in the park, with archaeological exhibits, Victoriana, crafts and natural history.

Brora

Brora, five miles up the coast from Golspie, is a small tourist resort with good salmon fishing and an 18-hole golf course. The harbour, once used by fishing boats, is now a haven for pleasure craft. In the middle of the 19th century, crofters sailed from here to New Zealand, to start fresh lives away from the threat of eviction during the Clearances. **Hunter's of Brora** (open weekdays) are woollen mills, renowned for their yarn and tweed in many parts of the world.

There are two brochs, one either end of Brora, the best being about three miles north between the road and the sea. It has domed chambers in the walls and outworkings. Two headless skeletons were excavated from the site in 1880. There is hardly a hill or hummock in this area that is not crowned by some sort of fort or broch and there are less Gaelic-derived names as you go north and more with Nordic origins.

Helmsdale

Helmsdale, 10 miles north of Brora, is a fishing and holiday town where road and railway part company.

The ruin of 15th-century **Helmsdale Castle** (always accessible) overlooks the pretty, natural harbour. It was within these innocent-looking walls, in 1567, that Isobel Sinclair poisoned the Earl and Countess of Sutherland, so that her son might inherit the earldom. This somewhat drastic solution failed, however, because her son drank the poison and died with them.

The castle was rebuilt in the early 19th century by the Duke of Sutherland who, having evicted the crofters from his lands, tried to make amends by re-settling them. The streets are laid out in neat geometric parallels, named after the Duke's estates.

Timespan Heritage Centre (open daily, Easter–Sept: adm), left and left again off the main road into the village, is a gem. It traces the history of man in the Kildonan area from the stone circles, cairns and brochs of pre-history, through Norse invasion, the Clearances, herring fishing, gold rush and crofting to the present—including local celebrity, Barbara Cartland, who has a holiday house in the area. It is extremely well done in film and animated tableaux, and supplies many good aids to the imagination.

The River Helmsdale is rich in salmon and trout, and there is a 9-hole golf course.

Suisgill

An alternative route north from Helmsdale goes inland on the A897, 38 miles up to Melvich on the north coast. This route through **Strath of Kildonan** is wild, windswept, treeless moorland, broken by delightful river valleys. Suisgill, 10 miles from Helmsdale was the centre of a mini gold rush towards the end of the 19th century, and a considerable amount of gold was panned from the rivers. Ask in the Helmsdale Tourist Information Centre for details of the Goldrush Heritage Tour. Kildonan lost four-fifths of its population in the first half of the 19th century, during the Highland Clearances. Now it is sparsely populated with shooting lodges and sheep farms, along the Helmsdale—one of Scotland's top fishing rivers. Several years ago, there was a bout of 'lodge burnings', thought to be the work of drunks or Scottish Nationalists, which left a number of smoking shells. Suisgill Lodge was one of the victims and all that is left is one end of the house and a complete wilderness replaces what was once a beautiful garden. **Strath Halladale**, running north from Strath Kildonan on this road, is green and fertile, fed by many rivers and burns: attractive farmland for the invading Vikings so many years ago.

Ord of Caithness

Going on up the A9 from Helmsdale, the scenery becomes more dramatic, with ravines and steep cliffs as the road climbs to a high plateau with spectacular views from the Ord of Caithness about four miles beyond Helmsdale. No superstitious Sinclair will cross the Ord on a Monday since that Monday in 1513 when the men of the clan passed this way to fight with James IV at Flodden, from which not one of them returned. There are often red deer up here, especially in the early morning or at dusk.

There is a broch at Ousdale, a couple of miles beyond the Ord, where the main road runs inland for a while. Take the track out to the old hamlet of Badbea, two miles east on the cliffs. Crofters took refuge here during the Clearances and stories are told of the beasts and the children having to be tethered, to prevent them from being blown into the sea.

The 15th-century castle visible from the road at **Dunbeath**, five miles north (private), was captured by Montrose in 1650. Six miles to the west, at **Braemore**, a monument was erected after the air crash here that killed the Duke of Kent in 1942. The Dunbeath Highland Games are held in July.

Laidhay Croft Museum, two miles north of Dunbeath (open daily Easter–Sept: adm), shows a typical Victorian croft house, looking cosier, perhaps, than it was in reality. These interiors are excellent for displaying domestic detail, but not so good at conveying the damp, cold, smoky atmosphere, when rats ran around the floor and animals shared the living space. There is also a collection of farm implements in an outhouse, some of which, like the peat-cutters, are still used today.

Clan Gunn Museum and Heritage Centre (open June–Sept, Mon–Sat: adm) is in the old parish church, a couple of miles further north, beyond **Latheron** with its picturesque harbour. The A895 is an alternative but less spectacular route north to Thurso, which goes inland from Latheron.

Turn off the broad thoroughfare, flanked by sturdy, dignified houses, in **Lybster**, four miles north of Latheron. Dip down to the delightful harbour, scooped out of rock to provide a perfect haven for the large fishing fleet that once plied from here in the 19th century. The fleet is reduced now to a few lobster boats and a number of pleasure craft, but the atmosphere is still very much that of a fishing community, with piles of creels and fishing gear, and the salty tang of the sea.

Inland from Lybster a minor road joins the A895 north to Thurso. **Shepherdstown Nature Reserve**, two miles along this road, is a treasure trove of wildlife. A few miles further on is the Ardvanish Standing Stone Circle. This ritual site in the form of an unusual truncated oval may once have contained as many as 60 stones. Less than a mile west of here, on the main road up from Latheron, is Rangag Broch, dating from 150 BC, once 40 or 50 ft high.

Five miles to the east, on the minor road north from **Clyth**, beyond Lybster, the **Grey Cairns of Camster** date from around 2500 BC. They have been restored and there are explanation boards. The smoothly rounded cairn is one of the best of its kind on the mainland. Its original entrance passage is still intact. Both animal and human remains were excavated from this site.

A couple of miles' walk to the east reaches the **Hill o' Many Stanes**, dating from the early Bronze Age. This fascinating fan of stones has ribs, each rib containing about eight or more stones, numbering some 200 in all. This could have been a ritual site for burials, like other henges, or some form of astronomical calculation, lined up with the stars. Whatever its purpose, it is an eerie feeling to stand on this lonely, windswept moor, and try to picture how it must have been for those early settlers, once so numerous in this northern corner.

In **Ulbster**, seven miles up the A9 from Lybster, a flight of 365 stone steps twists steeply down the cliff to the old harbour. Now disused and overgrown, it was once used by fishing fleets to moor and unload their catches, among the cheerful bustle and raucous banter of the fishermen and the teams of women working at the gutting. The steps are only for the sure-footed; they can be extremely slippery.

Wick

Wick, so called from the Viking word *vik* meaning 'bay or creek', is a substantially built sea port and tourist centre, stretching round the sweep of Wick Bay, 15 miles northeast of Lybster. There is a harbour, airport and railway terminal. Norse pirates were drawn to Wick by the shelter of its bay at the mouth of the river, and by the magnet of the rich farmland that beckoned from the west. Created a Royal Burgh in 1140, it was only properly developed in the 19th century, by the British Fisheries Society, who commissioned Telford to design a model village for them at Pulteneytown. It is difficult to believe, now, that 1122 herring boats once plied from the complex of three harbour basins, before the decline of the herring stock and the development of vast factory ships. White fish trawlers still use the harbour.

The Heritage Museum (open June–Sept, daily except Mon: adm), near the harbour, tells the fishing story of Wick. It contains a wonderful collection of displays including a fishing boat, working lighthouse, kippering kilns, blacksmith shop, coopering shop and fishing gear.

Carnegie Library has a small museum (open during library hours: admission by donation) displaying the history of the area, with its domestic and farming life.

Caithness Glass Factory (open daily except Sun: free) is to the south of the town. Visitors can watch the craftsmen fashioning molten glass, shaping it and engraving it. This factory was established in the slump of the herring industry to offer alternative employment for the fishermen. It is interesting to notice that in this land so full of echoes of the Norse occupation, the designs of the glass are distinctively Scandinavian.

Also south of the town is the shell of **Old Wick Castle** (always accessible) three storeys high on a rock promontory, and known to seamen as the 'Auld Man o' Wick'. Having no water supply, the castle was unable to withstand lengthy sieges and was abandoned in the 16th century.

Look out for the **Brig o' Trams** nearby, a spectacular natural rock arch formed by the erosion of sea and weather.

There are more spectacularly shaped rocks three miles to the north along the cliffs, at **Noss Head**. It is possible to drive but it is also a glorious walk, buffetted by the wind.

From the point it isn't far to walk to **Sinclair and Girnigoe Castles** (always accessible). These two dramatic ruins extend from a keep and were lived in as one dwelling by the Sinclairs, Earls of Caithness, for 200 years. The eastern part is 15th century, the western, 17th century. The jagged ruin seems to grow up out of horizontally layered rock on a cliff above a sheltered cove. Ghosts lurk in these history-soaked walls: in 1570 the 4th Earl of Caithness, suspecting his son of plotting to kill him, imprisoned him in the dungeons for seven years till he died of 'famine and vermine'.

The great sandy sweep of **Sinclair's Bay** leads north along coastland believed to be among the earliest inhabited in Scotland. Excavations revealed that Middle Stone Age man existed here in large numbers, on the fertile hinterland.

Less than 8 miles north of Wick, a detour left goes to **Lyth**, where, in a tiny community, you will find an 'Arts Centre'. The old school house has been converted, and there is a not always outstanding range of paintings, ceramics, sculpture, photography, etc on show.

The tall, slender tower on top of the cliff at **Keiss**, eight miles north of Wick, is all that remains of Keiss Castle, home of William Sinclair, founder of the first Baptist church in Scotland.

John Nicolson Museum (open daily except Sun: adm) in the former schoolhouse at **Auckengill**, beyond the north arm of Sinclair's Bay, deals with the fascinating archaeology of this area. John Nicolson was a 19th-century antiquarian who lived in the house opposite the museum and spent his life studying local history.

The ruin of 12th-century **Bucholie Castle**, a mile north, was stronghold of Sweyn Aslefson, a Norse pirate whose name features often in the old Norse sagas. A 10th-century Viking settlement is in the process of excavation, a mile further north at **Freswick**.

John o' Groats

Although it is neither the most northerly, nor the most easterly tip of Britain, John o' Groats, 17 miles north of Wick, is loosely accepted as the northeastern extremity, linked diagonally to Lands End, 876 miles away in the southwest, which is in fact neither the most southerly, nor the most westerly tip of the country.

Stop on the summit of the final curve of the moor and look down. It is a bleak, scattered village, washed by the Pentland Firth whose islands are sometimes so close you can almost jump the gap. It is a marvellous vista—the edge of the world.

The small settlement, given over to supplying the needs of the dozens of tourists who come here, got its curious name from a Dutchman, Jan de Groot, who established a ferry link with the newly acquired Orkney Islands, in 1496, under the rule of James IV. There are several explanations for the octagonal house he built, with eight doors, no longer standing but represented by the octagonal tower on the hotel which is believed to stand on the site of de Groot's house. One explanation is that he wanted to provide shelter from every point of the fierce wind for his waiting passengers. A nicer theory is that when his eight sons squabbled over who should take precedence at the dinner table, he decided to settle the dispute by having an octagonal table and eight doors, so that each son had his own entrance and no one, or everyone, sat at the head of the table.

Duncansby Head

Boat trips run from the harbour to Duncansby Head, two miles east, the true 'top right-hand corner' where many different species of sea birds throng the dramatic cliffs. A road runs out to the lighthouse on the cliffs, from which the only limit to the view over the Pentland Firth in clear weather, is the keenness of your eye. The 12-knot tide rip here is a notorious hazard to shipping: over 400 wrecks have been recorded in only the last 150 years. Going back to the days of Viking longboats, the total number of wrecks must be enormous.

Once away from the inoffensive blemishes of tourism, this coastline is perfect for those who like wild and lonely places and extremes of weather.

WHERE TO STAY AND EAT
Royal Hotel, Fortrose, tel 0381 20236, stands very prominently on the corner of Union Street, rather 'central' but the food is all right, the staff are friendly, and it's cheap. Also cheap, **Royal Hotel** in Dingwall, tel 0349 62130, is not very peaceful but the comfort and service is reasonable. **Conon Hotel**; Conon Bridge, tel 0349 61500, is an attractive inn by the River Conon, cheap and renowned for its fishing. They are friendly and obliging and the food isn't bad.

Ord House Hotel, Muir of Ord, tel 0463 870492, is a charming old family house, a listed building in 20 acres of lovely garden and woodland. Moderately priced, it's hospitable, comfortable and friendly. **Marine Hotel**, Rosemarkie, tel 0381 20253, overlooks the sea, and its terraced lawns run down to a sandy beach. Prices on application. If you want a meal out on the Black Isle, **Le Chardon** in Cromarty, tel 03817 471, is an excellent gourmet-food restaurant in charming bistro-style atmosphere. Very reasonable. Or try **The Anchor and Chain**, on the north shore of the Beauly Firth, see above.

Castle Hotel, Portmahomack, tel 086287 263, is a cheap, friendly little hotel with panoramic views over the Dornoch Firth.

Royal Hotel, Tain, tel 0862 2013, is quite comfortable, right in the middle of the town, though the decor in some of the public rooms is a bit overpowering. It's moderately priced and the food is quite good. Also moderately priced, **Morangie Hotel**, Tain, tel 0862 2281, has a good reputation for comfort and is more secluded. **Bridge Hotel**, Bonar Bridge, tel 08632 204, is friendly and cheap.

Burghfield House Hotel, Dornoch, tel 0862 810212, has been run by the same family since 1946, is cheap and known for its good food. **Dornoch Hotel**, Dornoch, tel 0862 810351, is an imposing seaside hotel overlooking the golf course; solid, old fashioned, comfortable, moderately priced. Also moderately priced, **Dornoch Castle**, tel 0862 810261, is very special. This 400-year-old castle was formerly the Bishop's Palace and reeks of history. Its restaurant is one of the best in the area and the cellar is good. There is a sunny terrace and formal garden, and a 16th-century panelled bar overlooking the Square. **Royal Golf Hotel**, Dornoch, tel 0862 810283, is on the golf course; large, moderately priced and comfortable, with reasonable food.

Links Hotel, Brora, tel 0408 21225, is close to the golf course, moderately priced, serves decent food, and is comfortable and friendly.

Forsinard Hotel, tel 06417 221, perhaps the most remote hotel in Britain, right in the heart of the Flow Country, is a haven of peace and a paradise for nature lovers. Moderately priced, comfortable and relaxed, it is open mid-April to mid-October. **Golf Links Hotel** Golspie, tel 04083 3408, is another good refuge for golfers. As well as being on the golf course, it is 300 yards from the beach and cheap. **John o' Groats House Hotel**, tel 095581 203, is the most northerly hotel on the mainland. What it lacks in sophistication, it makes up for in fresh air, and it's cheap. **Portland Arms Hotel**, Lybster, tel 05932 208/255, is an early 19th-century attractive and comfortable hotel; cheap, with friendly staff and good food.

John o' Groats to Durness

This is an end-of-the-world highway, with detours into great tracts of barren wasteland to the south.

Castle of Mey, seven miles west of John o'Groats, was built around the middle of the 16th century for the Earl of Caithness and bought by the Queen Mother in 1956. The gardens are open on certain days in the summer in aid of charity.

Dunnet Head, nine miles further on, is the most northerly point of Scotland's mainland. Walk out to the tip on a carpet of pink thrift, laced with tormentil, trefoils, wild thyme, yellow saxifrage, purple butterwort and many other wild flowers. You'll see lots of puffins, those endearing birds with comic tuxedo garb and vivid striped beaks, burrowing in the turf. The view from Dunnet Head is memorable particularly at sunrise or sunset. The village is a scattering of houses near the vast, clean sweep of Dunnet Bay.

The tower of the charming little white church, with its saddle-backed roof, dates from the 14th century, a pre-Reformation survivor adding continuity to a place where nothing seems to have changed much over the years.

The fishing is good here, both sea, river and loch. A halibut weighing 210 lbs was caught here with rod and line in 1975.

Castlehill Harbour, six miles south of Dunnet Point, is the main centre for the Caithness Flagstone industry.

Thurso

Thurso, 20 miles west of John o' Groats, is a large, thriving holiday resort and an important fishing port, built on the River Thurso. Elegant 18th-century houses built of brown sandstone surround a central square, with a long, narrow harbour. The name stems from the Norse *Thors—a* meaning 'river of the God Thor'. This important Viking stronghold reached its zenith in the 11th century under Thorfinn, who defeated King Duncan's nephew in 1040 in a mighty battle at Thurso. The town was the chief trading port between Scotland and Scandinavia in the Middle Ages.

Thurso Folk Museum (open June–Sept, daily except Sun: adm), in the High Street, has a good collection of exhibits of local interest, including a reconstruction of a croft house kitchen, whose homely equipment was often just as efficient as its modern counterparts. The Pictish 'Ulbster Stone' is in the museum, with intricate carved symbols.

St Peter's Church, near the harbour, dates from the 12th or 13th century. It was restored in the 17th century and used for worship until 1862. Some of the original stone can be seen in the curious choir—a semicircular apse within a square end.

Harald Tower, just over a mile's walk along the coast to the northeast, was built in the early 19th century as a burial place for the Sinclairs. It stands on the grave of Harald, Earl of Caithness, a mighty war lord who ruled over half Caithness and Orkney, killed in battle nearby in 1196.

There are good shops in the town, plenty of places to stay, an 18-hole golf course, and splendid walks all around.

Scrabster Harbour, two miles round the bay, is the terminal for the car ferry, *St Ola*, to Stromness in the Orkneys. It is an invigorating two-hour trip and on Mondays and Thursdays in the summer it links with special bus tours to make a pleasant day excursion, returning to Scrabster in the evening.

St Mary's Chapel, at **Crosskirk**, six miles to the west, dates from the 12th century, a simple little kirk with its chancel linked to the nave by a small doorway.

Dounreay

The tourist office in Thurso arranges tours of Britain's prototype Fast Reactor Power Station at Dounreay, eight miles west of Scrabster. There is a Visitor Exhibition here for anyone with a scientific turn of mind. In a strange way this vast modern complex is not offensive to the eye in a land of such contrasts.

A few miles west, the A897 branches off south back to Helmsdale through Strath Halladale and Strath of Kildonan, into the heart of the Flow Country.

Just outside **Melvich**, a couple of miles on round the coast, is the **Split Stone of Melvich**. An old woman was returning from a shopping trip when she was chased by the devil. She ran round and round this stone and escaped: the devil was so furious he split it in two. Parts of **Portskerra Fort**, a mile or so beyond Melvich on the point, rise 80 ft sheer from the shore.

At **Strathy Point**, 12 miles west of Dounreay, the sea has carved fabulous arches and caverns in the cliffs. The variety of the coastal scenery is amazing; there are many types of rock, sandy beaches, sheltered bays and the restless sea, licking the feet of the cliffs. There is good birdwatching here and lots of wild flowers.

To the west is **Armadale Bay**, with a lovely sandy beach and between the next two points, **Ardmore** and **Kirtomy**, the sea has carved out a natural tunnel from the cliffs. On **Farr Point**, three miles west, **Borve Castle** was a stronghold of the Clan Mackay in medieval times. It was destroyed by the Earl of Sutherland's army in 1515.

Bettyhill

Bettyhill, 10 miles on, named after Elizabeth, first Duchess of Sutherland, is at the top of Strath Naver. The Strath Naver Museum (open June–Sep, daily except Sun: donation) is in a converted church. It gives a fascinating insight to the Strath Naver chapter of the Highland Clearances (see 'Topics', pp. 37–8). The museum is extremely well laid out, and it is interesting to think that the minister may have read out eviction notices from his pulpit here.

The B873, to the south, runs through **Strath Naver**, where many croft houses went up in flames during those troubled times and where people died of exposure, huddled against the ruins of their homes. This too is Flow Country. About five miles down and accessible only on foot, there is a particularly attractive wooded gorge.

Invernaver National Nature Reserve, two miles south of Bettyhill, is a gold mine for nature lovers. It is situated around the mouth of the River Naver, with the finest collection of mountain and coastal plants in the north. Among the rarer birds that breed here are greenshank, ring ouzel and twite. On the edge of the reserve, on a plateau, is **Baile Marghait**, once a Neolithic community, with graves, hut circles and a broch.

Tongue

Tongue, 12 miles west of Bettyhill, is held by some to be the most attractive place on this northern coast; it has a very special charm. The ruin of **Castle Varrich** dominates the town, once a Norse stronghold in the days when the Vikings occupied these lands.

The **Kyle of Tongue**, crossed by a causeway, is a long, shallow inlet from the wild sea outside, so shallow that at low tide you can walk out to Rabbit Island, at its mouth. The lane up the west side winds among sandy bays, cliffs, weirdly shaped rocks and islands, remote and lovely.

The **North Coast Adventure Centre** in Tongue organizes watersports and hill walking. This includes climbing Ben Loyal, 2504 ft high, its four jagged peaks dominating the skyline five miles to the south.

From Tongue, the A836 goes south through the heart of the Flow Country, past lovely Loch Loyal, 38 miles to Lairg.

Loch Eriboll, 10 miles west of Tongue, is a sea loch running 10 miles inland, very deep and beautiful. This was one of the subjects of a prophecy by the Brahan Seer, early in the 17th century. He named Loch Eriboll as a place where a war would end one day. In 1945, German submarines came into the loch to surrender, at the end of the Second World War.

There are the remains of several ancient settlements around here. About a mile north of Laid School on the west side of the loch, there is a souterrain, complete and untouched, with curved steps leading down to a round chamber. You need a torch for this earth house, which floods after heavy rain.

Durness is the gateway to Cape Wrath and the top left-hand corner (see p. 420).

WHERE TO STAY AND EAT
On the whole, the standard of places to stay or eat on this coast isn't great. The best are solid and respectable without too many frills.

Northern Sands Hotel, Dunnet, tel 084785 270, is on the coast, five minutes from the sandy beach. Each of the nine rooms has a bathroom; cheap and friendly. **Ulbster Arms Hotel**, Halkirk, tel 084783 206, stands on Thurso River five miles south of Thurso in Flow Country. The bad news is there are only five public bathrooms between 31 bedrooms, but it's very cheap, the staff are amiable and it's lovely and remote. A bit more expensive, **Forss Hotel**, tel 084786, about five miles west of Thurso is quite nice, in extensive woodland overlooking the river. **Berriedale Arms Hotel**, Mey, tel 084785 244, is an attractive old inn near the Queen Mother's castle. One bathroom between four bedrooms, and cheap. **Royal Hotel**, Traill Street, Thurso, tel 0847 63191, is in the town centre, and not over-endowed with style. However, it's cheap, offers game and sea fishing and the staff are obliging.

Bettyhill Hotel, tel 06412 202, has panoramic views of the sea and the hills, and the hospitality is wonderfully old fashioned. Bathrooms are scarce, but it is a lovely place and cheap. **Farr Bay Inn**, Bettyhill, tel 06412 230, is a charming early 19th-century inn with good views and near a sandy beach. Prices on application. **Borgie Lodge Hotel**, Skerray, tel 06412 332, is a well established fishing hotel in a nice old family house in attractive grounds. Prices on application. **Tongue Hotel**, tel 084755 206/7, is a family-run Victorian hotel which has kept its original character, including a paucity of bathrooms. Nice views and reasonable food. Prices on application. **Ben Loyal Hotel**, Tongue, tel 084755 216, overlooks Kyle of Tongue and Ben Loyal. The staff are very pleasant and it's cheap.

Part XV

THE ISLANDS

Callanish Standing Stones

There are hundreds of islands off the coast of Scotland, but this chapter only deals with the main inhabited ones, served by public transport. For the rest you need your own boat, a good knowledge of seamanship and navigation and many years of leisure. Each one has its own, special magic, each one is 'intire of it selfe'. (See also The Islands of Strathclyde, p. 222.) A native of Eriskay can feel homesick living a mile away across the sound in South Uist. Almost untouched by the distractions and bright lights of an increasingly materialistic world, the islanders tend to build their lives around God and the Church—a Church that varies, depending on the island, from Catholic to extreme Presbyterian. Slow to change, insular communities represent a distillation of the past.

The Western Isles

> *From the lone shieling on the misty island*
> *Mountains divide us, and a waste of seas*
> *Yet still the blood is strong, the heart is Highland*
> *And we, in dreams, behold the Hebrides.*
>
> —Canadian Boat Song

Skye and the Small Isles lie close to the west coast between Ardnamurchan Point and Gairloch. They are separated from the Outer Hebrides by the Sea of the Hebrides and the Minch, a notoriously capricious channel treated with respect by prudent mariners.

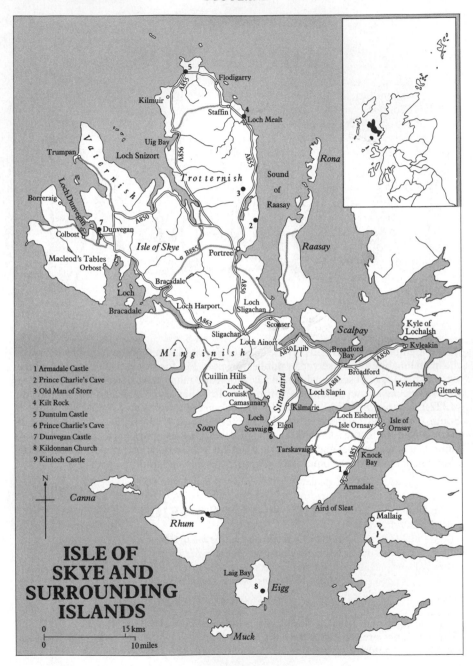

Flodigarry
Kilmuir
Staffin
Loch Mealt
Uig Bay
Loch Snizort
Trumpan
Vaternish
Trotternish
Rona
Sound
of
Raasay
Borreraig
Loch Dunvegan
Dunvegan
Colbost
Isle of Skye
Macleod's Tables
Orbost
Portree
Raasay
Bracadale
Loch Harport
Loch Sligachan
Loch
Bracadale
Sconser
Scalpay
Kyle of
Lochalsh
Sligachan
Loch Ainort
Luib
Broadford
Bay
Kyleakin
Minginish
Broadford
Cuillin Hills
Loch
Coruisk
Camasunary
Strathaird
Loch Slapin
Kilmarie
Kylerhea
Glenelg
Soay
Loch
Scavaig
Elgol
Loch Eishort
Isle Ornsay
Isle of
Ornsay
Tarskavaig
Knock
Bay
Aird of Sleat
Armadale
Mallaig

1 Armadale Castle
2 Prince Charlie's Cave
3 Old Man of Storr
4 Kilt Rock
5 Duntulm Castle
6 Prince Charlie's Cave
7 Dunvegan Castle
8 Kildonnan Church
9 Kinloch Castle

N

Canna

Rhum

ISLE OF
SKYE AND
SURROUNDING
ISLANDS

Laig Bay
Eigg

Muck

0   15 kms
0   10 miles

First known to be populated around 3800 BC, the Hebrides are rich in archaeological sites, many of which are yet to be dug. Mesolithic man gave way to Neolithic, who came in boats made of animal hide, bringing skills and culture, and leaving burial cairns as evidence of his existence. Gaelic immigrants from Europe arrived, with Celtic arts, building brochs and mysterious stone circles, practising a Druid religion, worshipping nature gods, until the first Christian missionaries arrived from Ireland early in the 6th century. The Norsemen arrived at the end of the 8th century and remained until the defeat of King Haakon by Alexander III at Largs in 1263. After this the islands were ceded to the Scottish Crown. But stronger than the authority of the Crown was the Lordship of the Isles. Chiefs as powerful as kings paid no heed to a government who ruled from the east of mainland Scotland.

A succession of Stewart kings tried to whip in the arrogant clans of the Western Isles, but they clung to their own traditions. A patriarchal clan system existed, with every member of the clan family being independent and equal in status, looking to their chief for guidance and justice but not for oppression. This was the foundation of that proud independence that still endures in Hebrideans today, a truly classless pride that endured even the suppression of the clans, after Culloden, and, in the 19th century, the appalling depopulation of the Highland Clearances.

The islands to the south of Benbecula never quite caught up with the Reformation and are entirely Catholic: North Uist, Harris and Lewis, and Skye embraced the Reformed church with such enthusiasm that even today visitors must be careful not to offend their strong Sabbatarianism.

Most island families have their own croft, or smallholding, their tenancy carefully controlled by the Crofters Commission, brought about in 1886 by public indignation after the Highland Clearances. But crofting is a hard life in the islands. With only a few acres, poor markets and expensive freight, few can exist solely on its returns. Crofting is therefore usually an auxiliary occupation, during weekends and days off from more lucrative employment such as building, fishing, and public works.

The old thatched croft houses have mostly been replaced by modern bungalows, but some are still occupied. In the old 'black houses' the byre was usually part of the dwelling, with the peat fire on a raised platform in the middle of the room, its smoke escaping through a hole in the roof. Black houses are only seen now as folk museums, restored and authentic in design, but probably misleadingly cosy in atmosphere. No museum can duplicate the reality: the vermin, the pervading damp, the smell from the byre and heavy pall of smoke.

Electricity transformed living conditions, but it brought with it the television, which has effectively killed the ceilidh tradition. In the old days, when a crofting township was totally communalistic, the day's work was done on a cooperative basis and in the evenings whole communities gathered together round the fire in one of the black houses, to listen to music and poetry and to tell the old sagas. Attempts have been made to capture some of this ancient folklore and imprison it on paper, but it was a living thing, passed verbally from generation to generation, embroidered and altered year by year: its true spirit cannot be appreciated except by ear. Gaelic is still the first language for most people in the Outer Hebrides, but an influx of non-Gaelic speakers means that the children of today are growing up speaking English in the playground.

Those who go to the islands for their holidays enjoy outdoor life: walking, climbing, birdwatching, wild flowers, boating, fishing. Whatever the weather, and it is often good, each day is an adventure. Walk five miles to an isolated beach, collect driftwood and make a fire using dried heather twigs as kindling. Cook sausages on the stones and wash them down with peat-coloured water from a burn. Collect mussels from rocks below the high tide and rake cockles out of the white sand. Have a quick swim, diving into deep water as clear as glass (whatever people may say about the proximity of the Gulf Stream, the waters of the Minch are icy). Pick wild mushrooms from the grassy hillsides.

There are no smart shops: only general foodstores which stock most things from boots to butter. There are a few craft shops and weavers, and a post office here and there. Portree and Stornoway have more sophisticated shops, but on the whole, people who enjoy shopping tend to stay on the mainland. For public entertainment, there may be a local ceilidh or concert in the village halls to mark a particular occasion, and there are Games in the summer on most of the islands. Otherwise, evenings are spent in front of a peat fire with a good book, or listening to the tales of local people, who can still tell much of the old folk lore, and who will often make music for you.

SKYE

Speed bonnie boat like a bird on the wing,
Onward the sailors cry;
Carry the lad that's born to be king
Over the sea to Skye.

—from *Skye Boat Song*

On the map, Skye looks like a great, misshapen claw, its pincers being lumpy peninsulas, separated by fiord-like inlets, surrounded by many islands. From the distance, Skye's outline is dominated by the Cuillins in the middle, a massive range of pointed peaks, training ground for international climbers, and by Macleod's Tables, two distinctive, flat-topped hills further north.

Skye is the most touristy of the Western Isles because of its accessibility, but tourism has not yet spoiled it. However, in 1991 the Scottish Office approved a long-disputed plan to build a 700 m toll bridge between Kyle of Lochalsh and Kyleakin—the longest single-span bridge outside Australia. This will improve communications dramatically for the locals. Whether they will appreciate this in a few years' time, when Skye has become a Bonnie Prince Charlie Theme Park, remains to be seen. Off the main road there are still rural communities quite untouched by the influx of knapsacks and campers. Gaelic is no longer the first language, though it is still spoken, and road signs are bilingual. Attempts are made in certain parts to revive the old language, sometimes somewhat self-consciously by incomers who have learnt it as a subject. Portree is the only town on the island, a lively little place, busy in the summer.

GETTING TO SKYE
By sea: Ferries run continually during daylight hours, from Kyle of Lochalsh to Kyleakin, taking only a few minutes to cross. There are plans afoot to make this a

24-hour service by summer 1991. There is a summer ferry service from Mallaig to Armadale, taking half an hour, and a limited service from Glenelg to Kylerhea. Ferries also run from Uig to the Outer Isles.

By train: Trains run from Inverness to Kyle of Lochalsh—the Kyle Line, one of the most beautiful in Britain. Just as scenic is the West Highland Line, from Glasgow to Mallaig, connecting with the ferry to Armadale.

By road: Once on the island, there is a limited bus service and you can hire cars.

TOURIST INFORMATION

Tourist Information Centre, Meall House, Portree, Isle of Skye, tel 0478 2137. Open all year.

Open May–September: Broadford: tel 047 12 361; Kyle of Lochalsh: tel 0599 4276; Shielbridge: tel 0599 81 264.

Ferry Information: Caledonian MacBrayne Ltd, Uig (for Western Isles), tel 047042 219; Kyleakin (for Kyle of Lochalsh), 0599 4482; Armadale (for Mallaig), tel 047 14248.

WHAT TO SEE

Kyleakin, the ferry terminal, stands round a small bay overlooked by a fragment of a ruin on a knoll; a jagged double tooth, familiar from postcards. The 12th-century relic was once a Mackinnon stronghold: **Castle Maol** or Moil, or Dun-na-Kyne. A story is told of one of its earliest inmates, Saucy Mary, a Norwegian princess, who somehow managed to stretch a barrier across the Kyle in order to levy tolls from passing ships. There are several hotels and a shop, and a constant flow of traffic using the ferries. From Kyleakin, the road runs west along the coast. About four miles along, a very minor road leads southeast across lonely moor to **Kylerhea** and the ferry back to Glenelg.

A couple of miles on past the turning to Kylerhea, the A851 leads south to the **Sleat Peninsula**, a Macdonald stronghold (pronounced like the slates on the roof). **Isle Oronsay** is an attractive hamlet, on the east coast of the peninsula, nine miles across heather-carpeted moor, looking across the Sound of Sleat into the mouth of Loch Hourne. There is a pleasant hotel and a bar, whose landlord, a recent student of Gaelic, encourages his customers to speak Gaelic. The Isle of Oronsay is just off the hotel with a lighthouse and a ruined chapel dedicated to the Columbian monk, Oran.

Knock Bay is three miles on. Knock Castle (always accessible), an overgrown ruin on a rocky peninsula, was held by the Macdonalds on condition they were always ready to receive the king or one of his representatives. Watch out for the *glaistig* who haunts this ruin—a female sprite who graciously accepts libations of milk.

Armadale Castle, another three miles south, was built by Gillespie Graham in 1815. Much of it was demolished and the rest has been imaginatively restored. It is now the **Clan Donald Centre** (open daily, April–Oct: adm), with an excellent Museum of the Isles Exhibition, telling the story of Clan Donald and the Lords of the Isles in an audio-visual show. It stands in lovely grounds with a mature arboretum, nature trails and a children's play area. There is a well-stocked book and gift shop, and a restaurant.

A ferry runs from Armadale Pier to Mallaig, in the summer, taking half an hour: book ahead through Caledonian MacBrayne. Look out for **Ragamuffin** by the Armadale quay, an unprepossessing looking hut that is an Aladdin's Cave of the most beautiful hand- and machine-knitted woollen garments.

441

The road goes on another five miles to **Aird of Sleat** with glorious views across the sound. A couple of miles' walk reaches the lighthouse on the southern tip of the peninsula where there is a sandy beach and more good views. Returning on the same road, take the narrow, twisting lane to the west, a mile north of Armadale. It runs for five miles through woodland and moor, past lochans and mossy glades among silver birches, out to the west coast of Sleat.

Tiny settlements cluster round coves and sandy beaches. The road goes north from **Tarskavaig** about two miles to **Dunsgiath Castle** (always accessible). This is one of the oldest fortified headlands in the Hebrides, home of the Macdonalds until the late 16th century. Little remains now but stacks of stones on a rock 40 ft high, overlooking Loch Eishort. Celtic legend tells of Scathac the Wise, Queen of Skye in the Dark Ages, who held court here and preached the arts of peace and war to Cuchullin, an Ossianic hero. Cuchullin went off to a foreign land to practise his newly learnt arts, leaving his beautiful wife Bragela weeping in vain at Dunsgiath, on 'The Isle of Mist'. He never returned.

Another two miles north, at **Ord**, the views, particularly of the Cuillins across Loch Eishort, and southwest to the Isle of Rhum, are magnificent, especially when there is one of those staggering red sky sunsets.

From here, it is 15 miles or so to **Broadford**, rejoining the road a couple of miles short of Isle Oronsay. Broadford, though small, is a busy place on a crossroads. It has hotels, shops and, inevitably, groups of people bowed under knapsacks. A new baker attached to the General Store makes delicious bread and cakes.

Take the narrow, cul-de-sac road 14 miles southwest to Elgol. **Elgol** is a scattered village with more splendid views and from here you can get a boat across Loch Scavaig to **Loch Coruisk**. A half-hour stop gives time to walk across ice-smoothed rocks to the inland loch, long, deep and dark, surrounded by the peaks of the Cuillins. In the evening, the sun goes down behind the hills sending up great shafts of colour and refracted light, made more dramatic by the proximity of the hills. For the energetic, another way is out along the Camasunary track, from **Kilmarie**, about three miles before Elgol. It is an easy walk over stony ground through bracken and heather, with just one tricky bit called The Bad Step where care is needed.

Anyone fortunate enough to be exploring by boat should put into the perfect natural harbour in the island of **Soay** off the entrance to Loch Scavaig. The remains of the shark factory on the quay were established after the Second World War by the author Gavin Maxwell. His subsequent book, *Harpoon at a Venture*, is compelling reading, telling about these waters in the days when sharks and whales were so plentiful in the Minch that at times the water was literally black with them.

Continuing round the coast from Broadford, the road follows the coast, looping round long inlets, zig-zagging up the hills. In a thatched cottage in **Luib**, seven miles northwest on Loch Ainort, **Old Skye Crofter's House** is a folk museum (open daily except Sun, April–Sept: adm) furnished in the style of a croft house 100 years ago. From Luib there is an easy but delightful four-mile walk due south along the river in Strath Mor, between the rounded paps of the red Cuillins, to the east and the strong black ridge leading from mighty Blaven to the west.

Continuing north, the main hazard for golfers on the 9-hole course at **Sconser**, six miles further on, is sheep.

The Cuillins

There is a delightfully old-fashioned hotel at the head of **Loch Sligachan**, five miles west of Sconser. It sits on the junction of the east and west routes to the north and is popular with fishermen and anyone planning to climb in the Cuillins. Here, surrounded by the sound of falling water, the Cuillins reign supreme. Whether capped with snow, their lower slopes mottled and smeared like camouflage jackets; or in mist, elusive and eerie; or shrouded by swirling cloud; or in brilliant sunshine against a postcard-blue sky, they always present a challenge. Only experienced climbers, with proper equipment, should attempt to conquer these mountains, which have claimed many lives over the years.

The road up the east coast, nine miles north from Sligachan to Portree, runs through valleys, pine woods and moorland past fast-flowing rivers and burns. Just south of Portree, a minor road goes out to the east coast overlooking the Sound of Raasay, with lovely views and sheltered bays below the cliffs.

Portree is a busy little tourist resort and the only town on Skye. Bus excursions run from here to many of the island's beauty spots. It is an attractive town, built round a natural harbour with the houses rising steeply from the water, neat and brightly painted. The name Portree is derived from the Gaelic for King's Port, after a visit by James V, in 1540, when he came to the Islands in an attempt to win the allegiance of the Lords of the Isles. It was in a room in what is now the Royal Hotel that Prince Charles took his leave of Flora Macdonald. He repaid her half-a-crown she had lent him, gave her a miniature of himself, and said: 'For all that has happened, I hope, Madam, we shall meet in St James yet.' He bowed and kissed her hand: a fugitive with a bundle of clean shirts, a chicken, a bottle of whisky and a bottle of brandy tied at his waist, and £30,000 reward on his head. Such is the romance of Scotland.

Portree is the stage for: Skye Week, in June, with every sort of Scottish entertainment both indoors and out; the Portree Show, in July; Portree Folk Festival in mid-August, the Skye Highland Games also in August, and the Portree Fiddlers Rally in September.

The Skye Woollen Mill has excellent cashmere and lambswool products at reduced prices, as well as a coffee lounge. Fishermen should visit **The West Highland Crofters Shop**, down by the pier, for fishing tackle, flies and fishing permits. Fishing permits can also be obtained from Anderson, MacArthur and Co, Somerled Square.

Going northeast from Portree up the **Trotternish Peninsula**, Prince Charles' Cave is about three miles north, out on the coast, where the prince hid during his escape. The best way to get to the cave is by boat.

The Old Man of Storr

The Old Man of Storr is about seven miles north of Portree, to the west of the road and is another of those landmarks made familiar by photographs. The easiest walk up is through the forestry woods along maintained paths, rather than up the steep, southerly grass slopes. The Old Man is the tallest of a group of mighty towers and pinnacles of basaltic rock, the Storr Ridge. He is over 180 ft high and 40 ft in diameter: a great weathered stack, undercut and pointed at the top, like a giant fir cone.

In 1891, on the shore below the Old Man of Storr, a hoard of treasure was unearthed; a most remarkable collection of silver neck rings, brooches, bracelets and beaten ingots, together with many 10th-century coins, some from Samarkand. It is believed they must have been left there by a Norseman, who presumably died before he could return to claim them. These treasures are now in the Antiquities part of the Royal Museum of Scotland, in Queen Street, Edinburgh.

There is good trout fishing in the stocked **Storr Lochs**, from bank or boat.

Loch Mealt

The road twists and turns up the east coast, with views across the islands of Rona and Raasay, to the Highland skylines of Dundonnel, Torridon and Applecross on the mainland, south to the Cuillins and west to the Quiraing ridge. Stop at the car park at Loch Mealt, seven miles north of The Old Man of Storr, where the road comes to the brink of the cliff. The loch drains in a sheer 300 ft white cascade, plummeting into the cobalt sea. Extreme care should be taken here and vertigo sufferers should not even think of approaching the edge. On the north side of Loch Mealt, the **Kilt Rock**, whose vertical columns of basalt over horizontal strips of grey and white oolite, look like the pleats and pattern of a kilt.

The Quiraing is two miles west of Staffin and you must scramble up quite a slope to get into it. Great pillars of basaltic rock surround an emerald-green grass amphitheatre, like a surreal Gothic cathedral. Cattle used to be driven here for safety during raids in the old days. It is hard to find and difficult to get to, but once there it is a magic place with stunning views.

Flodigarry, about three miles north of Staffin, is the house where Flora Macdonald lived after her marriage to Captain Allan Macdonald of Kingsburgh. It stands beside the Flodigarry Hotel, whose terrace gives lovely views across to the Ross-shire coast.

Duntulm Castle

This is a jagged ruin, less than five miles to the west. The castle, with a water gate, stands in an easily defended position on a precipitous cliff on the northwest coast. Built on the site of an earlier fortress, it was a stronghold of the Macdonalds of Sleat, under the authority of James VI during his attempts to discipline the Hebridean chiefs at the turn of the 16th century. Sir Donald Gorme Macdonald of Sleat was ordered to maintain his fortress in good condition, to restrict his household to six gentlemen, to limit his consumption of wine to four tuns (1008 gallons) a year, and to produce three of his kinsmen, annually, as surety for his good behaviour. The family left the castle after a nursemaid dropped the laird's infant son out of a window into the sea. The luckless nursemaid was punished for her carelessness by being cast adrift in an open boat full of holes.

Kilmuir

Scotland's most endearing heroine, Flora Macdonald, is buried below a simple white Celtic cross in the windswept churchyard at **Kilmuir**, a couple of miles further south. They say her shroud is a sheet on which Prince Charlie slept when he was hidden at Kingsburgh House. Flora smuggled the Prince, disguised as her maid, Betty Bourke, from Loch Uskavagh in Benbecula, to Skye. For this act of courage she was briefly imprisoned. She lived with her family in North Carolina for some years, but returned to Kingsburgh for the last decade of her life, dying at the age of 68. A portrait of her by Allan Ramsay shows a woman with large eyes and a calm, fine-boned face of classic

Scottish beauty. Dr Johnson, who was a guest of Flora and her husband at Kingsburgh in 1773, wrote of her: 'Flora Macdonald, a name that will be mentioned in history, and if courage and fidelity be virtues, mentioned with honour. She is a woman of middle stature, soft features, gentle manners and elegant presence.'

From the churchyard you can look out across the entrance to Loch Snizort to the west, to where Flora and the Prince came on their daring voyage.

Kilmuir has a popular agricultural show in August.

The Skye Cottage Museum (open daily except Sun, April–Sept: adm) is close to the churchyard. It consists of a group of cottages with a 'black house', farming and domestic implements and a splendid collection of documents and photographs, giving a good idea of what life was like in the old days of crofting. The green plain stretching away to the south is known as the Granary of Skye. It was once a loch, over which the Macdonalds of Sleat and the Macleods of Vaternish frequently fought for ownership.

Monkstadt House
Monkstadt House, four miles south of Kilmuir, is now virtually a ruin. This was the home of Sir Alexander Macdonald of Sleat, who supported the Hanoverian cause. Flora and the Prince landed here, while the house was occupied by Hanoverian troops. Fortunately, Macdonald was away ingratiating himself with the Duke of Cumberland at Fort Augustus, and his wife, Lady Margaret, was a staunch Jacobite. The Prince hid in the grounds, where he was served by Macdonald of Kingsburgh, who brought him food and wine under the noses of the soldiers. (Sir Alexander is reputed to have made a fast buck by shipping Highlanders to the Caribbean as slaves.)

Uig Bay
Uig Bay, three miles to the south, lies below a green amphitheatre of hills, its long pier cutting across it like an outflung arm. The tiny hamlet of Uig is made busy by ferry traffic, for this is the terminal for the steamer to the Outer Isles. If you are lucky, one of the fishing boats that use the pier may have berthed with a load of scampi, and may agree to sell you a bagful, scooped up off a great pile on deck. Anyone with a portable camping stove should boil these for just a few moments and eat them while still warm, accompanied by a slice of locally baked brown bread from the village shop.

Loch Snizort Beag
At Borve, 11 miles south of Uig, take the right turn (west) and stop in **Skeabost**, about three miles along, a pretty hamlet at the head of Loch Snizort Beag. Below the stone bridge the river branches round a rocky island, now reached by a bridge. (Take the road to the village hall; by the stone bridge on the right, a path leads to the new bridge.)This was the site of an ancient Christian settlement, probably founded by St Columba, whose name it bears, and among the tumble of weeds is the ruin of a Celtic chapel and a collection of old gravestones carved with effigies of Crusaders, in chain mail. **Skeabost Hotel** offers salmon fishing and they do an excellent eat-as-much-as-you-want buffet lunch.

Annait
Annait is the site of the oldest Christian settlement in these parts. The wall and foundations of a small chapel and the monks' cells are scattered across a green

promontory between two deep gulleys. In this wild and lonely place the only sound is the piping of skylarks, the chatter of running water and the wind.

At **Trumpan,** the scant remains of a church have an unholy history. In 1579, the Macleods were attending a service in the church when they were attacked by their bitter enemies, the Macdonalds of South Uist, who massacred them, setting fire to the church and burning the congregation. One woman, cutting off a breast in order to escape through a window, managed to get away and warn the remainder of the Macleod clan. When the Macdonalds returned to their boats they were massacred by the alerted Macleods.

Dunvegan

From the road south towards Dunvegan the outline of Macleod's Tables dominate the horizon 10 miles away to the southwest. It is said that when Alasdair Crottach Macleod went to the court of King James V, at Holyrood in Edinburgh in the 16th century, he was asked somewhat patronizingly whether he was impressed by the grandeur of the palace. He replied that he saw nothing to compare for grandeur with his own domain in Skye. When James V then visited Skye, trying to rally support from the Hebridean clans, Macleod gave an open-air banquet for him, on the lower of the two 'tables', lit by his kilted clansmen, each holding aloft a flaming torch. 'My family candlesticks', he told the king, with a sweep of his hand. One can only hope it was a fine day, and that the monarch was supplied with a good horse or some stout walking shoes.

Dunvegan Castle (open daily except Sun, Easter–mid-Oct: adm) is five miles southwest of Fairy Bridge. Seat of the Macleods since at least 1200, it is a massive castle on a rock, with 'country house' windows which soften its otherwise fortress-like stature. From every angle it seems to show a different face, each one grey, formidable and impressive. Today it is approached by a bridge over a ravine which once formed a perfect dry moat. In the old days the only way in was from the sea, through a watergate on to the rocks.

The castle contains family heirlooms, pictures, arms, original furnishings, documents and relics. The history of the Macleods can be traced back 30 generations to their Norse ancestry. The *pièce de résistance* is the Fairy Flag, a frail scrap of faded and worn silk, shot with gold thread and marked with crimson 'elf spots'. Legend tells of the Macleod who fell in love with a fairy, hundreds of years ago. The lovers were forced to part (at Fairy Bridge, to the north) and the fairy left the flag as a coverlet for their child. This flag had the power to save the Macleod Clan from destruction three times and only if waved in a genuine crisis. It has been used twice: once at Trumpan (see above), helping the Macleods to massacre the marauding Macdonalds of South Uist, and once during a famine, caused by cattle plague.

Boat cruises run from the jetty below the castle to the little islands where seals bask on the rocks. Dunvegan has a Gala Day, in August and the Dunvegan Show, also in August. Look out for the excellent craft shop just outside Dunvegan on the Portree road.

The Durinish Peninsula

The Durinish Peninsula, topped by Macleod's Tables, stretches away west of Loch Dunvegan. Macleod's Maidens, only visible if you walk or go by sea, are off the southern tip eight miles south of Dunvegan. These three basalt stacks are called after the wife and daughters of a Macleod, who drowned here in a shipwreck.

The Orbost Art Gallery

The Orbost Art Gallery, three miles south of Dunvegan on the east side of the peninsula, has modern exhibitions in the summer. Five miles further north, the **Colbost Folk Museum** (open daily except Sun, Easter–Sept: adm) is a thatched 'black house' with peat fire in the middle of the room and all the implements and furnishings of the 19th century. There is also an illicit whisky still, once common all over the Highlands. The museum includes a watermill, three miles to the west at Glendale. Also on this road, two miles north of Colbost, is the Piping Centre at Borreraig. Here, a cairn marks the site of the piping school where the hereditary pipers to the Macleods, the MacCrimmons of Durinish, lived and taught piping for 300 years.

Carry on west to Loch Pooltiel, with its sheltered anchorage, and then on to **Neist Point**, the most westerly point in Skye. Park at the top and walk down to the lighthouse.

Going south on the main road from Dunvegan, after about eight miles look carefully up to the left as you drop down into Bracadale. **Dun Beag** (always accessible), one of the best brochs in Skye, seems to grow out of the hillside and would be easy to miss. It is only a few minutes climb over springy turf and stones to this 2000-year-old relic, which once stood 40 or 50 ft high. This refuge, once used by farmers and herdsmen, has double walls, braced by a honeycomb of chambers and galleries, with cells and passages and stairways, and traces of outbuildings.

To complete a circular tour of Skye, the road southeast runs along the northern edge of the Cuillins, dappled with brown, tan, grey, blue and ochre; 14 miles back to Sligachan and the route to the mainland.

A detour west from Drynoch takes you to Talisker, home of Skye's malt whisky. To the south, there are glorious sands and coastal and hill walks at Glen Brittle.

Raasay

The island of Raasay can be reached by ferry from Sconser. It is a 15-mile strip, sheltered and fertile, once the hiding place of the fugitive Prince Charlie, who spent a couple of nights in a shepherd's hut. Dr Johnson visited the island during his tour of the Hebrides with Boswell and was lavishly entertained at Raasay House, built by the Macleods in 1746. The house and land were badly neglected by an absentee landlord in the 1970s, giving rise to much publicity and local outrage. It now houses the Raasay Outdoor Centre.

Castle Brochel

Castle Brochel (always accessible) is a ruin on a rock on the eastern shore. It has a lovely setting overlooking a bay, with the hills of Torridon massing on the eastern horizon. Boswell, exploring this ruin, discovered that it contained a privy—a convenience that was sadly lacking in Raasay House where they were staying. He pointed this out to their host: 'You take very good care of one end of a man, but not of the other.'

The island has a ruined chapel dedicated to St Moluag of Lismore, with a carved Celtic cross, and the remains of a ruined broch, Dun Borodale. A nice, easy walk goes up

SCOTLAND

the Inverarish Burn to the flat topped volcano-like Dunn Caan, then west along the track to join the coastal road.

WHERE TO STAY AND EAT

Broadford Hotel, Broadford, tel 04712 204/5, is a comfortable, friendly hotel on the edge of the village, moderately priced, and the food isn't too bad. **Duntulm Castle Hotel,** tel 047052 213, is in a glorious position, high above Score Bay, looking across to the outer isles. Open April to October, it is cheap. Moderately priced **Greshornish House Hotel,** near Edinbane, tel 047082 266/255, is a former family home in a glorious position, in 12 acres overlooking the loch. There are log fires, a four-poster, fishing, riding, tennis, croquet and snooker. Watch out for the food: it has its off days, and can arrive on the plate a little too fresh from the freezer. **Dunringell Hotel,** Kyleakin, tel 0599 4180, is a cheap, reasonably comfortable hotel in attractive grounds.

Cuillin Hills Hotel, Portree, tel 0478 2003, overlooks Portree Bay and is comfortable, hospitable and moderately priced. Also moderately priced, **Rosedale Hotel,** Portree, tel 0478 2531, is right on the waterfront overlooking the harbour, and is very friendly. **Royal Hotel,** Portree, tel 0478 2525, is not quite as it was the day Prince Charlie took his leave of Flora Macdonald in one of its parlours, but the older part has plenty of character and it's cheap. **Viewfield House Hotel,** Portree, tel 0478 2217, is on the outskirts of Portree as you come in from the south. Run by the family for whom it has always been home, it stands in attractive grounds and still feels more like a welcoming, comfortable country house than a hotel. Open from May to mid-October, it is cheap. Moderately priced **Sconser Lodge Hotel,** tel 047852 333, was a Victorian shooting lodge, at the mouth of Loch Sligachan, looking across to Raasay Island. **Kinloch Lodge Hotel,** Isle Oronsay, tel 04713 214/333, is another Victorian shooting lodge overlooking the sea, owned and run by Lord and Lady Macdonald. The magic touch of Lady Macdonald, who writes cookery books, is very evident in the delicious food. Open from March to January, it's expensive by Skye standards. **Hotel Eilean Iarmain,** Isle Oronsay, tel 04713 332, is right on the water and moderately priced. It's a lively place, in spite of the somewhat self-conscious Gaelic encouraged by the non-local owner/landlord.

Torvaig House Hotel, Knock Bay, Sleat, tel 04713 231, is a friendly place on the bay, in lovely grounds, moderately priced with good food. **Sligachan Hotel,** tel 047852 204, is friendly, old-world, cheap and easy-going, ideally placed for the Cuillins. **Ferry Inn Hotel,** Uig, tel 047042 242, is even cheaper; a charming old inn with a great atmosphere and not too many frills. **Isle of Raasay Hotel,** tel 047862 222/226, overlooking the Sound of Raasay, is moderately priced, friendly and fairly comfortable.

Of the many bed and breakfast places, two are specially recommended and both are cheap: Mrs Flora Cumming, Eilean Dubh, Edinbane, tel 047082 218, is so welcoming and hospitable it is like going to stay with an old friend. At Mrs B. La Trobe's house in Fiordham, Ord, tel 04715 226, the sea laps below the dining room whose picture windows look west to the setting sun. Take your own wine if you want dinner.

It is often more fun to rent a self-catering house. There are many to choose from. The cream of them all is at Braes, high above the Narrows of Raasay south of Portree. This is a charming, cosy, family house, sleeping six to seven people with everything anyone

448

could wish for. It looks across Isle of Raasay to the mainland and is very reasonable. Book: c/o Mrs Bengough, Rosewood, Harrowbarrow, Nr Callington, Cornwall, PL17 8JH, tel 0579 51124.

The Small Isles: Rhum, Eigg, Canna and Muck

GETTING THERE
Caledonian MacBrayne run a seasonal service to all four islands from Mallaig. For details write to Caledonian MacBrayne, The Ferry Terminal, Gourock, Renfrewshire, PA19 1QP, tel 0475 34531. Murdo Grant runs regular cruises from Arisaig at Easter and from May–September; less frequently out of season. His boat, *MV Shearwater*, is fast and comfortable and takes 130 people. He will also charter; tel 06875 224.

TOURIST INFORMATION
Fort William and Lochaber Tourist Board, Cameron Square, Fort William, tel 0397 3781.

RHUM

Rhum is a squashed-diamond shaped island, rising to a massive hump; another unmistakable landmark for sailors, eight miles west of Sleat in Skye. Inhabited since the Stone Age, its population of over 400 was reduced to one family in 1826, to make way for one sheep farm of 8000 sheep. Deer were then introduced and it became a private sporting estate until the Nature Conservancy acquired it in 1957. It is now an 'outdoor laboratory' trying to discover how the Hebrides can best support wildlife and human beings.

The name Rhum is thought to come from the Greek *rhombos*, referring to the rhomboid shape. The chief interest of the island is its geology: special permission must be obtained from the Nature Conservancy warden to visit most parts of the island.

A herd of half-wild golden-brown ponies preserved on Rhum are said to be descended from the survivors of a Spanish galleon which was part of the Armada wrecked off these coasts in 1588. There are also wild goats, golden eagles and plenty of deer.

The imposing red sandstone castle that looks across the bay is Kinloch Castle, built in 1901 by the owners of the estate, the Bulloughs of Lancashire. It is now a hotel with the atmosphere of a baronial seat, all the original furnishings, and very good food. The hotel is owned by the Nature Conservancy Council and is frequently written up in quality magazines. One of the features is the extremely rare electric 'orchestrarian', a wonderful Heath Robinson contraption whose parts represent a full orchestra, activated by a vast library of pre-set cylinders, each programmed with a well-known tune. All the working components can be seen in action, in a huge glass chamber in the hall.

For further information about the Kinloch Castle Hotel ring 9687 2037. Prices vary from cheap to expensive.

EIGG

Eigg, privately owned, is an idyllic holiday island about four miles southeast of Rhum, with chalets and cottages to let. Shaped like an upturned boat, or a crouching lion, surrounded by clear, sparkling water, it is a magic place, both in sunshine, or in storm. About six miles by four, it is dominated by the huge black hump of the Sgurr.

Walk up from the little harbour in the southeast, round the bay to the east to the ancient burial ground at Kildonnan Church. This is the resting place of Macdonalds who were once holders of the island. A broken Celtic cross, a scattering of grave stones and a ruin overgrown with nettles are all that remains.

An aura of tragedy still hangs over *Uamh Fhraing*, a cave southwest of the pier, easily reached by a path from Galmisdale—torch advised. In 1577 some Macleods were forced to shelter from storm on Eigg. Due to constant feuding over disputed land, the Macdonalds were not hospitable. The Macleods left and returned later to take revenge. The Macdonalds took shelter in this cave and the landing party found one old woman, whose life they spared. But as they were putting out to sea, they saw a scout, sent from the cave to see if they had gone. They rushed back, found the cave and lit a fire in the mouth of it, suffocating the 398 inhabitants. Sir Walter Scott is said to have found bones here in 1814 and taken a souvenir away with him. Several people have seen ghosts here.

Palm trees and flame trees thrive in this paradise island and there are lovely walks. Go up to the northwest corner, the glorious Bay of Laig, with 'Singing Sands' (the *Camas Sgiotaig*). The sands make a curious keening sort of song in certain conditions.

WHERE TO STAY
Both the following are cheap, friendly and hospitable: **Laig Farm Guest House**, tel 0687 82437, is a farmhouse overlooking Rhum and Skye near the Singing Sands, and **Seaview Guest House**, tel 0687 82433, a working croft overlooking the Sgurr and Laig Bay. For information about self-catering places, write to: Eigg Holiday Bookings, Maybank, Udny, Ellon, Aberdeenshire, tel 06513 2367. There are five chalets, eight cottages and three houses, all different prices.

CANNA

Sometimes called 'the Garden of the Hebrides', Canna lies less than five miles off the west coast of Rhum. The highest point of this long thin island is only 690 ft above sea level. Compass Hill, 458 ft, in the north, is so called because of the magnetic rock in it that can distort the true readings of a ship's compass. Canna is charming; serene and lonely, with a good harbour. The remains of a Celtic nunnery that once flourished here can still be seen, and the ruined tower near the harbour was owned by a Lord of the Isles who is reputed to have imprisoned his beautiful wife in it, suspecting her of infidelity.

WHERE TO STAY
The National Trust for Scotland have a very nice guest house on the island, but members get priority. Apply to National Trust for Scotland, 5 Charlotte Square, Edinburgh, EH2 4DU, tel 031 226 5922.

MUCK

Muck, seven miles south of Rhum, is the smallest of the group known as the Small Isles, its strange name being derived from the Gaelic *muc*, pig. It is a green, pretty little island with lovely sandy beaches. Bed and breakfast can be had from Mrs Martin, Godag House, tel 0687 2371.

The Outer Hebrides

Of all Scotland's islands, the Outer Hebrides seem to evoke the deepest nostalgia; its exiles to suffer the strongest pangs of homesickness. There is no specific explanation. The distinctive tang of peat-smoke, the nasal cadence of Gaelic, the wild flowers on the machair, the cry of the curlew, the fundamental faith, the humour; these and many other things cast an unbreakable spell.

The Long Island, as the entire chain is sometimes called, runs about 130 miles from the Butt of Lewis in the north, down to Barra Head in the south. Its main islands include Lewis and Harris, North Uist, Benbecula, South Uist, Eriskay, Barra Berneray, Scalpay and Vatersay.

Each is unique, with dialects that differ even between the moorlands of Lewis and mountains of Harris. Gaelic still lives, the first language for many and fighting to remain so. North of Benbecula is almost entirely Presbyterian; south is almost entirely Catholic. All the islanders are famous for the warm hospitality and friendliness they offer to strangers.

It is picture-postcard scenery: miles of white sand; acres of machair, rich in wild flowers; rugged mountains and bleak moorland. The east coast is indented by long sea lochs that provide shelter for boats in bad weather. An aerial photograph reveals a land broken up by a vast number of lochs and lochans which once provided waterways throughout the islands. The climate is unpredictable.

Tourists should note that all road signs are now only in Gaelic, except in Benbecula where they are bi-lingual, and are often difficult for strangers to pronounce and to translate into the more familiar anglicised version. For example, if you saw *Taobh a Deas Loch Aineort* you might not realise you had reached South Locheynort. In this guide, the Gaelic translantion is given where it differs from the anglicised. The Western Isles Tourist Board have published an excellent leaflet with all the names in both English and Gaelic, well worth arming yourself with.

GETTING TO THE OUTER HEBRIDES
By sea: Ferries run from Ullapool to Stornoway in Lewis; from Uig in Skye to Tarbert in Harris and Lochmaddy in North Uist; from Oban to Castlebay in Barra and Lochboisdale in South Uist. The timetable changes for winter and summer and is constantly under review. Apply to Caledonian Macbrayne, The Ferry Terminal, Gourock PA19 1QP, tel 0475 34531.

Local boats run between the smaller islands. Their timetables are sometimes subject to tides and sometimes they do extra runs to connect with other services. Details of these times are available locally and through the tourist information centres.

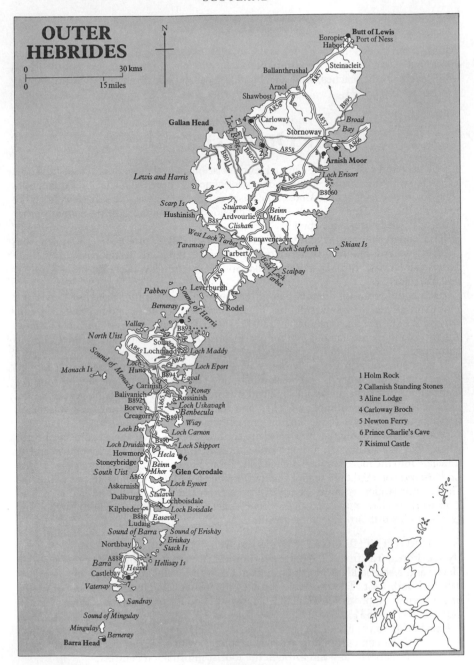

OUTER HEBRIDES

0 ————————— 30 kms

0 ————————— 15 miles

N

Butt of Lewis
Eoropie ● Port of Ness
Habost

Steinacleit

Ballanthrushal

Arnol
Shawbost

Gallan Head

Carloway

A857

B895

Stornoway

Broad
Bay

A866

Loch Roag

A858

1
Arnish Moor

Lewis and Harris

A859

Loch Erisort

B8060

Scarp Is

Stulaval

3

Beinn
Mhor

Hushinish

B887

Ardvourlie

Clisham

Shiant Is

West Loch Tarber

Bunaveneader

Taransay

Loch Seaforth

Scalpay

Tarbert

A859

East Loch Tarbet

Leverburgh

Pabbay

Berneray

Rodel

Vallay

5

B893 . . . .

North Uist

Sollas

A865

Lochmaddy

Loch Maddy

Loch
Huna

A867

Loch Eport

Monach Is

B894

Eaval

Carinish

Ronay

Balivanich

B892

Rossinish

Borve

B865

Loch Uskavagh

Creagorry

Benbecula

B891

Wiay

Loch Bee

Loch Carnon

Loch Druidibeg

B890

Loch Skipport

Howmore

Hecla

6

Stoneybridge

Beinn
Mhor

Glen Corodale

South Uist

A865

Loch Eynort

Askernish

Daliburgh

Stulaval

Lochboisdale

Kilpheder

Loch Boisdale

B888

Easaval

Ludaig

Sound of Barra

Sound of Eriskày

Eriskay

Northbay

Stack Is

A888

Barra

Heaval

Hellisay Is

Castlebay

Vatersay

7

Sandray

Sound of Mingulay

Mingulay

Berneray

Barra Head

1 Holm Rock
2 Callanish Standing Stones
3 Aline Lodge
4 Carloway Broch
5 Newton Ferry
6 Prince Charlie's Cave
7 Kisimul Castle

By air: British Airways operate a daily service (except Sundays) from Glasgow/Inverness to Stornoway, Lewis, and from Glasgow to Benbecula. Apply to British Airways, Buchanan Street, Glasgow, tel 041 889 1311. Loganair operate a daily service from Glasgow to Barra, and a Glasgow to Stornaway service, Mon–Fri. They also operate an inter-island service between Stornoway, Lewis, Benbecula and Barra. Charter flights can be arranged. Write to Loganair Ltd, Glasgow Airport, Abbotsinch, Renfrewshire, tel 041 889 1311.

Public transport in the islands is operated through local garages, supplemented by the post office Post Bus Service. For visitors wanting to explore at random, a car is essential. Cars can be hired locally; consult the Tourist Office for more information.

TOURIST INFORMATION

Western Isles Tourist Board, 4 South Beach Street, Stornoway, Isle of Lewis, tel 0851 3088, open all year.
Open Easter–September:
Harris: Pier Road, Tarbert, tel 0859 2011;
North Uist: Pier Road, Lochmaddy, tel 08763 321;
South Uist: Pier Road, Lochboisdale, tel 08784 286;
Barra: Main Street, Castlebay, tel 08714 336.

LEWIS (Eilean Leodhais)

Lewis and Harris are joined to form one island. Lewis, the largest of all the outer isles, has mountains in the southwest, undulating moor in the middle, thousands of lochs, especially in the southeast, green fertile croftland and many fine beaches. A common sound throughout both Lewis and Harris is the 'clackety-clack' of the Harris Tweed looms in the weavers' own homes.

Stornoway

Stornoway (Steornabhagh), the largest town and administrative centre for the Western Isles, is an attractive place on the east coast. It forms a sturdy metropolis with a busy harbour, brightly painted houses, reasonable shops and plenty of amenities. After the First World War, the rich industrialist Lord Leverhulme bought the island and tried to develop it in order to improve the economy for the benefit of the people. His motives were entirely philanthropic but came to nothing. Economic recession caused failure of the herring markets, particularly in Europe, and Lord Leverhulme did not understand the importance of letting crofters have their own plots of land. He offered to give the island to the people, having lost a considerable sum of money trying to establish a strong fishing industry, but they refused to accept his gift. Stornoway Town Council, however, accepted the land of the Stornoway Parish, including croftland, the town itself, the castle and grounds. The Stornoway Trust was formed, a unique form of land ownership in the Highlands. It is administered by elected Trustees so the crofters are their own landlords and at the same time, tenants of the Stornoway Trust, democratically administered by themselves.

The picturesque harbour, with fishing boats and all the clutter of the waterfront, is the focus of the town. The grounds of **Lewis Castle** are now a public park and golf course. The castle is closed, awaiting decisions from the local authority, Comhairle nan Eilean. The original Lewis Castle, near the present ferry terminal, was the stronghold of the Macleods and was destroyed by Cromwell.

Museum nan Eilean—Western Isles Museum (open daily except Sunday, afternoons only in winter: free) is in the Old Town Hall, with good local history displays. Also in the Town Hall, open daily except Sunday, is the award-winning **An Lanntair Gallery**, with exhibitions by local artists and themes of local interest.

About four miles south of the castle, on the edge of Arnish Moor, a cairn commemorates the night Prince Charlie spent here, while trying to negotiate for a boat during his fugitive days after Culloden. (Such was rumour in those days that when one of his three companions, Donald Macleod, went ahead of him into Stornoway to make arrangements, he found large numbers of armed Mackenzies preparing to fight off the Prince and an estimated army of 500 Highlanders.)

On New Year's Day 1919, a troop ship, the *Iolaire*, hit Holm Rock on the other side of the harbour and sank, drowning 200 men returning from the war.

East of Stornoway, past the airport, a narrow neck of land connects **Point** (an Rubha) to the rest of Lewis. It is also called the Eye (or Ui) Peninsula, after a Norse word meaning narrow ford or isthmus. 14th-century **St Columba's Church**, at the western end of Point, is the burial ground of the Macleod chiefs. There is some fine carving in the church which was last used in 1828.

North of Stornoway, **Back** (Am Bac) and **North Tolsta** (Tolastadh) have fertile croft land, steep cliffs and large white beaches, unique on the east coast of the Western Isles. At the end of the road is Lord Leverhulme's 'Bridge to nowhere', the beginning of the road he hoped to build between Tolsta and Ness to complete the coastal road.

The Butt of Lewis (Rubha Robhanais) is a bleak headland on the northern tip of the island, 27 miles from Stornoway by road, and topped by a lighthouse. This is a birdwatcher's dreamland: shags, cormorants, puffins, razorbills, guillemots, terns, kittiwakes, fulmars, gulls, oystercatchers, plovers, redshanks, greenshanks are just a few of the birds whose calls echo among the cliffs.

The 'Ness' (Nis) district just to the south is known as one of the most densely populated rural areas in Britain, with a hotel, a tearoom (open in the summer), and a very active football and social club. There are good beaches here, particularly the one near the harbour at Port of Ness. On the road out to the lighthouse, the old *feannagan* or inappropriately named Lazy Beds can be seen clearly, characteristic of the old type of agriculture throughout the islands. There was nothing lazy about the hard work that went into digging these strips and fertilizing them with seaweed carted in heavy creels.

At **Eoropie**, (Eoropaidh) the little hamlet southwest of the lighthouse, is the restored 12th-century **St Moluag's Chapel**, known as Teamphull Mhor and built on the site of an early Christian chapel. The key for this charming little place is in the shop. Episcopal services are held occasionally and there is a strong feeling of the simple, uncomplicated faith that keeps such a remote church alive.

About 10 miles down the A857, the 20 ft monolith, **The Thrushel Stone** (Clach an Truiseal), is the largest single stone in Scotland, a relic from pre-historic settlers. This and the burial cairn within a stone circle surrounded by bleak moorland at **Steinacleit**, about a mile or so away, have a marvellously primal atmosphere.

About eight miles further on, at **Arnol**, there is the **Black House Museum** (open daily except Sun: adm). It gives a splendid example of how crofting families lived, with exhibits of implements and simple furnishings, until as recently as the Second World War. At **Bragar** a mile beyond Arnol, look out for a gateway beside the road made of the massive jaw bone of an 80 ft blue whale that came ashore in the bay here in 1920. It had been harpooned and the harpoon hangs from the centre of the arch.

Shawbost (Siabost) Folk Museum (open daily except Sun: donation box) is a couple of miles further on. Here there is a splendid exhibition covering the old way of life in Lewis. It includes a restored Norse watermill about a mile to the west. The entire museum was set up by pupils of the school. There is a modern Harris Tweed Mill, open to visitors, in Shawbost.

Between Shawbost and Carloway (Carlabhagh), there are beautiful sheltered beaches at **Dalbeg** (Dail Beag) and **Dalmore** (Dail Mor), down two turnings off the A857.

In **Carloway**, five miles southwest of Shawbost, drive out to the end of the Gearrannan road. Here is a typical village street of black houses, in traditional style, one of which has been renovated and is a Gatliff Trust Hostel. Stop on the way to watch John MacGregor at work in his weaving shed and buy a length of his Harris Tweed.

Carloway Broch is always accessible. On the northern shore of East Loch Roag, a couple of miles south of the village, it is the best preserved broch in the Hebrides, on a wonderful site overlooking the sea. Its only rival for age and preservation is Mousa Broch in Shetland. Part of it rises to about 30 ft; a reassuring shelter for those families who 2000 years ago crowded inside the massive walls to take refuge from invaders.

Callanish (Calanais) Standing Stones

The Callanish Standing Stones, always accessible, are five miles southeast of Carloway along the northern shore of East Loch Roag. They rank in importance with Stonehenge, being one of the most complete pre-historic sites in Britain. The stones are laid out to depict a Celtic cross with a burial cairn at the centre, approached from north and south by avenues of pillars. Traces of cremated bones were found in the cairn. The central pillar casts its shadow along the entrance passage into the grave only at sunset on the days of the equinox. It is a most dramatic place, set in moorland overlooking the loch and surrounded by hills. It stirs the imagination, conjuring the burial of some priest-king with the elaborate ritual practised in the centuries before Christianity. A mini-museum, open in the summer, gives details of the stones. There is also a tea room. On a clear day **Flannan Islands** can be seen, 15 miles to the west. In 1900 a gale raged at Christmas and all three of the lighthouse-keepers vanished without trace.

After Callanish, the B8011 branches south at **Garynahine** (Gearraidh Na H-Aibhne) for **Bernera** (Bearnaraigh) and **Uig**. The island of Bernera is reached by a 'bridge over the Atlantic', built in 1953. The men of Bernera were agitators in the period leading up to the 1886 crofters' revolt, when they marched with their grievances to the landlord, Sir James Matheson, in his castle in Stornoway. **Bosta Beach**, on the northern tip, is well worth a visit. Go on down the B8001 and explore the district around Uig, which has some of the most beautiful scenery in the islands.

The famous **Lewis Chessmen**, made of walrus ivory, were discovered in 1831, in the sands of **Ardroil** (Eadar Dha Fhadhail), a few miles south of Gallan Head. Of Norse origin, they are thought to have been buried here to save them from plunder, by nuns living in a Benedictine convent at Brenish at the end of the road. Replicas can be bought all over the islands. The original chessmen are divided between the British Museum and the Scottish National Museum.

This is grand walking country—along the coast to the Uig Hills and south to the hills of Harris.

Going south from Stornoway towards Harris, the road goes through the 'Lochs' area and a detour east on the B8060, down to **Lemreway**. The land is split by deep sea lochs and masses of little lochans, surrounded by heathery hills.

HARRIS (Eilean Hearadh)

Aline Lodge, at the head of Loch Seaforth (Shiophoirt), marks the boundary between Harris and Lewis. Harris is divided into north and south by a narrow isthmus at Tarbert (Tairbeart), between East and West Loch Tarbert. North Harris has outstanding mountain scenery and the west coast of South Harris has lovely machair and huge white sandy beaches. The east coast of South Harris is a complete contrast, with a rugged, stony landscape. Although geographically one island, Lewis and Harris are effectively divided by the high range of hills along the border, and are always referred to as separate islands.

The moors of Lewis give way to the hills of Harris, dominated by Clisham, at 2600 ft the highest mountain in the Western Isles. Although not as impressive as the mainland Munros, these hills provide excellent hill walking and attractive walks in their glens.

Tarbert (An Tairbeart)

Tarbert, Harris's main village, at the head of East Loch Tarbert on the east coast, is a thriving centre with good shops and the ferry terminal for Skye and North Uist. It is a good base for fishermen, both for salmon, sea trout and trout, and for sea fishing. There are local tweed suppliers who welcome visitors to watch Harris Tweed being woven.

Scalpay (Scalpaigh), at the entrance to East Loch Tarbet, was where Prince Charlie stayed whilst trying to arrange a boat from Stornoway. He and his three companions spent four nights here as guests of the tenant, Donald Campbell. It was here that the only recorded attempt to betray the Prince for the £30,000 reward offered for his capture was made. John Macaulay (grandfather of the historian Lord Macaulay) was the Presbyterian minister in South Uist. A zealous Whig on a Catholic island, he sent word to his father, Aulay MacAulay, who was minister in Harris. He warned him of the Prince's arrival and urged him to contact Colin Mackenzie, the minister in Stornoway, and arrange to have the fugitive arrested. A boatload of armed men, led by Aulay, duly landed on Scalpay 'with a determined resolution to seize the Chevalier and secure the bribe offered by the Government'. They reckoned without Donald Campbell who, although not a Jacobite, was deeply aware of his obligations as a Highlander and a host. He refused the offered bribe and dismissed the invaders with bitter scorn; they slunk away, ashamed. Donald Campbell's house is now the Free Church Manse.

The footpath east from Tarbert to Scalpay road was until now the only access by land to the little village of Rhenigadale (Reinigeadal). The new road down from Maraig will transform the lives of this community.

When weather permits, boat cruises run from Tarbert to the **Shiant Islands** 12 miles to the east, a wonderful wild cliff-land with masses of birds.

North of Tarbert it was at **Ardvourlie Castle**, now a guest house, on the west side of the loch, that the Prince landed to walk the rest of the way to Arnish.

The road to the west from Tarbert runs through 14 miles of lovely scenery with views out to sea, among hills sliced by cascading burns and carpeted in heather. There was a whaling station along this road, at **Bunaveneadar** (Bun Abhainn Eadarra), built by Norwegians in 1912, when whales were plentiful in these waters. Salmon can be seen trying to jump the falls where Loch Leosaidh pours down a cliff into the sea, about eight miles further on. The beaches at **Hushinish** (Huisinis), another five miles on, at the end of the road, are magnificent. **Scarp,** the island off the tip at Hushinish, is best known because in 1934 it was to be the recipient of a very advanced method of postal delivery: mail was to be sent by specially designed rocket. A special stamp was issued, coveted by philatelists, and the first rocket was fired. Unfortunately it exploded, as rockets tend to, destroying the mail and the project.

The roads down the east and west coasts of South Harris are so different it is fun to travel them both. The east coast road is a tortuous single track through a bleak, stony landscape. The tiny cultivated patches were painstakingly built up by people evicted from the fertile west coast who were forced to live here and try to make a living from fishing. Many of the inhabitants are now Harris Tweed weavers. Stop at **Plocrapool** (Plocrabol) to see Marion Campbell spinning and handweaving tweed in the old way. There is a Youth Hostel at Stockinish (Stocinis), open in the summer, and a guest house half-way down at **Likisto**.

At **Rodel** (Roghadal), on the southern tip, the church of St Clements dates from the 12th century and has some intriguing carved kilted figures on its tower. Among the tombs there is one of Alastair Crotach, the Macleod chief from Dunvegan who entertained James V at Macleod's Tables.

On the main road, round the west side, the first expanse of coast is the huge **Luskintyre Beach** (Losgaintir), and from here on there are lovely beaches and sea views all the way down to Leverburgh.

Leverburgh (An T-ob/Tob), on the south coast, a couple of miles northwest of Rodel, was developed by Lord Leverhulme after his plans for Stornoway had collapsed. He put a great deal of money into improving the harbour building a large pier, houses, kippering sheds, roads and lighthouses. But he died a year after the local fishing industry began to flourish, and with him died the drive and energy needed to keep things going as he had planned.

A passenger ferry runs from Leverburgh to North Uist and Berneray.

BERNERAY (Bearnaraigh)

As well as the ferry from Leverburgh, a car ferry runs to Berneray from Otternish in North Uist. It is a lovely, fertile island, its people living by crofting and fishing. They have a lively Community Centre and tea and snacks are served in the Community Hall.

WHERE TO STAY
Baile-Na-Cille, Timsgarry, Uig, Isle of Lewis, tel 085175 242, is a converted 18th-century manse in a superb position overlooking Uig Sands. Closed in January, it is cheap, simple but very comfortable with good country cooking. **Cross Inn**, Ness, Isle of Lewis, tel 085181 378, is an attractive old inn with lovely views, very cheap and friendly. **Caberfeidh Hotel**, Manor Park, Stornoway, Isle of Lewis, tel 0851 2604, is a modern, purpose-built monstrosity at the upper end of the moderate price range; comfortable if characterless. **Seaforth Hotel**, Stornoway, Isle of Lewis, tel 0851 2740, is another eyesore, but a bit cheaper, friendly and comfortable.

Scarista House, Scarista, Isle of Harris, tel 085985 238, is a delightful Georgian manse in lovely surroundings, backed by hills and overlooking a sandy beach. Moderate to expensive, this is unquestionably the pick of the bunch. Very comfortable, with peat fires and a good library, interesting food and a quite extensive wine list. **Harris Hotel**, Tarbert, Isle of Harris, tel 0859 2154, is a friendly, relaxed place, cheap and comfortable. About the same price, **Ardvourlie Castle Guest House**, Isle of Harris, tel 0859 2307, is a splendid, rather gaunt house overlooking the loch where Prince Charlie landed after his narrow escape from the avaricious minister, Macaulay, on Scalpay. There is a larger choice of accommodation in the brochure.

NORTH UIST (Uibhist a Tuath)

North Uist is about 17 miles long and 13 wide and a great deal of it is water. Wild peat moors cover the eastern side, with gentler green farmland to the west and glorious sandy beaches.

Lochmaddy (Loch Na Madadh) is the island port; a sprawling village with a sheltered harbour. It has several shops, a bank, hotel, and guest houses. Some say the three rocks at the harbour entrance look like crouching dogs and, indeed, the port's name comes from the Gaelic for dog—*madadh*.

A road circles the island, an attractive drive through a series of crofting and fishing communities. Peat bogs flank the road, with rows of neatly stacked peat bricks, waiting to be transported to the houses. Almost all the outer isles use this free fuel, each croft having its own 'hag', supplemented by calor gas and, in recent years, electricity. The peat is cut in spring and stacked on the site until dry enough to cart. It is then built into great piles beside the houses, and used both on open fires and in Rayburn stoves for the rest of the year.

There are several pre-historic remains to look at round the island. About three miles west from Lochmaddy going anti-clockwise, there are three standing stones on the slope of **Blashaval** (Blathaisbhal). These are known as the Three False Men, said to be three men from Skye who were turned to stone by a witch as punishment for deserting their wives.

Five miles west of Lochmaddy a small road goes four miles north to **Newton Ferry** (Port Nan Long). In a loch on the right of this road, just before its end, is a well preserved fortress, **Dun-an-Sticir**, reached by a causeway and occupied as late as 1601. A car ferry runs from Newton Ferry to Berneray, and a passenger ferry to Harris.

Eilean-an-Tighe is a rocky islet in Loch-nan-Geireann, back on the circular road, two miles west. It was the site of a Neolithic potters' workshop, the oldest to be excavated in western Europe. The pottery found here was of a very high quality, better than that of later times, and there was so much of it that the factory must have supplied a large area.

In **Sollas** (Solas), three miles west, a medieval settlement is being excavated. This district was the scene of one of the 'episodes' of the Highland Clearances. In 1849 Lord Macdonald, 4th Baron of the Isles, was faced with debts of around £200,000 due mainly to the decline of the kelp industry. Among other schemes to find the money to pay off his creditors, he decided to evict some 600 people from the overcrowded uneconomic area around Sollas and rent the land to sheep farmers. Since the potato famine in 1846, the people had been living well below subsistence level, but they loved their land and resisted eviction physically during some extremely unfortunate skirmishes with the Sheriff's officers and police. Eventually they were forced to give in, but for various reasons there was a three-year delay before they were shipped off to Canada—in a frigate carrying smallpox germs below decks.

Valley (Bhalaigh), pronounced Varlie, is an island at the entrance to a wide, shallow bay running north and west from Sollas. Here stands a big Victorian house sadly dying of neglect, inhabited only by birds and the occasional dead sheep. You can walk out to Valley at low tide, but watch out for the flood tide: it is very easy to get cut off.

Black House

459

Follow the road about four miles round the coast westwards to **Huna**. Here, a footpath goes two miles east across the moor, to a chambered cairn on **Clettraval**. This was built before peat covered the land, in the days when birchwood copses grew here. A fort was built over it in the Iron Age, from which pottery was excavated and found to be the same as that made in the factory at Eilean-an-Tighe.

At **Balranald** (Baile Raghaill), stretching out to the most westerly tip of the island at **Ard an Runair**, there is an important RSPB reserve supporting one of the highest densities of breeding waders in Britain. Altogether, 183 species of bird have been recorded on the reserve. Visitors are asked to report to the RSPB cottage on arrival.

Unival is a hill north of the road, six miles southeast of Huna. Walk across the moor, up its eastern flank, on the west side of Loch Huna to another chambered burial cairn with a small cist.

A couple of miles further down, the road forks, south to the right and northeast to the left. The left-hand road completes the circle of the island and takes in two of its greatest treasures.

Pobull Fhinn

Two miles along this road back to Lochmaddy, a track to the right is signposted to Langlass Lodge Hotel, less than a mile away. Park at the hotel and take the footpath up behind it, a 10-minute climb through heather, bracken and bog-myrtle. On the hillside is an oval of standing stones called Pobull Fhinn (Finn's People), a pre-historic site deeply overlaid with mysticism. It is believed this may have been one of the sites where, hundreds of years before Christ, an annual ritual included the ceremonial sacrifice of the king.

Barpa Langass

Back on the road, continue less than a mile northeast. On the right, on the shoulder of Ben Langass there is a grey lump, obviously man-made, shaped like a squashed beehive. This is Barpa Langass—a truly magnificent and amazingly well preserved burial cairn, the tomb of a chieftain, thought to date from about 1000 BC. Visitors are not encouraged to crawl through the tunnel into the cairn, both for their own safety and for the preservation of the site. Great stone slabs line the interior and there are traces of where other cells may have led off the main chamber.

From here it is about six miles on to Lochmaddy, to complete the circle of the island. Going back southwest, to the fork, go left. **Carinish** (Cairinis) is two miles down the road, with some of the most interesting, though by no means the oldest, remains in North Uist.

Teampull-na-Trionaid (Trinity Temple) is a ruin on the top of a knoll on the Carinish promontory at the southern end of the island. A large building with a detached side chapel reached by a vaulted passage, this early 13th century church was regarded as an important seat of learning for the training of priests.

The last battle to be fought in Scotland using just swords and bows and arrows was the Battle of Carinish, in 1601, between the Macdonalds of Uist and Macleods of Harris. The cause of the battle appears to have been the insulting behaviour by one of the Macdonalds, who divorced his Macleod wife and sent her home. The Macleods descended on Carinish in a wild frenzy, but in the furious battle that ensued all but two of them were killed. **Feith-na-Fala** (The Field of Blood) marks the site of the battle, just north of the Carinish Inn.

Ben Lee, 896 ft high southeast of Lochmaddy, gives a marvellous view of the island with its mass of lochs and great expanses of moorland, peat and hill.

WHERE TO STAY
Langlass Lodge Hotel, Locheport, North Uist, tel 08764 285, is a converted shooting lodge overlooking Loch Langlass, remote peaceful and cheap. The food is first class. Also cheap, **Lochmaddy Hotel**, North Uist, tel 08763 331, is convenient for the ferry terminal; a comfortable, old-established fishing hotel with friendly staff. There are also quite a few bed and breakfast and self-catering places, listed in the tourist information brochure.

BENBECULA (Beinn Na Faoghla)

Benbecula is linked to the south of North Uist by over three miles of causeway. The low-tide route across North Ford by foot, once the only way, is extremely dangerous for those who don't know the path. Locals tell hair-raising stories of lost travellers and quicksands. Rocky bays and inlets surround the causeway, washed by the ever-changing tides.

The Gaelic name means 'the mountain of the fords'. The only mountain is Rueval in the east, a small round hillock only 409 ft high, but with good views from the top. The island is flat and waterlogged, with a fertile strip on the west side. The main road cuts through the middle with minor roads off to the east and a circular road round the west coast, to the airport.

Benbecula is the home of the British Army, which runs the rocket range to the south. In the northwest corner there is a large army base—a rash of utility buildings, hardly designed to please the eye. The airport is just beside the army camp, at **Balivanich**.

Near the airfield are the remains of St Columba's Chapel, dating from early Christian times. There is a well close by, now marked by a cairn, where people came to drink the holy water.

Benbecula was part of the patrimony of the Macdonalds of Clanranald from the 13th to 19th centuries, when the lands were sold off to pay impatient creditors. Most of the ruins are of Clanranald origins.

At **Nunton,** two miles south of Balivanich, there is a ruined chapel which belonged to a nunnery whose nuns were brutally massacred when the building was destroyed during the Reformation. The stones of a large-ish farmhouse by the road came from the nunnery.

Borve Castle, a gaunt ruined keep near the road four miles south of Balivanich, was scene of many a bloody skirmish. A Clanranald stronghold, it was finally burnt down by clansmen who opposed their chief and supported Hanoverian George II. The scant remains of the castle chapel can still be seen nearby.

461

Wiay, an island off the southeast tip of Benbecula, is a bird sanctuary supporting snipe, duck, geese and swans.

It was from **Rossinish**, on the northeast corner, that Prince Charlie sailed 'over the sea to Skye' disguised as gawky Betty Bourke, the servant of Flora Macdonald.

A new Community School has recently been built at **Liniclate** on the southern end of the island. It is a huge place with swimming pool, superb sports facilities, restaurant, library and museum, serving children throughout the islands, some of whom previously had to board on the mainland for their education. It is also open to the public, and has been the cause of hot dispute between Presbyterians and Catholics over Sunday opening.

Keen shoppers must visit **D. MacGillivray and Co**, at Balivanich opposite the high cone-shaped water tank at the airport. Inside the unpretentious building is an Aladdin's Cave of tweed and woollen products and some fantastic bargains. It's the sort of place you pop into to buy a pair of socks and stagger out of, hours later, laden with parcels.

WHERE TO STAY
Creagorry Hotel, Creagorry, tel 0870 2024, is an old inn with a newish extention, cheap, and known for its convivial bar. **Dark Island Hotel**, Liniclate, tel 0870 2414/2283, is a modern hotel with very obliging staff and reasonable food. Prices range from cheap to moderate. **Inchyra Guest House**, also at Liniclate, tel 0870 2176, is cheap, comfortable and gives a very warm welcome. There is a self-catering bungalow, sleeping six, at Liniclaite; apply Mrs Shepherd, Heisker, Liniclate, tel 0870 2235. There are several bed and breakfasts listed in the brochure.

SOUTH UIST (Uibhist a Deas)

A straight causeway links Benbecula with South Uist, less than half a mile across South Ford: a white strand that yields an abundant harvest of cockles at low tide. When the tide is out there is usually at least one stooped figure scooping the molluscs into a bucket.

South Uist is about 20 miles long and seven wide at the widest point, with mountains and long sea lochs to the east; sand and machair to the west; peat bog and moorland in between. Ben Mhor, less than half way down in the east, is the highest peak at 2034 ft. A roadside shrine to the Virgin Mary, just south of the causeway, seems to be a gentle reminder that you have left the Presbyterian north and are on the threshold of the Catholic south.

In **Iochdar**, just down the road to the west, look out for Mrs Johnson's amazing bus, completely decorated with shells, and her partly shell-covered house. The main road runs straight from north to south, mostly single track, with an occasional stretch of fast, new highway—somewhat unnerving as it narrows abruptly and often without warning, back to the old road. Lateral roads branch off like the veins of a leaf and lead to the many crofting townships that scatter the island.

The first road to the east, a mile south of the causeway, goes out two miles to **Loch Carnan**, a beautiful fiord-type sea loch with a pier for large boats.

Three miles to the south, the main road becomes a causeway and crosses **Loch Bee**, one of the largest swan reserves in Britain. The area of marshland to the east is a nature reserve, the breeding ground of many wildfowl including greylag geese. The hill on the left, just south of Loch Bee, is **Rueval**, crested by a futuristic contraption which is an Army Range Head. Rocket targets can often be seen off the west coast, and you will hear the muffled bang of firing.

On the western slope of Rueval, clearly seen from the road, there is a classically beautiful statue by Hew Lorimer of Our Lady of the Isles. Carved from white granite, it stands high on the hillside, the Child held up on His mother's shoulder. The clean-cut simplicity of the statue seems to embody the deep faith that exists in these islands.

The next road east, a mile south, runs four miles out to **Loch Skipport** (Loch Sgioport) where there is a deep water anchorage, a salmon farm and a skeleton pier; another lovely fiord-like sea loch.

Less than two miles further south on the main road, beyond the road west to **Drimisdale** (Dreumasdal), there is a small loch with an island and a ruined castle. A submerged causeway runs out to the island. Beware! Some of its wobbly stones have been known to topple the unwary into the dark peaty water of the loch. The ruined castle is **Caisteal Bheagram**, a 15th- or 16th-century keep that was once a mighty Clanranald stronghold. The present Captain of Clanranald recently led a large team of experts in an attempt to map out the original layout of the castle, revealing that its foundations cover almost all the island.

A mile south, the side road runs west a mile to **Howmore** (Tobha Mor), where there is an ancient burial ground and early Christian stones. The Church of Scotland still has its old central communion pew here.

Ormaclete Castle (Ormacleit) (always accessible) is three miles to the south on the western machair, in a farm steading between the main road and the sea. This massive keep was built in seven years between 1701 and 1708 as a home for the Clanranald chief. Only seven years after its completion, it was accidentally burnt down, on the day of the Battle of Sheriffmuir in which the chief was killed.

Hecla, 1988 ft, and **Ben Mhor**, 2034 ft, rise to the east of the road, from which they can be approached over a wasteland of bog. The summits can dangerous in high winds, especially the terrifying sharp serrated edge of Ben Mhor, with dizzying drops off the far side.

To the south a road runs east to Loch Eynort (Loch Aineort), another lovely sea loch, cutting deep into the east coast, and a starting point for some lovely walks as far north as Loch Skipport. Ben Mhor can also be reached from here, and **Glen Corodale**, about four miles northeast of the end of the road. A good map is essential. This wild country north of Loch Eynort, among the hills and glens of Ben Mhor and Hecla, was where Prince Charlie took refuge for a while, hiding in a cave in a shieling. The cave is marked on the map but is very difficult to find; this whole area is only accessible on foot or by boat. In the summer of 1980 Hercules the bear, star of several television advertisements, went for a swim with his owner off this coast. Freedom went to his head and he escaped. He was missing for three weeks, during which time frantic bear-hunting went on. He was finally recaptured, weighing a mere fraction of his normal weight, having been too domesticated to cope with life in the wild.

Three miles south of the turning to Loch Eynort, a road runs west, signposted to **Milton** (Gearraidh Bhailteas) where a cairn marks the place where Flora Macdonald was born in 1722. Flora's father was a tacksman. She was tending her brother's cattle in the shieling about three miles from here when the Prince was brought to her needing help.

Askernish (Aisgernis), a mile south, has a 9-hole golf course on the machair where players must dodge sheep and plovers' nests among the dunes. The South Uist Games take place on the golf course in July usually followed by a dance or a concert in the church hall. Everyone on the island turns out for the games, where, as well as piping, dancing and all the traditional sports, there are jovial gatherings of spectators among the parked cars and in the beer tent.

Daliburgh (Dalabrog) is a very quiet village on the crossroads west of Lochboisdale. The road to the west leads to the parish church of St Peters, a large, simple building, weathered and unadorned. This is the living heart of the island, filled to capacity at every Sunday mass and well attended throughout the week, as indeed are the other churches that support it to the north and south.

Northwest of St Peters is what must be one of the most beautiful, lonely burial grounds in the country, on the edge of the machair, overlooking the wild Atlantic.

The road east from Daliburgh goes three miles to the port of **Lochboisdale** (Loch Baghasdail), with a hotel, bank, shop, police station and harbour. It is at its busiest early in the morning and late at night, for then the Caledonian MacBrayne ferry comes and goes, turning the quay into a bustling place, with a wonderful atmosphere and a babble of Gaelic voices. A few visiting yachts anchor in the small bay in the summer and the hotel overlooking the harbour, with its excellent reputation for fishing and for food, attracts many visitors. Towering over the northern shore of Loch Boisdale is **Beinn Choinnich**. There is a challenging race to its summit every year for the young men of the area, who may take whatever route they choose to the top.

A mile south of Daliburgh a small road runs about two miles west to **Kilpheder** (Cille Pheadair), then a track leads out on to the machair to an Iron Age Pictish wheel house. This is a communal dwelling with a central hearth with cells radiating from it like the spokes of a wheel, elaborate drainage systems and storage places sunk into the floor.

A good map and a 10-mile walk (round-trip) are needed to discover one of the most enchanted secret places in Scotland. Two miles south of Daliburgh, a road runs east for two miles through **South Lochboisdale** (Taobh A Deas Loch Baghasdail) to a parking bay at the end. From here a map is needed to follow a faint track over hills and moor, along Lochs Kerrsinish, Marulaig and Moreef, a total of five miles southwest to the coast. **Bun Struth** is a loch joined to the sea by a narrow passage of sheer rock, surrounded by hills. It is a forgotten corner, inaccessible except by boat or on foot, peopled only by sheep and birds and the ghosts of the people who once lived in the now ruined croft houses that lie scattered over the valley. When the tide is out the loch is higher than the sea, draining over a shelf of rock in the entrance passage and marooning boats until the next tide, which comes in through the passage fast and hard. Golden eagles can often be seen, gliding on the wind above the hills north of Loch Marulaig.

All this southeastern foot of the island is good walking country, and the views from the summits of the hills are spectacular. On a clear day you can see Ardnamurchan Point on the mainland. The road out to the west, opposite that to South Lochboisdale, leads to a white beach with the gloomy remains of a once flourishing seaweed factory, a ghostly shell of flapping corrugated iron and scrap. A few years ago any islander could cut seaweed—a laborious job—and sell it to this factory, where it was processed into alginates for use in a large number of products ranging from soap to cosmetics. Now, any seaweed that is harvested is collected in lorries and shipped to factories on the mainland. The white beach runs for miles in a great sweep of sand where keen eyes will spot tiny pink cowrie shells. Its surface is so hard cars can drive on it. The wide fringe of machair is famous for its glorious carpet of wild flowers in the summer. Opposite the seaweed factory there is a small conical island called **Orosay**, accessible at low tide and with lovely views. In westerly gales spray has been known to break over its top.

The road south climbs to the wedge-shaped church at **Garrynamonie** (Gearraidh Na Monadh), built in 1963 and much nicer inside than out. It has an enamelled mosaic behind the side altar and some beautiful Stations of the Cross designed by a priest from Barra, Father Calum McNeil. Here, as in the other churches, you can hear mass in Gaelic, with a haunting almost Moorish chant from the choir.

At the end of the road, five miles south of Daliburgh, is the **Pollachar Inn** (Pol A Charra) overlooking one of the most beautiful views in Scotland: across the sound to Barra and east to Eriskay. The inn is a great place for local atmosphere and stories of the past.

Ludag is a couple of miles east along the south coast, and ferries run from the pier here to Eriskay (cars) and Barra (passengers only). A lovely sandy bay beyond at **South Glendale** (Gleann Dail a Taobh) dries out at low tide and makes an excellent picnic spot, sheltered all round by turf-covered rocks. East of the bay, along the rocky shore and below the water, lies part of the wreck of the *Politician*, immortalized as the *Cabinet Minister* by Compton Mackenzie in his book, *Whisky Galore*. The true story was only slightly embroidered in the novel. The ship was carrying 20,000 cases of whisky to America in 1941, at a time when whisky was scarce in the islands. Magnetic minerals in the rocks distorted the compass readings and she went off course, riding over Hartamul, the rock at the entrance to the Sound of Eriskay, and finishing up against the cliff. The islanders made a valiant attempt to 'rescue' the whisky, thwarted by the bureaucracy of the customs and excise department, and not a few families still own a much-valued 'Polly bottle'. Stories are still told, with a twinkle and a knowing shake of the head, of animals reeling down the road, and of bottles dug up on the machair that have been buried for years.

South Uist is littered with places where Prince Charlie is said to have sheltered. He certainly hid for a time in the jagged, ruined castle on Calvay Island, at the entrance to Loch Boisdale, clearly seen from the ferry.

ERISKAY (Eirioshaigh)

For some, the tiny island of Eriskay is the jewel of them all. A car ferry runs from Ludag in South Uist but as the road is barely two miles long it is hardly worth taking a car across. The boat runs a mile across the sound to **Haun** (Haunn), a smiling village of freshly painted white cottages with roofs of bright blue, pink, green and red, sheltered by hills. The church, perched high above the harbour, is the heart of the island. It was built in 1903 by Father Allan MacDonald, the man who wrote down the folklore and many of the songs of the Hebrides. The altar is shaped like the prow of a ship, worshipped at by a community whose existence has always been shaped by the sea. The ship's bell outside, beyond the church, was rescued from the *Derflinger*, one of the German ships that sank in Scapa Flow in 1919.

Just beyond the village on the western shore there is a delightful crescent of sand called Prince Charlie's Bay. This was where the prince landed from France on 23 July 1745 and where he spent his first night on Scottish soil. The black house he stayed in was only pulled down in 1902. Its smoky interior drove him out into the fresh air several times during the night, drawing reproofs from his host. It was a simple place, like all the others of its kind, with cupboard beds, hens running over the earth floor, and wooden trunks holding the family possessions. The pretty pink convolvulus, called Prince Charlie's Rose, in the machair round Prince Charlie's Bay, is said to have been introduced here from a seed dropped from his shoe.

The **Stack Islands** lie just off the southern tip of Eriskay. There is a rock creek on the main island where boats can land in calm weather. It is then a scramble to climb the precipitous cliff to the Weaver's Castle at the top. Here a notorious Macneil lived, a much-feared wrecker and pirate. He built the castle as a hideout, and stole a girl from a shieling in South Uist to be his wife and the mother of a large number of sure-footed children.

WHERE TO STAY

Borrodale Hotel, Daliburgh, South Uist, tel 08784 444, stands on the crossroads in Daliburgh, and provides the centre of island life. It is cheap, comfortable and friendly and the food is good. **Lochboisdale Hotel**, South Uist, tel 08784 332, looks over Loch Boisdale by the ferry terminal. It has always been a popular fishing hotel and has a reputation for good food. Prices range from cheap to moderate. 17th-century **Polochar Inn**, Kilbride, South Uist, tel 08784 215, has one of the best views in Scotland, is cheap and has a very convivial bar. (Five bedrooms share one bathroom.) It is open from April to October. **The Grianaig Guest House**, Garryhallie, South Uist, tel 08784 406, is just north of Daliburgh not far from the golf course. It is a comfortable, modern house, cheap and well run with good food. At the north end of the island there is **Orasay Inn**, Lochcarnan, tel 08704 298, a small, family-run hotel, cheap with good food. There are a number of bed and breakfasts, listed in the brochure.

For those who prefer the freedom of self-catering, **Boisdale House**, South Lochboisdale, tel 08784 314 or 09856 219, is a family holiday house by the water, sleeping 12 and cheap.

BARRA (Eilean Barraigh)

Ringed by a number of smaller islands, four miles south of South Uist at the nearest point, Barra has a unique charm and atmosphere. One road circles the main part of the island, with an arm running north to the airport and Scurrival Point. Beautiful beaches, rich croftland and a hilly interior make up this compact haven, which took its name from St Barr of Cork, who converted its people to Christianity. Barra is crammed with magnificent views: seascapes and landscapes that have inspired a large number of artists.

No one arriving in the boat from Oban forgets their first sight of Castlebay (Bagh A Chaisteil). **Kisimul Castle** (open May–Sept, Wed and Sat afternoons: adm) stands on a rock in the middle of the harbour. Built in 1060, it is one of Scotland's oldest castles, a splendid sight in any weather but most romantic when silhouetted against a half-dark sky on a summer night. The Macneils acquired the castle as a reward for fighting for Robert Bruce at Bannockburn. This clan was famous for its lawlessness, piracy and arrogance: A clansman from Barra is said to have declared, 'The reason there was no Macneil on Noah's Ark is that the Macneil had a boat of his own'. Kisimul was virtually destroyed by fire at the end of the 18th century. It remained in ruins until the 45th chief of the Macneil clan, returning from his adopted homeland in America, restored it to its present excellent condition.

Neat little shops and houses line the road that climbs from the harbour in **Castlebay**, overlooked by the lovely statue of the Blessed Virgin and Child on the southern shoulder of **Heavel**—at 1260 ft, Barra's highest peak. The statue was erected in 1954 during the Marian Year and carved from Carrara marble; another symbol of the deep faith that governs the lives of these islands.

Like all the islands, Barra has its ancient remains. Going clockwise, two miles west from Castlebay, the standing stones beside the road past the Isle of Barra Hotel are said to mark the grave of a Norse pirate. A mile inland from the chapel at **Gariemore**, a mile further north, is **Dun Bharpa**, a large chambered cairn beyond the hamlet, surrounded by standing stones.

On the eastern side of the peninsula at the north end of the island, four miles beyond Gariemore and past North Bay, the great sweep of white sand is the landing strip for the daily Loganair air service. Two square miles of dazzling cockle-shell strand, the **Traigh Mhor** is washed twice a day by the tide and provides a firm touchdown for the little plane that comes droning in like a bumble bee, its timetable as flexible as the tide.

The house at the end of this great strand was the home of Compton Mackenzie, the writer who caught the spirit of the Highlands more perceptively than anyone. He is buried in the graveyard at **Eoligarry** (Eolaigearraidh), just to the north. Here among the ruins of a chapel are burial slabs said to have arrived from Iona as ballast in an ancient galley.

Another famous name can be seen in the cemetery: that of John Macpherson, better known to lovers of Gaeldom as 'The Coddy' who died here in his native island in 1955. *Tales from Barra*, recorded in both Gaelic and English, is a large collection of folk tales told by the Coddy in his inimitable voice; a delight for exiled Scots all over the world and well worth getting.

A grassy mound is all that remains of Eoligarry House, a three-storey house built by the Macneils after Kisimul Castle burned down in 1795. It was a substantial ruin until very recently.

Isle of Vatersay (Bhatarsaigh) just off the south of Barra, and now linked by causeway, is an enchanted island with beautiful beaches.

The other islands off Barra are each a delight for anyone with access to a boat. Golden eagles and a number of black rabbits greet visitors to **Hellisay**, off the east coast. The birds are magnificent, the wild flowers a constant delight, the sea so clear that 20 ft of water seems no more than a few inches.

WHERE TO STAY
Castlebay Hotel, tel 08714 223, is comfortable and very friendly, with prices from cheap to moderate. **Clachan Beag Hotel**, Castlebay, tel 08714 279, is cheap and full of local atmosphere, with a very friendly staff. **Craigard Hotel**, Castlebay, tel 08714 200, is also cheap, serves nice food and the staff are obliging. **Isle of Barra Hotel**, Tangusdale, tel 08714 383, is purpose built, in a glorious position overlooking a crescent of white sand. Moderately priced and comfortable, it has good food and a nice easy-going atmosphere. There are also self-contained apartments. There are a number of bed and breakfast and self-catering places, listed in the brochure.

ST KILDA

St Kilda, consisting of four islands and a few great rock stacks, is the most westerly of the British Isles apart from Rockall. These lonely islands are owned by the National Trust for Scotland. A small detachment of Gunners man a missile tracking-station, but otherwise they are unpopulated. **Outer Hebrides Yachts**, 33 Cromwell St, Stornoway, operate regular trips to St Kilda.

The history is one of decline brought about by isolation in a world obsessed by centralization and conformity. There is evidence of human occupation as far back as the Iron Age with the remains of a pottery and earth house. A small, patriarchal, strongly Presbyterian society subsisted here, paying its rent with meat, feathers and oil from sea birds. They were often cut off by storms. The population of about 200 in the 18th and 19th centuries remained fairly constant, except for a smallpox epidemic in 1727, kept in check by puerperal fever. The introduction of money and visitors from the mainland reduced their self-reliance and many of the younger ones left. In 1930 the able members of the community, attracted by the lure of the outside world and dragged down by hardship, persuaded the older ones they should move to the mainland, and a mass emigration took place.

Some of the houses, at Village Bay on Hirta, have been preserved, with their cleits—beehive-shaped cells of rough stone that were the islanders' larders and store-rooms. The careful design of these cleits allowed air and wind to circulate inside and preserve the meat of the sea birds. It also kept clothes and gear dry. *The Life and Death of St Kilda* by Tom Steel gives an excellent account of its history.

The Northern Isles

Although separated by 60 miles or so of ocean and very different in character, Orkney and Shetland have a common history and tend to be bracketed together. Norsemen called them the 'Nordereys'.

Both groups—about 70 Orkney islands, and 100 Shetland islands—were inhabited in the Stone Age. The Picts colonized them in the 1st century AD and were subjected to continual harassment from the Vikings for centuries until the Norse King, Harold

Harfagri, annexed them in 875. When Harold succeeded to the throne of Norway in about 860, large parts of his kingdom didn't recognize the authority of the Crown—like the Lords of the Scottish Isles. Harold was in love with a Princess Gyda, daughter of one of the rebel 'kings', and she refused to marry him until he had conquered all Norway. He vowed that he would not cut his hair, or his beard, until he'd done this. He must have been a very hairy bridegroom when he claimed his bride, 10 years later. All the dispossessed '*jarls*', or minor kings, took refuge in Orkney and Shetland and from here proceeded to raid Norway in wild Viking raids. King Harold, exasperated, collected up a fleet and sailed down to put an end to their antics. He landed at what is now Haraldswick, in Unst, in Shetland and declared all the islands to be a 'Jarldom'. The Norse occupation of these islands is recorded in romantic, stirring sagas, handed down over the years. *The Orkneyinga Saga* is one of the best known.

By the 13th century, although still under Norse rule, the islands were presided over by Scots' earls. When Princess Margaret of Norway and Denmark became betrothed to James III of Scotland, her father, King Christian I, pledged the islands to Scotland, as part of her dowry in 1468. Scotland formally annexed them in 1472 and since then they have been part of Scotland.

Norse place names still predominate and the people of these northern islands are a blend of Norse and Scots, very different in character to the dreamy Celts of the Hebrides. They are extremely friendly, extrovert and stolid, industrious and mainly Presbyterian. Their accent is sing-song: the old 'Norn' language disappeared during the 18th century, although some phrases have remained and when the Islanders talk among themselves they use many words more akin to Norwegian than English.

The coming of the oil boom struck hard at established roots, bringing innovations that were not always popular, but on the whole the Islanders managed to retain their old way of life.

ORKNEY

Orkney's 70 or so islands are six miles off the north coast of Scotland on a level with Leningrad. They extend 53 miles from north to south and about 23 from west to east: Oslo is closer than London. Nineteen of them are inhabited, and when an Orcadian talks of the Mainland, he means Mainland Orkney—the big island. (The Mainland of Scotland is 'the sooth'.) Orkney means 'seal islands', the *ey* being Norse for islands: no one talks of The Orkneys, just Orkney.

First impressions are of emerald green plateaux of turf above sheer rock cliffs and sandy beaches, fertile farmland and sparkling sea. Apart from Hoy, nothing is higher than 900 ft. A great dome of clear sky seems to shed an ethereal greenish light. Sunsets in May and June are fantastic. At midsummer the sun is above the horizon for $18\frac{1}{4}$ hours and it is possible to read a book outside all through the night. This Midsummer Twilight is called 'Grimlins', from the Norse word *Grimla*, to glimmer or twinkle.

St Magnus Festival in Kirkwall in June is a week of music, drama and art, rapidly growing in popularity and attracting companies from many countries. The standard is

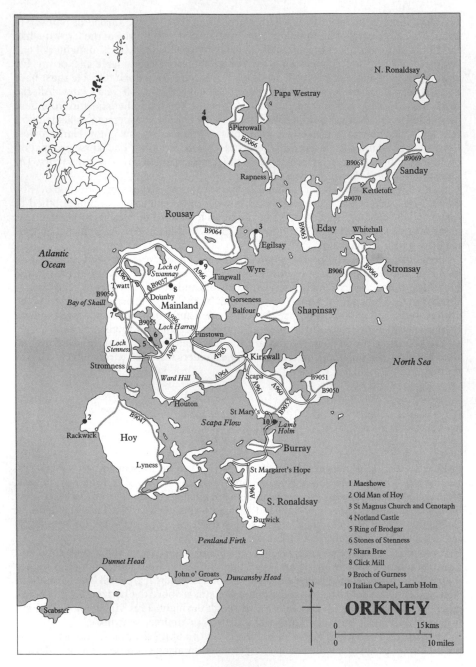

N. Ronaldsay

Papa Westray

Pierowall
B9066
Rapness

B9068
B9069
Sanday
Kettletoft
B9070

Rousay
B9064
3
Egilsay
Eday
Whitehall
B9063

Atlantic
Ocean

Wyre
B9061
B9060
Stronsay

9
A966
Tingwall

Loch of
Swannay
B9057
8
Twatt
B9056
Dounby
Mainland
Gorseness
Balfour
Shapinsay

Bay of Skaill
7
B9055
6
A986
Loch Harray
Finstown

Loch
Stenness
5
A965
A965
Kirkwall

North Sea

Stromness
A964
Ward Hill
Scapa
A961
A960
B9051
B9050

Houton
B9052

St Mary's
St Magnus
2
B9047
Scapa Flow
10
Lamb
Holm

Rackwick
Hoy
Burray

Lyness
St Margaret's Hope

A961
S. Ronaldsay

Burwick

Pentland Firth

Dunnet Head
John o' Groats
Duncansby Head

N

Scabster

1 Maeshowe
2 Old Man of Hoy
3 St Magnus Church and Cenotaph
4 Notland Castle
5 Ring of Brodgar
6 Stones of Stenness
7 Skara Brae
8 Click Mill
9 Broch of Gurness
10 Italian Chapel, Lamb Holm

ORKNEY

0   15 kms
0   10 miles

470

high. For two weeks in July there is a **Craftsmen's Guild** in Kirkwall, with demonstrations of local craftwork. Stromness has a **Folk Festival** in May and a **Shopping Week** in July. Although there is plenty of accommodation, it is wise to book well in advance.

SPORT

Birdwatching is almost compulsive. One in six of all seabirds breeding in Britain nests in Orkney. The long-eared owl is an endearing resident: his 'ears' are elongated head feathers and have nothing to do with hearing. His low, moaning hoot is an eerie sound at night. There are short-eared owls, who hunt by day over the moors; red-throated divers, so graceful until they come in to land; razorbills with their fascinating courtship displays and refusal to build nests; puffins, whose brightly coloured bills are a weapon and a spade with which to dig burrows in the turf. For **botanists** the wild flowers are a joy: tiny Primula Scotica, a survivor from the last Ice Age; grass of Parnassus, whose honey-scented white flowers litter the marshland; bog pimpernel, oysterplant, bog asphodel, and many more. For general **naturalists** there is the unique Orkney vole to look out for, a sweet little round ball of fur. There are otters—Kirkwall must be about the only town to display a red triangular road sign saying: Otters Crossing 100 yds.

Fishermen leave Orkney with enough fishing stories to keep them happy till they return. Brown trout are the best in Britain and fishing is free, thanks to Norse law. Sea angling is also good. **Water sports** include perfect waters for **sub-aqua** diving, especially wreck-diving around Scapa Flow. **Archaeologists** will find more pre-historic remains than anwhere else in Scotland, some in a remarkable state of preservation: brochs, standing stones, burial cairns—an average of three sites per square mile. It is beyond the scope of this book to describe each of the many hundreds of historic sites and antiquities that pepper Orkney. The Tourist Board's Information Office, in Broad Street, Kirkwall, has brought out a first-class free booklet on what to see, and you are strongly advised to get hold of it.

Walking is an endless delight and visitors are urged to venture further than the Mainland. The other islands are easy to get to and each has a different charm. There is also **pony-trekking** and **golf**.

GETTING THERE

By sea: P&O operate a daily roll-on, roll-off car ferry service (except on Sundays) from Scrabster near Thurso to Stromness on Mainland Orkney, sailing time 2 hours. They also have a Saturday boat from Aberdeen taking 8 hours. Thomas and Bews run passenger boats from John o' Groats to Burwick in the summer, crossing time 45 minutes, no bookings. Orkney Ferries run a new roll-on, roll-off car ferry from Gill's Bay, crossing time 45 minutes, no bookings.

By air: British Airways operate a daily service from Glasgow, Inverness and Aberdeen to Kirkwall. Loganair operate a daily service from Glasgow, Edinburgh, Inverness and Wick.

On arrival, there is an excellent inter-island air service (the shortest flight, between Westray and Papa Westray, taking only a minute in good conditions), as well as ferries. It is easy to hire cars and there are causeways to some of the islands. Careful planning is needed, to make best use of the transport available. The people in the tourist office are very helpful and will advise on the best tours to take, and give up-to-date opening times.

TOURIST INFORMATION
Orkney Tourist Board Information Centre, Broad Street, Kirkwall, tel 0856 2856.
Ferry Terminal, Stromness, tel 0856 850716 (limited hours Oct–April).

Mainland

Kirkwall is the capital of Orkney and one of the earliest established Norse trading towns, referred to in *The Orkneyinga Saga* as Kirkjuvagr, 'Church-bay-of-the-Vikings', indicating that the Norsemen found an Early Christian church here when they arrived. It is a cheerful, bustling, sturdy town; an ideal centre from which to explore these fascinating islands.

Kirkwall has its own unique 'Ba' Game', loosely described as football. It is played on Christmas and New Year's Day, between the 'trsuppies' and 'trsdoonies' and often involves as many as 150 men from either end of the town. If the ball finishes up in the harbour it is victory for the 'trsuppies': if it reaches the goal at the old castle, then the 'trsdoonies' win. The game can last all day and dates from Norse times.

St Magnus Cathedral (open daily except Sun when it is only open for worship: free) dominates the town. It is a massive red sandstone cruciform building, founded in 1137. St Magnus, who was murdered in 1116, and whose canonization may have been more political than spiritual, was the uncle of Jarl Rognvald Kilson, the founder of the cathedral. The bones of both these men now lie below the columns of the central bay of the choir. They were discovered, hidden in chests, during repair work in this century. The cathedral has been carefully restored: the rose window is modern but the east window dates from 1511. Although still called a cathedral the services are Church of Scotland.

The old part of the town clusters round the cathedral, with the ruin of the 12th-century **Bishop's Palace** (open daily except Fri afternoons and Sat in winter: adm) next door to it. It was here that poor old King Haakon of Norway died, having struggled back this far from his defeat by Alexander III at Largs in 1263.

Across the road from the Bishop's Palace is the still beautiful ruin of the **Earl's Palace** (open daily except Fri afternoons and Sat in winter: adm) built by forced labour for a much loathed tyrant, Earl Patrick Stewart, at the beginning of the 17th century. The palace is L-shaped, with attractive angle-turrets, once described as 'the most mature and accomplished piece of Renaissance architecture in Scotland'. Earl Patrick was Steward of Orkney and Shetland and entirely corrupt. He was finally executed for his awful crimes against humanity, having been granted a week's reprieve so that he could learn the Lord's Prayer.

Tankerness House Museum (open daily except Sun: adm) is in a well-restored 16th-century merchant's town house, with an attractive courtyard and garden. The fascinating history of Orkney, over 4000 years, is displayed here.

The Library (open daily except Sun: free), founded in 1683, is the oldest public library in Scotland and has an excellent Orkney Room, for anyone wanting to go more deeply into the history of the island.

Among the other things to visit in the town are the **Silver Works** and the two malt whisky distilleries, **The Highlands Park Distillery** and **Scapa Distillery**, all of which welcome visitors, free, on weekdays.

Stromness, about 17 miles west of Kirkwall, is the only other proper town in Orkney. This pretty place with a sheltered harbour has houses dating from 1716. It was once a principal port on the sailing route round the north of Scotland and base for the Hudson Bay Company ships. Many local men went to do contract work in Canada. The houses, many of them with their own jetties, seem to jostle each other aside, to get the best position along the mile of waterfront. Stromness is the terminal for the car ferry from Scrabster. There is a Traditional Folk Festival in May and a Shopping Week in July, when all the shops compete for your business and offer many a good bargain.

Pier Arts Centre (open daily except Mon: free) is in well-restored 18th-century buildings, with exhibitions of modern paintings.

Stromness Natural History Museum (open daily except Thurs afternoons and Sun: small fee) has collections of birds, fossils, shells and butterflies. There are also exhibitions covering whaling, fishing, the Hudson Bay Company, Scapa Flow and the German fleet.

Scapa Flow is a great inlet to the south of Mainland, surrounded by protective islands; a perfect deep-water anchorage up to 10 miles wide, adapted as the main base of the Grand Fleet in 1912. At the end of the First World War, the German navy sailed their fleet into Scapa, having surrendered. Then, on 21 June 1919, on the order of Rear Admiral Ludwig von Reuter, the whole fleet of 74 warships was scuttled. At the beginning of the Second World War a German U-boat crept through the defences and sank the *Royal Oak*, after which the Churchill Barriers were erected, making the anchorage almost impregnable.

Scapa is very popular with sub-aqua divers and its clear water offers great scope for wreck diving. There are good supplies of air obtainable locally.

The following is a small selection of some of the very many historic, and pre-historic antiquities that there are to be seen in Orkney. Do consult the tourist office in Broad Street, Kirkwall, for more detailed information and advice as how best to fit in as much as possible.

Maes Howe

Maes Howe (open daily: adm) is 10 miles west of Kirkwall, just off the main road to Stromness. It is a huge Stone Age burial cairn, unquestionably the most outstanding in Britain. The passage into the cairn, made of huge single slabs of stone, is so aligned that a shaft of sunlight pierces its 36 ft length into the chamber on only one day a year, that of the winter solstice. Burial cells lead off the main chamber which has massive stone buttresses in each corner.

When Maes Howe was first excavated, in 1861, the cells were found to be empty and this fact, together with runic Viking inscriptions on the walls, misled archaeologists into thinking the tomb was Norse. Then it became obvious that the structure dates back many centuries before that and probably to around 2700 BC. The Vikings came, much later, sacking the tombs and leaving their graffiti on the walls.

In fact the graffiti are just as fascinating as the much older cairn. There are references to treasure, and to the Crusades and a collection of sex slogans that are as modern as any today: 'Thorny was bedded, Helgi says so,' reads one; 'Ingigerd is the best of them all,' says another. There is an excellent guide book on sale at the site. Beside the car park is **Tormiston Mill**, a restored 19th-century water mill with a restaurant and a craft centre.

The Ring of Brodgar
The Ring of Brodgar (always accessible) is on the narrow neck of land between Harray and Stenness Lochs, four miles northwest of Maes Howe. From the original 60 stones, 36 remain. They are precisely set, being 6° apart, with a surrounding ditch cut from bedrock, as much as 9 ft deep and 27 ft wide, crossed by two causeways. These stones date from about 1560 BC and are believed to be some sort of lunar observatory, a splendid reminder that those Stone Age men may have been primitive but they certainly weren't stupid.

The Stones of Stenness
The Stones of Stenness (always accessible) date from around the third millennium BC, and only four stones remain of the original circle. Excavations uncovered an almost square setting of horizontal stones, scattered with fragments of cremated bones, charcoal and shards of pottery, indicating that this must have been some sort of cremation and burial site. The two outlying stones, the Barnhouse and the Watch Stone, were probably associated with this circle, as must have been the many cists and cairns that have been unearthed in this area.

Skara Brae
Skara Brae (open daily: adm) is five miles northwest of the Stones of Stenness, on the west coast and on the southern arm of the sandy sweep of **Bay of Skaill**. This was a Stone Age settlement, hit by a massive storm that buried it in sand for about 4000 years. Another storm then blew away some of the sand to reveal the village to archaeologists. It is unique, giving an insight into the whole way of life of those pre-historic tribes, rather than just revealing a burial cairn which only tells a fraction of their story. Careful excavation has un-sanded about six of the original 10 one-roomed houses, and a workshop, with covered passages from one to another and a communal paved courtyard.

Lack of wood meant they used stone for their furniture and the old bed platforms, cupboards, hearths, fish tanks and tables can still be seen, as well as a fascinating collection of tools and implements. Recent progress in carbon-dating means that more and more information is coming to light about those mysterious settlers and there is an excellent guide book with up-to-date findings. A small museum gives more details. Midden (rubbish heap) excavations have revealed that the inhabitants of this earliest fishing village in Scotland were also farmers.

The only surviving **Click Mill** is beyond Dounby, about eight miles northeast of Skara Brae (always accessible). It is a horizontal water wheel, built in about 1800 from an earlier design, and so called from the noise it makes as it turns. It is preserved in working order, although the pond has been drained.

Gurness
On the wild, windswept headland at **Gurness,** five miles northeast of the Click Mill, there is the best broch in Orkney (open daily: adm). A booklet describes the very complicated layout of the site. It was built as a broch and then added to over the centuries by the Norsemen, and includes many domestic buildings, Norse longhouses, partitioned chambers and a well.

Islands South of Mainland

Lamb Holm, linked by a mile of causeway, south of Mainland, has a heart-stirring little chapel, called **The Italian Chapel**. created out of Nissen huts by Italian prisoners-of-war during the Second World War. They were building the Churchill Barrier, after the sinking of the *Royal Oak* and made the chapel in their spare time, using scrap metal. It is a miracle of faith, with delicate wrought-iron tracery, and frescoes, whose artist, Dominico Chiocchetti, returned in 1960 to restore the original work.

South Ronaldsay, joined to Lamb Holm by four miles of causeway, across Burray, has a picturesque village with a poignant memory—St Margaret's Hope. In 1290, the seven-year-old Princess Margaret, Maid of Norway, died of sea sickness in the ship bringing her from Norway, to marry Prince Edward of England. (The marriage had been planned as a way of uniting Britain.) The ship, bearing the wasted body of the little princess, put in to St Margaret's Hope.

Hoy, the largest island apart from Mainland, about three miles south of Stromness, is the only one that is not flat. Ward Hill rises to 1500 ft. **The Old Man of Hoy** is an incredible rock stack, 450 ft high, on a promontory above the sea. This is a favourite challenge to serious rock climbers, a towering pinnacle of horizontally layered rock. **St John's Head**, on northwest Hoy, is part of a 1140 ft high vertical cliff, teeming with sea birds and many rare plants.

Islands North of Mainland

Birsay and Brough of Birsay are less than a mile off northwest Mainland and it is possible to walk out at low tide. Here there are the remains of Early Christian and Norse settlements.

Rousay, a couple of miles northeast of Mainland, has a burial cairn at **Midhowe**. This cairn has a long chamber, 76 ft by 7 ft, with 24 burial cells leading off it, in which the remains of 25 human bodies were found. Another tomb on Rousay, **Taversoe Tuick**, is unusual because it is two-storied. One tomb sits on top of the other, each with its own entrance passage. Rousay also has also a very well-preserved broch, with a complex of cells, cubicles, passages, stairs and doorways, and outbuildings.

Wyre, a mile southeast of Rousay, has the ruin of a 12th-century stone castle, one of the oldest in Scotland, known as **Cubbie Roo's Castle** and probably the stronghold of a Norse robber baron. There is also a ruined 12th-century chapel, St Mary's.

Egilsay, is two miles east of Rousay. **St Magnus' Cenotaph** marks the site of the murder of Jarl Magnus in 1116, after whom the cathedral in Kirkwall is named. The ruin of St Magnus' Church dominates this small, low-lying island, with a tall, tapering round tower at the west end. This design is of Irish origin, indicating close contact between Ireland and Orkney during Viking times. It was probably built in the 12th century, and its walls still stand to their full height. The tower, nearly 50 ft high, was once taller still and it seems to beckon from all round. Magnus was killed on the order of his rival, Earl Haakon, who wanted sole power over Orkney. Egilsay has a large proportion of southerners in its small population.

On **Eday**, four miles to the east of Egilsay, there are chambered tombs and an Iron Age dwelling that was once a roundhouse with radial divisions inside, dating from several centuries BC.

Westray, seven miles north of Rousay, has the formidable ruin of **Noltland Castle**, built in 1560 by Gilbert Balfour, Master of the Household to Mary, Queen of Scots. Its design is Z-plan, with all-round visibility and an almost extravagant provision of gun loops. It was burned by Covenanters in 1650.

Papa Westray, 2 miles off the northeast tip of Westray, is so called from the hermits who lived in the cells here. This island was part of an important Norse family estate in the 11th and 12th centuries and archaeologists discovered the remains of Neolithic settlements which have provided valuable clues to the lifestyle of those ancient inhabitants.

North Ronaldsay is the most northern island of Orkney, 15 miles east of Papa Westray and 32 miles northeast of Kirkwall. It is surrounded by a sea dyke designed to keep the unique breed of sheep off the grass, so that they feed from the rich seaweed on the shore. The meat of these small, sturdy animals has a distinctive flavour.

WHERE TO STAY
Ayre Hotel, Ayre Road, Kirkwall, tel 0856 3001, is on the waterfront overlooking Kirkwall Bay near the main shopping area. Moderately priced, it is comfortable and friendly. Also moderately priced, **Kirkwall Hotel**, Harbour Street, tel 0856 2232, overlooks the harbour in the town centre, is obliging and has good food. **Barony Hotel**, Birsay, tel 085672 327, is on the shores of Boardhouse Loch, with views of the village and the Brough of Birsay. Open from May to September it is cheap and offers free trout fishing. **Merkister Hotel**, Harray, is a splendid place on the edge of Loch Harray. It's cheap, specializes in trout fishing holidays and is open April to October. **Merry Dancers Inn** Eday, tel 08572 221, is a dear little cottage overlooking Calfsound and Calf of Eday. It only has three bedrooms and one bathroom, but it is cosy and has a licence and is ridiculously cheap. There are plenty more, and dozens of bed and breakfast and self-catering places, all detailed in the brochure. For something a bit different, try **Wildabout**, Inner Urrigar, Costa, Evie, tel 0856 75 307. Michael and Jenny Hartley run week-long 'Wildlife, Environmental' Holidays with every day planned to take you round the sights of Orkney.

SHETLAND

Sixty miles north of Orkney and half way to Norway, Shetland has its own character, very different from that of Orkney although they share much of their history. In spite of being on the same latitude as Greenland, Shetland's climate is startlingly mild because of the Gulf Stream, with plenty of sunshine in early summer and less rain than the Western

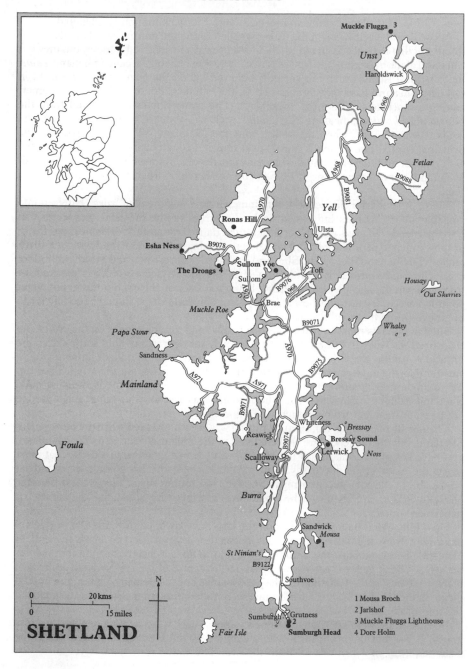

Muckle Flugga 3

Unst

Haroldswick

A968

Fetlar

B9088

Yell

B9081

A970

Ronas Hill

A968

Ulsta

Esha Ness

B9078

Sullom Voe

Toft

The Drongs 4

Sullom

B9076

A968

Housay

Out Skerries

Brae

Muckle Roe

B9071

Whalsy

Papa Stour

A970

Sandness

Whiteness

A971

Bressay

Mainland

A971

Reawick

B9074

Bressay Sound

B9071

Lerwick

Noss

Foula

Scalloway

Burra

Sandwick

Mousa

1

St Ninian's

B9122

Southvoe

N

Grutness

2

Sumburgh

Sumburgh Head

Fair Isle

| 0 | 20 kms |
| 0 | 15 miles |

SHETLAND

1 Mousa Broch
2 Jarlshof
3 Muckle Flugga Lighthouse
4 Dore Holm

Isles. Of the 100 islands in the archipelago, only 15 are continuously inhabited.

According to Tacitus, when the Romans sailed round the north coast of Scotland and found out that Britain was an island, they 'discovered and subdued' Orkney but they left Shetland alone because of the wild seas that lay between them. He called Shetland *Thule*, that mythical island which the ancients believed lay on the edge of the world. As in Orkney, Shetland has long summer nights, the 'simmer dim' twilight of midsummer, adding a touch of timelessness to holidays. The name Shetland is derived from the Norse word *hjaltland*, meaning Highland. Locals talk about Shetland, never the Shetlands. As in Orkney, when they talk about the Mainland, they are referring to the principal island. The terrain is mostly peat bog and rough highland hillside, carpeted with heather and turf and dotted with many small lochs. Ronas Hill in the northwest of Mainland, is the highest point, at 1475 ft, and nowhere is more than three miles from the sea.

There is wonderful cliff scenery with long winding inlets, called 'voes', battered into amazing arches, fissures and jagged stacks. Few trees survive the gale-force winds that lash the islands. There is a fair bit of agriculture: dairy farming and vegetable crops thrive in the south and central Mainland and sheep-farming is important, including the black and brown Shetland sheep. The Shetland cabbage is salt resistant and grown as a fodder crop. Shetland knitwear is world famous: in the old days the wool was plucked, or 'roo'ed' from the sheep's neck by hand, being too fine for shears, but this is no longer common except for the odd show animal. A true Shetland shawl should be so fine it can be drawn through a wedding ring.

Shetland ponies roam over the hills, originally mini draughthorses on the crofts and then bred for work in coalmines, with 'as much strength as possible and as near the ground as can be got'. The skeleton of one was found in the middle of Jarlshof Broch, smaller than the modern breed. They are not strictly wild as they are all owned. They run on common grazing and efforts are made to improve the breed by introducing good Shetland stallions to run with them. Their tail hair was used as fishing lines and it used to be illegal to steal hair from another man's horse.

The old life of crofting, fishing and knitting was greatly changed when the oil boom hit Shetland, but the oil depots are well confined to the Sullom Voe area, on the Mainland, and have not spoiled the rest of the islands, while bringing a new prosperity that must make life a lot easier for many. Hugh MacDiarmid, the poet, said: 'It is indeed impossible to eke out a decent living in Shetland by crofting alone. That is the difference between Orkney and Shetland: the Orcadian is a farmer with a boat, the Shetlander is a fisherman with a croft.'

Up-Helly-Aa is held in Lerwick, on the last Tuesday in January and is a wonderful hang-over from the Viking days. This pagan fire festival used to mark the end of Yule-tide and symbolize the desire for the sun to appear again after the long winter nights. A Viking galley is carried to a park in the centre of the town amidst a forest of blazing torches, and set alight while the people sing 'The Norseman's Home' as a funeral dirge. In the old days blazing barrels of tar were rolled through the streets and carried to the tops of the hills.

Because they were such good seamen, Shetlanders were very vulnerable to press gangs. It was not unknown for a whole community of able bodied young men to be snatched away in a furtive raid from the sea. The fiddle tune 'Jack is yet alive' was composed for a Shetlander who had been press-ganged, served his time, and returned to a family who had written him off long ago. Fiddle music is still very popular throughout the islands.

The seascapes are unforgettable: sudden glimpses of an island-dotted sea with dramatic rocks and cliffs, and glorious beaches, suffused by an extraordinary clarity of light. The colours must have influenced the natural shades used in the knitwear, particularly those in the Fair Isle designs.

SPORT

Shetland has more or less the same activities as Orkney. For **ornithologists**, the bird life is just as rewarding, with vast colonies of sea birds, both northern and migrant. Among the many hundred species to be seen is the dear little Shetland wren, 'stinkie', even smaller than her more common cousin. As if to make up for her stature, her formal name is *Troglodytes Troglodytes Shetlandicus*. Fair Isle, half way to Orkney, has an observation station and is famous as a staging post for migrants. For **botanists** the wild flowers are marvellous with around 500 species of plants to discover. Because much of the pasture is untreated, many that have become rare elsewhere have survived, including the rather hideous large Australian daisy. There are Arctic flowers, the American Mondey Flower, and the tiny blue Caucasus from Asia Minor. For **naturalists** there are also vast quantities of seals to watch, basking on the rocks, known locally as 'selkies' (too many of them, in fact, due to culling restrictions). Otters can be seen, around small rocks and skerries in the remoter coastal areas. Whales, killer whales, sharks, dolphins and porpoises can all be seen off the coast. **Trout fishing** is excellent, in the lochs, of which there are more than 300, and there are some salmon. **Sea angling** is first class and fishermen catch cod, halibut and many other white fish. Porbeagle shark of up to 450lbs have been caught in local waters and the current European record of a 226.5 lb skate is held by Shetland. There is a wealth of pre-historic remains for **archaeologists**, all types of **water sports** and **walks** galore. **Pony trekking** is an excellent way of exploring and there are six **hang gliding** centres.

GETTING THERE

By air: British Airways operate four flights a day from Aberdeen. These connect with flights to and from Glasgow, Edinburgh, Manchester, Birmingham, Belfast and London. They also operate a daily service from Inverness, via Orkney. Loganair run a daily flight from Edinburgh.

By sea: P&O Scottish Services operate a passenger and car ferry service, overnight, five times a week from Aberdeen to Lerwick, including a weekend crossing via Orkney. From June to August, the Tuesday night boat also goes via Orkney. For information and booking write or phone P&O Ferries, PO Box 5, Jamieson's Quay, Aberdeen, tel 0224 572615. P&O Scottish Ferries are also agents for the Smyril Line which operates from the end of May to the end of August, between Norway, Shetland, Faroe, Iceland and Denmark—the only ferry connection between a Scottish port and the Continent.

There are good bus and taxi services from the airport, as well as plenty of hire cars. Shetland roads are good and the inter-island ferries are excellent. The ferries between Mainland and Yell, North Yell and Unst, Unst and Fetlar, Mainland and Whalsay are all roll-on, roll-off. There is also a good inter-island air service.

TOURIST INFORMATION
Shetland Tourist Organization, Information Centre, Lerwick, tel 0595 3434.

Mainland

Mainland is by far the biggest of the islands, its chief town being **Lerwick**, Britain's most northerly town, so called from the Norse *leir-vik* meaning clay creek. Looking over sheltered Bressay Sound, Lerwick has always been a refuge for seafarers. In spite of its geographical isolation it is a lot more up-to-date and cosmopolitan than many of the towns in the Highland region of Scotland. It was a stopping-off port for Norsemen: King Haakon re-provisioned his fleet here on the way to defeat at Largs in 1263.

Lerwick was always important for fishing: not only are the home waters productive but it lies on the edge of the valuable northern fishing fields. Dutch fishing fleets were based here in the 17th century and by the 18th century the export of salt fish was thriving. In the 17th century the town became important as a base for the British Navy. Fort Charlotte was built in 1665 to protect the Sound of Bressay from the Dutch.

The buildings that grew up round the port were sturdy and compact, designed to withstand violent storms. Many of them were the town houses of Scottish lairds who succeeded the Norsemen and found winter conditions rather bleak in the outlying countryside.

The *Dim Riv* is a replica Norse longship, over 40 ft long, and she takes visitors on trips round the harbour in the summer. The harbour is a lively, bustling place with a picturesque waterfront, and charmingly haphazard, flagstoned Commercial Street, straggling up behind. This is the main shopping centre of the town, and the steep, narrow lanes around it are said to cover a network of secret tunnels and passages used by smugglers in the past. Boat trips run from Victoria Pier, to cruise round the coast in the summer. Look out for the distinctive Shetland sailing dinghy, a local design with the elegant double prow effect of the Viking longboats. They can be seen in most of the harbours around Shetland and are raced in local regattas.

Fort Charlotte (open daily: free) built by Cromwellian troops, was partly burned by the Dutch in 1673. It was repaired and restored in 1781 and garrisoned during the Napoleonic wars. It is the only Cromwellian military building still intact in Scotland.

The **Town Hall**, above Commercial Street, in Hillhead, is a great Victorian-Gothic building, partly resembling a church, with tower and rose window. It is a splendid building with four corner turrets, a central oriel window and stained-glass windows on the upper floor. These enclose the main hall and depict a fascinating parade of the history of Shetland, beginning with the Scandinavian conquest in 870. There are full-length figures of Norway's King Harald Harfagri, the conqueror of the islands, and Rognvald, Jarl of More, to whom Harald offered the first earldom. The windows go on through all the main events in Shetland's story and include one of the Maid of Norway, who died at sea nearby.

Shetland Museum (open daily except Sun: free) is opposite the Town Hall. It has four galleries devoted to the history of man in Shetland, from pre-historic times to the present. Look out for the fascinating **Papil Stone**, dating from the 7th century, showing a procession of papas, or priests, one of whom is on a horse. Other exhibits include the history of Shetland knitting, and the history of the island's marine and fishing past. There are also replicas of the treasure found on St Ninian's Isle.

These beautiful islands are a great inspiration to artists and there are exciting exhibitions of local art and crafts in the **Shetland Workshop Gallery** (open daily: free) in Burns Lane.

Clickhimin Broch (always accessible) is on the western outskirts of the town, on an island in a loch, reached by a causeway. It is 65 ft in diameter, its walls 18 ft thick and 15 ft high, on a massive stone platform. Excavations on this site suggest that it may have been a late Bronze Age settlement.

A frequent car ferry crosses to the island of **Bressay** just east of Lerwick, and from here a boat crosses the 200 yds to the bird sanctuary on **Noss**. (It is only open to the public from mid-May to the end of August.) Among the many birds to be seen on Noss are a colony of gannets—those great yellow-headed Solon Geese who dive from great heights to fish.

Scalloway is Mainland's other town, in an attractive bay seven miles west of Lerwick. It was the capital until 200 years ago and is still an important fishing port. There is a small but extremely interesting local **Museum** in the middle of the town, which has, among other things, a detailed history of the Shetland Bus. During the Second World War, small Norwegian fishing boats crossed to Nazi-occupied Norway to carry out sabotage or to land secret agents and bring back refugees. 'To take the Shetland Bus' meant to escape from Norway. **Lunna House**, in northeast Mainland, now a guest house, was the original headquarters of this Norwegian Resistance Movement, before it was transfered to Scalloway where more facilities were available. *The Shetland Bus* by David Howarth, recently reprinted, gives a good account of the whole operation.

Scalloway Castle (always accessible) dominates the town, a forbidding ruin built by Earl Patrick Stewart in 1600. Stewart was the notorious despot who tyrannized Orkney and Shetland until he was executed. Built in medieval style, the roofless shell, with corner turrets and gables, stands on a narrow promontory by the water. The Earl is said to have hung his victims from an iron ring in one of the chimneys. The castle was, not surprisingly, left to rot after the earl's death.

Scalloway, much older than Lerwick, retains a quiet, old-fashioned atmosphere. There are bridges across to the islands of **Tronda** and **Burra** just to the south. Scalloway is at the southern end of the agricultural valley of **Tingwall**, so called after the site of the old Norse parliament, or *thing*, at the north end of **Tingwall Loch**, reached by stepping stones.

At **Whiteness,** seven miles north of Scalloway, the **Hjaltasteyn Workshop** (open weekdays: free) is where local semi-precious stones are polished and mounted in silver and enamel. Not far north, at **Weisdale**, Shetland Silvercraft also make high quality Celtic and Viking design jewellery.

South of Lerwick

Mousa Broch (open daily: free) on **Mousa Island**, is one of Shetland's main archaeological treasures. A boat runs, weather permitting, from **Sandwick**, 11 miles south of Lerwick. Mousa Island, a mile offshore, is inhabited only by sheep and ponies, and its broch is the best preserved in existence. It is a thrilling experience to climb its steps, walking in the footsteps of its Pictish builders 2000 years ago. Over 50 ft in diameter, 45 ft high, with walls that taper from 12 ft to 7 ft in thickness, this was one of the smallest of the brochs and probably one of the latest. Galleries honeycomb its double walls and stairways lead to a parapet round the top. This broch illustrates clearly how the builders tapered the walls inwards to within about 10 ft of the top and then sloped them outwards, making it impossible for invaders to climb up.

Mousa appears romantically in two of the old sagas. In 1150, a Norwegian Prince Erland abducted a famous beauty and held her in the broch until her son, a Jarl, unable to storm the impregnable fortress, had to consent to their marriage. Another saga tells of a young man called Bjorn, who brought Thora, whom he had seduced, to Mousa in 900 and here they set up home together.

St Ninian's Isle is four miles southwest of Sandwick, off the west coast of Mainland. You can walk to it along a glorious white crescent of sand, called a 'tombolo', that forms a causeway. Here are the foundations of a 12th-century chapel (always accessible), buried by sand for many hundreds of years. In 1958, Aberdeen University began excavating the site and discovered not only the foundations of the chapel, but also a Bronze Age burial ground and the remains of a pre-Norse church.

Under a stone slab in the chapel nave they found a hoard of 8th-century Celtic silver, now in the Royal Museum of Scotland, in Queen Street, Edinburgh, with a replica collection in the museum in Lerwick. It is believed that this wonderful hoard was buried by the monks who lived here, probably during an invasion threat from Vikings. The treasure includes silver bowls, delicate brooches and a Communion spoon. Lengthy litigation followed the finding, it being disputed whether the Crown could claim treasure in a land where Udal law still applies.

The Shetland Croft Museum (open daily except Mon, 1 May–30 Sept: adm) is at **Boddam** on the east coast of Mainland, five miles south of Sandwick. The museum is a restored croft house, typical of the mid-19th century. Inside the very cosy cottage is the original driftwood furniture and all the domestic utensils, giving an excellent picture of how crofters lived in the last century. There is also the old watermill, down the hill by the burn.

Sumburgh, with the airport, is at the southern tip of Mainland, 27 miles south of Lerwick. The modern, clean-cut buildings at the airport present a remarkable contrast to the antiquity of Jarlshof, just next door.

Jarlshof (open daily except closed Tues and Wed afternoon in winter: adm) was a name invented by Sir Walter Scott in his stirring book *The Pirate*. He visited the island in 1814, was impressed by the laird's hall, and wrote his story round it. He was not to know how misleading this name was to prove, because it was not until 1905 that a violent storm revealed that this was a site that had been occupied for over 3000 years, by seven distinct civilizations of which the Norse Jarls were by far the most recent.

The remains of these village settlements, from Bronze Age to Viking, are sprawled over a low green promontory by the sea. The first house dates from the early or middle part of the second millennium BC. It would be impossible to sort out the various ages and purposes of the conglomeration of stones without the excellent explanations displayed, and the very helpful guide book. The Bronze Age huts include cattle stalls and a metal workshop; the Iron Age settlement has two earth houses and a broch. The three

8th-century wheel houses are fascinating: thought to be family dwellings, they consist of a number of individual recesses separated as if by the spokes of a wheel, all around a central hearth. A confusion of longhouses is all that is left of the Norse occupation. It was the now ruined medieval farmhouse that Sir Walter used as his setting. There is a fascinating little museum, with some of the things that have been dug from the site as well as good ground plan and an interpretive display showing the history of Jarlshof.

North of Lerwick

Sandness is about 25 miles northwest of Lerwick and from here a boat runs to **Papa Stour**, a couple of miles off the coast. The boats only go three times a week so day trips aren't possible. The sea caves are believed to be the finest in Britain, but you will need to hire a boat locally to see them properly. The scent from the wild flowers on Papa Stour was said to be so strong that fishermen could fix their position from it if caught in fog out at sea.

Lunna is about 18 miles north of Lerwick as the crow flies, out on the east coast. When Lunna House, now a small hotel, was the original headquarters of the Norwegian Resistance, the barns and outhouses were used as an arsenal. Lunna Kirk is one of the oldest Shetland churches still in use. Built in 1753, it is a charming old building with a leper squint, for lepers to listen to the service and receive Communion.

At **Brae**, about 23 miles north of Lerwick, a very narrow neck of land, called **Mavis Grind** prevents the northwest corner of Mainland from being an island. You can stand on this 'anchor cable' of land and throw a stone one way into the Atlantic, and the other way into the North Sea.

Sullom Voe Oil Terminal (pronounced Soolem), with its complex of buildings and jetties, is on the peninsula of **Calback Ness**, seven miles northeast of Brae, joined to Mainland by reclaimed land. The terminal is tucked away so discreetly that you are hardly aware of it. **Firth**, nearby, was built to house the oil men. **Toft** is four miles east of Sullom Voe and from here the car ferry crosses to **Yell**, three miles northeast.

This northern part of Mainland is dominated by **Ronas Hill**, Shetland's highest point, 1475 ft high, 10 miles north of Brae, and well worth climbing for marvellous views.

Eshaness, on the coast of Mainland, 15 miles northwest of Brae, has precipitous cliffs and breathtaking views of the **Drongs**, a collection of weird stacks carved by the force of the ocean. These stacks include a huge natural arch called the **Dore Holm**.

The island of **Yell**, to the north, is mostly peat moor. It was described by Eric Linklater as 'dull and dark and one large peat bog'. Although the second largest of the Shetland islands, it has suffered from depopulation and is rather depressing. A Minister of the Kirk once said: 'Yell is Hell, but Unst—Oh! Unst!'

Unst is Britain's most northern island, with the **Muckle Flugga** lighthouse on a rock just off its northern tip. The lighthouse was built by Robert Louis Stevenson's father, and while he was designing and building it, his son stayed on Unst, dreaming up the story of *Treasure Island*. Unst supports a number of Shetland ponies and it has wonderful cliff scenery. Philatelists can get a special frank on their letters at Britain's most northerly post office in **Haroldswick**, in northeast Unst, the place where Harald Harfagri landed from Norway to subdue the troublesome Vikings.

Fetlar, east of Yell and much smaller, derives its name from the Norn name for 'fat land' and is the most fertile of the islands, with a large number of birds. The rare snowy owl bred in Fetlar until 1975, when the resident male died. Now, although they no longer breed there, visiting females can still be seen. They have a buzzard-like flight and distinctive white plumage. Another of Fetlar's rare visitors is the red-necked phalarope, a dear little bird with a long, needle-like beak, who spins round on the water to stir up insects. The whimbrel, rather like a smaller curlew, usually a coastal migrant, nests on Fetlar and can be seen combing the shore for molluscs and worms with its long curved beak.

Whalsay, a couple of miles off northeast Mainland, is important for fishing and fish processing. On the pier there is a 17th-century Hanseatic trading booth. The Hanseatic League merchants, pioneers of today's Common Market, came to Shetland to trade, buying fish and salting it for export, until salt tax was introduced in 1712. The Baltic traders set up booths like this one, from which they offered fine cloth, fishing tackle, exotic foods, tobacco, fruit and gin at a farthing a pint, in exchange for fish, butter, wool and fish oil. It is intriguing to look at this quiet, peaceful place and picture what it was like when the merchants haggled and bartered from their booths.

Whalsay has two pre-historic sites: the **Standing Stones**, at Yoxie, and the **Benie Hoose,** thought to have been the dwelling for the Druid priests who were responsible for the ceremonies performed around the standing stones.

Foula is an island 27 miles west of Mainland, with dramatic cliff scenery and a colony of skuas. Still inhabited, it is often cut off in bad weather. This was the last place where Norn was spoken, in the 19th century.

FAIR ISLE

Fair Isle is 24 miles southwest of Sumburgh on Mainland, and boats run to it from Grutness Pier, on Sumburgh Head. These aren't day trips: there is a three-day stay on the island before the next boat back. Alternatively, Loganair operate two flights from Tingwall Airport on Mondays, making a day's outing possible. Fair Isle, the 'Far Isle' of the Vikings, half way between Orkney and Shetland, is a buffer between the Atlantic and the North Sea. It must be the most gale-battered island in Britain, presenting a tough challenge to the 60-odd people who live there. The bird population is enormous, preserved by the warden of the **Observatory**. Over 300 species have been recorded on Fair Isle; as well as resident colonies, it is a regular staging post for many migratory birds.

Although bleak, Fair Isle is magnificent, with needle-sharp rocks pounded by ferocious seas, and sheer cliffs topped by green turf and wild flowers. Paying guests can stay at the Observatory in the summer.

Fair Isle knitting is internationally renowned. There is a thriving island cooperative of men and women who work machines and hand finish only 200 orders of Fair Isle jumpers, scarves, hats and gloves a year. These are only sold on the island. Each jersey takes seven hours to finish by hand. The designs date back to Viking times, possibly influenced by the Moorish patterns learnt from the survivors of a Spanish Armada shipwreck, in 1588, who were given shelter by the islanders.

WHERE TO STAY

There are dozens to choose from, to suit all tastes and pockets, all detailed in the brochure. **Queens Hotel**, Lerwick tel 0595 2826, is right on the water in attractive Commercial Street, picturesque, old fashioned and very comfortable, at the top of the moderate price range. For the same price, **Lerwick Hotel**, tel 0595 2166, 10 minutes' walk from the town centre, is a hideous modern building with a glorious view over Breiwick Bay and Bressay Island. What it lacks in style and character however it makes up for in comfort and service. **Shetland Hotel**, Holmsgarth Road, Lerwick, tel 0595 5515, is another modern horror, opposite the ferry terminal. It is expensive, comfortable and well run with a friendly staff. Moderately priced, **Grand Hotel**, Lerwick, tel 0595 2826, is in Commercial Street in the centre of the town, with an imposing castellated tower. **Sumburgh Hotel**, tel 0950 60201, close to the airport and next to Jarlshof, is an old laird's house, with lots of character moderately priced and very friendly. **Westings Hotel**, Wormdale, Whiteness, tel 059584 242, is a small, family-run hotel with gorgeous sea views. Easy-going, friendly and moderately priced. More expensive, **Busta House**, Busta, tel 080622 506, is a large old country house, full of character, with good food and wine and a selection of 120 malt whiskies. Much cheaper, **St Magnus Bay Hotel**, Hillswick, tel 080623 372/3, is a charming Norwegian-style hotel overlooking the bay, comfortable and hospitable. For a really cosy, friendly bed and breakfast, try Mrs W. J. Hutchison, Orablaa, 3 Twageos Road, Lerwick, tel 0595 3417.

Fair Isle Bird Observatory Lodge, tel 03512 258, is idyllic. The building itself is modern and unbeautiful but it offers the perfect island/wildlife holiday for anyone interested in birds, nature and hospitality. Open from April to October, its 12 bedrooms share one bathroom, its staff are relaxed and friendly and its outlook sublime. It is cheap, with full board.

GLOSSARY

Aber—mouth of: confluence of (rivers)
Advocate—barrister
Aird—point, promontory
Allt—stream
An—of the
Aros—dwelling
Athole brose—delicious drink made from whisky, honey, oatmeal and cream, left to soak and squeezed through a cloth: once tasted, never forgotten
Auch—field
Auld—old
Ay—island
Aye—yes
Bairn—child
Bal—town, home
Ban—fair
Bannock—oatmeal pancake-ish scone-ish cake
Bap—bread roll
Bard—poet
Barr—crest
Beag—small
Bealach, balloch—mountain pass
Bean—woman
Ben, beinn—mountain
Bhlair—plain
Blether—talk nonsense
Bogle—frightening ghost
Bothy—rough hut, temporary accommodation
Brae—hill
Bramble—blackberry
Branks—bridle, halter
Braw—fine
Breeks—trousers
Bridie—pie made with circle of pastry folded over filling of meat , onions, vegetables, etc.
Brig—bridge
Broch—pre-historic round stone tower with hollow walls, enclosing cell-like galleries, and stairways, ften built round a well, purpose only guessed at, probably dwelling for chief and refuge for clan in times of danger

Burn—stream
Byre—barn
Cadger—pedlar
Cailleach—old woman
Cairn—stone monument
Callan(t)—youth
Cam—crooked
Canny—prudent
Caolas—firth
Capercailzie—wood-grouse
Car—curve
Ceann—head
Ceilidh—informal social gathering among neighbours, often with spontaneous singing, music, story telling, etc.
Chanter—double-reeded pipe on which bagpipe tune is played
Chum—(verb) to accompany as a friend: 'I'll chum you to the party.'
Cil—church
Clach—stone
Cladach—beach
Clarty—dirty
Claymore—sword
Cleg—horsefly
Close—shared entry to tenement, enclosure, courtyard
Cnoc—hillock
Collie—sheepdog, wood
Corbie—crow
Corrie—hollow
Crack—conversation
Craig—rock
Crannog—small man-made island dating from Iron Age. Stones piled on wooden base with easily defended single dwelling on top, often reached by a sunken causeway
Creel—pannier-type basket, also lobster pot
Croft—smallholding
Crowdie—soft cheese
Cuddy—donkey
Cul—recess
Cutty—short (cutty sark, short petticoat; cutty stool, stool of repentance)

Dal—field
Dalr—valley
Damph—deer, steer
Daunder—saunter
Ding—knock, beat
Dominie—schoolmaster
Doo—dove
Doo'cot—dovecot
Dour—dry, humourless
Douse—sweet, gentle
Dram—officially one eighth fluid ounce: commonly generous tot of whisky
Dreich—dreary, boring
Drochit—bridge
Dross—coal dust
Drove road—tracks used for herding (droving) cattle or sheep to market, often long distances
Druim, drum—ridge
Dubh—dark, black
Dun—hillfort
Dux—best pupil
Dyke—wall of stones or turf
Dysart—hermit's retreat, desert
Eaglais—church
Eas—waterfall, gorge
Eilean—island (*see* Ay
Eldritch—elfin, weird, ghostly, strange,
Ey—island
Factor—land agent, usually of private estate
Fada—long
Fail—rock
Fank—sheepfold
Fash—trouble, upset, 'dinna fash yersel', 'don't getcher knickers in a twist'
Feat—man
Feu—feudal tenure of land with rent paid in kind or money
Fey—susceptible to supernatural influence
Fillebeg—kilt
Fionn—gleaming, white
Firth—wide mouth of river, estuary
Flit—remove, move house
Fou—full (of drink)
Fraoch—heather
Gab—mouth, talk
Gearr—short
Geo—chasm

Gil—ravine
Girdle—iron baking tray
Glass—grey
Glen—valley
Gleo—mist
Gobha—blacksmith
Gorm—blue, green
Gowk—fool
Greet—cry
Grieve—farm manager
Haar—drizzle, soft rain, mist
Harling—rough-cast facing to walls
Haver—talk nonsense
Heugh—hillock
Hog—unshorn lamb
Hogmanay—New Year's Eve
Holm—low ground by river, islet in river
Hope—bay
How—burial mound
Howe—low-lying ground, hollow
Howff—meeting place, refuge, burial ground
Howk—dig
Ilk—same, of that ilk—surname and name of property the same
Inch—island
Inver—mouth of river
Jougs—iron neck collar used as instrument of public punishment
Kail—cabbage
Kailyard—cabbage patch, back yard
Keek—peep
Kelpie—water-sprite, water-horse
Ken—know
Kenspeckle—easily recognizable, conspicuous
Kil—burial place, church
Kin—head (of loch, river)
Kirk—church
Knock, knowe—knoll, hillock
Kye—cattle
Kyle—strait, narrow channel between two points of land
Lag, laggan—hollow, dip
Laird—owner of estate
Land—tenement
Larach—site of ruin
Larig, learg—mountain pass
Law—round hill
Leac—flagstone

487

Leana—plain
Liath—grey
Links—dunes
Linn, linne—pool
Lis—garden on site of fortress
Loan—lane
Loch, lochan—lake, small lake
Lug—ear
Lum—chimney
Machair—sand-peat lowland bordering
 seashore
Maol—bare headland
Manse—minister's house (ecclesiastical)
March—boundary
Meikle—large
Mon—moor
Mor—great
Moy—plain
Muc, muic—sow
Muckle—large
Mull—promontory
Na, nam, nan—of the
Neeps—turnips (bashed neeps—mashed
 turnips). Turnips in Scotland refer to
 English swedes
Neuk—nose
Ob, oba, oban—bay
Ochter—high
Pit—dip
Plenishing—furniture, domestic equipment
Ploy—activity
Poke—bag
Policies—grounds within an estate
Poll—pool
Provost—mayor
Puddock—frog
Quaich—shallow, two-handled drinking bowl
Rath—fort
Reek—smoke
Reidh—smooth
Rig—ridge
Ross—peninsula
Roup—auction
Ru, rhu, row, rubha—point
Sark—shift, shirt
Saugh—willow
Scunner—dislike
Selkie—seal
Sgeir, skerry—sea, rock

Sgor, scuir, sgurr—sharp rock
Sheiling—hut for summer pasture
Sherrif—county court judge
Shinty—hockey
Siccar—certain
Siller—silver (money)
Slochd—hollow, grave
Sonsie—bonnie
Soutar—cobbler
Spittal—hospice
Stob—stake, point
Strath—broad valley
Strone—nose, promontory
Struan, struth—stream
Swither—vacillate
Syne—ago
Tarbert, tarbet—isthmus
Tassie—cup
Thing—parliament, council
Thole—endure
Thrang—thronged
Thrawn—awkward
Tigh—house
Tir—land
Tobar—well
Tocher—dowry
Tod—fox[ep]Toom—empty
Tom—hillock
Torr—hill
Tow—rope
Tulloch, tilly, tully—knoll
Uachdar—upper, high
Uamh—cave
Uig—sheltered bay
Uisge, esk—water
Uisge beatha—water of life (whisky)
Unco—strange, very
Usquebaugh—whisky
Vennel—alley
Voe—narrow bay, fiord
Wean—child
Weems—caves
Whaup—curlew
Whinn—gorse
Wick, vik—bay
Wight—strong
Wynd—alley
Yett—gate

CLANS AND FAMILIES

Gaelic *clann* means offspring, family, stock, race, derived from Latin *planta*—sprout, scion.

When Robert the Bruce released Scotland from the English yoke in 1314 he opened the field for tremendous power-struggles between the leading clans. Some became too-powerful, others sank into obscurity. Many families, too weak to survive alone, sought the protection of stronger neighbours; some of these took the name of their adopted chief, others retained their own names. Thus many clans have 'septs' and dependents. Clans amalgamated for strength: the Clan Chattan Confederation consisted of a large number of clans who joined forces under Mackintosh hegemony. The chiefs of the Highland clans ruled with total disregard to the authority of the Crown, as did the powerful Border families. The final Jacobite rebellion, in 1745–56, resulted in the death of the old clan system. (See also Clans and Tartans, in 'Topics'.)

Today, although all that is left is the clan name, there remains a pride and sense of loyalty so strong that descendents come from all over the world to visit the land of their ancestors. This is a list of the main clans and families, with the address (where there is one), of the clan secretary, or clan centre, who will send more information if required. Names not included will be those of septs, or clan branches. Anyone seriously seeking their roots should get hold of *The Clan Almanac*, by Charles Maclean, published by Lochar, a comprehensive little book which lists, among other things, the septs and dependents of the main clans so if you are called Abbot, for instance, you find you were part of the Macnab clan. Mac, and Mc mean son of, as of course does any name ending in son.

Anderson: son of Andrew, Highland version MacAndrew. They came from Badenoch and their motto is Stand Sure. In the 15th century they were part of the Clan Chattan Confederation. Clan Chattan Secretary, Dyunmaglash, Westhill, Inverness-shire.

Armstrong: the original, armour-bearer to a King of Scots, saved his king, fallen in a battle, by lifting him onto his horse. He was given land as a reward and named Strong-arm. They were Borderers and their motto *Invictus maneo* means I remain unvanquished. One of their descendents, Neil, was the first man on the moon. Clan Secretary, Brieryshaw, Langholm, Dumfriesshire.

Baird: from an old Scots word meaning sumptuous dress. They came from Aberdeenshire and their motto *Dominus fecit* means The Lord made. John Logie Baird invented television.

Barclay: derived from the Berkeley family who came over with William the Conqueror. They settled in Aberdeenshire and Kincardineshire and their motto *Aut agere aut mori*, means Either action or death.

Blair: from Gaelic *blar*—field, battle field; motto: *Amo Probos*—'I love the righteous'. An ancient family, one branch having roots in Renfrew, Ayr and Wigtown; and another in

Perth, Fife and Angus. The Barony of Blair, in Ayrshire, was granted by William the Lion in the 12th century. When the two branches competed for chieftainship, James VI settled the dispute by appointing the oldest man in either family to be chief. Thus the honour alternates, depending upon seniority. Clan Secretary, 15 Brompton Terrace, Perth.

Brodie: from their Norman ancestor, de Brothie. They settled in Morayshire and their motto is Unite. Clan Secretary, Brodie Castle, Forres, Moray.

Bruce: from the French town Brix—Adam de Brus came over with William the Conqueror. They lived in Annandale, Clackmannan and Elgin and their motto, *Fuimus*, means We have been. Robert the Bruce won independence for Scotland at the Battle of Bannockburn in 1314; Thomas Bruce, 7th Earl of Elgin and 11th Earl of Kincardine, 1766–1841, rescued the decorated sculptures on the Parthenon from vandalism and installed them in the British Museum as *The Elgin Marbles*, now periodic bones of contention.

Buchanan: from Gaelic *mac-a-Chanonaich*—son of the canon. They lived around Loch Lomond and their motto is *Clarior hinc honos*—Brighter hence the honour. James Buchanan was 15th President of the United States in 1856, and strongly in favour of slavery. Clan secretary, Brechin Robb, 24 George Square, Glasgow.

Cameron: from Gaelic *cam-shorn*—hook nose. They lived in Northern Argyll and Locheil. Their mottos, translated from Gaelic, are: unite; For King and Country; and Sons of the hounds come here and get flesh. Among their many illustrious ancestors were Sir Ewen Cameron—the Great Locheil, 1629–1719, a leading Royalist; and Sir Donald Cameron—Gentle Locheil, one of Bonny Prince Charlie's chief supporters. The Cameron Highlanders, now amalgamated with the Seaforth Highlanders to become The Queen's Own Highlanders, were raised by Sir Alan Cameron in 1793. Their Clan Centre is at Aberchalder, Loch Eil, and the new Clan Cameron Museum is at Achnacarry. Clan Secretary, 78 Milton Road West, Edinburgh.

Campbell: from Gaelic *cam-beul*—crooked mouth. They came from Argyll, Cawdor, Loudoun and Breadalbane. Their various mottos are: Forget not; Follow me; Be mindful; I byde my tyme. Their roots go back to the legendary Ossianic sagas, and they supported the government against the Jacobites. The Duke of Argyll is their chief and the clan centre is Inverary Castle, Argyll.

Chisholm: means a water meadow which produces milk good for cheese-making. They lived in Roxburghshire and Berwickshire and later moved to Inverness-shire. Their motto, *Feros ferio* means I am fierce with the fierce. Clan Secretary, 21 Blytheswood Square, Glasgow.

Colquhoun: pronounced *kerhoon*, the name comes from the Barony, in Dunbartonshire and they lived around Loch Lomond. Their motto, *Si je puis*—If I can, was said by one of their ancestors, to James I, when ordered to capture Dumbarton Castle. (He did.)

Cumming: derived from the herb cummin, which is their emblem. They come from Roxburghshire, Buchan, Badenoch and Altyre and their motto is Courage. The Comyns came to Scotland during the reign of Malcolm Canmore in the 11th century, and it was

Sir John Comyn—The Red Comyn, who was murdered by Robert the Bruce in order to gain the Crown. Clan Secretary, House of Altyre, Forres.

Douglas: from Gaelic *dubh glais*—black water. They lived in Lanarkshire, Galloway, Dumfriesshire and Angus and were as powerful as kings in the Middle Ages. Their motto, *Jamais arrière*, means Never behind. Archibald Douglas became known as Bell-the-cat, from his undertaking to kill the much-despised favourites of James III. Sir James Douglas was killed in 1330, while honouring his promise to take Robert the Bruce's heart to the Holy Land.

Drummond: derived from Drymen, near Stirling. They came from Perthshire and their motto is Gang (go) warily.

Duncan: more properly Clan Donnachaidh—Brown Warriors. They came from Atholl and Lundie in Fife and their motto is *Disce parti*—learn to suffer. Donnaichaidh Clan Secretary, 127 Rose Street, South Lane, Edinburgh.

Elliot: (there are 70 different spellings) probably from Old-English Aelfwald—Elf Ruler, which became the christian name Elward. They were one of the strongest of the Border families and their mottos are *Soyez sage*—Be wise, and *Fortiter et Recte*—With Strength and Right. Jane Elliot wrote the poignant lament for Flodden, 'The Flowers of the Forest', in the 18th century. T. S. Eliot's poetical works are internationally famous. Clan Secretary, Redheugh, Newcastleton, Roxburghshire.

Erskine: from the Barony of Erskine in Renfrewshire. They lived around Alloa and their motto is *Je pense plus*, I think more. John Erskine, 11th Earl of Mar was known as Bobbing John during the Jacobite rebellions because, although nominally a Jacobite, he kept changing sides.

Farquharson: the Gaelic *fearchar* means dear one, and they came from Aberdeenshire and Invercauld. Their motto is *Fide et Fortitudine*—By Fidelity and Fortitude. They were part of the Clan Chattan Confederation. Clan Chattan Secretary, Dyunmaglash, Westhill, Inverness-shire.

Ferguson: Fergus founded the Scottish kingdom of Dalriada and they inhabited the lands of Argyll, Perthshire, Dumfries, Galloway and Raith. Their motto is *Dulcius ex asperis*—Sweeter after difficulties. They are one of the oldest clans of Scotland. Clan Secretary, Pendle Cottage, Dunigoyne, Glasgow.

Forbes: from Gaelic *forba*—field or district. They were powerful in Aberdeenshire and their motto is Grace me guide. Clan Secretary, Balforbes, Lonach, Donside, Aberdeenshire.

Fraser: of Norman derivation, from *fraises*—strawberry flowers. Originally they were in East Lothian, then Aberdeenshire. Their motto is *Je suis prest*—I am ready. They gained property in Ross-shire through marriage, raised 600 men to fight for Prince Charlie at Culloden and suffered in the subsequent reprisals. Simon Fraser, Lord Lovat, known as the Old Fox, was beheaded at the age of 80 for his Jacobite leanings. Clan Secretary, Balblair House, Beauly, Black Isle, Ross-shire.

Gordon: from Gordon in Berwickshire where they settled, as Anglo-Normans, in the 12th Century. They became very powerful in the northeast: Strathbogie, Deeside and around Aberdeen, and their chief was called Cock of the North. Their mottos are *Animo non Astutia*—By Courage, not Craft; and *Bydand*—Remaining. Among their famous scions were the 19th-century hero, General 'Chinese' Gordon, and George Gordon, Lord Byron. Clan Secretary, Harlaw House, Harlaw Hill, Prestonpans, East Lothian.

Graham: Anglo-Saxon origin—*graeg ham*, meaning grey home. William de Graham came to Scotland with David I, who gave him lands and the family became prominent in the Wars of Independence. Their lands included those north of Glasgow, Loch Katrine, part of Perthshire, and around Dundee and Montrose. Their motto is *Ne Oublie*—Do not forget. Among their greatest ancestors were *the* Montrose, that gallant Royalist who was brutally hung for his loyalty to the Crown, in 1650; Graham of Claverhouse—Bonnie Dundee—hero of Killiecrankie in 1689, and James Graham, 3rd Duke of Montrose who helped to repeal the Act of Proscription in 1782. Clan Secretary, 23 Ardmillan Terrace, Edinburgh.

Grant: derived from the French *grand*—great. Their origins are disputed: some say the first Grant was a Nottinghamshire squire married into an Inverness-shire family; some that they were descended from Kenneth MacAlpine, some that they are descended from MacGregors. Their lands were Strathspey, Rothiemurchas, Glen Moriston and Loch Ness and their motto is Stand fast. General Ulysses Grant was the 18th President of the United States, in 1868. Clan Secretary, 18 Great Stewart Street, Edinburgh.

Gunn: possibly from Gunni, in the Norse sagas, or from Gaelic *guineach*, meaning fierce, or of Pictish descent. Their lands were in Caithness and Sutherland and their motto is *Aut Pax Aut Bellum*—Either Peace or War. Neil M. Gunn, who died in 1973, son of a Caithness skipper, is said by many to have been Scotland's greatest novelist. Clan Secretary, 22 Muirhouse Gardens, Edinburgh.

Hamilton: derived from Hameldone, meaning crooked hill, in England, whence came Walter Fitz-Gilbert to lands in Renfrewshire and Arran during the Wars of Independence. Their motto is Through. Patrick Hamilton, 1498–1528, was the protomartyr of the Scottish Reformation. Clan Secretary, Lennoxlove, Haddington, East Lothian.

Hay: derived from La Haye, in Normandy, which stemmed from *haie*, meaning hedge. Their lands were Aberdeenshire and Tweedale and their motto is *Serva jugum*—Keep the yoke. Clan Secretary, 12 St Peter's Place, Edinburgh. Clan Centre, Delgatie Castle, Turriff, Grampian.

Henderson: in Gaelic, this clan is MacEanruig, anglecized as MacKendrick. Their lands were Caithness and Glencoe and their motto is *Sola Virtus nobilitat*—Virtue alone ennobles.

Home: pronounced Hume, derived from Gaelic *uamh*—cave. Their lands were the Borders and their motto is A Home, a Home! Among their scions were David Hume, the great philosopher of the Scottish Enlightenment, Sir Alec Douglas-Home, Prime minister of Britain in 1963, and his brother William, playwright.

Innes: meaning greens. Innes was a town in Morayshire for which the family received a royal charter in the 12th century. Their motto is *Be traist*—Be faithful. Clan Secretary, 35 East Clarmont Street, Edinburgh.

Johnstone: derived from John's *toun*—homestead; the Gaelic for John is Iain, giving MacIain. There are various spellings but Johnson is uncommon in Scotland. They were a powerful Border family and also had lands in Aberdeenshire. Their mottos are *Numquam non paratus*—Never unprepared, and Light thieves all.

Keith: from the town of Keith in Banffshire. Their lands stretched from East Lothian to Caithness and they held the hereditary office of Great Marischal of Scotland from the 12th to the 18th centuries. Their motto is *Veritas vincit*—Truth conquers. Clan Secretary, North Dykes, Kilbirnie, Ayrshire.

Kennedy: from Gaelic *ceann eitigh*—grim-headed—or possibly from *ceann dubh*—black-headed. Their lands were in Ayrshire, Lochaber and Skye and their motto is *Avise la Fin*—Consider the end. Their best known descendent was John F. Kennedy, 35th President of the United States, assassinated in 1963. The seat of their chief, The Marquess of Ailas, is Culzean Castle.

Kerr: pronounced *kar*, the name is derived from the Norse *kjarr* meaning brushwood. They were an Anglo-Norman family who came to Scotland in the 12th century. Their lands were Roxburghshire and their motto is *Sero sed serio*—Late but in earnest. Legend has the Kerrs left-handed so they reversed the spiral of their staircases to allow space for the left sword-arm.

Lamont: derived from Lawman, Lawgiver; MacKeracher is the Highland version. Their lands were in Argyll and Cowal and their motto is *Nec parcas nec spernas*—Neither spare nor dispose. Clan Secretary, 17 Broomhall Loan, Edinburgh.

Leslie: taken from the barony of Leslie in Aberdeenshire which they adopted in the reign of William the Lion. Their motto is Grip fast.

Lindsay: Lindsey means Linden (lime tree) Island. They came to Scotland with David I and became very powerful, with lands in the Borders and in Angus. Their motto is *Endure Fort*—Endure with Strength. Clan Secretary, 112 Corsebar Road, Paisley.

Livingstone: from Livingstone in West Lothian where they held land, as well as in the Trossachs and Lorne. Their motto is *Si je puis*—If I can. Clan Secretary, Bachuil, Isle of Lismore, Oban, Argyll.

Logan or MacLennan: Logan is in Lothian, with MacLennan as the Highland version. Their lands were in Lothian, Berwickshire and Easter Ross and their motto is The Ridge of Tears.

MacAlister: son of Alasdair, Gaelic for Alexander, who was descended from the great Somerled. Their lands were Kintyre, Arran and Bute and their motto is *Fortiter*—Boldly. Clan Centre, Glenbarr Abbey, Kintyre, Strathclyde.

MacAlpin: Alpins claim descent from 9th-century King Alpin and Dunstaffnage was their traditional home, though the race had no land. Their motto is *Cuimhnich bas Ailpein*—Remember the death of Alpin.

MacArthur: the MacArthurs were the senior branch of the Campbell clan, taking their name from Arthur Campbell in 14th century. Their lands were Argyll, Cowal and Skye and their mottos are *Fide et Opera*—By Fidelity and Work—and *Eisd! O eisd!*—Listen! O listen! John MacArthur emigrated to Australia in the 18th century and became known as the Father of New South Wales. Douglas MacArthur was the brilliant American military leader, Commander in chief of UN Forces in 1950. Clan Secretary, 14 Hill Park Road, Edinburgh.

MacAulay: son of Olaf, who was King of Man and the Isles in the 13th century. Their lands were Dunbartonshire, Isle of Lewis, Sutherland and Ross. Their motto is *Dulce Periculum*—Danger is sweet. Thomas Babington, Ist Lord MacAulay, was the well known 19th-century writer and historian. Rose MacAulay, who died in 1958, was a leading novelist and writer. Clan Secretary, Cameron Loch Lomond Ltd, Alexandria, Dumbartonshire.

MacBean: son of Beathan, or from the Gaelic *bheann*—fair skin—or from King Donald Ban, from whom they claim descent. Donald Ban was the son of Duncan, murdered by MacBeth. Their lands were in Inverness-shire and their motto is Touch not the catt bot a targe (without a shield). Gallant Gillies MacBean was a General at Culloden who breached a gap in a wall with his enormous body and killed 14 Hanoverians before he was himself slain.

MacBeth: derived from the Gaelic for Son of Life. Their lands were in Morayshire and Perthshire and their most famous ancestor, King MacBeth 1040–57, was very different from Shakespeare's character: a wise, generous, pious ruler, the last of the Gaelic kings.

MacCallum: *callum* is Gaelic for tonsured dove, implying disciple of St Columba whose emblem was the Dove of Peace. Their lands were in Argyll and their mottos are *In ardua petit*—He has tried difficult things—and *Deus refugium nostrum*—God is our refuge.

Macdonald: Domhnull is Gaelic for World Ruler. Donald of Islay was grandson of Somerled, Lord of the Isles and Ragnhildis,daughter of King Olaf of Man. Clan Donald was the largest and most powerful of the clans, with a number of branches, reigning supreme in the northwest Highlands and Islands. There are a variety of spellings, including MacDonnell. (Mac was not used in the surname until the 16th century). It is the commonest Mac name in Scotland. The main branches were: Sleat in Skye, Clanranald in Moidart, Glengarry, Keppoch in Lochaber, and Glencoe. They were staunch Jacobites and Royalists, fiercely claiming their position on the right wing of any battle, given them by Robert the Bruce at Bannockburn and still held at Culloden. Their mottos include: *Per mare per terras*—By land and by sea; *Fraoch eilean*—The heathery isle; My hope is constant in thee; *Dh'aindeoin co'theireadh e*—Gainsay who dare; *Creag an Fhitich*—the Raven's Rock; and *Dia's naomh Aindrea*—God and St Andrew. Clan Centre, Armadale Castle, Sleat, Skye. Clan Secretary, Ceadach, 39 Redford Road, Edinburgh.

MacDougal: from the Gaelic *dubh gall* meaning dark stranger. Their lands were Lorne and their motto is *Buaidh no bas*—To conquer or die. They fought against Robert the Bruce in the Wars of Independance, and with the Hanoverians at Culloden. Clan Secretary, Dunollie Castle, Oban, Argyll.

MacDuff: from the Gaelic *mac dubh*—son of the dark one. Their lands were in Fife, Lothian, Strathbran and Strathbogie and their motto is *Deus juvat*—God assists. Although there aren't many MacDuffs today they spawned a number of other clans: a

MacDuff earl was known as *Mac an toiseach*—son of the chief, which became MacIntosh, for example. Clan Secretary, 5 Sidlaw Road, Glasgow.

MacEwan: son of Ewan, who flourished in the 13th century. Their lands were Cowal, Lennox and Galloway and their motto is *Reviresco*—I grow strong.

MacFarlane: son of Partholon, whose father, Sear, took over Ireland after the Flood. Their lands were around Loch Lomond, Tarbert and Arrochar and their motto is *Loch Sloigh*—Loch Sloy.

MacFie: derived from the Gaelic *Dubhshith*, meaning peaceful dark one, the MacFies are a branch of the Clan Alpine. Their lands were Colonsay and their motto is *pro rege*—for the king. Clan Secretary, 120 Cockburn Crescent, Balerno, Midlothian.

MacGillivray: *gillie bhrath* is Gaelic for servant of judgement and the clan belonged to the Clan Chattan Confederation. Their lands were in Mull, Lochaber and Morven, and later in Inverness-shire. Their motto is Dunmaghlas, the name of the chief's castle. MacGillivray of Dunmaglass led the Clan Chattan at Culloden. Clan Secretary, Dunlichty, 7 Cramond Park, Edinburgh.

MacGregor: *grioghair* is Gaelic for Gregory and they claim descent from Griogar, son of 8th-century King Alpin. Some prefer to claim Pope Gregory the Great as their forefather. Whatever the truth, they all claim royal descent. Their lands were in Argyll and Perthshire and their motto is *S'rioghal mo dhream*—Royal is my race. Their name was first proscribed 'under pain of death' after a bloodthirsty massacre of the Colhuhouns in 1603, and again by William III. Many changed their names. Rob Roy MacGregor, immortalized by Walter Scott, was their most famous ancestor. Clan Secretary, 14 Lockharton Avenue, Edinburgh.

MacInnes: *aonghais* is Gaelic for unique choice and they were an ancient Celtic clan. Their lands were Morven and Ardnamurchan and their motto is *Irid Ghibht dhe Agus an Righ*—Through the Grace of God and the King. Clan Secretary, 35 East Claremont Street, Edinburgh.

MacIntosh: see **Mackintosh** and **MacDuff**.

MacIntyre: *an-t-saoir* is Gaelic for son of a carpenter and the clan is said to have taken this name from one who chopped off his thumb to stop a leak in a Macdonald chief's galley. Their lands were Kintyre, Glenoe and Badenoch and they were part of the Clan Chattan Confederation. Their motto is *Per ardua*—Through difficulties. Clan Chattan Secretary, Dyunmaglash, Westhill, Inverness-shire.

MacKenzie: *coinneach* is Gaelic for fair or bright and was a popular Celtic forename, anglecized as Kenneth. MacKenzie lands were in Ross and Cromarty and the Isle of Lewis. Their mottos include *Luceo no uro*—I shine, not burn; *Tulach Ard*—The High Hillock; and *Cuidich 'n righ*—Save the King. Traditionally they provided most of the men in the Seaforth Highlanders, now amalgamated with the Cameron Highlanders to form The Queen's Own Highlanders. Sir Compton MacKenzie, who died in 1972 aged 89, was a well-known writer, particularly of Scottish novels including *Whisky Galore*. Clan Secretary, 1b Downie Place, Musselburgh, Midlothian.

MacKinnon: Kinnon derives from 13th-century Fingan and the MacKinnons were the family of St Columba, part of the Clan Alpin. Their lands were Iona and North Mull;

then Skye and Arran and their mottos are *Audentes fortuna iuvat*—Fortune favours the brave; and *Cuimhnich bas Ailpein*—Remember the death of Alpin. Clan Secretary, 222 Darnley Street, Pollockshiels, Glasgow.

MacKintosh: *toiseach* was Gaelic for tribal leader or thane and the clan descended from the MacDuffs. MacKintosh, originally the leading family of the Clan Chattan Confederation. Their lands were Inverness-shire and their motto is Touch not the cat bot (without) a glove. Brave, beautiful, Jacobite Lady Anne MacKintosh, known as Colonel Anne, won also the name Heroine, in 1745, when she masterminded the Rout of Moy, ousting 1500 of Cumberland's troops with a mere five men. Charles MacKintosh, 1766–1843, invented the waterproof coat, and Charles Rennie MacKintosh, 1868–1928 was a leading architect and designer. Clan Secretary, Moy Hall, Moy, Inverness-shire.

MacLachlan: Lachlan was a Celtic forename derived from the Gaelic Lochlann meaning Norway and the clan claims descent from Niall of the Nine Hostages, High King of Ireland, who won land in Argyllshire. They later spread to Lochaber, Perthshire and Stirlingshire. Their motto is *Fortis et Fidis*—Brave and Trusty. MacLachlan of MacLachlan, Prince Charles' ADC, died at Culloden in 1746. Clan Secretary, Tigh-na-Croft, Enochdhu, Blairgowrie, Angus.

MacLaine of Lochbuie: *ghille Eoin* is Gaelic for servant of John and they claim descent from Lachlans and MacLeans. Their lands were Lochbuie and their motto is *Vincere vel mori*—conquer or die.

MacLaren: from the Gaelic, son of Lawrence. Their lands were Strathearn and Balquhidder and their motto is The Boar's Rock. Clan Secretary, 1 Inverleith Place, Edinburgh.

Maclean: *gille Eoin* is Gaelic for servant of John and they claim descendency from the Kings of Dalriada. Their lands were Morvern, Mull, Coll and Tiree and their mottos are *Bas no Beatha*—death of life; and *Fear eile airson Eachairn*—Another for Hector. Among their many distinguished scions were Lord Maclean of Duart and Morvern who died in 1990 and was, among other things, Lord Chamberlain to the Queen, and Sir Fitzroy Maclean of Dunconnell, diplomat, soldier and acclaimed writer. Clan Secretary, 12 Elie Street, Glasgow.

Macleod: *liotr* was old Norse for ugly; *leod* was Saxon for prince. They claim descent from Olaf the Black, King of Man and the Islands in the 13th century, and their lands were Skye, Lewis and Harris. Hold fast is their motto. Dame Flora Macleod was a famous 20th-century chief and Lord Macleod of Fuinary is renowned for having restored Iona Abbey and established the present community there. Clan Secretary, 38 Ravelston Gardens, Edinburgh.

MacMillan: *mhaolain* is bald one, meaning tonsured and therefore priest, so their origins were ecclesiastical. Their lands were Lochaber, Argyll and Galloway and their motto is *Miseris succurrere disco*—I learn to succor the distressed. John MacMillan 1670–1753, founded the Reformed Presbyterian Church; Kilpatrick MacMillan invented the bicycle in 19th century; Sir Harold MacMillan was Prime Minister of Britain from 1957 to 1963, and nicknamed Super Mac. Clan Centre, Finlaystone, Langbank, Renfrewshire. Clan Secretary, 21 Huntley Gardens, Edinburgh.

MacNab: from *aba* meaning abbot, the MacNabs are descended from the Abbot of Glendochart, in the time of David I. Their lands were Glendochart and Loch Tay and their motto is *Timor omnis abesto*—Let fear be far from all. Raeburn's magnificent painting of *The MacNab*, was of the 12th chief, Francis, 1734–1816, a remarkable eccentric, described by one as 'a herculean Highlander'. Clan Secretary, Finlarig, Killin, Perthshire.

MacNaughton/MacNachtan: *neachdainn* is Gaelic for pure one and they can be traced back to Pictish royalty. Their lands were Strathtay, Lewis and Argyll and their motto is I hope in God. The Clan Centre is at Dunderaive Castle, near Inveraray. Clan Secretary, 2 Douglas Crescent, Edinburgh.

MacNeil: descended from the O'Neills who were High Kings of Ireland. Their lands were Barra, Gigha, Knapdale and Colonsay and their motto is Vincere vel mori—To conquer or die. Clan Secretary, 34 Craigleith Hill Avenue, Edinburgh.

MacNicol or Nicholson: son of Nicol, tracing their ancestry back to the dark ages. Their lands were Sutherland, Skye and Argyll and their motto is *Sgorra Bhreac*—Skorrybreck. Ben Nicholson, who died in 1982, was a famous artist, and William Nicholson 1781–1844 was a well-known portrait painter.

MacPherson: *phearsoin* was Gaelic for parson. They were part of the Clan Chattan Confederation and trace their ancestry to Ferchar, King of Lorne, who died in 697. Staunch Jacobites, they arrived too late for the Battle of Culloden. Their land was Badenoch and their motto is Touch not the cat bot (without) a glove. James MacPherson, 1736–96, caused public dispute with his 'translations' of the Ossianic poems. Clan Secretary, 39 Swanson Avenue, Edinburgh.

MacQuarrie: *guadhre* is Gaelic for noble one and they trace their roots to the Clan Alpine and Saint Columba's family. Their lands were Ulva and their motto, *An t'arm breac dearg*, means the red tartaned army. Major General Lachlan Macquarie, 1761–1824, became Governer of New South Wales and was called Father of Australia. Lachlan and Macquarie Rivers and Macquarie Island were called after him.

MacQueen: from the Norse *sweyne*, or Gaelic *shuibhne*, meaning good going. They were strong members of the Clan Chattan Confederation, with close Macdonald connections. Their lands were Skye, Lewis, Argyll and Lanarkshire and their motto is Constant and faithful. Steve MacQueen, the actor, was a descendant. Clan Chattan Secretary, Dyunmaglash, Westhill, Inverness-shire.

MacRae: means son of grace, probably of ecclesiastical origin. Known as the 'Wild MacRaes', they were hereditary Constables of Eilan Donan Castle for the MacKenzies of Kintail, now restored by one of their descendants. Their lands were Beauly and Kintail and their motto is *Fortitudine*—With Fortitude. Clan Secretary, 6 Gardiners Crescent, Edinburgh.

Malcolm: followers of St Columba. Their lands were in Argyll, Fife, Lochore and Dumfriesshire. Their motto was *Deus refugium nostrum*—God is our refuge, and is now *In ardua petit*—He aims at difficult things. Clan Secretary, Duntrune Castle, Kilmelford, Lochgilphead, Argyll.

Matheson: *mhathain* is Gaelic for bear and, traditionally, the Clan of the Bear helped Kenneth MacAlpin against the Picts in 843. Their lands were Lochalsh and Sutherland and their motto is *Fac et Spera*—Do and hope. Clan Secretary, Burnside, Duirnish, Kyle of Lochalsh, Ross-shire.

Maxwell: from Maxwell on the River Tweed, derived from Maccus's Wiel, they were a powerful Border family descended either from 11th-century Maccus, King of Man and the Isles, or from Norman settlers. Their lands were in Nithsdale and their motto is *Reviresco*—I flourish again.

Menzies: correctly pronounced *mingiz*, from Mesnières in Normandy. Although of Anglo-Norman origin they became Gaelicized. Their lands were Atholl, Weem, Aberfeldy and Glendochart and their mottos are *Vil God I Zal*—Will God I shall; and *Geal 'us dearg a suas*—Up with the white and red. Robert Menzies (mispronounced, as spelt) was Prime Minister of Australia from 1939–41. Menzies introduced the larch to Scotland. Clan Secretary, 1 Belford Place, Edinburgh. Clan Museum, Castle Menzies, Aberfeldy, Tayside.

Moncreiffe: from Gaelic *monadh craoibhe*—hill of the sacred bough, descended from Maldred, brother of King Duncan. Their lands were in Perthshire and their Lairds were traditionally Archers of the Sovereign's bodyguard. Sir Iain Moncrieffe of that Ilk, who died in 1988, was renowned as an historian, bon viveur and genealogist. Clan Secretary, Easter Moncreiffe, Perthshire.

Montgomery: from Montgomerie, in Normandy, the family are descended from Anglo-Norman Robert de Montgomery, who came to Scotland in the 12th century. Their lands were Eglinton, Ardrossan and Kintyre and their motto is *Gardez bien*—Look well. Their most famous scion was 'Monty', the Field Marshall who defeated Rommel in the desert in the Second World War. Clan Secretary, c/o P.O. Box 6, Saltcoats, Ayrshire.

Morrison: *ghille Mhoire* is Gaelic for servant of Mary, presumably of ecclesiastical origin, and they trace their ancestors to the MacLeods of Dunvegan in 13th century. Their lands were Lewis, Sutherland, Skye and Harris. Hebridean Morrisons are well-known pipers today. Clan Secretary, Ruchdi, by Loch Maddy, Isle of North Uist.

Munro: from the Gaelic *Rothach*—man from Ro, thought to be from the River Roe in Ireland. Their lands were in Easter Ross, their motto is Dread God and their war-cry, Castle Foulis Ablaze!, refers to the beacon that used to be lit on the chief's castle to summon the clan to arms. They were Whigs, supporting the Government against the Jacobites. Sir Hector Munro of Novar, 1726–1805, was a famous Anglo-Indian General. Another Hector, 1870–1916, was the novelist and short-story writer, Saki; and Neil Munro who died in 1930 was a Scottish writer.

Murray: from Moray, the place-name meaning settlement by the sea. They are descended from Pictish Mormaers, with lands in Morayshire and Perthshire. Their motto is *Tout pret*—All ready. Andrew Murray, who died in 1338, was Regent of Scotland; Lord George Murray was a Jacobite general, believed by some to have been a traitor at Culloden; John Murray, 1745–93, founded the famous publishing house. Clan Secretary, 204 Bruntsfield Place, Edinburgh.

Napier: descended from the ancient earls of Lennox; legend has it that one, having been particularly brave in battle, was ordered by his King to change his name to 'Nae peer'! Their lands were Gosford, Fife and Midlothian and their mottos are *Sans tache*—Without stain; and *To vincula frange*—To break bones. John Napier, 1550–1617, invented logarithms.

Ogilvie: from Brythonic *ocel fa*—high plain. Ogilvie Earls of Airlie descend directly from the Earls of Angus, and were granted lands in Angus by William the Lion. Their motto is *A fin*—To the finish. St John Ogilvie, 1579–1615, was a Scottish Jesuit martyr, canonized in 1976. The present chief, the Hon Angus Ogilvie, is married to Princess Alexandria.

Ramsay: meaning wild-garlic island. The family is descended from an Anglo-Norman, Simund de Ramesie, who was granted lands in Lothian by David I. Their lands were Dalhousie and Perthshire, and their motto is *Ora et labor*—Pray and work. Allan Ramsay, 1685–1758, was a poet; another Allan, 1713–84, was the renowned portrait-painter.

Robertson: the eponymous Robert was Robert Riabbhach (Grizzled Robert) Duncanson, 4th Chief of Clan Donnachaidh, and the Robertsons of Struan are one of the earliest known families in Scotland. Struan was their land and their mottos are: *Virtutis Gloria Merces*—Glory is the reward of valour; and *Garg'n uair dhuis gear*—Fierce when raised. Clan Secretary, 29 Lauriston Gardens, Edinburgh.

Rose: descended from the Norman family de Rose and first recorded in Scotland in the reign of Alexander II. Their lands were Strathnairn and Ross-shire and their motto is Constant and true. Clan Secretary, Kilravoch Castle, Nairnshire.

Ross: the Gaelic *ros* is a headland; Brythonic *ros* is a moor. They are descended from Fearchar Mac-an-t-Sagairt of Applecross, created Earl of Ross in 1234. Their lands were Ross-shire, Ayrshire and Renfrewshire and their motto is *Spem successus alit*—Success nourishes hope. Clan Secretary, 57 Barnton Park View, Edinburgh.

Scott: the Scoti was the Irish tribe who gave Scotland its name. The family descend from Uchtred, filius Scoti—son of a Scot—in the 12th century, and were one of the most powerful Border families. Their lands were in the Borders and Fife and their best-known scions were Sir Walter, the 19th-century writer; Captain (Robert Falcon) Scott, the arctic explorer who died so tragically at the South Pole in 1912; and Sir Peter Scott, his son, the ornithologist, artist and broadcaster.

Scrymgeour: from French *eskermisor*—sword-fencer or skirmisher. Their ancestor Alexander 'Schyrmeschar' was royal banner-bearer, hanged by Edward I in 1306. Their lands were in Argyll and Fife and their motto is Dissipate. Clan Secretary, 21 Braid Farm Road, Edinburgh.

Shaw: possibly derived from the *Gaelic* seaghdha—pithy. Principal members of the Clan Chattan Confederation, they were probably descended from 14th-century Shaw Macduff, founder of the MacIntosh clan. Their land was Strathspey and their motto is *Fide et Fortitudine*—By Fidelity and Fortitude. George Bernard Shaw, 1856–1950, the dramatist, writer and critic, was descended from a Dublin branch. Clan Secretary, Tordarroch House, Tordarroch, Inverness-shire.

Sinclair: from the French St Clair sur Elle, in Normandy, whence came William de Sancto Claro in the 12th century, receiving the barony of Roslin. Their lands were in Midlothian, Orkney and Caithness, and they were jarls of Orkney in 14th century. Their motto is Commit thy work to God. Clan Secretary, 2 Shandon Road, Edinburgh.

Skene: from Skene in Aberdeenshire, they are descended from Robertsons of Struan. Their lands were in Aberdeenshire, granted by the king in 11th century. Their motto is *Virtutis regia merces*—A palace the reward of bravery.

Stewart: derived from High Steward. Walter Fitz-Allan, an Anglo-Norman, came to Scotland in the 12th century and was given land and the greatest office in the realm—Steward of Scotland. The family provided Scotland with 14 sovereigns, five of whom also reigned in England. Stewart became Stuart for Mary, Queen of Scots, because there is no 'w' in French. Their lands were Renfrewshire, Teviotdale, Lauderdale, Appin and Ardshiel and their motto is *Virescit vulnere virtus*—Courage grows strong at a wound. Probably the best known Stuart was the one who never got to the throne, Prince Charles Edward, 1720–88. Clan Secretary, 48 Castle Street, Edinburgh.

Sutherland: Sudrland was the Norman name for Sutherland, to the south of Caithness. The clan is descended from early inhabitants of Sutherland, which was granted to them in 1228. Clan Secretary, Donrobin Castle, Golspie, Sutherland.

Urquhart: derived from Brythonic *air cairdean*—at the woods, the name of the district where the family originated. William of Urquhart was hereditary sheriff of Cromarty during the reign of Robert the Bruce. Their lands were in Ross-shire and Inverness-shire and their motto is Mean, speak and do well. Thomas Urquart, 1611–60, who claimed descent from Adam, was a brilliant translator of Rabelais and is said to have died of laughter, on hearing of the Restoration. Clan Secretary, Bigram, Port of Monteith, Stirlingshire.

Wallace: derived from Wallenses, the mediaeval word for the Welsh who peopled Strathclyde, from whom the Wallaces are descended. Their lands were Ayrshire and Renfrewshire and their motto is *Pro Libertate*—For Liberty. William Wallace fought for Scottish independence, paving the way for Robert the Bruce.

SCOTTISH REGIMENTS

Scotland is rightly proud of the seven regiments that make up the Scottish Division. Perhaps because of their war-like ancestors, Scots have always had the reputation for being the bravest in battle, their war-memorials the longest. On parade, because of their colourful uniforms and their pipes and drums, Scottish regiments draw the largest crowds. Within the Scottish Division, administered from Edinburgh, each regiment is a closeknit family, retaining its separate identity, uniform, traditions and customs.

The Royal Scots (The Royal Regiment), recruit mainly in Lothian, Edinburgh and Tweeddale. The oldest infantry regiment in the British Army, The Royal Scots were raised by Sir John Hepburn in 1633, for service under Louis XIII in France. They claimed and won precedence over all others in the French Service, challenged by the Regiment of Picardy, who declared that they had been on duty on the night of the Crucifixion. 'If we had been on guard' retorted the colonel of the Royal Scots, 'we should not have slept at our posts', thus gaining the regiment its famous nickname 'Pontius Pilate's Bodyguard'.

The Royal Highland Fusiliers (Princess Margaret's Own Glasgow and Ayrshire Regiment). In 1678, Charles Erskine, 5th Earl of Mar, raised The Earl of Mar's Regiment to subdue the fanatical Covenanters in the southwest shires of Scotland. They became the Scots Fusiliers in 1695 and gained their present title in 1959 when they were amalgamated with the Highland Light Infantry.

The Kings Own Scottish Borderers recruit across the south of Scotland. They were raised in 1689 by David Earl of Leven, when the citizens of Edinburgh were alarmed at the Jacobite threat. They fought at Killiecrankie, Sheriffmuir and Culloden. They are also one of six infantry regiments to have 'gained immortal glory' at the Battle of Minden in 1759, and now wear red roses on 1 August, Minden Day, to commemorate the tradition that the soldiers picked roses as they advanced through gardens during the battle.

The Black Watch (The Royal Highland Regiment), recruits from Angus, Perthshire, Fife and Dundee. The Black Watch was originally raised as six independent companies to police the Highlands after the first Jacobite rebellions, and was then formed into one regiment with the addition of four more companies, in 1739. Their name comes from the dark colour of their tartan (compared to the red coats and white trousers of the other regiments of that period), and from their duty to 'Watch the Highlands'. They were busy 'watching' on the Continent, in 1745, which may have contributed to Bonnie Prince Charlie's early success in raising an army of Jacobites to his father's standard and marching south as far as Derby. They wear a plume of red feathers in their bonnets—the red hackle—said to originate from recapturing guns lost to the enemy.

The Queen's Own Highlanders (Seaforth and Camerons) recruit from the Northern Highlands. They are descended from three Highland regiments raised in the late 18th century for service in the American and French Revolutionary Wars. The 72nd and 78th Highlanders were raised by Chiefs of Clan MacKenzie, mainly from Ross-shire and Lewis, and became the Seaforth Highlanders. The 79th Cameron Highlanders were raised by Alan Cameron of Erracht, mainly from Lochaber and North Argyll, and were honoured with the title Queen's Own by Queen Victoria in 1873. The regiments amalgamated to become The Queen's Own Highlanders in 1961.

The Gordon Highlanders recruit in Grampian. They were raised by the Duke of Gordon in 1794 with the help of his beautiful wife Jean, who donned a regimental jacket and bonnet and toured her husband's estates, placing a guinea between her lips and kissing each man who came forward to enlist. They wear black buttons on their spats in tribute to Sir John Moore who was killed in the moment of victory at the battle of Corunna in 1809. One of their achievements was capturing the Heights of Dargai on the Northwest Frontier of India in 1897, driven on by the skirl of the pipes played by Piper Findlater, who, shot through both ankles, continued to play the regimental march 'The Cock of the North' throughout the battle.

The Argyll and Sutherland Highlanders (Princess Louise's) recruit in Argyllshire and eastwards. They were formed in 1881 by the amalgamation of two Highland Regiments, the 91st and 93rd, which had been raised at the end of the 18th century for foreign service. They earned the nickname The Thin Red Line at Balaklava in 1854. The 93rd Sutherland Highlanders were ordered to the Heights above the town by Sir Colin Campbell and commanded to form a line against the full might of the Russian Cavalry. 'There is no retreat from here, you must die where you stand,' they were told. They advanced, fired two volleys and routed the Russians, suffering only two casualties. They won glory in Aden in 1967 and later conducted a successful campaign to avoid disbandment.

SCOTTISH MONARCHS

Kenneth Macalpine: 832–860
Constantine I: 863–879
Constantine II: 863–877
Donald I: 892–900
Donald II: 900–943
Malcolm I: 943–954
Kenneth II: 954–994
Malcolm II: 1005–1034
Duncan I: 1034–1040
Macbeth: 1040–1057
Malcolm III, Canmore: 1057–1093
Donald Bane: 1093 (six months)
Duncan II: 1094 (six months)
Donald Bane (again) and Edmund: 1094–1097
Edgar: 1097–1107
Alexander I: 1107–1124
David I: 1124–1153
Malcolm IV, the Maiden: 1153–1165
William I, the Lion: 1165–1214
Alexander II: 1214–1249
Alexander III. 1249–1286
Margaret, Maid of Norway: 1286–1290
Interregnum
John Balliol: 1292–1296
Interregnum

Bruces
Robert I: 1306–1329
David II: 1329–1371

Stewarts
Robert II: 1371–1390
Robert II: 1390–1406

Regent Albany: 1406–1419
Regent Murdoch: 1419–1424
James I: 1424–1437
James II: 1437–1460
James III: 1460–1488
James IV: 1488–1513
James V: 1513–1542
Mary: 1542–1567
James VI/I: 1567–1625
Charles I: 1625–1649
The Commonwealth: 1649–1660
Charles II: 1660–1685
James VII/II. 1685–1688
William and Mary: 1689–1694
William (alone): 1694–1702
Anne: 1702–1714

Hanoverians
George I: 1714–1727
George II: 1727–1760
George III: 1760–1820
George IV: 1820–1830
William II/IV: 1830–1837

Saxe-Coburg-Gotha
Victoria: 1837–1901
Edward I/VII: 1901–1910

Windsors
George V: 1910–1935
Edward II/VIII: 1935–1936
George VI: 1936–1952
Elizabeth I/II: 1952–

CHRONOLOGY

82	Defeat of Picts at battle of Mons Graupius by Roman Agricola.
141	Building of Antonine Wall.
397	Founding of Christian church at Whithorn by St Ninian.
410	Departure of Romans from Britain.
500	Invasion of Scotland by Irish Scots, settlement of Dalriada.
563	Landing of St Columba in Iona, conversion of Picts to Christianity.
794	Invasion of Hebrides by Norsemen.
844–60	Kenneth Macalpine unites Picts and Scots.
1034	Whole of Scotland united into one kingdom under Duncan I.
1040	Duncan I murdered by Macbeth who is in turn murdered by Malcolm Canmore.
1057–93	Anglicizing of Scotland under Queen Margaret.
1102	Western Isles granted to Magnus of Orkney.
1124–53	David I founds many abbeys and burghs, grants land to Normans.
1174	William the Lion forced to acknowledge supremacy of Henry II.
1200	Beginning of Auld Alliance of Scotland and France against England.
1214	Alexander II, Golden Age of Scottish history.
1263	Battle of Largs, defeat by Alexander III of King Haakon of Norway. Annexation of the Hebrides.
1286	Death of Alexander III, succeeded by Maid of Norway.
1290	Death of Maid of Norway at sea on her way to Scotland.
1291	Edward I arbitrates between Robert Bruce and John Balliol. Balliol gets crown.
1296	Balliol renounces his crown in favour of Edward I.
1297–98	William Wallace stirs up resistance, defeats Edward at Stirling Bridge, and is defeated at Falkland. Goes into hiding.
1305	Capture and execution of William Wallace.
1306	Robert Bruce slays John Comyn and is crowned at Scone.
1307	Edward I dies.
1314	Battle of Bannockburn, Bruce defeats English.
1326	First Scottish Parliament at Cambuskenneth.
1346	Battle of Neville's Cross. David II taken prisoner by English.
1371	Robert Stewart crowned, Robert II, first Stewart King.
1406	James I captured, Regency of Duke of Albany.
1414	Foundation of St Andrews, Scotland's first university.
1450–55	Struggle for supremacy between Stewarts and Douglases. Douglases crushed by James II.
1469	Orkney and Shetland pledged to James III as part of dowry of his wife, Margaret of Denmark.
1476	Overthrow of Lords of the Isles.
1495	Perkin Warbeck claims English throne, encouraged by James IV.
1513	Battle of Flodden, death of James IV.
1528	Burning of Patrick Hamilton, proto–martyr of Reformation.
1538	Marriage of James V to Marie de Guise.

1542	Defeat of Scots at Solway Moss, death of James V, accession of his infant daughter, Mary.
1544	Rough Wooing, devastation of Lowland Scotland by Henry VIII.
1546	Burning of George Wishart, murder of Cardinal Beaton.
1554	Regency of Marie de Guise.
1557	Signing of first Protestant Covenant.
1558	Marriage of Mary to Dauphin of France, Francis II.
1559	John Knox preaches Reform.
1565	Marriage of Mary to Darnley.
1566	Birth of James VI.
1567	Murder of Darnley, marriage of Mary to Bothwell, defeat, imprisonment and abdication.
1568	Mary, finally defeated leaves Scotland.
1587	Mary executed.
1600	The Gowrie conspiracy, a squalid attempt to abduct James VI in dubious circumstances.
1603	Accession of James VI to English throne making him James VI/I (VI of Scotland, I of England). Establishment of Episcopacy in Scotland.
1637	Riots of Edinburgh against Charles I's Episcopacy.
1638	Signing of National Covenant to uphold Presbyterian worship.
1643	Signing of Solemn League and Covenant recognized by English Parliament.
1645	Battle of Philiphaugh. Defeat of Royalist Montrose by Covenanters under Leslie.
1649	Execution of Charles I, Charles II proclaimed King in Scotland.
1650	Signing of Covenants by Charles II. Invasion of Scotland by Cromwell.
1653	United Parliament at Westminster.
1660	Restoration of Monarchy.
1662	Renunciation of Covenants by king and re-establishment of Episcopacy.
1666	Start of the Killing Times, persecution of Covenanters.
1688	James VII/II tries to restore Catholicism. He is deposed in favour of William and Mary.
1689	Highlanders, under Claverhouse, Bonnie Dundee, defeat King's army at Killiecrankie.
1692	Massacre of Glencoe.
1698	Failure of Darien Scheme.
1707	Union of Parliaments.
1715	Rebellion in favour of the Old Pretender.
1736	The Porteous Riot, Scots rebel against English domination.
1745/6	Final Jacobite rebellion. Defeat of Prince Charles Edward Stuart at Battle of Culloden. Repression of Highlands. Soon followed by the beginning of the Highland Clearances which lasted for over 100 years and depopulated the Highlands.
18th/19th century	Scottish Enlightenment
1845–6	Irish potato famine spreads to Scotland causing starvation and terrible hardship.
1947	Founding of Edinburgh International Festival, putting Scotland back on the cultural map.
1970s	North Sea Oil industry developed.
1979	Scotland rejected devolution in a referendum.

BIOGRAPHICAL NOTES

The following names are mentioned in the text but are not necessarily explained.

Adam, William and his four sons, John, Robert, James and William. Renowned Scottish-born architects, Robert, 1728–92 being the best known.

Adamnan, Saint. *c.* 624–704. Ninth Abbot of Iona and biographer of St Columba.

Barrie, Sir James. 1860–1937. Novelist and playwright. Born in Kirriemuir which he renamed Thrums in a series of novels. *Peter Pan* was one of his best-known works. Belonged to the Kailyard school of writers who sentimentalized small-town life in Scotland.

Bean, Sawney. Apocryphal 17th-century cannibal who lived with his incestuously-bred family in a cave in Ayrshire, existing on the flesh and gold of unwary travellers.

Beaton, (1) David. 1494–1546. Cardinal and Archbishop of St Andrews. Notorious for persecution of Reformers. Burned George Wishart for heresy and was murdered in revenge in St Andrews Castle. (2) James. 1470–1539. Uncle of (1). Archbishop of Glasgow, then St Andrews. Opponent of the Reformation and responsible for death of Patrick Hamilton, proto-martyr.

Boswell, James. 1740–95. Scottish lawyer, writer and admirer of prominent people. Met Dr Johnson in 1763 and toured Hebrides with him in 1773. Wrote *Life of Samuel Johnson*. A volatile, promiscuous man given to fits of depression. Of great value to anyone visiting Scotland is to read his *Journal of a Tour of the Hebrides*, in conjunction with Dr Johnson's account.

Bothwell, James Hepburn. Earl of, 1537–78. Powerful and ambitious. Closely involved in murder of Mary, Queen of Scots' husband, Darnley. Abducted Mary, raped her and married her after quick divorce from his wife. Escaped when Mary was deposed. Imprisoned in Denmark where he died insane.

Brahan, Seer. Coinneach Odhar. 17th century. Given gift of second sight after falling asleep on a fairy hill. Made astonishing prophecies, many of which have been fulfilled; some of which may yet be. Murdered by Countess of Seaforth having told her of her husband's infidelity.

Bridie, James. 1888–1951. Pseudonym of Osborne Henry Mavor, dramatist. Born in Glasgow, qualified as a doctor and served in R.A.M.C. in both world wars. His plays include *The Anatomist, Dr Angelus* and *A Sleeping Clergyman*. Amusing, extravagant, thought-provoking and entertaining.

Bryce, David. 1803–76. Edinburgh architect whose speciality was Scottish Baronial, most evident in Fettes College.

Burns, Robert. 1754–96. Born at Alloway in Ayrshire of humble parents and rose to become lionized as Scotland's greatest vernacular poet. Renowned almost as much for his enthusiastic love life and 'joi de vie' as for his verse. Among the many classics he wrote were 'Tam o' Shanter', 'My Love is like a Red, Red Rose', 'A Man's a Man, for a' That' and 'Auld Lang Syne'.

Columba, Saint. *c.* 521–97. Of royal Irish blood, he was exiled from Ireland for ecclesiastical plagiarism, settled in Iona in 563 and founded a religious community, launching-pad for missionaries who then converted Scotland to Christianity.

Cromwell, (1) Oliver. 1599–1658. Led Parliamentarians in England's civil war and was responsible for execution of Charles I. (2) Thomas. 1485–1540. *Malleus monachorum*, Hammer of the Monks. Rose from humble beginnings with help from Cardinal Wolsey. Ingratiated himself with Henry VIII, encouraging his first divorce and promising to make him rich. Very active in suppression and dissolution of monasteries; served in many high offices before losing favour by encouraging marriage to Anne of Cleves whom Henry disliked. Sent to the tower and beheaded.

Cumberland, William Augustus. Duke of, 1721–65. Fat son of George II, defeated Prince Charles at Culloden 1746, winning nickname of Butcher Cumberland for his brutality.

Douglas. Ancient Scottish family, often so powerful that they were a threat to the Crown. Divided into the Black Douglases and the Red Douglases, they appear for better or worse throughout Scottish history. The Black Douglases were finally subdued by James II. The Red Douglases, who 'rose upon the ruins of the Black' held considerable power until deposed by James V.

Dundee, Graham of Claverhouse. Viscount 'Bonnie Dundee'. 1649–89. Royalist and notorious persecutor of Covenanters. Led early Jacobite rebellion after James VII/II was deposed, and was killed defeating William's army at Killiecrankie.

Duns Scotus, Johannes, *c.* 1265–1308. One of the greatest of the medieval scholars, joined Franciscans, studied and lectured on philosophy and theology in Oxford, Paris and Cologne.

Fingal, or Fionn MacCumhail, *c.* 3rd century. Legendary Irish warrior and hunter, dominating Gaelic sagas. His band of men were the original Fenians, defending Ireland against invasion. Traditionally father of Ossian.

Hamilton, Patrick. 1502–28. Proto-martyr of Scottish Reformation, influenced by Erasmus and Luther. He returned to his native Scotland and was burned for heresy by Archbishop James Beaton at St Andrews. In spite of his youth, he was titular Abbot of Ferne.

Hertford, Edward Seymour. Earl of, 1506–52. Leading aggressor in Henry VIII's 'Rough Wooing' of Scotland, to punish them for cancelling marriage between Mary, Queen of Scots, and Henry's son, Edward. He was responsible for appalling destruction to many of Scotland's finest Lowland buildings, including the Border abbeys.

Hogg, James. 1770–1835. Protégé of Sir Walter Scott, known as the Ettrick shepherd. Prolific poet and novelist.

Johnson, Samuel. 1709–84. English lexicographer, critic and poet, whose reputation as a man and a conversationalist is as great as his literary fame. Dogmatic, unreasonable, humble, pious and loveable, his account of his tour of the Hebrides with James Boswell, in 1773, makes marvellous reading and is full of acute observations on life in the Highlands after Culloden and the Act of Proscription.

Jones, John Paul. 1747–92. Born in Kirkcudbrightshire, son of a gardener. He received commission in American Navy and returned to harass the English, but always with honour. Stories are told of his chivalrous treatment of his victims.

Knox, John. *c.* 1505–72. Leading Scottish Reformer. Spent 19 months as French galley-slave, returning to preach fiery iconoclastic sermons in Perth and St Andrews in 1559 which led to destruction of monasteries. Minister of St Giles in Edinburgh, during which time he tangled with Mary, Queen of Scots. The phrase 'monstrous regiment of women' was coined from his pamphlet called: 'The First Blast of the Trumpet Against the Monstrous Regiment of Women'. Although dogmatic, he had a keen sense of humour. As a 51-year-old-widower, he married a girl of 16.

Lauder, Sir Harry. 1870–1950. Mill boy and miner who became a much-loved writer and interpreter of Scottish songs, including 'The Road to the Isles'.

Leslie, David. 1601–82. Scottish Covenanter and General. Defeated Montrose at Battle of Philiphaugh. Supported Charles II in 1650 and was defeated by Cromwell at Dunbar. Imprisoned in Tower of London till Restoration of Monarchy, and then made Lord Newark.

Lorimer, Sir Robert. 1864–1929. Architect responsible for Thistle Chapel in St Giles Cathedral, Scottish War Memorial in Edinburgh Castle, and restoration of many castles and abbeys.

Macdonald, Flora. 1722–90. Born in South Uist. Tacksman father died when she was two. Adopted at 13 by Lady Clanranald, wife of chief of clan, and brought up in Skye. She smuggled Prince Charlie from Benbecula to Skye, disguised as her maid, Betty Burke, thus helping to save his life. Was imprisoned for a year on a troopship. Married son of Macdonald of Kingsburgh and entertained Dr Johnson during his tour of Hebrides in 1773. Emigrated with family to North Carolina where her husband became a brigadier-general in American War of Independence. Returned to Scotland in 1779 and died at Kingsburgh.

Mackintosh, Charles Rennie. 1868–1928. Architect, born in Glasgow, exercising considerable influence on European design. His style was simple and uncluttered. The best example of his work is Glasgow School of Art.

Macpherson, James. 1736–96. Scottish poet who 'translated' the Ossianic poems. Many believed that these works were genuine and they were certainly of great value, but others, including Dr Johnson, doubted their authenticity and it is now believed that James M. (not Dr. J.) collected a quantity of Gaelic material and composed his own poems from them. In their own right, whatever the source, they are a valuable and beautiful contribution to Gaelic past.

Monk, George. 1608–69. Parliamentary General in Scotland, fighting for Cromwell at Dunbar and then Governor of Scotland in 1653–58. When Cromwell died he saw that the only way to heal the turmoil in Britain was to restore the Monarchy and he was instrumental in bringing Charles II back to the throne.

Monmouth, Duke of. 1649–85. Bastard son of Charles II by Lucy Waters, he claimed that his parents had been married and raised a revolt against James VII/II, for which he was executed.

Moray, James Stuart. Regent, 1531–70. Bastard son of James V, half-brother to Mary, Queen of Scots. Sided with Lords of the Congregation and became Regent on Mary's abdication. Shot while riding through Linlithgow.

Ossian. 3rd-century Gaelic bard, possibly son of Fingal, chief of the Fenians, semi-mythical military body said to have been raised for defence of Ireland against Norse. Countless tales told. (See Macpherson, above)

Queensberry. 'Old Q' 4th Duke. 1724–1810. Notorious gambler, despoiled many tree plantations in Scotland, to pay his debts.

Ramsay, Allan. 1686–1758. Scottish poet, best known for 'The Gentle Shepherd'.

Ramsay, Allan. 1713–84. Son of above. Famous portrait painter.

Rob Roy, Robert MacGregor. 1671–1734. Known as Rob Roy (Red Robert) from colour of his hair. Romanticized by Walter Scott as philanthropic Robin Hood, he was in fact a cattle-raider and smuggler. Died peacefully, having been imprisoned in London and pardoned.

Scott, Sir Walter. 1771–1832. Prolific poet and novelist. Remarkable for his efforts to pay off debts of £130,000 after collapse of his publisher, hence the amazing volume of his work. He also did much for Scotland after the despair that followed Culloden. It was he who organized the search for the Scottish Regalia, and he who organized the State Visit of George IV.

Stevenson, Robert. 1772–1850. Scottish engineer responsible for many important light-houses, including Bell Rock.

Stevenson, Robert Louis. 1850–94. Grandson of above and son of another engineer. Prolific writer, best known for *Treasure Island, Kidnapped, The Master of Ballantrae*, and *Dr Jekyll and Mr Hyde*.

Telford, Thomas. 1757–1834. Scottish engineer famous for his bridges, of which many still exist, his roads and his canals including the Caledonian Canal.

Thomas the Rhymer. c. 1220–97. Thomas Learmont of Erceldoune (Earlston), Scottish seer and poet, many of whose prophecies were fulfilled. Said to have lived with the Fairy Queen for three years in the Eildon Hills. He foretold the death of Alexander III at his wedding feast.

Wade, George. 1673–1748. English general, sent to Scotland in 1724 to try to bring the Highlands under control. Built a system of metalled roads and bridges that opened up the north.

Warbeck, Perkin. 1474–c. 1499. Claimed to be one of the princes murdered in the Tower. Put forward by English Yorkists as rightful king. Made three futile 'invasions', was caught and executed. He was in fact the Son of a Flemish boatman.

Wishart, George. c. 1513–46. Scottish reformer, burned by Cardinal David Beaton in St Andrews, for which the cardinal was later murdered.

Wolf of Badenoch. died 1394. Bastard son of Robert II, Alexander Stewart, Earl of Buchan. Also known as 'Big Alastair, Son of the King'. Brutal and merciless, terrorizing the countryside from his castles of Ruthven and Lochindorb. Excommunicated by Bishop of Elgin in 1390 for which he destroyed Elgin Cathedral and much else.

SUGGESTED READING

The following are some recommended books which will prove valuable companions to anyone visiting Scotland.

A Concise History of Scotland, Fitzroy Maclean
Scotland's Story, Tom Steel
A History of the Scottish People 1560–1830, T. C. Smout
A Century of the Scottish People, 1830–1950
The Lion in the North, John Prebble
Mary, Queen of Scots, Antonia Fraser
Bonnie Prince Charlie, Fitzroy Maclean; latest biography, beautifully written and entirely unbiased.
The Prince in the Heather, Eric Linklater (Prince Charlie's escape after Culloden)
In Search of Scotland, H. V. Morton
In Scotland Again, H. V. Morton (These two were written in 1929 and 1933 and are as fresh and readable today as then.)
A Description of the Western Islands of Scotland M.Martin. James Thin reprinted a facsimile of this 1716 gem.
A Hundred Years in the Highlands, Osgood Mackenzie
The Life and Death of St Kilda, Tom Steel
A Companion to Scottish Culture, David Daiches
The Highland Clans, Sir Iain Moncreiffe of that Ilk. Not quite so 'readable' but an erudite book of great value.
A Journey to the Western Islands, Samuel Johnson
Journal of a Tour to the Hebrides, James Boswell
(These two can be obtained in one volume and should be read together. They are fascinating to read as you visit the places they went to.)
The Drove Roads of Scotland, A. R. B. Haldane
Highland Drove, John Keay (An account of droving cattle today using the old methods and routes. Good descriptions.)
Highland Folk Ways, I. F. Grant
Memoires of a Highland Lady, Elizabeth Grant
The Fringe of Gold, Charles MacLean (Wonderful collection of anecdotes about the fishing villages of the east coast.)
The Islands of Western Scotland, W. H. Murray
The Prophecies of the Brahn Seer, Alexander Mackenzie
A Macdonald for the Prince, Alasdair Maclean (The story of Neil MacEachen, native of Uist and father of Napoleon's Marshal Macdonald.)
Tales of a Grandfather, Walter Scott (The history of Scotland as told by Walter Scott to his young grandson. Delightful.)

Edinburgh: A Travellers' Companion, (ed) David Daiches (Excellent new anthology of historical accounts of the city, its life and customs.)
Scotland: An Anthology, Paul Harris (Delightful, idiosycratic literary collection covering all aspects of Scotland.)
The Sobieski Stuarts, H. Beveridge
The House of Elrig, Gavin Maxwell (About his childhood in Galloway). Also *Harpoon at a Venture; Ring of Bright Water; The Rocks Remain; Raven Seek Thy Brother.* (All describe Maxwell's fascinating life in the Western Highlands.)
A Description of the Western Islands of Scotland, Martin Martin (James Thin have reprinted a facsimile of the 1716 edition of this bewitching collection of observations.)
The Discovery of the Hebrides, Elizabeth Bray.
The Highlands, Calum I. Maclean (Charming reminiscenses, recently reprinted to include an introduction by his brother Sorley, the poet, with outstanding photographs by his nephew, Cailean.)
Reflections on Scotland, Ian Wallace (A traveller's scrap-book, by the well-known Scottish singer.)
Scottish Highland Estate: Preserving an Environment, Michael Wigan.

Novels
Whisky Galore, and anything else by Compton Mackenzie
Walter Scott's vast output includes: *Waverley*, his first novel, about Jacobites; *Redgauntlet*, about how Prince Charlie returned to Scotland to try his luck once more; *Fair Maid of Perth*, set in Perth at the end of the 14th century; *Old Mortality*, about Covenanters; and *Rob Roy*
The Song of the Forest, Colin Mackay (A beautiful piece of contemporary writing, giving a picture of life in the Dark Ages.)
The Sound of the Sea, also by Colin Mackay and equally well written
Consider the Lilies, Iain Crichton Smith, charming, sad story about the Clearances
No Mean City, A. MacArthur
Shetland Bus, David Howarth
King Hereafter, Dorothy Dunnet
A Scots Quair, Lewis Grassic Gibbon
Lanark, Alasdair Gray
The Inn at the Edge of the World, Alice Thomas Ellis
Sea Music, David Profumo
Kidnapped, Robert Louis Stevenson, and *Catriona* (based on the story of the Appin murder).

Poetry
Poems and Songs of Robert Burns, edited and introduced by James Barke.
From Wood to Ridge, Sorley Maclean (A collection of his haunting poems, in Gaelic and English.)
Poetic Gems Selected From the Works of William McGonagall, Poet and Tragedian (Scotland's worst poet—compulsive reading.)
Anything by Hugh MacDiarmid

Light Relief
The Old Man of Lochnagar, HRH The Prince of Wales

INDEX

Note: Page references in *italics* indicate illustrations; those in **bold** indicate maps.

Well of Tarlair 378
Wemyss Bay 191, 227
West Highland Way 29, 279
West Kilbride, museum 192
West Wemyss 292
Westerkirk 115
Western Isles 437–49
 tourist information 441
Westray 476
Whalsay 484
Whinnyfold 373
whisky 34
 in Grampian 361–2, 364–6
 in Highlands 426
 in Islands 473
 in Strathclyde 193–4, 206,
 219, 229–30

in Tayside 306, 314, 331, 336
White Corries chairlift 221
Whiteadder Reservoir 157
Whitehills 379
Whitekirk 132–3
Whithorn,
 prehistoric sites 3, 50, 108
 Priory and Museum 108
Whiting Bay 225
Wiay island 462
Wick 12, 430–2
Wigtown 107
Wilkie, David 174, 304
William the Lion 52
 in Borders 83
 in Central region 270
 in Dumfries and Galloway 99

in Grampian 345, 353, 371
 in Highlands 423
 in Tayside 313, 316, 321, 322
windsurfing 187, 337
Wolf of Badenoch 330, 367,
 509
Wood of Cree 94
Woodland Centre 89
Wren's Egg Stone Circle 109
Wyre 475

Yell island 483
Yellow Craig 135
Younger Botanic Garden 210
youth hostels 32, 402, 410, 415,
 417, 426, 457

INDEX OF CLAN NAMES

Barclay 371
Brodie 382
Cameron 61, 123, 408
Campbell 212–14, 220–1, 234,
 268, 278, 279, 401, 402,
 456
Chattan 313
Colquhoun 208
Cumming 383
Cunningham 189
Douglas x, 100–1, 124, 133,
 150, 166, 201, 270, 286–7,
 311, 314, 423, 507
Farquharson 356, 357, 358
Forbes 359, 360, 370, 377, 394
Fraser 376, 400
Galbraith 266
Gordon 105, 125, 341, 345,
 364, 371, 380
Graham 319
Hamilton 105, 201, 202
Hay 372

Irvine 354
Johnstone 119
Kennedy 198, 199, 297, 298,
 425
Kerr 150
Lovat 414
Macarthur 221
MacCrimmon 447
MacDonald 57, 60–1, 207,
 230, 400, 402, 407, 416,
 424, 441–2, 444–6, 450,
 460–1
Macdonell 399
MacDougall 240
Macduff 302
MacGregor 207, 208, 277, 278
MacIan 406
Mackay 427, 435
Mackenzie 404, 405, 416, 423
MacLaren 278
Maclean 57, 234, 235, 237, 240,
 268

Macleod 61, 406, 418, 446,
 447, 450, 454, 457, 460–1
Macmillan 187, 216
MacNab 278, 279
Macneil 466, 467
McNeill 216, 425
MacPherson 364
Macrae 405
MacSween 216
Maxwell 98, 116, 117, 119, 190
Menzies 334
Murray 427
Ogilvy 379, 380
Rose 391
Ross 426
Scott of Buccleuch 149
Sinclair 429, 431, 434
Stewart 198, 220, 240, 401, 472
Stuart 291

Other Cadogan Guides available from your local bookshop or from UK or USA direct:
From the UK: Cadogan Books, Mercury House, 195 Knightsbridge, London SW7 1RE.
From the US: The Globe Pequot Press, 138 West Main Street, Chester, Connecticut 06412.

Title

Australia ☐
Bali ☐
Berlin ☐
The Caribbean ☐
Ecuador, The Galapagos & Colombia (available Oct 1991) ☐
Greek Islands (2nd Edition) ☐
India (2nd Edition) ☐
Ireland ☐
Italian Islands (2nd Edition) ☐
Italy ☐
Mexico (available Sept 1991) ☐
Morocco ☐
New York ☐
Northeast Italy ☐
Northwest Italy ☐
Portugal ☐
Prague ☐
Rome ☐
South Italy ☐
Southern Spain: Andalucía & Gibraltar ☐
Spain (2nd Edition) ☐
Thailand & Burma ☐
Tunisia (available June 1992) ☐
Turkey (2nd Edition) ☐
Tuscany, Umbria & The Marches (2nd Edition) ☐
Venice ☐

Name

Address

Post Code

Date   Order Number

Special Instructions

Please use these forms to tell us about the hotels or restaurants you consider to be special and worthy of inclusion in our next edition, as well as to give any general comments on existing entries. Please include your name and address on the order form on the reverse of this page.

Hotels

Name ....

Address ....

Tel... Price of double room ....

Description/Comments ....

....

....

Name ....

Address ....

Tel... Price of double room ....

Description/Comments ....

....

....

Name ....

Address ....

Tel... Price of double room ....

Description/Comments ....

....

....

Name ....

Address ....

Tel... Price of double room ....

Description/Comments ....

....

....

Restaurants

Name ....

Address ....

Tel... Price per person ....

Description/Comments ....

....

....

Name ....

Address ....

Tel... Price per person ....

Description/Comments ....

....

....

Name ....

Address ....

Tel... Price per person ....

Description/Comments ....

....

....

Name ....

Address ....

Tel... Price per person ....

Description/Comments ....

....

....

General Comments

RAC HOTELS

The following is a list of RAC appointed hotels in Scotland.

Aberdeen Grampian (Aberdeenshire).

★★★★ **Bucksburn Moat House,** Old Meldrum Rd, Bucksburn, AB2 9LN ✆(0224) 713911 Tx: 73108 Fax: (0224) 714020

★★★★ **Caledonian Thistle,** Union Terr, AB9 1HE ✆(0224) 640233 Tx: 73758 Fax: (0224) 641627 &

★★★★ **Copthorne,** 122 Huntly St, AB1 1SU ✆(0224) 630404 Tx: 739707 Fax: (0224) 640573

★★★★ **Skean Dhu,** Souterhead Rd, Altens, AB1 4LE ✆(0224) 877000 Tx: 739631& Fax: (0224) 896964

♨ ★★★ **Ardoe House,** Blairs, South Deeside Rd, AB1 5YP ✆(0224) 867355 Tx: 739413 Fax: (0224) 861283

★★★ **Dyce Skean Dhu,** Farburn Ter, AB2 0DW ✆(0224) 723101 Tx: 73473 Fax: (0224) 722965

★★★ **Stakis Tree Tops,** 161 Springfield Rd, AB9 2QH ✆(0224) 313377 Tx: 73794 Fax: (0224) 312028

★★★ **Westhill,** Westhill, AB3 6TT ✆(0224) 740388 Tx: 739925 Fax: (0224) 744354

★★ **Ferryhill House,** Bon Accord St, AB1 2UA ✆(0224) 590867

Aberdeen Airport Grampian (Aberdeenshire).

★★★★ **Holiday Inn,** Riverview Dr, Farburn, Dyce AB2 0AZ ✆(0224) 770011 Tx: 739651 Fax: (0224) 722347 &

★★★★ **Skean Dhu,** Argyll Rd, AB2 0DU ✆(0224) 725252 Tx: 739239 Fax: (0224) 723745 &

Aberdour Fife.

★★★ **Woodside,** High St, KY3 0SW ✆(0383) 860328 Tx: 721656 Fax: (0383) 860920

Aberfeldy Tayside (Perthshire).

♨ ★★★ **Moness House,** PH15 2DY ✆(0887) 20446 Fax: (0887) 20062

★★ **Weem,** Weem, PH15 2LD ✆(0887) 20381

Guinach (Highly Acclaimed), Urlar Rd, PH15 2ET ✆(0887) 20251.

Aberlady Lothian (East Lothian).

★★ **Kilspindie House,** Main St, EH32 0RE ✆(087 57) 682 &

Achnasheen Highland (Ross & Cromarty).

♨ ★★ **H Ledgowan,** IV22 2EJ ✆(044 588) 252 Tx: 75431 Fax: (044 588) 240

Airdrie Strathclyde (Lanarkshire).

★★ **Tudor,** 39 Alexandra St, ML6 0BA ✆(0236) 64144 Fax: (0236) 47589

Annan Dumfries & Galloway (Dumfriesshire).

★ **Corner House,** 78 High St, DG12 6DL ✆(046 12) 2754

Anstruther Fife.

★★★ **Craw's Nest,** Bankwell Rd, KY10 3DA ✆(0333) 310691 Tx: 727049 Fax: (0333) 312216 &

★★ **Smugglers Inn,** High St East, KY10 3DQ ✆(0333) 310506

Arbroath Tayside (Angus).

★★ **Seaforth,** Dundee Rd, DD11 1QF ✆(0241) 72232

Ardeonaig Central (Perthshire).

★★ **Ardeonaig,** FK21 8SU ✆Killin (056 72) 400

Ardlui Strathclyde (Dunbartonshire).

★★ **Ardlui,** G83 7EB ✆Inveruglas (030 14) 243 Fax: (030 14) 268

Ardrossan Strathclyde (Ayrshire).

★★ **Blair Lodge,** 20 South Cres, KA20 8EA ✆(0294) 68436

Auchencairn Dumfries & Galloway (Kirkcudbrightshire).

♨ ★★★ **R Balcary Bay,** DG7 1QZ ✆(055 664) 217

Auchterarder Tayside (Perthshire).

★★★★★ **The Gleneagles,** PH3 1NF ✆(0764) 62231 Tx: 76105 Fax: (0764) 62134 &

♨ ★★★ **Duchally,** PH3 1PN ✆(0764) 63071

Aultbea Highland (Ross & Cromarty).

★★ **Aultbea,** IV22 2HX ✆(044 582) 201 Fax: (044 582) 214

★★ **Drumchork Lodge,** IV22 2HU ✆(044 582) 242

Aviemore Highland (Inverness-shire).

★★★★ **Stakis Four Seasons,** Aviemore Centre, PH22 1PF ✆(0479) 810681 Tx: 75213 Fax: (0479) 810862

★★★ **Aviemore Highlands** (formerly Post House), Aviemore Centre, PH22 1PJ ✆(0479) 810771 Tx: 57643 Fax: (0479) 811473

★★★ **Red MacGregor,** Main Rd, PH22 1RH ✆(0479) 810256 Fax: (0479) 810685

★★★ **Stakis Coylumbridge,** PH22 1QN ✆(0479) 810661 Tx: 75272 Fax: (0479) 811309

Ayr Strathclyde (Ayrshire).

★★★★ **Fairfield House,** 12 Fairfield Rd, KA7 2AS ✆(0292) 267461 Tx: 778833 Fax: (0292) 261456

♨ ★★★ **Belleisle House,** Doonfoot, KA7 4DU ✆(0292) 42331 Fax: (0292) 45325

★★★ **Caledonian,** Dalblair Rd, KA7 1UG ✆(0292) 269331 Tx: 776611 Fax: (0292) 610722

★★★ **Kylestrome,** Miller Rd, KA7 2AX ✆(0292) 262474

★★★ **Pickwick,** 19 Racecourse Rd, KA7 2TD ✆(0292) 260111 Fax: (0292) 43174

★★★ **Savoy Park,** 16 Racecourse Rd, KA7 2UT ✆(0292) 266112 Fax: (0292) 611488

★★★ **Station,** Burns Statue Sq, KA7 3AT ✆(0292) 263268 &

★★ **Ayrshire and Galloway,** 1 Killoch Pl, KA7 2AE ✆(0292) 262626

★★ **R Burns Monument,** Monument Rd, Alloway, KA7 4PQ ✆(0292) 42466 Fax: (0292) 611295

★★ **Chestnuts,** 52 Racecourse Rd, KA7 2UZ ✆(0292) 264393 Fax: (0292) 264393

★★ **Gartferry,** 44 Racecourse Rd, KA7 2UY ✆(0292) 262768

★★ **Old Racecourse,** 2 Victoria Park, KT7 1HT ✆(0292) 262873 &

Ballachulish Highland (Argyll).

★★★ **Ballachulish,** PA39 4JY ✆(085 52) 606 Tx: 94013696 Fax: (085 52) 629

Ballater Grampian (Aberdeenshire).

★★★★ **H C R Craigendarroch,** Braemar Rd, Royal Deeside, AB3 5XA ✆(033 97) 55858 Tx: 739952 Fax: (033 97) 55447

♨ ★★★ **Darroch Learg,** Braemar Rd, AB3 5UX ✆(033 97) 55443 Fax: (033 97) 55443

★★★ **Glen Lui,** Invercauld Rd, AB3 5RP ✆(033 97) 55402 Fax: (033 97) 55545

★★ **Monaltrie** (formerly Invercauld Arms), 5 Bridge Sq, AB3 5QJ ✆(033 97) 55417 Fax: (033 97) 55180

Balloch Strathclyde (Dunbartonshire).

★★ **Balloch,** G83 8LQ ✆Alexandria (0389) 52579 Fax: (0389) 55604

Balmacara Highland (Ross & Cromarty).

★★ **Balmacara,** IV40 8DH ✆(059 986) 283 Fax: (059 986) 329 &

Banavie Highland (Inverness-shire).

★★★ **Moorings,** Fort William, PH3 7LY ✆Corpach (0397) 772 797 Fax: (0397) 772 797

Banchory Grampian (Kincardineshire).

♨ ★★★★ **H C R Invery House,** Feughside, AB3 3NJ ✆(0224) 321371 Tx: 73225 Fax: (0224) 311162 &

♨ ★★★ Banchory Lodge, Dee St, AB3 3HS
☎(033 02) 2625 Fax:(033 02) 5019

♨ ★★★ H C Raemoir, AB3 4ED
☎(033 02) 4884 Tx: 73315 Fax:(033 02) 2171 &

★★★ Tor-na-Coille, Inchmarlo Rd, AB3
4AB ☎(033 02) 2242 Fax:(033 02) 4012

★★ Burnett Arms, 25 High St, AB3 3TD
☎(033 02) 4944 Tx: 739925 Fax:(0224) 744354

Banff Grampian (Banffshire).

★★★ Banff Springs, Golden Knowes Rd,
AB4 2JE ☎(026 12) 2881 Fax:(026 12) 5546

Barrhead Strathclyde (Renfrewshire).

★★ Dalmeny Park, Lochlibo Rd, G78 1LE
☎041-881 9211

Barrhill Strathclyde (Ayrshire).

♨ ★★★★ R Kildonan, KA26 0PU
☎(046 582) 360 Fax:(046 582) 292 &

Bathgate Lothian (West Lothian).

★★★ Golden Circle, Blackburn Rd, EH48
2EL ☎(0506) 53771 Tx: 72606

Bearsden Strathclyde

★★ Burnbrae, Milngavie Rd, G61 3TA
☎041-942 5951

Beattock Dumfries & Galloway

♨ ★★★ Auchen Castle, DG10 9SH
☎(068 33) 407

♨ ★★ Beattock House, DG10 9QB
☎(068 33) 402

Beauly Highland (Inverness-shire).

★★ Lovat Arms, Main Street, IV4 7BS
☎(0463) 782313 Fax:(0463) 782313

★★ Priory, The Square, IV4 7BX ☎(0463)
782309 Fax:(0463) 782531

Biggar Strathclyde (Lanarkshire).

♨ ★★★★ Shieldhill, Quothquan,
ML12 6NA ☎(0899) 20035 Tx: 777308
Fax:(0899) 21092

Birnam Tayside (Perthside).

★★★ Birnam, PH8 0BQ ☎(035 02) 462
Tx: 57515 Fax:(03502) 8979

Blairgowrie Tayside (Perthshire).

♨ ★★★ H C Altamount House, Coupar
Angus Rd, PH10 6JN ☎(0250) 3512

★★ Angus, Wellmeadow, PH10 6NQ
☎(0250) 2838 Tx: 76526 Fax:(0250) 5289

★★ Rosemount Golf, Golf Course Rd,
PH10 6LJ ☎(0250) 2604

Boat of Garten Highland (Inverness-shire).

★★★ The Boat, PH24 3BH ☎(047 983) 258
Tx: 9401 3436 Fax:(047 983) 414

Bonar Bridge Highland (Sutherland).

★★ Bridge, Ardgay, IV24 3EB ☎(086 32) 204

Bothwell Strathclyde (Lanarkshire).

★★★ Bothwell Bridge, 89 Main St,
G71 8LN ☎(0698) 852246 Tx: 776838

★★ Silvertrees, Silverwells Cres, G71 8DP
☎(0698) 852311 Fax:(0698) 852311

Bridge of Allan Central
(Stirlingshire).

★★★ Royal, Henderson St, FK9 4HL
☎(0786) 832284 Fax:(0786) 834377

Bridge of Cally Tayside (Perthshire).

★★ Bridge of Cally, PH10 7JJ ☎(025 086)
231

Brora Highland (Sutherland).

★★★ Links, KW9 6QS ☎(0408) 21225
Tx: 75242 &

★★★ Royal Marine, KW9 6QS ☎(0408)
21252 Tx: 76165 Fax:(08212) 446

Buckie Grampian (Banffshire).

★★ Cluny, 2 High St, AB5 1AL ☎(0542)
32922

Busby Strathclyde (Lanarkshire).

★★ Busby, Field Rd, G76 8RX ☎041-644
2661

Bute, Isle of See Isle of Bute

Callander Central (Perthshire).

♨ ★★★ R Roman Camp, off Main St,
FK17 8BG ☎(0877) 30003 Tx: 9312132123
Fax:(0877) 31533 &

★★ Dalgair House, Main St, FK17 8BQ
☎(0877) 30283

★★ Glenorchy, Leny Rd, FK17 8AL ☎(0877)
30329

★ H C R Lubnaig, Leny Feus, FK17 8AS
☎(0877) 30376

Campbeltown Strathclyde (Argyll).

★★ Royal, Main St, PA28 6AG ☎(0586)
52017

★★ R Seafield, Kilkerran Rd, PA28 6JL
☎(0586) 54385

★ Ardshiel, Kilkerran Rd, PA28 6JL ☎(0586)
52153

Canonbie Dumfries & Galloway
(Dumfriesshire).

★★ Cross Keys, DG14 0SY ☎(054 15) 382

Carfraemill Borders (Berwickshire).

★★ Carfraemill, Oxton by Lauder, TD2
6RA ☎(057 85) 200 Tx: 336587

Carnoustie Tayside (Angus).

★★ Glencoe, Links Parade, DD7 7JF ☎(0241)
53273.

Castle Douglas Dumfries &

★★ Douglas Arms, King St, DG7 1DB
☎(0556) 2231

♨ ★★ Urr Valley (formerly Ernespie
House), Ernespie Rd, DG7 3JG ☎(0556) 2188
Fax:(0556) 2188

★★ Imperial, King St, DG7 1AA ☎(0556)
2086

Clarencefield Dumfries & Galloway.

Clydebank Strathclyde.

★★★ Patio, 1 South Av, Clydebank Business
Park, G81 2RW ☎041-951 1133
Fax:041-952 3713 &

Coatbridge Strathclyde (Lanarkshire).

★★★ Coatbridge, Glasgow Rd, ML5 1EL
☎(0236) 24392

Colliston Tayside (Angus).

♨ ★★★ Letham Grange, Arbroath
DD11 4RL ☎Gowanbank (024 189) 373
Fax:(024 189) 414

Colmonell Strathclyde (Ayrshire).

★ Boar's Head, Main St, KA26 0RY
☎(0468 588) 272

Comrie Tayside (Perthshire).

★★ Comrie, Drummond St, PH6 2DY
☎(0764) 70239

Connel Strathclyde (Argyll).

★★ Falls of Lora, PA37 1PB ☎(063 171) 483
Fax:(063 171) 694

Contin Highland (Ross & Cromarty).

♨ ★★ Craigdarroch Lodge, Strathpeffer,
IV14 9EH ☎Strathpeffer (0997) 21265 &

Craigellachie Grampian.

★★★ Craigellachie House, AB3 9SS
☎(0340) 881 204 Fax:(0340) 881253

Crail Fife.

★ Croma, 33 Nethergate Rd, KY10 3TU
☎(0333) 50239

Creetown Dumfries & Galloway
(Kirkcudbrightshire).

★★ Ellangowan, DG8 7JF ☎(067 182) 201

Crieff Tayside (Perthshire).

★★ Crieff, 45 East High St, PH7 3JA ☎(0764)
2632 Tx: 779980 Fax:(0786) 50034

♨ ★★ H Cultoquey House, PH7 3NE
☎(0764) 3253

★★ Locke's Acre, Comrie Rd, PH7 4BP
☎(0764) 2526

★★ H R Murray Park, Connaught Terr,
PH7 3DJ ☎(0764) 3731 Fax:(0764) 5311

★ H Gwydir House, Comrie Rd, PH7
4BP ☎(0764) 3277

Crinan Strathclyde (Argyll).

★★★ R Crinan, PA31 8SR ☎(054 683) 261
Fax:(054 683) 292 &

Crocket Ford Dumfries & Galloway
(Kirkcudbrightshire).

★★ Galloway Arms, Stranraer Rd, DG2
8KA ☎(055 669) 240

★★ Royal, Marine Ter, IV11 8YN ☎(038 17)
217

Crossmichael Dumfries & Galloway
(Kirkcudbrightshire).

♨ ★★ Culgruff House, DG7 3BB
☎(055 667) 230

Cullen Grampian (Banffshire).

★★★ Seafield Arms, Seafield St, AB5 2SG
☎(0542) 40791

★★ Cullen Bay, AB5 2XA ☎(0542) 40432
Fax:(0542) 40900

Cumnock Strathclyde (Ayrshire).

★★ Dumfries Arms, 54 Glaisnock St,
KA18 1BY ☎(0290) 20282

★★ Royal, 1 Glaisnock St, KA18 1BP (0290)
20822

Dalry Dumfries & Galloway
(Kirkcudbrightshire).

♨ ★★ Milton Park, DG7 3SR ☎(064 43) 286

Dalry Strathclyde.

P P Dalry, Kilbirnie Rd, KA24 5JS
☎(029 483) 5135

Dingwall Highland (Ross & Cromarty).
★★ **National,** High St, IV15 9HA ✆(0349) 62166 Fax: (0349) 65178

Dolphinton Strathclyde (West Lothian).
♨ ★★★ H C R **Dolphinton House,** West Linton, EH46 7AB ✆(0968) 82286 Fax: (0899) 20456

Dornoch Highland (Sutherland).
★★★ **Royal Golf,** Grange Rd, IV25 3LG ✆(0862) 810283 Tx: 75300
★★ **Burghfield House,** IV25 3HW ✆(0862) 810212 Fax: (0862) 810404
★★ **Dornoch Castle,** Castle St, IV25 3SD ✆(0862) 810216

Doune Central (Perthshire).
★★ **Woodside,** Stirling Rd, FK16 6AB ✆(0786) 841237

Drummore Dumfries & Galloway (Wigtownshire).
★ **Queen's,** Mill St, DG9 9PS ✆(077 684) 300

Drymen Central (Stirlingshire).
★★★ **Buchanan Arms,** Main St, G63 0BQ ✆(0360) 60588 Fax: (0360) 60943
★★ **Winnock,** The Square, G63 0BL ✆(0360) 60245 Fax: (0360) 60267

Dulnain Bridge Highland (Moray).
★★★ **Muckrach Lodge,** PH26 3LY ✆(047 985) 257

Dumbarton Strathclyde (Dunbartonshire).
★★ **Dumbuck,** Glasgow Rd, G82 1EG ✆(0389) 34336 Tx: 778303 Fax: (0389) 34336

Dumfries Dumfries & Galloway (Dumfriesshire).
★★★ **Cairndale,** English St, DG1 2DF ✆(0387) 54111 Tx: 777530 Fax: (0387) 50555
♨ ★★★ **Hetland Hall,** Carrutherstown, DG1 4JX ✆(0387) 84201 Tx: 776819 Fax: (0387) 84211
★★★ **Station,** Lovers Walk, DG1 1LT ✆(0387) 54316 Tx: 778654 Fax: (0387) 50388
★★ **Skyline,** 123 Irish St, DG1 2NP ✆(0387) 62416
★ **Swan,** Kingholm Quay, DG1 4SU ✆(0387) 53756

Dunbar Lothian (East Lothian).
★★ **Bayswell,** Bayswell Park, EH42 1AE ✆(0368) 62225 Fax: (0368) 62225
★★ **Redheugh,** Bayswell Park, EH42 1AE ✆(0368) 62793

Dundee Tayside (Angus).
★★★★ **Stakis Earl Grey,** Earl Grey Pl, DD1 4DE ✆(0382) 29271 Tx: 76569 Fax: (0382) 200072
★★★ **Angus Thistle,** 101 Marketgait, DD1 1QU ✆(0382) 26874 Tx: 76456 Fax: (0382) 22564
★★★ **Invercarse,** 371 Perth Rd, DD2 1PG ✆(0382) 69231 Tx: 76608 Fax: (0382) 644112
★★★ **Queen's,** Nethergate, DD1 4DU ✆(0382) 22515 Fax: (0382) 202668

★★★ **Swallow,** Kingsway West, DD2 5JT ✆(0382) 641122 Tx: 76694 Fax: (0382) 568340

Dundonnell Highland (Ross & Cromarty).
★★★ C **Dundonnell,** IV23 2QS ✆(085 483) 204 Fax: (085 483) 366

Dunfermline Fife.
★★★ **Elgin,** Charlestown, KY11 3EE ✆(0383) 872257
★★★ **Keavil House,** Crossford, KY12 8QW ✆(0383) 736258 Tx: 728227 Fax: (0383) 621600
★★★ **King Malcolm Thistle,** Queensferry Rd, KY11 5DS ✆(0383) 722611 Tx: 727721 Fax: (0383) 730865
★★★ **Pitbauchlie House,** Aberdour Rd, KY11 4PB ✆(0383) 722282 Tx: 727756 Fax: (0383) 620738
★★★ **Pitfirrane Arms,** Main St, Crossford, KY12 8NJ ✆(0383) 736132 Tx: 728255 Fax: (0383) 621760

Dunkeld Tayside (Perthshire).
♨ ★★★★ **Stakis Dunkeld House,** PH8 0HX ✆(035 02) 771 Tx: 76657 Fax: (035 02) 8924
★★ **Atholl Arms,** Bridge St, PH8 0AQ ✆(035 02) 219

Dunnet Highland (Caithness).
★★ **Northern Sands,** KW14 8XD ✆Barrock (084 785) 270

Dunoon Strathclyde (Argyll).
★★ **Abbeyhill,** Dhalling Rd, PA23 8EA ✆(0369) 2204
★★ **Argyll,** Argyll St, PA23 7NE ✆(0369) 2059
★★ **Esplanade,** West Bay, PA23 7HU ✆(0369) 4070 Fax: (0369) 4070

Duntocher Strathclyde (Dunbartonshire).
★★ **Duntocher** (formerly Maltings), Dumbarton Rd, G81 6DP ✆(0389) 75371

East Kilbride Strathclyde (Lanarkshire).
★★★ **Bruce,** Cornwall St, G74 1AF ✆(035 52) 29771 Tx: 778428 Fax: (035 52) 42216
♨ ★★★ R **Crutherland,** Strathaven Rd, G75 0QZ ✆(035 52) 37633
★★★ **Stuart,** Cornwall Way, G74 1JS ✆(035 52) 21161 Tx: 778504 Fax: (035 52) 64410

East Linton Lothian (East Lothian).
★★ C **The Harvesters,** EH40 3DP ✆(0620) 860395

Edinburgh Lothian (Midlothian).
See also UPHALL
★★★★★ **Caledonian,** Princes St, EH1 2AB ✆031-225 2433 Tx: 72179 Fax: 031-225 6632
★★★★★ **Edinburgh Sheraton,** 1 Festival Sq, Lothian Rd, EH3 9SR ✆031-229 9131 Tx: 72398 Fax: 031-228 4510
★★★★ **Carlton, Highland,** North Bridge, EH1 1SD ✆031-556 7277 Tx: 727001

Fax: 031-556 2691
★★★★ **George,** George St, EH2 2PB ✆031-225 1251 Tx: 72570 Fax: 031-226 5644
★★★★ **Hilton International,** Belford Rd, EH4 3DG ✆031-332 2545 Tx: 727979 Fax: 031-332 3805
★★★★ **Scandic Crown,** 80 High St, EH1 1TH ✆031-557 9797 Tx: 727298 Fax: 031-557 9789
★★★★ **Swallow Royal Scot,** 111 Glasgow Rd, EH12 8NF ✆031-334 9191 Tx: 727197 Fax: 031-316 4507
★★★ **Albany,** 39 Albany St, EH1 3QY ✆031-556 0397 Tx: 727079
★★★ **Barnton Thistle,** 562 Queensferry Rd, EH4 6AS ✆031-339 1144 Tx: 727928 Fax: 031-339 5521
★★★ **Braid Hills,** 134 Braid Rd, EH10 6JD (2½ m S on A702). ✆031-447 8888 Tx: 72311 Fax: 031-452 8477
★★★ **Capital Moat House,** Clermiston Rd, EH12 6UG ✆031-334 3391 Tx: 728284 Fax: 031-334 9712
★★★ **Crest,** Queensferry Rd, EH4 3HL ✆031-332 2442 Tx: 72541 Fax: 031-332 3408
★★★ **Ellersly House,** Ellersly Rd, Murrayfield, EH12 6HZ ✆031-337 6888 Tx: 727239 Fax: 031-313 2543
★★★ C R **Howard,** 36 Great King St, EH3 6QH ✆031-557 3500
★★★ **King James Thistle,** St James Centre, EH1 3SW ✆031-556 0111 Tx: 727200 Fax: 031-557 5333
★★★ **Mount Royal,** 53 Princes St, EH2 2DG ✆031-225 7161 Tx: 727641 Fax: 031-220 4671
★★★ **Old Waverley,** 43 Princes St, EH2 2BY ✆031-556 4648 Tx: 727050 Fax: 031-557 6316
★★★ **Post House,** Corstorphine Rd, EH12 6UA ✆031-334 0390 Tx: 727103 Fax: 031-334 9237
★★★ H C **Roxburghe,** 38 Charlotte Sq, EH2 4HG ✆031-225 3921 Tx: 727054 Fax: 031-220 2518
★★ **Clarendon,** 18 Grosvenor St, EH12 5EG ✆031-337 7033 Tx: 72450 Fax: 031-346 7606
★★ **Hailes,** 2 Wester Hailes Centre, EH11 2SW ✆031-442 3382
★★ **Harp,** St John's Rd, Corstorphine, EH12 8AX (3½ m W A8). ✆031-334 8235
★★ **Iona,** 17 Strathearn Pl, EH9 2AL ✆031-447 5050 Fax: 031-452 8574
★★ **Lady Nairne,** 228 Willowbrae Rd, EH8 7NG ✆031-661 3396 Fax: 031-652 2789
★★ **Murrayfield,** 18 Corstorphine Rd, EH12 6HN ✆031-337 1844 Fax: 031-346 8159
★★ **Royal Ettrick,** 13 Ettrick Rd, EH10 5BJ ✆031-228 6413 Fax: 031-229 7330

Edzell Tayside (Angus).
★★★ **Glenesk,** High St, DD9 7TF ✆(035 64) 319 Fax: (035 64) 7333
★★ **Panmure Arms,** 52 High St, DD9 7TA ✆(035 64) 420

Elgin Grampian (Moray).

★★★ **Eight Acres,** Sheriff Mill, IV30 3UL ☎(0343) 543077 Fax: (0343) 540001

★★ **St Leonards,** Duff Av, IV30 1QS ☎(0343) 547350 &

Erskine Strathclyde (Renfrewshire).

★★★ **Crest,** PA8 6AN ☎041-812 0123 Tx: 776877 Fax: 041-812 7642 &

Ettrickbridge Borders (Selkirkshire).

♨ ★★★ **Ettrickshaws Country House,** TD7 5HW ☎(0750) 52229

Falkirk Central (Stirlingshire).

★★★ **Stakis Park,** Camelon Rd, Arnothill, FK1 5RY ☎(0324) 28331 Tx: 776502 Fax: (0324) 611593

Fochabers Grampian (Moray).

★★ **Gordon Arms,** 80 High Street, IV32 7DH ☎(0343) 820508 Fax: (0343) 820300

Forres Grampian (Moray).

★★ **Park,** Victoria Rd, IV36 0BN ☎(0309) 72328

★★ H **Ramnee,** Victoria Rd, IV36 0BN ☎(0309) 72410

Fort Augustus Highland (Inverness).

★★★ **Lovat Arms,** Main Rd, PH32 4BE ☎(0320) 6206

★★ **Inchnacardoch Lodge,** PH32 4BL ☎(0320) 6258

Fortingall Tayside (Perthshire).

★★ **Fortingall,** By Aberfeldy, PH15 2NQ ☎Kenmore (088 73) 367

Fort William Highland (Inverness-shire).

♨ ★★★★ **Inverlochy Castle,** Torlundy, PH33 6SN ☎(0397) 2177 Tx: 776229

★★★ **Mercury,** Achintore Rd, PH33 6RW ☎(0397) 3117 Tx: 778454

★★★ **Grand,** Gordon Sq. PH33 6DX ☎(0397) 2928 Fax: (0397) 5060

★★ **Nevis Bank,** Belford Rd, PH33 6BY ☎(0397) 705721 Tx: 94016892 Fax: (0397) 706275

Fraserburgh Grampian (Aberdeenshire).

★★ **Alexandra,** High St, AB4 5HE ☎(0346) 28249

Freuchie Fife.

★★ **Lomond Hills,** High St, KY7 7EY ☎Falkland (0337) 57329 Fax: (0337) 58180

Gairloch Highland (Ross & Cromarty).

★★★ **Creag Mor,** Charleston, 1V21 2AH ☎(0445) 2068 Fax: (0445) 2044

★★ **Old Inn,** IV21 2BD ☎(0445) 2006

Galashiels Borders (Selkirkshire).

♨ ★★★ C **Kingsknowes,** Selkirk Rd, TD1 3HY ☎(0896) 58375

★★ **Abbotsford Arms,** 63 Stirling St, TD1 1BY ☎(0896) 2517

Garve Highland.

★★ **Garve,** IV23 2PR ☎(099 74) 205

★★ **Inchbae Lodge,** Inchbae, IV23 2PH ☎Aultguish (099 75) 269

Gatehouse-of-Fleet Dumfries & Galloway (Kirkcudbrightshire).

♨ ★★★★ **Cally Palace,** DG7 2DL ☎(055 74) 341 Fax: (055 74) 522

★★★ **Murray Arms,** Main St, DG7 2HY ☎(055 74) 207 Fax: (055 74) 370

Giffnock Strathclyde.

★★★ R **MacDonald Thistle,** Eastwood Toll, G46 6RA ☎041-638 2225 Tx: 779138 Fax: 041-638 6231

★★ **Redhurst,** Eastwood Mains Rd, G46 6QE ☎041-638 6465 Fax: 041-620 0419

Girvan Strathclyde (Ayrshire).

★★ **Kings Arms,** Dalrymple St, KA26 0DU ☎(0465) 3322

★★ **Westcliffe,** Louisa Dr, KA26 9AH ☎(0465) 2128

★ **Hamilton Arms,** 12 Bridge St, KA26 9KH ☎(0465) 2182

Glamis Tayside.

★★★ **Castleton House,** Forfar, DD8 1SJ ☎(030 784) 340 Fax: (030 784) 506

Glasgow Strathclyde (Lanarkshire).

★★★★ **Albany,** Bothwell St, G2 7EN ☎041-248 2656 Tx: 77440 Fax: 041-221 8986

★★★★ **Holiday Inn,** Anderston, Argyle St, G3 8RR ☎041-226 5577 Tx: 776355 Fax: 041-221 9202 &

★★★★ **Hospitality Inn,** Cambridge St, G2 3HN ☎041-332 3311

★★★★ **Stakis Grosvenor,** Grosvenor Terr, Great Western Rd, G12 0TA ☎041-339 8811 Tx: 776247 Fax: 041-334 0710

★★★ **Central,** Gordon St, G1 35F ☎041-221 9680

★★★ **Crest,** Argyle St, G2 8LL ☎041-248 2355 Tx: 779652 Fax: 041-221 1014

★★★ **Ewington** 132 Queen's Dr, G42 8QW ☎041-423 1152 Fax: 041-422 2030

★★★ **Stakis Ingram,** 201 Ingram St, G1 1DQ ☎041-208 4401 Fax: 041-226 5149

★★★ **Swallow,** 517 Paisley Rd, G51 1RN ☎041-427 3146 Tx: 778795 Fax: 041-427 4059

★★★ **Tinto Firs Thistle,** 470 Kilmarnock Rd, G43 2BB ☎041-637 2353 Tx: 778329 Fax: 041-633 1340

★★ **Newlands,** 290 Kilmarnock Rd, G43 2XS ☎041-632 9171

★★ **Sherbrooke,** 11 Sherbrooke Av, G41 4PG ☎041-427 4227 Fax: 041-427 5685 &

★ **Dunkeld** 10–12 Queen's Dr, G42 8BS ☎041-424 0160

Glasgow Airport (Abbotsinch) *See* Renfrew.

Glenborrodale Highland (Argyll).

♨ ★★★★ **Glenborrodale Castle,** Ardnamurchan, Acharacle, PH36 4JP ☎(097 24) 266 Tx: 778815 Fax: (097 24) 224

Glencaple Dumfries & Galloway (Dumfriesshire).

★★ **Nith,** DG1 4RE ☎(038 777) 213

Glencoe Highland (Argyll).

★★ **King's House,** PA39 4HY (12 m SE A82), ☎Kingshouse (085 56) 259

Glenrothes Fife.

♨ ★★★ **Balgeddie House,** Balgeddie Way, KY6 3ET ☎(0592) 742511 Fax: (0592) 621702

★★ **Albany,** 1 North St, KY7 5NA ☎(0592) 752292 Fax: (0592) 756451

Glenshiel Highland (Ross & Cromarty)

★★ **Kintail Lodge,** IV40 8HL. ☎(059 981) 275

Golspie Highland (Sutherland).

★★ **Golf Links,** Church St, KW10 6TT ☎(040 83) 3408

★★ **Sutherland Arms,** Main St, KW10 6SA ☎(040 83) 3234

Gourock Strathclyde.

★★★ **Stakis Gantock,** Cloch Rd, PA19 1AR ☎(0475) 34671 Tx: 778584 Fax: (0475) 32490

Grantown-on-Spey Highland (Moray).

★★★ **Garth,** Castle Rd, PH26 3HN ☎(0479) 2836 Tx: (0479) 2116

★★ **Seafield Lodge,** Woodside Av, PH26 3JN ☎(0479) 2152 Fax: (0479) 2340

★ **Dunvegan,** Heathfield Rd, PH26 3HX ☎(0479) 2301

Greenlaw Borders (Berwickshire).

♨ ★★ H **Purves Hall,** TD10 6UJ ☎Leitholm (089 084) 558

Greenock Strathclyde (Renfrewshire).

★★★ **Tontine** 6 Ardgowan Sq, PA16 8MG ☎(0475) 23316

Gretna Dumfries & Galloway.

★★ **Gretna Chase,** CA6 5JB ☎(0461) 37517

★★ **Royal Stewart,** Glasgow Rd, CA6 5DT ☎(0461) 38210

★★ **Solway Lodge,** CA6 5DN ☎(0461) 38266 Fax: (0461) 37791

Gullane Lothian (East Lothian).

★★ **Queen's,** Main St, EH31 2AS ☎(0620) 842275

Hawick Borders.

★★ **Elm House,** 17 North Bridge St, TD9 9BD ☎(0450) 2866

★★ C **Kirklands,** West Stewart Pl, TD9 8BH ☎(0450) 72263

♨ ★★ **Mansfield House,** Weensland Rd, TD9 9EL ☎(0450) 73988 Fax: (0450) 72007

Helensburgh Strathclyde (Dunbartonshire).

★★★ **Commodore,** 112 West Clyde St, G84 8ES ☎(0436) 76924 Tx: 778740

Huntly Grampian.

♨ ★★ **Castle,** AB5 4SH ☎(0466) 2696 Fax: (0466) 2641

Imchnadamph Highland.

★★ **Inchnadamph,** IV27 4HN ☎Assynt (057 12) 202

Inveraray Strathclyde (Argyll).

★★ **Great Inn**, PA32 8XB ☎ (0499) 2466
Fax: (0499) 2421

Invergarry Highland (Inverness-shire).

⚑ ★★★ **Glengarry Castle**, PH35 4HW
☎ (080 93) 254 Fax: (080 93) 207

Invermoriston Highland.

★★ **Glenmoriston Arms**, Glenmoriston,
IV3 6YA ☎ Glenmoriston (0320) 51206

Inverness Highland.

⚑ ★★★ **Bunchrew House**, Bunchrew, IV3
6TA ☎ (0463) 234917 &

★★★ **Caledonian**, 33 Church St, IV1 1DX
☎ (0463) 235181 Tx: 75232 Fax: (0463) 711206

★★★ Ⓒ **Kingsmills**, Culcabock Rd,
IV2 3LP ☎ (0463) 237166 Tx: 75566
Fax: (0463) 225208 &

★★★ **Mercury**, Millburn Rd, IV2 3TR
☎ (0463) 239666 Tx: 75377 Fax: (0463) 711145

★★★ **Palace**, Ness Walk, IV3 5NE ☎ (0463)
223243 Tx: 777210

★★★ **Station**, Academy St, IV1 1LG ☎ (0463)
231926 Tx: 75275 Fax: (0463) 710705 &

★★ **Cumming's**, Church St, IV1 1EN
☎ (0463) 232531 Fax: (0463) 236541

★★ **Drumossie**, Old Perth Rd, IV1 2BE
☎ (0463) 236451 Tx: 75138

★★ **Glen Mhor**, 10 Ness Bank, IV2 4SG
☎ (0463) 234308 Tx: 75114 &

★★ **Lochardil**, Stratherrick Rd, IV2 4LF
☎ (0463) 235995

★★ **Loch Ness House**, Glenurquhart Rd,
IV3 6JL ☎ (0463) 231248

★★ **Muirtown**, 11 Clachnaharry Rd,
IV3 6LT ☎ (0463) 234860 &

Invershin Highland.

★★ **Invershin**, IV27 4ET ☎ (054 982) 202

Inverurie Grampian.

★★★ **Strathburn**, Burghmuir Dr, AB5 9GY
☎ (0467) 24422 Fax: (0467) 25133

★★ **Gordon Arms**, Market Pl, AB5 9SA
☎ (0467) 20314 Fax: (0467) 21792

Irvine Strathclyde (Ayrshire).

★★★★ **Hospitality Inn**, Roseholme,
Annick Water, KA11 4LD ☎ (0294) 74272
Tx: 777097 Fax: (0294) 77287 &

⚑ ★★★ Ⓗ Ⓒ Ⓡ **Montgreenan Mansion
House**, Montgreenan Estate, KA13 7QZ
☎ Kilwinning (0294) 57733 Tx: 778525
Fax: (0294) 85397

★★ **Redburn**, 65 Kilwinning Rd, KA12 8SU
☎ (0294) 76792

ISLE OF ARRAN

Blackwaterfoot Strathclyde (Bute).

★★★ **Kinloch**, Brodick, KA27 8ET
☎ Shiskine (077 086) 444 Fax: (077 086) 447

Brodick Strathclyde (Bute).

⚑ ★★★ Ⓡ **Auchrannie Country House**,
KA27 8BZ ☎ (0770) 2234 Fax: (0770) 2812

★★ **Douglas**, KA27 8AW ☎ (0770) 2155

Kilmory Strathclyde (Bute).

★★ Ⓗ **Lagg**, KA27 8PQ ☎ Sliddery (077 087)
255

ISLE OF BARRA

Barra, Isle of Western Isles (Inverness-shire).

★★ **Isle of Barra**, Tangusdale Beach,
Castlebay, PA80 5XW ☎ Castlebay
(087 14) 383 Fax: (087 14) 385

ISLE OF HARRIS

Western Isles (Inverness-shire).

★★ **Harris**, Tarbert, PA85 3DL ☎ Harris
(0859) 2154 Fax: (0859) 2281

ISLE-OF-ISLAY

Bowmore Strathclyde (Argyll).

★★ **Lochside**, Shore St, PA43 7LB ☎ (049 681)
244

Port Askaig Strathclyde (Argyll).

★★ **Port Askaig**, PA46 7RD ☎ (049 685) 245

ISLE OF JURA

Craighouse Strathclyde.

★★ **Jura**, PA60 7XU ☎ Jura (049 682) 243

ISLE OF LEWIS

Stornoway Western Isles (Ross & Cromarty).

★ **Royal**, Cromwell St, PA87 2DG ☎ (0851)
2109

ISLE OF MULL

Craignure Strathclyde.

★★★ **Isle of Mull**, PA65 6BB ☎ (068 02) 351
Tx: 778215 Fax: (068 02) 462

Tobermory Strathclyde (Argyll).

★★★ **Western Isles**, PA75 6PR ☎ (0688) 2012
Fax: (0688) 2297

★ **Mishnish**, PA75 6NU ☎ (0688) 2009
Fax: (0688) 2462

ISLE OF SKYE

Ardvasar Highland (Inverness-shire).

★★ Ⓗ **Ardvasar**, IV48 8RS ☎ (047 14) 223

Broadford Highland (Inverness-shire).

★★ **Broadford**, IV49 9AB ☎ (047 12) 204/5 &

Isle Ornsay Highland (Inverness-shire).

★★ **Duisdale**, Isle Ornsay, Sleat, IV43 8QW
☎ (047 13) 202

★ **Eilean Iarmain**, Camus Croise, IV43 8QR
☎ (047 13) 332 Tx: 75252

Portree Highland (Inverness-shire).

★★ **Rosedale**, Quay Brae, IV51 9DB ☎ (0478)
3131

★★ **Royal**, Bank St, IV51 9LU ☎ (0478) 2525

★ Ⓗ **Isles**, Somerled Sq, IV51 9EH ☎ (0478)
2129

Skeabost Bridge Highland

⚑ ★★★ **Skeabost House**, IV51 9NR
☎ (047 032) 202

Teangue Highland (Inverness-shire).

★★ **Toravaig**, IV44 8RJ ☎ Isle of Ornsay
(047 13) 231

Uig Highland (Inverness-shire).

★★ **Uig**, IV51 9YE ☎ (047 042) 205 &

★ **Ferry Inn**, IV51 9XP ☎ (047 042) 242

ISLE OF SOUTH UIST

Lochboisdale Western Isles,
(Inverness-shire).

★★ **Lochboisdale**, PA81 5TH ☎ (087 84) 332

Keith Grampian (Banffshire).

★★ **Royal**, Church Rd, AB5 3BR ☎ (054 22)
2528

Kelso Borders (Roxburghshire).

★★★ **Cross Keys**, 36 The Square, TD5 7HL
☎ (0573) 23303 Fax: (0573) 25792

★★★ **Ednam House**, Bridge St, TD5 7HT
☎ (0573) 24168

★ **Bellevue House**, Bowmont St, TD5 7DZ
☎ (0573) 24588. &

Kenmore Tayside (Perthshire).

★★★ **Kenmore**, Village Sq, PH15 2NU
☎ (088 73) 205 Fax: (088 73) 262

Kilchrenan Strathclyde (Argyll).

⚑ ★★★ Ⓗ Ⓒ Ⓡ **Ardanaiseig**, Taynuilt,
020PA35 1HE ☎ (086 63) 333 Fax: (086 63) 222

⚑ ★★★ **Taychreggan**, Lochaweside by
Taynuilt, PA35 1HQ ☎ (086 63) 211

Kildrummy Grampian
(Aberdeenshire).

⚑ ★★★ Ⓗ Ⓒ **Kildrummy Castle**,
AB3 8RA ☎ (097 55) 71288 Tx: 94012529
Fax: (097 55) 71345

Kilfinan Strathclyde.

★★ Ⓗ Ⓡ **Kilfinan**, Tighnabruaich, PA21
2EP ☎ (070 082) 201 Fax: (070 082) 205

Killearn Central (Stirlingshire).

★★ **Black Bull**, 2 The Square, G63 9NG
☎ (0360) 50215

Killiecrankie Tayside (Perthshire).

★★ **Killiecrankie**, PH16 5LG ☎ (0/96) 3220
Fax: (0796) 2451

Killin Central (Perthshire).

★★ **Bridge of Lochay**, Bridge of Lochay,
FK21 8TS ☎ (056 72) 272

Kilmarnock Strathclyde (Ayrshire).
563) 39090

★★★ **Howard Park**, 136 Glasgow Rd,
KA3 1UT ☎ (0563) 31211 Tx: 53168
Fax: (0563) 27795 &

Kilmelford Strathclyde (Argyll).

★★ **Cuilfail**, Oban, PA34 4XA ☎ (085 22) 274

Kinclaven Tayside (Perthshire).

⚑ ★★★ Ⓒ **Ballathie House**, Kinclaven by
Stanley, PH1 4QN ☎ Meikleour (025 083) 268
Tx: 76216 Fax: (025 083) 396 &

Kingseat Fife.

★★ **Halfway House**, Main St, KY12 0TG
☎ (0383) 731661 Fax: (0383) 621274

Kingussie Highland (Inverness-shire).

★★ 🄷 **Columba House,** Manse Rd, PH21 1JF ☎(0540 661) 402

★★**Royal,** 29 High St, PH21 1HX ☎(0540) 661898, 661236

Kinloch Rannoch Tayside.

★★★**Loch Rannoch,** PH16 5PS ☎(088 22) 201 Fax: (088 22) 203

Kinross Tayside.

★★★**Green,** KY13 7AS ☎(0577) 63467 Tx: 76684 Fax: (0577) 63180

★★★**Windlestrae,** KY13 7AS ☎(0577) 63217 Fax: (0577) 64733

★★ **Bridgend,** 253 High St, KY13 7EN ☎(0577) 63413 Fax: (0577) 64769

★★**Kirklands,** 20 High St, KY13 7AN ☎(0577) 63313

Kirkcaldy Fife.

★★★**Dean Park,** Chapel Level. ☎(0592) 261635 Tx: 727071

★★★**Parkway,** Abbotshall Rd, KY2 5DG ☎(0592) 262143 Tx: 728256 Fax: (0592) 200433

Kirkcudbright Dumfries & Galloway (Kirkcudbrightshire).

★★**Selkirk Arms,** Old High St, DG6 4JG ☎(0557) 30402 Fax: (0557) 31639

Kirkmichael Tayside (Perthshire).

★★**Aldchlappie,** PH10 7NS ☎Strathardle (025 081) 224

★★**Log Cabin,** PH10 7NB ☎Strathardle (025 081) 288 &

Kyle of Lochalsh Highland (Ross & Cromarty).

★★★**Lochalsh,** Ferry Road, IV40 8AF ☎(0599) 4202 Tx: 75318 Fax: (0599) 4881

Laggan Highland (Inverness-shire).

★★★**Gaskmore House,** by Newtonmore, PH20 1BS ☎(052 84) 250 &

Laide Highland (Ross & Cromarty).

★**Ocean View,** Achnasheen, 1V22 2ND ☎(044 582) 385

Lairg Highland (Sutherland).

★★★**Sutherland Arms,** Main Rd, IV27 4AT ☎(0549) 2291 Fax: (0549) 2261

Langbank Strathclyde (Renfrewshire).

▲▲ ★★★ 🆁 **Gleddoch House,** PA14 6YE ☎(047 554) 711 Tx: 779801 Fax: (047 554) 201

Langholm Dumfries & Galloway (Dumfriesshire).

★★**Eskdale,** Market Pl, DG13 0JH ☎(038 73) 80357

Largs Strathclyde (Ayrshire).

★★**Elderslie,** Broomfields, KA30 8DR ☎(0475) 686460

★★**Glen Eldon,** 2 Barr Cres, KA30 8PX ☎(0475) 673381

★★**Queen's,** North Promenade, KA30 8QW ☎(0475) 675311 Fax: (0475) 675313

★★**Springfield,** North Bay, KA30 8QL ☎(0475) 673119

Leslie Fife.

★★**Rescobie,** Valley Dr, KY6 3BQ ☎Glenrothes (0592) 742143.

Letham Fife.

▲▲ ★★★ **Fernie Castle,** Ladybank, nr Cupar, KY7 7RU ☎(033 781) 381 Fax: (033 781) 422

Linwood Strathclyde (Renfrewshire).

★★ **Golden Pheasant,** Moss Rd, PA3 3HP ☎Johnstone (0505) 21266

Lochearnhead Central (Perthshire).

★★ **Clachan Cottage,** FK19 8PU ☎(056 73) 247

Lochgilphead Strathclyde (Argyll).

★★ **Stag,** PA31 8NE ☎(0546) 2496

Lochinver Highland (Sutherland).

★★★ 🄷 🄲 **Inver Lodge,** IV27 4LU ☎(057 14) 496 Tx: 75206 Fax: (057 14) 395

Lochmaben Dumfries and Galloway (Dumfries-shire).

★★**Balcastle,** High St, nr Lockerbie, DG11 1NG ☎(0387) 810239

Lockerbie Dumfries & Galloway (Dumfriesshire).

▲▲ ★★★ **Dryfesdale,** DG11 2SF ☎(057 62) 2427 &

▲▲ ★★★ **Lockerbie House,** DG11 2RG ☎(057 62) 2610 Fax: (057 62) 3046

★★★ **Queens,** Annan Rd, DG11 2RB ☎(057 62) 2415 Fax: (057 62) 3901

★★ **Somerton House,** Carlisle Rd, DG11 2DR ☎(057 62) 2583

Lundin Links Fife.

★★**Lundin Links,** Leven Road, KY8 6AP ☎(0333) 320207 Fax: (0333) 320930

Macduff Grampian.

★★**Highland Haven,** Shore St, AB4 1UB ☎(0261) 32408 Fax: (0261) 33652

Mallaig Highland (Inverness-shire).

★★**Marine,** Station Rd, PH41 4PY ☎(0687) 2217

★★**West Highland,** PH41 4QZ ☎(0687) 2210 Fax: (0687) 2130

Markinch Fife.

▲▲ ★★★★ **Balbirnie House,** KY7 6NE ☎(0592) 610066

Maryculter Grampian.

▲▲ ★★★ **Maryculter House,** Southdeeside Rd, AB1 0BB ☎(0224) 732124 Tx: 739579 Fax: (0224) 735510 &

Maybole Strathclyde (Ayrshire).

▲▲ ★★★ 🆁 **Ladyburn,** Ladyburn, KA19 7SG ☎(065 54) 585

Melrose Borders (Roxburghshire).

★★ 🄲 **Burt's,** Market Sq, TD6 9PN ☎(089 682) 2285 Fax: (089 682) 2870

★★ **George & Abbotsford,** High St, TD6 9PD ☎(089 682) 2308 Fax: (089 682) 3363

Melvich Highland (Sutherland).

★★**Melvich,** nr Thurso, KW14 7YJ ☎(06413) 206

Milngavie Strathclyde (Dunbartonshire).

★★★ **Black Bull Thistle,** Main St, G62 6BH ☎041-956 2291 Tx: 778323

Fax: 041-956 1896

Moffat Dumfries & Galloway (Dumfriesshire).

★★★ **Moffat House,** High St, DG10 9HL ☎(0683) 20039 Fax: (0683) 21288 &

★★★ **Annandale Arms,** High St, DG10 9HF ☎(0683) 20013

★★ **Balmoral,** High St, DG10 9DL ☎(0683) 20288

★★ **Star,** 44 High St, DG10 9EF ☎(0683) 20156

Moniaive Dumfries & Galloway (Dumfriesshire).

▲▲ ★★ **Woodlea,** DG3 4EN ☎(084 82) 209

Monymusk Grampian (Aberdeenshire).

★★ **Grant Arms,** AB3 7HJ ☎(046 77) 226

Morar Highland (Inverness-shire).

★★ **Morar,** PH40 4PA ☎Mallaig (0687) 2346 Fax: (0687) 2130

Motherwell Strathclyde (Lanarkshire).

★★★ **Garrion,** 73 Merry St, ML1 1JN ☎(0698) 64561

Muir of Ord Highland.

★★ **Ord Arms,** Great North Rd, IV6 7XR

Nairn Highland (Nairnshire).

★★★ **Newton,** Inverness Rd, IV12 4RX ☎(0667) 53144 Tx: 739248 Fax: (0667) 54026

★★★ **Windsor,** Albert St, IV12 4HP ☎(0667) 53108 &

★★ **Alton Burn,** Alton Burn Rd, IV12 5ND ☎(0667) 52051

★★ **Carnach House,** Delnies, IV12 5NT ☎(0667) 52094

★ **Blenheim House,** Crescent Rd, IV12 4NB ☎(0667) 52019

Nethy Bridge Highland (Inverness-shire).

★★★ **Nethybridge,** PH25 3DP ☎(047 982) 203 Fax: (047 982) 686 &

New Abbey Dumfries & Galloway (Kirkcudbrightshire).

★ **Abbey Arms,** DG2 8BU ☎(038 785) 215

New Galloway Dumfries & Galloway (Kirkcudbrightshire).

★ **Ken Bridge,** DG7 3PR ☎(064 42) 211

★ **Kenmure Arms,** High St, DG7 3RL ☎(064 42) 240

Newtonmore Highland.

★★ **Mains,** Main St, PH20 1DE ☎(054 03) 206

★★ **Weigh Inn,** Main St, PH20 1DD ☎(054 03) 203

Newton Stewart Dumfries & Galloway (Wigtownshire).

▲▲ ★★★★ 🆁 **Kirroughtree,** DG8 6AN ☎(0671) 2141 &

★★★ **Bruce,** Queen St, DG8 6JL ☎(0671) 2294

★★ **Crown,** Queen St, DG8 6JW ☎(0671) 2727

North Berwick Lothian (East Lothian).

6

★★★ **Marine,** Cromwell Rd, EH39 4LZ
☎(0620) 2406 Tx: 72550 Fax: (0620) 4480

★★ **Nether Abbey,** Dirleton Av, EH39 4BQ
☎(0620) 2802

★★ **Point Garry,** West Bay Rd, EH39 4AW
☎(0620) 2380

OBAN Strathclyde (Argyll).

★★★ **Alexandra,** Corran Esplanade,
PA34 5AA ☎(0631) 62381 Fax: (0631) 64497

★★★ **Caledonian,** Station Sq, PA34 5RT
☎(0631) 63133 Tx: 777210

★★★ **Columba,** North Pier, Esplanade,
PA34 5QD ☎(0631) 62183 Tx: 728256
Fax: (0631) 64683

★★ **Lancaster,** Corran Esplanade, PA34 5AD
☎(0631) 62587

★★ **Rowan Tree,** George St, PA34 5NX
☎(0631) 62954

★ **King's Knoll,** Dunollie Rd, PA34 5JH
☎(0631) 62536

Old Rayne Grampian (Aberdeenshire).

★ **Lodge,** AB5 6RY ☎(046 45) 205

Onich Highland (Inverness-shire).

★★★ **H** **Lodge on the Loch,** Creag Dhu,
PH33 6RY ☎(085 53) 237 Tx: 94013696
Fax: (085 53) 463 &

★★★ **Onich,** PH33 6RY ☎(085 53) 214
Fax: (085 53) 484

★★ **R** **Allt-Nan-Ros,** PH33 6RY ☎(085 53)
210 Fax: (085 53) 462

★★ **Loch Leven,** PH33 6SA ☎(085 53) 236

ORKNEY ISLANDS

Stromness

★★ **Stromness,** 15 Victoria St, KW16 3AA
☎(0856) 850298

Paisley Strathclyde (Renfrewshire).

★★ **Rockfield,** 125 Renfrew Rd, PA3 4EA
☎041-889 6182 Fax: 041-389 9526

★★ **Stakis Watermill,** Lonend, PA1 1SR
☎041-889 3201

Peebles Borders (Peeblesshire).

★★★ **Hydro,** EH45 8LX ☎(0721) 20602
Fax: (0721) 22999

★★★ **Park,** Innerleithen Rd, EH45 8BA
☎(0721) 20451 Tx: 72568 Fax: (0721) 22999

★★★ **Tontine,** High St, EH45 8AJ ☎(0721)
20892

▲▲ ★★ **H** **C** **R** **Cringletie House,** EH45
8PL ☎(072 13) 233

▲▲ ★★ **Venlaw Castle,** Edinburgh Rd,
EH45 8OG ☎(0721) 20384

Perth Tayside (Perthshire).

▲▲ ★★★ **Huntingtower,** Crieff Rd, PH1 3JT
☎(0738) 83771 Tx: 76204

★★★ **Isle of Skye Osprey,** Dundee Rd,
PH2 7AB ☎(0738) 24471 Tx: 76185

★★★ **Lovat,** Glasgow Rd, PH2 0LT
☎(0738) 36555 Tx: 76531 Fax: (0738) 43123

★★★ **Newton House,** Glencarse, PH2 7LX
☎(073 886) 250 Fax: (073 886) 717

★★★ **Queen's,** Leonard St, PH2 8HB
☎(0738) 25471 Tx: 76531 Fax: (0738) 38496

★★★ **Royal George,** Tay St, PH1 5LD
☎(0738) 24455 Fax: (0738) 30345

★★★ **Salutation,** South St, PH2 8PH
☎(0738) 30066 Tx: 76357 Fax: (0738) 33598

★★★ **Stakis City Mills,** West Mill St,
PH1 5QP ☎(0738) 28281 Tx: 778704
Fax: (0738) 43423

★★ **Station,** Leonard St PH2 8HE ☎(0738)
24141 Tx: 76481 Fax: (0738) 39912 &

Peterhead Grampian (Aberdeenshire).

★★★ **Waterside Inn,** Fraserburgh Rd, AB4
7BN ☎(0779) 71121 Tx: 739413
Fax: (0779) 70670

Pitlochry Tayside (Perthshire).

★★★ **Atholl Palace,** Atholl Rd, PH16 5LY
☎(0796) 2400 Tx: 76406 Fax: (0796) 3036

▲▲ ★★★ **Pine Trees,** Strathview Terr, PH16
5QR ☎(0796) 2121 Fax: (0796) 2460

★★★ **Pitlochry Hydro,** Knockard Rd, PH16
5JH ☎(0796) 2666

★★★ **Scotland's,** Bonnethill Rd, PH16 5BT
☎(0796) 2292 Tx: 76392 Fax: (0796) 3284

★★ **Acarsaid,** Atholl Rd, PH16 5BX ☎(0796)
2389

★★ **Airdaniar,** Atholl Rd, PH16 5QL
☎(0796) 2266

★★ **Birchwood,** East Moulin Rd, PH16
5DW ☎(0796) 2477

★ **Castlebeigh,** Knockard Rd, PH16 5HJ
☎(0796) 2925

★★ **Claymore,** Atholl Rd, PH16 5AR
☎(0796) 2888

★★ **Craigvrack,** West Moulin Rd, PH16
5EQ ☎(0796) 2399 &

★★ **Dundarach,** Perth Rd, PH16 5DJ
☎(0796) 2862 &

Plockton Highland (Ross & Cromarty).

★★ **H** **C** **Haven,** Innes St, IV52 8TW
☎(059 984) 223

Polmont Central.

★★★ **Inchyra Grange,** Grange Rd, FK2 0YB
☎(0324) 711911 Tx: 777693 Fax: (0324) 716134

Portpatrick Dumfries & Galloway

★★★ **Fernhill,** Heugh Rd, DG9 8TD
☎(077 681) 220 Fax: (077 681) 596

★★ **Mount Stewart,** South Cres, DG9 8LE
☎(077 681) 291

★★ **Portpatrick,** DG8 8TQ ☎(077 681) 333

Port William Dumfries & Galloway (Wigtownshire).

▲▲ ★★★ **R** **Corsemalzie House,** DG8 9RL
☎(098 886) 254

★★ **Monreith Arms,** The Square, DG8 9SE
☎(098 87) 232

Prestwick Strathclyde (Ayrshire).

★★★ **Carlton Toby,** 187 Ayr Rd, KA9 1TP
☎(0292) 76811 Fax: (0292) 76811

★★ **North Beach,** 5 Links Rd, KA9 1QG
☎(0292) 79069

★★ **St Nicholas,** 41 Ayr Rd, KA9 1SY
☎(0292) 79568

★ **Auchencoyle,** 13 Links Rd, KA9 1QG
☎(0292) 78316

Renfrew Strathclyde (Renfrewshire).

★★★★ **Excelsior,** Abbotsinch, PA3 2TR
☎041-887 1212 Tx: 777733
Fax: 041-887 3738

★★★ **Dean Park,** Glasgow Rd, PA4 8YB
☎041-886 3771 Tx: 779032
Fax: 041-885 0681

★★★ **Glynhill,** Paisley Rd, PA4 8XB ☎041-886 5555 Tx: 779536
Fax: 041-885 2838

★★★ **Stakis Normandy,** Inchinnan Rd, PA4
9EJ ☎041-886 4100 Tx: 778897
Fax: 041-885 2366

Rhu Strathclyde (Dunbartonshire).

★★ **Ardencaple,** Shore Rd, G84 8LS
☎(0436) 820200 Fax: (0436) 821099

Rockcliffe Dumfries & Galloway (Kirkcudbrightshire).

▲▲ ★★★ **Baron's Craig,** DG5 4QF
☎(055 663) 225 &

▲▲ ★★ **Clonyard House,** Colvend,
DG5 4QW ☎(055 663) 372 &

Rosebank Strathclyde (Lanarkshire).

★★★ **Popinjay,** ML8 5QB ☎Crossford
(055 586) 441 Fax: (055 586) 204

Rosyth Fife.

★★ **Gladyer Inn,** Heath Rd, KY11 2BT
☎(0383) 419977

Rothes Grampian (Moray).

▲▲ ★★★ **C** **Rothes Glen,** IV33 7AH
☎(034 03) 254

Rutherglen Strathclyde (Lanarkshire).

★★ **Burnside,** East Kilbride Rd, G73 5EA
☎041-634 1276 Fax: 041-634 1223 &

St Andrews Fife.

★★★★ **Rusack's,** Pilmour Links, KY16 9JQ
☎(0334) 74321 Fax: (0334) 77896

★★★ **R** **Rufflets,** KY16 9TX ☎(0334) 72594
Fax: (0334) 78703

★★★ **H** **C** **St Andrews Golf,** The Scores
☎(0334) 72611 Tx: 94013267 Fax: (0334) 72188

★★★ **Scores,** The Scores, KY16 9BB ☎(0334)
72451 Tx: 94012061 Fax: (0334) 73947

★★ **Ardgowan,** 2 Playfair Terr, KY16 9HX
☎(0334) 72970

★★ **Parkland,** Kinburn Castle, Double
Dykes Rd, KY16 9DS ☎(0334) 73620

St Fillans Tayside (Perthshire).

★★★ **Four Seasons,** PH6 2NF ☎(076 485)
333

Sanquhar Dumfries & Galloway (Dumfriesshire).

★ **Nithsdale,** High St, DG4 6DJ ☎(0659)
50506

Scone Tayside (Perthshire).

▲▲ ★★★ **H** **C** **R** **Murrayshall House,**
Tayside PH2 7PH ☎(0738) 51171 Tx: 76197
Fax: (0738) 52595

Scourie Highland (Sutherland).

★★ **H** **Scourie,** IV27 4SX ☎(0971) 2396
Fax: (0971) 2423

SHETLAND ISLANDS

Brae Mainland.

▲▲ ★★★ Busta House, ZE2 9QN ✆(080 622) 506 Tx: 9312100218 Fax: (080 622) 588

Lerwick Mainland.

★★★Shetland, Holmsgarth Rd, ZE1 0PW ✆(0595) 5515
Tx: 75432 Fax: (0595) 5828 &

★★ Grand, Commercial St, ✆(0595) 2826 Fax: (0595) 4048

★★ Queens, Commercial St, ZE1 0AB ✆(0595) 2826 Fax: (0595) 4048

Skelmorlie Strathclyde.

▲▲ ★★★ H C Manor Park, St Phillans, PA17 5HE ✆(0475) 520832

South Queensferry Lothian.

★★★ Forth Bridges Moat House, Forth Bridge Road, EH30 9SF ✆031-331 1199 Tx: 727430 Fax: 031-319 1733 &

★★ R Hawes Inn, Newhalls Rd, EH30 9TE ✆031-331 1990

Spean Bridge Highland.

★★ H Letterfinlay Lodge, Letterfinlay, PH34 4DZ (7½ m N of Spean Bridge on A82) ✆(039 781) 622

★★ Spean Bridge, PH34 4ES ✆(039 781) 250 &

Stanley Tayside (Perthshire).

★★ Tayside, Mill St, PH2 0QL ✆(0738) 828249 Fax: (0738) 33449

Stepps Strathclyde (Lanarkshire).

★★★ Garfield House, Cumbernauld Rd, G33 6HW ✆041-779 2111 Fax: 041-779 2111

Stirling Central (Stirlingshire).

★★★ Golden Lion, King St, FK8 1BD ✆(0786) 75351 Fax: (0786) 72755

★★★ Terraces, 4 Melville Terr, FK8 2ND ✆(0786) 72268 Tx: 778025 Fax: (0786) 50314

★★ Garfield, Victoria Sq, FK8 2QZ ✆(0786) 73730

Stirling Highland, Spittal St. ✆(Central reservations) 041-332 6538.

Stonehaven Grampian (Kincardineshire).

★★★ Commodore, Cowie Park, AB3 2PZ ✆(0569) 62936 Tx: 739111 Fax: (0569) 66179

Stoneykirk Dumfries & Galloway (Wigtownshire).

★★ Torrs Warren, DG9 9DH ✆Sandhead (0776 83) 204

Strachur Strathclyde (Argyll).

★★★ H R Creggans Inn, PA27 8BX ✆(036 986) 279 Tx: 777694 Fax: (036 986) 637 &

Stranraer Dumfries & Galloway (Wigtownshire). *See also* Stoneykirk.

★★★★ North West Castle, Cairnryan Rd, DG9 8EH ✆(0776) 4413 Tx: 777088 Fax: (0776) 2646

Strathaven Strathclyde (Lanarkshire).

★★★ Strathaven, Hamilton Rd, ML10 6SZ ✆(0357) 21778 Tx: 776496 Fax: (0357) 20789

Strathblane Central (Stirlingshire).

★★ Kirkhouse Inn, G63 9AA ✆(0360) 70621

Strathpeffer Highland (Ross & Cromarty).

★★ Highland, IV14 9AN ✆(0997) 21457 Tx: 75160

★★ H R Holly Lodge, IV14 9AR ✆(0997) 21254

★★ Mackay's, The Square, IV14 9DC ✆(0997) 21542

Strontian Highland (Argyll).

▲▲ ★★ H C R Kilcamb Lodge, PH36 4HY ✆(0967) 2257

Symington Strathclyde (Lanarkshire).

★★★ Tinto, ML12 6PQ ✆Tinto (089 93) 454 Fax: (089 93) 520

▲▲ ★★★ Wyndales House, nr Biggar, ML12 6JU ✆Tinto (089 93) 207

Tain Highland.

★★★ Mansfield, Scotsburn Rd, IV19 1PR ✆(0862) 2052

★★★ H Morangie House, Morangie Rd, IV19 1PY ✆(0862) 2281

★★★ Royal, High St, IV19 1AB ✆(0862) 2013 Fax: (0862) 3450

Tarbert Strathclyde (Argyll).

▲▲ ★★★ Stonefield Castle, Loch Fyne, PA29 6YJ ✆(0880 820) 836 Tx: 776321 Fax: (0880 820) 929

★★ Anchor, PA29 4YJ ✆(088 02) 577

Taynuilt Strathclyde (Argyll).

★★ Brander Lodge, Bridge of Awe, PA35 1HT ✆(086 62) 243 Fax: (086 62) 273

★★ Polfearn, PA35 1JQ ✆(086 62) 251 &

Thornhill Dumfries & Galloway (Dumfriesshire).

★★ Buccleuch & Queensberry, Drumlanrig Rd, DG3 5LU ✆(0848) 30215

★★ George, Drumlanrig Rd, DG3 5LU ✆(0848) 30326

▲▲ ★★ R Trigony House, Closeburn, DG3 5EZ ✆(0848) 31211

Thurso Highland (Caithness).

★★Pentland, Princes St, KW14 7AA ✆(0847) 63202

★★ Royal, Traill St, KW14 8EH ✆(0847) 63191 &

★★ St Clair, Sinclair St, KW14 7AJ ✆(0847) 66481

Tongue Highland (Sutherland).

★★ Ben Loyal, IV27 4XE ✆(084 755) 216

Troon Strathclyde (Ayrshire).

★★★★ Marine Highland, Crosbie Rd, KA10 6HE ✆(0292) 314444 Tx: 777595 Fax: (0292) 316922 &

★★★ Piersland House, Craig End Rd, KA10 6HD ✆(0292) 314747 Fax: (0292) 365613

★★ Ardneil, St Meddans St, KA10 6NU ✆(0292) 311611

★★ Craiglea, South Beach, KA10 6EG ✆(0292) 311366

★★ South Beach, South Beach, KA10 6EG ✆(0292) 312033

Turnberry Strathclyde.

★★★★★ Turnberry, Maidens Rd, KA26 9LT ✆(0655) 31000 Tx: 777779 Fax: (0655) 31706 &

★★★ H R Malin Court, KA26 9PB ✆(0655) 31457 Fax: (0655) 31072

Tweedsmuir Borders (Peeblesshire)

★★ Crook Inn, ML12 6QN ✆(089 97) 272

Ullapool Highland (Ross & Cromarty).

★★★ Mercury, North Rd, IV26 2UD ✆(0854) 2314

★★★ Royal, Garve St, IV26 2SY ✆(0854) 2181 Fax; (0854) 2951

★★ Harbour Lights, Garve Rd, IV26 2SX ✆(0854) 2222

Uphall Lothian.

▲▲ ★★★ Houstoun House, EH52 6JS ✆(0506) 853831 Fax: (0506) 854220

Walkerburn Borders (Peeblesshire).

▲▲ ★★★ H Tweed Valley, Galashiels Rd, EH43 6AA ✆(089 687) 636 Fax: (089 687) 639

West Wemyss Fife.

★★ Belvedere, Coxstool, KY1 4SL ✆(0592) 54167

Whitebridge Highland (Inverness-shire).

★★Whitebridge, IV1 2UN ✆Gorthleck (045 63) 226

Whithorn Dumfries & Galloway (Wigtownshire).

★★Queen's Arms, Isle of Whithorn, DG8 8LF ✆(098 85) 369
ntury building at head of fishing village.

Wick Highland (Caithness).

★★ Mackays, Union St, KW1 5ED ✆(0955) 2323

Wishaw Strathclyde (Lanarkshire).

★ Coltness, Coltness Rd, ML2 7EX ✆(0698) 381616

Wormit Fife.

▲▲ ★★ Sandford Hill, Newport-on-Tay, DD6 8RG ✆Newport-on-Tay (0382) 541802

Key to symbols

★	hotel rating
▲▲	country house hotel
	RAC Hotel Awards
H	Hospitality
C	Comfort
R	Restaurant quality
⛊	Tankard award for inns